MOON

NORTHERN
CALIFORNIA

ELIZABETH LINHART VENEMAN

© AVALON TRAVEL

NORTHERN
CALIFORNIA

PACIFIC OCEAN

NEVADA
CALIFORNIA

0   25 km
0   25 mi

Point Reyes
National
Seashore

Bodega Bay
Point Reyes
Sonoma
Santa Rosa
Calistoga
128
Napa
Fairfield
Vacaville
Davis
80
SACRAMENTO
99
Lodi
Jackson
16
49
Eldorado
88
San Andreas
Angels Camp
4
Stanislaus
National
Forest
Dardanelle
4
395
182
338
Bridgeport
Lee
Vining
Mono
Lake
167
359
Hawthorne
395
6
Benton
Bishop

San Rafael
San Francisco
101
Oakland
Walnut
Creek
Concord
Rio Vista
80
Pleasanton
Livermore
Tracy
4
Stockton
120
Modesto
132
Turlock
Merced
49
Mariposa
140
Groveland
Sonora
108
Yosemite
National
Park
Yosemite Village
120
Oakhurst
Mammoth
Lakes
120

Half Moon Bay
Pigeon Point
Palo Alto
101
35
Santa
Cruz
17
Watsonville
San Jose
101
Gilroy
Morgan
Hill
152
San Luis
Reservoir
Los Banos
165
152
59
Chowchilla
Madera
145
Fresno
41
168
Millerton
Lake
Kings
Canyon
National
Park
Pine Flat
Reservoir
Sierra
National
Forest
180

Point Sur
Monterey
Carmel
Big Sur
1
Salinas
Hollister
25
King
City
101
Los Padres
National
Forest
Cambria
1
Paso
Robles
46
Morro Bay
San Luis Obispo
41
Cholame
Coalinga
198
Avenal
33
46
58
Buttonwillow
5
Wasco
Delano
65
99
Selma
Kingsburg
Hanford
Lemoore
269
180
Kettleman City
41
43
Tulare
198
Visalia
190
245
Porterville
155
Bakersfield
178
58
Sequoia
National
Forest
Sequoia
National
Park
180
Kings
Canyon
National
Park

OCEAN

NORTHERN CALIFORNIA

Contents

DISCOVER
Northern California

If you're torn between the beach or the mountains, city nightlife or quaint historic towns, wining and dining or roughing it, then Northern California is your ultimate destination—rich in history and dense in culture, amid some of the most scenic landscapes in the world. Yosemite, Lake Tahoe, Big Sur, and San Francisco are on most travelers' bucket lists. But beyond these headlining pleasures are lesser-known discoveries: towering coast redwoods, historic ghost towns, an active volcano, pounding surf, and gold rush-era mines.

Culturally, San Francisco is the beating heart of Northern California. Fine art, radical ideas, and world-class cuisine mix easily in this cosmopolitan city that loves its politics as much as its nightlife. In Wine Country, culture meets nature where locals enjoy life one sip at a time. Sacramento, the sometimes cantankerous capital, is surrounded by the historic Gold Country, dotted with mines and preserved 19th-century towns that reveal the state's early days—and the events that shaped it into the dynamic place it is now.

Clockwise from top left: McWay Falls; San Francisco; Mono Lake; giant sequoias; Santa Cruz Beach Boardwalk; St. Francis Winery.

Wide-open spaces draw visitors and locals to climb Yosemite's granite peaks, hike among redwoods in Sequoia and Kings Canyon, surf the beaches of Santa Cruz, scale the spines of Shasta, Lassen, and Whitney, ski the slopes of Tahoe, and dip their toes into the sea in Big Sur.

Whether you're a visitor discovering its wonders for the first time or a seasoned native exploring its hidden treasures, enchanting Northern California awaits.

Clockwise from top left: Carmel Mission; Haight Street in San Francisco; Hearst Castle; Napa Valley Wine Train.

10 TOP EXPERIENCES

1 **Golden Gate Bridge:** Nothing beats the view from **San Francisco**'s famous and fascinating bridge (page 49).

2 **Point Reyes National Seashore:** Acres of unspoiled grassland, forest, and beaches make this one of the most diverse parks in the **San Francisco Bay Area** (page 89).

3 **Wine Tasting:** California's beautiful vineyards are renowned worldwide. Oenophiles will hit the **Napa** and **Sonoma Valleys** (page 133) wine regions.

>>>

4 **Wander amid Redwoods:** No visit to California is complete without cruising along the **Avenue of the Giants** (page 198), camping in the **Redwood State and National Parks** (page 225), or hiking in **Sequoia National Park** (page 404) or **Muir Woods** (page 84).

5 **Scale Mount Shasta:** Numerous trails circle this dazzling glacier-topped **mountain peak** that beckons from every angle for miles around (page 261).

>>>

6 **Emerald Bay:** This "underwater" park offers perfect entry into **Lake Tahoe**'s sparkling blue waters (page 279).

<<<

7 **Rafting in Gold Country:** Gold was discovered here in the American River in 1848. Today, this river offers a new reward with thrilling whitewater perfect for rafting (page 331).

>>>

8 **Yosemite Valley:** The famous valley is filled with iconic monuments like **El Capitan** and **Bridalveil Fall.** Hike **Half Dome** or the **Mist Trail** for the best perspective of this natural playground (page 357).

<<<

9 **Monterey Bay Aquarium:** Gorgeous Monterey Bay is famous for its sealife, best experienced at its world-renowned aquarium (page 430).

>>>

10 **Cruise the Big Sur Coast Highway:** With jutting cliffs, crashing surf, and epic views, this scenic, twisty drive is iconic (page 460).

<<<

Planning Your Trip

Where to Go

San Francisco

The politics, the culture, the food—these are what make San Francisco world-famous. Dine on cutting-edge **cuisine** at high-end restaurants and offbeat food trucks, tour classical and avant-garde **museums**, bike through **Golden Gate Park** to explore its hidden treasures, and stroll along **Fisherman's Wharf** where barking sea lions and loud street performers compete for attention.

Surrounding San Francisco is a region as diverse as the city itself. To the north, **Marin** offers wilderness seekers a quick reprieve from the city, while ethnic diversity and intellectual curiosity give the **East Bay** a hip urban edge. On the southern **Peninsula,** beaches and farmland are within quick driving distance of the entrepreneurial culture of Silicon Valley and **San Jose.**

Wine Country

Northern California's Wine Country is famous for a reason. This is the place to pamper yourself with excellent wines, fantastic food, and luxurious spas. **Napa** offers all of the above in spades, while **Sonoma** is the place to catch a bit of history and to enjoy a mellower atmosphere. The **Russian River** adds redwoods and a bit of river-rafting to the mix.

North Coast

For deserted beaches, towering redwoods, and scenic coastal towns, cruise north along **The Redwood Coast.** Explore Russian history at Fort Ross on the grassy bluffs of the **Sonoma Coast** or be romanced by **Mendocino's** small-town charm and nearby wineries.

Shasta and Lassen

At the southern end of the volcanic Cascade Range are geologic wonders alongside plentiful outdoor recreation. Rent a houseboat on **Shasta Lake** or spend a few days climbing or skiing dramatic **Mount Shasta.** You can traverse nearby lava tunnels or travel south to hike through boiling mud pots and fumaroles at **Lassen Volcanic National Park.**

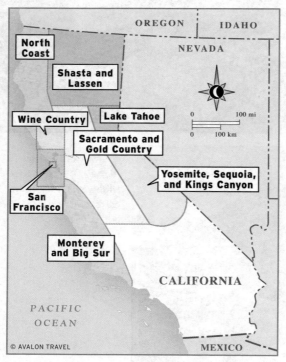

Lake Tahoe

Bright blue skies, granite mountaintops, and evergreen forests surround jewel-like Lake Tahoe. Glossy hotels and casinos line the South Shore, while the low-key North and West Shores beckon with quiet beaches and miles of hiking, biking, and ski trails. The Truckee-Donner area adds a bit of Old West flavor to the outdoor scene, while the East Shore specializes in uninhibited good times.

Sacramento and Gold Country

The political epicenter of California is the gold rush-era town of Sacramento. History abounds here as well as on the winding scenic highways that crisscross Northern Gold Country. Tour abandoned mines, raft some high-octane white water, go wine-tasting in the Shenandoah Valley, or explore the caves, caverns, and big trees of Southern Gold Country.

Yosemite, Sequoia, and Kings Canyon

The work of Ansel Adams and John Muir made Yosemite a worldwide icon. Thousands crowd into Yosemite Valley to view the much-photographed Half Dome, Bridalveil Fall, and El Capitan. On the eastern side of the Sierra, Mono Lake and Mammoth Lakes provide more scenic wilderness to explore.

Aside from the dramatic rugged terrain, the real draws to Sequoia and Kings Canyon are the giant sequoias in the General Grant Grove and the General Sherman Tree. Visit the Giant Forest Museum, take an invigorating hike up to Moro Rock, and duck into glittering Crystal Cave, which is as beautiful as its name suggests.

Monterey and Big Sur

Some of the most beautiful and adventure-filled coastline in the world is along Highway 1—the Pacific Coast Highway. Go surfing and wine-tasting in Santa Cruz. Witness gray whales and sea lions off the rugged Monterey Bay, and then explore their environment at the Monterey Bay Aquarium. Camp and hike the unspoiled wilderness of Big Sur, and then tour grandiose Hearst Castle in San Simeon.

Mount Lassen

Know Before You Go

When to Go

Northern California's best feature is its all-season appeal. Yosemite's waterfalls are at their peak in **spring,** when the crowds are lighter. This is also a great time to visit Big Sur—lodging rates drop, as do the number of visitors, while blooming wildflowers make for colorful road trips.

"The coldest winter I ever spent was a summer in San Francisco"—a quote falsely attributed to Mark Twain—still holds true as the wind and fog that blows through the city June-August surprises unsuspecting visitors. Regardless, **summer** remains Northern California's travel season; expect crowds at popular attractions, wineries, national parks, and campgrounds.

Fall is a wonderful time to visit as the summer crowds have left but winter rain and snow have not yet closed Yosemite, Shasta, or Tahoe. September in particular is San Francisco's "summer," with warm sunny days and little summer fog.

In **winter,** Tahoe draws crowds for skiing and snowboarding. Unfortunately, it also draws heavy traffic along I-80, which can close due to snow and related accidents. Yosemite's roads likewise close in winter, including Highway 120 and the Tioga Pass, which links the Eastern Sierra to the west entrance of the park. Heavy rains can also flood Wine Country roads, leaving travelers stranded (although there are worse places to be stuck).

Transportation

The most central place to **fly** into is San Francisco International Airport (SFO), but you can avoid some of the hassle of this large facility by flying into smaller airports in Oakland, San Jose, or even Sacramento.

Unless your trip is focused on San Francisco, plan to **rent a car** to explore the rest of the region. Winter drivers should carry **tire chains** for unexpected snows in the high Sierra.

Advance Reservations

Book **hotels** early and buy **tickets** for popular attractions in advance, especially in summer. If you plan to visit any big-name restaurants, make those reservations early as well. Lodging and **campground reservations** are particularly essential in Yosemite and Big Sur.

Summer fog is likely along the coast and pretty much guaranteed in San Francisco, making the air damp and chilly. Bring **layered clothing,** especially a wind-resistant coat and a warm sweater, as well as sunscreen.

Visiting the United States from abroad, you'll need your **passport** and possibly a **visa.**

Best Day Trips

Many of California's most famous destinations are within a short drive of **San Francisco.** Less than two hours away, **Wine Country** is one of the best day trips out of San Francisco. You can indulge and pamper yourself all day and still have time to fall asleep in the city that night. While only a few hours away from San Francisco, **Big Sur** and **Yosemite** are better suited to an overnight stay or a weekend getaway.

Three Days in San Francisco

Day 1

Start your day with breakfast at the **Ferry Building.** Grab a latté at **Blue Bottle Café** or graze from one of the many on-site vendors before taking a stroll along **Fisherman's Wharf.** Near Pier 39, buy ferry tickets to **Alcatraz** to tour the former island prison. Back at the foot of Beach and Hyde Streets, board the Powell-Hyde **cable car** and hop off for some window-shopping at **Union Square.**

In the afternoon, head west to explore verdant **Golden Gate Park.** The fabulous **de Young Museum** is directly across from the **California Academy of Sciences.** Art lovers and science geeks can part ways here or squeeze in a trip to enjoy both! Near Golden Gate Park, visit the **Haight,** the hippie enclave made famous in the 1960s. Enjoy the finely crafted cocktails and nibbles at **Alembic** or head back downtown to splurge on dinner at **Farallon.**

Ferry Building

End the day with martinis at the swank **Top of the Mark.**

Day 2

North Beach is home to **Mama's on Washington Square,** whose specialty "m'omelettes" have made this joint a local favorite for decades. After brunch, stop in at **City Lights,** the legendary Beat generation bookstore, then enjoy an old-school cappuccino at **Caffé Trieste.** Work off that omelet with a climb to the top of **Coit Tower** to catch a great view of the city skyline—look west to find crooked **Lombard Street.**

Spend the afternoon in the hip Mission District. Order an authentic Mission burrito at **La Taqueria** or sweets from **Tartine Bakery.** History buffs should visit the 18th-century **Mission Dolores.** End your stay in the Mission with thin-crust pizzas and classic cocktails at **Beretta.**

Day 3

Get an early start for breakfast at popular **Dottie's True Blue Café.** Spend a few hours discovering the world of science at the **Exploratorium** or, if the weather cooperates, explore the **Presidio** and take a stroll along **Crissy Field.** Stop for coffee and a snack at **Warming Hut Bookstore & Café,** then it's off to the ultimate San Francisco photo-op on the **Golden Gate Bridge.**

At night, grab a place in line for California fusion dishes served dim sum-style at **State Bird Provisions.**

Marin Day Trip

Extend the love affair with a side trip to wander the redwoods in Marin. **Muir Woods National Monument** comprises acres of staggeringly beautiful redwood forest nestled just north of San Francisco. The **Muir Woods Visitors Center** is a great place to begin your exploration. Hike the **Redwood Creek Trail,** a paved boardwalk through the beautiful trees; pick up a self-guided trail leaflet at the visitors center and follow the interpretive numbers along the way to learn about the flora and fauna of this unique ecosystem.

Golden Gate Park

Family Fun

California has a host of attractions for kids and parents alike. Following are some favorites:

- **Fisherman's Wharf:** Kids can dine on decadent sundaes at Ghirardelli Square, play vintage games at the Musée Mécanique, and have their mind blown at the **Exploratorium** (page 44).

- **California Academy of Sciences:** This kid-friendly, interactive environment has a three-story rainforest, live animals, and a planetarium (page 51).

- **Charles M. Schulz Museum:** This kid-centric museum celebrates the *Peanuts* comic creator (page 147).

- **Trees of Mystery:** This kitschy North Coast stop is a great place to let the family out for some good cheesy fun (page 228).

- **Ed Z'berg Sugar Pine Point State Park:** Vacationing families love to swim around the boulder-strewn beach (page 292).

- **California State Railroad Museum:** It's train buff heaven, with wooden tracks and trains, exquisite model train sets, and a collection of 21 restored cars (page 318).

- **Columbia State Historic Park:** At this perfectly preserved Gold Rush-era town, kids can pan for gold, ride a 100-year old stagecoach, and sample 19th-century confectionery at an old-time candy kitchen (page 346).

- **Mammoth Lakes:** With endless opportunities for hiking and camping, boating and fishing, and biking and skiing, this Eastern Sierra gem has all the ingredients for a perfect family vacation (page 385).

- **Santa Cruz Beach Boardwalk:** With 34 rides, the Boardwalk has been thrilling kids and grownups alike since 1907 (page 415).

- **Monterey Bay Aquarium:** A dazzling array of local sealife includes a Kelp Forest, playful otters, and glowing jellyfish (page 430).

beach day

After your hike, fill up on British comfort food at the **Pelican Inn.** Dark wood and a long trestle table give a proper Old English feel to the dimly lit dining room. It's just a short walk from the restaurant to lovely **Muir Beach,** perfect for wildlife-watching and beachcombing. End the day with oysters and drinks at the Farley Bar at **Cavallo Point Lodge.** Snag a blanket and a seat on the porch to watch the fog roll in over the Golden Gate Bridge.

Two Days in Wine Country

The Napa Valley is less than 100 miles north of San Francisco, making it a popular day-trip destination. If you plan to tour Wine Country, choose one region to explore. **Napa** and **Sonoma** are closest to San Francisco, about one hour's drive. Traffic on the winding two-lane roads in these regions can easily become clogged with wine-tasting day-trippers, especially on weekends. To avoid the crowds, try to get an early start or visit on a weekday. Note that most wineries close by 4pm, and some are open only by appointment.

One Day in Napa
50 MILES, 1-1.5 HOURS
FROM SAN FRANCISCO
Get your bearings in downtown Napa, where you can sample some excellent vintages and pick up picnic supplies at the **Oxbow Public Market.** Hop onto Highway 29 and cruise to the **Robert Mondavi Winery,** an excellent place to begin your Wine Country exploration. Unpack your

Napa Valley

picnic basket at the historic **Bale Grist Mill** in St. Helena, followed by a visit to the **Culinary Institute of America** to browse its expansive bookstore.

After a full day of wine-tasting, give your taste buds a rest with dinner at the **Sam's Social Club,** where the festive atmosphere is favorite among locals, in laid-back Calistoga. From Calistoga, the drive back to San Francisco will take 1.5-2 hours.

Overnight: Spend the night at **Dr. Wilkinson's Hot Springs Resort** where you can greet the next morning with a spa treatment before spending a second day exploring Sonoma.

One Day in Sonoma
40-50 MILES, 1-1.5 HOURS
FROM SAN FRANCISCO
From Napa, Highway 121 winds west through the Carneros wine region. Stop off for a bit of Carneros chardonnay at gorgeous **Cuvaison,** where you can practically touch the vineyards

Julia Pfieffer Burns State Park

from the handsome tasting room, or head all the way over for the famous bubbly at **Gloria Ferrer,** with views to match. From Highway 121, Highway 12 twists north into Sonoma. Stretch your legs in Sonoma Plaza and explore the charming downtown area. Stop in at the **Sonoma Mission** for a bit of history, then grab a lunch at **the girl & the fig,** housed in the historic Sonoma Hotel.

After lunch, continue up the valley to Glen Ellen. Learn about biodynamic farming on the tractor-led tour at **Benziger Family Winery,** or cozy up with a delicate pinot at the homey tasting room of the **Eric Ross Winery.** Finish your tasting tour with a big merlot at red wine specialist **St. Francis Winery,** where a friendly atmosphere is combined with stunning picture windows. Then head to **The Fig Café** and savor some heavenly French bistro fare. San Francisco is a little over an hour away.

Overnight: Spend the night at the **Sonoma Hotel** on the plaza in Sonoma.

Three Days in Monterey and Big Sur

Monterey and Big Sur are popular day trips from the San Francisco Bay Area and the scenic coastal drive along Highway 1 is not to be missed.

One Day in Monterey Bay
112 MILES, 2 HOURS FROM SAN FRANCISCO
Attractions in Santa Cruz and Monterey, plus the charm of Carmel, can easily fill your itinerary.

From San Francisco, take U.S. 101 south to Highway 17 through the redwoods to the laid-back town of Santa Cruz. Ride the rides on the **Santa Cruz Beach Boardwalk** and dig your toes in the sand on the beach. Once you've gotten your fill of sun, continue an hour south to Monterey and the **Monterey Bay Aquarium.** Dine at **Montrio,** or splurge at **Aubergine** in quaint Carmel.

The state's big-name attractions can draw endless crowds. These hidden gems offer a more intimate perspective.

- Tickets to **Alcatraz** sell out months in advance. **Angel Island State Park** has greater recreation options, the same spectacular views, and fewer crowds—all for the price of a ferry ride.

- **Napa** and **Sonoma** earn accolades for their fantastic wines, but the tiny towns can barely accommodate all the traveling oenophiles. The Gold Country's **Shenandoah Valley** is relatively unexplored, lined with excellent wineries and plenty of Gold Rush history.

- **Tahoe**'s beaches are often swarmed in summer. Head instead to **Donner Memorial State Park,** where lovely Donner Lake offers a peaceful spot far from Tahoe's crowds.

- **Yosemite Valley** can resemble an overflowing parking lot in summer, when visitors risk being turned away. Just south, **Sequoia and Kings Canyon National Parks** offer towering redwoods and scenic canyons, and share the same granite cliffs as their more famous neighbor.

- The views of the **Big Sur Coast** can take your breath away—if the winding road is open and

Trinidad

passable. If not, cruise north along Highway 1 to the artsy town of **Mendocino** or the secluded headlands around **Trinidad.**

Overnight: The delightful **Cypress Inn** in Carmel provides a quick launch to the coastal wonders of Big Sur the next day.

Two Days in Big Sur
140 MILES, 3 HOURS FROM SAN FRANCISCO

Big Sur captures the best qualities of the California coast: windswept beaches and pounding surf, verdant state parks with majestic redwoods, and the literary solitude of the Beats. Although possible to do as a day trip, two days will allow you to better enjoy the splendor of this region.

Part of Big Sur's appeal is the drive along Highway 1, the Pacific Coast Highway, lined with historic bridges, pastures of grazing sheep, and breathtaking cliffs. The **Bixby Bridge** marks the official entrance to Big Sur. Stop at **Pfeiffer Big Sur State Park** to hike through the redwoods to Pfeiffer Falls, or walk the short trail to **McWay Falls** farther south in **Julia Pfeiffer Burns State Park.** Thumb through the books at **Henry Miller Memorial Library,** drink in the sunset at **Nepenthe,** and don't miss breakfast at **Deetjen's.**

Overnight: Deetjen's has rustic accommodations in a historic setting, or pitch a tent at **Pfeiffer Big Sur State Park.** Make reservations in advance for both on summer weekends.

Yosemite National Park

Three Days in Yosemite and Tahoe

From San Francisco, it's just a four-hour drive to either **Lake Tahoe** or **Yosemite National Park;** from Sacramento, they are even closer. Combine a trip to both in summer by crossing through Yosemite via the Tioga Pass Road (Hwy. 120). On the eastern side of the Sierra, scenic U.S. 395 leads north almost to the Nevada border, and road-trippers can take forested Highway 89 west to its junction with U.S. 50 to continue to South Lake Tahoe.

One Day in Yosemite
200 MILES, 4 HOURS FROM SAN FRANCISCO

From the north, **Yosemite National Park** is most easily accessed from Highway 120 through the Big Oak Flat Entrance.

In **Yosemite Valley,** hop on board the Valley Shuttle for a scenic car-free exploration of the sights, especially **Bridalveil Fall, El Capitan,** and **Half Dome.** The best way to experience

Yosemite's beauty is on one of its many trails; enjoy a leisurely stroll around **Mirror Lake,** scale a waterfall on the **Mist Trail,** or test your powers of endurance on the way to **Upper Yosemite Fall.** Afterward, reward your efforts with a pit stop at the **Majestic Yosemite Hotel** bar to soak in the valley views.

Overnight: It takes advance planning to score a campground reservation in Yosemite Valley, especially in summer. Try your luck with one of the first-come, first-served campgrounds such as **Camp 4** or **Tuolumne Meadows** (summer only)—but be sure to get there before noon.

Two Days in Yosemite

Highway 120 becomes Tioga Road as it continues east through Yosemite's high country. This seasonal road is only open late spring to late fall; plan your trip in the shoulder seasons (spring and fall) to avoid the crowds. Along the way, gape at jaw-dropping vistas from **Olmsted Point,** gaze at

Lake Tahoe

crystal-clear alpine lakes and grassy **Tuolumne Meadows,** and explore some of Yosemite's rugged high-elevation backcountry on hikes to **Cathedral Lakes.** Tioga Road peaks at Tioga Pass as it leaves the park, descending to the arid desert along U.S. 395. Here, abandoned ghost towns like **Bodie State Historic Park** and saline **Mono Lake** characterize the drier Eastern Sierra.

One Day in Tahoe
190 MILES, 3-4 HOURS FROM SAN FRANCISCO OR YOSEMITE VALLEY

U.S. 50 enters the Tahoe region on the popular **South Shore** of Lake Tahoe. Stop in at one of the casinos across the **Nevada** state line, or take in the lay of the land on the **Heavenly Gondola.** Highway 89 heads west to glittering **Emerald Bay,** where you can hike the **Rubicon Trail** to **Vikingsholm Castle.** Continue north on Highway 89 to reach the **North and West Shores,** which hold Tahoe's legendary ski resorts and sunny beaches. The lively center of **Tahoe City** has plenty of restaurants, hotels, and campgrounds to keep you close to the lake for the night.

Overnight: Spend the night at the **Sunnyside**

Resort in Tahoe City, or camp at General Creek Campground in **Sugar Pine Point State Park** (reservations recommended in summer).

Two Days in Tahoe

In the morning, take Highway 89 east to **Truckee.** Along the way, take a stroll along the **Truckee River,** or stop and shop along the main street in Truckee. While in Truckee, enjoy the Old West vibe and stop for lunch at the **Bar of America,** a Truckee institution since 1974. On your way home, check out the **Donner Memorial State Park.** While the park history tells a grim tale, the hiking trails around the lake are quite beautiful. After your last taste of the Sierra, it is 184 miles back to San Francisco (3.5 hours) or 100 miles to Sacramento (2 hours).

Tahoe in Winter

Nothing says winter like sliding down the slopes at Tahoe. Numerous ski resorts line the lake and mountains. **Heavenly** rules the roost on the South Shore, while **Squaw Valley** draws snowboarders and skiers on the North and West

Shores. Cross-country skiers should head to **Royal Gorge** in the Truckee-Donner area.

Highway 89 and U.S. 50 are the main arteries to the Tahoe area, and they can become congested and blocked by snow into spring. Bring tire chains and plenty of patience—in inclement weather, it can take up to eight hours to drive here from San Francisco.

Classic Road Trips

The classic tour of Northern California is behind the wheel. Don't miss a chance to drive up the **Pacific Coast Highway,** with its quaint towns, giant redwoods, and untamed beaches. Cruising down **Highway 49** in the Gold Country is another favorite, where mining towns, some seemingly preserved in amber, detail California's boom-time beginnings. Shasta and Lassen, with their glaciers, steaming fumaroles, and beautiful desolation, celebrate the state's wild side. To add to the experience, a multitude of **scenic two-lane highways** makes driving from one destination to the next a treat in and of itself.

Cruise the North Coast

Crashing surf, towering redwoods, and rocky beaches typify the rugged Northern California coast. Highway 1 and U.S. 101 twist apart and converge again for almost 400 miles from San Francisco to Crescent City, culminating in one of the state's best and most scenic road trips.

San Francisco to Mendocino
170 MILES, 4-5 HOURS

From San Francisco, travel north over the Golden Gate Bridge to the Bay Area's playground, Marin County. Following Highway 1, stop for a short hike amid coastal redwoods at **Muir Woods**

Point Reyes National Seashore

northern spotted owl in Muir Woods

National Monument before continuing north past Stinson Beach to **Point Reyes National Seashore,** where a wealth of hiking and biking opportunities await. Slurp oysters at **Hog Island Oyster Co.** or stock up on gourmet cheese at **Cowgirl Creamery** for a picnic later. Just an hour north lies **Bodega Bay,** where Alfred Hitchcock's *The Birds* was filmed. January-May you may even spot whales off the coast.

Guerneville makes a fun detour inland from Highway 1. Spend the night at **Creekside Inn & Lodge** and dip your toes—or a canoe—in the **Russian River.** Back on Highway 1, stop for a dose of history at **Fort Ross State Historic Park,** a reconstructed Russian fort. As Highway 1 winds north, the artsy enclave of **Mendocino** beckons. Wander through the **Mendocino Coast Botanical Gardens** and consider spending the night at one of the many quaint B&Bs.

The Redwood Coast
175 MILES, 3-4 HOURS

Highway 1 rejoins U.S. 101 in Leggett and enters the famed Redwood Coast. From **Humboldt Redwoods State Park** near Garberville to **Del Norte Coast Redwoods** south of Crescent City, this 150-mile stretch is rich with hiking and camping opportunities. Cruise the **Avenue of the Giants** and pitch a tent in **Humboldt Redwoods State Park** or snag a campsite at **Prairie Creek Redwoods. Del Norte Coast Redwoods State Park** is the last of the redwoods before **Crescent City.**

Go Wild in Shasta and Lassen

These northern peaks and parklands are some of the state's most spectacular and least visited. Mount Shasta is a paradise for outdoor enthusiasts year-round. You can hike or climb to the summit in the summer and ski down its slopes in winter. Shasta Lake, by contrast, is best in summer, when boating, fishing, and waterskiing can fully be enjoyed. Because of its high elevation and rocky terrain, Mount Lassen's roads are closed late fall to spring, making it a mid- to late-summer destination.

Most services are found in Redding and Red Bluff, which are also the best access points from I-5. Each destination can be a road trip in itself, but you can also make a loop via **Highway 89.** It is a thrilling way to see both peaks and to make the most of a trek this far north.

Sacramento to Mount Shasta
220 MILES, 3.5-4 HOURS

From Sacramento, it takes about 2.5 hours

driving north on I-5 to get to the small city of **Redding,** the gateway for both **Shasta Lake** and **Mount Shasta.** From Redding, continue north on I-5 for just eight miles until you come to Shasta Lake. Turn west on Highway 151 to explore looming **Shasta Dam.** After marveling at its size, head over to the other side of I-5 to experience another kind of wonder, this one made by the hand of nature, and tour the **Lake Shasta Caverns.**

Next, take advantage of what Shasta Lake does best: watery summertime fun. Head over to the **Bridge Bay Resort** where you can rent all you need to go boating, waterskiing, or fishing out on the lake's many fingers and inlets. Rent a room for the night or make the most of your time on the lake by renting a houseboat.

From Shasta Lake, head north on I-5 for 40 miles to **Castle Crags State Park,** where you can try your hand at rock climbing and scale granite faces, domes, and spires. Or you can hike

Mount Shasta

the **Crags Trail to Castle Dome,** a 5.5-mile round-trip with spectacular views.

Next stop is Mount Shasta, only 15 miles up I-5, where more climbing and hiking opportunities await. The **Gray Butte Trail** is a moderate 3.4-mile hike to this small peak, but if the big peak is too irresistible, you can opt for a multiday trek summiting **Mount Shasta.** Winter offers equally fun outdoor adventures, when you can spend all day skiing and snowboarding at **Mount Shasta Ski Park.**

After a full day on the hiking, climbing, or skiing trails, snag a campsite at **Lake Siskiyou Beach and Camp** or opt for a greater indulgence and reward at the **Shasta Mount Inn Retreat & Spa.**

Mount Shasta to Lassen
100 MILES, 2 HOURS
Once you have had your fill of Mount Shasta, head east on Highway 89. The scenic two-lane road winds through mountainous terrain and across wild rivers. One of the best sights along the way is **McArthur-Burney Falls,** claimed to be the most beautiful waterfall in California. This can either be a quick stop, as the falls are near the parking lot, or you can take the time to do a short hike nearby.

You'll enter **Lassen Volcanic National Park** shortly after leaving McArthur-Burney Falls. Because you are entering from the north, you can make a quick stop at the **Loomis Museum** before pressing south to **Lassen Peak;** the beauty and the views on the trail make the effort worthwhile. Nearby is another treat—**Bumpass Hell**—where you can hike surrounded by smoking fumaroles and boiling mud pots.

Camp at either **Manzanita Lake** or **Summit Lake Campgrounds.** From the park, it is less than 200 miles (3-3.5 hours) back to Sacramento.

Gold Country Ramble

A tour through Gold Country is a road trip rich in history, beautiful scenery, outdoor adventure, and even wine-tasting. **Highway 49** runs for 127 miles through the heart of Gold Country from Nevada City to Jamestown. Sacramento is near the northern Gold Country and a great place to start a historic tour. You can easily extend this trip to Yosemite via Highway 120 (2 hours) or continue east on U.S. 50 in Placerville to reach Lake Tahoe in a mere 1.5 hours.

Sacramento to Northern Gold Country
60 MILES, 1-1.5 HOURS
In **Sacramento,** start your day early with a tour of the **Capitol Building** and see where all the big decisions are made. Walk over to **Old Sacramento** and the **California State Railroad Museum,** where the history of the gold rush and the golden era of the railroad come alive. To really drink in the atmosphere, step into **Fat City Bar and Café** to enjoy comfort food served in a 19th-century dining room, or head over to the hip Midtown district to **Mulvaney's Building & Loan** and sample Sacramento's epicurean renaissance.

Take I-80 east for 32 miles until you reach Auburn in Northern Gold Country, then detour north on Highway 49 for 23 miles to **Grass Valley.** Stop at the **Empire Mine State Historic Park** and get a feel for the toil, hardship, dreams, and occasional wild luck that shaped the Gold Country. Charming Grass Valley offers food and shopping, or go straight to **Nevada City,** only three miles away, and spend the afternoon strolling its narrow streets. The **Outside Inn** offers unique guest rooms that border the creek, and **Three Forks Bakery and Brewery** serves some of the best food in Gold Country.

Sacramento

Northern to Southern Gold Country
100 MILES, 2-3 HOURS

Fuel up with breakfast in **Auburn** at **Awful Annie's** then head south on Highway 49 for one hour to **Placerville.** Take a thrilling white-water rafting trip on the American River near **Coloma,** or tour **Marshall Gold Discovery State Historic Park,** the site where James Marshall discovered gold in 1848. Next, hit the wineries and orchards around **Apple Hill** and taste the Gold Country's best vintages. Consider staying nearby at the **Historic Cary House Hotel.**

It is 60 winding miles from Placerville down Highway 49 to **Angels Camp,** the heart of Southern Gold Country. Visit the **Angels Camp Museum and Carriage House,** which beautifully showcases 30 carriages and wagons

from the gold rush era. Grab a bite at the **Angels Creek Café,** then venture east for eight miles on Highway 4 to **Murphys** and descend 162 feet below the ground into **Mercer Cavern,** then taste some wine along Murphys' Main Street.

Head down to **Columbia,** where most of downtown is part of the **Columbia State Historic Park.** Stroll the preserved streets of this gold rush boomtown to get a feel for what life was like when the mines operated. Stick around for dinner at the **Columbia City Hotel Restaurant,** where fine dining meets Old West elegance.

Accommodations await a short jog west on Highway 108 in **Jamestown,** where the **National Hotel** has been in operation since 1859. Enjoy a hearty brunch at the restaurant downstairs before returning to Sacramento (2 hours, 114 miles).

San Francisco

T he regular grid pattern found on maps of San Francisco leaves visitors unprepared for the precipitous inclines and stunning water views in this town built on 43 hills.

Geographically and culturally, San Francisco is anything but flat, and what level ground exists might at any moment give way. While earthquakes remake the land, social upheavals play a similar role, reminding locals that the only constant here is change. In the 1950s, the Beats challenged postwar conformity and left a legacy of incantatory poems and independent bookstores. The late 1960s saw a years-long Summer of Love, which shifted consciousness as surely as quakes shift tectonic plates. Gay and lesbian liberation movements sprung forth in the 1970s, as did a renewed push for women's rights. Since then, a vibrant culture of technological innovation has taken root and continues to rapidly evolve as groundbreaking companies and tech visionaries choose to make the city their home.

Although San Francisco is one of the most visited cities in the United States, it often seems like a provincial village, or a series of villages that share a downtown and a roster of world-class icons. Drive over the Golden Gate or the Bay Bridge as the fog is lifting and your heart will catch at the ever-changing beauty of the scene. Stand at the base of the Transamerica Pyramid, hang off the side of a cable car, or just walk through the neighborhoods that make the city more than the sum of its parts. Despite the hills, San Francisco is a city that cries out to be explored on foot.

PLANNING YOUR TIME

Spend at least one weekend in San Francisco and focus your time downtown. Union Square makes a great base, thanks to its plethora of hotels, shops, and easy access to public transportation, but it can be fairly dead at night.

With a full week, you can explore Golden Gate Park's excellent museums—the de Young and the California Academy of Sciences—hike the trails of the Presidio, take a scenic, foggy stroll across the Golden Gate Bridge, and dive into the Mission's hip culinary culture.

Previous: San Francisco skyline; farm land on the Peninsula. Above: redwood trees.

Highlights

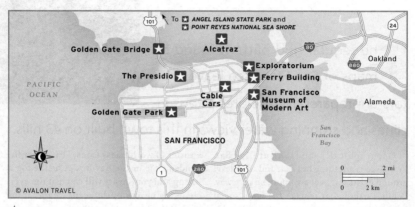

★ **Cable Cars:** Nothing is more iconic than climbing San Francisco's steep hills on a historic cable car (page 36).

★ **Ferry Building:** The 1898 Ferry Building has been renovated and reimagined as the foodie mecca of San Francisco (page 37).

★ **San Francisco Museum of Modern Art:** After a massive renovation, SFMOMA showcases some of modern art's greatest hits with a space dedicated to photography (page 38).

★ **Exploratorium:** Kids and adults love to explore San Francisco's innovative and interactive science museum (page 44).

★ **Alcatraz:** Spend the day in prison at the historically famous former maximum-security penitentiary in the middle of the bay (page 44).

★ **The Presidio:** The original 1776 El Presidio de San Francisco is now a public park filled with hiking trails, beaches, and historic buildings (page 48).

★ **Golden Gate Bridge:** Nothing beats the view from one of the most famous and fascinating bridges in the country (page 49).

★ **Golden Gate Park:** The city's park is home to the stunning de Young Museum, the inventive California Academy of Sciences, and the historic San Francisco Botanical Gardens (page 51).

★ **Angel Island State Park:** This unique park in the middle of the bay is filled with history, wilderness, and great views (page 81).

★ **Point Reyes National Seashore:** Point Reyes is home to tule elk, desolate beaches, dairy farms, lighthouses, and remote wilderness trails (page 89).

San Francisco Bay Area

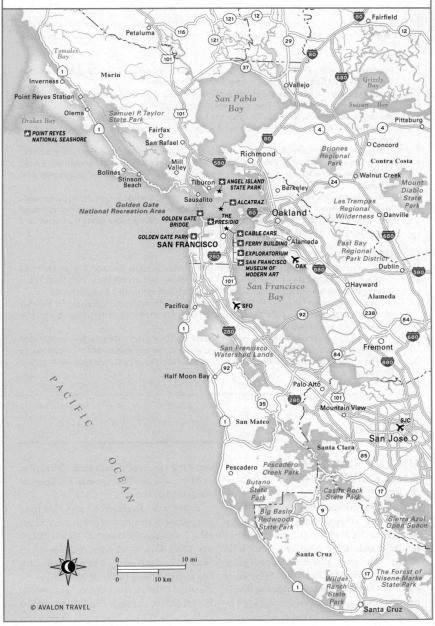

© AVALON TRAVEL

Two Days in San Francisco

San Francisco may only be roughly seven miles long and seven miles wide, but it packs in historic neighborhoods, iconic landmarks, and dozens of stomach-dropping inclines within its small area.

DAY 1

Start your day at the **Ferry Building**. Graze from the many vendors, including **Blue Bottle Café, Cowgirl Creamery,** and **Acme Bread Company.**

After touring the gourmet shops, catch the Muni F line to Jefferson Street and take a stroll along **Fisherman's Wharf.** Stop into the **Musée Mécanique** to play a few coin-operated antique arcade games. Near Pier 39, catch the ferry to **Alcatraz**—be sure to buy your tickets well in advance. Alcatraz will fill your mind with amazing stories from the legendary island prison.

After you escape from Alcatraz, follow Columbus Avenue to **North Beach,** and wander the streets of **Chinatown.** Browse **City Lights,** the legendary Beat generation bookstore, then toast their iconoclasm at neighboring **Vesuvio,** a colorful watering hole and former Beat hangout.

Next comes pizza at **Tony's Pizza Napoletana,** on Washington Square. Now you are ready to enjoy the talented performers, silly jokes, and gravity-defying hats of the long-running theater production *Beach Blanket Babylon*. If theater is not your thing, take a cab to the Mission and grab a cocktail at **Beretta,** followed by a show at **The Chapel.**

DAY 2

Fortify yourself for a day of sightseeing with a hearty breakfast at **Brenda's French Soul Food.** Next, drive or take a cab to the **Cliff House** where you can walk the **Lands End Trail,** investigating the ruins of the former Sutro Baths and exploring the city's rocky coastline.

Continue south to **Golden Gate Park** and delve into art at the fabulous **de Young Museum** or science at the **California Academy of Sciences.** Stroll the serene **Japanese Tea Garden** and get a snack at the Tea House.

For dinner, your options are legion. Head to the Fillmore District for California dim sum at **State Bird Provisions,** to the Mission District for traditional Mexican cuisine at **La Taqueria,** to hip Hayes Valley for beer and bratwurst at **Suppenküche,** or to Castro favorite, **Anchor Oyster Bar.**

Sights

UNION SQUARE AND DOWNTOWN
★ **Cable Cars**

A San Francisco icon, the **cable car** (www.sfmta.com) was originally conceived by Andrew Smith Hallidie as a safer alternative for traveling the steep, often slick hills of San Francisco. Cable cars ran as regular mass transit from 1873 into the 1940s, when buses and electric streetcars began to dominate the landscape. Dedicated citizens, especially "Cable Car Lady" Friedel Klussmann,

saved the cable car system from extinction, and the cable cars have become a rolling national landmark.

Today you can ride the cable cars from one tourist destination to another for $7 per ride. A full-day **"passport" ticket** ($22/1 day, $33/3 days, $43/7 days, includes streetcars and buses) is worth it to run around the city all day. Routes run from Nob Hill to the Financial District, from Union Square along Powell Street, through Chinatown, and to Fisherman's Wharf. Take a seat or grab one of the exterior poles and hang on! Cable cars have open-air seating only, making for a chilly ride on foggy days.

The cars get stuffed to capacity on weekends and during weekday rush hours. Expect an hour wait for a ride at any of the turn-around points on a weekend or holiday. But a ride on a cable car from Union Square down to the Wharf is more than worth the wait. The views from the hills down to the bay inspire wonder even in lifetime residents. To learn a bit more, make a stop at the **Cable Car Museum** (1201 Mason St., 415/474-1887, www.cablecarmuseum.org, 10am-6pm daily Apr.-Oct., 10am-5pm daily Nov.-Mar., free), the home and nerve center of the entire fleet.

Grace Cathedral

The iconic **Grace Cathedral** (1100 California St., 415/749-6300, www.gracecathedral.org, 8am-6pm daily) is many things to many people. The French Gothic-style edifice, completed in 1964, attracts architecture lovers by the thousands with its facade, stained glass, and furnishings. The labyrinths—replicas of the Chartres Cathedral labyrinth in France—appeal to meditative walkers seeking spiritual solace. Concerts featuring world music, sacred music, and modern classical ensembles draw audiences from around the bay and farther afield.

To view some of the church's lesser-seen areas, sign up for the 1.5-hour **Grace Cathedral Grand Tour** (415/749-6316, 10am, days vary, $25).

★ Ferry Building

Restored to its former glory, the 1898 **San Francisco Ferry Building** (1 Ferry Bldg., 415/983-8030, www.ferrybuildingmarketplace.com, 10am-7pm Mon.-Fri., 8am-6pm Sat., 11am-5pm Sun., businesses hours vary) stands sentinel at the end of Market Street at the water's edge. Its peaked 245-foot clock tower beckons foodies and commuters alike to the white Beaux Arts building. Inside the main lobby, photos and interpretive plaques bring the history of the Ferry Building to life.

Along the interior Nave (main corridor), shops hawk top-tier artisanal food and drinks. Grab a baguette from **Acme Bread Company** (shop #15, 7am-7:30pm Mon.-Fri., 8am-7pm Sat.-Sun.) and a selection of cheeses at **Cowgirl Creamery** (shop #17, 10am-7pm Mon.-Fri., 8am-6pm Sat., 10am-5pm Sun.) for a quick snack, or gorge on a scoop of bourbon caramel ice cream from **Humphry Slocombe** (shop #10, 11am-9pm Sun.-Fri.,

cable car

8am-9pm Sat.) while strolling the high-end kitchenwares at Sur La Table (store #37, 9am-6:30pm Mon.-Fri., 8am-6:30pm Sat., 10am-6:30pm Sun.).

Outside, the Farmers Market (415/291-3276, 10am-2pm Tues. and Thurs., 8am-2pm Sat.) is filled with rows upon rows of stalls overflowing with fresh organic produce and sustainably raised meats.

Amid this foodie paradise, the Ferry Building still operates as a commute hub, with ferry service via the Blue and Gold Fleet (www.blueandgoldfleet.com), Golden Gate Ferry (http://goldengateferry.org), and San Francisco Bay Ferry (https://sanfranciscobayferry.com).

★ San Francisco Museum of Modern Art

After a three-year renovation, SFMOMA (151 3rd St., 415/357-4000, www.sfmoma.org, 10am-5pm Fri.-Tues., 10am-9pm Thurs., adults $25, seniors $22, students 19-24 $19, children 18 and under free) is an architectural wonder with 45,000 square feet filled with giant installations. The museum's expansive permanent collection includes work from Henri Matisse, Shiro Kuramata, Wayne Thiebaud, Richard Diebenkorn, and Chuck Close, as well exciting visiting exhibits such as works by Robert Rauschenberg and Louis Bourgeois's giant spiders.

The Pritzker Center for Photography hosts the largest space dedicated to photographic art in the country. Wander outside amid the 3rd-floor sculpture terrace or ascend to the 5th floor to walk across the Oculus Bridge and take in the building's stunning design.

Contemporary Jewish Museum

Inside a striking geodesic structure, the Contemporary Jewish Museum (736 Mission St., 415/655-7800, www.thecjm.org, 11am-5pm Fri.-Tues., 11am-8pm Thurs., adults $14, seniors and students $12, children 18 and under free) hosts a wide range of events and performances, including lectures, family art making, and traveling exhibitions such as a retrospective of Stanley Kubrick and the art of Rube Goldberg.

Museum of the African Diaspora

Explore that which connects us at the Museum of the African Diaspora (685 Mission St., 415/358-7200, www.moadsf.org, 11am-6pm Wed.-Sat., noon-5pm Sun., adults

Grace Cathedral

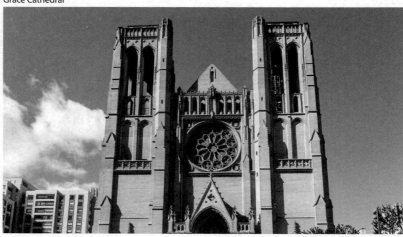

$10, seniors and students $5, under 13 free), a museum dedicated to our collective connection to Africa, the birthplace of humanity. Four main galleries host a variety of rotating exhibits on subjects from Carnival and the performance art of the Caribbean to an oral history exhibit of San Francisco's Bayview neighborhood.

Yerba Buena Gardens

Yerba Buena Gardens (750 Howard St., 415/820-3550, http://yerbabuenagardens. com, 6am-10pm daily) are an oasis of green in SoMa's museum district. Verdant lawns host public art and performances. A variety of attractions include the **Yerba Buena Center for the Arts** (700 Howard St., 415/978-2700, www.ybca.org, 11am-6pm Tues.-Wed. and Fri.-Sun., 11am-8pm Thurs., $10), a gallery space filled with contemporary art that also hosts live theater, dance, and musical performances.

The **Children's Creativity Museum** (221 4th St., 415/820-3320, https://creativity. org, 10am-4pm Wed.-Sun., $13, under 2 free) is where children merge fun with technology, coding robots and making stop-motion films. Other attractions include the 1906 **Le Roy Carousel** (221 4th St., https://creativity.org, 10am-5pm daily, $4, $3 with museum pass), an **ice-skating rink** (750 Folsom St., 415/820-3521, www.skatebowl.com, daily, hours vary, adults and children 6-54 $12, seniors 55 and older, $10, children under 6 $7, skate rentals $5), and a **bowling alley** (750 Folsom St., 415/820-3541, www.skatebowl.com, daily, hours vary, $22-27/hour).

NORTH BEACH AND FISHERMAN'S WHARF

North Beach has long served as the Little Italy of San Francisco, a fact still reflected in the restaurants in the neighborhood. North Beach truly made its mark in the 1950s when it was, for a brief time, home to many writers in the Beat generation, including Jack Kerouac, Gary Snyder, and Allen Ginsberg.

Keeping the flame alive, the **Beat Museum** (540 Broadway, 415/399-9626, www.kerouac.com, 10am-7pm daily) exhibits first editions, letters, and memorabilia of the era, along with regular readings by contemporary poets.

Chinatown

The massive Chinese migration to California began almost as soon as the news of easy gold in the mountain streams made it to East Asia. In San Francisco, Chinese immigrants carved out a thriving community at the border of **Portsmouth Square,** then center of the young city, which eventually became known as Chinatown. Along with much of San Francisco, the neighborhood was destroyed in the 1906 earthquake and fire.

Today visitors see the post-1906 visitor-friendly Chinatown that was built after the quake, particularly if they enter through the **Chinatown Gate** (Grant Ave. and Bush St.) at the edge of Union Square. In this historic neighborhood, beautiful Asian architecture mixes with more mundane blocky city buildings to create a unique skyline. Small alleyways wend between the touristy commercial corridors, creating an intimate atmosphere.

Coit Tower

Built in 1933 as a monument to benefactor Lillie Hitchcock Coit's beloved firefighters, **Coit Tower** (1 Telegraph Hill Blvd., 415/249-0995, http://sfrecpark.org, 10am-6pm daily May-Oct., 10am-5pm daily Nov.-Apr., entrance free, tours $5-8, call for tour times) has beautified the city just as Coit intended. Inside the art deco tower, the walls are covered in the restored frescoes painted in 1934 depicting city and California life during the Great Depression. Ride the **elevator** (adults $8, seniors and youth $5, children 5-11 $2, under 5 free) to the top and on a clear day you can see the whole city.

To get there, walk up Telegraph Hill Boulevard through Pioneer Park. When exiting, descend down either the Filbert or Greenwich steps to see the lovely cottages and gardens of beautiful **Telegraph Hill.**

San Francisco

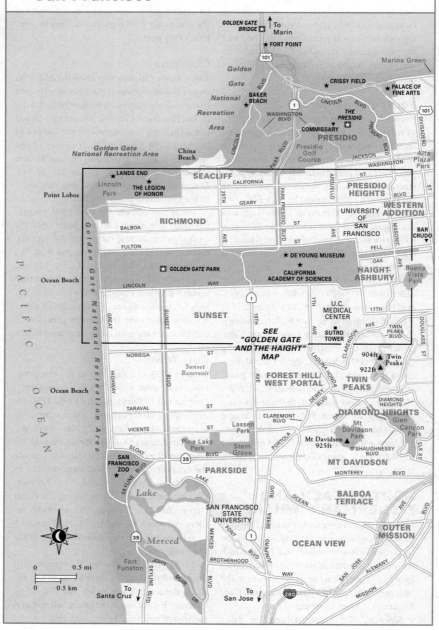

GOLDEN GATE
BRIDGE → To
         Marin
★ FORT POINT
101
Marina Green
Golden
Gate
★ CRISSY FIELD
★ PALACE OF
FINE ARTS
National
BAKER
BEACH
LINCOLN   BLVD
101
Recreation
WASHINGTON
BLVD
THE
PRESIDIO
Area
COMMISSARY
PRESIDIO
Golden Gate
National Recreation Area
China
Beach
Presidio
Golf
Course
JACKSON
WASHINGTON
Alta
Plaza
Park
★ LANDS END
SEACLIFF
CALIFORNIA
PRESIDIO
HEIGHTS
Lincoln
Park
THE LEGION
OF HONOR
25TH
GEARY
PARK PRESIDIO
ARGUELLO
BLVD
Point Lobos
WESTERN
ADDITION
UNIVERSITY
OF
SAN
FRANCISCO
MASONIC
BAR
CRUDO
RICHMOND
BALBOA
AVE
ST
BLVD
AVE
FELL
OAK
FULTON
DE YOUNG MUSEUM
HAIGHT-
ASHBURY
Buena
Vista
Park
Ocean Beach
GOLDEN GATE PARK
CALIFORNIA
ACADEMY OF SCIENCES
LINCOLN
WAY
7TH
U.C.
MEDICAL
CENTER
17TH
AVE
TWIN
PEAKS
BLVD
DOUGLASS
ST
SUNSET
19TH
CLARENDON
SUTRO
TOWER
SEE
"GOLDEN GATE
AND THE HAIGHT"
MAP
904ft ▲ Twin
922ft ▲ Peaks
NORIEGA
ST
LAGUNA HONDA
AVE
FOREST HILL
WEST PORTAL
TWIN
PEAKS
Sunset
Reservoir
DEWEY
BLVD
DIAMOND
HEIGHTS
TARAVAL
ST
CLAREMONT
BLVD
DIAMOND HEIGHTS
Mt
Davidson
Park
Glen
Canyon
Park
VICENTE
ST
Lassen
Park
PORTOLA
DR
ELK ST
Pine Lake
Park
Stern
Grove
Mt Davidson ▲
925ft
O'SHAUGHNESSY
BLVD
SAN
FRANCISCO
ZOO
SLOAT
SKYLINE BLVD
35
LAKE
BLVD
MT DAVIDSON
MONTEREY
BLVD
PARKSIDE
BALBOA
TERRACE
Lake
OCEAN
AVE
Merced
SAN FRANCISCO
STATE
UNIVERSITY
MERCED
FONT
BLVD
JUNIPERO
SERRA
BLVD
SAN
JOSE
ALEMANY
AVE
BLVD
OUTER
MISSION
35
OCEAN VIEW
Fort
Funston
JOHN
MUIR
DR
SKYLINE
BLVD
BROTHERHOOD
WAY
1
280
MISSION
→ To
Santa Cruz
→ To
San Jose

PACIFIC

OCEAN

Ocean Beach

Golden Gate National Recreation Area

0   0.5 mi
0   0.5 km

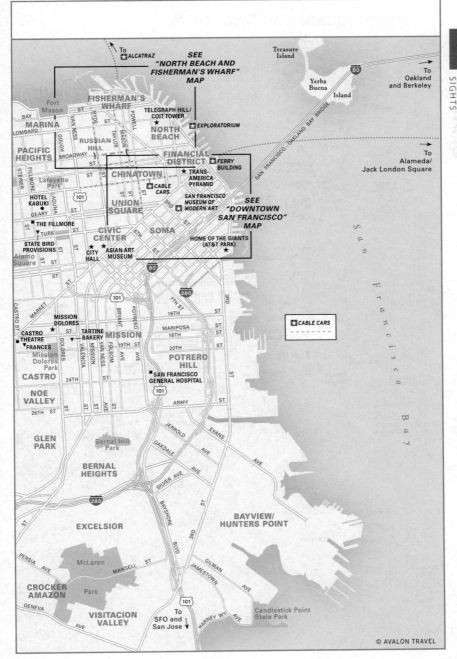

To **★**ALCATRAZ

SEE
"NORTH BEACH AND
FISHERMAN'S WHARF"
MAP

Treasure
Island

Yerba
Buena
Island

→ To
Oakland
and Berkeley

Fort
Mason

**FISHERMAN'S
WHARF**

TELEGRAPH HILL/
COIT TOWER
★ EXPLORATORIUM

BAY

MARINA

LOMBARD

**PACIFIC
HEIGHTS**

**RUSSIAN
HILL**

BROADWAY

**NORTH
BEACH**

**FINANCIAL
DISTRICT** **★** FERRY
BUILDING

→ To
Alameda/
Jack London Square

SAN FRANCISCO OAKLAND BAY BRIDGE

CHINATOWN

★ CABLE
CARS

★ TRANS-
AMERICA
PYRAMID

Lafayette
Park

STEINER

HOTEL
KABUKI

FILLMORE
LAGUNA

GEARY

**UNION
SQUARE**

SAN FRANCISCO
MUSEUM OF
★ MODERN ART

SEE
"DOWNTOWN
SAN FRANCISCO"
MAP

■ THE FILLMORE

TURK

**CIVIC
CENTER**

SOMA

S a n

STATE BIRD
PROVISIONS

Alamo
Square

★ CITY
HALL

★ ASIAN ART
MUSEUM

HOME OF THE GIANTS
(AT&T PARK)
★

F r a n c i s c o

MARKET

7TH ST

3RD

★ CABLE CARS

B a y

CASTRO ST

MISSION
DOLORES

CASTRO
THEATRE
■ FRANCES

TARTINE
BAKERY

MISSION

16TH
ST
MARIPOSA
18TH
ST
20TH

POTRERO

BRYANT

DOLORES

VALENCIA

MISSION

VAN NESS
AVE

FOLSOM

19TH
ST

**POTRERO
HILL**

Mission
Dolores
Park

CASTRO

24TH

■ SAN FRANCISCO
GENERAL HOSPITAL

**NOE
VALLEY**

26TH ST

ARMY

**GLEN
PARK**

Bernal Hill
Park

JERROLD

EVANS

**BERNAL
HEIGHTS**

OAKDALE

AVE

AVE

EXCELSIOR

SILVER AVE

BAYSHORE

3RD

**BAYVIEW/
HUNTERS POINT**

PERSIA

AVE

McLaren

MANSELL ST

JAMESTOWN

AVE

**CROCKER
AMAZON**

GENEVA

Park

GILMAN

AVE

Candlestick Point
State Park

**VISITACION
VALLEY**

AVE

To
SFO and
San Jose ↓

HARNEY WY

© AVALON TRAVEL

Union Square and Downtown

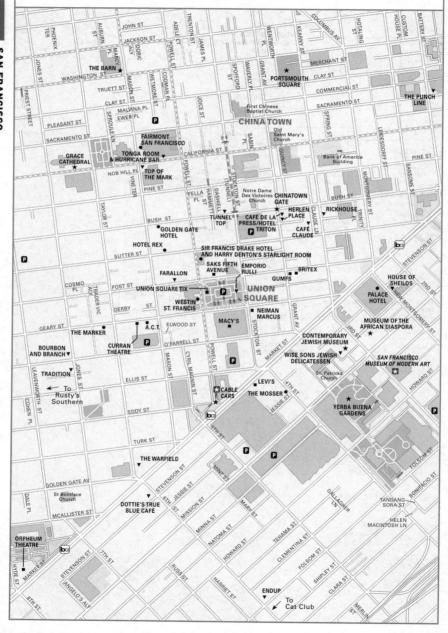

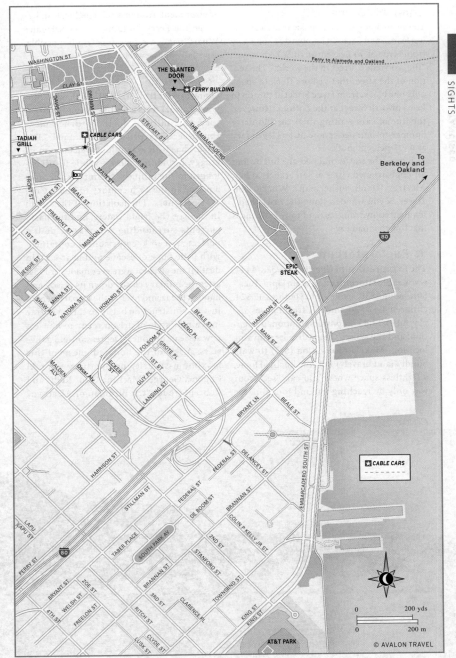

Lombard Street

You've no doubt seen it in postcards and movies: **Lombard Street** (Lombard St., one-way from Hyde St. to Leavenworth St.), known as "the crookedest street in the world." The section of the street that visitors flock to spans only one block, from Hyde Street at the top to Leavenworth Street at the bottom. However, the line of cars waiting their turn to drive bumper-to-bumper can be just as legendary as its 27 percent grade.

Bypass the traffic and take the hill by foot for unobstructed vistas of San Francisco Bay, Alcatraz Island, Fisherman's Wharf, Coit Tower as you wander along the brick steps, manicured hydrangeas, and tony residences that line the roadway.

★ Exploratorium

The **Exploratorium** (Pier 15, 415/528-4444, www.exploratorium.edu, 10am-5pm Tues.-Sun., adults $30, seniors and youth 13-17 $24, children 4-12 $20, under 4 free) houses 150 playful exhibits on physics, motion, perception, and the senses that utilize its stunning location. Make a reservation ($15) to walk blindly (and bravely) into the Tactile Dome, a lightless space where you can "see" your way only by reaching out and touching the environment around you. The location between the Ferry Building and Fisherman's Wharf makes a crowd-free trip impossible, especially on the weekends.

★ Alcatraz

Going to **Alcatraz** (415/561-4900, www.nps.gov/alcatraz) feels a bit like going to purgatory; this military fortress-turned-maximum-security prison, nicknamed "The Rock," has little warmth or welcome on its craggy, forbidding shores. While it still belonged to the military, the fortress became a prison in the 19th century to house Civil War prisoners. The isolation of the island in the bay, the frigid waters, and the nasty currents surrounding Alcatraz made it a perfect spot to keep prisoners contained, with little hope of escape and near-certain death if the attempt were ever made. In 1934, after the military closed down its prison and handed the island over to the Department of Justice, construction began to turn Alcatraz into a new style of prison ready to house a new style of prisoner: Depression-era gangsters. A few of the honored guests of this maximum-security penitentiary were Al Capone, George "Machine Gun" Kelly, and Robert Stroud, "the Birdman of Alcatraz."

Alcatraz

The prison closed in 1963, and in 1964 and 1969 occupations were staged by Indians of All Tribes, an exercise that eventually led to self-determination for North America's original inhabitants.

Today, Alcatraz is part of the Golden Gate National Recreation Area and the island welcomes millions of visitors each year. Highlights include audio cell-house tours, interpretive walks, and informative video presentations.

GETTING THERE

To see Alcatraz, you must book a tour 90 days to one week in advance with **Alcatraz Cruises** (Pier 33, 415/981-7625, www.alcatrazcruises.com, 8:45am-7:45pm daily). All tours depart from Pier 33 for the ferry ride to the island and most sell out far in advance. Choose from the following:

The basic **Day Tour** (daily, adults $38, seniors $35.75, children 12-17 $37.25, children 5-11 $23.25, children under 5 free; family pack $114.75) includes a self-guided audio tour and allows you to explore the island at your own pace.

The **Behind the Scenes Tour** (4.5-hours, Thurs.-Mon., adults $90, seniors $83.75, children 12-17 $86, children under age 12 not permitted) is docent-led.

The chilling **Night Tour** (2.5 hours, Thurs.-Mon., adults $45, seniors $41.75, children 12-17 $44, children 5-11 $26.75, children under 5 free) visits the prison at sunset and has been voted one of the best tours in the Bay Area.

The company also offers a combined **Alcatraz and Angel Island Tour** (5.5 hours, Sat.-Sun. Mar.-Oct and daily June-Oct. 1, adults $71.50, seniors $69.50, children 12-17 $71.50, children 5-11 $48.25, children under 5 free), which hops between both islands.

Pier 39

Pier 39 (www.pier39.com) hosts a wealth of restaurants, shops, and attractions. Start with the unusual **Aquarium of the Bay** (415/623-5300, www.aquariumofthebay.com, 9am-8pm

daily summer, 10am-6pm daily fall-spring, adults $27, seniors $21, children 4-12 $17, children under 4 free). A 300-foot, clear-walled tunnel lets visitors see thousands of species native to the San Francisco Bay, including sharks, rays, and plenty of fish. For a special treat, take the **Behind the Scenes** (45 minutes, 1pm Mon.-Thurs., 1pm and 4pm Fri.-Sun., $17, ages 8 and up) or **Feed the Sharks** (75 minutes, 2:30pm Tues., Thurs., and Sun., $27, ages 8 and up) tours.

Farther down the pier, get close (but not *too* close) to the local colony of **sea lions.** These big, loud mammals tend to congregate at K-Dock in the West Marina. The best time to see them is in winter, when the population grows to the hundreds. To learn more about the sea lions, visit the interpretive center on Level 2 of the **Sea Lion Center** (415/623-5300, http://bayecotarium.org 10am-5pm daily, free).

A perennial family favorite, the **San Francisco Carousel** (10am-9pm daily, $5/ride) is painted with beautiful scenes of the city. Ride moving horses and carriages while looking out onto the pier. Kids love the daily shows (showtimes vary, free) by local street performers—jugglers, magicians, stand-up comedians—at the adjacent stage.

Fisherman's Wharf

Fisherman's Wharf (Beach St. from Powell St. to Van Ness Ave., www.fishermanswharf.org) sprawls along the waterfront and inland several blocks, drawing tourists to its dime-store attractions, souvenir shops, and pricey seafood eateries. Despite its tourist mecca status, the Wharf encompasses important (and fun) pieces of San Francisco's heritage, including the **Fisherman's and Seaman's Memorial Chapel** (Pier 45, 415/674-7503) and the **Musée Mécanique** (Pier 45, 415/346-2000, www.museemecanique.org, 10am-7pm Mon.-Fri., 10am-8pm Sat.-Sun., free), an arcade dating more than a century old.

Fisherman's Wharf is reachable by the Muni F line and the Hyde-Powell cable car.

North Beach and Fisherman's Wharf

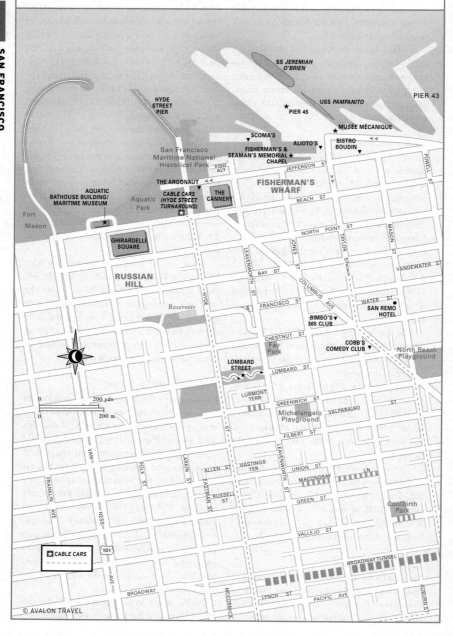

SS JEREMIAH O'BRIEN

USS PAMPANITO

PIER 43

HYDE STREET PIER

★ PIER 45

MUSÉE MÉCANIQUE

▼ SCOMA'S

BISTRO BOUDIN ▼

ALIOTO'S ▼

San Francisco Maritime National Historical Park

FISHERMAN'S & SEAMAN'S MEMORIAL ★ CHAPEL

FISH ALY

JEFFERSON ST

POWELL ST

THE ARGONAUT ◄◄ ▼

FISHERMAN'S WHARF

AQUATIC BATHOUSE BUILDING/ MARITIME MUSEUM

CABLE CARS (HYDE STREET TURNAROUND) ★

THE CANNERY

BEACH ST

Aquatic Park

Fort Mason

GHIRARDELLI SQUARE

NORTH POINT ST

JONES ST

TAYLOR ST

MASON ST

RUSSIAN HILL

VANDEWATER ST

LEAVENWORTH ST

BAY ST

COLUMBUS AVE

Reservoir

HYDE ST

FRANCISCO ST

WATER ST

SAN REMO HOTEL

BIMBO'S 365 CLUB ▼

CHESTNUT ST

COBB'S COMEDY CLUB ▼

North Beach Playground

Fay Park

LOMBARD STREET ★

LOMBARD ST

0   200 yds

0   200 m

LURMONT TERR

GREENWICH ST

VALPARAISO

ST

Michelangelo Playground

FILBERT ST

LEAVENWORTH ST

VAN NESS AVE

POLK ST

LARKIN ST

ALLEN ST

HASTINGS TER

EASTMAN ST

RUSSELL ST

UNION ST

MACONDRAY

LN

FRANKLIN AVE

GREEN ST

Coolbirth Park

VALLEJO ST

BROADWAY TUNNEL

★ CABLE CARS

101

BROADWAY

MCCORMICK

LYNCH ST

PACIFIC AVE

AUBURN ST

© AVALON TRAVEL

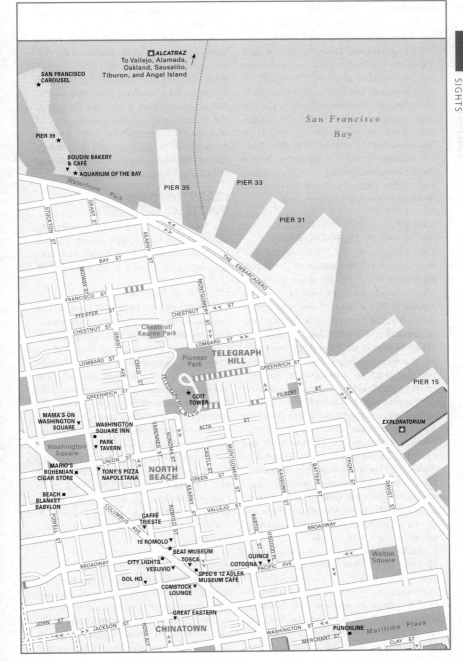

★ ALCATRAZ
To Vallejo, Alameda,
Oakland, Sausalito,
Tiburon, and Angel Island

SAN FRANCISCO
CAROUSEL

San Francisco
Bay

PIER 39

BOUDIN BAKERY
& CAFÉ
★ AQUARIUM OF THE BAY

Waterfront   Park

PIER 35

PIER 33

PIER 31

THE EMBARCADERO

STOCKTON ST

GRANT ST

KEARNY ST

BAY ST

MIDWAY ST

FRANCISCO ST

MONTGOMERY ST

PFEIFFER ST

CHESTNUT ST

CHESTNUT ST

GRANT AVE

CHILD ST

Chestnut/
Kearny Park

LOMBARD ST

PIER 15

LOMBARD ST

Pioneer
Park

TELEGRAPH
HILL

GREENWICH ST

GREENWICH ST

TELEGRAPH HILL BLVD

★ COIT
TOWER

FILBERT   ST

EXPLORATORIUM

MAMA'S ON
WASHINGTON
SQUARE

WASHINGTON
SQUARE INN
● PARK
TAVERN

VARENNES   ST

SONOMA ST

ALTA   ST

ST

CASTLE ST

MONTGOMERY   ST

SANSOME   ST

BATTERY   ST

FRONT   ST

DAVIS T

Washington
Square

UNION   ST

NORTH
BEACH

GREEN   ST

MARIO'S
BOHEMIAN ■
CIGAR STORE

▼ TONY'S PIZZA
NAPOLETANA

KEARNY   ST

VALLEJO   ST

BEACH ■
BLANKET
BABYLON

COLUMBUS AVE

ROMOLO ST

POWELL ST

CAFFÉ
TRIESTE

BROADWAY

BARTOL   ST

OSGOOD PL

Walton
Square

BROADWAY

15 ROMOLO ▼

BEAT MUSEUM

CITY LIGHTS ■
VESUVIO ▼

TOSCA ▼

QUINCE ▼

COTOGNA ▼

PACIFIC   AVE

DOL HO ▼

★ SPEC'S 12 ADLER
MUSEUM CAFÉ

COMSTOCK ▼
LOUNGE

★ GREAT EASTERN

JOHN   ST

JACKSON   ST

ROSS ALY

CHINATOWN

WASHINGTON   ST

PUNCHLINE ■

Maritime   Plaza

MERCHANT   ST

CLAY   ST

GHIRARDELLI SQUARE

Ghirardelli Square (900 North Point St., www.ghirardellisq.com), pronounced "GEAR-ah-DEL-ee," began its life as a chocolate factory in 1852, but has since reinvented itself as an upscale shopping, dining, and living compound. The Ghirardelli Chocolate Manufactory (900 North Point St., 415/474-3938, www.ghirardelli.com, 9am-11pm Sun.-Thurs., 9am-midnight Fri.-Sat.) is the descendant of the original 1852 chocolatier and anchors the corner of the square. Browse the rambling shop picking up truffles, wafers, and candies, then get in line at the ice-cream counter to order a hot fudge sundae.

SAN FRANCISCO MARITIME NATIONAL HISTORICAL PARK

The real gem of the Wharf is the San Francisco Maritime National Historical Park (415/561-7000, www.nps.gov/safr), which spreads from the base of Van Ness Avenue to Pier 45 and is filled with attractions. Start at the visitors center (499 Jefferson St., 415/447-5000, 9:30am-5pm daily), housed in the brick Argonaut Hotel, where rangers can help you make the most of your visit. Inside, exhibits include an immense Fresnel lighthouse lens and engaging displays that recount San Francisco's history.

Walk down to the Aquatic Park (Van Ness Ave., sunrise-sunset, free), a protected crescent-shaped beach ideal for swimming and sandy fun. Facing the beach, the 1939 art deco Aquatic Bathhouse Building (900 Beach St., 415/561-7100, www.nps.gov/safr, 10am-4pm daily, adults $10, children under 16 free) houses the Maritime Museum, where you can see a number of rotating exhibits alongside its brilliant WPA murals

Walk east along the beach toward Hyde Street Pier (9:30pm-5pm daily, $10, children under 16, free), a permanent dock of historical ships. The shiniest jewel of the collection is the 1886 square-rigged Balclutha, a three-masted schooner with excellent historical exhibits below deck. There are also several steamboats, including the workhorse

ferry paddle-wheel Eureka and an old tugboat, the Eppleton Hall.

At Pier 45 (off Jefferson), World War II buffs can feel the claustrophobia of the submarine USS Pampanito (415/775-1943, www.maritime.org, 9am-close daily, adults $20, seniors and students $12, children 6-12 $10, children under 6 free, family $45) or the expansiveness of the Liberty ship SS Jeremiah O'Brien (415/544-0100, www.ss-jeremiahobrien.org, 9am-4pm daily, adults $20, seniors and students $12, children 6-12 $10, children under 6 free, family $45).

MARINA AND PACIFIC HEIGHTS

The Marina and Pacific Heights are wealthy neighborhoods with a couple of yacht harbors, plenty of open space, great dining, and shopping that only gets better as you go up the hill.

Palace of Fine Arts

The Palace of Fine Arts (3301 Lyon St.) was originally meant to be nothing but a temporary structure—part of the Panama-Pacific International Exposition in 1915. But the lovely building designed by Bernard Maybeck won the hearts of San Franciscans, and a fund was started to preserve the palace beyond the exposition. Through the first half of the 20th century, efforts could not keep it from crumbling, but in the 1960s and 1970s, serious rebuilding work took place.

Today the Palace of Fine Arts stands proud, strong, and beautiful. It houses the Palace of Fine Arts Theatre (415/563-6404, www.palaceoffinearts.org), which hosts events nearly every day, from beauty pageants to conferences to children's musical theater performances.

★ The Presidio

A visit to the Presidio (www.nps.gov/prsf) reminds visitors that this used to be an army town. Capping the northwest end of the city, the Presidio has been a military installation since 1776. When defense budgets shrank at the end of the Cold War, the military turned it over to the National Park Service, making it a historical park in 1994.

Start at the **visitors center** (210 Lincoln Blvd., 415/561-4323, 10am-5pm daily) in the beautiful Main Post, which also houses an interpretive museum and exhibits. Across the parade grounds is the **Walt Disney Family Museum** (104 Montgomery St., 415/345-6800, www.waltdisney.org, 10am-6pm daily, adults $25, seniors and students $20, children 6-17 $15, children under 6 free) and George Lucas's **Letterman Digital Arts Center** (Chestnut St. and Lyon St., www.lucasfilm.com), where you can snap a photo with a life-size Yoda statue. More history can be found along the bay at **Crissy Field,** which includes the World War II grass airfield, and Civil War-era fortifications at the breathtaking **Fort Point** (end of Marine Dr., 415/504-2334, www.nps.gov/fopo, 10am-5pm Fri.-Sun.).

★ Golden Gate Bridge

People come from the world over to see and walk along the **Golden Gate Bridge** (U.S. 101/Hwy. 1 at Lincoln Blvd., 415/921-5858, http://goldengatebridge.org, southbound cars $7.75, pedestrians free). A marvel of human engineering constructed in 1936 and 1937, the suspension bridge spans the narrow "gate" from which the Pacific Ocean enters the San Francisco Bay. Pedestrians are allowed on the **east sidewalk** (5am-6:30pm daily Nov.-Apr., 5am-9pm daily Apr.-Oct.) for the 1.7-mile trek across the bridge. On a clear day, the whole bay, Marin Headlands, and city skyline are visible. Cyclists are allowed on both sidewalks (check website for times).

Stop at the **Golden Gate Bridge Welcome Center** (415/426-5220, www.parksconservancy.org, 9am-6pm daily) in the visitor plaza at the southern end of the bridge to learn the history and engineering of the bridge or warm up at the adjacent **Round House Café** (415/426-5228, www.parksconservancy.org, 9am-5pm daily).

CIVIC CENTER AND HAYES VALLEY

The Civic Center is the heart of San Francisco. Not only is the seat of government here, but so are venerable high-culture institutions: the War Memorial Opera House and Davies Symphony Hall, home of the world-famous San Francisco Symphony. As the Civic Center melts into Hayes Valley, you'll find fabulous

The Presidio

Mission Murals

In the early 1930s, artist Diego Rivera was commissioned to paint three murals in San Francisco (at City College, the Art Institute, and the City Club). The mural tradition continued and was brought to the Mission District by the Chico art movement of the 1960s and 1970s. Today, murals fuse politics and art throughout the Mission. The most concentrated collection of murals can be found at:

- **Balmy Alley** (24th and 25th Sts., Treat Ave. and Harrison St.): This pedestrian alley is crowded with dynamic art that reflects current political conversations.

- **Clarion Alley** (17th and Sycamore Sts., Valencia and Mission Sts.): Gritty murals reflect a sense of political urgency and illustrate themes of immigration, gentrification, and inclusivity.

- **Women's Building** (18th St., Linda and Lapidge Sts., Valencia St.): This is one of the city's largest murals, *MaestraPeace*. After nearly 25 years, the work still impresses.

To learn more, join a walking tour by **Precita Eyes** (1-2.5 hours, 415/285-2287, www.precitaeyes. org, Sat.-Sun., adults $8-20, children $3-6), a nonprofit the promotes and support public art.

hotels and restaurants serving both the city's politicos and the well-heeled.

City Hall

San Francisco's **City Hall** (1 Dr. Carlton B. Goodlett Place, 415/554-6139, www.sfgov.org, 8am-8pm Mon.-Fri., free) is a stately Beaux-Arts building with a gilded dome. It houses the mayor's office and much of the city's government. Inside you'll find a combination of historical grandeur and modern accessibility. Tours are available (415/554-6139, 10am, noon, 2pm daily, free) at the Docent Tours desk kiosk near the Goodlett Place lobby.

Asian Art Museum

Across from City Hall is the **Asian Art Museum** (200 Larkin St., 415/581-3500, www. asianart.org, 10am-5pm Tues.- Sun., adults $15, seniors and students $10, children 13-17 $10, children under 13 free). Inside you'll have an amazing window into the Asian cultures that have shaped and defined San Francisco and the Bay Area. The second and third floors are packed with art from across Asia, while the ground floor features rotating exhibits. The breadth and diversity of the museum is staggering, with everything from a Chinese gilded Buddha dating from AD 338 to modern Korean couture.

Alamo Square

At this area's far western edge sits **Alamo Square** (Hayes St. and Steiner St.), possibly the most photographed neighborhood in San Francisco. Among its stately Victorians are the famous **"painted ladies,"** a row of brilliantly painted and immaculately maintained homes. From the lovely Alamo Square Park, the ladies provide a picturesque foreground to the perfect view of the Civic Center and the rest of downtown.

MISSION AND CASTRO

Castro is the heart of gay San Francisco, complete with nightlife, festivals, and LGBT community activism. With its mix of Latino immigrants, working artists, hipsters, and tech workers, the Mission is a neighborhood bursting at the seams with idiosyncratic energy. While the heart of the neighborhood is Latin American, with delicious burritos and *pupusas* around every corner, it is also the go-to neighborhood for the tech economy with luxury condos, pricey boutiques, and international restaurants.

Mission Dolores

Mission San Francisco de Asís, or **Mission Dolores** (3321 16th St., 415/621-8203, www.mis-siondolores.org, 9am-4:30pm daily May-Oct.,

9am-4pm daily Nov.-Apr., adults $7, seniors and students $5), was founded in 1776. The mission is the oldest intact building in the city, having survived the 1906 earthquake and fire, the 1989 Loma Prieta quake, and more than 200 years of use. Guests can visit the Old Mission Museum, the rose garden and cemetery, and the Basilica, which houses artifacts from the Native Americans and Spanish of the 18th century.

GOLDEN GATE PARK AND THE HAIGHT

The neighborhood surrounding the intersection of Haight and Ashbury Streets (known as "the Haight") is best known for the wave of countercultural energy that broke out in the 1960s. Haight Street terminates at the entrance to San Francisco's gem—Golden Gate Park.

★ Golden Gate Park

Golden Gate Park (Stanyan St. at Fell St., 415/831-2700, www.golden-gate-park.com) is one of the city's most enduring treasures. Its 1,000-plus acres include lakes, forests, formal gardens, windmills, museums, a buffalo pasture, and plenty of activities. Enjoy free concerts in the summer, hike in near solitude in the winter, or spend a day wandering and exploring scores of cultural sights.

DE YOUNG MUSEUM

The **de Young Museum** (50 Hagiwara Tea Garden Dr., 415/750-3600, http://deyoung. famsf.org; 9:30am-5:15pm Tues.-Sun., adults $15, seniors $10, students $6, children under 18 free) is staggering in its size and breadth. View paintings, sculpture, textiles, ceramics, "contemporary crafts" from all over the world, with rotating exhibits that range from King Tut to the exquisite Jean Paul Gaultier collection.

The museum's modern exterior is wrapped in perforated copper, while the interior incorporates pockets of manicured gardens. Poking out of the park's canopy is a twisted tower that offers a spectacular 360-degree view of the city and the bay. Down below, a lily pond and sculpture garden are surrounded by sphinxes and dripping wisteria. Entrance to the tower, lily pond, and art garden is free.

CALIFORNIA ACADEMY OF SCIENCES

A triumph of the sustainable scientific principles it exhibits, the **California Academy of Sciences** (55 Music Concourse Dr., 415/379-8000, www.calacademy.org, 9:30am-5pm Mon.-Sat., 11am-5pm Sun., adults $36; students, seniors, and children 12-17 $31;

the de Young Museum

Golden Gate Park and the Haight

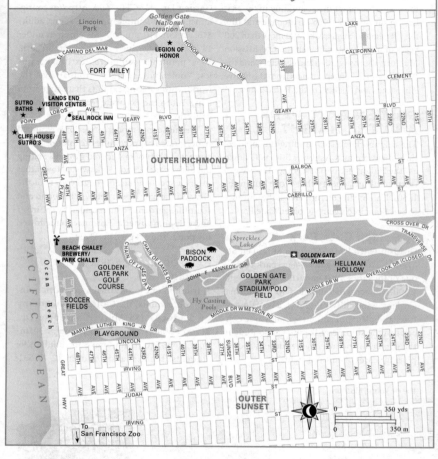

children 4-11 $26; children 3 and under free) is a guiding light of ecological perfection. From the grass-covered roof to the underground **aquarium,** visitors can explore every part of the universe. Wander through a steamy endangered **rainforest** contained inside a giant glass bubble, or travel through an all-digital outer space in the high-tech **planetarium.** More studious nature lovers can spend days examining every inch of the **Natural History Museum,** including exhibits like the 87-foot-long blue whale skeleton.

The Academy of Sciences takes pains to make itself kid-friendly, with interactive exhibits, thousands of live animals, and endless opportunities for learning. On **Thursday nights** (6pm-10pm, $15), the academy is an adults-only zone; DJs spin music and the café serves cocktails by renowned mixologists.

JAPANESE TEA GARDEN
The **Japanese Tea Garden** (75 Hagiwara Tea Garden Dr., 415/752-4227, http://japaneseteagardensf.com, 9am-6pm daily

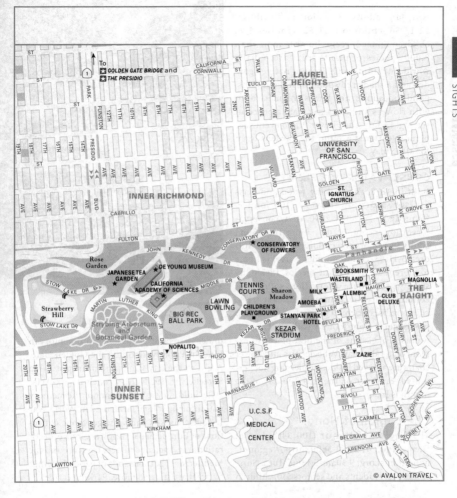

© AVALON TRAVEL

Mar.-Oct., 9am-4:45pm daily Nov.-Feb., adults $9, seniors and youth 12-17 $6, children 5-11 $2, children under 5 free) is a haven of peace and tranquility within the park, particularly in spring. The planting and design of the garden began in 1894 for the California Exposition. Today the flourishing garden displays a wealth of beautiful flora, including stunning examples of rare Chinese and Japanese plants. As you stroll along the paths, you'll come upon sculptures, bridges, ponds, and even traditional

tsukubai (a tea ceremony sink). Take one of the docent-led **tours** and conclude your visit with tea and a fortune cookie at the teahouse.

SAN FRANCISCO
BOTANICAL GARDEN

The 55-acre **San Francisco Botanical Garden** (1199 9th Ave. at Lincoln Way, 415/661-1316, www.sfbotanicalgarden.org, 7:30am-6pm daily Mar.-Sept., 7:30am-5pm daily Oct.-Nov. and Feb., 7:30am-4pm

Nov.-Jan., adults $8, seniors and children 12-17 $6, children 5-11 $2, families $18, children under 5 free) is home to more than 8,000 species of plants from around the world, including a California natives garden and a shady redwood forest. Fountains, ponds, meadows, and lawns are interwoven with flowers and trees to create a peaceful setting. In July, the Flower Piano event sees pianos scattered around the gardens open for all to play.

CONSERVATORY OF FLOWERS

Built in 1878, the striking wood and glass **Conservatory of Flowers** (100 John F. Kennedy Dr., 415/831-2090, www.conservatoryofflowers.org, 10am-4:30pm Tues.-Sun., adults $9, seniors and children 12-17 $6, children 5-11 $3, children under 5 free) is home to more than 1,700 plant species. Inside the steamy greenhouse, exotic flora spill out of containers, twine around rainforest trees, climb trellises reaching the roof, and rim deep ponds where eight-foot lily pads float on still waters. This is one of the best places to explore on a rainy day. Wheelchairs and power chairs are allowed inside; strollers are not permitted. Entrance on the first Tuesday of the month is free.

The Legion of Honor

The Legion of Honor (100 34th Ave. at Clement St., 415/750-3600, http://legionofhonor.famsf.org, 9:30am-5:15pm Tues.-Sun., adults $15, students and seniors $10, children

Japanese Tea Garden

under 18 free) sits on its lonely promontory in Lincoln Park overlooking the Golden Gate. A gift to the city from philanthropist Alma Spreckels in 1924, this French Beaux-Arts-style building was built to honor the memory of California soldiers who died in World War I. Today visitors can view gorgeous collections of European paintings, sculpture, decorative arts, ancient artifacts from around the Mediterranean, thousands of paper drawings by great artists, and more. Parking is free.

Entertainment and Events

NIGHTLIFE
Bars and Clubs
UNION SQUARE AND DOWNTOWN

The ritzy Union Square and Nob Hill neighborhoods are better known for shopping than for nightlife, but a few upscale bars hang in there. At the **Tonga Room & Hurricane Bar** (950 Mason St., 415/772-5278, www. tongaroom.com, 5pm-11:30pm Sun. and Wed.-Thurs., 5pm-midnight Fri.-Sat.), an over-the-top tiki theme adds a whimsical touch to the stately Fairmont Hotel on Nob Hill. The 1940s-era lounge—with its fruity rum drinks served in coconuts, its "rainstorms," and its floating stage—is a historical landmark.

The views and drinks from the **Top of the Mark** (InterContinental Mark Hopkins, 999 California St., 415/392-3434, www.intercontinentalmarkhopkins.com, 4:30pm-11:30pm Mon.-Thurs., 4:30pm-12:30am Fri.-Sat., 5pm-11:30pm Sun.) draw visitors from around the world. The cocktail lounge/restaurant serves light meals and a champagne brunch on Sunday (10am-1:30pm, adults $99, children 4-12 $65). Live bands play most nights. The enforced dress code is business casual.

A bit grungier, the **Tunnel Top** (601 Bush St., 415/235-6587, http://tunneltop.bar, 4:30pm-2am Mon.-Sat., 5pm-2am Sun.) sits perched atop the Stockton Tunnel near Union Square and is popular with industry types. Expect stiff drinks (the mojitos are excellent), DJs, and a chill vibe with couches and secluded tables upstairs.

Harry Denton's Starlight Room (450 Powell St., 21st Fl., 415/395-8595, www.harrydenton.com, 6pm-midnight Tues.-Thurs., 5pm-2am Fri.-Sat., cover $15) brings the flamboyant side of San Francisco downtown. Enjoy a cocktail in the early evening or a nightcap and post-theater dessert in this truly old-school nightclub.

The **Rickhouse** (246 Kearny St., 415/398-2827, www.rickhousesf.com, 5pm-2am Mon., 3pm-2am Tues.-Fri., 6pm-2am Sat.) craft cocktails are made from long-forgotten spirits and fresh ingredients. Sit in the all-wood bar to sample a Rye Maple Fizz or a massive rum punch served in a hollow clamshell. Get here early or you may not get in at all.

Bourbon and Branch (505 Jones St., 415/346-1735, www.bourbonandbranch.com, 6pm-2am daily, reservations suggested) is a must for lovers of the brown stuff. Tucked behind a nameless brown door, this resurrected 1920s-era speakeasy evokes its Prohibition-era past with secret passwords, a hidden library, and an art deco vibe.

A mainstay since 1959, the **Edinburgh Castle** (950 Geary, St., 415/885-4074, 5pm-2am daily) supports obscure and rising literary talents, hosts indie bands, pub quizzes, and cultural events, and serves a mean fish-and-chips.

The original 1908 incarnation of the **House of Shields** (39 New Montgomery St., 415/284-9958, www.thehouseofshields.com, 2pm-2am Mon.-Fri., 3pm-2am Sat.-Sun.) was an illegal speakeasy during the Prohibition era. Today, this downtown bar serves upscale cocktails (with upscale prices) in its gorgeous interior. The huge happy hour crowd thins out after 8pm.

It's dark, it's dank, and it's very, very Goth. The **Cat Club** (1190 Folsom St., 415/703-8965, www.sfcatclub.com, 9pm-3am Tues.-Sat., 9pm-midnight Sun., cover $6-10) is pretty energetic on '80s dance nights, with a friendly crowd, decent bartenders, strong drinks, and easy access to smoking areas. Each of the two rooms has its own DJ, which somehow works perfectly even though they're only a wall apart from each other.

The **DNA Lounge** (375 11th St., 415/626-1409, www.dnalounge.com, 9pm-5am daily, cover varies) hosts live music, DJs, and dance parties like Bootie. It's also one of the few clubs that's open late, and it has a 24/7 pizza joint next door.

NORTH BEACH AND FISHERMAN'S WHARF

North Beach is famous for its watering holes. Its most iconic is **Vesuvio** (255 Columbus Ave., 415/362-3370, www.vesuvio.com, 8am-2am Mon.-Fri., 7am-2am Sat.-Sun.) for the simple reason that Jack Kerouac loved it. Not much has changed since then, except its jukebox, which has only gotten better.

Spec's 12 Adler Museum Café (12 William Saroyan Pl., 415/421-4112, 4:30pm-2am Mon.-Fri., 5pm-2am Sat.-Sun.) is a tiny dive bar filled with an amazing array of knickknacks and good vibes. A local favorite, it has changed little since it was a sailors' bar in the 1960s.

Comstock Saloon (155 Columbus Ave., 415/617-0071, www.comstocksaloon.com,

4pm-midnight Sat.-Thurs., noon-midnight Fri.) has a retro-fresh cocktail menu that recalls the city's early days. The heavy, ornate bar and an offbeat menu conjure the 1860s, making it feel both modern and relevant.

Hidden up a steep alley, **15 Romolo** (15 Romolo Place, 415/398-1359, www.15romolo.com, 5pm-2am Mon.-Fri., 3pm-2am Sat., 11:30am-2am Sun.) serves fab cocktails with an edgy jukebox and a mellow crowd. The small bar gets crowded during Sunday brunch; come on a weeknight for a quiet drink and a small bite.

CIVIC CENTER AND HAYES VALLEY

Channeling a shipwreck in the middle of the Caribbean, the cocktail menu at hipster **Smuggler's Cove** (650 Gough St., 415/869-1900, http://smugglerscovesf.com, 5pm-1:15am daily) reads like an index of rum drinks from the heyday of tiki bars.

The **Rickshaw Stop** (155 Fell St., 415/861-2011, www.rickshawstop.com, hours vary, cover $7-25) welcomes live music, dancing, and club nights to its cavernous bar, stage, and dance floor. A quirky balcony area is complete with comfy old sofas.

MISSION AND CASTRO

Trick Dog (3010 20th St., 415/471-2999, www.trickdogbar.com, 3pm-2am daily) turns craft cocktails into art. The changing menu resembles a record album, children's book, or an airline pamphlet, listing odd, yet amazing combinations of specialty spirits and unusual ingredients (think: seaweed, lychee). The bar is located in an old, rehabilitated factory turned light, stylish, and rustic.

Excellent draft beers, tasty barbecue, and a motorcycle-inclined crowd give **Zeitgeist** (199 Valencia St., 415/431-6891, http://zeitgeistsf.com, 9am-2am daily) a punk rock edge. This Mission favorite endears with a spacious outdoor beer garden and Friday barbecues.

Blackbird (2124 Market St., 415/503-0630, www.blackbirdbar.com, 3pm-2am Mon.-Fri., 2pm-2am Sat.-Sun.) draws a mixed crowd to its Castro location. The specialty cocktails are mixed and then aged in either oak or bourbon barrels for up to two months. There are also carbonated cocktails on tap, a cool interior, and a pool table.

GOLDEN GATE PARK AND THE HAIGHT

The dimly lit **Toronado** (547 Haight St., 415/863-2276, www.toronado.com, 11:30am-2am daily) maintains one of the finest beer selections in the city, with a changing roster of several dozen microbrews on tap, including many hard-to-find Belgian ales.

Haight Street crowds head out in droves to the **Alembic** (1725 Haight St., 415/666-0822, www.alembicbar.com, 4pm-midnight Mon.-Tues., 4pm-2am Wed.-Fri., noon-2am Sat., 2pm-midnight Sun.) for artisanal cocktails laced with American spirits. On par with the whiskey and bourbon menu is the cuisine: Wash down beef-tongue sliders with a Sazerac.

Discover your inner Sinatra at **Club Deluxe** (1511 Haight St., 415/552-6949, www.clubdeluxe.co, 4pm-2am Mon.-Fri., 2pm-2am Sat.-Sun.). Order something classic at this dark retro-style bar while listening to live jazz or watching burlesque.

Gay and Lesbian

Since 1973, **The EndUp** (401 6th St., 415/896-1075, https://theendupsf.com, 11pm-4am Thurs., 10pm-8am Fri., 10pm-6am Sat., 6am-noon and 10pm-3am Sun., cover varies) has been where late-night revelers have, well, ended up. The mixed crowd dances and parties until dawn. On Sunday, the party starts *at* dawn with DJs for "Sunrise Sunday."

The Stud (399 9th St., 415/863-6623, www.studsf.com, 5pm-2am Sun.-Thurs., 5pm-4am Fri.-Sat.) has been around for more than 50 years, hosting karaoke, drag shows, musical acts, and DJs nightly.

The balcony of **The Lookout** (3600 16th St., 415/431-0306, www.lookoutsf.com, 3:30pm-2am Mon.-Fri., 12:30pm-2am Sat.-Sun., cover to $10) overlooks the iconic Castro neighborhood, with primo people-watching as you sip industrial-strength concoctions and nibble on bar snacks and pizza.

Live Music

Opened in the late 1960s, **The Fillmore** (1805 Geary Blvd., 415/346-3000, www.thefillmore. com) ignited the careers of such legends as Santana and the Grateful Dead. Major acts still pass through here, and the Fillmore remains a local favorite of music lovers for its balcony seating, comfortable bar, and intimate stage setting.

The **Great American Music Hall** (859 O'Farrell St., 415/885-0750, www.slimspresents.com) is the oldest venue in the city with great acts, casual balcony seating, a small stage, ample bars, and ornate architectural detailing. Located in a dodgy neighborhood, it's is well worth the effort.

Started by rock veteran Boz Scaggs in 1988, **Slim's** (333 11th St., 415/255-0333, www. slims-sf.com) fills the alternative pop niche in the city. Dinner tickets are the only way to score an actual seat, and when it's crowded, it can be difficult to see the small stage.

The Independent (628 Divisadero St., 415/771-1421, www.theindependentsf.com) shares the city's indie rock mantle with Slim's, with well-known and emerging acts at a small, no-frills venue.

Seeing live music at **The Chapel** (777 Valencia St., 415/551-5157, www.thechapelsf. com) is like to going to church. Indie rockers play beneath 40-foot-high arched ceilings in this former 1914 chapel, while the **Chapel Bar** (7pm-2am daily) pours drinks to locals and ticket holders.

The beautiful and ornate **Warfield** (982 Market St., 415/345-0900, http://thewarfieldtheatre.com) books acts ranging from Bill Maher to alternative rock. Reserve limited table seating on the lower level or balcony seats, or opt for standing room orchestra below the stage.

A favorite venue for locals, **Bimbo's 365 Club** (1025 Columbus Ave., 415/474-0365, www.bimbos365club.com) remains a beloved elder statesman with a midcentury vibe. You'll see major acts such as Chris Isaak, the White Stripes, and Adele.

The **SFJAZZ Center** (201 Franklin St., 866/920-5299, http://sfjazz.org, hours vary Tues.-Sun.) is a stunning 35,000-square-foot space in Hayes Valley with state-of-the-art acoustics. Steep seating brings the large audience close to the performers for a small-club feel. Major acts have included Herbie Hancock and the Afro-Cuban All Stars.

Comedy

The **Punch Line** (444 Battery St., 415/397-7573, www.punchlinecomedyclub.com, times and cover varies) is an elegant and intimate venue that's earned its top-notch reputation with stellar headliners such as Amy Schumer, Marc Maron, and Dave Chappelle. An on-site bar keeps the audience primed.

Cobb's Comedy Club (915 Columbus Ave., 415/928-4320, www.cobbscomedy.com, times and cover varies, two-drink minimum) has played host to star comedians such as Sarah Silverman and Margaret Cho since 1982. The 425-seat venue offers a full dinner menu and a bar.

THE ARTS
Theater

For same-day, half-price, no-refund tickets to shows across the city, stop at **Union Square TIX** (Union Square, 415/433-7827, www.tix-bayarea.com, 10am-6pm daily).

Near Union Square, the **American Conservatory Theater** (A.C.T., 415 Geary St., 415/749-2228, www.act-sf.org, shows Tues.-Sun., $22-95) puts on a season filled with big-name, big-budget productions and high-value musicals. Expect American classics by the likes of Sam Shepard and Harold Pinter as well as intriguing new works.

The **Curran Theatre** (445 Geary St., 415/358-1220, www.sfcurran.com, $105-250), next door to A.C.T., is a state-of-the-art stage for classic, high-budget musicals, such as *Jersey Boys, Wicked,* and *Chicago.*

In the mid-Market area, both the **Orpheum Theatre** (1192 Market St.,

888/746-1799, www.shnsf.com, $60-250) and **Golden Gate Theatre** (1 Taylor St., 888/746-1799, www.shnsf.com, $60-250) run touring productions of popular Broadway musicals.

There's one live show that's always different, yet it's been running continuously since 1974. *Beach Blanket Babylon* (678 Green St., 415/421-4222, www.beachblanketbabylon.com, shows Wed.-Sun., $30-155) mocks pop culture as it continuously evolves to take advantage of tabloid treasures.

Classical Music and Opera

Davies Symphony Hall (201 Van Ness Ave., 415/864-6000, www.sfsymphony.org) is home to Michael Tilson Thomas's world-renowned San Francisco Symphony. Loyal patrons flock to performances that range from the classic to the avant-garde.

The **War Memorial Opera House** (301 Van Ness Ave., 415/621-6600, www.sfwmpac.org), a Beaux-Arts-style building designed by Coit Tower and City Hall architect Arthur Brown Jr., houses the **San Francisco Opera** (415/864-3330, http://sfopera.com) and **San Francisco Ballet** (415/865-2000, www.sfballet.org). Tours are available (415/552-8338, hourly 10am-2pm Mon., $5-7).

Cinema

The **Castro Theatre** (429 Castro St., 415/621-6120, www.castrotheatre.com, $10-13) is a grand movie palace from the 1920s that has enchanted San Francisco audiences for almost a century. The theater hosts revival double features (from black-and-white films through 1980s classics), musical movie sing-alongs, live shows, and even the occasional book signing. The Castro also screens current releases and documentaries about queer life in San Francisco.

The **AMC DINE-IN Kabuki 8** (1881 Post St., www.amctheatres.com, $13-15) offers a modern, upscale moviegoing experience with reserved seating, a full-service dinner brought to your seat, and a selection of beer, wine, and cocktails (age 21 and over). The eight screens show mostly big blockbuster Hollywood films, plus a smattering of independents.

FESTIVALS AND EVENTS

San Francisco is host to numerous events year-round. Following are some of the biggest that are worth planning a trip around.

During the **Chinese New Year Parade** (Chinatown, www.chineseparade.com, Feb.), Chinatown celebrates the lunar new year with a parade of costumed dancers, floats, firecrackers, and the Golden Dragon.

Join rowdy, costumed revelers for **Bay to Breakers** (Embarcadero to Great Highway, www.baytobreakers.com, May), a 12K run/walk/stumble across the city through Golden Gate Park to a massive street party at Ocean Beach.

One of the year's biggest parades is the **San Francisco LGBT Pride Parade and Celebration** (Market St., www.sfpride.org, June). Hundreds of thousands of people of all orientations take to the streets for this quintessentially San Franciscan party-cum-social justice movement.

Golden Gate Park is host to two wildly popular summer music festivals. **Outside Lands** (www.sfoutsidelands.com, Aug., $150/one-day pass, $375/three-day pass) is a three-day music festival that floods the park with revelers, food trucks, and hundreds of bands. Headliners have included Radiohead, LCD Soundsystem, Kanye West, Metallica, Neil Young, and Elton John. The park barely recovers in time for **Hardly Strictly Bluegrass** (www.hardlystrictlybluegrass.com, late Sept. or early Oct., free), a free music festival celebrating a wide variety of bluegrass sounds, from Lucinda Williams and Emmylou Harris to Bella Fleck and Yo La Tengo.

Shopping

UNION SQUARE

For the biggest variety of department stores and high-end international designers, plus a few select boutiques, locals and visitors alike flock to Union Square (bounded by Geary St., Stockton St., Post St., and Powell St.). The shopping area includes more than just the square proper: Designer and brand-name stores cluster for several blocks, and down alleys in all directions.

The big guys anchor Union Square. Macy's (170 O'Farrell St., 415/397-3333, www.macys. com, 10am-9pm Mon.-Sat., 11am-7pm Sun.) has two immense locations, one for women's clothing and another for the men's store and housewares. Neiman Marcus (150 Stockton St., 415/362-3900, www.neimanmarcus.com, 10am-7pm Mon.-Wed. and Fri.-Sat., 10am-8pm Thurs., noon-6pm Sun.) is a favorite among high-budget shoppers, and Saks Fifth Avenue (384 Post St., 415/986-4300, www.saksfifthavenue.com, 10am-7pm Mon.-Wed., 10am-8pm Thurs.-Sat., noon-7pm Sun.) adds a touch of New York style to funky-but-wealthy San Francisco.

Gumps (135 Post St., 415/982-1616, www. gumps.com, 10am-6pm Mon.-Sat., noon-5pm Sun.) has been a San Francisco institution to the city's well-heeled since 1861. You'll find everything from stationery to silver, fine jewelry to toys. Come at Christmas when the store's ornament selection far outshines anywhere else's.

Levi's (815 Market St., 415/501-0100, www.levi.com, 9am-9pm Mon.-Sat., 10am-8pm Sun.) is a home-grown San Francisco company that is now a household name. Its three-floor flagship store offers incredible customization services while featuring new music and emerging art.

Britex Fabrics (117 Post St., 415/392-2910, www.britexfabrics.com, 10am-6pm Mon.-Sat.) draws designers, quilters, DIYers, and costume geeks to its legendary monument to fabric. Four floors are crammed floor-to-ceiling with bolts of fabric, swaths of lace, and rolls of ribbon.

NORTH BEACH

Founded by Lawrence Ferlinghetti, City Lights (261 Columbus Ave., 415/362-8193, www.citylights.com, 10am-midnight daily) opened in 1953 as an all-paperback bookstore with a decidedly Beat aesthetic, focused on selling modern literary fiction and progressive political tomes. As the Beats flocked to San Francisco, the shop put on another hat—that of publisher. Allen Ginsberg's *Howl* was published by the erstwhile independent, which never looked back. Today City Lights continues to sell and publish the best of cutting-edge fiction and nonfiction. The store is still in its original location, though it's expanded somewhat since the '50s. Expect to find your favorite genre paperbacks, intriguing new works, and thought-provoking nonfiction.

MARINA AND PACIFIC HEIGHTS

The shopping is good in the tony Marina and its elegant neighbor Pacific Heights. Chestnut and Union Streets cater to the Marina's young and affluent residents with plenty of clothing boutiques and makeup outlets.

Fillmore Street is the other major shopping corridor, funkier than its younger Marina neighbors, with a great variety of consignment stores selling high-end clothes, shoes, and antiques. The best is Goodbyes (3483 Sacramento St., 415/674-0151, http:// goodbyessf.com, 10am-6pm Mon.-Wed. and Fri.-Sat., 10am-7pm Thurs., 11am-5pm Sun.), where you'll find last season's designer threads for reasonable prices. Goodbyes dominates Sacramento Street with three locations: the Women's Store (3483 Sacramento St., 415/674-0151), the Women's Sale Store (3464

Sacramento St., 415/346-6388), and the **Men's Store** (3462 Sacramento St., 415/346-6388).

HAYES VALLEY

Shopping goes upscale in Hayes Valley, but a unique counterculture creativity still permeates. This is a fun neighborhood to get your stroll on, with art galleries, clothing boutiques, upscale housewares, and lovely cafés.

Paolo Iantorno's boutique **Paolo Shoes** (524 Hayes St., 415/552-4580, http://paoloshoes. com, 11am-7pm Mon.-Sat., 11am-6pm Sun.) showcases his collection of handcrafted shoes. All leather and textiles are conscientiously selected and then inspected to ensure top quality.

Housed inside an Airstream is the beautiful collection of handmade tableware by **MM Clay** (315 Linden St., 415/601-9152, www. mmclay.com, 11am-6pm Wed.-Sun.), made and designed by Mary Mar Keenan. Keenan's wares are found on the tables of some of the city's best restaurants.

For something intimate, stop by **Alla Prima** (539 Hayes St., www.allaprimalingerie.com, 415/864-8180, 11am-7pm Mon.-Sat., noon-5pm Sun.) where the beauty and selection of the lingerie is matched by its quality. To get a corset made, make an appointment at **Dark Garden** (321 Linden St., 415/431-7684, www. darkgarden.com, 11am-5pm Sun.-Thurs., 11am-6pm Fri., 10am-6pm Sat.), or just browse the collection of high-end sexy couture.

MISSION

Valencia Street is one of the most vibrant and diverse neighborhood for shoppers in the city. Vintage threads can be found at **Painted Bird** (1360 Valencia St., http://shoppainted. com, 415/401-7027, 11am-8pm daily), which has a small, but good selection of clothes, shoes, and jewelry.

Far from your typical five and dime, **Five and Diamond** (510 Valencia St., 415/255-9747, www.fiveanddiamond.com, noon-8pm daily) features off-the-wall art, unusual clothing, and downright scary jewelry. Make an appointment to get a tattoo or purchase some keen body jewelry.

Author Dave Eggers's tongue-in-cheek storefront at **826 Valencia** (826 Valencia St., 415/642-5905, www.826valencia.org, noon-6pm daily) doubles as a pirate supply shop and youth literacy center. While you'll find plenty of pirate booty, you'll also find a good stock of literary magazines and books. Almost next door, quirky **Paxton Gate** (824 Valencia St., 415/824-1872, www.paxtongate.com, 11am-7pm Sun.-Wed., 11am-8pm Thurs.-Sat.) is an atypical gift shop with garden supplies, books, candles, and fossilized creatures. Kids will love **Paxton Gate's Curios for Kids** (766 Valencia St., 415/252-9990, 11am-7pm Sun.-Wed., 11am-8pm Thurs.-Sat.), filled with toys, games, and science activity sets for all ages.

HAIGHT-ASHBURY

The **Haight-Ashbury** shopping district has a few bargains left in its remaining thrift shops. Originally a vaudeville theater, the capacious **Wasteland** (1660 Haight St., 415/863-3150, www.shopwasteland.com, 11am-8pm Mon.-Sat., 11am-7pm Sun.) has a traffic-stopping art nouveau facade, a distinctive assortment of vintage hippie and rock-star threads, and a glam-punk staff.

Housed in an old bowling alley, **Amoeba** (1855 Haight St., 415/831-1200, www.amoeba. com, 11am-8pm daily) is a larger-than-life record store that promotes every type of music imaginable. Many of Amoeba's staff are musicians themselves and knowledgeable in the business.

The award-winning **Booksmith** (1644 Haight St., 415/863-8688, www.booksmith. com, 10am-10pm Mon.-Sat., 10am-8pm Sun.) boasts a helpful and informed staff, a fabulous magazine collection, and Northern California's preeminent calendar of readings by internationally renowned authors.

Make for the glam at **Piedmont Boutique** (1452 Haight St., 415/864-8075, www.piedmontboutique.com, 11am-7pm daily). The narrow store beneath two giant legs is a riot of color, filled with feather boas, sequined shorts, fantastic wigs—and those who wear them.

Sports and Recreation

BEACHES
Ocean Beach

Ocean Beach (Great Hwy., parking at Sloat Blvd., Golden Gate Park, and the Cliff House, www.nps.gov) is a four-mile stretch of sand that forms the breakwater for the Pacific Ocean along the west side of the city. It's so large, you're likely to find a sandy spot—and maybe even a parking space—except perhaps on that rarest of occasions in San Francisco, a sunny, warm day. Tides and rip currents make the beach a dangerous place for swimming; only experienced surfers should tackle the waves. Bonfires are a welcome tradition (Burning Man was born here); bring your own firewood and use one of the fire rings between stairwells 15 and 20.

Aquatic Park

The beach at Aquatic Park (Beach St. and Hyde St., www.nps.gov/safr) sits at the west end of the Fisherman's Wharf tourist area, and swimming is popular here. Triathletes and hard-core swimmers brave the frigid waters in the protected cove. More sedate visitors can sit and enjoy a cup of coffee, a newspaper, and some people-watching.

Baker Beach

Baker Beach (Lincoln Blvd., www.nps.gov/prsf) is best known for its scenery—and that doesn't just mean the lovely views of the Golden Gate Bridge. The north end of Baker is a clothing-optional (i.e., nude) beach. But plenty of beach lovers wear clothes while flying kites, playing volleyball, throwing a Frisbee, and strolling on the beach. Swimming should be avoided; the currents are strong and dangerous as it's so close to the Golden Gate. Baker Beach is small and can get crowded in summer.

PARKS
Golden Gate Park

The largest park in San Francisco is Golden Gate Park (main entrance at Stanyan St. and Fell St., 415/831-2700, www.goldengate-park.com). In addition to housing popular sights like the Academy of Sciences, the de Young, and the Japanese Tea Garden, the park is San Francisco's unofficial playground. There a children's playground (Martin Luther King Jr. Dr. and Bowling Green Dr.), tennis courts, a golf course, fly-casting pools, and a model yacht club. Stow Lake (415/702-1390, http://stowlakeboathouse.com, 9am-5pm daily, $22-38/hour) rents paddleboats, and the park even has its own bison paddock. Locals fill the park on weekends with in-line skating, biking, hiking, and even Lindy Hopping. John F. Kennedy Drive, east of Transverse Drive, closes to motorists (Sat., Apr.-Sept.; Sun. year-round) for pedestrian-friendly fun.

Crissy Field

With beaches, wetlands, and a wide promenade, Crissy Field (Marina Blvd. and Baker St., 415/561-4323, www.nps.gov/prsf) is the place to enjoy a sunny day. Bike along the bay, take a picnic to the grassy airfield, or turn the kids loose at the protected beaches. Finish your exploration of Crissy Field at Fort Point (end of Marine Dr., 415/504-2334, www.nps.gov/fopo, 10am-5pm Fri.-Sun.) beneath the Golden Gate Bridge, or grab a coffee and shop for souvenirs at the aptly named Warming Hut (983 Marine Dr., 415/561-3040, www.parksconservancy.org, 9am-5pm daily, $5-12).

Lands End

Rising above rugged cliffs and beaches, the three-mile Lands End Trail (Merrie Way, 415/561-4700, www.nps.gov/goga) feels wild, but is perfect for hiking. The trail runs from El Camino Del Mar near the Legion of Honor to the ruins of the Sutro Baths, with auxiliary trails leading down to little beaches. Look for the remains of three shipwrecks on the rocks of Point Lobos at low tide.

Grab a cup of hot chocolate at the stunning **Lands End Lookout visitors center** (680 Point Lobos Ave., 415/426-5240, www.parks-conservancy.org, 9am-5pm daily) when your hike is finished.

Mission Dolores Park

Mission Dolores Park (Dolores St. and 19th St., 415/554-9521, http://sfrecpark. org), also called Dolores Park, is a favorite of Castro and Mission District denizens. Bring a blanket to sprawl on the lawn and people-watch, and grab a picnic lunch from one of the excellent nearby eateries. Music festivals and cultural events often spring up on weekends.

BIKING

In San Francisco, bicycling is a religion. The high church of that religion is the **San Francisco Bike Coalition** (415/431-2453, www.sfbike.org), which provides workshops, hosts events, and is an excellent resource for cycling through the city.

A popular trek is the ride across the **Golden Gate Bridge** (3.4 miles) and back. This is a great way to see the bridge and the bay for the first time, and it takes only an hour or two to complete. For a longer (and more strenuous) adventure, continue past the bridge into the town of Sausalito (8 miles) or Tiburon (16 miles), then ride the ferry back to the city (bikes are allowed on board).

Paved trails and promenades line **Crissy Field** to Fort Mason, Fisherman's Wharf, and the Ferry Building, all the way to **AT&T Park** on the Embarcadero. It's flat and wonderfully bikeable.

The paved paths of **Golden Gate Park** (main entrance at Stanyan St. and Fell St., 415/831-2700, www.golden-gate-park.com) connect its various museums and attractions and extend all the way to Ocean Beach.

Bike Rentals
Blazing Saddles (2715 Hyde St., 415/202-

8888, www.blazingsaddles.com, $8-9/hour, $32-60/day) rents bikes (including tandem, kids' bikes and trailers, and electric bikes) and offers tips on where to go. Their guided tours (10am daily, three hours, adults $55, children $35, reservations required) travel through San Francisco and across the Golden Gate Bridge into Marin County. With six locations (one in Union Square, the rest in Fisherman's Wharf/North Beach), it's easy to find a cruiser.

Golden Gate Tours & Bike Rentals (1816 Haight St., 415/922-4537, www.goldengate-parkbikerental.com, 9:30am-6:30pm daily, $8-9/hour, $30-38/day) has a rental kiosk at the park entrance. Other locations include Fisherman's Wharf and the Ferry Building.

Golden Gate Park Bike and Skate (3038 Fulton St., 415/668-1117, http://golden-gateparkbikeandskate.com, 10am-6pm Mon.-Fri., 10am-7pm Sat.-Sun. summer, 10am-5pm Mon.-Fri., 10am-6pm Sat.-Sun., winter) rents bikes ($5/hour, $25/day), disc golf bags, and skates near the de Young Museum.

WHALE-WATCHING
With day-trip access to the marine sanctuary off the Farallon Islands, whale-watching is a year-round activity in San Francisco. **San Francisco Whale Tours** (Pier 39, 415/706-7364, www.sanfranciscowhaletours.com, tours daily, $45-99, advance purchase required) offers six-hour trips to the Farallons (Sat.-Sun.), with almost-guaranteed whale sightings on each trip. Shorter whale-watching trips along the coastline run weekdays; the 90-minute trips see elephant seals and sea lions. Kids love the chance to spot whales, sea lions, and pelicans. Children ages 3-15 are welcome (for reduced rates); however, children under age three are not permitted for safety reasons.

SPECTATOR SPORTS
AT&T Park (24 Willie Mays Plaza, 3rd St. and King St., 415/972-2000) is home to baseball's **San Francisco Giants** (www.mlb.com/gi-ants, Apr.-Sept. or Oct.). As the Giants win

championships, tickets become harder to come by—and more expensive—but the food and views are worth it.

NBA champions the **Golden State** **Warriors** (www.nba.com/warriors) are scheduled to play at the **Chase Center Arena** (www.chasecenter.com), near the AT&T Park, for the 2019-2020 NBA season.

Food

UNION SQUARE AND DOWNTOWN
Bakeries and Cafés

Blue Bottle Café (66 Mint Plaza, 415/495-3394, www.bluebottlecoffee.net, 6:30am-7pm daily, $5-10) is a popular coffee chain with multiple locations around the city. The Mint Plaza location is the only café with a full food menu. Other locations include the Ferry Building, Chinatown (628 California St.), and the original venue in Hayes Valley (315 Linden St.).

Café de la Presse (352 Grant Ave., 415/398-2680, www.cafedelapresse.com, 7:30am-9pm Mon.-Fri., 8am-9pm Sat.-Sun., $4-31) is a 1930s-style French bistro serving breakfast, lunch, and dinner. Those in need of a relaxing espresso or glass of wine are welcome to take a table and drink in the atmosphere.

Breakfast and Lunch

At **Dottie's True Blue Café** (28 6th St., 415/885-2767, www.dottiestruebluesf.com, 7:30am-3pm Mon. and Thurs.-Fri., 7:30am-4pm Sat.-Sun., $9-17), the menu is simple: classic egg dishes, light fruit plates, and an honest-to-goodness blue-plate special for breakfast as well as salads, burgers, and sandwiches for lunch. The service is friendly and the portions are huge. Expect an hour wait for a table at this locals' mecca, especially on weekend mornings.

Wise Sons Jewish Delicatessen (736 Mission St., 415/655-7887, http://wisesonsdeli.com, 11am-2pm Mon.-Fri., 11am-3pm Sat.-Sun., $4-16) serves standard deli favorites such as Reuben and pastrami sandwiches, as well as soups, salads, and some of the best bagels in the city. Seating spills out onto Jessie Plaza.

Asian

At ★ **The Slanted Door** (1 Ferry Plaza, Ste. 3, 415/861-8032, http://slanteddoor.com, 11am-10pm Mon.-Sat., 11:30am-10pm Sun., $21-48), owner Charles Phan utilizes organic local ingredients in both traditional and innovative Vietnamese cuisine, creating a unique dining experience. The light afternoon tea menu (2:30pm-4:30pm daily) is the perfect pick-me-up.

California Cuisine

The menu at **Herlen Place** (334 Grant Ave., 415/391-0207, http://herlenplace.com, 8am-9pm daily, $12-17) is tailored around a diverse and carefully curated list of organic and biodynamic wines. Standouts include the fennel tart, vegetable tempura, and whole roasted cauliflower. Fuel up for a day of shopping with eggs Benedict a mimosa at this casual and friendly place.

French

Hidden in a tiny alley that looks like it might have been transported from Saint-Michel in Paris, ★ **Café Claude** (7 Claude Ln., 415/392-3505, www.cafeclaude.com, 11:30am-10:30pm Mon.-Sat., 5:30pm-10:30pm Sun., $14-29) serves classic brasserie cuisine to French expatriates and Americans alike. Enjoy a glass of sancerre at the zinc bar while listening to live jazz, or sit in the colorful dining room with a plate of coq au vin or steak tartare.

Seafood

Make reservations in advance to dine at San Francisco legend ★ **Farallon** (450 Post St., 415/956-6969, www.farallonrestaurant. com, 5:30pm-9:30pm Mon.-Thurs. and Sun., 5:30pm-10pm Fri.-Sat., $36-45). Dark, cave-like rooms are decorated in an underwater theme—complete with the unique Jellyfish Bar. Chef Mark Franz has made Farallon a 20-year icon that keeps gaining ground. Seafood dominates the pricey-but-worth-it menu.

One of the very first restaurants established in San Francisco during the gold rush in 1849, the ★ **Tadich Grill** (240 California St., 415/391-1849, www.tadichgrill.com, 11am-9:30pm Mon.-Fri., 11:30am-9:30pm Sat., $23-46) still serves fresh-caught fish and classic miner fare. The menu combines perfectly sautéed sand dabs, octopus salad, and the Hangtown Fry, an oyster and bacon frittata. Mix that with the business lunch crowd in suits, out-of-towners, and original dark wooden booths from the 1850s and you've got a fabulous San Francisco stew of a restaurant. Speaking of stew, the Tadich cioppino enjoys worldwide fame—and deserves it, even in a city that prides itself on the quality of its seafood concoctions.

Southern

There will be a line out the door of ★ **Brenda's French Soul Food** (652 Polk St., 415/345-8100, http://frenchsoulfood.com, 8am-3pm Mon.-Tues., 8am-10pm Wed.-Sat., 8am-8pm Sun., $11-19). People come in droves to this Tenderloin eatery for its delectable and filling New Orleans-style breakfasts, although lunch and dinner are also popular. Unique offerings include crawfish beignets, an andouille sausage omelet, and beef cutlet and grits.

Southern hospitality North Carolina-style is found at ★ **Rusty's Southern** (750 Ellis St., 415/683-6974, http://rustyssf.com, 5pm-10pm Tues.-Wed., 10am-2:30pm and 5pm-10pm Thurs.-Sun., $17-21). Barbecue, catfish, hush puppies, and buttermilk-fried chicken are served with fresh ingredients and the

sophisticated beer and wine pairs well with the cuisine.

Steak

How could you not love a steak house with a name like **Epic Roasthouse** (369 Embarcadero, 415/369-9955, www.epicroasthouse.com, 11:30am-2:30pm and 5pm-9:30pm Mon.-Thurs., 11:30am-2:30pm and 5pm-10pm Fri., 11am-2:30pm and 5pm-10pm Sat., 11am-2:30pm and 5pm-9:30pm Sun., $34-90)? Come for the wood-fired grass-fed beef; stay for the prime views over San Francisco Bay. The Epic Roasthouse sits almost underneath the Bay Bridge, where the lights sparkle and flash over the deep black water at night. On weekends, the steak house offers an innovative brunch menu complete with hair-of-the-dog cocktails.

NORTH BEACH AND FISHERMAN'S WHARF
Bakeries and Cafés

There is much talk about sourdough bread in San Francisco, but Boudin's, which was started in 1849 by French immigrants, is the original. Tourists at Boudin's **Bakers Hall** (160 Jefferson St., 415/928-1849, www.boudinbakery.com, 8am-10pm Sun.-Thurs., 8am-10:30pm Fri.-Sat., $10-16) can order a steaming bowl of clam chowder in a fresh bread bowl and watch how the bread is made in its demonstration bakery. Upstairs, have a more formal dinner at **Bistro Boudin** (415/351-5561, 11:30am-9pm Sun.-Thurs., 11:30am-10pm Fri.-Sat., $16-40), which serves elegant American food and a whole host of oysters in its dark wood dining room overlooking the wharf. Boudin has another café location at Pier 39 (Space 5 Q, 9am-8pm daily, $10-16).

Widely recognized as the first espresso coffeehouse on the West Coast, family-owned **Caffé Trieste** (601 Vallejo St., 415/392-6739, www.caffetrieste.com, 6:30am-11pm daily, cash only) first opened its doors in 1956 and is rumored to be where Francis Ford Coppola penned the original *The Godfather* screenplay.

Sip a cappuccino and munch on Italian pastries at this treasured North Beach institution.

Breakfast

★ **Mama's on Washington Square** (1701 Stockton St., 415/362-6421, www.mamas-sf. com, 8am-3pm Tues.-Sun., $9-18, cash only) is legendary for breakfast—and so is the line. Starting from down the block, the line flows through the heart of the restaurant to the counter where you place your order, then wait for a table to open up. To minimize your wait, arrive at Mama's when it opens or go after noon.

California Cuisine

Park Tavern (1652 Stockton St., 415/989-7300, http://parktavernsf.com, 5:30pm-9pm Mon., 5:30pm-10pm Tues.-Thurs., 5:30pm-11pm Fri., 10am-11pm Sat., 10am-10pm-Sun., $17-42) serves meat and fish dishes as well as exquisite appetizers in its elegant dining room. For a low-key meal, sit at the bar and order a cocktail and the Marlow Burger.

Chinese

One of the many great dim sum places in Chinatown is the ★ **Great Eastern** (649 Jackson St., 415/986-2500, www.greateasternsf.com, 10am-11pm Mon.-Fri., 9am-11pm Sat.-Sun., $19-30). The menu includes dim sum and standard Chinese favorites. Write down everything you want and hand the list to your waiter—your choices will be served tableside. Reservations are strongly recommended.

Italian

North Beach is San Francisco's version of Little Italy. One of the last holdouts from North Beach's heyday is **Mario's Bohemian Cigar Store** (566 Columbus Ave., 415/362-0536, 10am-11pm daily, $11-17). Not much has changed has changed in this slender café since it opened in 1972, except that it no longer sells tobacco. There are just a few tables and stools at the bar, where the bartender/server/cook pulls espresso, pours beer and wine, and

prepares personal pizzas and focaccia sandwiches baked in a tiny oven.

Nine-time World Pizza Champion Tony Gemignani runs ★ **Tony's Pizza Napoletana** (1570 Stockton St., 415/835-9888, www.tonyspizzanapoletana.com, noon-10pm Mon., noon-11pm Wed.-Sun., $19-30), where four different pizza ovens cook eight distinct styles of pizza. The chef's special Neapolitan-style pizza margherita is simple pizza made to perfection.

Founded in 1919, **Tosca** (242 Columbus Ave., 415/986-9651, http://toscacafesf.com, 5pm-2am daily, $18-32) is one of North Beach's best Italian restaurants. Take a seat at the bar and step back in time as you order the house cappuccino—made with armagnac, bourbon, chocolate ganache, and absolutely no coffee—while you wait for excellent plates of pasta and fish.

Quince (470 Pacific Ave., 415/775-8500, www.quincerestaurant.com, 5:30pm-9pm Mon.-Thurs., 5pm-9pm Fri.-Sat., $275) is a fine-dining Italian restaurant spotlighting chef-owner Michael Tusk's celebrated pastas. In the exposed-brick dining room, the tasting menu features such delicacies as caviar, white truffle, and abalone with black garlic. In the salon, choose from the à la carte caviar menu. Expect impeccable service and specialty cocktails made tableside.

Neighboring **Cotogna** (490 Pacific Ave., 415/775-8508, www.cotognasf.com, 11:30am-10:30pm Mon.-Thurs., 11:30am-11pm Fri.-Sat., 5pm-9:30pm Sun., $20-68) is also owned by Tusk. Dressed down, with a chic farm-table look, Cotogna offers excellent pizzas, classic meat dishes, and Tusk's signature pastas.

Seafood

Dungeness crabs enjoy celebrity status in San Francisco. The season usually runs November-June, but the freshest crabs are caught and cooked from the start of the season through New Year's. Italian seafood restaurant **Alioto's** (8 Fisherman's Wharf, 415/673-0183, www.aliotos.com, 11am-10pm Sun.-Thurs., 11am-11pm Sat.-Sun., $19-53) serves whole cracked Dungeness in the traditional style. They've also got crab soups, salads, sandwiches, and stews.

Locals have a soft spot for **Scoma's** (1965 Al Scoma Way, Pier 47, 415/771-4383 or 800/644-5852, https://scomas.com, 3pm-9pm Mon.-Thurs., 11:30am-10pm Fri.-Sat., 11:30am-9pm Sun., $11-55), a seafood restaurant with white-tablecloths and high prices.

MARINA AND PACIFIC HEIGHTS
Bakeries and Cafés
Le Marais Bistro and Bakery (2066 Chestnut St., 415/359-9801, www.lemaraisbakery.com, 7am-7pm daily, $10-16) reflects the highly polished farm-to-table dining scene of the next generation. You'll find plenty of the buttery indulgences plus French brasserie classics.

Squeeze into tightly packed **Jane** (2123 Fillmore St., 415/931-5263, http://janeonfillmore.com, 7am-6pm daily, $5-14) for coffee and avocado toast. This small, but chic café serves a selection of light breakfast dishes and a host of elegant salads and hot-pressed sandwiches.

Asian
Kiss Seafood (1700 Laguna St., 415/474-2866, 5:30pm-9:30pm Wed.-Sat., $38-70) is a tiny restaurant (12 seats in total) that boasts some of the freshest fish in town. The lone chef prepares all the fish himself, possibly because of the tiny size of the place. Reservations are a good idea.

California Cuisine
Chef Traci Des Jardins took over the 1895 mess hall in the Presidio's historic Main Post and turned it into the **Commissary** (Presidio, 101 Montgomery St., 415/561-3600, www.thecommissarysf.com, 5:30pm-9pm Mon.-Thurs., 5:30pm-9:30pm Fri.-Sat., $30-42). The cuisine is a blend of San Francisco and Spanish influences that utilizes such ingredients as cod, anchovies, chorizo, and peppers.

There is no escaping the hipster cred of

★ **State Bird Provisions** (1529 Fillmore St., 415/795-1272, http://statebirdsf.com, 5:30pm-10pm Sun.-Thurs., 5:30pm-11pm Fri.-Sat., $30). This unpretentious restaurant excels in carefully crafted California fusion dishes served dim sum-style. The friendly servers can slow their brisk pace to help pair beer or wine with your meal.

The Progress (1529 Fillmore St., 415/673-1294, http://theprogress-sf.com, 5:30pm-10pm Sun.-Thurs., 5:30pm-11pm Fri.-Sat., $17-36), next door to State Bird, serves similarly celebrated eclectic cuisine in a fine-dining setting.

Food Trucks
To get the very best food truck experience, plan a Sunday afternoon at the **Off the Grid Presidio Picnic** (Presidio, Main Post Lawn, 415/339-5888, http://offthegridsf.com, 11am-4pm Sun., mid-Mar.-Nov., $7-17), where six trucks, 17 tents, and two carts roving through the crowds sell everything from Bloody Marys to Vietnamese soup. The Presidio Picnic is a party with live DJs and plenty of dogs, kids, hipsters, Frisbees, and picnic blankets.

CIVIC CENTER AND HAYES VALLEY
French
A Parisian brasserie with a retro-modern look, **Absinthe** (398 Hayes St., 415/551-1590, www.absinthe.com, 11:30am-11pm Mon.-Wed., 11:30am-midnight Thurs.-Fri., 11am-midnight Sat., 11am-10pm Sun., $18-31) serves the notorious "green fairy" along with upscale French bistro fare and the best french fries in the city.

German
★ **Suppenküche** (525 Laguna St., 415/252-9289, www.suppenkuche.com, 5pm-10pm Mon.-Fri., 10am-2:30pm and 5pm-10pm Sat.-Sun., $19-22) brings a taste of Bavaria to the Bay Area. For dinner, expect German classics such as spaetzle, pork, sausage. You name it, they've got it, and it will harden your arteries right up. Suppenküche also has a popular **Biergarten** (424 Octavia St., http://

biergartensf.com, 3pm-9pm Mon.-Sat., 1pm-7pm Sun.) two blocks away.

MISSION AND CASTRO
Bakeries and Cafés
Locals love the artful pastries and panini made on the legendary bread of ★ **Tartine Bakery** (600 Guerrero St., 415/487-2600, www.tartinebakery.com, 8am-7pm Mon., 7:30am-7pm Tues.-Wed., 7:30am-8pm Thurs.-Fri., 8am-8pm Sat.-Sun., $5-15). A line snakes out the door and around the block any time of day. To snag a loaf of bread, order it in advance (not kidding).

Around the corner from Tartine, **Bi-Rite Creamery & Bakeshop** (3692 18th St., 415/626-5600, http://biritecreamery.com, 11am-10pm daily) satisfies your sweet tooth. The ice cream is made by hand with organic milk, cream, and eggs. Flavors change daily.

American
Café Flore (2298 Market St., 415/621-8579, www.cafeflore.com, 7:30am-10pm Mon.-Fri., 9am-11pm Sat., 9am-8pm Sun., $8-28) has been a Castro mainstay since 1973. The food is good, unfussy, and reasonably priced. Order the eggs Benedict for brunch or the Wagyu steak and frites for dinner. Part of the place's charm is the somewhat ramshackle wood building and lush outside garden patio.

Blush (476 Castro St., 415/558-0893, www.blushwinebar.com, 4pm-midnight Mon.-Tues., 4pm-12:30am Wed.-Thurs., 4pm-1:30am Fri., 3pm-1:30am Sat., 3pm-midnight Sun., $13-16) is a slim, classy wine bar with a French country feel. Expect a robust international wine list and a menu of shareable bites—from charcuterie boards to oysters—plus warm sandwiches, salads, and ravioli imported from the French Alps.

French
★ **Frances** (3870 17th St., 415/621-3870, 5pm-10pm Sun. and Tues.-Thurs., 5pm-10:30pm Fri.-Sat., $30-34) wins rave reviews for its California-inspired French cuisine. The short-but-sweet menu is locavore friendly and changes daily; temptations include caramelized Atlantic scallops and bacon beignets. Reservations are strongly advised.

Italian
Delfina (3621 18th St., 415/552-4055, www.delfinasf.com, 5:30pm-10pm Mon.-Thurs., 5:30pm-11pm Fri.-Sat., 5pm-10pm Sun., $10-31) gives Italian cuisine a hearty California twist. From the antipasti to the entrées, the dishes speak of local farms and ranches, fresh seasonal produce, and the best Italian American taste that money can buy.

In the same building, ★ **Pizzeria Delfina** (415/437-6800, 11:30am-10pm Mon. and Wed.-Thurs., 5pm-10pm Tues., 11:30am-11pm Fri., noon-11pm Sat., noon-10pm Sun., $14-22) is casual and low-key, with excellent antipasti and the best pizza in the Mission.

The bar menu at **Beretta** (1199 Valencia St., 415/695-1199, www.berettasf.com, 5:30pm-1am Mon.-Fri., 11am-1am Sat.-Sun., $13-17) consistently wins rave reviews and is hard to pass up, particularly as the restaurant doesn't take reservations for parties under six and the only place to wait is at the bar. Order a Rattlesnake, then a pizza to suck up the venom of that bite.

Mexican
Much of the rich heritage of the Mission district is Hispanic, thus leading to the Mission being *the* place to find a good taco or burrito. **La Taqueria** (2889 Mission St., 415/285-7117, 11am-9pm Wed.-Sat., 11am-8pm Sun., $7-13) makes the best burrito in the city. Critics rave, as do locals grabbing dinner on their way home.

Seafood
For great seafood in a lower-key atmosphere, head for the ★ **Anchor Oyster Bar** (579 Castro St., 415/431-3990, www.anchoroysterbar.com, 11:30am-10pm Mon.-Sat., 4pm-9:30pm Sun., $12-38), an institution in the Castro since 1977. The raw bar features different varieties of oysters, while the dining

room serves seafood, including local favorite Dungeness crab.

GOLDEN GATE PARK AND THE HAIGHT
California Cuisine

Magnolia (1398 Haight St., 415/864-7468, http://magnoliapub.com, 11am-10pm Mon.-Thurs., 11am-11pm Fri., 10am-11pm Sat., 10am-10pm Sun., $16-26) began its life channeling the spirit of the Grateful Dead into its strong beer and laid-back pub fare. To match its muscular beers, the excellent menu is meat-heavy, with a whole section of sausages. The aesthetic is dark and brooding, tapping into the neighborhood's Victorian past. Selections include oysters, bread pudding, flat iron steak, and, for dessert, a stout ice cream float.

Nopa (560 Divisadero St., 415/864-8643, http://nopasf.com, 6pm-midnight Mon.-Thurs. 6pm-1am Fri., 11am-2:20pm and 6pm-1am Sat., 11am-2:30pm and 6pm-midnight Sun., $25-41) serves hip, farm-to-table comfort food on long communal tables. Expect quality ingredients, a global sensibility, and excellent execution. Reservations are essential.

★ **Bar Crudo** (655 Divisadero St., 415/409-0679, 5pm-10pm Sun. and Tues.-Thurs., 5pm-11pm Fri.-Sat., $14-28) is an ideal way to end a day of exploring Golden Gate Park. Inside the light interior, dine on delicate bites of raw fish, light salads, and roasted crab, or soak in the oyster-heavy happy hour. The breadth of the beer selection is astounding.

The **Beach Chalet Brewery** (1000 Great Hwy., 415/386-8439, www.beachchalet.com, 11am-9:30pm Mon.-Thurs., 11am-10pm Fri., 10am-10pm Sat., 8am-10pm Sun., $17-30) is an attractive brewpub and restaurant directly across the street from Ocean Beach. Out back, sister restaurant **Park Chalet** (http://parkchalet.com, noon-9pm Mon.-Thurs., noon-10pm Fri., 11am-10pm Sat., 10am-9pm Sun., $15-27) offers a similar menu with outdoor seating and jumping live music on the weekends.

One of the most famous locations in San Francisco is the ★ **Cliff House** (1090 Point Lobos Ave., 415/386-3330, www.cliffhouse. com). The high-end eatery inhabiting the famed facade is **Sutro's** (11:30am-9:30pm Mon.-Thurs., 11:30am-10pm Fri.-Sat., 11am-9:30pm Sun., $29-49), where expensive plates of steak, lamb, and salmon are best with a glass of California wine. The more casual (and affordable) **Bistro** (9am-3:30pm and 4:15pm-9:30pm Mon.-Sat., 8:30am-3:30pm and 4:15pm-9:30pm Sun., $20-40) serves big bowls of cioppino at an ornately carved zinc bar. The **Lounge** (9am-10:30pm Sun.-Thurs., 9am-11:30pm Fri.-Sat.) is the best deal in the house, where you can sip coffee and drinks without all the fuss.

French

One of the best places in the Haight is in the pocket neighborhood of Cole Valley. Dripping with charm, ★ **Zazie** (941 Cole St., 415/564-5332, www.zaziesf.com, 8am-2pm and 5pm-9pm Mon.-Thurs., 8am-2pm and 5pm-9:30pm Fri., 8am-3pm and 5pm-9:30pm Sat., 8am-3pm and 5pm-9pm Sun., $9-34), a tiny French bistro, is known mainly for brunch. Benedicts, croque monsieur, coq au vin, and boeuf bourguignon go down perfectly with either a latte or Kir Royale.

Mexican

Nopalito (1224 9th Avenue, 415/233-9966, www.nopalitosf.com, 11:30am-10pm daily, $9-24) serves artfully plated traditional Mexican food with bright flavors and local ingredients in an atmosphere that feels fresh. Choose from a slate of margarita, Mexican coffee, and tequila drinks to wash it all down. A second location (306 Broderick St., 415/535-3969) serves the Divisadero corridor.

Accommodations

Both the cheapest and most expensive hotels tend to be in Union Square and downtown. Consistently cheaper digs can be had in the neighborhoods surrounding Fisherman's Wharf. You'll find the most character in the smaller boutique hotels, but plenty of big chain hotels have at least one location in town if you prefer a known quantity.

Valet parking and overnight garage parking can be excruciatingly expensive. Check with your hotel to see if they have a "parking package" that includes this expense.

UNION SQUARE AND DOWNTOWN

Union Square has the greatest concentration of hotels. Those closest to the top of Nob Hill or to Union Square proper are the most expensive.

$150-250

The ★ **Golden Gate Hotel** (775 Bush St., 415/392-3702 or 800/835-1118, $150-225) offers small, charming rooms with friendly, unpretentious hospitality. You'll find a continental breakfast every morning in the hotel lobby. There are only two rates: the higher rate ($225) gets you a room with a private bathroom, while the lower rate ($150) gets you a room with a bath down the hall.

The Mosser's (54 4th St., 415/986-4400 or 800/227-3804, www.themosser.com, $152-342) inexpensive rooms have European-style shared baths in the hallway and bright modern decor that nicely complements the century-old building. Pricier options include bigger rooms with private baths. With a rep for cleanliness and pleasant amenities, including morning coffee and comfy bathrobes, this hotel provides visitors with a cheap crash space in a great location convenient to sights, shops, and public transportation.

The Marker (501 Geary St., 415/292-0100 or 844/736-2753, www.jdvhotels.com, $199-389) shows the vibrant side of San Francisco. Big rooms are whimsically decorated with bright colors, while baths are luxurious and feature cushy animal-print bathrobes. Friendly service comes from purple-velour-coated staff, who know the hotel and the city and will cheerfully tell you all about both. Chair massage complements the free wine and cheese in the large, open guest lounge.

The ★ **Hotel Triton** (342 Grant Ave., 800/808-0290, www.hoteltriton.com, $179-329) adds a bit of whimsy and eco-chic to the stately aesthetic of Union Square. Jerry Garcia decorated a room here, and Häagen-Dazs tailored its own suite, complete with an ice cream-stocked freezer case in the corner. You'll find the rooms tiny but comfortable and well stocked with ecofriendly amenities and bath products. The flat-panel TVs offer a 24-hour yoga channel, and complimentary yoga props can be delivered to your room on request.

Hotel Rex (562 Sutter St., 415/433-4434 or 800/433-4434, www.viceroyhotelsandresorts.com, $180-279) channels San Francisco's literary side, evoking a hotel in the early 1900s when bohemians such as Jack London, Ambrose Bierce, and even Mark Twain roamed and ruminated about the city. Rooms are bright, comfortable, spacious, and decorated with the work of local artists and artisans. The dimly lit **Library Bar** serves breakfast and dinner, and drinks in the evening. Valet parking is available, as is use of the hotel's bicycles.

Rock-and-roll decadence is the theme at **Hotel Zeppelin** (545 Post St., 415/563-0303, www.viceroyhotelsandresorts.com, $194-423), where some of the 196 rooms have record players. You'll find a high-end style, techy conveniences, and loaner bikes and electric scooters. The restaurant and bar serves breakfast, lunch, and dinner, plus drinks late into the night.

Hotel Nikko (222 Mason St., 415/394-1111, www.hotelnikkosf.com, $194-343) offers all the amenities and convenience of a classic midcentury hotel with swank San Francisco style. All 532 rooms in the 22-story building burst with color and Japanese touches. Take a dip in the glassed-in hotel pool, walk your pooch on the sky-high dog run, or enjoy a nightcap in the hotel bar.

A San Francisco legend, the **Clift** (495 Geary St., 415/775-4700, www.clifthotel.com, $188-400) has a lobby worth walking into. The high-ceilinged industrial space is devoted to modern art. Yes, you really are supposed to sit on the antler sofa and the metal chairs. By contrast, the rooms are almost spartan in their simplicity, with colors meant to mimic the city skyline. Stop in for a drink at the **Redwood Room,** done in brown leather and popular with a younger crowd.

Over $250

At the 1904-built **Westin St. Francis** (335 Powell St., 415/397-7000 or 888/627-8546, www.westinstfrancis.com, $250-500), the hotel's robber-baron past is evident as soon as you walk into the immense lobby. The hotel's two wings are the original section, called the Landmark Building, and the 1972 renovation is The Tower. There are 1,200 rooms, making it the largest hotel in the city. Rooms in the historical section are loaded with lavish charms like ornate woodwork and chandeliers, while the modern rooms are large and sport fantastic views of the city and the bay and have use of the famous glass elevators.

Designed by Julia Morgan in the Beaux-Arts style, the ★ **Fairmont San Francisco** (950 Mason St., 415/772-5000, www.fairmont.com, $259-509) opened shortly after the 1906 earthquake. The Fairmont has historical rooms and a Tower addition; large Tower rooms feature marble baths and even more spectacular views than the historical rooms.

The grande dame of San Francisco hotels, **Palace Hotel** (2 New Montgomery St.,

415/512-1111, www.sfpalace.com, $265-395) opened its doors in 1875 to be gutted by fires following the 1906 earthquake. It was rebuilt and reopened in 1909. In 1919, President Woodrow Wilson negotiated the terms of the Treaty of Versailles over lunch at the Garden Court. Today guests take pleasure in beautiful bedrooms and a lavish indoor pool. A meal in the exquisite Garden Court dining room is a must, though you may forget to eat as you gaze upward at the stained-glass domed ceiling.

NORTH BEACH AND FISHERMAN'S WHARF
Under $150

The **San Remo Hotel** (2237 Mason St., 415/776-8688 or 800/352-7366, www.sanremohotel.com, $99-259) is one of the best bargains in the city. The rooms boast the simplest of furnishings and decorations. None have telephones or TVs, and the bathrooms are located down the hall. Downstairs, Fior d'Italia is the oldest Italian restaurant in the country and has a generous happy hour seven days a week.

The ★ **Fisherman's Wharf Hostel** (Fort Mason Bldg. 240, 415/771-7277, www.sfhostels.com/fishermans-wharf, dorm $40-55, private room $110-159) sits in a historic military building in beautiful Fort Mason. The best amenities (aside from the free linens and breakfast) are the views of the bay and Alcatraz, the sweeping lawns and mature trees all around the hostel, and easy proximity to San Francisco's attractions.

$150-250

The **Washington Square Inn** (1660 Stockton St., 415/981-4220 or 800/388-0220, www.wsisf.com, $199-259) looks more like a small, elegant hotel than a B&B. The inn offers 16 rooms with queen or king beds, private baths, flat-screen TVs, and free Wi-Fi. Standard rooms are "cozy" in the European style; some have spa bathtubs, while others have views of Coit Tower and Saints Peter and Paul Church. All enjoy a generous daily continental breakfast.

Over $250

In a district not known for its luxury, the **Argonaut** (495 Jefferson St., 415/563-0800 or 800/790-1415, www.argonauthotel.com, $395-510) in Fisherman's Wharf stands out. Housed in an exposed-brick 1907 warehouse, the hotel embraces its nautical connections to the nines. Many rooms have great views of the bay, and its location is ideal, only steps away from Aquatic Park, Pier 45, Ghirardelli Square, and the excellent Maritime Museum.

MARINA AND PACIFIC HEIGHTS
$150-250

The rooms at the ★ **Marina Motel** (2576 Lombard St., 415/921-9406, www.marinamotel.com, $160-254) may be small, but the place is big on charm. This friendly little motel, decorated in French-country style, welcomes families with kids and dogs. Ask for the room type that best suits your needs when you make your reservations; you can even have one with a full kitchen.

The stately **Queen Anne Hotel** (1590 Sutter St., 415/441-2828, www.queenanne.com, $134-244) is Victorian through and through. Sumptuous fabrics, ornate antiques, and rich colors in the rooms and common areas add to the feeling of decadence and luxury in this boutique bed-and-breakfast. Small, moderate rooms offer attractive accommodations on a budget, while superior rooms and suites are more upscale. Continental breakfast is included, as are a number of high-end services.

Over $250

The **Hotel del Sol** (3100 Webster St., 415/921-5520, www.thehoteldelsol.com, $279-310) embraces its origins as a 1950s motor lodge. Rooms are decorated in bright, bold colors with whimsical accents; family suites and larger rooms have kitchenettes. There's a heated courtyard pool and the ever-popular free parking. The Marina locale offers trendy cafés, restaurants, bars, and shopping within walking distance.

The ★ **Inn at the Presidio** (42 Moraga Ave., 415/800-7356, www.innatthepresidio.com, $295-405) is inside Pershing Hall in the center of the Presidio. Built in 1903, the large brick building has classic rooms and suites (some with fireplaces) with subtle contemporary furnishings that complement the framed photos and Presidio memorabilia sprinkled throughout. On-site amenities include a complimentary breakfast buffet, wine and cheese reception, free Wi-Fi, a covered front porch with rocking chairs overlooking the Main Post, and an outdoor deck with fire pit. There is self-parking ($8) or take advantage of the PresidiGo shuttle.

Tucked in with the money-laden mansions of Pacific Heights, ★ **Hotel Drisco** (2901 Pacific Ave., 800/634-7277, www.hoteldrisco.com, $360-450) offers elegance to discerning visitors. You get quiet, comfy rooms that include a "pillow menu"; continental breakfast with a latte, smoked salmon, and brie; hors d'oeuvres and a glass of wine in the evening; and bicycles on loan.

In Japantown, the ★ **Hotel Kabuki** (1625 Post St., 415/922-3200, www.jdvhotels.com, $299-349) has stylish rooms with Japanese accents in a handsome Eichler building. The hotel is stocked with modern amenities and posh comforts like rainforest showers, loaner bikes, and complimentary passes to Kabuki Springs and Spa.

CIVIC CENTER AND HAYES VALLEY
$150-250

At the **Chateau Tivoli** (1057 Steiner St., 415/776-5462 or 800/228-1647, www.chateautivoli.com, $195-300), the over-the-top colorful exterior matches the American Renaissance interior decor perfectly. Each of the nine unique rooms and suites showcases an exquisite style evocative of the Victorian era. Most rooms have private baths, though the two least expensive share a bath.

Located in Hayes Valley a few blocks from the Opera House, the **Inn at the Opera** (333 Fulton St., 888/298-7198, www.

shellhospitality.com, $229-329) promises to have guests ready for a swanky night of San Francisco culture. French interior styling in the rooms and suites once impressed visiting opera stars and now welcomes guests from all over the world.

The Parsonage (198 Haight St., 415/863-3699, www.theparsonage.com, $240-280) is a classy Victorian bed-and-breakfast with an elegance that fits in with the Hayes Valley chic. Rooms are decorated with antiques, and baths have stunning marble showers. Enjoy pampering, multicourse breakfasts, and brandy and chocolates when you come "home" each night.

Muted colors, cluttered patterns, and modern amenities make accommodations at Proper (1100 Market St., 415/735-7777, www.properhotel.com, $166-251) unique. If the prices are too high, opt for the cozy Bunk Rooms (from $166), which only have room enough for a bunk bed. Downstairs, a stylish restaurant and bar serves breakfast, lunch, and dinner, plus a variety of craft cocktails.

MISSION AND CASTRO
Under $150

At the Inn on Castro (321 Castro St.,

415/861-0321, www.innoncastro.com, $135-265), you've got all kinds of choices. You can pick an economy room with a shared bath, a posh private suite, or a self-service apartment. Once ensconced, you can chill out on the cute patio, or go out into the Castro to take in the legendary entertainment and nightlife. The self-catering apartments can sleep up to four and have fully furnished and appointed kitchens and dining rooms. Amenities include LCD TVs with cable, DVD players, and colorful modern art.

GOLDEN GATE PARK AND THE HAIGHT
$150-250

The Stanyan Park Hotel (750 Stanyan St., 415/751-1000, www.stanyanpark.com, $179-323) graces the Upper Haight area across the street from Golden Gate Park. This renovated 1904-1905 building, listed on the National Register of Historic Places, shows off its Victorian heritage both inside and out. Rooms can be small but are elegantly decorated, and a number of multiple-room suites are available. All 36 rooms include free Wi-Fi and flat-screen TVs, but for a special treat, ask for a room overlooking the park.

Transportation and Services

AIR

San Francisco International Airport (SFO, 800/435-9736, www.flysfo.com) is 13 miles south of San Francisco in the town of Millbrae. You can easily get a taxi ($40) or other ground transportation into the city from the airport. BART is available from SFO's international terminal, but Caltrain is only accessible via a BART connection from SFO. Car rentals are also available. Some San Francisco hotels offer complimentary shuttles from the airport.

As one of the 30 busiest airports in the world, SFO has long check-in and security lines and dreadful overcrowding on major

travel holidays. Plan to arrive at the airport two hours prior to departure for domestic flights and three hours prior to an international flight.

TRAIN AND BUS

Amtrak (www.amtrak.com) does not run directly into San Francisco, but several lines reach the Bay Area at stations in Emeryville, Oakland, and San Jose. These include *Capitol Corridor* (Bay Area to Sacramento and Auburn), the *Coast Starlight* (Seattle to Los Angeles via the Bay Area), the *San Joaquin* (Southern California and Central Valley via Bay Area), and the *California Zephyr*

(Emeryville to Chicago). Amtrak runs buses from its Bay Area stations into downtown San Francisco.

Greyhound (200 Folsom St., 415/495-1569, www.greyhound.com) offers bus service to San Francisco from all over the country.

CAR

The **Bay Bridge** (toll $5-7) links I-80 to San Francisco from the east. (Note that Bay Bridge tolls will increase annually through 2025.). The **Golden Gate Bridge** (toll $7.75) connects Highway 1 from the north. From the south, U.S. 101 and I-280 snake up the peninsula and into the city.

Get a detailed map and directions to drive into San Francisco—the freeway interchanges, especially surrounding the east side of the Bay Bridge, can be confusing, and the traffic congestion is legendary. For traffic updates and route planning, visit **511.org** (www.511.org).

Car Rental

All the major car rental agencies have a presence at the **San Francisco Airport** (SFO, 800/435-9736, www.flysfo.com). In addition, most reputable hotels can offer or recommend a car rental. Rates tend to run $60-120 per day and $250-600 per week (including taxes and fees), with discounts for weekly and longer rentals.

Parking

Parking a car in San Francisco can easily cost $50 per day or more. Most downtown and Union Square hotels do not include free parking with your room. Expect to pay $35-65 per night for parking, which may not include in-and-out privileges.

Street parking meters cost up to $4.50 per hour, often go late into the night, and charge during the weekends. At least many now take credit cards. Unmetered street parking spots are as rare as unicorns and often require residential permits for stays longer than two hours during the day. Lots and garages fill up quickly, especially during special events.

MUNI

The **Muni** (www.sfmta.com, adults $2.75, youth and seniors $1.35, children under 4 free) transit system can get you where you want to go as long as time isn't a concern. Bus and train tickets can be purchased from any Muni driver; underground trains have ticket machines at the entrance. Exact change is required, except on the cable cars ($7), where drivers can make change for up to $20. A **Visitor Passport** ($22/1 day, $33/3 days, $43/7 days) offers unlimited rides.

BART

Bay Area Rapid Transit, or **BART** (www.bart.gov, fares range $4-10 one-way), is the Bay Area's metropolitan underground system. Sadly, there's only one arterial line through the city. However, service directly from San Francisco Airport into the city runs daily, as does service to Oakland Airport, the cities of Oakland and Berkeley, and many other East Bay destinations. BART connects to the Caltrain system and San Francisco Airport in Millbrae. See the website for route maps, schedules (BART usually runs on time), and fare information.

To buy tickets, use the vending machines found in every BART station. If you plan to ride more than once, you can add money to a single ticket and then keep that ticket and reuse it for each ride.

Caltrain

This traditional commuter rail line runs along the peninsula into Silicon Valley, from San Francisco to San Jose, with limited continuing service to Gilroy. **Caltrain** (800/660-4287, www.caltrain.com, one-way $3.75-15) Baby Bullet trains can get you from San Jose to San Francisco in an hour during commuting hours. Extra trains are often added for San Francisco Giants, San Francisco 49ers, and San Jose Sharks games.

You must purchase a ticket in advance at the vending machines found in all stations. The main Caltrain station in San Francisco is at the corner of 4th and King Streets, within walking distance of AT&T Park and Moscone Center.

Taxis and Ride Shares
You'll find taxis around all the major tourist areas of the city. If you have trouble hailing a cab, try **City Wide Dispatch** (415/920-0700, www.citywidetransit.com). Uber and Lyft vehicles are equally ubiquitous.

SERVICES
Tourist Information
The main San Francisco **Visitor Information Center** (900 Market St., 415/391-2000, www.sanfrancisco.travel; 9am-5pm Mon.-Fri., 9am-3pm Sat.-Sun., May-Oct.; 9am-5pm Mon.-Fri., 9am-3pm Sat., Nov.-Apr.) can give you information about attractions and hotels as well as discounted tickets for various museums and attractions. The Market Street location (just below Hallidie Plaza at Powell Street) has brochures in 14 different languages and a few useful coupons.

To save money, consider using a **City Pass** (888/330-5008, www.citypass.com, adults $89, children 5-11 $69), which includes a cable car and Muni passport, a ferry cruise, and entrance to the Academy of Sciences, Aquarium of the Bay, the Exploratorium,

and the SFMOMA for nine days. A **Go Card** (800/887-9103, www.smartdestinations.com, adults $69-155, children 3-12, $55-115) offers a variety of passes from one to multiday, with access to nearly 30 attractions.

Emergency Services
The central station of the **San Francisco Police Department** (766 Vallejo St., 415/315-2400, www.sf-police.org) is between North Beach and Chinatown.

San Francisco boasts a large number of full-service hospitals. Downtown, **St. Francis Memorial Hospital** (900 Hyde St., 415/353-6000, www.dignityhealth.org) has an emergency department, as does **St. Mary's Medical Center** (450 Stanyan St., 415/668-1000, www.dignityhealth.org).

Dignity Health has a several Urgent Care clinics (www.gohealthuc.com) for nonemergencies: North Beach (170 Columbus Ave., 415/965-8050, 8am-8pm Mon.-Fri., 9am-5pm Sat.-Sun.), the Marina (3259 Pierce St., 415/965-7942, 8am-8pm Mon.-Fri., 9am-5pm Sat.-Sun.), Lower Pacific Heights (1801 Divisadero St., 415/965-7944, 8am-8pm Mon.-Fri., 9am-5pm Sat.-Sun.), and the Castro (2288 Market St, 415/964-4855, 8am-8pm Mon.-Fri., 9am-5pm Sat.-Sun.).

North Bay

Marin County, in the North Bay, is San Francisco's backyard. Beginning with the Marin Headlands at the terminus of the Golden Gate Bridge, there is a nearly unbroken expanse of wildlands from San Francisco Bay to Tomales Bay. Here you'll find rugged cliffs plunging into the Pacific, towering redwoods, and verdant pastures.

MARIN HEADLANDS
The Marin Headlands lie north of San Francisco at the end of the Golden Gate Bridge. The land here encompasses a wide swath of virgin wilderness, former military

structures, and a historical lighthouse. You can cross the Golden Gate Bridge and explore Marin County on a day trip, but you may spend more time in the car than strolling beaches and forests. To better enjoy the parks and hiking trails, plan an early start.

Vista Point
At the north end of the Golden Gate Bridge, the aptly named **Vista Point** offers views from the Marin Headlands toward San Francisco. If you dream of walking across the **Golden Gate Bridge** (5am-6:30pm daily Nov.-Apr., 5am-9pm daily Apr.-Oct.), be sure

to bring a warm coat as the wind and fog can really whip through. The bridge is 1.7 miles long, so a round-trip walk will turn into a 3.4-mile hike. Bikes are allowed daily 24 hours on the west side. Bicycle riders may also use the east side but must be careful to watch for pedestrians. Dogs are never allowed on either side.

To reach Vista Point, take U.S. 101 north across the Golden Gate Bridge. The first exit on the Marin County side is Vista Point; turn right into the parking lot. This small parking lot often fills early.

Marin Headlands Visitors Center

A great place to start your exploration of the headlands is at the **Marin Headlands Visitors Center** (Field Rd. and Bunker Rd., 415/331-1540, www.nps.gov/goga, 9:30am-4:30pm daily) in the old chapel at Fort Barry. The park rangers can give you the current lowdown on the best trails, beaches, and campgrounds in the Headlands. Grab a complimentary coffee and peruse the displays highlighting the park's human and natural history, as well as the small but well-stocked bookstore.

Point Bonita Lighthouse

The **Point Bonita Lighthouse** (415/331-1540, www.nps.gov/goga, 12:30pm-3:30pm Sat.-Mon.) has been protecting the headlands for more than 150 years. You'll need some dedication to visit Point Bonita, since it's only open a few days each week and there's no direct access by car. A 0.5-mile trail with steep sections leads from the parking lot and trailhead on Field Road. Along the way, you'll pass through a hand-cut tunnel chiseled from the rock by the builders of the lighthouse, then over the bridge that leads to the building. Point Bonita was the third lighthouse built on the West Coast and is now the last staffed lighthouse in California. Today the squat hexagonal building shelters automatic lights, horns, and signals.

Marine Mammal Center

Inspired by the ocean's beauty and want to learn more about the animals that live in it? Visit the **Marine Mammal Center** (2000 Bunker Rd., 415/289-7325, www.marine-mammalcenter.org, 10am-4pm daily, free) at Fort Cronkhite in the Marin Headlands. The center is a hospital for sick and injured seals and sea lions. Visitors are free to wander around and look at the educational displays to learn more about what the center does, but the one-hour docent-led tours (daily, times vary by season, adults $9, seniors and children 5-17 $5, children under 5 free) explain the program in greater depth. Visitors will also get an education on the impact of human activity on marine mammals and maybe a chance for close encounters with some of the center's patients.

Nike Missile Site

Military history buffs jump at the chance to tour a restored Cold War-era Nike missile base, known in military speak as SF-88. The **Nike Missile Site** (Field Rd. past the Headlands Visitors Center, 415/331-1453, www.nps.gov/goga, 12:30pm-3:30pm Sat.) is the only such restored Nike base in the United States. Volunteers lead tours at 12:45pm and 1:45pm on the first Saturday of the month. On the tour, you'll see the fueling area, the testing and assembly building, and even take a ride on the missile elevator down into the pits that once stored missiles built to defend the United States from the Soviet Union. As restoration work continues, the tour changes as new areas become available to visitors.

Hiking

The Marin Headlands is some of the most beautiful landscape in the state, with unparalleled views of the Golden Gate Bridge and the Pacific Ocean.

From the Marin Headlands Visitors Center parking lot (Field Rd. and Bunker Rd.), the **Lagoon Trail** (1.75 miles, easy) encircles Rodeo Lagoon and gives bird-watchers an eagle's-eye view of the egrets, pelicans, and

North Bay

SEE
"POINT REYES
NATIONAL SEASHORE"
DETAIL

TOMALES
POINT

★ POINT REYES
NATIONAL
SEASHORE

Tomales Bay

★ POINT REYES
HISTORIC
LIGHTHOUSE

Inverness

Point Reyes
Station

LIMANTOUR RD

Olema

Philip Burton

Golden Gate
NRA

Wilderness

Area

SHORELINE HWY

BOLINAS-
FAIRFAX RD

Bolinas

Bolinas
Lagoon

Bolinas Bay

PACIFIC

Stinson
Beach

OCEAN

Farallon
Islands

Muir Beach

SEE
"MARIN
HEADLANDS"
DETAIL

Sausalito

GOLDEN GATE ⊞
BRIDGE

Golden
Gate Park

SAN FRANCISCO

0   4 mi
0   4 km

© AVALON TRAVEL

1

TOMALES-
PETALUMA RD

PETALUMA VALLEY FORD RD

116

101

STONEY POINT
RD

PETALUMA HILL RD

ADOBE RD

CHILENO
VALLEY RD

Laguna
Lake

BODEGA AVE

Petaluma

MARSHALL

SHORELINE HWY

PETALUMA RD

Soulajule
Reservoir

POINT REYES RD

LAKEVILLE HWY

Petaluma
River

Nicasio
Reservoir

PETALUMA

NOVATO

NICASIO VALLEY RD

Stafford
Lake

BLVD

101

Novato

To
Vallejo
→

Samuel P.
Taylor SP

SIR FRANCIS DRAKE BLVD

LUCAS VALLEY RD

37

San
Geronimo

Kent
Lake

Fairfax

NORTH SAN PEDRO
RD

San
Pablo
Bay

San
Anselmo

San
Rafael

China Camp
State Park

Kentfield

San Pablo Strait

Mount
Tamalpais
State Park

Mill
Valley

Corte Madera

RICHMOND-
SAN RAFAEL BRIDGE

Muir Woods →
National Monument

Tennessee
Valley

Richardson Bay

131

Tiburon

580

Richmond

ANGEL ISLAND
STATE PARK

Treasure
Island

Berkeley

101

1

101

80

Marin Headlands

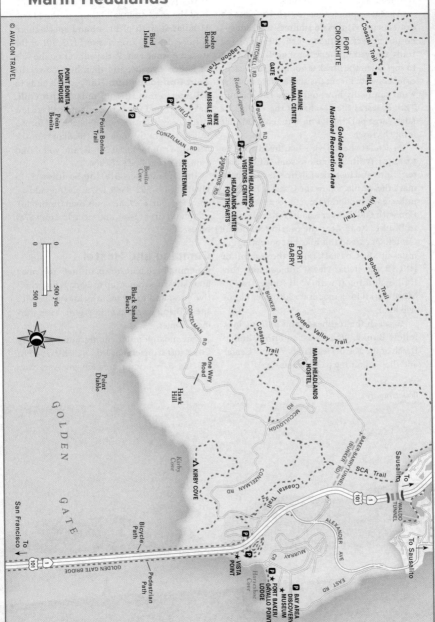

© AVALON TRAVEL

POINT BONITA
LIGHTHOUSE

Point
Bonita

Point Bonita Trail

Bird
Island

Rodeo
Beach

Lagoon Trail

Rodeo Lagoon

FORT
CRONKHITE

MITCHELL RD

GATE

MARINE
MAMMAL CENTER

Coastal Trail

HILL 88

BUNKER RD

NIKE
MISSILE SITE

FIELD RD

CONZELMAN RD

SIMONDS RD

MARIN HEADLANDS
VISITORS CENTER

HEADLANDS CENTER
FOR THE ARTS

BICENTENNIAL

Golden Gate
National Recreation Area

Miwok Trail

FORT
BARRY

Bobcat Trail

Bonita
Cove

Black Sands
Beach

Point
Diablo

CONZELMAN RD

One Way
Road

Hawk
Hill

Coastal Trail

BUNKER RD

Rodeo Valley Trail

MARIN HEADLANDS
HOSTEL

MCCULLOUGH RD

KIRBY COVE

Kirby
Cove

CONZELMAN RD

Coastal Trail

BAKER-BARRY TUNNEL (BUNKER RD)

SCA Trail

To
Sausalito

WALDO
TUNNEL

101

1

GOLDEN

GATE

To
San Francisco

Bicycle
Path

Pedestrian
Path

GOLDEN GATE BRIDGE

101

To
San Francisco

VISTA
POINT

Horseshoe
Cove

MURRAY CIR

FORT BAKER/
CAVALLO POINT
LODGE

BAY AREA
DISCOVERY
MUSEUM

ALEXANDER AVE

EAST RD

To Sausalito

0   500 yds
0   500 m

other seabirds that call the lagoon home. The trailhead is near the restrooms.

An easy spot to get to, **Rodeo Beach** draws many visitors on summer weekends— do not expect solitude on the beach or the trails, or even in the water. Locals come out to surf when the break is going, while beach-combers watch from the shore. Note that the wind can really howl out here. The Lagoon Trail accesses the beach, but there is also a fairly large parking lot on Bunker Road that is much closer.

At Rodeo Beach is a trailhead for the **Coastal Trail.** To explore some of the battery ruins and historical signposts that pockmark these hills, follow the Coastal Trail (1.5 miles, easy-moderate) north to its intersection with Old Bunker Road Trail and return to Bunker Road near the Marine Mammal Center. Or extend this hike by continuing 2.3 miles up the Coastal Trail to the summit of **Hill 88** and stellar views. You can loop this trail by linking it with Wolf Ridge Trail to Miwok Trail for a moderate 3.8-mile round-trip hike.

To reach the trailheads and parking lots, follow Bunker Road west to either Rodeo Beach or the Marin Headlands Visitors Center and their adjoining parking lots.

Biking

If you prefer two wheels to two feet, you'll find the road and trail biking in the Marin Headlands both plentiful and spectacular. A fun ride leads from just off U.S. 101 at the Rodeo Avenue exit. Park your car on the side of Rodeo Avenue, and then bike down the short **Rodeo Avenue Trail,** which ends in a T intersection after 0.7 mile at **Alta Trail.** Take a left, and access to **Bobcat Trail** is a few yards away. Continue on Bobcat Trail for 2.5 miles straight through the Headlands to the **Miwok Trail** for just 0.5 mile, and you'll find yourself out at Rodeo Beach.

In San Francisco, **Blazing Saddles** (2715 Hyde St., 415/202-8888, www.blazingsaddles. com, $8/hour, $32/day) rents road (from $48), mountain (from $48), and electric (from $78) bikes.

Camping and Hostel

Camping here requires planning: You must book sites in advance (up to 30 days for primitive sites, and three months for full-service sites). Bring warm camping gear, even during summer.

The most popular campground is **Kirby Cove** (off Conzelman Rd., 415/331-1540 or 877/444-6777, www.recreation.gov, Apr.-Nov.,

Rodeo Beach

reservations required, $30). Five secluded and shaded campsites provide a beautiful respite complete with bay views and a private beach. Getting there requires a one-mile hike from the parking lot. Make reservations well in advance for summer weekends; this popular campground fills fast.

The **Bicentennial Campground** (Battery Wallace parking lot, 415/331-1540 or 877/444-6777, www.recreation.gov reservations required, Mar.-Dec., $20) boasts three campsites easily accessible from the parking lot. Each site can accommodate a maximum of three people in one tent, and there's no water available or fires allowed on-site. A nearby picnic area has barbecue grills that campers can use to cook.

A 2.5-mile hike from the Tennessee Valley Trailhead leads to **Hawk Campground** (reservations 415/331-1540, reservations required, free) with three primitive sites. Your reward for the work of packing in all your gear and water is a near-solitary camping experience. Amenities include chemical toilets but no water, and fires are not allowed.

For budget accommodations indoors, the **Marin Headlands Hostel** (Bldg. 941, Fort Barry, 415/331-2777, www.norcalhostels.org/marin, dorm $31-37, private room $105-132) has full kitchen facilities, Internet access, laundry rooms, and a rec room. Surprisingly cozy and romantic, the hostel is sheltered in the turn-of-the-20th-century buildings of Fort Barry, creating a unique atmosphere. With the headlands right outside your door, there is no lack of activities or exploration opportunities.

Transportation

The Marin Headlands are just north of the Golden Gate Bridge on Highway 1 and U.S. 101. Traffic can be heavy on beautiful weekend days, particularly in the headlands, so plan to get here early.

At the north end of the bridge, the Alexander Avenue exit offers two options for exploring the headlands. To reach the Marin Headlands Visitors Center and Nike Missile Site, turn left onto Bunker Road and travel through the one-way tunnel. If the Bonita Lighthouse is your first stop, follow Alexander Avenue right and travel under the highway to Conzelman Road, which leads up the hill along the southern edge of the headlands overlooking the Golden Gate. Keep in mind that many of the roads are very narrow and become one-way in places.

SAUSALITO

A former commercial fishing town and home to a World War II shipyard, the affluent town of Sausalito still has a few old cannery buildings and plenty of docks, most of which are now lined with pleasure boats. Bridgeway, the main drag, runs along the shore, and the concrete boardwalk is perfect for strolling and biking. Farther north is the heart of working Sausalito, where the lovely waterfront Dunphy Park is rarely crowded, and the city's famous houseboats retain their character. To the south, the main strip eventually leads to Fort Baker, with views of the city.

In town, the **San Francisco Bay Model** (2100 Bridgeway, 415/332-3871, www.spn.usace.army.mil, 9am-4pm Tues.-Fri., 10am-5pm Sat.-Sun., summer; 9am-4pm Tues.-Sat., winter; free) is a scale hydraulic model that demonstrates how the currents and tides of the bay and the Sacramento-San Joaquin River Delta affect the bay and estuary surrounding San Francisco.

Fort Baker

Fort Baker (435 Murray Circle, Sausalito, 415/331-1540, www.nps.gov/goga, sunrise-sunset daily) is a 335-acre former Army Post established in 1905. With the transfer of many of the Bay Area's military outposts to parkland and civilian use, Fort Baker was handed over to the Golden Gate National Recreation Area. The location, just east of the Golden Gate Bridge, secluded in a shallow valley, makes it a great destination to enjoy city views and a wind-free beach. The fort includes many elegant homes with large porches centered around the oval parade grounds.

Most of the historic structures are part of the Cavallo Point Lodge and its two restaurants. Download the Cell Phone Walking Tour, an audio tour of the fort available in one- or three-hour formats.

Bay Area Discovery Museum

Surrounded by Fort Baker, the **Bay Area Discovery Museum** (557 McReynolds Rd., Sausalito, 415/339-3900, www.baykids-museum.org, 9am-4pm Tues.-Fri., 10am-5pm Sat., 9am-5pm Sun., adults and children 1 and up $15, seniors and babies 6-11 months $14, first Wed. of the month free) is a surefire hit with the younger set. The indoor-outdoor space is filled with the stuff that excites kids' imaginations—a train room, a tot room, an art studio, frequent story times, and a "construction site" where they can don hard hats and dig to their heart's content. Most of the exhibits are directly related to the museum's location.

Food

Sausalito's main drag is full of places to eat. Most are expensive, reflecting the quality of the view and not necessarily the food. Fortunately, there are some standouts. A sidewalk café across the street from the waterfront, **Copita Tequileria y Comida** (739 Bridgeway, 415/331-7400, www.copitares-taurant.com, 11:30am-9:30pm Mon.-Thurs., 11:30am-10:30pm Fri., 11am-10:30pm Sat., 11am-9:30pm Sun., $11-19) serves upscale Mexican food such as oyster tacos and slow-cooked carnitas alongside a variety of tangy ceviche. The noise level and long wait on sunny summer or weekend days may beat out the restaurant's other charms.

Fish (350 Harbor Dr., 415/331-3474, www.331fish.com, 11:30am-8:30pm daily, $9-23, cash only) can hook you up with some of the best sustainable seafood in the North Bay, in a charming, unpretentious café overlooking the water. Fresh wild fish prepared using a California-style mix of international cooking techniques results in amazing dishes.

Cibo (1201 Bridgeway, 415/331-2426, www. cibosausalito.com, 7am-5pm daily, $8-17) sits in the hip center of Sausalito. In crisp modern surroundings, this café serves a number of breakfast dishes, hot and cold panini, hearty salads with locally sourced ingredients, and a rich array of coffee drinks and boutique sodas.

Snag a blanket and a seat on the porch to watch the fog roll in over the Golden Gate Bridge at ★ **Farley Bar** (Cavallo Point Lodge, 601 Murray Circle, Fort Baker, Sausalito, 415/339-4751, www.cavallopoint. com, 11am-11pm Sun.-Thurs., 11am-midnight Fri.-Sat., $10-28). With cocktails, wine, and oysters, Farley is the perfect end to a day of hiking. Inside the lodge, **Murray Circle Restaurant** (415/339-4751, www.ca-vallopoint.com; 7am-11am, 11:30am-2pm, and 5:30pm-9pm Mon.-Thurs.; 7am-11am, 11:30am-2pm, and 5:30pm-10pm Fri.; 7am-2:30pm, and 5:30pm-10pm Sat.; 7am-2:30pm and 5:30pm-9pm Sun.; $25-60) has a menu based on the best Marin produce, seafood, meat, and dairy, with touches from cuisines around the world.

Accommodations

The Gables Inn (62 Princess St., 415/289-1100 or 800/966-1554, www.gablesinnsau-salito.com, $190-545) opened in 1869 and is the oldest B&B in the area. Although this inn honors its long history, it has also kept up with the times, adding rooms with panorama bay views and flat-screen televisions, Internet access, and luxurious baths to all 16 rooms. Genial innkeepers serve a buffet breakfast each morning and host a wine and cheese soiree each evening.

With a checkered history dating back to 1915, the **Hotel Sausalito** (16 El Portal, 415/332-0700, www.hotelsausalito.com, $175-395) was a speakeasy, a bordello, and a home for the writers and artists of the Beat generation. Today this tiny boutique hotel, with its yellow walls and wrought-iron beds, evokes the Mediterranean coast.

For a taste of the Marin good life, stay at Sausalito's **Inn Above Tide** (30 El Portal, 415/332-9435 or 800/893-8433, www.

innabovetide.com, $405-885). The inn sits over the edge of the water looking out at the San Francisco skyline and most rooms have private decks that show off sublime views. Guests love the smart upscale furnishings, the stand-alone fireplaces, and the rooms with oversize bathtubs set by windows.

★ **Cavallo Point Lodge** (601 Murray Circle, Fort Baker, Sausalito, 415/339-4700 or 888/651-2003, www.cavallopoint.com, $449-813) offers a stay in beautiful historical homes that feature early 20th-century woodwork and wraparound porches, but 21st-century amenities such as lush carpets, beds dressed in organic linens, flat-screen TVs, wireless Internet, gas fireplaces, and bathtubs so deep you can get lost. Cavallo Lodge also has eco-chic accommodations in its newer two-story buildings. You'll find floor-to-ceiling windows framing spectacular views, radiant floor heating, and private porches. The lodge has excellent environmental credentials and is dog-friendly. The excellent Murray Circle Restaurant and Farley Bar are on-site.

Transportation

Sausalito is north of San Francisco just over the Golden Gate Bridge; it is easily accessible by bicycle on side roads or by car on U.S. 101. Take U.S. 101 and exit at Alexander Avenue; turn left for Fort Baker or stay right for downtown Sausalito. In town, the narrow oceanfront main road gets very crowded on weekends; park and walk instead. Street parking is mostly metered.

The ferry is a great way to get to Sausalito from San Francisco. Two companies make the trip daily, which takes up to an hour. The **Blue and Gold Fleet** (415/705-8200, www.blueandgoldfleet.com, 11am-6:15pm Mon.-Fri., 11am-7:30pm Sat.-Sun., adults $12.50, seniors and children $7.50, children under age 5 free) makes the trip from Pier 41. Largely serving commuters, the **Golden Gate Ferry** (415/455-2000, http://goldengate.org, 7:10am-7:50pm Mon.-Fri., 10:40am-6:45pm Sat.-Sun., adults $12, seniors and children $6, children under age 5 free) leaves from the Ferry

Building, closer to downtown San Francisco. Bikes can be taken on both.

TIBURON

Tiburon's small downtown backs onto a popular marina. Aside from the views, one of the greatest draws to Tiburon is its proximity to Angel Island, the largest island in the bay and one of the most unique state parks around.

★ Angel Island State Park

Angel Island (415/435-1915 or 415/435-5390, www.parks.ca.gov, 8am-sunset daily, admission included with ferry rate) has a long history, beginning with regular visits (though no permanent settlements) by the Coastal Miwok people. During the Civil War the U.S. Army created a fort on the island in anticipation of Confederate attacks from the Pacific. The attacks never came, but the Army maintained a presence here. Later, the Army built a Nike missile base on the island to protect San Francisco from possible Soviet attacks. (The missile base is not open to the public but can be seen from roads and trails.)

Start your visit at the lovely **visitors center** (9:30am-4:30pm daily) in Ayala Cove. Then explore **Camp Reynolds,** the West Garrison built during the Civil War, and **Fort McDowell,** a large base that served as a point of discharge during World War II.

IMMIGRATION STATION

Angel Island's history also has a sobering side. Between 1910 and 1940, it served as an immigration station for inbound ships and as a concentration camp for Chinese emigrants attempting to escape turmoil in their homeland. Europeans were waved through, but Chinese were herded into barracks as government officials scrutinized their papers. After months and sometimes years of waiting, many were sent back to China. Poetry lines the walls of the barracks, expressing the despair of the immigrants who had hoped for a better life. The **Immigration Station** (415/435-5537, 11am-3pm Wed.-Sun., adults $5, children 6-17 $3, children under 6 free) is open to visitors;

docent-led tours are also available (11am and 12:30pm Wed.-Sun., adults $7, children 5-11 $5).

RECREATION

Perimeter Road (5 miles, moderate) passes all Angel Island's points of interest and is a popular bike ride. Hikers can get off the beaten path and scale Mount Livermore via either the **North Ridge Trail** or the **Sunset Trail** (4.5 miles round-trip, moderate). At the top, enjoy gorgeous bay views. For the best experience, make a loop by taking one trail up the mountain and the other back down. **Bike rentals** (415/435-3392, http://angelisland.com, daily, $15-25/hour, $60-90/day) are available at Ayala Cove.

FOOD

Angel Island Café (415/435-3392, http://angelislandsf.com, 10am-2pm Mon.-Tues., 10am-3pm Wed.-Fri., 10am-4pm Sat.-Sun. Apr. and Oct., 10am-3pm Mon.-Fri., 11am-4pm Sat.-Sun. May-Sept., $8-14) serves hot sandwiches, wraps, salad, soup, and an inventive kids menu. In summer, nearby **Angel Island Cantina** (11:30am-4:30pm Sat.-Sun., $8-14) serves burgers, tacos, oysters, beer, wine, and pitchers of mimosas and sangria.

Boxed lunches are also available for an alfresco lunch at one of Angel Island's many scattered picnic tables.

CAMPING

Camping is available at nine primitive **campsites** (800/444-7275 or www.reserve-california.com, $30) that fill up quickly; successful campers reserve their sites six months in advance. Each "environmental site" is equipped with food lockers (a must), surprisingly nice outhouses, running water, and a barbecue. You must bring your own charcoal, as wood fires are strictly prohibited. The three **Ridge Sites** sit on the southwest side of the island, known to be fairly windy; the six **East Bay** and **Sunrise Sites** face the East Bay. Despite the dramatic urban views, camping here is a little like backpacking; plan on walking up to 2.5 miles from the ferry to your campsite.

GETTING THERE

The harbor at Tiburon is the easiest place to access Angel Island out in the middle of San Francisco Bay. The private **Angel Island-Tiburon Ferry** (415/435-2131, http://angelislandferry.com, 10am-3pm Mon.-Fri., 10am-5pm Sat.-Sun. May-Sept., 10am-1pm

Angel Island

Mon.-Tues., 10am-3pm Wed.-Fri., 10am-5pm Sat.-Sun. Oct., 10am-3pm Sat.-Sun. Nov.-Feb., 10am-1pm Wed.-Fri., 10am-3pm Sat.-Sun. Mar., 10am-1pm Mon.-Tues., 10am-3pm Wed.-Fri., 10am-4pm Sat.-Sun. Apr., adults $15, seniors $14, children 6-12 $13, children 3-5 $5, children under 3 free, bicycles $1, cash only) can get you out to the island in about 10 minutes and runs several times a day.

You can also take the **Blue and Gold Fleet** (415/705-8200, www.blueandgoldfleet.com, one-way adults $9.75, seniors and children 5-11 $5.50, children under 5 free) to Angel Island from San Francisco's Pier 41. Blue and Gold ferries begin sailing at 9:45am daily from San Francisco, and the last ferry back departs at 3:40pm Monday-Friday and 4:15pm Saturday-Sunday. Both ferries accommodate bicycles.

An hour-long **tram tour** (415/897-0715 or 415/435-3392, http://angelislandsf.com, daily Apr.-Oct., Sat.-Sun. Nov.-Feb., adults $16.50, seniors $15, children 6-12 $10.50) navigates the island or opt for a docent-led two-hour **Segway tour** (415/897-0715 or 415/435-3392, http://angelislandsf.com, daily, $68).

Food and Accommodations

The lovely **Waters Edge Hotel** (25 Main St., 415/789-5999, www.marinhotels.com, $289-519) is a boutique lodge that lives up to its name. You can stumble right out of your room onto the dock and over to the Angel Island ferry. Inside, you'll love the feather beds, cushy robes, a fireplace, and breakfast delivered to your room each morning.

Sam's Anchor Café (27 Main St., 415/435-4527, www.samscafe.com, 11am-5pm Mon., 11am-11pm Tues.-Thurs., 11am-midnight Fri., 9:30am-midnight Sat., 9:30am-11am Sun., $18-29) sits on the water with a large glassed-in deck and specializes in seafood and wine. Catch some rays over oysters on the half shell, fish-and-chips, or a burger. At night, the place becomes a bit fancier, with white tablecloths and low lighting inside.

Guaymas (5 Main St., 415/435-6300, www.guaymasrestaurant.com, 11:30am-8:30pm Sun.-Thurs., 11:30am-9pm Fri.-Sat., $16-30) has big plates of Mexican favorites, a prime spot on the water, and a generous happy hour (4pm-7pm daily).

For a casual breakfast or lunch, **Caffè Acri** (1 Main St., 415/435-8515, www.caffeacri.com, 6am-6:30pm Mon.-Fri., 7am-6:30pm Sat.-Sun., $5-13) anchors the main drag.

Transportation

Tiburon is located on a peninsula about eight miles north of the Golden Gate Bridge. From San Francisco, take U.S. 101 north to the Tiburon Boulevard (CA 131) exit. Stay to the right and follow the road along the water for nearly six miles until you reach the small downtown area. Parking is limited to 2 hours in town near the docks. Four downtown lots offer hourly parking ($4-15/day)

Tiburon is very walkable and a great destination via ferry from San Francisco. The **Blue and Gold Fleet** (415/705-8200, www.blueandgoldfleet.com) runs multiple daily trips (30-45 minutes, 9:45am-10pm Mon.-Fri., 11am-10pm Sat.-Sun., adults $12.50, seniors and children 5-11 $7.50, children under 5 free) to Tiburon from San Francisco's Pier 41.

MILL VALLEY

Mill Valley is a gateway to Marin's most breathtaking parkland—from the bayside marshlands to the slopes of Mount Tamalpais. Continue past the turnoff to Highway 1 along Miller Avenue to reach the charming downtown tucked in a redwood valley. The small square is filled with cute shops, galleries, and great food.

Hiking and Biking

As U.S. 101 enters Marin County, the Mill Valley/Stinson Beach exit leads west through unincorporated Tamalpais Valley. One of the most popular—and crowded (especially on summer weekends)—places to hike is the **Tennessee Valley Trailhead** (end of Tennessee Valley Rd.). A quick hike from the trailhead can take you out to the **Haypress Campground** (about one mile, moderate), which has picnic tables and pretty views. For a nice long hike, take the **Old Springs Trail** (1.3 miles) down to the **Miwok Trail.** Turn right, and after 0.3 mile, take another right at **Wolf Ridge Trail** (0.7 mile) to the **Coastal Trail.** Taking a right, you'll intersect the **Tennessee Valley Trail** after 1.3 miles, which, taking another right toward the east, leads you back to the trailhead (1.4 miles).

The Tennessee Valley Trailhead has many multiuse trails designated for bikers as well as hikers. The **Valley Trail** (four miles roundtrip) takes you down the Tennessee Valley and all the way out to Tennessee Beach. A longer ride runs up the **Miwok Trail** (two miles) northward, also accessed by Tennessee Valley Road. Turn southwest onto the **Coyote Ridge Trail** (0.7 mile); then catch the **Coastal Fire Road** (1.4 miles) the rest of the way west to Muir Beach.

To reach the Tennessee Valley Trailhead, take the Mill Valley/Stinson Beach exit off U.S. 101 and drive 0.6 mile, passing under the freeway. Continuing straight through the light then turn left on Tennessee Valley Road. Drive two miles to the trailhead.

Food and Accommodations

The **Mill Valley Inn** (165 Throckmorton Ave., 415/389-6608 or 855/334-7946, www. marinhotels.com, $279-340) is the only hotel in downtown Mill Valley. The inn offers 25 rooms, including private cottages. Rooms in the Creekhouse have a historical feel and overlook the creek, and all main building rooms have French doors that open onto private patios. Furnishings are classic yet contemporary, and some rooms have fireplaces.

★ **Mill Valley Beerworks** (173 Throckmorton Ave., 415/888-8218, http:// millvalleybeerworks.com, 5:30pm-9pm Mon., 5:30pm-9:30pm Tues.-Thurs., 5:30pm-10:30pm Fri., 11:30am-3pm and 5:30pm-10:30pm Sat., 11:30am-3pm and 5:30pm-9pm Sun., $18-26) tailors a local, seasonal menu to pair with its eight handcrafted beers or a flight of four ($12). Communal seating allows for sociable dining. A bar in the back overlooks the stainless-steel fermentation tanks.

After a day hiking nothing beats a burrito. **Avatars Punjabi** (15 Madrona St., 415/381-8293, http://avatars-restaurant-mill-valley. sites.tablehero.com, 11am-8pm daily, $7-10) burritos are filled with garbanzo beans, basmati rice, herb salsa, fruit chutney, yogurt, and tamarind sauce, or opt for a more traditional rice plate. The small shop mostly caters to takeout orders, but there are a few tables.

Fill up *before* a day of hiking at **Kitchen Sunnyside** (31 Sunnyside Ave., 415/326-5159, 8am-2:30pm Mon.-Fri., 8am-3pm Sat.-Sun., $9-17). Order hearty a breakfast of Benedicts, scrambles, breakfast tacos, and Dungeness hash or get a burger at lunch.

MUIR WOODS NATIONAL MONUMENT

Established in 1908 and named for naturalist and author John Muir, **Muir Woods National Monument** (1 Muir Woods Rd., 415/388-2596, www.nps.gov/muwo, 8am-sunset daily, adults $10, children under 16 free, reservations required: $8/vehicle, $3/shuttle) comprises acres of staggeringly beautiful redwood forest. More than six miles of trails wind through the redwoods and accompanying Mount Tamalpais area, crossing verdant creeks and the lush forest. These are some of the most stunning—and accessible—redwoods in the Bay Area.

The visitors center is a great place to begin your exploration. The **Muir Woods Visitors Center** (8am-sunset daily) abuts the main parking area and marks the entrance to Muir Woods. In addition to maps, information, and advice about hiking, you'll also find a few amenities. Inside the park is the **Muir Woods Trading Company** (415/388-7059, www.muirwoodstradingcompany.com, 9am-5:30pm daily, closing hours vary, $3-12) where you can purchase souvenirs and an organic lunch. Along the trails, rangers lead informative tours.

Muir Woods National Monument

Hiking

Many lovely trails crisscross the gorgeous redwood forest. First-time visitors should follow the wheelchair- and stroller-accessible **Redwood Creek Trail** (one mile, easy). Leading from the visitors center on an easy and flat walk through the beautiful redwoods, this trail has an interpretive brochure (pick one up at the visitors center) with numbers along the way that describe the flora and fauna. Hikers can continue the loop on the **Hillside Trail** for an elevated view of the valley.

One of the first side trails off the Main Trail is the **Canopy View Trail** (3 miles, moderate). Some advice: Either bring water or pick up a bottle at the visitors center before starting up the trail. The trail climbs through the redwoods for 1.3 miles until its junction with **Lost Trail.** Turn right on Lost Trail and follow it downhill for 0.7 mile to **Fern Creek Trail.** Bear left onto the Fern Creek Trail for a lush and verdant return to the Main Trail. Along

the way you'll see the much-lauded Kent Tree, a 250-foot-tall Douglas fir.

It's easier to avoid the crowds by following the Main Trail to its terminus with the **Bootjack Trail** (6.4 miles, moderate). The Bootjack Trail climbs uphill for 1.3 miles before its junction with the **TCC Trail.** Bear left for the TCC Trail and meander through the quiet Douglas firs. At 1.4 miles, the trail meets up with the **Stapleveldt Trail;** turn left again to follow this trail for 0.5 mile to **Ben Johnson Trail,** which continues downhill for 1 more mile to meet up with the Main Trail.

You may notice signs in this area for the **Dipsea Trail,** an out-and-back hike to Stinson Beach. This is a strenuous, unshaded 7.1-mile hike, and the only way back is the way you came—but uphill.

Getting There

Muir Woods is accessed via the long and winding Muir Woods Road. From U.S. 101, take the Stinson Beach/Highway 1 exit. On Highway 1, also named the Shoreline Highway, follow the road under the freeway and proceed until the road splits in a T junction at the light. Turn left, continuing on Shoreline Highway for 2.5 miles. At the intersection with Panoramic Highway, make a sharp right turn and continue climbing uphill. At the junction of Panoramic Highway and Muir Woods Road, turn left and follow the road 1.5 twisty miles down to the Muir Woods parking lots on the right.

PARKING

Reservations (800/410-2419, https://go-muirwoods.com, private vehicle $8, shuttle $3 pp, children under 16 free) are required to park and are based on time of arrival. Once parked, you may stay until the park closes. Reservations are accepted up to 90 days in advance and demand is high—book early. Print out your reservation confirmation before arrival as there is no cell reception in the park.

SHUTTLE

The **Muir Woods Shuttle** (415/226-0855, www.marintransit.org/routes/66.html, reservations 800/410-2419, https://gomuirwoods.com, summer daily, Sat.-Sun. Sept-mid-June, $3 round-trip, children under 16 free) departs from three points in Sausalito (including the Sausalito ferry terminal) to the Muir Woods entrance. Bikes are not allowed on the shuttles, but bike parking is available at two shuttle locations. Reservations are accepted up to 90 days in advance and demand is high—book early.

MUIR BEACH

Few California coves can boast as much beauty as **Muir Beach** (south of the town of Muir Beach, www.nps.gov/goga, sunrise-sunset daily). From the overlook above Highway 1 to the edge of the ocean beyond the dunes, Muir Beach is a haven for both wildlife and beachcombers; many trails lead from the beach into the surrounding headlands. The south side of the beach houses the windswept picnic grounds, while the north cove attracts nudists.

To take it all in, head to **Muir Beach Overlook** (1.5 miles north of Pacific Way, turn out on left side), where a 0.5-mile walk leads to breathtaking views of plunging cliffs, crashing surf, and the wide Pacific. The overlook is not for those with vertigo. Picnic tables are available, though it is often windy.

Hiking

Ka'asi Road Trail (0.5 mile, easy) crosses the 450-foot-long pedestrian bridge over the Redwood Creek floodplain, connecting to Pacific Way near the Pelican Inn. For a longer hike, turn south on the **Coastal Trail** to **Pirates Cove Trail** (1.5 miles one-way, moderate), where you can scramble down to secluded Pirates Cove.

Food and Accommodations

The ★ **Pelican Inn** (10 Pacific Way, Muir Beach, 415/383-6000, www.pelicaninn.com, $242-316) has provided shelter and sustenance to this corner of Marin for 40 years. The historical ambience shines with big-beam construction, canopy beds, and lovely portrait prints. The seven cozy rooms each come with private baths and full English-style breakfast, but no TVs or phones. For lodgers and daytrippers, the **restaurant** (11:30am-9:30pm Mon.-Fri., 8am-9:30pm Sat.-Sun., $11-36) serves pints of beer, beef Wellington, shepherd's pie, and fish-and-chips.

Getting There

Muir Beach is directly off Highway 1. The most direct route is to take U.S. 101 to the Stinson Beach/Highway 1 exit and follow Highway 1 (also called Shoreline Highway) for 6.5 miles to Pacific Way (look for the Pelican Inn). Turn left onto Pacific Way and continue straight to the Muir Beach parking lot. If arriving from Muir Woods, simply continue on Muir Woods Road down to the junction with Highway 1 and turn right onto Pacific Way.

MOUNT TAMALPAIS STATE PARK

Mount Tamalpais State Park (801 Panoramic Hwy., Mill Valley, 415/388-2070, www.parks.ca.gov, 7am-sunset daily, day-use parking $8) boasts stellar views of the San Francisco Bay Area—from Mount St. Helena in Napa down to San Francisco and across to the East Bay. The Pacific Ocean fills the western view, including a unique vista of the distant Farallon Islands, while on a clear day you can just make out the foothills of the Sierra Nevada to the east.

The **East Peak Visitors Center** (end of East Ridgecrest Blvd., 11am-4pm Sat.-Sun.), located at the top of Mount Tam, houses a small museum and gift shop as well as a picnic area with tables and restrooms. The **Pantoll Ranger Station** (3801 Panoramic Hwy. at Pantoll Rd., 415/388-3653, 8am-4pm daily) anchors the western and larger edge of the park and provides hikers with maps and camping information.

Enjoy the views without setting out on the trail at the **Bootjack Picnic Area** (Panoramic

Mount Tamalpais

visitors center, make the climb up to **Gardner Fire Lookout** for stellar views from the top of Mount Tam's East Peak (2,571 feet). Stop at the **Gravity Car Barn** (noon-4pm Sat.-Sun.), a replica and small museum dedicated to the train that once brought intrepid travelers to the summit.

PANTOLL

The Pantoll Ranger Station is ground zero for some of the best and most challenging hikes in the park. The **Old Mine Trail** (0.5 miles, easy) is an accessible trail that leads to a lovely lookout bench and the Lone Tree Spring. Ambitious hikers can continue on the **Dipsea Trail** (1.4 miles, moderate), making it a loop by turning right on the **Steep Ravine Trail** (3.8 miles, moderate) as it ascends through lush Webb Creek and gorgeous redwoods back to the Pantoll parking lot.

The **Dipsea Trail** (7.3 miles round-trip, strenuous) is part of the famous Dipsea Race Course (second Sun. in June), a 7.4-mile course renowned for both its beauty and its challenging stairs. The trailhead that begins in Muir Woods, near the parking lot, leads through Mount Tam all the way to Stinson Beach. Hikers can pick up the Dipsea on the Old Mine Trail and come back via the **Steep Ravine Trail** (3.8 miles, moderate-strenuous). A common but longer loop is to take the **Matt Davis Trail** (across Panoramic Hwy. from the Pantoll parking area) west all the way to Stinson Beach and then return via the Dipsea Trail to Steep Ravine Trail (7 miles, strenuous). This is a long, challenging hike, especially on the way back, so bring water and endurance. Sections of the Dipsea Trail are often impassible in winter. Check trail conditions before going.

ROCK SPRINGS

A variety of trails lead off the historic **Mountain Theater** (E. Ridgecrest Blvd. at Pantoll Rd., 415/383-1100, www.mountainplay.org, May-June, $20-40), an outdoor theater built in the 1930s that hosts plays and **astronomy talks** (www.friendsofmttam.

Hwy.), which has tables, grills, water, and restrooms. The small parking lot northeast of the Pantoll Ranger Station fills quickly and early in the day.

Hiking

Mount Tam's 60-plus miles of hiking trails are divided into three major sections: the East Peak, the Pantoll area, and the Rock Springs area. Each of these regions offers a number of beautiful trails, so grab a map from the visitors center or online to get a sense of the options. For additional hikes, visit the **Friends of Mount Tam** (www.friendsofmttam.org).

EAST PEAK

The charming, interpretive **Verna Dunshee Trail** (0.75 mile, easy) offers a short, mostly flat walk along a wheelchair-accessible trail. The views are fabulous, and you can get a leaflet at the visitors center that describes many of the things you'll see along the trail. Turn this into a loop hike by continuing on Verna Dunshee counterclockwise; once back at the org, date and times vary). To get there, cross Ridgecrest Boulevard and take the **Mountain Theater Fire Trail** to Mountain Theater. Along the top row of the stone seats, admire the vistas while looking for **Rock Springs Trail** (it's a bit hidden). Once you find it, follow Rock Springs Trail all the way to historical West Point Inn. The views here are stunning, and you'll see numerous cyclists flying downhill on Old Stage Road below. Cross this road to pick up Nora Trail, following it until it intersects with **Matt Davis Trail.** Turn right to reach the Bootjack day-use area. Follow the **Bootjack Trail** right (north) to return to the Mountain Theater for a 4.6-mile loop.

In winter, be sure to visit **Cataract Falls** (3 miles, easy-moderate). From the trailhead, follow Cataract Trail for a short bit before heading right on Bernstein Trail. Shortly, turn left onto Simmons Trail and continue to Barth's Retreat, site of a former camp that is now a small picnic area with restrooms. Turn left on Mickey O'Brien Trail (a map can be helpful here), returning to an intersection with the Cataract Trail. It's worth the short excursion to follow Cataract Trail to the right through the Laurel Dell picnic area and up to Cataract Falls. Enjoy a picnic at Laurel Dell before returning to Cataract Trail to follow it down to the Rock Springs trailhead.

Food and Accommodations

When the **West Point Inn** (100 Old Railroad Grade Rd., Mill Valley, 415/388-9955, www. westpointinn.com, Tues.-Sat., adults $50, children under 18 $25) was built in 1904, guests would take the old train to its doorstep. Today it's a two-mile hike on a dirt road. The inn has no electricity; instead, it's lit by gaslights and warmed by fires in the large fireplaces in the downstairs lounge and parlor. There are seven rooms upstairs and five rustic cabins nearby. Guests must bring their own linens, flashlights, and food, which can be prepared in the communal kitchen. May-October, the inn hosts a monthly Sunday pancake breakfast (9am-1pm, adults $10, children $5). The wait can be long, but it's a lot of fun.

Boasting terrific views, **Mountain Home Inn** (810 Panoramic Hwy., 415/381-9000, www.mtnhomeinn.com, $179-329) was built during the heyday of the railroad. With 10 rooms, many with jetted tubs, wood-burning fireplaces, and private decks, the inn specializes in relaxation. Slip downstairs for a complimentary breakfast or dine in the cozy and warmly lit **dining room** (11:30am-7pm Mon.-Fri., 8am-11am and 11:30am-7pm Sat.-Sun., $10-30). The three-course prix fixe **dinner** (5:30pm-8:30pm Wed.-Sun., $45) requires reservations.

Camping

With spectacular views of the Pacific Ocean, it's no wonder that the rustic accommodations at ★ **Steep Ravine** (800/444-7275, www.reservecalifornia.com, cabins $100, campsites $25) stay fully booked. On the namesake ravine are six primitive campsites and nine cabins. Each rustic cabin comes equipped with a small woodstove, a table, a sleeping platform, and a grill. The campsites have a table, a fire pit, and a food locker. Restrooms and drinking water are nearby. To reserve a cabin or campsite, you need to be on the phone at 8am six months before the date you intend to go.

If you want to camp within hiking distance of the top of the mountain, the **Pantoll** and **Bootjack Campgrounds** (Panoramic Hwy., 415/388-2070, www.parks.ca.gov, first-come, first-served, $25) each have 15 sites with drinking water, firewood, and restrooms. Camping here is first-come, first-served, paid for at the ranger station, so get here early. The sites are removed from the parking lots, which means that you'll need to haul in all your gear; it also makes for a peaceful campground.

Transportation

Panoramic Highway is a long and winding two-lane road across the Mount Tamalpais area and extending all the way to Stinson Beach. Take Highway 1 to the Stinson Beach exit, and then follow the fairly good signs up the mountain. Turn right at Panoramic Highway at the top of the hill. Follow the road for five winding miles until you reach the Pantoll Ranger Station. To get to the East Peak Visitors Center, take a right on Pantoll Road, and another right on East Ridgecrest Boulevard. To access the park from Stinson Beach, turn on Panorama Highway at the T intersection with Highway 1 just south of town.

STINSON BEACH

The primary attraction at Stinson Beach is the tiny town's namesake: a broad 3.5-mile sandy stretch of coastline that's unusually congenial to visitors. **Stinson Beach** (415/388-2595, www.nps.gov, 9am-sunset, daily) is the favorite destination for San Franciscans seeking some surf and sunshine. On hot and sunny days, the parking lot fills before noon. Lifeguards are on duty Memorial Day through Labor Day.

Stinson Beach Surf and Kayak (3605 Hwy. 1, 415/868-2739, www.stinsonbeach-surfandkayak.com, weekdays by appointment, 9:30am-6pm Sat.-Sun., $20-45/day) rents surfboards, kayaks, boogie boards, and stand-up paddleboards, plus a wetsuit, which you will certainly need.

Food and Accommodations

The **Sandpiper Inn** (1 Marine Way, 415/868-1632, www.sandpiperstinsonbeach.com, $145-300) has six rooms and five cabins. Two of the rooms have kitchenettes and all have gas fireplaces and comfortable queen beds. The individual redwood cabins offer additional privacy, bed space for families, and full kitchens.

Stinson Beach Motel (3416 Shoreline Hwy. 1, 415/868-1712, www.stinsonbeach-motel.com, $105-259) features eight vintage-y beach bungalow-style rooms that sleep 2-4 guests each. Some of the blue-themed rooms have substantial kitchenettes; all have private baths, garden views, and TVs.

The **Sand Dollar Restaurant** (3458 Hwy. 1, 415/868-0434, www.stinsonbeachrestaurant.com; 11am-9pm daily, bar open later, $19-26) serves more land-based dishes than

seafood, except for its popular cioppino. The dining room is constructed out of three old barges, and there is a pretty patio when the weather is nice.

With the vibe of a seaside hamburger joint, ★ **Parkside Café** (43 Arenal Ave., 415/868-1272, www.parksidecafe.com, 6am-9pm daily, $16-30) is the perfect place to stop with your feet still sandy from the beach. Order the local rock cod tacos, the burger on a brioche bun, or a half-dozen oysters on the half shell. Pizzas are also available, as is homemade bread.

Getting There

Take the Stinson Beach exit off U.S. 101 and follow Shoreline Highway (Hwy. 1) until it descends into Stinson Beach, a little over 10 miles. Most of the town is strung along the highway, and signs make it easy to navigate to the beach. Traffic can be a huge problem on weekend days, with backups that stretch for miles. Your best bet is to drive in on a weekday or in the evening.

TOP EXPERIENCE

★ POINT REYES NATIONAL SEASHORE

The Point Reyes area boasts acres of unspoiled grassland, forest, and beach. Cool weather presides even in the summer, but the result is lustrous green foliage and spectacular scenery. **Point Reyes National Seashore** (1 Bear Valley Rd., 415/464-5100, www.nps.gov/pore, dawn-midnight daily) stretches between Tomales Bay and the Pacific and from Bolinas to Tomales Point. Dedicated hikers can trek from the bay to the ocean or from the beach to land's end. The protected lands shelter a range of wildlife. In the marshes and lagoons, a wide variety of birds—including three different species of pelicans—make their nests. The pine forests shade shy deer and larger elk. A few ranches and dairy farms operate inside the park. Grandfathered in at the time the park was created, these sustainable, generations-old family farms give added character and historical depth to Point Reyes.

Side Trip to Bolinas

Agate Beach

Bolinas is a town that does not want to be found. Locals wary of tourist development routinely remove road signs to hide their hometown from visitors. Surrounded by beaches, wetlands, and Point Reyes National Seashore, this "nature-loving town" is reluctant to join the outside world.

BEACHES

Longboarders and beginning surfers will love the breaks at **Bolinas Beach** (end of Wharf Rd.), which are protected from big swells. At **2 Mile Surf Shop** (22 Brighton Ave., 415/868-0264, www.2milesurf.com, 10am-5pm daily Nov.-Apr., 9am-6pm daily May-Oct.) you can rent surfboards ($40/day), boogie boards ($15/day), and wetsuits ($15/day) or take surf lessons ($60/1.5 hours, $150/day).

Agate Beach (Elm Rd., www.marincounty.org, sunrise-sunset daily) is an ideal spot at low tide. The two-mile-long beach is filled with tidepools home to hermit crabs, sea anemones, and chitons, while beautiful agate stones hide deep in the sand. (Taking rocks, shells, and marinelife is strictly prohibited.)

FOOD

The **Coast Café** (46 Wharf Rd., 415/868/2298, 11am-3pm and 5pm-8pm Tues.-Thurs., 11am-3pm and 5pm-9pm Fri., 8am-9pm Sat.-Sun., $18-32) is decorated with surf boards, fishing poles, and faded fishing buoys. They serve a menu filled with oysters, burgers, fried fish, french fries, and homemade blackberry pie. The menu at **11 Wine Bar Bistro** (11 Wharf Rd., 415/868-1133, 8am-noon Sun.-Mon. and Wed., 8am-noon and 5pm-9pm Thurs.-Sat., $14-18) has wood-fired pizzas and elegant entrées, which are served in a stylish interior.

GETTING THERE

From Stinson Beach, take Highway 1 north. At the end of Bolinas Lagoon, make the first left onto Olema Bolinas Road. Keep left and follow the road all the way into town to the junction of Wharf Road and Brighton Avenue.

The Point Reyes area includes the pocket Tomales Bay State Park, and the tiny towns of Olema, Point Reyes Station, and Inverness.

Visitors Centers

The **Bear Valley Visitor Center** (1 Bear Valley Rd., 415/464-5100; 10am-5pm Mon.-Fri., 9am-5pm Sat.-Sun., Mar-Nov.; 10am-4:30pm Mon.-Fri., 9am-4:30pm Sat.-Sun., Nov.-Feb.) acts as the central visitors center for Point Reyes National Seashore. In addition to maps, flyers, and interpretive exhibits, the center houses a short video introducing the region. You can also talk to park rangers, either to ask advice or to obtain beach fire permits and backcountry camping permits.

The **Ken Patrick Visitors Center** (Drakes Beach, 415/669-1250, 9am-5pm daily summer; 9:30am-4:30pm Sat.-Sun. fall-spring) sits right on the beach in a building made of weathered redwood. Its small museum focuses on the maritime history of the region. It's also the location for the annual Sand Sculpture event.

Point Reyes Lighthouse

The rocky shores of Point Reyes make for great sightseeing but incredibly dangerous maritime navigation. In 1870 the first lighthouse was constructed on the headlands. Its first-order Fresnel lens threw light far enough for ships to avoid the treacherous granite cliffs. Yet the danger remained, and soon after, a lifesaving station was constructed alongside the light station. It wasn't until the 20th century, when a ship-to-shore radio station and newer lifesaving station were put in place, that the Point Reyes shore truly became safer for ships.

The **Point Reyes Lighthouse** (Sir Francis Drake Blvd., 415/669-1534, www.nps.gov/pore, 10am-4:30pm Fri.-Mon.) still stands today on a point past the visitors center, accessed by descending a sometimes treacherous, cold, and windblown flight of 300 stairs, which often closes to visitors during bad weather. Still, it's worth a visit. The Fresnel lens and original machinery all remain in place, and the adjacent equipment building contains foghorns, air compressors, and other safety implements from decades past. Check the website for information about twice-monthly special events when the light is switched on.

GETTING THERE

The lighthouse is 19 miles west of the Bear Valley Visitor Center on Sir Francis Drake Boulevard. Parking can be difficult, and the area is extremely popular. To alleviate congestion, the park closes Sir Francis Drake Boulevard at the South Beach Junction on winter weekends. Visitors must take a **shuttle** (9:30am-3pm Sat.-Sun. late-Dec.-mid-Apr., adults $7, children under 16 free) from Drakes Beach. Tickets are available at the Kenneth C. Patrick Visitor Center.

Tomales Bay State Park

At the northeast edge of the Point Reyes Peninsula, pine forests shroud **Tomales Bay State Park** (1100 Pierce Point Rd., 415/669-1140, www.park.ca.gov, 8am-sunset daily, $8), home to four lovely beaches. Protected from the wind and waves by the Inverness Ridge to the west, the beaches are calm, gently sloping, and partially secluded. All require a walk from the parking lots, but the walks are scenic, taking you through meadows and forest.

There are also places to picnic or hike. An easy one-mile trail leads to the **Jepson Memorial Grove,** home to the last virgin groves of bishop pine trees in California. Access is via the Jepson Trail, which leads to **Heart's Desire Beach,** perhaps the most popular beach in the park.

Hiking

To list all the hikes in Point Reyes would require a book in itself. For a taste of what the area has to offer, start at the Bear Valley Visitor Center and pick up maps and trail information for the rest of the park. Across from the visitors center, the accessible **Earthquake Trail** (0.6 mile, easy) is dotted with informative displays illustrating the unique geology

Point Reyes National Seashore

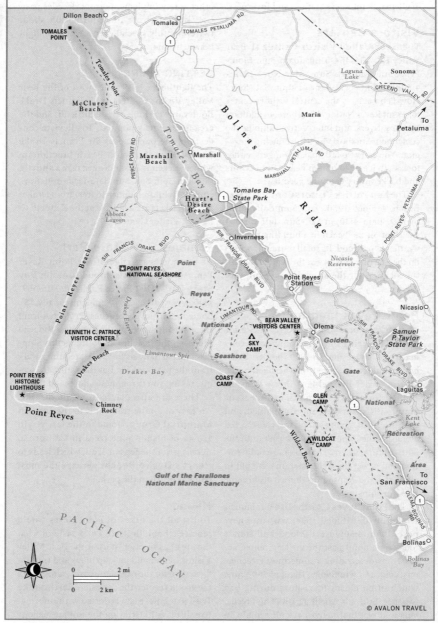

© AVALON TRAVEL

of Point Reyes. Trails are accessed along four main roads (south to north): Mesa Road in Bolinas, Limantour Road, Sir Francis Drake Boulevard, and Pierce Point Road.

BOLINAS
The very south end of Point Reyes backs into the small town of Bolinas where Mesa Road leads to the Palomarin Trailhead at Palomarin Beach. Here, you can pick up the **Coastal Trail**, which offers both day hikes and overnight backpacking trips to **Wildcat Camp** (5.5 miles one-way, permit required). Day hikers can follow the trail out past Bass Lake, Pelican Lake, and **Crystal Lake** (8.2 miles round-trip, easy to moderate). In spring, continue on to Wildcat Camp to see **Alamere Falls** (11 miles round-trip, easy-moderate) crashing into Wildcat Beach.

BEAR VALLEY
From the visitors center, the **Bear Valley Trail** runs south all the way to the ocean and the dramatic perch above **Kelham Beach** (8.2 miles round-trip, moderate). For a shorter hike, follow Bear Valley Trail to **Divide Meadow,** for a moderate 3.2-mile out and back.

Bear Valley Trail also provides access to **Mount Wittenberg** (2 miles, strenuous), though there is an easier trailhead off Limantour Road. This is the highest point in the park (1,407 feet), and you'll feel it on the climb up. From Bear Valley Trail, turn right at the intersection with Mount Wittenberg Trail and follow it to the top. Hikers can return via either the **Meadow Trail** (turn left on Sky Trail, then left again on Meadow Trail) or take **Z Ranch Trail** (left) to return via **Horse Trail** for a 5- or 6.1-mile loop.

LIMANTOUR ROAD
Limantour Road is north of the Bear Valley Visitor Center: Take Bear Valley Road north and turn west on Limantour Road. One of the first trailheads along this road is for the Sky Trail. The Sky Trail provides easier access to **Mount Wittenberg** (4.3 miles, moderate-strenuous) with the bonus of passing by Sky Camp, one of the area's most popular hike-in campgrounds.

Limantour Road eventually passes Point Reyes Hostel, where you'll find the trailhead for the **Coast-Laguna Loop** (5 miles, easy-moderate). Follow Coast Trail down to Drakes Bay, where it hugs the shoreline until reaching **Coast Camp,** another backpacking campsite. From Coast Camp, take **Fire Lane**

Bear Valley Visitor Center

Trail north to **Laguna Trail** and return to Limantour Road. You may have to walk along Limantour toward the hostel to reach your car. Birders will want to make a beeline for the **Limantour Spit Trail** (2 miles, easy). From the parking lot at Limantour Beach, it's a quick hike to the beach; look for a spur trail headed west.

SIR FRANCIS DRAKE BOULEVARD
The Estero Trailhead is off Sir Francis Drake Boulevard, shortly after the junction with Pierce Point Road. **Estero Trail** offers several options for hikers. For a short two-mile hike, follow the trail to Home Bay and turn around there. You can extend the hike to **Sunset Beach** (7.8 miles round-trip, moderate), which overlooks Drakes Estero, or continue farther to **Drakes Head** (9.4 miles round-trip), via Estero Trail and **Drakes Head Trail,** with views overlooking Estero de Limantour and Drakes Bay.

Sir Francis Drake Boulevard continues rolling through pastures south and west until it ends at the Point Reyes Lighthouse. From the parking area on Chimney Rock Road, just south of the Point Reyes Lighthouse, follow the **Chimney Rock Trail** (1.6 miles, easy) through grassy cliffs to a wooden bench at the tip of the peninsula. The views of the Pacific and the Point Reyes coast are stunning even though the wind tends to whip mercilessly here.

December through March, the southwest end of Drakes Beach becomes a rookery for elephant seals. The **Elephant Seal Overlook** is a 0.2-mile stroll from the trailhead. During birthing season, docents (11am-4pm Sat.-Sun.) are on hand with binoculars and spotting scopes to answer questions.

PIERCE POINT ROAD
Splitting off from Sir Francis Drake Boulevard at Tomales Bay State Park, Pierce Point Road extends to the northern end of the peninsula, where windswept sandy beaches, lagoons, and tule elk await. The trek to **Abbots Lagoon** (2-3 miles round-trip) is an easy hike that will

be a hit with bird lovers. From there, Pierce Point Road continues north to another hiking option at **Kehoe Beach** (one mile, easy), where a gravel trail descends to the beach. (Note that this is the only trail in Point Reyes where leashed dogs are permitted.)

Pierce Point Road runs almost to the tip of Tomales Point. From the trailhead at Pierce Point Ranch, there are two hiking options. For a short and easy hike to the beach, follow **McClures Beach Trail** (1.3 miles, easy) to explore tidepools bordered by granite cliffs. A bit longer, **Tomales Point Trail** (9.5 miles round-trip, moderate) is a wide, smooth path through the middle of the Tule Elk Reserve to a viewpoint at Bird Rock. From Bird Rock, the "trail" to Tomales Point becomes tricky and less defined, but is worth it for the views. This area is susceptible to erosion; exercise caution on the bluffs.

Biking
Most paved roads in Point Reyes are open to bicycles and cars. Stop at Bear Valley Visitor Center for tips on the best routes and information on any trail closures. In the park, bikes are restricted to certain trails.

From the Five Brooks Trailhead on Highway 1, you can opt for the challenging **Stewart Trail** (6.7 miles, strenuous) to Wildcat Beach or head south on the **Olema Valley Trail** (5 miles, easy). Add some challenge to the ride by making it a loop and take either Randall or McCurdy Trail east across Highway 1 to the **Bolinas Ridge Trail.** Follow the trail to its terminus at Sir Francis Drake Boulevard for a 19-21-mile ride, then take Highway 1 back to the trailhead.

Kayaking
The calm water of Tomales Bay practically begs to be explored by kayak. **Blue Waters** (12944 Sir Francis Drake Blvd., Inverness, 415/669-2600, www.bwkayak.com, 9am-4pm Sat.-Sun., weekdays by appointment) rents kayaks ($60-85/2 hours, $80-125/day) and stand-up paddleboards ($30/hour, $80/day). All rentals are available for one hour and up to

48 hours, for those who want to kayak camp. Kayak tours ($78-98) include the bay, Drakes Estero in Point Reyes, full moon, and bioluminescent trips. Tours generally last 4-6 hours. **Point Reyes Outdoors** (11401 Hwy. 1, Point Reyes Station, 415/663-8192, www.pointreyesoutdoors.com) provides a wide variety of kayak tours ($75-120), including bioluminescent tours, kayak camping, and bioluminescence camping trips ($184). Tours last 3-6 hours and include a gourmet picnic. For solitude, rent a stand-up paddleboard ($65/4 hours, $85/6 hours, reservations required) and spend the day on the water.

Horseback Riding

Five Brooks Ranch (8001 Hwy. 1, 3 miles south of Olema, 415/663-1570, www.fivebrooks.com, 9am-5pm daily, $50-210) can get you saddled up to ride through Point Reyes's wide variety of ecosystems on tours that last 1-6 hours. The most popular tour is up to an ospreys' nest along Inverness Ridge, then dropping down for a peaceful amble along Olema Creek.

Food

West Marin is famous for its agricultural bounty. Inside the soot-colored **Sir and Star at the Olema** (10000 Sir Francis Drake Blvd., Olema, 415/663-1034, http://sirandstar.com, 5pm-9pm Wed.-Sun., $28-32), expect dishes such as quail, oysters, lamb tenderloin, and buffalo ice cream gracing the slim menu. The highly stylized interior includes taxidermy animals, bouquets of dried kelp, and Shakeresque furniture.

The star of the Point Reyes Station restaurant scene is the ★ **Station House Café** (11180 Hwy. 1, Point Reyes Station, 415/663-1515, www.stationhousecafe.com, 8am-8pm Sun.-Tues. and 8am-9pm Thurs.-Sat., $17-29), which is both casual and upscale. Since 1974, the Station House has been dedicated to serving comfort food with ingredients that reflect the area's agrarian culture. The popovers are worth a visit alone.

Head north on Highway 1 and be rewarded with beautiful views and a meal at ★ **Nick's Cove** (23240 Hwy. 1, Point Reyes Station, 415/663-1033, www.nickscove.com, 11am-8pm Sun.-Thurs., 11am-9pm Fri.-Sat., $24-34). Overlooking the bay in an expansive and weathered redwood building, Nick's well-designed menu includes light nibbles, high-end dishes, an expansive kids menu, and a spectacular bar. A long deck and a boathouse are out back, perfect to explore with restless little ones.

Stop for a cup of coffee and a pastry at the **Bovine Bakery** (11315 Hwy. 1, Point Reyes Station, 415/663-9420, 6:30am-5pm Mon.-Fri., 7am-5pm Sat., 7am-4pm Sun., $4-8), where you can pick up a loaf of bread, cookies, and even a slice of pizza for your picnic basket. Add cheese to your lunch at **Cowgirl Creamery** (80 4th St., Point Reyes Station, 415/663-9335, www.cowgirlcreamery.com, 10am-5pm Wed.-Sun.), just around the corner, where, you'll find the stellar Red Hawk and Mount Tam. Also located in the barn is the **Cowgirl Cantina** (10am-5pm Wed.-Sun., $6-17), a takeout deli counter and espresso bar, which serves hot and cold sandwiches made with local ingredients.

Locals get their lunch at ★ **Inverness Park Market** (12301 Sir Francis Drake Blvd., Inverness Park, 415/663-1491, https://invernessparkmarket.com, 7am-8pm Mon.-Thurs., 7am-9pm Fri.-Sat., 8am-8pm Sun., $7-13), which has a great selection of deli sandwiches. It is also a full-service market, so you can grab any other essentials. After your hike, swing back for a pint at the market's **Tap Room** (4pm-8pm Mon.-Thurs., 4pm-9pm Fri., 8am-9pm Sat., 8am-8pm Sun., $8-16) where you'll find a hearty menu of burgers, fish tacos, noodle bowls, and even breakfast bites on the weekend. For a drink with a bit of local color, slip through the swinging doors of the **Old Western Saloon** (11201 Hwy. 1, Point Reyes Station, 415/663-1661, 10am-2am daily), a crusty old West Marin haunt.

Barbecuing oysters at **Hog Island** (20215 Hwy. 1, Point Reyes Station, 415/663-9218, www.hogislandoysters.com, 9am-5pm daily) is a Bay Area tradition—so much so that you need to reserve a table and grill. Or simply swing by to grab a dozen oysters and enjoy them at one of the picnic spots in Point Reyes National Seashore. Harvested in Tomales Bay, Hog Island's oysters grace many upscale Bay Area menus.

Across the bay in Inverness, the sun-drenched **Saltwater Oyster Depot** (12781 Sir Francis Drake Blvd., Inverness, 415/669-1244, www.saltwateroysterdepot.com, 5pm-9pm Mon. and Thurs.-Fri., noon-9pm Sat.-Sun., $17-28) serves a variety of oysters prepared different ways, in addition to hearty fare such as pork chops and risotto.

Accommodations

The ★ **Point Reyes Seashore Lodge** (10021 Hwy. 1, Olema, 415/663-9000 or 800/404-5634, www.pointreyesseashorelodge. com, $200-440) offers both budget and luxury lodging in its 22 rooms. Charming rooms are individually decorated with modern furnishings and have private baths; some have whirlpool tubs and fireplaces. Larger suites offer kitchens and private patios. Two cottages ($305-440) that sleep four people are a relative bargain. The Farm House Restaurant, Bar, and Deli adjoin the hotel, providing plenty of food and drink options. A hot breakfast is complimentary with all stays.

The five-room **Point Reyes Station Inn** (11591 Hwy. 1, Point Reyes Station, 415/663-9372, www.pointreyesstationinn.com, $135-225) drips with turn-of-the-20th-century charm. Rooms feature vaulted ceilings, large windows, and glass doors leading to private porches. All but one have fireplaces and private en-suite baths. A communal hot tub is in the garden, and the continental breakfast features eggs from the inn's own chickens.

Fantastic hiking and lush natural scenery is at your door at **Point Reyes Hostel** (1390 Limantour Spit Rd., Point Reyes Station, 415/663-8811, www.norcalhostels.org/reyes, $29-130), located one mile from Limantour Beach. Accommodations are spare but comfortable; choose from affordable dorm rooms

(adults $29-35, children under 12 $14-17) or a private room ($105-130). The hostel has a communal kitchen, three lounge areas, and bicycle storage.

Manka's Inverness Lodge (30 Callendar Way, Inverness, 415/669-1034, www.mankas. com, $225-635) is not so much a lodge as a slightly funky compound dressed in an ethereal combination of hunting lodge and Arts and Crafts styles. Stay in the lodge or annex, or in one of the additional cabins scattered throughout.

Constructed of natural wood with fanciful flourishes, ★ **Motel Inverness** (12718 Sir Francis Drake Blvd., Inverness, 415/236-1967 or 866/453-3839, www.motelinverness.com, $135-345) is more like a classic lodge than a typical motel. Rooms open onto the serene wetlands bordering the bay. Some are suites with decks and kitchenettes; others are cozy and economy style. Inside the main lodge is a grand lounge with an antique pool table and a great stone fireplace.

Camping

Four small campgrounds offer a place to pitch a tent at **Point Reyes National Seashore** (877/444-6777, www.recreation. gov, $20). All are hike-in sites that require reservations up to six months in advance. **Sky Camp** (11 sites, 1.4 miles, moderate) is the closest to the Bear Valley Visitor Center and accessed via a trail on Limantour Road. Near the end of Limantour Road is the trailhead for **Coast Camp** (12 sites) to which you can take the moderate 1.8 miles Laguna and Firelane Trails, or the easy, but longer Coast Trail (2.7 miles). **Wildcat Camp** (five sites) is set away from the beach along the Coastal Trail, reachable from Bear Valley (6.3 miles, moderate) or from Palomarin in Bolinas (5.5 miles, easy). The most secluded campground is **Glen Camp** (12 sites), a healthy 4.6 miles from the Bear Valley Trailhead. All campsites have a pit toilet, a water faucet, a picnic table, a charcoal grill, and a food locker.

You'll find more traditional car camping

at **Samuel P. Taylor State Park** (8889 Sir Francis Drake Blvd., Lagunitas, 800/444-7275, www.reservecalifornia.com, $35). Nestled in the redwood forest are 59 campsites with grills, bear boxes, picnic tables, and flush toilets and showers nearby. The Orchard Hill sites are larger and offer more privacy than the cramped Creekside sites.

Transportation and Services

Point Reyes is only about an hour north of San Francisco by car, but getting here can be quite a drive. From the Golden Gate Bridge, take U.S. 101 north to just south of San Rafael. Take the Sir Francis Drake Boulevard exit toward San Anselmo. Follow Sir Francis Drake Boulevard west for 20 miles to the small town of Olema and Highway 1. At the intersection with Highway 1, turn right (north) to Point Reyes Station and the Bear Valley Visitor Center.

A slower but more scenic route follows Highway 1 into Point Reyes National Seashore and provides access to the trails near Bolinas in the southern portion of the park. From the Golden Gate Bridge, take U.S. 101 north to the Mill Valley/Stinson Beach exit. Follow Shoreline Highway for almost 30 miles through Stinson Beach and past Bolinas Lagoon to the coast. From the lagoon, it's 11 miles north to Point Reyes Station. Expect twists, turns, and slow going as you approach Point Reyes.

You can get gas only in Point Reyes Station, and don't expect any cell service. There are full-service grocery stores in Point Reyes Station at **Palace Market** (11300 Hwy. 1, Point Reyes Station, 415/663-1016, www.palacemarket.com, 8am-8pm Sun.-Thurs., 8am-9pm Fri.-Sat.) and in Inverness at **Inverness Store** (12784 Sir Francis Drake Blvd., Inverness, 415/669-1041, 9am-7pm daily).

East Bay

Across the bay, the cities of Berkeley and Oakland rival San Francisco in cultural diversity, radical thinking, and cutting-edge gastronomy.

Note that the East Bay is spread out and is often clogged by commuter traffic in the afternoon. Oakland and Berkeley offer easier access via the BART commuter rail system and have concentrated sights in their downtown areas.

BERKELEY

Berkeley has long been known for its radical, liberal, progressive activism. The youthful urban culture tends to revolve around the University of California, Berkeley. Yet, the spirit of the 1960s is alive and well on the slightly grungy **Telegraph Avenue,** where students, street kids, and tourists browse eclectic shops, independent bookstores, and record stores.

University of California, Berkeley

Berkeley is a college town and, fittingly, the **University of California, Berkeley** (www.berkeley.edu) offers the most interesting places to go and things to see. As an introduction to the school, take a guided **campus tour** (510/642-5215, www.berkeley.edu, 10am daily, by reservation only, free). To get a great view of the campus from above, take an elevator ride up the **Campanile** (10am-3:45pm Mon.-Fri., 10am-4:45pm Sat., 10am-1:30pm and 3pm-4:45pm Sun., adults $3, seniors and children 3-17 $2, children under 3 free, cash only), formally called Sather Tower.

Stop in at the **Lawrence Hall of Science** (1 Centennial Dr., 510/642-5132, www.lawrencehallofscience.org, 9am-4pm Tues.-Fri., 10am-5pm Sat.-Sun., adults $12, seniors and students $10, children under 3 free) for a look at the latest exhibits and interactive displays. Stroll through an astounding array of wild plants from around the world, at the **University of California Botanical Garden** (200 Centennial Dr., 510/643-2755, http://botanicalgarden.berkeley.edu, 9am-5pm daily, adults $12, seniors $10, children 7-17 $7, children under 7 free). Both are located high in the hills behind campus and offer great views across the bay.

Entertainment and Events

There's a reasonable variety of evening entertainment to be had in Berkeley. The major regional theater is the **Berkeley Repertory Theatre** (2025 Addison St., 510/647-2949, www.berkeleyrep.org, Tues.-Sun., $30-100), which puts on several unusual shows, from world premieres of edgy new works to totally different takes on old favorites.

The big-name acts come to the **Greek Theater** (2001 Gayley Rd., 510/548-3010, www.apeconcerts.com), an outdoor amphitheater constructed in the classic Greek style on the UC Berkeley campus. **The Starry Plough** (3101 Shattuck Ave., 510/841-0188, www.thestarryplough.com, 4pm-2am Mon.-Sat., 2pm-2am Sun., cover varies) is an Irish pub with a smallish stage setup. Fabulous Celtic rock groups, folk musicians, and indie bands play here almost every day of the week.

Jupiter (2181 Shattuck Ave., 510/843-8277, www.jupiterbeer.com, 11:30am-12:30am Mon.-Thurs., 11:30am-1:30am Fri., noon-1:30am Sat., noon-11:30pm Sun.) serves excellent wood-fired pizzas and a wide selection of locally brewed beer in their outdoor beer garden as jazz ensembles play or DJs spin the night away.

Sports and Recreation

Berkeley's backyard is the all-encompassing **Tilden Regional Park** (Grizzly Peak Blvd., 888/327-2757, www.ebparks.org, 5am-10pm daily). Within its more than 2,000 acres, the park has a celebrated botanical garden, the swimmable Lake Anza and its sandy beaches, an antique carousel, and miniature steam trains, perfect to thrill the little ones. Tilden

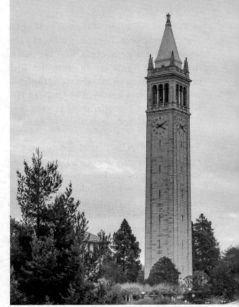
the Campanile on the UC Berkeley campus

also offers scores of hiking and mountain biking trails that almost convince you that you are in absolute wilderness, except for the breathtaking views of the Bay Area. Taking a trail map is advisable, as multiple trails crisscross one another, allowing for more adventure but also potential confusion.

For a simple stroll, take the **Jewel Lake Nature Trail** (one mile, easy), located in the Nature Area of the park. From the parking lot, the trail heads north along Wildcat Creek and out to Jewel Lake. For a more rigorous climb, the **Wildcat Peak/Laurel Canyon Loop** (3.5 miles, moderate) leaves from the same trailhead behind the Environmental Education Center. Spend some time on the **Bay Area Ridge Trail** (3.5 miles, moderate), a pleasant loop that starts at the Quarry Trailhead off Wildcat Canyon Road. Take **Wildcat Canyon Trail** to **Seaview Trail** and turn right. After some time, the trail changes names to **East Bay Skyline National Trail** and **Bay Area Ridge Trail**. At **Upper Big Springs Trail**, take a right back down the mountain. After nearly one mile, take a left on **Quarry Trail;** it will take you back to the parking lot.

Tilden offers many roads and trails for cyclists. The paved roads snaking through the park (Wildcat Canyon Rd., Grizzly Peak Blvd., and South Park Dr.) twist and turn while gaining and losing enough elevation to keep any cyclist busy.

North of Tilden, the equally large **Wildcat Canyon Regional Park** (5755 McBryde Ave., Richmond, 510/544-3092, www.ebparks. org, sunrise-sunset daily) is filled with wide fire roads, all of which are open to cyclists. Wildcat Canyon has fewer trails than Tilden, but it's quieter, and the trails traverse a more challenging topography and allow for longer treks. To best access the bike trails, park at the **Alvarado Trailhead** (5755 McBryde Ave., Richmond) at the north entrance of the park. From here you can take a variety of loops that allow you to see most of the park and some ridge-top views. Be advised that bikes are restricted on some trails that border Tilden Park in the south.

Food

With Alice Waters at the helm, ★ **Chez Panisse** (1517 Shattuck Ave., 510/548-5525, www.chezpanisse.com, $75-125) has been leading the charge of California cuisine based on fresh organic and local ingredients, executed with French precision since the 1970s. Every dinner is prix fixe, and there are two seatings per evening (5:30pm and 8pm Mon.-Sat.). You'll need to make reservations up to one month in advance ($50 cancelation fee). Eating at the upstairs **café** (510/548-5049, 11:30am-2:45pm and 5pm-10:30pm Mon.-Thurs., 11:30am-3pm and 5pm-11pm Fri.-Sat., $22-31) is a bit more relaxed. The food is just as good, and the casual atmosphere is less intimidating.

A worker-owned co-op since 1971, ★ **Cheese Board Collective** (1504 Shattuck Ave., 510/549-3183, http://cheese-boardcollective.coop, 7am-1pm Mon., 7am-6pm Tues.-Fri., 8am-5pm Sat., under $10) is

filled with the best fresh bread, pastries, and cheese around. At the counter are up to 400 different cheeses, which the clerks encourage customers to taste. Step next door and stand in line with the locals for a slice or a whole pie at the Cheese Board's **pizzeria** (1512 Shattuck Ave., 11:30am-3pm and 4:30pm-8pm Tues.-Sat., $3-22), where one type of pizza is made daily with organic and vegetarian toppings.

Comal (2020 Shattuck Ave., 510/926-6300, www.comalberkeley.com, 5:30pm-10pm Sun.-Thurs., 5:30pm-11pm Fri.-Sat., $11-21) brings the vibrant flavors of Oaxaca to downtown Berkeley. Rich sauces, fresh ingredients, and fire-roasted meat fill the rotating menu. The hip interior, expansive patio with fire pit, and an excellent selection of beer, wine, and cocktails keeps the atmosphere lively.

Step into dimly lit **Ippuku** (2130 Center St., 510/665-1969, www.ippukuberkeley.com, 5pm-10pm Sun. and Tues.-Thurs., 5pm-11pm Fri.-Sat., $20-30), an *izakaya*-style bar where soba and charcoal-grilled *yakitori* are specialties. Expect a wide selection of Japanese whiskeys and *shochu* to wash it all down.

Accommodations

Spend a weekend in the charming Claremont district by booking a room at ★ **Mary's Bed and Breakfast** (47 Alvarado Rd., 510/848-1431, http://marys-bedandbreakfast.com, weekend two-day minimum, $175). The Craftsman-style home has been meticulously maintained and is elegantly decorated with antiques from the period. Three rooms with private baths are available, as is an apartment for longer stays. A deluxe continental breakfast is served daily in the dining room. Mary's is within walking distance of the Claremont Hotel's spa and restaurant.

The **Hotel Durant** (2600 Durant St., 510/845-8981, www.hoteldurant.com, $160-220) has it all: location, views, and style. Get a room on the upper floors for a view of Oakland, San Francisco, or the bay. From here, you can walk (or take a complimentary bike) to the university, Telegraph Avenue, and the Elmwood shopping district.

Since 1915, the **Claremont Club & Spa** (41 Tunnel Rd., 510/843-3000, www.fairmont.com, $254-350) has catered to the rich and famous. No two of the 279 elegantly furnished rooms look quite the same, so you'll have a unique experience even in this large resort hotel. The real focus at the Claremont is fitness and pampering. A full-fledged health club, complete with yoga, Pilates, and spin classes, takes up part of the huge complex. And the full-service **spa,** which offers popular body treatments plus aesthetic services, finds favor with visitors and locals alike.

Transportation and Services

Berkeley is north of Oakland, along the east side of the San Francisco Bay. To drive into Berkeley, take the Bay Bridge from San Francisco, then merge onto I-80 East. Major roads in town include San Pablo, Ashby, Shattuck, Telegraph, and University Avenues. Parking in Berkeley can be frustrating. If you're visiting for the day or for an evening show, consider taking BART to avoid the parking hassle.

BART (www.bart.gov, fares range $4-10 one-way) is a major form of transit in the Bay Area. The Downtown Berkeley station is located underneath Shattuck Avenue. Other stations in the city include North Berkeley and Ashby. **AC Transit** (510/891-4777, www.actransit.org, adults $2.25, seniors and children 5-18 $1.10, day pass adults $5, seniors and children 5-18 $2.50) is the local bus service, offering routes that connect the East Bay and San Francisco (adults $4.50, seniors and children 5-18 $2.20).

The closest airport is **Oakland International Airport** (OAK, 1 Airport Dr., Oakland, 510/563-3300, www.flyoakland.com). From the Oakland airport, you can rent a car, catch a cab, or take BART ($9-10) from the terminals to the BART Coliseum/Airport station. If you fly into San Francisco, you can take BART from SFO to Berkeley.

OAKLAND

Oakland is the biggest city in the East Bay. Although its reputation hasn't always been perfect, a great deal of downtown urban renewal has made it a visitor-friendly place with plenty of attractions, accommodations, and exceptional food.

Oakland Museum of California

The **Oakland Museum of California** (1000 Oak St., 510/318-8400, www.museumca.org, 11am-5pm Wed.-Thurs., 11am-9pm Fri., 10am-6pm Sat.-Sun., adults $16, students and seniors $11, children 9-17 $7, children under 9 free) has launched itself into the stratosphere of must-see museums. Its multidisciplinary approach tells California's story through art, history, and science. Within its modernist concrete walls you'll be able to see Thiebaud's and Diebenkorn's take on the urban California landscape, a rare and authentic Ohlone basket, and a casting of a once-endemic mastodon. The museum also hosts special themed exhibits that complement its three-pronged approach.

The museum's **Blue Oak** (11am-4pm Wed.-Fri., 10am-6pm Sat.-Sun., $8-12) café serves wine, espresso, and a selection of salads and sandwiches. The central grassy courtyard is a great space to enjoy the Oakland sunshine and let kids burn off some energy.

Chabot Space and Science Center

One of the most spectacular sights in the East Bay, **Chabot Space and Science Center** (10000 Skyline Blvd., 510/336-7373, www.chabotspace.org, 10am-5pm Wed.-Sun., adults $18, seniors, students, and children 13-18 $15, children 3-12 $14) makes science and space super-cool. Up in the Oakland Hills, the Chabot complex includes observatories, a planetarium, a museum, and the Megadome theater, all open to the public (most Bay Area observatory telescopes are private). If your visit runs long, grab a bite to eat and a cup of coffee at the on-site café.

Entertainment and Events

BARS AND CLUBS

Luka's Taproom & Lounge (2221 Broadway, 510/451-4677, www.lukasoakland.com, 11:30am-midnight Sun.-Wed., 11:30am-2am Thurs.-Sat.) is a restaurant during the day, then a lounge and dance club at night. With a separate room for DJs and dancing; another space reserved just for pool and a 45-playing jukebox; and the Taproom, with its brasserie-style food, 16 beers on tap, and full bar, almost everyone can find something to enjoy at Luka's.

The kids (or the kid in you) will love noisy **Plank** (98 Broadway, 510/817-0980, http://plankoakland.com, 11am-midnight daily) in Jack London Square. Inside you'll find a bowling alley, an arcade, and pool tables. Outside, bocce ball courts and a beer garden overlook the Oakland Harbor. There is a full bar and the menu is affordable and eclectic.

The **Era Art Bar** (19 Grand Ave., 510/832-4400, www.oaklandera.com, 4:30pm-10pm Mon.-Thurs., 4:30pm-1:30am Fri., 9pm-1:30am Sat.) is as carefully crafted with eclectic furnishings, blown-glass chandeliers, and rotating art shows as its craft cocktails. Evenings are usually booked with DJs, live music, and unusual acts.

A muscular devotion to beer is on tap at **Beer Revolution** (464 3rd St., 510/452-2337, http://beer-revolution.com, noon-11pm Sun.-Thurs., noon-midnight Fri.-Sat.) at the edge of Jack London Square. Select from a dizzying array of beer on tap that changes daily (hourly!) to enjoy on the patio.

With only 40 beers on tap, **Mad Oak Bar and Yard** (135 12th St., 510/843-7416, www.madoakbar.com, 3pm-12:30am Sun.-Wed., 3pm-2am Thurs.-Sat.) mixes its love of beer with other spirits best enjoyed on the patio or roof deck. A rotating line up of pop-up restaurants occupies the kitchen, serving street food to the hungry.

LIVE MUSIC

Yoshi's (510 Embarcadero W., 510/238-9200, www.yoshis.com, 5:30pm-9pm Mon.-Wed., 5:30pm-10pm Fri.-Sat., 5pm-9pm Sun., shows 8pm and 10pm daily) has a sushi restaurant in one room and the legendary jazz club next door, so it's possible to enjoy the sushi without attending the concert, or vice versa.

The renovated **Fox Theater** (1807 Telegraph Ave., 510/302-2250, www.thefoxoakland.com) attracts big names to this city landmark. Originally opened in 1928 and designed in the Moorish style, the theater is now in league with some of the more venerated venues across the bay. Past acts in this intimate venue have included Sufjan Stevens, the Pixies, and 2 Chainz. It also has a bar and café where you can get champagne with your fish tacos.

A grand Oakland venue, the **Paramount Theatre** (2025 Broadway, 510/465-6400, www.paramounttheatre.com) is a 1931 art deco beauty home to the Oakland Symphony, the Oakland Ballet, and a variety of contemporary music and comedy acts. When there is no live performance, the theater hosts evenings of classic cinema.

Sports and Recreation

The jewel of Oakland is the 140-acre **Lake Merritt** (650 Bellevue Ave., 510/238-7275, www.oaklandca.gov), a tidal lagoon. Surrounding the lake is a parkland with walking trails, manicured gardens, a bandstand, and kayak rentals. At the edge of the lake, **Children's Fairyland** (699 Bellevue Ave., 510/452-2259, www.fairyland.org; 10am-4pm Mon.-Fri., 10am-5pm Sat.-Sun., summer; 10am-4pm Wed.-Sun., spring-fall; 10am-4pm Fri.-Sun., winter; $10) provides hours of entertainment and diversion for children ages 1-100.

Oakland is home to the **Oakland A's** (http://oakland.athletics.mlb.com), who play Major League baseball at the Oakland Coliseum (7000 Coliseum Way, www.coliseum.com).

Food

In Jack London Square, you can't walk 10 yards without running into a restaurant.

For pizza overlooking the water, **Forge** (66 Franklin St., 510/268-3200, 11am-9:30pm Mon.-Thurs., 11am-10:30pm Fri.-Sat., 11am-9pm Sun., $14-18) makes wood-fired Neapolitan-style pizza. Toppings vary from classic to inventive. Burgers, salads, and barbecue round out the eclectic menu. Cocktails, craft beer, and wine by the glass are available.

There's no place more Oakland than the ★ **Home of Chicken and Waffles** (444 Embarcadero W., 510/836-4446, http://homeofchickenandwaffles.com, 11am-midnight Mon.-Thurs., 11am-4am Fri.-Sat., 10am-midnight Sun., $8-18), which serves up good ol' Southern comfort food late into the night. Specialties of the house include the gooey mac and cheese, true Southern sides (lots of grits), and chicken and waffles.

★ **Nido Kitchen** (444 Oak St., 510/444-6436, 11am-3pm and 5pm-9:30pm Tues.-Thurs., 11am-3pm and 5pm-10pm Fri., 10am-3pm and 5pm-10:30pm Sat., 10am-3pm Sun., $10-26) earns raves for its Mexican farm-to-fork cuisine. Expect quirky twists on traditional favorites like blue-corn quesadillas and halibut ceviche with pomegranate in the festive interior.

Many believe that the best pizza in the Bay Area can be found in Temescal at ★ **Pizzaiolo** (5008 Telegraph Ave., Oakland, 510/652-4888, www.pizzaiolooakland.com, 8am-noon and 5:30pm-10pm Mon.-Thurs., 8am-noon and 5:30pm-10:30pm Fri.-Sat., 9am-1pm Sun., $15-29) where the pies are always fire-roasted, thin-crusted, and topped with ingredients both traditional and inventive. Despite the fanfare, Pizzaiolo retains a casual vibe with simple wood tables, an open kitchen, and a cool patio.

Across from the Fox Theater, **Duende** (468 19th St., 510/893-0174, 5:30pm-9:30pm Sun.-Mon. and Wed.-Thurs., 5:30pm-10:30pm Fri.-Sat., $20-26) is a great beginning to a night on the town. The Spanish-style food, tapas, and family platters are ideal to share. Slake your thirst with a glass of Spanish *rojo* or one or 15 sherries.

Michelin-starred dining awaits at **Commis** (3859 Piedmont Ave., 510/653-3902, http://commisrestaurant.com, 5:30pm-9:30pm Wed.-Sat., 5pm-9pm Sun., $159), in the swank Piedmont neighborhood. Enjoy eight artful courses of inventive bites that capture the flavor of California. Drink in the atmosphere at the **CDP Bar** (5pm-11:30pm Wed.-Sat., 4:30pm-11:30pm Sun., $9-22) next door, with bubbly and light nibbles.

Jack London Square

Accommodations

Hotel Jack London Square (233 Broadway, 510/452-4565, www.zhoteljacklondonsquare. com, $179-189) offers comfortable digs for reasonable rates. In addition to its clean and modestly stylish decor, the hotel has standard amenities such as complimentary Wi-Fi plus an exercise room and an outdoor pool perfect for relaxing during summer days. The hotel is within easy walking distance of Oakland's waterfront.

Compact, but packed with character and bright colors, **Waterfront Hotel** (Jack London Square, 10 Washington St., 510/836-3800 or 888/842-5333, www.jdvhotels.com, $169-339) boasts stellar views, a heated outdoor pool, sauna, and complimentary wine in the afternoons. Some of the more luxurious rooms have private balconies where you can sip your coffee in the morning.

★ **The Washington Inn** (495 10th St., Oakland, 510/452-1776, www.thewashingtoninn.com, $139-159) brings a hint of European elegance to Oakland. Rooms are smartly decorated in a refined style that highlights the 1913 landmark building while giving it a boutique hotel vibe. Downstairs, the white-tablecloth **Seison** (510/832-7449, www.seison.com, 5pm-9pm Mon.-Sat., $14-18) serves classic California fare and serious cocktails.

With all the amenities of a higher-priced chain motel, the **Bay Breeze Inn** (4919 Coliseum Way, 510/536-5972, www.baybreezeinnoakland.com, $70-159) offers both comfort and convenience. Located just down the street from the Oakland Coliseum and only a few miles from Oakland Airport, this is the perfect place to stay if you're into baseball, live concerts, or just need to be near the airport.

Transportation and Services

Oakland is across the bay from San Francisco and borders Berkeley to the south. It's accessible by car from San Francisco via I-80 (toll) over the Bay Bridge. From I-80, I-580 borders Oakland to the east and north, and I-880 runs along the bay on the west. Try to avoid driving I-80, I-880, or I-580 during rush hour (7am-10am and 4pm-7pm).

The **Oakland International Airport** (OAK, 1 Airport Dr., Oakland, 510/563-3300, www.flyoakland.com) sees less traffic than San Francisco's airport and has shorter security lines and fewer delays. Alaska, Delta, JetBlue, Southwest, and Spirit service the airport.

BART (Bay Area Rapid Transit, www.bart. gov) offers public transportation from San Francisco to the East Bay. The 12th Street/ Oakland City Center station is convenient to downtown Oakland, with trains to 19th Street, Lake Merritt, Rockridge, and the Oakland Airport. BART fares ($4-10 one-way) are based on distance. Ticket machines at the station accept cash and debit or credit cards are.

AC Transit (510/891-4777, www.actransit. org, adults $2.25, seniors and children 5-18 $1.10, day pass adults $5, seniors and children 5-18 $2.50) transbay bus routes connect the East Bay and San Francisco (adults $4.50, seniors and children 5-18 $2.20).

The Peninsula

The San Francisco Peninsula encompasses the coastal area from Pacifica down to Año Nuevo State Park and inland to Palo Alto along the San Francisco Bay. Many Bay Area locals enjoy the small-town atmosphere in Half Moon Bay and Pescadero along with the unspoiled beauty of the dozens of miles of undeveloped coastline. Peak seasons include October's pumpkin season and summer.

MOSS BEACH

Between San Francisco and Half Moon Bay on Highway 1, Moss Beach is one of several residential towns that line the coast south of the imposing Devil's Slide. There is little here besides stunning scenery, a few small businesses, and the Fitzgerald Marine Reserve. North of Moss Beach is the lovely Montara, and south is the Half Moon Bay Airport, El Granada, Princeton, and then Half Moon Bay.

Fitzgerald Marine Reserve

The 32-acre **Fitzgerald Marine Reserve** (200 Nevada Ave., Moss Beach, 650/728-3584, http://parks.smcgov.org, 8am-sunset daily) is considered one of the most diverse intertidal zones in the Bay Area. On its rocky reefs, you can hunt for sea anemones, starfish, eels, and crabs—there's even a small species of red octopus. The reserve is also home to egrets, herons, an endangered species of butterfly, and a slew of sea lions and harbor seals that enjoy sunning themselves on the beach's outer rocks. Rangers are available to answer any questions and, if need be, to remind you of tidepool etiquette (including a strict no-dog policy). For the best viewing, come at low tide (www.protides.com). For a more leisurely and drier experience, numerous trails crisscross the windswept bluffs and through sheltering groves of cypress and eucalyptus trees.

Montara State Beach

North of Moss Beach is **Montara State Beach** (2nd St. and Hwy. 1, Montara, www.parks.ca.gov, 650/726-8819, 8am-sunset daily), one of the most beautiful beaches in this area. It is as popular with tidepool visitors, surfers, and anglers as it is with picnickers and beachcombers. For those who want

Montara State Beach

a heart-pounding hike instead of a stroll on the beach, cross Highway 1 to the trailhead at **McNee Ranch.** Fire roads crisscross this eastern section of the state park, but the big hike is eight miles up **Montara Mountain** (1,900 feet), through California chaparral. Parking is in a small dirt lot directly across Highway 1 from the parking lot at Montara Beach. McNee Ranch is also a popular mountain biking area, and dogs are welcome on leash.

Devil's Slide Trail

The moniker for this former stretch of Highway 1 between Pacifica and Montara is no joke. For nearly 75 years, white-knuckled motorists braved the thin asphalt hugging the sheer cliffs that plunged into the churning Pacific hundreds of feet below. Once the Tom Lantos Tunnel was completed, this former hellish road was converted to the 1.3-mile, multiuse **Devil's Slide Trail** (Hwy. 1 between Pacifica and Montara, 650/355-8289, http://parks.smcgov.org/devils-slide-trail, 8am-sunset daily). Today, you can enjoy spectacular views of the Farallon Islands and migrating whales. Parking lots sit on either end of the trail and have clean bathrooms.

Food and Accommodations

Tucked away in the cypress and pine forest of Moss Beach, **Seal Cove Inn** (221 Cypress Ave., Moss Beach, 650/728-4114 or 800/995-9987, www.sealcoveinn.com, $325-425) is a highly regarded 10-room B&B. Outside, the gabled roof, climbing ivy, and expansive gardens let guests know they have entered the inn's rarified world. The pampering extends to private decks and fireplaces, a complimentary breakfast brought to your room, and an evening wine social.

The **Point Montara Lighthouse Hostel** (16th St. and Hwy. 1, Montara, 650/728-7177, www.norcalhostels.org, dorm $33-36, private room $83-128, nonmembers add $3/night) offers great views in the shared dorm rooms (either coed or gender-specific), each with 3-6

beds. Enjoy use of the shared kitchen, common areas with wood-burning fireplaces, the eclectic garden perched on the cliff, and the private cove beach. Other amenities include Wi-Fi, laundry facilities, and complimentary linens.

The **Moss Beach Distillery** (140 Beach Way, Moss Beach, 650/728-5595, www.mossbeachdistillery.com, noon-8pm Mon.-Thurs., noon-8:30pm Fri.-Sat., 11am-8pm Sun., $16-37) is famous for its hearty portions of comfort food, friendly (though sometimes slow) service, and for the spine-tingling stories of the Blue Lady, the distillery's legendary ghost. But the real draw is the terrace overlooking the ocean.

Swing by **Gherkin's Sandwich Shop** (171 7th St., Montara, 650/728-2211, www.eatgherkins.com, 9am-7pm daily, $4-10) for a picnic lunch. You'll find oddities like the Ooey Gooey, with peanut butter, Nutella, and marshmallows, and hallowed favorites like the BLT, burgers, and pastrami and swiss. Sides include garlic fries and macaroni salad.

Poised above Montara Beach, ★ **La Costanera** (8150 Cabrillo Hwy., Montara, 650/728-1600, www.lacostanerarestaurant.com, 5pm-9pm Tues.-Thurs. and Sun., 5pm-10pm Fri.-Sat., $21-39) is a sophisticated Peruvian restaurant and the only eatery on this part of the coast to earn a Michelin star. There are a variety of ceviche options to choose from, and the bar menu offers hearty plates that can serve as a light dinner.

HALF MOON BAY

Half Moon Bay retains its character as an "ag" town. Strawberries, artichokes, and Brussels sprouts are the biggest agricultural crops, along with flowers, pumpkins, and Christmas trees, making the coast a destination for holiday festivities. Four miles north are Pillar Point Harbor and the neighboring blue-collar town of **Princeton-by-the-Sea,** where hardworking anglers haul in crab, salmon, and herring, with local businesses catering to their needs.

Beaches

The beaches of Half Moon Bay draw visitors from over the hill and farther afield all year long. **Half Moon Bay State Beach** (www.parks.ca.gov, 650/726-8819 or 650/726-8820, parking $10/day) encompasses three discrete beaches stretching four miles down the coast, each with its own access point and parking lot. **Francis Beach** (95 Kelly Ave.) has the most developed amenities, including a good-size **campground** (50 sites, reservations 800/444-7275 or www.reservecalifornia.com, $35) with grassy areas to pitch tents and enjoy picnics, a visitors center, and indoor hot showers. **Venice Beach** (Venice Blvd., off Hwy. 1) offers outdoor showers and flush toilets. **Dunes Beach** (Young Ave., off Hwy. 1) is the northernmost major beach in the chain and the least developed.

Linking the beaches is the popular **Coastside Trail** (www.parks.ca.gov), which extends five miles from Pillar Point Harbor to Poplar Beach. Beyond the Poplar Beach parking lot (end of Poplar St., $2/hour), the trail turns to dirt and crosses into the **Wavecrest Open Space.** This is a great place to spot herons, egrets, and gray whales off the coast during their spring migration.

Sports and Recreation

SURFING

It's hard to miss the surfers while driving down Highway 1. The most popular surfing spot is appropriately named **Surfers Beach,** just south of Princeton. The break is long and small, perfect for beginners. In the summer you're likely to see "surf camps" (the coast's answer to kids' summer camp) as kids practice paddling, standing up on their board, and taking a wave. More experienced surfers tend to pick **Kelly, Montara,** and **Dunes Beaches,** where the waves are bigger and more unpredictable and the currents challenging. Of course, nothing can touch **Mavericks Break,** west of Pillar Point Harbor. Formed by unique underwater topography, the giant waves are the site of the legendary **Mavericks Surf Contest,** for which the top surfers in the

world are given 48 hours' notice to compete on the peak of the winter swells. The deadly break is a half-mile offshore, keeping it a safe distance from anyone not seasoned enough to survive it.

If the waves prove too tempting to resist, **Cowboy Surf Shop** (2830 N. Cabrillo Hwy., Half Moon Bay, 650/726-6968, www.cowboy-surfshop.com, 10am-6pm daily, surfboard $20/day, wetsuit $10/day) can rent you what you need and provide plenty of advice.

KAYAKING AND WHALE-WATCHING

Join naturalists at the nonprofit **Oceanic Society** (800/326-7491 or 415/256-9604, www.oceanicsociety.org, Sat.-Sun. Jan.-Apr., adults and children 8 and older $59) for whale-watching expeditions during the annual migration. During the three-hour trip, you may see gray whales, sea lions, harbor porpoises, and the occasional humpback whale. The *Queen of Hearts* (Pillar Point Harbor, 510/581-2628, www.fishingboat.com) offers whale-watching trips (Jan.-Apr., $50), in addition to deep-sea salmon fishing (Apr.-Nov., $100), shallow-water rock fishing (Apr.-Dec., $88-92), Farallon Island rock fishing (call for season, $95), and deep-sea albacore fishing (July-Oct., call for rates).

One of the coolest ways to see the coast is from the deck of a sea kayak. Many kayak tours with the **Half Moon Bay Kayaking Company** (2 Johnson Pier, 650/773-6101, www.hmbkayak.com, 10am-4pm daily summer, 10am-4pm Wed.-Mon., $85-150) require no previous kayaking experience; all tours are roughly three hours and the company offers tours geared toward kids. Rental kayaks are available ($25-50/hour, $75-150/day), as are stand-up paddleboards ($25/hour, $75/day). The price of the rental includes a wetsuit, life jacket, and basic instruction.

Half Moon Bay Art & Pumpkin

Nearly 250,000 people trek to Half Moon Bay for the **Half Moon Bay Art & Pumpkin Festival** (650/726-9652, www.miramarevents.com, Oct.) with live music, food, artists' booths, contests, kids' activities, an adults' lounge area, and a parade. Perhaps the best-publicized event is the pumpkin weigh-off, which takes place before the festivities begin. Farmers bring their tremendous squash in on flatbed trucks from all over the country to determine which is the biggest of all. The winner gets paid per pound, a significant prize when the biggest pumpkins weigh more than 1,000 pounds.

Food

★ **Pasta Moon** (315 Main St., 650/726-5125, www.pastamoon.com, 11:30am-2pm and 5:30pm-9pm Mon.-Thurs., 11:30am-2pm and 5:30pm-9:30pm Fri., noon-3pm and 5:30pm-9:30pm Sat., noon-3pm and 5:30pm-9pm Sun., $19-40) is the godmother of Coastside fine dining, serving updated Italian cuisine with an emphasis on fresh, light dishes. The wood-fired pizzas are particularly good and affordable, as are any of the pasta dishes, created with house-made noodles. The bar and lounge hums with live jazz, offering an urbane evening out.

The brightly painted **Chez Shea** (408 Main St., 650/560-9234, www.chez-shea.com, 11am-3pm and 5pm-8pm Mon.-Thurs., 11am-3pm and 5pm-8:30pm Fri., 10am-4pm and 5pm-8:30pm Sat., 10am-4pm and 5pm-8pm Sun., $17-19) serves an eclectic mix of comfort food from Spain, Mexico, Lebanon, Italy, and South Africa. Order the mezza platter, with a wonderful array of dipping sauces, or the shwarma platter, with lean strips of seasoned beef and lamb. A kid's menu offers American staples.

The virtual parking lot out front on Highway 1 speaks to the golden touch of **Sam's Chowder House** (4210 N. Cabrillo Hwy., Pillar Point Harbor, 650/712-0245, www.samschowderhouse.com, 11:30am-9pm Mon.-Thurs., 11:30am-9:30pm Fri., 11am-9:30pm Sat., 11am-9pm Sun., $15-38). This is the place to get seafood and soak in the surf and sun. Facing the water you'll find ample views and plentiful decks with Adirondack chairs and fire pits, where you can sip cocktails, slurp down oysters, and indulge in

steaming plates of whole lobster, seafood paella, and seared tuna.

Stop into the **Moonside Bakery & Café** (604 Main St., 650/726-9070, www.moonsidebakery.com, 7am-4pm Sun.-Thurs., 7am-5pm Fri.-Sat., $5-15) for breakfast pastries and espresso or a casual lunch.

Accommodations

Half Moon Bay offers several lovely bed-and-breakfasts and one luxury resort hotel.

The **Ritz-Carlton Half Moon Bay** (1 Miramontes Point Rd., 650/712-7000, www.ritzcarlton.com, $700) has a top-tier restaurant, Navio; a world-class day spa; and posh rooms that are worth the rates. If you can, get a room facing the ocean. While you're here, enjoy free access to the spa's bathing rooms, an outdoor hot tub overlooking the ocean, tennis courts, and the basketball court. Two distinguished golf courses make this a favorite destination for serious golfers.

For a personal lodging experience, try the **Nantucket Whale Inn** (779 Main St., 650/726-1616, www.nantucketwhaleinn.com, $169-429). Each of the seven rooms has a nautical theme, along with flat-screen TVs, fancy toiletries, refrigerators, and coffeemakers. Most rooms have an en-suite bath. Guests enjoy a hot complimentary breakfast that can be delivered to the room (advance notice).

Built out of weathered redwood, the ★ **Cypress Inn** (407 Mirada Rd., 650/726-6002, www.cypressinn.com, $229-472) is a neat compound where most rooms come with fireplaces, private decks, jetted tubs, and fridges. A full-service breakfast and a cocktail hour are offered in the Main House. The inn is an easy bike ride to downtown Half Moon Bay.

Transportation

Half Moon Bay is on Highway 1 about 45 minutes south of San Francisco. From San Francisco, take I-280 south to Highway 92 west to Half Moon Bay and Highway 1. You can also take the scenic route by following Highway 1 directly south from San Francisco.

Parking in downtown Half Moon Bay is usually easy—except if you're in town during the Pumpkin Festival. Your best bet is to stay in town with your car safely stowed in a hotel parking lot before the festival.

PESCADERO AND VICINITY

South of Half Moon Bay, the coast turns wild and agricultural. You'll pass by fields of artichokes atop coastal bluffs, state park beaches, and towering redwoods further inland. Pescadero is the largest town between Half Moon Bay and Santa Cruz, a tiny dot on the coast with one main street, several small farms—and the legendary Duarte's Tavern.

Sights

San Gregorio is a one stop sign town of rolling rangeland, neat patches of colorful crops, and century-old homes, including a one-room schoolhouse and an old brothel. Its beating heart is the **San Gregorio General Store** (Hwy. 84 and Stage Rd., 650/726-0565, www.sangregoriostore.com, 10:30am-6pm Mon.-Thurs., 10:30am-7pm Fri., 10am-7pm Sat., 10am-6pm Sun.), open since 1889. Like at any good country store, you'll find a collection of books, a variety of cast-iron cookery,

oil lamps, work pants, and raccoon traps. On weekends the store is packed with out-of-towners, and live music keeps things moving.

South of Pescadero is **Pigeon Point Lighthouse** (210 Pigeon Point Rd., at Hwy. 1, 650/879-2120, www.parks.ca.gov, 8am-sunset daily, visitors center 10am-4pm Wed.-Mon. June-Aug., 10am-4pm Thurs.-Mon. Sept.-May, free). First lit in 1872, Pigeon Point is one of the most photographed lighthouses in the United States. Its hostel still shelters travelers, and visitors can marvel at the incomparable views from the point. In winter, look for migrating whales from the rocks beyond the tower.

Beaches

San Gregorio State Beach (650/726-8819, www.parks.ca.gov, 8am-sunset daily, $8) stretches out beyond the cliffs to create a spot perfect for contemplative strolling. San Gregorio is clothing-optional at the far north end and a local favorite in the summer, despite the regular appearance of fog. Picnic tables and restrooms cluster near the parking lot but can be hampered by the wind.

Pomponio State Beach (650/726-8819, www.parks.ca.gov, 8am-sunset daily, $8) sits halfway between San Gregorio and

San Gregorio General Store

Pescadero. Its breaks sometimes lure surfers, while its stretch of sandy beach is popular with families.

Pescadero State Beach (Hwy. 1 at Pescadero Rd., 650/879-2170, www.parks. ca.gov, 8am-sunset daily, $8) encompasses the wetlands, rocky shore, and small stretch of sand at the mouth of Pescadero Creek. The near-constant winds make it less than ideal for picnics or sunbathing, but bird lovers flock to **Pescadero Marsh Natural Preserve** across the highway. This protected wetland is home to a variety of avian species, including great blue herons, snowy egrets, and northern harriers, with trails and bridges crisscrossing throughout.

South of Pescadero, pint-size **Bean Hollow State Beach** (Hwy. 1, 650/879-2170, www. parks.ca.gov, 8am-sunset daily, $8) is a cozy cove with a crescent-shaped stretch of sand and a rocky outcropping great for tidepooling. Avoid swimming; rip currents and heavy surf make it much more dangerous than it appears.

Año Nuevo State Park

Año Nuevo State Park (1 News Years Creek Road at Hwy. 1, south of Pescadero, 650/879-2025, reservations 800/444-4445, www.parks. ca.gov, 8am-sunset daily, $10/car) is world-famous as the winter home and breeding ground of once-endangered elephant seals. The reserve also has extensive dunes, marshland, and excellent bird habitat. The beaches and wilderness are open year-round. The elephant seals start showing up in late November and stay to breed, birth pups, and loll on the beach until early March. Visitors are not allowed down to the elephant seal habitats on their own and must sign up for a guided walking tour (reservations 800/444-4445 or www. reservecalifornia.com, 8:45am-2:45pm daily Dec.-Mar., $7, under 4 free). Once you see two giant males crashing into one another in a fight for dominance, you won't want to get too close. Book your tour at least a day or two in advance since the seals are popular with both locals and travelers.

Butano State Park

Beautiful **Butano State Park** (1500 Cloverdale Rd., 650/879-2040, www.parks. ca.gov, 8am-sunset, $8) follows Little Butano Creek into the mountains, where it is home to old-growth redwoods, 40 miles of hiking trails, and a campground. The **Little Butano Creek Trail** (3 miles, easy-moderate), makes a great half-day loop when connected with the fire road. For a longer hike with great views, take the **Canyon Loop** (9.5 miles, strenuous) from the Jackson Flats trailhead at the small visitors center. To reach the backpacker Trail Camp and the abandoned landing field at the top of the ridge, turn left on the Indian Trail for a one mile out and back. Or, turn right on Indian Trail and follow it to the Olmo Fire Road. Take the Año Nuevo Trail back to the trailhead.

Food

★ **Duarte's Tavern** (202 Stage Rd., 650/879-0464, www.duartestavern.com, 7am-8pm Sun.-Thurs., 7am-8:30pm Fri.-Sat., $8-26) is famous for its artichoke soup and olallieberry pie. For the best experience, sit in the bar, where locals of all stripes are shoulder to shoulder with travelers, sharing conversation and a bite to eat. Pick out a selection from the outdated jukebox and order a Bloody Mary, garnished with a pickled green bean.

Inside the gas station across the street, **Mercado & Taqueria De Amigos** (1999 Pescadero Creek Rd., 650/879-0232, 9am-9pm daily, $6-13 cash only) has been written up by the *New York Times* and is rumored to be the best taqueria between San Francisco and Santa Cruz. Squeezed in next to coolers of beer and energy drinks, the open kitchen prepares excellent shrimp burritos, *al pastor* tacos, and not-too sweet *horchata*. You'll find mainly locals here, most speaking Spanish, and the wait can be long.

Espresso has arrived in Pescadero with **Downtown Local** (231 Stage Rd., 650/879-9155, 8am-5pm Mon.-Fri., 8am-5:30pm Sat.-Sun., $5). You'll find coffee, a few sweets, home-brewed kombucha, and a quirky collection of 1960s and 1970s ephemera.

For a slice of pie, **Pie Ranch** (2080 Hwy. 1, 12 miles south of Pescadero, 650/879-9281, noon-5pm Mon.-Fri., 10am-5pm Sat.-Sun., $5) is the spot. The nonprofit works to educate kids about farming and cooking, while whipping up some delicious desserts.

Accommodations and Camping

Pigeon Point Hostel (210 Pigeon Point Rd., at Hwy. 1, 650/879-0633, http://norcalhostels. org/pigeon, dorm adults $28-32, children $14-16, private room $82-186) has simple but comfortable accommodations, both private and dorm-style. Amenities include a kitchen, free Wi-Fi, and beach access. Linens are provided, but the biggest draw is a hot tub perched above the pounding surf. Check in early to reserve a spot (4pm-10:30pm, max. four people, $8 pp).

At **Costanoa Lodge and Campground** (2001 Rossi Rd., at Hwy. 1, 650/879-1100 or 877/262-7848, www.costanoa.com, campsite $42-55, rooms $80-385), lodging options include pitching a tent in the campground, staying in a tent or log-style cabins, or renting a whirlpool suite. A small general store offers s'mores fixings and souvenirs while "comfort stations" provide outdoor fireplaces, private indoor-outdoor showers, baths with heated floors, and saunas that are open 24 hours to all guests.

The best camping on the coast is at ★ **Butano State Park** (1500 Cloverdale Rd., 650/879-2040, www.parks.ca.gov, reservations 800/444-7275 or www.reservecalifornia.com, Apr.-Nov., $35), with 21 drive-in sites and 18 walk-in campsites. The few amenities include clean restrooms, fire pits, bear boxes, drinking water, and pit and flush toilets. The walk-in sites are particularly beautiful nestled in a glen of redwoods.

Farther inland, past the tiny town of Loma Mar, is **Memorial Park** (9500 Pescadero Creek Rd., 650/879-0238 or 650/363-4021, https://parks.smcgov.org, year-round, $25-30) with 158 campsites. Each site accommodates up to eight people and has a fire pit, picnic tables, and a metal locker to store food and sundries. Drinking water, flush toilets, coin-operated showers, and a general store are within the park. Memorial boasts an amphitheater and swimming holes.

Transportation

Pescadero is 17 miles south of Half Moon Bay. At Pescadero State Beach, Highway 1 intersects Pescadero Road. Turn east on Pescadero Road and drive two miles to the stop sign (the only one in town). Turn left onto Stage Road to find the main drag. Parking is free and generally easy to find on Stage Road or in the Duarte's parking lot. On weekends, you may need to park down the road a ways.

Silicon Valley

Palo Alto, San Jose, and the Santa Clara Valley form the trifecta known as Silicon Valley, home to tech-media giants and the wizards who run them. Palo Alto owes much of its prosperity and character to Stanford University, an incubator for some of Silicon Valley's great talents and entrepreneurs. Sprawled across the south end of Silicon Valley, San Jose proudly claims the title of biggest city in the Bay Area. It is the workhorse of the valley's high-tech industry and is home to eBay, Cisco, Adobe, IBM, and many others.

SIGHTS
Stanford University

Stanford University (University Ave., Palo Alto, 650/723-2560, www.stanford. edu) is one of the top universities in the world, and fewer than 10 percent of the high school students who apply each year are accepted. The **visitors center** (295 Galvez St.,

650/723-3335, www.stanford.edu, 8:30am-5pm Mon.-Fri., 10am-5pm Sat.-Sun.) is in a handsome one-story brick building; inside, well-trained staff can help you with campus maps and tours (11:30am and 3:30pm daily). Definitely download or procure a map of campus before getting started on your explorations, as Stanford is infamously hard for newcomers to navigate.

For a taste of the beauty that surrounds the students on a daily basis, begin your tour with **The Quad** (Oval at Palm Dr.) and **Memorial Church.** Located at the center of campus, these architectural gems are still in active use. Classes are held in the quad every day, and services take place in the church each Sunday. Almost next door to the Quad is **Hoover Tower** (650/723-2053, 10am-4pm Tues.-Sat., adults $4, seniors and children under 13 $3, cash only), the tall tower that's visible from up to 30 miles away. For great views of the Bay Area, head up to its observation platform.

On the other side of the Quad, just past the Oval, is the **Cantor Arts Center** (328 Lomita Dr. at Museum Way, 650/723-4177, www.museum.stanford.edu, 11am-5pm Mon., Wed., and Fri.-Sun., 11am-8pm Thurs.). This free art museum features both permanent collections of classic paintings and sculpture donated by the Cantors and other philanthropists, along with traveling exhibitions. One of the center's highlights is the **Rodin Sculpture Garden,** pieces cast in France from Rodin's originals that include *The Burghers of Calais* and *The Gates of Hell.* The most famous member of this collection, *The Thinker,* can be found in the Susan and John Diekman Gallery inside the museum.

San Jose Museum of Art

The highly regarded **San Jose Museum of Art** (110 S. Market St., San Jose, 408/271-6840, www.sjmusart.org, 11am-5pm Tues.-Sun., adults $10, seniors $8, students $6, children 7-17 $5, children under 6 free) is right downtown. Housed in a historical sandstone building that was added to in 1991, the beautiful

light-filled museum features modern and contemporary art. Its permanent collection focuses largely on West Coast artists, but major retrospectives of works by the likes of Andy Warhol, Robert Mapplethorpe, and Alexander Calder come through often, giving the museum a broader scope. As a bonus, the Museum Store offers perhaps the best gift shopping in downtown San Jose. The **café** (8am-3:30pm Tues.-Fri., 11am-3:30pm Sat.-Sun.), with both an indoor lounge and outside sidewalk tables, is a great place to grab a quick bite.

Tech Museum of Innovation

The **Tech Museum of Innovation** (201 S. Market St., San Jose, 408/294-8324, www.thetech.org, 10am-5pm daily, adults $24, seniors and children 3-17 $19) brings technology of all kinds to kids, families, and science lovers. The interactive displays at the Tech invite touching and letting children explore and learn about medical technology, computers, biology, chemistry, physics, and more, using all their senses. The **IMAX theater** (additional $5/adults, $4/seniors and children 3-17) shows films dedicated to science, learning, technology, and adventure (and the occasional blockbuster).

Winchester Mystery House

For good old-fashioned haunted fun, stop in at the **Winchester Mystery House** (525 S. Winchester Blvd., San Jose, 408/247-2101, www.winchestermysteryhouse.com, 9am-5pm daily), a huge bizarre mansion built by famous eccentric Sarah Winchester. Kids love the doors that open onto brick walls, stairwells that go nowhere, and oddly shaped rooms, while adults enjoy the story of Sarah and the antiques displayed in many of the rooms. Sarah married into the gun-making Winchester family and became disturbed later in life by the death wrought by her husband's products. She designed the house to both facilitate communication with the spirits of the dead and to confound them and keep herself safe. Whether or not ghosts still haunt the

Scenic Drive: Skyline Boulevard

The San Andreas Fault splits the coastal and inland peninsula, with dramatic views and curves from aptly named **Skyline Boulevard (Hwy. 35).** Nestled amid redwoods, quaint and beautiful Woodside sits midway along Skyline at its junction with Highway 85. Nearby, Palo Alto provides easy access via U.S. 101.

SIGHTS AND ACTIVITIES

Skyline Boulevard is lined with numerous parks filled with excellent hiking and mountain biking trails. The road itself is popular with bicyclists and motorcycles on weekends. Following is a list of stops from north to south:

- **Filoli** (86 Cañada Rd., Woodside, 650/364-8300, www.filoli.org, 10am-5pm Tues.-Sun. June-Oct., adults $22, seniors $18, children 5-17 $11, children under 5 free) was the country manor of William Bowers Bourn II. Designed in 1917 in the Georgian style, the house reflects the rarefied world of the very wealthy. The gardens cover nearly 700 acres, 16 of which are carefully cultivated plots that celebrate American horticultural style and botanical diversity. Tours ($5) are available daily.

- **Purisima Creek Open Space** (Skyline Blvd., 4.5 miles south of Hwy. 92, www.openspace.org) has 4,711 acres of redwoods that stretch from Skyline down the coast. The 24 miles of trails are favorites for hikers and mountain bikers.

- **El Corte de Madera Creek Preserve** (Skyline Blvd., 2.7 miles north of Hwy. 84, www.openspace.org) offers 36 miles of multiuse trails and is favorite among cyclists. Look for the lacy Tafoni sandstone formations near the Fir Trail or hike the Timberview Trail to the remaining old-growth redwoods.

- **Huddart Park** (1100 Kings Mountain Rd., 650/851-1210, https://parks.smcgov.org) has picnic areas, hiking trails, group campsites, and an archery range.

- **Crystal Springs Trail** (Canada Rd. at Raymundo Dr., https://parks.smcgov.org) is an easy

mansion is a matter of debate and of faith—visit and make up your own mind.

Admission to the grounds is free, but to peek inside the house, you must book a **tour** (adults $39-49, seniors $32-42, children 6-12 $20, children 5 and under free). For an extra-spooky experience, take a Friday the 13th or Halloween flashlight tour (book early, as these tours fill up fast).

FOOD
San Jose

The center of San Jose's hip restaurant scene is San Pedro Square, the long narrow block of North San Pedro Street, east of West Santa Clara Street. At the **San Pedro Square Market** (87 N. San Pedro St., www.sanpedrosquaremarket.com, 7am-10pm daily), a variety of vendors serve everything from noodle bowls to ice cream cones.

Solid Mediterranean classics are served in a romantic setting at **71 Saint Peter** (71 N. San Pedro St., 408/971-8523, www.71saintpeter.com, 11am-9pm Mon.-Fri., 5pm-9pm Sat., $18-30). At **Firehouse No. 1 Gastropub** (69 N. San Pedro St., 408/287-6969, http://firehouse1.com, 11:30am-midnight Mon.-Wed., 11:30am-2am Thurs.-Fri., 4:30pm-2am Sat., 11am-midnight Sun., $19-39), meat-heavy comfort food complements a robust drink menu.

Mezcal (25 W. San Fernando St., 408/283-9595, http://mezcalrestaurantsj.com, 11:30am-8:30pm Mon.-Fri., 11:30am-9:30pm Tues.-Thurs., 11:30am-10:30pm Fri., 4pm-10:30pm Sat., 4pm-8:30pm Sun., $10-19) specializes in food

15-mile route that's perfect for a mellow afternoon bike ride. The trail starts in Woodside and follows Cañada Road past Filoli and the Pulgas Water Temple to the Crystal Springs Reservoir.

- **Portola Redwoods** (west of Hwy. 35 off Alpine Rd., 650/948-9098, www.parks.ca.gov, $10) is 2,800 lush acres of redwoods and waterfalls, with 18 miles of hiking trails, a campground (800/444-7275, www.reservecalifornia.com, Apr.-Nov., $35), and a visitors center (10am-4pm Thurs.-Sun.).

- **Castle Rock** (Hwy. 35 at Hwy. 9, www.parks.ca.gov, sunrise-sunset daily, $8) sits at one of the highest ridges in the Santa Cruz Mountains, drawing hikers, bikers, and climbers who love to scale its sandstone formations.

FOOD

Alice's Restaurant (Hwy. 35 at Hwy. 84, 650/851-0303, www.alicesrestaurant.com, 8am-8pm Mon.-Wed., 8am-9pm Thurs.-Sat., 8am-6:30pm Sun., $16-23) is located in the redwoods that were once home to Ken Kesey and the Merry Pranksters. A hangout for bikers and locals, the menu features burgers, garlic fries, and a slew of draft beers. The outside deck is a destination on sunny weekends.

The Village Pub (2967 Woodside Rd., 650/851-9888, http://thevillagepub.net, 11:30am-2:30pm and 5pm-10pm Mon.-Fri., 5pm-10pm Sat., 10am-2pm and 5pm-10pm Sun., $28-60) is a Michelin-starred restaurant serving French Mediterranean cuisine. The pub menu (11:30am-10pm Mon.-Fri., $18-24) offers budget options.

GETTING THERE

From San Francisco, take I-280 south to the Skyline/Highway 35 exit. At the stoplight, turn right as the road merges with Highway 92, then turn left onto Skyline Boulevard. From Half Moon Bay, Highway 92 connects east with Skyline Boulevard, or take Highway 1 south to San Gregorio and follow Highway 84 to its intersection with Skyline. From Palo Alto, take I-280 north to Highway 84 or Highway 92.

from the Oaxaca region of Mexico. The menu is full of mole, pork cracklings, and fresh fish, fruit, and vegetables.

Gombei (193 E. Jackson St., 408/279-4311, http://gombei.com, 11:30am-2:30pm and 5pm-9:30pm Mon.-Sat., $9-13), in Japantown, is known for traditional Japanese food at good prices. The menu is as minimal as the decor, with simple categories such as *udon*, tofu, and curry rice.

Little has changed at **Original Joe's** (301 S. 1st St., San Jose, 408/292-7030, www.original-joes.com, 11am-midnight daily, $14-24) since it opened in 1956. Veal parmigiana and pot roast share the menu with burgers, tuna melts, pasta, and steaks in a friendly and classic atmosphere. The full bar keeps it real.

Southwest of San Jose, ★ **Manresa** (320 Village Ln., Los Gatos, 408/354-4330, www.manresarestaurant.com, 5:30pm-9pm Wed.-Sun., tasting menu $275) is the Michelin-starred darling of the South Bay. The nightly tasting menu features such delicate oddities as panna cotta topped with abalone "petals." Surprisingly, they do accept walk-ins, but if you're looking for a special Saturday night, reserve now.

The Bywater (532 N. Santa Cruz Ave., Los Gatos, 408/560-9639, www.thebywaterca.com, 11am-10pm Tues.-Thurs., 11am-11pm Fri., 10am-11pm Sat., 10am-9pm Sun., $15-28) dresses Manresa's magic in New Orleans flavors and delivers it at a fraction of the price. Expect gumbo, po'boys, pork pie, and "oysters rock-a-fella" served in a shabby-chic interior with stiff drinks.

Palo Alto

The kitschy decor at the **Palo Alto Creamery** (566 Emerson St., Palo Alto, 650/323-3131, www.paloaltocreamery.com, 7am-10pm Mon.-Wed., 7am-11pm Thurs., 7am-midnight Fri., 8am-midnight Sat., 8am-10pm Sun., $10-16) feels like a genuine 1950s soda shop. The food runs to American classics, but what patrons really come for is the house-made ice cream.

At California-Japanese hybrid **Bird Dog** (420 Ramona St., 650/656-8180, 11am-2pm and 5pm-10pm Mon.-Fri., 5pm-10pm Sat., 5pm-9pm Sun., $22-38), delicate plates of Japanese specialties are accented with Northern California ingredients. The interior is as sophisticated as the food.

ACCOMMODATIONS
San Jose

The **Four Points Sheraton Downtown San Jose** (211 S. 1st St., 408/282-8800, https://four-points.starwoodhotels.com, $123-224) provides modern comfort at reasonable rates. Amenities include a restaurant and bar, outdoor bocce ball courts, free Wi-Fi, and a great central location.

The **Westin San Jose** (302 S. Market St., 408/295-2000 or 866/716-8180, www.westin-sanjose.com, $296-429) offers big-city-style accommodations in a historic hotel. Standard rooms are small but attractive, with a flat-screen TV, free Wi-Fi, plush robes, and turn-down service. The hotel's common areas are dressed in 1920s finery, harkening back to the opening of the original Hotel Sainte Claire.

The top-tier **Hotel Valencia Santana Row** (355 Santana Row, 408/551-0010 or 855/596-3396, www.hotelvalencia-santan-arow.com, $409-650) offers ultramodern elegance and convenience with an outdoor pool and hot tub, a slick lounge perched on the hotel's balcony, and the swank Oveja Negra Restaurant. Inside the rooms are Egyptian cotton sheets and lavish baths with upscale toiletries.

Palo Alto

Affordable lodgings near Palo Alto can be found in the serene farm setting of **Hidden Villa Hostel** (26870 Moody Rd., Los Altos Hills, 650/949-8648, www.hiddenvilla.org, Sept.-May, $29-64). Sustainably constructed, the hostel provides access to hiking trails, the surrounding organic farm, and the small wealthy town of Los Altos Hills. Reservations are required on weekends and a good idea even on weekdays.

Dinah's Garden Hotel (4261 El Camino Real, 650/493-2844 or 800/227-8220, www.di-nahshotel.com, $139-379) has basic rooms the size and shape of a motel, but the high-priced suites are something to behold. Attached to the hotel are both a casual poolside grill and an upscale seafood restaurant with a decidedly Asian bent.

The ★ **Creekside Inn** (3400 El Camino Real, 650/493-2411, www.creekside-inn.com, $145-379) provides garden accommodations set back a bit from the noisy road. The rooms are upscale with stylish fabrics and modern amenities like free Wi-Fi, fully stocked private baths, refrigerators, coffeemakers, in-room safes, and comfy bathrobes.

TRANSPORTATION AND SERVICES
Air

Travelers heading straight for Silicon Valley should fly into **Mineta San José International Airport** (SJC, 1701 Airport Blvd., 408/392-3600, www.flysanjose.com). This suburban commercial airport has shorter lines, less parking and traffic congestion, and is convenient to downtown San Jose.

Train

Amtrak (800/872-7245, www.amtrak.com) trains come into San Jose, and you can catch either the once-daily Seattle-Los Angeles *Coast Starlight* or the commuter *Capitol Corridor* to Sacramento at the **San Jose-Diridon Station** (65 Cahill St.). **Caltrain** (800/660-4287, www.caltrain.com, one-way $3.75-15) is a commuter rail line that runs from Gilroy to San Francisco, stopping at San Jose's Diridon Station and

Palo Alto (95 University Ave.) multiple times daily.

Public Transit

At Caltrain's Diridon station you can catch the **VTA Light Rail** (408/321-2300, www.vta.org, adults $2.25, children 5-18 $1), a streetcar network that serves San Jose and some of Silicon Valley as far north as Mountain View. The VTA also operates Silicon Valley **buses,** which can get you almost anywhere you need to go if you're patient enough.

Car

San Jose is 50 miles south of San Francisco via U.S. 101 or I-280 south; I-280 is much prettier but less convenient. Palo Alto lies about 20 miles north of San Jose and is accessed by U.S. 101, I-280, or Highway 82. Highway 87, sometimes called the Guadalupe Parkway, can provide convenient access to downtown San Jose and the airport. Avoid San Jose's freeways during **rush hour** (7am-9:30am and 4pm-7:30pm Mon.-Fri.).

Services

You'll find excellent care at the 24-hour emergency room at **Stanford University Hospital** (900 Quarry Rd., Palo Alto, 650/723-5111, http://stanfordhospital.org). For non-life-threatening emergencies, try **Palo Alto Medical Foundation Urgent Care Center** (795 El Camino Real, 650/321-4121, www.pamf.org, 7am-8pm daily). In San Jose, the **Good Samaritan Hospital** (2425 Samaritan Dr., 408/559-2011, https://goodsamsanjose.com) has 24-hour emergency services.

Wine Country

From the crest of each rolling hill, sunlight paints golden streaks on endless rows of grapevines that stretch in every direction for as far as the eye can see.

Trellises run alongside every road, with unpicked weeds beneath the vines and rosebushes capping each row. A heady aroma of earth and grapes permeates the area. Welcome to the Napa and Sonoma Valleys.

These grapevines are renowned worldwide for producing both top-quality vintages and economical table wines. Foodies also know the area as a center for stellar cuisine. Yountville, a tiny upscale town in the middle of Napa Valley, is the home of celebrity chef Thomas Keller. The food served at his French Laundry is legendary—as are the prices. Keller's influence helped to usher in a culinary renaissance. Today the lush flavors of local sustainable produce are available throughout the region.

Sonoma Valley has long played second fiddle to Napa in terms of prestige, but its wines are second to none. Russian River Valley wineries are often friendlier and less crowded, while the wineries in the southern Carneros region are few and far between. Each offers a more personal experience and the chance to sample unique varietals.

PLANNING YOUR TIME

Napa and Sonoma are the epicenter of Wine Country. Many visitors plan a **weekend in Napa,** with another **weekend** to explore **Sonoma and the Russian River.** During summer and fall, you'll find packed tasting rooms in the valley; even the smaller boutique labels do big business during the high season (May-Oct.). To avoid the crowds, plan to visit in **November** or **early spring.**

Highway 29, which runs through the heart of Napa Valley, gets jammed up around St. Helena and can be very slow on weekends. U.S. 101 slows through Santa Rosa during the weekday rush hour and late in the day on summer weekends. Downtown tasting rooms in Napa Valley and Sonoma can offer an alternative.

Previous: vineyards in Napa; Sonoma Mission. **Above:** Cabernet grapes.

Look for ★ to find recommended sights, activities, dining, and lodging.

Highlights

★ **Domaine Chandon:** This Yountville winery offers a gorgeous setting in which to sample its premier California sparkling wine (page 127).

★ **Robert Mondavi Winery:** The pioneer of the modern Napa Valley wine industry offers a great introduction to wine and the valley (page 130).

★ **Frog's Leap Winery:** Tour the organic and biodynamic vineyards at this down-to-earth winery known for its sense of fun—and excellent cabernets (page 130).

★ **Mumm:** This sophisticated yet easygoing winery excels in friendly service, sparkling wines, and generous pours (page 131).

★ **Calistoga Spas:** Sink into a relaxing bath or soak in a large mineral pool at this spa-centered town (page 136).

★ **Gundlach Bundschu Winery:** Pack a picnic and relax at the beautiful grounds at this local favorite (page 139).

★ **Cline Cellars:** Rhône varietals, lush gardens, a museum, and a historical adobe make Cline a must-stop in Carneros (page 141).

★ **Mission San Francisco Solano de Sonoma:** The final Spanish mission built in California is the centerpiece of Sonoma State Historic Park (page 141).

★ **Russian River:** Rafting, canoeing, and

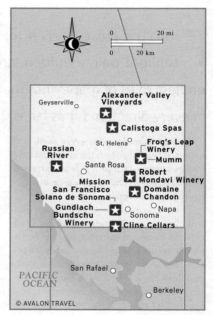

© AVALON TRAVEL

kayaking make this area as much a destination for outdoor enthusiasts as for wine fans (page 151).

★ **Alexander Valley Vineyards:** Visit the grave of Cyrus Alexander, who planted the first vineyards here, then taste decadent zinfandels surrounded by beautiful scenery (page 157).

Napa Valley

Napa Valley is home to hundreds of wineries, ranging from big names and historic houses that make millions of cases of wine annually to modest wineries turning out some of California's best vintages. It can be expensive and crowded in Napa, yet it's not hard to find pockets of rural tranquility off the beaten path.

NAPA

The blue-collar heart of Napa Valley is the city of Napa. The Napa River snakes through downtown, tempering the hot summer weather and providing recreation and natural beauty. Along the river, you'll find sparkling new structures with high-end clothiers and cutting-edge restaurants as well as the Oxbow Market.

Start at the **Napa Valley Welcome Center** (600 Main St., 707/251-5895 or 855/847-6272, www.visitnapavalley.com, 9am-5pm daily) for information about the best places to sip, stay, and sup in the valley, and pick up discount wine-tasting coupons. The center also sells the **Taste Napa Downtown** (www.donapa.com, $15) wine-tasting card, which is good for 12 downtown tasting rooms.

Wineries

The base of the valley has few wineries that host visitors without appointment. The best place to casually taste in Napa is the **Vintner's Collective** (1245 Main St., 707/255-7150, www.vintnerscollective.com, 11am-7pm daily, $40) in the historical Pfeiffer Building. A house of ill repute during its Victorian youth, it is now the public face of 31 different wineries and winemakers. The standard tasting includes a flight of six wines.

MARK HEROLD WINE

Next to the Oxbow Market, **Mark Herold Wine** (710 1st St., 707/256-3111, www.markheroldwines.com, noon-7pm daily, tasting

$20-60) is fun for both the casual sipper and the hard-core oenophile. The tasting room is filled with beakers and test tubes, and the pours are a heady selection of great, approachable wines. (Herold is known for his cabernets.)

TREFETHEN

Trefethen (1160 Oak Knoll Ave., 866/895-7696, www.trefethen.com, 10am-4:30pm daily, tasting $25-35) offers both history and outstanding chardonnay. The renovated tasting room is in the original Eshcol Winery, which was built in 1886 and is listed on the National Register of Historic Places. **Tours** (Mon.-Fri., $45 by appointment) include a tasting in the demonstration vineyard.

Entertainment and Events

The historical **Napa Valley Opera House** (1030 Main St., 707/880-2300, http://nvoh.org) hosts comedians, jazz ensembles, and musical acts—you can count on something going on nearly every night of the week. The building itself is also a treat, with antique tile floors, curving banisters, a café, and two lounges that make the 500-seat venue feel intimate.

The **Uptown Theatre** (1350 3rd St., 707/259-0123, www.uptowntheatrenapa. com) is a great place to see a show. Originally opened in 1937, this art deco theater hosts acts from Lindsey Buckingham to the Pixies.

The live music at **Silo's** (Napa Mill, 530 Main St., 707/251-5833, www.silosnapa. com, cover charge up to $25) is an eclectic mix that includes everything from jazz to stand-up comedy and Johnny Cash tribute bands. There is a decent wine list and a small food menu.

Shopping

The south end of Main Street has some flashy buildings with equally flashy clothiers, but the place to go is the **Historic Napa Mill** (Main

Wine Country

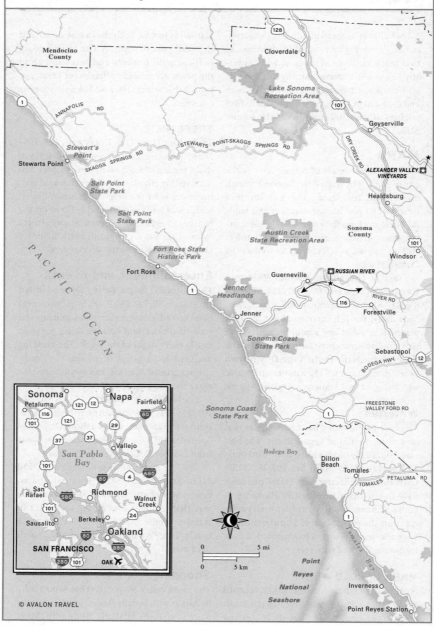

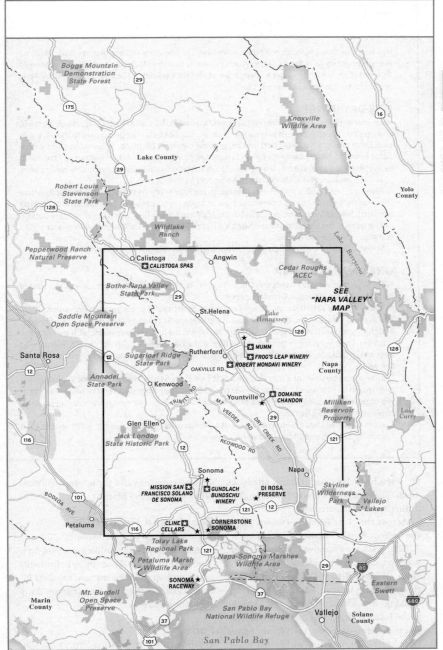

Boggs Mountain
Demonstration
State Forest

29

175

Knoxville
Wildlife Area

16

Lake County

29

Yolo
County

Robert Louis
Stevenson
State Park

128

Wildlake
Ranch

Pepperwood Ranch
Natural Preserve

Calistoga
CALISTOGA SPAS

Angwin

Cedar Roughs
ACEC

**SEE
"NAPA
VALLEY"
MAP**

Bothe-Napa Valley
State Park

29

St. Helena

Lake
Hennessey

128

Saddle Mountain
Open Space Preserve

Santa Rosa

12

Sugarloaf Ridge
State Park

Rutherford

MUMM
FROG'S LEAP WINERY
ROBERT MONDAVI WINERY

128

Napa
County

12

OAKVILLE RD

Annadel
State Park

Kenwood

Yountville

DOMAINE
CHANDON

Milliken
Reservoir
Property

Lake
Curry

116

Glen Ellen

Jack London
State Historic Park

12

29

121

TRINITY RD

MT. VEEDER RD

DRY CREEK RD

REDWOOD RD

Sonoma

Napa

Skyline
Wilderness
Park

Vallejo
Lakes

101

BODEGA AVE

MISSION SAN
FRANCISCO SOLANO
DE SONOMA

GUNDLACH
BUNDSCHU
WINERY

DI ROSA
PRESERVE

121

12

Petaluma

116

CLINE
CELLARS

CORNERSTONE
SONOMA

Tolay Lake
Regional Park

121

Napa-Sonoma Marshes
Wildlife Area

29

80

Eastern
Swett

680

Petaluma Marsh
Wildlife Area

SONOMA
RACEWAY

37

Marin
County

Mt. Burdell
Open Space
Preserve

San Pablo Bay
National Wildlife Refuge

Vallejo

Solano
County

37

101

San Pablo Bay

Two Days in Napa and Sonoma

Napa and Sonoma are about one hour's drive from San Francisco and popular day trips. Traffic on the winding, two-lane Wine Country roads can easily become clogged, especially on weekends. To avoid the crowds, try to get an early start or visit on a weekday. Most wineries close by 4pm, and some are open only by appointment.

ONE DAY IN NAPA

In downtown Napa, get your bearings at the **Oxbow Public Market.** Shop, nibble pastries, and sip a cup of coffee, or just pick up some picnic supplies before hopping over to the Silverado Trail. Drive north to **Rutherford** and enjoy some bubbly at **Mumm,** followed by some cabernet at **Frog's Leap,** a famously fun and relaxed Napa winery. Get back on Highway 29 and lunch in St. Helena at **Farmstead,** where the excellent farm-to-table cuisine, rustic chic atmosphere, plus wine- and olive oil-tasting make it the perfect all-in-one stop.

Give your taste buds a rest and stroll through the **Culinary Institute of America,** where the country's top chefs are trained, or soak in some steamy mud at **Dr. Wilkinson's Hot Springs Resort** in easygoing **Calistoga.** Afterward, you'll be hungry, so take a table outside on the patio at the Michelin-starred **Sam's Social Club.** From Calistoga, the drive back to San Francisco will take two hours.

Stay the night at **Indian Springs** before spending a second day exploring Sonoma.

ONE DAY IN SONOMA

From Napa, Highway 121 winds west through the **Carneros wine region.** Stop off for a bit of bubbly at on the terrace at **Gloria Ferrer.**

From Highway 121, Highway 12 twists north into **Sonoma.** Stretch your legs in Sonoma Plaza and explore the charming downtown area. Stop in at the **Sonoma Mission** for a bit of history, and then grab lunch at **the girl & the fig,** housed in the historic Sonoma Hotel. If the sunshine is calling, you may want to get picnic supplies at the **Basque Boulangerie Café** and head over to **Gundlach Bundschu Winery,** which boasts some of the best picnic grounds in the valley.

Then it may be time for a short hike at **Jack London State Historic Park** in quaint Glen Ellen, north on Highway 12. Practically next door, **Benziger Family Winery** offers more tasting opportunities, plus tractor tours of its beautiful hilltop vineyards. Afterwards, dine at local luminary the **Glen Ellen Star.**

From Glen Ellen, head to downtown **Santa Rosa,** where you can catch U.S. 101 south to San Francisco, 52 miles and a little over an hour away.

St., www.historicnapamill.com), one block down. The former mill is now a shopping and dining center, decorated with rustic touches.

Across the river from downtown Napa, the **Oxbow Public Market** (610-644 1st St., 707/226-6529, www.oxbowpublicmarket.com, 9am-7pm daily) is the center of foodie culture. Grab a cup of **Ritual Coffee** and browse through the epicurean wares. Pick through cooking- and kitchen-related knickknacks at the **Napastak.** Or get lost in the myriad spices and seasonings at the **Whole Spice Company.** There is also a chocolatier, an olive oil company, and the in-house **Oxbow Wine and Cheese Market.**

Sports and Recreation

Napa Valley Paddle (680 Main St., 707/666-1628, http://napavalleypaddle.com, 9am-5pm Thurs.-Mon., Tues.-Wed. by appointment) rents stand-up paddleboards and kayaks ($75/half day) and offers 1.5-3 hour tours daily along the Napa River.

Food

Morimoto's (610 Main St., 707/252-1600,

Napa Valley

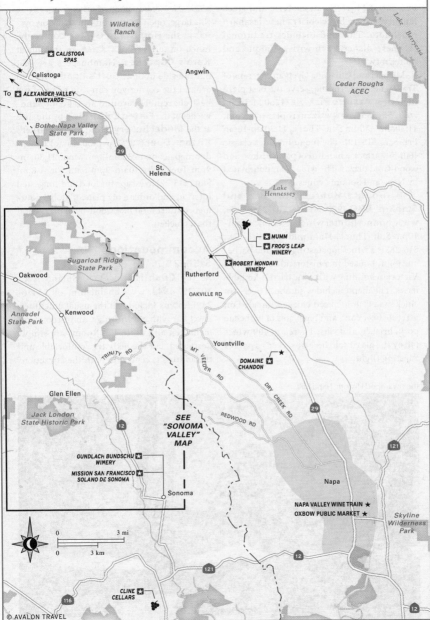

Wildlake
Ranch

CALISTOGA
SPAS

Calistoga

Angwin

To ALEXANDER VALLEY
VINEYARDS

Cedar Roughs
ACEC

Lake
Berryessa

Bothe-Napa Valley
State Park

29

St.
Helena

Lake
Hennessey

128

Sugarloaf Ridge
State Park

Oakwood

Annadel
State Park

Kenwood

MUMM
FROG'S LEAP
WINERY
ROBERT MONDAVI
WINERY

Rutherford

OAKVILLE RD

TRINITY RD

MT VEEDER RD

Yountville

DOMAINE
CHANDON

Glen Ellen

Jack London
State Historic Park

12

REDWOOD RD

DRY CREEK RD

**SEE
"SONOMA
VALLEY"
MAP**

29

121

GUNDLACH BUNDSCHU
WINERY

MISSION SAN FRANCISCO
SOLANO DE SONOMA

Sonoma

Napa

NAPA VALLEY WINE TRAIN ★
OXBOW PUBLIC MARKET ★

Skyline
Wilderness
Park

0   3 mi

0   3 km

121

12

116

CLINE
CELLARS

12

© AVALON TRAVEL

www.morimotonapa.com, 11:30am-2:30pm and 5pm-10pm Sun.-Thurs., 5pm-11pm Fri.-Sat., $24-46) is an esoteric and sleek Japanese eatery by celebrity chef Masaharu Morimoto. The food includes traditional Japanese dishes, each with a unique and modern twist.

Michael and Christina Gyetvan, veterans of Tra Vigne in St. Helena, serve the best pizza in town at **Azzurro Pizzeria** (1260 Main St., 707/255-5552, www.azzurropizzeria.com, 11:30am-9:30pm Sun.-Thurs., 11:30am-10pm Fri.-Sat., $15-19). The menu includes classic Italian starters, a handful of pasta dishes, and wood-fired pizzas. The wine list is dominated by Napa and Sonoma wines.

★ **Bounty Hunter Wine Bar and Smokin' BBQ** (975 1st St., 707/226-3976, www.bountyhunterwinebar.com, 11am-10pm Sun.-Thurs., 11am-midnight Fri.-Sat., $16-28) is a wineshop, tasting bar, and barbecue joint, housed in a historical brick-walled Victorian building with wine barrels for table bases. The menu includes gumbo, a beer-can chicken (a Cajun-spiced chicken impaled on a Tecate beer can), and big plates of barbecue pork, brisket, and ribs. There are 400 wines (40 by the glass) sold here or served as part of a tasting flight.

Across the Napa River is the ★ **Oxbow Public Market** (610-644 1st St., 707/226-6529, www.oxbowpublicmarket.com). Inside this large, open space, you can snack on oysters at the **Hog Island Oyster Company,** lunch on tacos from **C Casa,** or indulge at **Kara's Cupcakes.** Hamburgers are just out the side door at **Gott's Roadside,** and around the corner you can find some of the best charcuterie around in takeout sandwiches at the **Fatted Calf** or pizza by the slice at the **Model Bakery.** Head to the market's **Kitchen Door** (707/226-1560, www.kitchendoornapa.com, 11:30am-8pm Mon., 11:30am-9pm Tues.-Fri., 10am-9pm Sat., 10am-8pm Sun., $15-22) to escape the loud and congested interior, and order a big plate of global gourmet comfort food like wood-oven pizzas and roast chicken.

Accommodations
$150-250
At the **Chablis Inn** (3360 Solano Ave., 707/257-1944, www.chablisinn.com, $116-249), rooms include all the usual amenities: a wet bar with a minifridge, an in-room coffeemaker, and cable TV. Rooms are simply decorated, but the beds are comfortable and the address is central to both the attractions

the revamped Historic Napa Mill

of downtown Napa and the famous Highway 29 wine road. Dogs are welcome.

Napa Inn (1137 Warren St., 707/257-1444 or 800/435-1144, www.napainn.com, $169-339) comprises two Victorian houses in historical downtown Napa. You can walk to downtown shops and restaurants, and the Wine Train depot is a very short drive away. There are eight rooms and seven suites, each with period antiques and a bathroom. Breakfast is an event, with multiple courses served by candlelight. Talk to the inn well in advance to get one of the two pet-friendly rooms.

OVER $250

Napa's first and still most unique boutique hotel, the ★ **Napa River Inn** (500 Main St., Napa, 707/251-8500 or 877/251-8500, www.napariverinn.com, $210-399) has perhaps the best location in the city. Housed at the historical redbrick Napa Mill, it sits next to the river surrounded by shops, restaurants, and entertainment. The 66 rooms are spread across three buildings. All rooms are furnished in an eclectic mix of contemporary, Victorian, and nautical styles. Many have fireplaces, balconies, or views (which vary from a parking lot to the river). Complimentary hot breakfast is brought to your room.

★ **Blackbird Inn** (1755 1st St., 707/226-2450 or 888/567-9811, www.blackbirdinnnapa.com, $265-319) is an Arts and Crafts-style home that dates from the 1920s. Rooms come with TVs with DVD players and free wireless Internet access; some rooms have fireplaces and whirlpool tubs. Order breakfast brought to your room ($10), or stop by the lobby for a predinner drink and hors d'oeuvres.

Transportation and Services

Napa is the gateway to Wine Country. It is 50 miles north of the San Francisco Bay Area located at the intersections of Highways 12, 121, and 29.

CAR

Highway 29 runs north-south from the city of Napa. To reach Highway 29 from San Francisco, take U.S. 101 to Highway 37 in Novato. Take Highway 37 east to Highway 121, which intersects with Highway 29 north to Napa. From I-80, take Highway 37 west to Highway 29 north.

In Napa, the 1st Street exit leads to downtown.

BUS

The **VINE bus** (707/251-2800 or 800/696-6443, www.ridethevine.com, $1.60-5.50)

Oxbow Public Market

Leave the Car Behind

Napa has great alternatives that turn a day wine-tasting into an unforgettable adventure. Abandon your car and see the valley by train, bike, or hot-air balloon.

TRAIN

The **Napa Valley Wine Train** (1275 McKinstry St., Napa, 707/253-2111 or 800/427-4124, www.winetrain.com, $139-332) offers a relaxing experience aboard vintage train cars, where you can sit back and enjoy the food, wine, and views. The train runs from Napa to St. Helena and back. Along the way, dine on gourmet food and stop at wineries. Trips last 1.5-6 hours; advance reservations are strongly suggested.

BIKE

Get away from the highways and explore the wine roads on two wheels. Many upscale hotels offer loaner bikes, and bike rental shops are found throughout the valley.

- **Napa Valley Bike Tours** (6500 Washington St., Yountville, 707/251-8687, www.napavalleybiketours.com, 8:30am-5pm daily, tours $108-159, bike rentals $45-75/day) offers rentals and guided and self-guided tours.

- **St. Helena Cyclery** (1156 Main St., 707/963-7736, www.sthelenacyclery.com, 9:30am-5:30pm Tues.-Sat., 10am-5pm Sun. bike rentals $45-125) rents hybrid bikes and more advanced road bikes. Delivery is available to your hotel for a fee ($40-100).

- **Calistoga Bikeshop** (1318 Lincoln Ave., 707/942-9687, http://calistogabikeshop.com, 10am-6pm daily, tours $150-195 bike rentals $42-90/day) has rentals, guided tours, and self-guided tours. Tasting fees are included in the price.

HOT-AIR BALLOONING

Float serenely above it all in an early morning hot-air balloon tour. Beginning just after dawn, the whole experience lasts about four hours and usually includes a post-flight brunch.

- **Calistoga Balloons** (707/942-5758, www.calistogaballoons.com, $239-2,200) launches from the Calistoga area and offers a champagne breakfast afterward.

- **Balloons Above the Valley** (707/253-2222 or 800/464-6824, www.balloonrides.com, $219) offers tours that begin and end at the Oxbow Market in Napa. Brunch is available separately.

- **Napa Valley Balloons** (Yountville, 707/944-0228 or 800/253-2224, www.napavalleyballoons.com, $239) trips include a post-balloon lunch at Domaine Chandon.

provides bus service to downtown Napa from the El Cerrito BART station in the East Bay and from the Vallejo Ferry Terminal into Napa Valley.

NAPA VALLEY WINE TRAIN

The **Napa Valley Wine Train** (1275 McKinstry St., 800/427-4124, www.winetrain.com, $139-332) offers a relaxing sightseeing experience aboard vintage train cars, where you can sit back and enjoy the food, wine, and views. The train runs from Napa to St. Helena and back, a 36-mile, three-hour round-trip. Each package includes seating in a different historical railcar. Advance reservations are strongly suggested.

YOUNTVILLE

Yountville is the quintessential wine-loving town, filled with prestigious wineries, champagneries, and Michelin-starred restaurants.

Wineries
★ DOMAINE CHANDON

Domaine Chandon (1 California Dr., 888/242-6366, www.chandon.com, 10am-4:30pm daily, $20-25) is one of California's first big champagne houses. Choose the spacious tasting bar, leafy terrace, or lawn area to savor a flight of four wines (including two still), or pop a bottle to accompany a plate of carefully prepared appetizers for a wonderful afternoon.

ROBERT SINSKEY VINEYARDS

Robert Sinskey Vineyards (6320 Silverado Tr., 707/944-9090, www.robertsinskey.com, 10am-4:30pm daily, $40) is best known for its pinot noir and food-pairing program. Perched on a hill, the stone and redwood winery offers outside table service surrounded by lavender and wisteria. The kitchen prepares a menu of small bites made with ingredients from the vineyard's organic garden, served alongside a flight of current releases. The appointment-only tour ($95) includes a look in the cave and cellar, and discussions about the art of winemaking make a visit worthwhile.

STAG'S LEAP WINE CELLARS

Perhaps the most famous winery near Yountville is **Stag's Leap Wine Cellars** (5766 Silverado Tr., 866/422-7523, www.cask23.com, 10am-4:30pm daily, $45), which made the cabernet sauvignon that beat out the best French bordeaux in the now-famous 1976 blind tasting in Paris. It still makes outstanding single-vineyard cabernet. Such renowned wines command high prices, none more so than the Cask 23 cabernet, which retails at about $275. Appointment-only **tours** ($75) take in the pristine-looking cave system and its fascinating Foucault pendulum (for measuring the earth's rotation), before concluding with the estate tasting.

Sights

More about the history of Napa and the entire valley can be found at the **Napa Valley Museum** (55 Presidents Circle, 707/944-0500, www.napavalleymuseum.org, 11am-4pm Wed.-Sun., adults $10, seniors and youth 17 and under $5). It has a fascinating mix of exhibits exploring the valley's natural and cultural heritage. You'll learn about the modern wine industry with an interactive high-tech

WINE COUNTRY
NAPA VALLEY

Domaine Chandon

exhibit on the science of winemaking, as well as the local Native American tribes. You'll even find kid-friendly exhibits.

Entertainment and Events

At the **Lincoln Theater** (100 California Dr., 707/944-9900, http://lincolntheater.com, $10-125), a packed year-round season brings top-end live entertainment of all kinds to Wine Country. See touring Broadway shows, locally produced plays, and stand-up comedy. Although this large theater seats hundreds, purchase tickets in advance, especially for one-night-only performances.

Shopping

You'll find plenty of shops lining Yountville's main drag, but most of the action is around the giant brick **V Marketplace** (6525 Washington St., 707/944-2451, 10am-5:30pm daily). Built in 1870, the former winery and distillery building lends an air of sophistication to the little boutique stores selling everything from clothes and accessories to toys, art, and the usual Wine Country gifts. **V Wine Cellar** (709/531-7053, 10am-7pm daily) occupies 4,000 square feet selling fine boutique wines. It has a lounge and a tasting area within the shop.

Sports and Recreation

Biking is a popular way to get away from the highways and the endless traffic of the wine roads. **Napa Valley Bike Tours** (6500 Washington St., 70/251-8687, www.napavalleybiketours.com, 8:30am-5pm daily, tours $108-159, bike rentals $45-75/day) offers guided and self-guided tours; some tours include wine-tasting and meals. Bike rentals are also available.

Food

The tiny town of Yountville boasts perhaps the biggest reputation for culinary excellence in California. The reason for this reputation is restaurateur Thomas Keller's indisputably amazing ★ **The French Laundry** (6640 Washington St., 707/944-2380, www.

frenchlaundry.com, 5pm-8:45pm Mon.-Thurs., 11am-12:30pm and 5pm-8:45pm Sat.-Sun., by reservation only, $310). The menu, which changes often, offers two main selections: the regular nine-course tasting menu and the vegetarian nine-course tasting menu. The sommelier is at your beck and call to assist with a wine list that weighs several pounds. From the start of your meal, waiters and footmen ply you with extras—an *amuse-bouche* here, an extra middle course there—and if you mention that someone else has something on their plate that you'd like to try, it appears in front of you as if by magic. Finally, the desserts come . . . and come and come. Altogether, a meal at The French Laundry can run up to 13 courses and take four hours to eat.

If you can't get to The French Laundry, try another Thomas Keller option, **Bouchon** (6534 Washington St., 707/944-8037, www.bouchonbistro.com, 11am-midnight Mon.-Fri., 10am-midnight Sat.-Sun., $34-60). Reservations are still strongly recommended, but you should be able to get one just a week in advance. Bouchon's atmosphere and food suggest a Parisian bistro. Order traditional favorites such as the croque monsieur or steak frites, or opt for a California-influenced specialty salad or entrée made with local sustainable ingredients. For a pastry or sandwich, walk next door to the **Bouchon Bakery** (6528 Washington St., 707/944-2253, www.bouchonbakery.com, 7am-7pm daily). Locals and visitors flock to the bakery at breakfast and lunchtime, so expect a line.

★ **Ad Hoc** (6476 Washington St., 707/944-2487, 5pm-10pm Mon. and Thurs.-Sat., 9am-1:30pm and 5pm-10pm Sun., prix fixe menu $55) is Thomas Keller's fourth adventure in Yountville. The four-course rustic menu changes nightly, and you'll get no choices, but considering the quality of the seasonal fare, that's not a bad thing. The wine list is endowed with moderately priced Californian and international wines. Reservations are not required, but don't expect to walk in and get a table. For those on the go, the takeout window, **Addendum** (11am-2pm Thurs.-Sat.), means you can grab some of the most prestigious fried chicken in the culinary world.

A local favorite is **Bistro Jeanty** (6510 Washington St., 707/944-0103, www.bistro-jeanty.com, 11:30am-10:30pm daily, $21-41). The menu is a single page devoted to Parisian bistro classics. Tomato bisque served with a puff pastry shell, cassoulet, and coq au vin are all crafted with joy. Service is friendly and locals hang out at the bar, watching the TV tuned to a sports channel. Jeanty has two dining rooms, making walk-in dining easy on off-season weeknights. Make a dinner reservation on the weekend or in high season.

Accommodations

If you've come to Napa Valley for its high-wattage dining scene, you'll want to stay in Yountville if you can. Several inns are within stumbling distance of The French Laundry, which is convenient for gourmands who want to experience a range of wines with the meal.

$150-250

A French-style inn, the ★ **Maison Fleurie** (6529 Yount St., 707/944-2056, www.maison-fleurienapa.com, $160-365) offers the best of small-inn style for a reasonable nightly rate. It is in a perfect location for exploring Yountville by foot. The 13 rooms in this "house of flowers" have an attractive but not overwhelming floral theme. All guests enjoy a full breakfast each morning as well as an afternoon wine reception, fresh cookies, and complimentary access to the inn's bicycles.

Wake up to mouthwatering smells of Bouchon Bakery at cozy **Petit Logis Inn** (6527 Yount St., 707/944-2332, 877/944-2332, www.petitlogis.com, $145–310) next door. Each of the five rooms is decorated in warm cream colors with a fireplace, a jetted tub, and a fridge. Though breakfast is not included, it can be arranged at a nearby restaurant (fee).

OVER $250

At **The Cottages of Napa Valley** (1012 Darms Ln., 2 miles south of Yountville, 707/252-7810, www.napacottages.com, $305-575), you'll pay a princely sum to gain a home away from home in the heart of Wine Country. Each cottage has its own king bed, private garden, outdoor fireplace, and kitchenette. Every morning the quiet staff drops off a basket of fresh pastries from Bouchon Bakery and a pot of great coffee. A free shuttle will deliver you to your Yountville restaurant of choice for dinner.

The **Hotel Yountville** (6462 Washington St., 707/967-7900 or 888/944-2885, www.hotelyountville.com, $495-670) has a distinctively French farmhouse appeal. The 80-room hotel has a cobblestone exterior. Inside, each room has a four-poster bed, Italian linens, a fireplace, a spa tub, and French doors opening onto a private patio. Suites are also available with all the same amenities. There is a full-service spa and pool.

Transportation

Yountville is on Highway 29, nine miles north of Napa. Downtown Yountville is on the east side of Highway 29, and Washington Street is the main drag, connecting with Highway 29 at the south and north ends of town. To reach the heart of Yountville, exit on California Drive in the south and Madison Street in the north. The Yountville Cross Road will take you from the north end of town to the Silverado Trail.

To reach Yountville by bus, jump aboard the **VINE** (707/251-2800 or 800/696-6443, www.ridethevine.com, $1.60-5.50), which has routes running to Yountville daily. Around town, take the **Yountville Trolley** (www.ridethevine.com, 10am-11pm Mon.-Sat., 10am-7pm Sun., free). The trolley runs on a fixed track from Yountville Park along Washington Street to California Drive, near Domaine Chandon. The trolley also offers free pickup service (707/944-1234, after 7pm 707/312-1509).

OAKVILLE AND RUTHERFORD

Driving north along Highway 29, you might not even notice the tiny hamlets of Oakville and Rutherford. Both towns have tiny populations and neither has much in the way of a commercial or residential districts. Oakville is known for its Bordeaux-style varietals, while Rutherford has the distinction of growing some of the best cabernet grapes around.

Wineries

★ ROBERT MONDAVI WINERY

This sprawling mission-style complex, with its distinctive giant archway and bell tower, is considered the temple of modern Napa winemaking, with the late Robert Mondavi the high priest. The **Robert Mondavi Winery** (7801 Hwy. 29, Oakville, 888/766-6328, www.robertmondaviwinery.com, 10am-5pm daily, $5-30), started in the 1960s, has some very special wines (particularly the classic cabernet, chardonnay, and sauvignon blanc) that draw crowds. The impressive grounds and buildings are certainly highlights. Choose from a variety of tours ($25-50, reservations recommended), all of which include a tasting.

GRGICH HILLS WINERY

When winemaker Mike Grgich (then working for Calistoga's Chateau Montelena) took his California chardonnay to the Paris Wine Tasting of 1976 and entered it in the white burgundy blind-tasting competition, it won. French winemakers were incensed. They demanded that the contest be held again; Grgich's chardonnay won for a second time. This event has gone down in the lore of American winemaking as the 1976 Judgment of Paris. Today, **Grgich Hills Winery** (1829 St. Helena Hwy., Rutherford, 707/963-2784, www.grgich.com, 9:30am-4:30pm daily, $25-60), an entirely biodynamic winemaking operation, is still making some of the best wines in the valley. The best might be the descendants of Mike's legendary chardonnay—arguably the best chardonnay made in Napa or anywhere else. But don't ignore the reds; Grgich offers some lovely zinfandels and cabernets.

★ FROG'S LEAP WINERY

Frog's Leap Winery (8815 Conn Creek Rd., Rutherford, 707/963-4704, www.frogsleap.com, 10am-4pm daily by appt., $20-25) is known for environmental stewardship and organic wine production. This understated winery is housed in a historical red barn surrounded by vineyards and gardens. Tasting here is relaxing; sample a flight of four wines on the wraparound porch or inside the vineyard house, accompanied by cheese, crackers,

statue of St. Francis of Assisi at the Robert Mondavi Winery

Frog's Leap Winery

and jam. The highly recommended **tour** (one hour, by appointment only, $25) also provides a tasting of four wines, and each pour is enjoyed in a different spot along the tour route.

★ MUMM

Even for genuine wine aficionados, it's worth spending an hour or two at **Mumm** (8445 Silverado Tr., Rutherford, 707/967-7700, http://mummnapa.com, 10am-6pm daily, $25-35), a friendly and surprisingly down-to-earth winery on the Silverado Trail. Tastings take place at tables, in restaurant fashion. The prices may look very Napa Valley, but you'll get more wine and service for your money at Mumm. Each pour is three ounces of wine—some of it high-end—and you get three pours per tasting. Nonalcoholic gourmet grape sodas and bottled water are complimentary for designated drivers. Dogs are welcome in the tasting room, too.

For the best of the winery, join a **tour** (10am, 11am, 1pm, 3pm daily, no reservation necessary, $40) of the sample vineyard and the

production facility. The knowledgeable and articulate tour guides describe the process of making sparkling wine in detail. Tasting and a champagne flute are included in the price.

Food and Accommodations

Perched above the valley, off the Silverado Trail, ★ **Auberge du Soleil** (180 Rutherford Hill Rd., St. Helena, 707/963-1211 or 800/348-5406, www.aubergedusoleil.com, $750) is the ultimate in Wine Country luxury. The compound features dining options in addition to a pool, a fitness room, a store, and well-kept gardens accented by modern art. The rooms are appointed with Italian sheets, private patios, fireplaces, and TVs in both the living room and the bath. The main **restaurant** (7am-11am, 11:30am-2:30pm, 5:30pm-9:30pm daily, $110-150) serves exquisitely prepared French-Californian food. Request a table on the terrace for the best views, especially at sunset. The adjacent **Bistro & Bar** (11am-11pm daily, $19-68) offers braised short ribs, a plate of charcuterie, or a light salad, accompanied by a rotating and wide selection of wines.

For down-to-earth dining, often without the need of a reservation, the **Rutherford Grill** (1180 Rutherford Rd., Rutherford, 707/963-1792, www.hillstone.com, 11:30am-9:30pm Mon.-Thurs., 11:30am-10pm Fri., 11am-10pm-Sat., 11am-9:30pm Sun., $15-42) offers traditional steak house fare in a slightly corporate setting. It has become one of the most popular steak houses among Napa Valley residents and is a great place for a reliably cooked and aged steak paired with a Rutherford cabernet.

Since 1881, the ★ **Oakville Grocery** (7856 St. Helena Hwy., Oakville, 707/944-8802, www.oakvillegrocery.com, 6:30am-5pm Mon.-Thurs., 6:30am-6pm Fri.-Sun., $12) has stocked only the best food, wine, cheese, and goodies. Order a boxed lunch or a sandwich from the deli counter and enjoy it in the canopied picnic area. To find the grocery, look for the large Coca-Cola sign painted on the south side of the building.

Transportation

Oakville is four miles north of Yountville on Highway 29; Rutherford is another two miles north. Both can be easy to miss because of their loose organization and rural character. The Silverado Trail runs parallel to Highway 29 along this stretch. To reach it from Oakville, take Oakville Road east; in Rutherford, take Rutherford Road (Hwy. 128) east.

ST. HELENA

There are few Northern California towns as picturesque and well groomed as St. Helena. It is filled with fine eateries and quaint shops housed in historical buildings and surrounded by well-maintained Craftsman homes. The Napa campus of the Culinary Institute of America is a major employer in the area, as is the St. Helena Hospital. Highway 29 runs north-south through the center of town, which can give you a quick peek at the sights, but it's not so nice when sitting in traffic on a sunny weekend.

Wineries
HEITZ

One of the oldest wineries in the valley, **Heitz** (436 St. Helena Hwy., 707/963-3542, www.heitzcellar.com, 11am-4:30pm daily, free) brings sincere elegance to the glitz and glamour of Napa. The high-ceilinged tasting room is dominated by a stone fireplace with comfy chairs. Heitz's cabernets are well balanced and easy to drink, and though costly, they approach affordable by Napa standards. Most of the grapes used for these wines grow right in the Napa Valley.

HALL WINES

At **HALL Wines** (401 St. Helena Hwy. S., 707/967-2626, www.hallwines.com, 10am-5:30pm daily, $40) you'll notice two things. One is that the Halls are big fans of modern art and design; the other is that their winery is the first LEED Gold certified winery in California. The "winery complex" and tasting room has an industrial chic that's different from the typical chateau aesthetic. HALL offers highly rated wines to taste, but to really experience the grounds, book a spot on the **HALLmark Tour and Tasting** (daily, $40).

BERINGER VINEYARDS

The oldest continuously operating winery in Napa Valley, **Beringer Vineyards** (2000 Main St., 707/257-5771, www.beringer.com, 10am-5:30pm daily, $25-40) was established in 1876, and the entire estate, including the lavish and ornate Rhine House, was placed on the National Register of Historic Places in 2001. Beringer's reserve wines are sampled in the Rhine House; regular tastings are in the old winery building up the hill with several themed flights. Stroll in the beautiful estate gardens that stretch for acres on prime land. **Tours** (daily, reservation only, $30-55) show off the highlights of the vast estate and its winemaking facilities.

CHARLES KRUG WINERY

Charles Krug Winery (2800 Main St., 707/967-2229, www.charleskrug.com, 10:30am-5pm daily, tasting $20-45) opened the first tasting room in the valley in 1861. The winery started the Mondavi dynasty when it was purchased by Cesare Mondavi in 1943. Some structures are historic landmarks, including the stately Carriage House and giant redwood cellar building, home to a stylish tasting room. Tastings offer table service from a small bites menu of housemade salumi. **Tours** (10:30am Mon.-Fri., $75) are followed by a flight of three wines paired with artisanal cheese. For **lunch** (11am-4pm, Thurs.-Mon.), the outdoor pizza kitchen serves an alfresco meal on the stately grounds.

Sights
BALE GRIST MILL

Under the cool shade trees of the Napa hills, the gristmill at **Bale Grist Mill** (3315 St. Helena Hwy., 707/942-4575, www.parks. ca.gov, tours 10am-5pm Sat.-Sun., $5) is home to an 1846 redwood mill building and

Wine Tasting

Chardonnay: Most of the white wine made and sold in California is chardonnay. The grapes grow best in a slightly cooler climate, such as the vineyards closer to the coast. Most California chardonnays taste smooth and buttery and a bit like fruit, and they often take on the oak flavor of the barrels they sit in. Chardonnay doesn't keep (age), so most chards are sold the year after they're bottled and consumed within a few months of purchase.

- Best Place to Sample: **Grgich Hills Winery** (p. 130)

Sauvignon blanc: This pale-green grape is used to make both sauvignon blanc and fumé blanc wines. Sauvignon blanc grapes grow well in Napa, Sonoma, and other warm-hot parts of the state. The difference between a sauvignon blanc and a fumé blanc is in the winemaking more than in the grapes. Fumé blanc wines tend to have a strong odor and the taste of grapefruit; they pair well with fish dishes and spicy Asian cuisine. The California sauvignon blanc wine goes well with salads, fish, vegetarian cuisine, and even spicy international dishes.

- Best Place to Sample: **Hanna Winery** (p. 147).

Pinot noir: Pinot noir grapes do best in a cool coastal climate with limited exposure to high heat. Carneros and the Russian River Valley specialize in pinot noir, though many Napa and Sonoma wineries buy grapes from the coast to make their own versions. California vintners make up single-varietal pinot noir wines that taste of cherries, strawberries, and smoke.

- Best Place to Sample: **Robert Sinskey Vineyards** (p. 127) and **Merry Edwards Winery** (p. 150).

Zinfandel: These grapes grow best when tortured by their climate; a few grow near Napa, but most come from Dry Creek Valley. A true zinfandel is a hearty deep-red wine that boasts the flavors and smells of blackberry jam and the dusky hues of venous blood. Zinfandel often tastes wonderful on its own, but it's also good with beef, buffalo, and even venison.

- Best Place to Sample: **Ravenswood Winery** (p. 139)

Cabernet sauvignon: Cabernet sauvignon, a grape from the Bordeaux region of France, creates a deep, dark, strong red wine. The grapes that get intense summer heat make the best wine, which makes them a perfect fit for the scorching Napa Valley. In California, especially in Napa, winemakers use cabernet sauvignon on its own to brew some of the most intense single-grape wines in the world. A good dry cab might taste of leather, tobacco, and bing cherries. Cabs age well, often hitting their peak of flavor and smoothness more than a decade after bottling.

- Best Place to Sample: **Stag's Leap Wine Cellars** (p. 127)

its 36-foot-tall waterwheel. The grounds are open daily, and visitors can take a pleasant nature walk to the site of Dr. Edward Bale's old wheel and mill structures.

CULINARY INSTITUTE OF AMERICA

Napa Valley takes food very seriously, so it's fitting that the West Coast outpost of the **Culinary Institute of America** (CIA, 2555 Main St., 707/967-1100, www.ciachef.edu, 10:30am-6pm daily, tours $10) is housed in the fortress-like former Greystone Winery, one of

the grandest winery buildings in California. Hour-long cooking demonstrations (1:30pm Sat.-Sun., $25) are open to the public. Pop into the **Bakery Café** (10:30am-5pm daily) and browse the shelves of the **Spice Islands Marketplace** (707/967-2309, 10:30am-6pm daily), one of the best kitchen stores in the valley.

The on-site **Gatehouse Restaurant** (707/967-2300, 6pm-8:30pm Tues.-Sat.) is where students hone their skills with three- ($39) and four-course ($49) prix fixe dinners.

Food

Run by the Rutherford-based Long Meadow Ranch, ★ **Farmstead** (738 Main St., 707/963-4555, 11:30am-9:30pm Mon.-Thurs., 11:30am-10pm Fri.-Sat., 11am-9:30pm Sun., $19-31) takes the idea of farm-fresh to a new level. The ranch supplies many of the vegetables, herbs, olive oil, eggs, and grass-fed beef served at the restaurant. The restaurant is housed in a former nursery, where farm equipment has found new life as fixtures, fittings, and furnishings. Even the booths are covered in leather sourced from the ranch's cattle. The food hits the right balance of sophistication and familiarity. To escape the noisy barn, ask for one of the tables on the tree-shaded patio. Visit the ranch's **General Store** (11am-6pm daily) to taste its estate wines and its outdoor **Café** (7am-4pm daily) for coffee and a quick bite.

For Michelin-starred dining, make a reservation at romantic ★ **Terra** (1345 Railroad Ave., 707/963-8931, www.terrasrestaurant.com, 6pm-9:30pm Thurs.-Mon., $89-125) located in the historical stone Hatchery Building. The menu is French and Californian with Asian flourishes. Diners create their own prix fixe by selecting four ($89), five ($109), or six ($126) courses from the 17 savory dishes on the menu. For something more casual but with the same fusion flair, dine at adjacent **Bar Terra** (5:30pm-9:30pm Thurs.-Mon., $17-34), with its full liquor license and à la carte menu. Nibble on any one of Terra's signature dishes for considerably less.

The Cindy of **Cindy's Backstreet Kitchen** (1327 Railroad Ave., 707/963-1200, www.cindysbackstreetkitchen.com, 11:30am-9pm daily, $22-32) is Cindy Pawlcyn, who is credited with bringing casual-sophisticated dining to Napa Valley. The menu goes for homey charm, with large plates including meat loaf, wood-oven duck, and steak frites. Sandwiches can be ordered to go. The patio is a hive of activity at lunch and can require a wait.

Inside the relaxed **Pizzeria Tra Vigne** (1016 Main St., 707/967-9999, www.

Culinary Institute of America

travignerestaurant.com, 11:30am-9pm Sun.-Thurs., 11:30am-9:30pm Fri.-Sat., $15-21), the famous thin-crust Italian pizzas lure locals on many weekend nights. Wash it all down with a pitcher of any number of beers on tap. If you're traveling with kids, Pizzeria Tra Vigne is a great place.

Gott's Roadside (933 Main St., 707/963-3486, http://gotts.com, 8am-9pm daily, $10-20) is a classic roadside diner that has been around since 1949, but the burgers, fries, and milk shakes have been updated with local, organic ingredients. Gott's has earned three James Beard awards.

Fortunately for locals, the quick stop for a morning cup of joe also happens to be one of the most celebrated bakeries in the valley. Known chiefly for its bread, the **Model Bakery** (1357 Main St., 707/963-8192, www.themodelbakery.com, 6:30am-5pm Mon.-Sat. 7am-5pm Sun., $5-15) has been around since 1920. There are shelves of flour-dusted bread and display cases full of pastries, scones, and croissants. Sandwiches, wood-fired pizzas, and salads also make this an easy stop for lunch.

Accommodations

For the best rates, the **El Bonita Motel** (195 Main St. and Hwy. 29, 707/963-3216 or 800/541-3284, www.elbonita.com, $109-309) can't be beat. It's within walking distance of downtown and has a 1950s motel charm. The 42-room hotel wraps around a patio shaded by oak trees and filled with tables, chairs, and umbrellas. In the center are a pool, a hot tub, and a sauna. The rooms may not match the indulgence of other Napa inns, but they are clean, comfortable, and pet-friendly, with re-frigerators and microwaves; some even boast kitchenettes.

The **Hotel St. Helena** (1309 Main St., 707/963-4388, www.hotelsthelena.net, $159-300) is as central as can be, down a little alley off Main Street, right in the middle of town. The old Victorian building is full of original features and stuffed with knickknacks. The 18 rooms get some limited modern touches like air-conditioning, but you'll have to toler-ate temperamental plumbing and poor sound insulation. The four smallest and cheapest rooms share a bathroom. The best deals are the North Wing rooms, which are small but have private bathrooms.

In the thick of downtown St. Helena, the **Wydown Hotel** (1424 Main St., 707/963-5100, www.wydownhotel.com, $350) offers a break from Victorian excess. The 12 rooms are smartly decorated, while the lobby downstairs outdoes itself in urban chic. The small hotel has little in the way of luxury amenities, but it offers a convenient location and historical digs that are modern and stylish.

Transportation

St. Helena is on Highway 29 in the middle of Napa Valley, eight miles south of Calistoga. To reach the Silverado Trail from St. Helena, take Zinfandel Lane or Pope Street east.

To avoid the headache of driving, hop aboard the **VINE** (707/251-2800 or 800/696-6443, www.ridethevine.com, $1.60-5.50), which makes the trip from Napa multiple times daily.

CALISTOGA

Calistoga couldn't be more different from St. Helena, despite their proximity. Sporting a laid-back, mountain-town crunchiness, Calistoga is the land of great and affordable spas.

Wineries
CASTELLO DI AMOROSA

Driving up to **Castello di Amorosa** (4045 N. St. Helena Hwy., 707/967-6272, www.castello-diamorosa.com, 9:30am-6pm daily Mar.-Oct., 9:30am-5pm daily Nov.-Feb., general admis-sion adults 21 and over $25-30, children 5-20 $10), it is difficult to remember that it's a win-ery. Everything from the parking attendant directing cars through the crowded lot to the admission prices screams "Disneyland." And then there is the castle itself, complete with 107 rooms and eight floors, and made from 8,000 tons of stone and 850,000 European bricks.

Admission includes access to the main floors of the castle and a flight of five wines. **Tours** (2 hours, adults $40-45, children $30-35) include barrel tastings, a flight of current release wines (juice for kids), and a look at the armory and torture chamber.

STERLING VINEYARDS

Sterling Vineyards (1111 Dunaweal Ln., 800/726-6136, www.sterlingvineyards.com, 10am-5pm daily, general admission adults $32, youth under 21 $15, children 3 and under free) is more appealing for folks who are tour-ing Wine Country for the first time than for serious wine aficionados. Once you've stood in line and bought your tickets, a gondola ride up the mountain shows off Napa Valley at its best. Admire the stellar views of forested hills and endless vineyards.

CHATEAU MONTELENA

The beautiful French- and Chinese-inspired **Chateau Montelena** (1429 Tubbs Ln.,

707/942-5105, www.montelena.com, 9:30am-4pm daily, $30) will forever be remembered for putting Napa Valley on the map when its 1973-vintage chardonnay trounced the best French white burgundies at the famous 1976 Paris tasting. But if the wines aren't enough, the grounds are worth a visit. The stone chateau was built in 1882; the ornamental Chinese garden was added in 1965. The complex is centered around the lush five-acre Jade Lake, crisscrossed with lacquered bridges. Several tours (reservations required, $50) are available.

Sights and Events

Napa Valley has its own **Old Faithful Geyser** (1299 Tubbs Ln., 707/942-6463, www.oldfaithfulgeyser.com, 8:30am-7pm daily Mar.-Sept., 8:30am-6pm daily Oct., 8:30am-5pm daily Nov.-Feb., adults $15, seniors $13, children 4-12 $9, children under 4 free). Unlike its more famous counterpart, this geothermal geyser is artificial. In the 19th and early 20th centuries, more than 100 wells were drilled into the geothermal springs of the Calistoga area, and many created geysers. Old Faithful is one of the few that wasn't eventually capped, and it's the only one that erupts (60 feet) with clockwork regularity (roughly every 40 minutes). The cute petting zoo houses several fainting goats; that, plus a picnic area and a bocce court, make the wait with the kids easier.

The **Sharpsteen Museum of Calistoga History** (1311 Washington St., 707/341-2443, www.sharpsteen-museum.org, 11am-4pm daily, $3 donation) takes its name from its founder, Ben Sharpsteen, an Academy Award-winning animator for Disney who had a passion for dioramas. Go for the immense, exquisitely detailed dioramas depicting the 1860s Calistoga hot springs resort and life in 19th-century Calistoga. You'll also learn about the success and subsequent ruin of Sam Brannan, the Calistoga pioneer who was the first to build a hot springs resort in the area.

The **Napa County Fair** (1435 North Oak St., 707/942-5111, www.napacountyfair.org,

adults $12, children 7-12 $7, children under 7 free) is held every July 4th weekend at the Napa County Fairgrounds and is open to all.

★ Spas

For an old-school Calistoga spa experience, head down the main drag to **Dr. Wilkinson's Hot Springs Resort** (1507 Lincoln Ave., 707/942-4102, www.drwilkinson.com, 8:30am-3:45pm daily, $94-197). The spa is part of the perfectly preserved midcentury compound rigorously dedicated to health and relaxation opened by "Doc" Wilkinson in 1952. Doc's proprietary blend of Calistoga mineral water and volcanic ash, Canadian peat, and lavender is still the gold standard for the Calistoga mud bath today. "The Works" ($149) includes the mud bath (complete with a soothing mud mask for your face), mineral bath, sauna, and a blanket wrap, and is finished with a massage. The men's and women's spa areas are separated, and the whole experience is very down-to-earth, as are the prices. If you're a guest of the hotel, be sure to take a swim or a soak in one of the three mineral-water pools (there are two outdoor pools and one huge spa inside).

Four outdoor mineral pools are the main draw at **Calistoga Hot Springs Spa** (1006 Washington St., Calistoga, 707/942-6269, www.calistogaspa.com, 8:30am-4:30pm Tues.-Thurs., 8:30am-9pm Fri.-Mon., $99-183). Admission to the pools is included when booking a mud bath, a mineral bath, or a spa treatment.

Located on the original site of Brannan's resort, **Indian Springs** (1712 Lincoln Ave., Calistoga, 707/942-4913, www.indianspringscalistoga.com, 9am-9pm daily) specializes in 100-percent volcanic mud bath treatments ($95) using volcanic ash from its 16 acres of land. Mineral baths, massages, facials, and body treatments are also available. Indian Springs has an Olympic-size pool, built in 1913, that is fed by warm spring water. Spa customers can lounge by the pool ($25-50) or relax at the meditative Buddha Pond.

Sports and Recreation

BOTHE-NAPA STATE PARK

Bothe-Napa Valley State Park (3801 St. Helena Hwy., 707/942-4575, www.parks. ca.gov, sunrise-sunset, $8) boasts nearly 2,000 acres of oak woodlands and coastal redwoods. At 2,000-foot elevation, the park provides fantastic views of the valley and the Vaca Mountains. For an excellent hike with a backcountry feel, climb the **Coyote Peak Trail** (6.5 mile round-trip) to 1,170 feet and loop back via the Upper Ritchey Canyon Trail.

ROBERT LOUIS STEVENSON STATE PARK

Robert Louis Stevenson State Park (Hwy. 29, 707/942-4575, www.parks.ca.gov, sunrise-sunset daily) is named for the author who spent his honeymoon in a tiny cabin here. The park offers few amenities, but it does have a strenuous 11.2-mile round-trip trail to the top of Mount St. Helena. All that huffing and puffing is rewarded at the 4,300-foot summit, where great views of the valley unfold. The park also has picnic tables for a lovely outdoor lunch.

BIKING

Calistoga Bikeshop (1318 Lincoln Ave., 707/942-9687, http://calistogabikeshop.com, 10am-6pm daily, $42-90/day) offers guided tours, self-guided tours, and bike rentals. On the self-guided Calistoga Cool Wine Tour ($100), the bike shop books your tastings, pays the fees, picks up any wine you buy, and provides roadside assistance.

BALLOONING

Take in Calistoga's dramatic scenery from the air with **Calistoga Balloons** (707/942-5758, www.calistogaballoons.com, $239-2,200), the only company offering regular flights in the north end of Napa Valley. In addition to the vineyards, wineries, spas, and the charming town of Calistoga, you'll see Mount St. Helena and lush forested hills. A post-flight champagne breakfast follows.

Food

The beauty of Calistoga is how well the locals rub shoulders with the tourists. Just take a booth at the **Café Sarafornia** (1413 Lincoln Ave., 707/942-0555, http://cafesarafornia.com, 7am-2:30pm daily, $9-15) and see. Farmers and tradespeople sidle up next to out-of-towners for a down-home breakfast and bottomless cups of coffee. The huevos rancheros stand up to their claim of being the best and the Brannon Benedict is one-of-a-kind. Breakfast here may be the most expensive meal of the day in the otherwise quite affordable Calistoga.

Solbar (Solage Calistoga, 755 Silverado Tr., 877/226-0850, www.solagecalistoga.com, 7am-2:30pm and 5:30pm-9pm Sun.-Thurs., 7am-2:30pm and 5:30pm-9:30pm Fri.-Sat., $20-30) has earned a coveted Michelin star every year since 2009. The sleek dining room is a fine backdrop for innovative cuisine farm-to-table fare. A lounge menu offers a casual setting for oysters, the double Wagyu cheeseburger, and the legendary fish tacos ($14-21).

★ **Sam's Social Club** (1712 Lincoln Ave., 707/942-4969, http://samssocialclub.com, 8am-9pm Mon.-Wed., 8am-9:30pm Thurs.-Fri., 7:30am-9:30pm Sat.-Sun., $19-38) serves fresh, flavorful comfort food with an emphasis on farm-to-fork California cuisine. Dine outside under covered tables and an oak canopy or inside the stylish 1970s interior. Complement it all with a selection of Napa and Sonoma wines, a high-caliber cocktail, or a seasonal craft brew.

Accommodations

At the north end of Napa Valley, you'll find most of the hotel-and-spa combos plus plenty of mineral-water pools and hot tubs.

$150-250

The **Calistoga Inn** (1250 Lincoln Ave., 707/942-4101, www.calistogainn.com, $169) has been in operation since 1882, giving guests an old-school hotel experience complete with shared baths and showers. The inn provides some of the best bargain accommodations in

Napa Valley. Each of the 17 rooms is a cozy haven with a queen bed, simple but charming furnishings, and a view of the town. Amenities include a daily continental breakfast and an English pub downstairs that serves lunch and dinner. Make reservations in advance, especially in high season. The pub has live music four nights a week and gets loud on weekends.

The old-school **Hideaway Cottages** (1412 Fair Way, 707/942-4108, www.hideawaycottages.com, $180-315) is a collection of 1940s-era bungalows that retain their original details. Most have sitting rooms, full kitchens, and patios, all of which face the outdoor mineral pool and hot tub. In the interest of quiet, no pets or children under 18 are allowed. In the main house, built in 1877, guests pick up their complimentary "tote" breakfast, filled with fruit and pastries.

OVER $250

Embracing its midcentury charm, ★ **Dr. Wilkinson's Hot Springs Resort** (1507 Lincoln Ave., 707/942-4102, www.drwilkinson.com, $230-350) feels as though it is frozen in the 1950s. Options range from the motel's main rooms to bungalows with kitchens and rooms in the adjacent restored Victorian. Guests are welcome to use the pools, including the indoor hot mineral pool with its Eichleresque touches. In addition to complimentary bathrobes, all rooms have coffeemakers, refrigerators, and hypoallergenic bedding. Dr. Wilkinson's even has bathing suits on loan.

One of the prettiest spa resorts in Calistoga is **Indian Springs** (1712 Lincoln Ave., Calistoga, 707/942-4913, www.indianspringscalistoga.com, $199-479). Located on the site of Sam Brannan's original Calistoga resort, Indian Springs is best known for its charming cottages and bungalows, which have kitchenettes and patios. Amenities include on-site pools and massage services.

Solage Calistoga (755 Silverado Trail, 707/266-7531 or 888/974-0156, www.solagecalistoga.com, $360-700) has a compound of cottages and duplexes, with several places to soak and swim, plus a high-end spa and Michelin-star dining. Winding paths and prim gardens give the resort a quiet and private atmosphere. The 83 rooms are sleek in style with abundant amenities.

Transportation

Calistoga is eight miles north of St. Helena on Highway 29. In Calistoga, Highway 29 turns east, becoming Lincoln Avenue. It intersects with the Silverado Trail at the east end of town.

Highway 128 also runs through Calistoga, connecting to U.S. 101 north near Healdsburg. To reach Calistoga from U.S. 101 in Santa Rosa, take exit 494 off U.S. 101 labeled River Rd./Guerneville. Turn right on Mark West Springs Road and continue up the mountain. The road name changes to Porter Creek Road in the process. At the T intersection with Petrified Forest Road, turn left and travel a few miles until Highway 128. Turn right and follow Highway 128 south for one mile to Lincoln Avenue, Calistoga's main drag.

VINE (www.ridethevine.com, $1.60-5.50) buses make daily trips from Napa to Calistoga. In town, catch the **Calistoga Shuttle** (707/963-4229, www.ridethevine.com, 7am-9pm Mon.-Thurs., 7am-11pm Fri., 8:15-11pm Sat., 11am-9pm Sun. May-Nov.), an on-demand shuttle service available by phone. Wait times are roughly 15-20 minutes.

Sonoma Valley

The Sonoma and Carneros wine regions are in the southeast part of Sonoma Valley. The scenery features oak forests, vineyard-covered open spaces, and pristine wetlands bordering San Pablo Bay. The terminus of El Camino Real is in the small city of Sonoma, which includes the famed Sonoma Mission, historical sights, and a charming town square with plenty of shopping and great places to grab a bite.

SONOMA AND CARNEROS

Sonoma is one of the most idyllic towns in wine country. History weaves itself through town (literally) and the historic downtown plaza is still center of daily life, surrounded by tasting rooms, shops, and restaurants. South of Sonoma is the rolling grassland of Carneros, where cool-loving chardonnay and pinot noir are the principal varietals.

Sonoma Wineries
★ GUNDLACH BUNDSCHU WINERY
Not many wineries in California can boast that they won awards for their wines 100 years ago, but **Gundlach Bundschu Winery** (2000 Denmark St., 707/938-5277, www.gunbun.com, 11am-4:30pm daily Nov.-Apr., 11am-5:30pm daily May-Oct., $20) is one of them. The 19 Gundlach Bundschu wines entered into the 1915 Panama-Pacific International Exhibition all won medals. The tasting room is housed in one of the original stone winery buildings and filled with historic memorabilia.

Book a **seated tasting** (11am-4pm Fri.-Mon., May-Oct., $30) on the courtyard or opt for the **Winemaking Tour and Cave Tasting** (2:30pm Thurs.-Mon., reservations required, $40), which explores a 430-foot-long hillside cave. The picnic area boasts one of the nicest outdoor winery spaces in the valley.

RAVENSWOOD WINERY
Ravenswood Winery (18701 Gehricke Rd., Sonoma, 707/933-2332, www.ravenswood-wine.com, 10am-4:30pm daily, $25) prides itself on making "no wimpy wines." Zinfandel is Ravenswood's signature varietal, and the winery strives to make tasters of all types feel

the cave at Gundlach Bundschu

Sonoma Valley

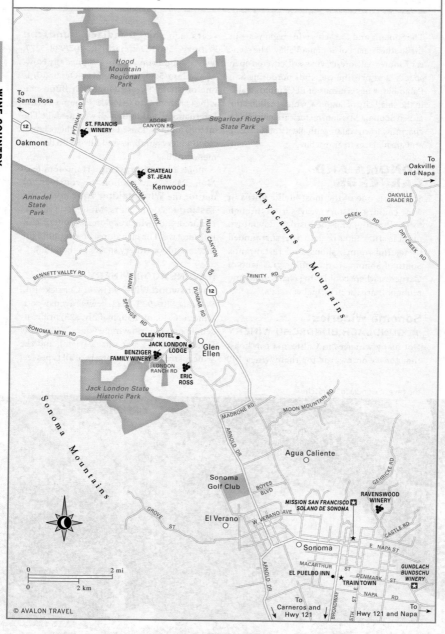

© AVALON TRAVEL

at home. The **tour** (10:30am, daily, reservation required, $30) is an entertaining start to the day and usually includes tasting of barrel samples.

Carneros Wineries
GLORIA FERRER
For a taste of some of Sonoma's upscale sparkling wines, visit the Spanish farmhouse-style tasting room at **Gloria Ferrer** (23555 Hwy. 121/Arnold Dr., Sonoma, 707/933-1917, www.gloriaferrer.com, 10am-5pm daily, $25-33). The champagnerie has the largest selection of sparkling wine in Carneros and also makes still wines. You can taste either by flight or by glass. If it gets crowded, snag a table on the outside terrace.

★ CLINE CELLARS
Cline Cellars (24737 Arnold Dr., Sonoma, 707/940-4030, www.clinecellars.com, 10am-6pm daily, free) specializes in Rhône-style wines. Tasting is free and takes place in a modest farmhouse with a wraparound porch, which dates from 1850. Natural springs feed the three ponds and help sustain the giant willow trees, magnolias, and colorful flower beds. The tasting room contains a small deli, and the wines include several picnic-friendly

options. Tours of the on-site **California Missions Museum** (10am-4pm daily) explore the area's history as a former Miwok Indian village.

CUVAISON
Cuvaison (1221 Duhig Rd., Napa, 707/942-2455, www.cuvaison.com, 10am-5pm daily, tasting $25) pours highly rated pinot noir and chardonnay in an indoor/outdoor tasting lounge. Cuvaison advertises their tasting room as appointment-only; call ahead to confirm.

Sights
★ MISSION SAN FRANCISCO SOLANO DE SONOMA
Mission San Francisco Solano de Sonoma (114 E. Spain St., 707/938-9560, www.parks.ca.gov, 10am-5pm daily, $3) is the northernmost Spanish mission in California. It's at the corner of the historical plaza in downtown Sonoma. The Sonoma Mission isn't the prettiest or most elaborate of the missions, but it's the last mission established and one of the first restored as a historical landmark. Visitors can see exhibits depicting the life of the missionaries and indigenous people who lived here. Outdoors is the Native American

Cuvaison

mortuary monument and a cactus "wall" that has been growing on the property since the mission era.

The mission is a central piece of **Sonoma State Historic Park,** which consists of five other historical attractions. The majority of the sights were built in the heyday of General Mariano Vallejo, the Mexican army commander who became a key figure in California's transition from Mexican province to statehood. The sites include the two-story adobe **Sonoma Barracks,** the old **Toscano Hotel,** and Vallejo's opulent home, **Lachryma Montis.** Tours are free with park admission and are available Saturday and Sunday.

TRAIN TOWN

Train Town (20264 Broadway, Sonoma, 707/938-3912, www.traintown.com, 10am-5pm daily June-Aug., 10am-5pm Fri.-Sun. Sept.-May, $2.75-6.75) is an amusement park, model railway, and petting zoo. Ride the 15-inch scale railroad that winds through 10 forested acres, take a spin on the roller coasters, or ride the vintage carousel and Ferris wheel. Rides are paid for with coupons, which add up quickly, so buy a Family Pack (six for $14.75).

DI ROSA PRESERVE

As Sonoma Valley yields to the open spaces of Carneros, history gives way to modern art. To visit the 217-acre **di Rosa Preserve** (5200 Sonoma Hwy., 707/226-5991, www.dirosapreserve.org, 10am-4pm Wed.-Sun., $5-15) is to enter an eclectic, artistic wonderland, where giant sculptures march up into the hills, a car hangs from a tree, and every indoor space is crammed with photographs, paintings, and video installations. Even nature seems to do its part to maintain the sense of whimsy as di Rosa's 85 peacocks (including two albinos) strut, screech, and occasionally crash-land around the galleries.

The preserve is on the north side of the Carneros Highway (Hwy. 121). Look for the two-dimensional sheep on the hillside. A $5 donation will get you into the Gatehouse Gallery, which displays rotating exhibits along with pieces from the permanent collection. To explore the property and indoor gallery space, join a **tour** (1.5-2 hours, $12-15).

CORNERSTONE SONOMA

Cornerstone Sonoma (23570 Arnold Dr., Sonoma, 707/933-3010, www.cornerstone-gardens.com, 10am-5pm daily) is a sprawling collection of shops, cafés, tasting rooms, and

Sonoma State Historic Park

gardens (1pm-4pm). The centerpiece is a nine-acre plot that's a showcase for dozens of well-known landscape architects.

The **Sonoma Valley Visitors Bureau** (707/996-1090, www.sonomacounty.com, 10am-4pm daily) also has a useful outpost here.

Sports and Recreation

The massive **Sonoma Raceway** (29355 Arnold Dr., Sonoma, 800/870-7223, www.racesonoma.com) motorsports complex hosts every sort of vehicular race possible, with several NASCAR events each year, various American Motorcyclist Association motorcycle races, an Indy car race, and a National Hot Rod Association drag race. Ticket prices vary widely; check the website for prices. The turnoff to Sonoma Raceway is near the intersection of Highways 37 and 121; traffic jams can last for hours. Check the race schedule online to avoid this area for at least four hours before or after a big race.

Sonoma Valley Bike Tours (1254 Broadway, Sonoma, 707/996-2453, http://sonomavalleybiketours.com, 8:30am-5pm daily, $39-78/day) rents bikes and offers self-guided tours and organized tours ($108-$144). Tasting room fees are not included.

The **Sonoma Valley Visitors Bureau** (453 1st St. E., 866/996-1090, www.sonoma-plaza.com, 9am-5pm Mon.-Sat., 10am-5pm Sun.) has a map of bike routes, including one that hits all the historical downtown sites.

Food
SONOMA
★ **the girl & the fig** (110 W. Spain St., 707/938-3634, www.thegirlandthefig.com, 11:30am-10pm Mon.-Thurs., 11am-11pm Fri., 8am-11pm Sat., 10am-10pm Sun., $16-32), right on Sonoma Plaza, is a valley institution. The French country menu includes main courses like free-range chicken and duck confit, Sonoma rabbit, and steak frites. The wine list focuses on Rhône varietals, with many from local Sonoma producers.

Traditional Portuguese eatery ★ **LaSalette** (452 1st St. E., 707/938-1927, www.lasalette-restaurant.com, 11:30am-2pm and 5pm-9pm Mon.-Fri., 11:30am-9pm Sat.-Sun. $22-36) has a simple, charming atmosphere with a wood-fired oven facing a bar and a large outdoor patio. The menu features fresh fish and hearty meat dishes plus some good meatless options.

The bustle of an open kitchen speaks to the success and creativity of **Oso** (9 E. Napa St.,

Cornerstone Sonoma

707/931-6926, http://ososonoma.com, 5pm-10pm Mon.-Wed., 11:30am-10pm Thurs. and Sun., 11:30am-11pm Fri.-Sat., $17-40). The menu is exclusively small plate, but portions are large and the California comfort fare is infused with international flavors. It's popular on weekends; call ahead for a table or walk in for seating at the bar.

Basque Boulangerie Café (460 1st St. E., 707/935-7687, http://basqueboulangerie.com, 6am-6pm daily, $5-12) serves a wide selection of soups, salads, and sandwiches to go. The line often snakes out the door on weekend mornings.

CARNEROS

For breakfast, ★ **The Boon Fly Café** (Carneros Inn, 4048 Sonoma Hwy., 707/299-4870, www.boonflycafe.com, 7am-9pm daily, $16-27) offers a gourmet take on hearty egg favorites. Wash it down with the signature bacon Bloody Mary. Lunch and dinner are just as good, with decadent salads and fried chicken.

Book a table at the **FARM** (Carneros Inn, 4048 Sonoma Hwy., 707/299-4880, www.farmatcarneros.com, 5:30pm-9pm Mon.-Thurs., 5:30pm-10pm Fri.-Sat., 10am-2pm and 5:30pm-9pm Sun., $20-49) for upscale California cuisine, complete with a chef's tasting menu ($115). More casual, the **bar** (4pm-11pm daily) serves lighter fare like burgers, flatbreads, and lobster risotto.

The Fremont Diner (2698 Fremont Dr., Hwy. 12/121, www.thefremontdiner.com, 8am-3pm Mon.-Wed., 8am-9pm Thurs.-Sun., $13-16) is a country café with a hip farm-to-fork ethos. You'll find hush puppies, grits, and fried chicken and waffles, all made from ingredients that are responsibly sourced from local farms.

Accommodations
SONOMA

In 1840, General Vallejo's brother built a home for his family on the town square. In the 1890s, it became a hotel, which would eventually become the **Swiss Hotel** (18 W. Spain St., 707/938-2884, www.swisshotelsonoma.com, $110-240). The five guest rooms have private bathrooms and plenty of modern amenities. The exterior and the public spaces retain the feel of the original adobe building.

The ★ **Sonoma Hotel** (110 W. Spain St., Sonoma, 707/996-2996 or 800/468-6016, www.sonomahotel.com, $150-210) is in a historic building right on Sonoma Plaza. Built in 1880, the hotel has bright and cozy rooms outfitted in trim Victorian fixtures with private baths.

Located just a few blocks from the square, **El Pueblo Inn** (896 W. Napa St., 707/996-3651, www.elpuebloinn.com, $189-249) has rooms facing a lush central courtyard with a pool and hot tub. Some boast adobe brick walls or lounge areas with fireplaces, but many are standard hotel accommodations—clean and modestly decorated. For the location and amenities it's a good deal, especially if you're traveling with kids.

CARNEROS

The Carneros Inn (4048 Sonoma Hwy., 707/299-4900, www.thecarnerosinn.com, $365-600) is an expansive cottage resort. The immense property has three restaurants, a spa, two pools, a fitness center, and a small market. Unpretentious cottages spread out in small clusters for acres, each group surrounding its own garden paths and water features. Inside, the cozy cottages sparkle with white linens, tile floors, and windows overlooking sizable private backyards with decks and comfy chaises.

Transportation and Services
The town of Sonoma is west of Napa via Highway 12 (also called Sonoma Highway). From the San Francisco Bay Area, take U.S. 101 north to Highway 37 east. At the intersection near Sonoma Raceway, turn left on Highway 121. To reach Sonoma, turn north on Highway 12; to continue to Carneros, head east.

The **Sonoma-Marin Area Rail Transit** (SMART, www.sonomamarintrain.org,

$3-12) offers daily rail service through Sonoma and Marin, including Santa Rosa (7 4th St.) and San Rafael (680 3rd St.). Payment is via Clipper card (http://clippercard.com) or eTicket; cash payments are not accepted on board.

The Sonoma Valley Visitors Bureau (707/996-1090, www.sonomacounty.com, 10am-4pm daily) has a useful outpost in Cornerstone Sonoma.

GLEN ELLEN AND KENWOOD

North of the town of Sonoma, the valley becomes more rural. The next hamlet on Highway 12 is Glen Ellen (pop. 784), surrounded by a couple of regional parks and Jack London State Historic Park. Despite having some excellent wineries, downtown Glen Ellen has not caught the Wine Country bug; instead, it feels like a sleepy farm town.

Wineries
ERIC ROSS WINERY

You can almost imagine author Jack London relaxing with a book in the cozy tasting room of the **Eric Ross Winery** (14300 Arnold Dr., 707/939-8525, www.ericross.com, 11am-4:30pm daily, $20), across the street from the Jack London Village complex. The bright red rustic building is thronged with visitors on summer weekends, but during the week you'll likely have the comfy leather sofa inside to yourself. The metal-topped corner tasting bar almost seems like an afterthought. The pinots in particular are worth trying, and there are usually two or three available to taste, each featuring classic Russian River complexity and smoothness.

BENZIGER FAMILY WINERY

With vines poking out from the hillside grass, free-range cockerels crowing, and rustic wooden buildings hidden among the trees, the mountainside **Benziger Family Winery** (1883 London Ranch Rd., Glen Ellen, 707/935-3000, www.benziger.com, 10am-5pm daily, $20) feels like the family-run operation that

it is. It's also the valley's only biodynamic winery.

To get a better understanding of biodynamic methods, hop aboard a 45-minute, tractor-drawn **wine tram tour** ($30, youth under 21 $10). You'll wind through the gorgeous and slightly wild-looking estate while learning about biodynamic principles, the natural environment, and winemaking in general. The tour concludes with stops at the winemaking facility and hillside storage cave, a special tasting of biodynamic wines, and a tasting back at the large commercial tasting room. It's the best tour in the valley for the money. Tours are offered every half hour 11am-3:30pm. Tram space is limited, so in the summer you should buy a ticket in advance. If you miss the tour, take the short (and free) Biodynamic Discovery Trail just off the parking lot.

CHATEAU ST. JEAN

White wine lovers will want to a stop at the cream-colored mansion of **Chateau St. Jean** (8555 Sonoma Hwy., Kenwood, 707/257-5784, www.chateaustjean.com, 10am-5pm daily, tasting $15-25) at the foot of the mountains. The multiple chardonnays, pinot blanc, riesling, and fumé blanc match the elegance of the surroundings, but lovers of reds won't miss out either with the highly rated Bordeaux-style red blend of five varietals. Flights of five are available in the spacious main tasting room, which has a small deli and countless Wine Country gifts. Enjoy the grounds on the nearby patio overlooking the valley and its vineyards.

ST. FRANCIS WINERY

Named to honor the Franciscan monks who are widely credited with planting California's first wine grapes, **St. Francis Winery** (100 Pythian Rd., Kenwood, 707/538-9463 or 888/675-9463, www.stfranciswine.com, 10am-5pm daily, $15) is a place for red wine lovers, particularly merlot, and fans of Spanish architecture. Windows run the length of the spacious tasting room and look out onto vineyards and mountains; escape into the garden if it gets crowded.

Picnickers are welcome on the sun-drenched patio across from the tasting room, but the tables just outside the picture windows are reserved for the charcuterie and wine pairing ($35, 11am-4pm daily, no reservation required) or the five-course lunch ($68).

Jack London State Historic Park

Visit **Jack London State Historic Park** (2400 London Ranch Rd., Glen Ellen, 707/938-5216, www.parks.ca.gov or http://jacklondonpark.com, 9:30am-5pm daily, $10), where author Jack London lived and wrote in the beginning of the 20th century. Docents lead tours of the park, which include talks on London's life and history. Explore the surviving buildings on London's prized Beauty Ranch or hike up Sonoma Mountain and check out the artificial lake and bathhouse. The pretty stone House of Happy Walls, a creation of London's wife, houses a small museum. There's no camping at the park.

The **Triple Creek Horse Outfit** (707/887-8700, www.triplecreekhorseoutfit.com, $75-220) offers guided horseback rides at Jack London State Historic Park. Tours take you through the writer's life in Sonoma County and the literary history of the region. At the conclusion of your ride, you'll be given complimentary tasting passes to Benziger and Imagery Estate wineries.

Food

★ **the fig café and winebar** (13690 Arnold Dr., Glen Ellen, 707/938-2130, www.thefigcafe.com, 5pm-close Mon.-Sat., 11am-close Sun., $12-25) is an offshoot of the popular the girl & the fig restaurant in Sonoma. Enjoy the same French bistro fare—grilled sandwiches, thin-crust pizzas, and braised pot roast—in a slightly scaled down interior.

★ **Glen Ellen Star** (13648 Arnold Dr., Glen Ellen, 707/343-1384, www.glenellenstar.com, 5:30pm-9pm Sun.-Thurs., 5:30pm-9:30pm Fri.-Sat., $14-32) serves locally sourced wood-oven pizzas, roasted meat and vegetables, and iron-skillet quick breads. It's comfort food with an urban sensibility. Reservations are encouraged, but patio and bar seating are available for walk-ins.

Accommodations

Attached to the redbrick Jack London Saloon and Wolf House Restaurant, the **Jack London Lodge** (13740 Arnold Dr., Glen Ellen, 707/938-8510, www.jacklondonlodge.com, $115-185) anchors central Glen Ellen. The 22-room lodge is modern, with a broad patio, a kidney-shaped pool, and groomed lawns. Vines draping the balcony add to the ambience, as do the hot tub and the creek running through the back of the property.

For historical lodgings, book a room, suite, or cottage at the ★ **Olea Hotel** (5131 Warm Springs Rd., Glen Ellen, 707/996-5131, www.oleahotel.com, $213-445), a B&B tucked away in Glen Ellen. Built at the turn of the 20th century, the property has since received a sleek update. Some rooms come with a stone fireplace, and others boast an expansive porch overlooking the well-maintained grounds. For more privacy, 300-square-foot cottages dot the property. Guests enjoy a hot two-course breakfast, use of an outdoor pool and hot tub, and complimentary wine-tasting in the lobby.

Pitch your tent at **Sugarloaf Ridge State Park** (2605 Adobe Canyon Rd., Kenwood, 800/274-7275, www.reservecalifornia.com, $35), which has 47 campsites with showers and free Wi-Fi at the park's visitors center.

Transportation

Glen Ellen is located just off Highway 12, seven miles north of Sonoma. Arnold Drive is the main street through town, and it runs south to Sonoma. To reach Glen Ellen from Santa Rosa, take Highway 12 east through Kenwood for about 15 miles.

Kenwood is located about 10 miles east of downtown Santa Rosa on Highway 12, and about five miles north of Glen Ellen. To reach Kenwood from U.S. 101 in Santa Rosa, take the exit for Highway 12 east.

Russian River Valley

The Russian River Valley covers about 150-square miles of forests, orchards, vineyards, and pastures. Running through the region is the mighty Russian River, which offers swimming, rafting, canoeing, and kayaking. Wineries line River Road, which parallels the river, as well as the Gravenstein Highway (Hwy. 116), named for the apples grown in this area.

SANTA ROSA

The largest city in Wine Country, Santa Rosa functions as a gateway to the Russian River Valley. This blue-collar city may be short on tasting rooms, but it has a variety of attractions, accommodations, and places to eat.

Wineries
HANNA WINERY

The specialty at **Hanna Winery** (5353 Occidental Rd., 707/575-3371, www.hannawinery.com, 10am-4pm daily, $10) is crisp, steel-fermented sauvignon blanc. A hit with critics, it's exactly what you want to drink while soaking in the sun, either on the winery's wraparound front porch or beneath the great live oak out front. Hanna offers a large tasting list, along with a reserve flight of the finest vintages.

KENDALL-JACKSON WINE CENTER

Kendall-Jackson Wine Center (5007 Fulton Rd., Fulton, 707/571-7500, www.kj.com, 10am-5pm daily, tasting $15) surprises even serious oenophiles with the quiet elegance of its tasting room and the extensive sustainable gardens and demonstration vineyards. In high season, make a reservation well in advance—KJ doesn't have many tables. **Tour** (1pm daily, $25) the gardens in spring and summer, and taste fresh wine grapes during the fall harvest.

Sights

In honor of former resident Charles Schulz and the *Peanuts* gang, the **Charles M. Schulz Museum** (2301 Hardies Ln., 707/579-4452, www.schulzmuseum.org, 11am-5pm Mon.-Fri., 10am-5pm Sat.-Sun. summer, 11am-5pm Mon. and Wed.-Fri., 10am-5pm Sat.-Sun. fall-spring, adults $12, seniors $8, children 4-18 $5, children under 4 free) exhibits original *Peanuts* strips, a large collection of Schulz's personal possessions, and an astonishing array of tribute artwork from other comic-strip artists and urban installation designers.

The **Pacific Coast Air Museum** (1 Air Museum Way, 707/575-7900, www.pacific-coastairmuseum.org, 10am-4pm Wed.-Sun., adults $10, seniors $7, children 6-17 $5, children under 6 free) is worth a visit. Learn about the history of aviation in the United States through interpretive and photographic exhibits. Many of the planes are examples of those that can be found on aircraft carriers today. Check out the funky Pitts aerobatic plane, the likes of which you'll see doing impossible-looking tricks during the museum's annual **Wings Over Wine Country Air Show** (Sept.).

If you love gardening, don't miss the **Luther Burbank Home and Gardens** (204 Santa Rosa Ave., 707/524-5445, www.luther-burbank.org; gardens 8am-dusk daily year-round, free; museum and tours 11am-3pm Tues. Apr.-Oct., $8.50-10). Using hybridization techniques, Luther Burbank personally created some of the most popular plants grown in California gardens and landscapes today. Burbank's own house, where he lived until 1906, is preserved along with a small greenhouse and the gardens as part of the 1.6-acre National and State Historic Landmark.

Sports and Recreation

Wine Country Balloons (707/538-7359 or 800/759-5638, www.balloontours.com, $225) maintains a fleet of balloons that can carry 2-16 passengers. Expect the total time to be

Russian River Valley

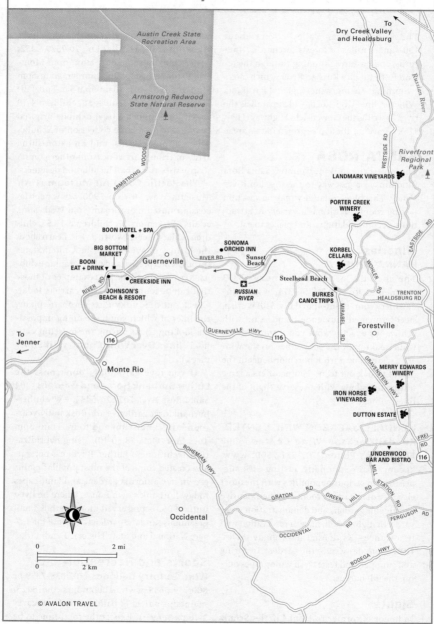

Austin Creek State
Recreation Area

Armstrong Redwood
State Natural Reserve

To
Dry Creek Valley
and Healdsburg

Russian River

ARMSTRONG WOODS RD

WESTSIDE RD

Riverfront
Regional
Park

LANDMARK VINEYARDS

**PORTER CREEK
WINERY**

EASTSIDE RD

BOON HOTEL + SPA

**BIG BOTTOM
MARKET**

**BOON
EAT + DRINK**

Guerneville

RIVER RD

**SONOMA
ORCHID INN**

Sunset
Beach

**KORBEL
CELLARS**

WOHLER RD

CREEKSIDE INN

RIVER RD

**JOHNSON'S
BEACH & RESORT**

**RUSSIAN
RIVER**

Steelhead Beach

**BURKES
CANOE TRIPS**

MIRABEL RD

TRENTON
HEALDSBURG RD

To
Jenner

GUERNEVILLE HWY

116

116

Forestville

Monte Rio

GRAVENSTEIN HWY

**MERRY EDWARDS
WINERY**

BOHEMIAN HWY

**IRON HORSE
VINEYARDS**

DUTTON ESTATE

FREI RD

116

**UNDERWOOD
BAR AND BISTRO**

MILL STATION RD

GRATON RD

GREEN HILL RD

FERGUSON RD

Occidental

OCCIDENTAL RD

BODEGA HWY

0   2 mi
0   2 km

© AVALON TRAVEL

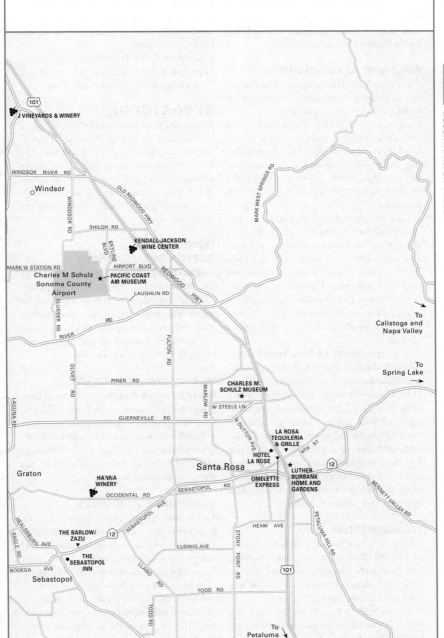

3-4 hours, with 1-1.5 hours in the air. You'll end your flight with brunch and a handful of wine-tasting coupons. Groups meet at **Kal's Kaffe Mocha** (397 Aviation Blvd.).

Food and Accommodations

Santa Rosa has all the familiar chain motels. In the Historic Railroad Square, **Hotel La Rose** (308 Wilson St., 707/579-3200, www. hotellarose.com, $175-290) offers historical and modern accommodations for very reasonable prices. In the stone-clad main building, guests will enjoy antique furniture and floral wallpaper, but across the street, the carriage house offers modern decor and amenities.

Get in line for breakfast, at the ★ **Omelette Express** (112 4th St., 707/525-1690, http://omeletteexpress.com, 6:30am-3pm daily, $10-14), a spot favored by locals. The very casual dining rooms are decorated with the front ends of classic cars, and the menu involves lots of omelets. Portions are huge and come with a side of toast made with homemade bread, so consider splitting with a friend.

The cavernous ★ **La Rosa Tequileria & Grille** (500 4th St., 707/523-3663, http://larosasantarosa.com, 11am-9pm Sun.-Thurs., 11am-1:30am Fri.-Sat., $10-19) is the place to go for a casual lunch downtown or a late night out with friends. The large restaurant has multiple dining rooms and a large back patio, each done up in a Mexican Gothic style with deep booths, luscious murals of roses, and collections of crucifixes. The classic south-of-the-border cuisine is excellent and delivered with artistic panache.

Transportation

Santa Rosa is 50 miles north of San Francisco on U.S. 101. Traffic gets congested, particularly during the morning and evening commutes and on summer afternoons. The side roads are seldom crowded.

To reach Santa Rosa from U.S. 101, take exit 489. West of the freeway is the historical Railroad Square, and downtown is on the east side. Wineries are on the west side of town and can be accessed by taking Highway 12 west as well as the U.S. 101 exits for River and Guerneville Roads.

Golden Gate Transit (415/455-2000, http://goldengatetransit.org, $13) runs buses between San Francisco and Santa Rosa.

SEBASTOPOL

Sebastopol is west of Santa Rosa, accessed by Highways 116 and 12. The heart of downtown (Sebastopol Ave./Hwy. 12 and Main St./Hwy. 116) contains shops where local artists sell their work, while the surrounding orchards give fragrance and beauty to the already scenic country roads, especially during the spring bloom.

Wineries

DUTTON ESTATE WINERY

Dutton Estate Winery (8757 Green Valley Rd., 707/829-9463, www.duttonestate.com, 10am-4:30pm daily, $15) barely hints at its highly rated wines. The winery specializes in pinot noir and chardonnay, which can be enjoyed with small bites or bring a bag lunch and picnic in the gorgeous vineyards.

MERRY EDWARDS WINERY

Merry Edwards Winery (2959 Gravenstein Hwy., 707/823-7466, www.merryedwards. com, 9:30am-4:30pm daily, free tasting) is one of California's leading and famous winemakers, best known for their pinot noirs. Members of Merry Edwards's tasting staff work with one party of tasters at a time.

IRON HORSE VINEYARDS

The rustic simplicity of **Iron Horse Vineyards** (9786 Ross Station Rd., 707/887-1507, www.ironhorsevineyards.com, 10am-4:30pm daily by appointment, $25-30) belies the pedigree of its sparkling wines, which have been served to presidents and have won accolades from wine critics since the 1970s. On Monday, **truck tours** (10am by appointment only, $50) are led by the winemaker, David Muskgard.

Food and Accommodations

There are not many places to stay in Sebastopol. Rooms at the **Sebastopol Inn** (6751 Sebastopol Ave., 707/829-2500, www.sebastopolinn.com, $119-269) have a refrigerator and microwave; all guests can enjoy the heated pool and hot tub. An on-site coffeehouse hosts live music on weekend afternoons. The location is an easy stroll to Sebastopol's shops and eateries.

The Barlow Complex houses Sebastopol's dining scene where ★ **ZaZu** (6770 McKinley St., 707/523-4814, http://zazukitchen.com, 5pm-10pm Mon. and Wed., 3pm-10pm Thurs., 11:30am-midnight Fri.-Sat., 9am-10pm Sun., $25-33) is known for its house-cured bacon and heirloom Black Pig salumi. The pork-heavy menu changes daily, and the wine list is locally sourced.

The **Underwood Bar and Bistro** (9113 Graton Rd., Graton, 707/823-7023, www.underwoodgraton.com, 11:30am-10pm Tues.-Sat., 5pm-10pm Sun., $23-35) is the best spot for a serious dinner. The menu leans French, with a Catalan dish here and an Italian dish there. An oyster menu and cheese plates perfectly accompany the decor and vibe.

Transportation

To reach Sebastopol from U.S. 101, take either the exit for Highway 12 west in Santa Rosa or the exit for Highway 116 west at Cotati, eight miles south of Santa Rosa. Highway 116 is the most direct route to continue to the Russian River from Sebastopol.

GUERNEVILLE

Most people come to Guerneville to float, canoe, or kayak the gorgeous Russian River. In addition to its busy summertime tourist trade, Guerneville is also a very popular gay and lesbian resort area. The rainbow flag flies proudly here, and the friendly community welcomes all.

Wineries

J VINEYARDS & WINERY

J Vineyards & Winery (11447 Old Redwood Hwy., Healdsburg, 707/431-3646, www.jwine. com, 11am-5pm daily, $20-75) loves the cutting edge of the California wine scene. J specializes in California-style sparkling wines, and its tasting room is a triumph of modern design. Tastings ($20) include generous pours of five wines. The more exclusive Bubble Room takes the tasting experience (and the price) up a notch.

KORBEL CELLARS

Korbel Cellars (13250 River Rd., Guerneville, 707/824-7000, www.korbel.com, 10am-4:30pm daily, free) is the leading producer of California champagne-style sparkling wines. The large, lush estate welcomes visitors with elaborate landscaping and attractive buildings, including a small area serving as a visitors center. Tours of the estate are offered several times daily. Korbel makes and sells a wide variety of high-end California champagnes, plus a few boutique still wines and brandies. The facility also has a full-service gourmet deli and picnic grounds.

★ Russian River

Guerneville and its surrounding forest are the center for fun on the river. In summer the water is usually warm and dotted with folks swimming, canoeing, or simply floating tubes serenely downriver amid forested riverbanks. **Burke's Canoe Trips** (8600 River Rd., Forestville, 707/887-1222, www.burkescanoetrips.com, Memorial Day-mid-Oct., $65) rents canoes and kayaks on the Russian River. The put-in is at Burke's Beach in Forestville; paddlers then canoe downriver 10 miles to Guerneville, where a courtesy shuttle picks them up. Burke's also offers overnight campsites for tents, trailers, and RVs.

On the north bank, **Johnson's Beach & Resort** (16215 1st St., Guerneville, 707/869-2022, www.johnsonsbeach.com, 10am-6pm daily May-Oct., parking $5, rentals $40) rents canoes, kayaks, pedal boats, and inner tubes for floating on the river. There is a safe, kid-friendly section of the riverbank that's roped off for small children; parents and beachcombers can rent beach chairs and umbrellas for use on the small beach. The boathouse sells beer and snacks.

Armstrong Redwoods

Armstrong Redwoods (17000 Armstrong Woods Rd., 707/869-2015, www.parks. ca.gov, 8am-sunset daily, $8/vehicle) is an easy five-minute drive from Guerneville. Take a fabulous hike—either a short stroll in the shade of the trees or a multiple-day backcountry adventure. The easiest walk to a big tree is the 0.1 mile from the visitors center to the tallest tree in the park, named the **Parson Jones Tree.** If you saunter another 0.5 mile, you'll reach the **Colonel Armstrong Tree;** another 0.25 mile more leads to the **Icicle Tree.**

Right next to Armstrong is the **Austin Creek State Recreation Area** (17000 Armstrong Woods Rd., 707/869-9177, www. parks.ca.gov, 8am-sunset daily, $8/vehicle). It's rough going on 2.5 miles of steep, narrow, treacherous dirt road to get to the main entrance and parking area; no vehicles over 20 feet long and no trailers of any kind are permitted. But once you're in, some great—and very difficult—hiking awaits you. The eponymous **Austin Creek Trail** (4.7 miles one-way) leads down from the hot meadows into the cool forest fed by Austin Creek. To avoid monotony on this challenging route, create a loop by taking the turn onto **Gilliam Creek Trail** (four miles one-way).

Entertainment and Events

Guerneville wouldn't be a proper gay resort town without at least a couple of good gay bars that create proper nightlife for visitors and locals. The most visible and funky-looking of these is the **Rainbow Cattle Company** (16220 Main St., Guerneville, 707/869-0206, www.queersteer.com, noon-2am daily). The Rainbow has cold drinks and hot men with equal abandon. Think cocktails in mason jars, wood paneling, and leather nights. This is just the kind of queer bar where you can bring your mom or your straight-but-not-narrow friends, and they'll have just as much fun as you will.

The **Stumptown Brewery** (15045 River Rd., 707/869-0705, www.stumptown.com, 11am-midnight Sun.-Thurs., 11am-2am Fri.-Sat.) is *the* place to hang out on the river. This atypical dive bar has a pool table, Naugahyde bar stools, a worn wooden bar crowded with locals, plus a deck out back overlooking the river. The brewery only makes a few of the beers sold on tap, but they are all great and

the Russian River

perfect to enjoy by the pitcher. Stumptown also serves a menu of burgers and grilled sandwiches; the food is a perfect excuse to stay put.

Held at Johnson's Beach in Guerneville, the **Russian River Jazz and Blues Festival** (707/869-1595, www.omegaevents.com, $50-80 each day, Sept.) is a two-day affair with jazz one day and blues the next. Much more than just a music festival, this event is the last big bash of the summer season. Camping at 37 sites is available at **Johnson's Beach** (707/869-2022, http://johnsonsbeach.com, $40 per night for two people, 2-night min.). Cabins ($135-145, 2-night min.) are also available.

Food

Pat's Restaurant (16236 Main St., 707/869-9905, www.pats-restaurant.com, 7am-3pm daily, $10) is a homey, casual diner where locals come to sit at the counter and have breakfast.

Big Bottom Market (16228 Main St., 707/604-7295, www.bigbottommarket.com, 8am-5pm Wed.-Mon., $10-14) serves French press coffee, freshly baked pastries, and biscuits so dense they can be a meal on their own. Pick up excellent cold and hot-pressed sandwiches, savory bread pudding, and a wide assortment of local wine.

Seaside Metal Oyster Bar (16222 Main St., 707/604-7250, http://seasidemetal.com, 5pm-9pm Sun. and Wed.-Thurs., 5pm-10pm Fri.-Sat., $10-24) has a slim menu of oysters, shellfish, and crudo plates of raw fish and savory veggies. Wash it all down with a selection from the large beer and wine menu.

★ **boon eat + drink** (16248 Main St., 707/869-0780, http://eatatboon.com, 11am-3pm and 5pm-9pm Sun.-Tues. and Thurs., 11am-3pm and 5pm-10pm Fri.-Sat., $17-28) is related to the nearby boon hotel + spa, where some of the vegetables are grown. Lunch consists of panini, small plates, and the grass-fed Boon burger. For dinner, hearty mains combine lamb shank with mint pesto or flat-iron steak with truffle fries.

Accommodations

You'll find a few dozen bed-and-breakfasts and cabin resorts in town. Many of these spots are gay-friendly, some with clothing-optional hot tubs.

The **Creekside Inn & Lodge** (16180 Neeley Rd., 707/869-3623 or 800/776-6586, www.creeksideinn.com, $109-300) is right beside the Russian River and just a few minutes' stroll to Guerneville's main street. The several acres of grounds include a main house with the cheapest rooms, a pool, and eight cottages, from studios to two bedrooms.

The experience at the ★ **Sonoma Orchid Inn** (12850 River Rd., 707/869-4466 or 888/877-4466, www.sonomaorchidinn.com, $149-249) is made by its amazing owners, who can not only recommend restaurants and spas, but also make reservations for you. The best rooms have microwaves and small fridges, while the budget rooms are tiny but cute, with private baths and pretty decorations. The Orchid is dog- and kid-friendly, clothing mandatory in the communal hot tub, and welcoming.

On the road to Armstrong Redwoods, **boon hotel + spa** (14711 Armstrong Woods Rd., 707/869-2721, www.boonhotels.com, $170-300) is minimal in the extreme, with a palette of white, slate, and chrome. Many of the 14 rooms have freestanding cast-iron fireplaces, private patios, and fridges, and all have large beds with fair-trade organic cotton sheets. There is a pool and hot tub (both saltwater), and plenty of facial and massage options. In the morning, wake up to a pressed pot of locally roasted coffee; in the evening, chill out with a cocktail by the pool.

Camping

There are numerous resort campgrounds along the Russian River. **Johnson's Beach & Resort** (16245 1st St., 707/869-2022, www.johnsonsbeach.com, $40) is a hive of summertime activity. The 37 campsites overlook the river beneath a sparse canopy of walnut and sycamore trees. Facilities include hot showers, laundry, and a game room. Cabins are also available ($135-145).

Primitive, creekside campgrounds are in **Austin Creek State Recreation Area** (17000 Armstrong Woods Rd., 707/869-2015, www.parks.ca.gov, $25). The road into the park through Armstrong Redwoods State Reserve ends at the **Bullfrog Pond Campground,** with 23 sites, toilets, and drinking water. No vehicles over 20 feet long are allowed. Camping is first-come, first-served; to register for a campsite, stop by the Armstrong Redwoods **park office** (17000 Armstrong Woods Rd., 707/869-2958, 11am-3pm daily).

Transportation

Guerneville is at the junction of Highway 116 and River Road. In downtown Guerneville, River Road becomes Main Street. The most direct access is via U.S. 101 north of Santa Rosa; take the River Road/Guerneville exit and follow River Road west for 15 miles to downtown Guerneville.

Alternatively, a more scenic and often less crowded route is to take U.S. 101 to Highway 116 near Cotati, south of Santa Rosa. Also called the Gravenstein Highway, Highway 116 winds about 22 twisty miles through Sebastopol, Graton, and Forestville to emerge onto River Road in Guerneville.

Dry Creek and Alexander Valley

The Russian River runs east then north to the charming Victorian town of Healdsburg. Sitting at the nexus of three American Viticultural Areas (AVAs), Healdsburg is an excellent place to explore the Russian River AVA, which produces pinot noir and chardonnay. Dry Creek AVA is famous for zinfandel and sauvignon blanc, while the Alexander Valley AVA produces cabernet sauvignon and merlot.

HEALDSBURG

Healdsburg is so charming it's easy to forget that people live and work here. The **Healdsburg Plaza** is one of the town's most treasured features and anchors the downtown area, while the wide and slow Russian River creates the town's natural southern border. Boutiques, chic restaurants, and galleries dot the town. Fresh paint brightens the historical storefronts and planters are filled with flowers and trailing vines.

Wineries
PORTALUPI

There are a number of tasting rooms in downtown Healdsburg, but if you go to one, make it **Portalupi** (107 North St., 707/395-0960,

www.portalupiwine.com, 11am-7pm daily, $10-20). You'll find Russian River lush and inky pinot noirs and zinfandel, as well as Italian barbera, a port made from carignane, and the Vaso di Marina, a blend of pinot noir, zinfandel, and cabernet sauvignon. As a nod to Jane Portalupi's grandmother, who used to make wine in her native village in Italy, the wine comes in a half-gallon glass jug. The sophisticated tasting room is filled with two large couches, perfect for relaxing as you taste a flight or enjoy a glass.

LANDMARK VINEYARDS

Landmark Vineyards (6050 Westside Rd., 707/433-6491, www.hopkilnwinery.com, 10am-5pm daily, $20) is home to an old hop kiln that is registered as a Historic Landmark. Inside the main kiln is an extensive wine-tasting bar with typical Wine Country varietals including Landmark's award-winning pinot noir. Tastings are comprised of six wines.

PORTER CREEK WINERY

Serious cork dorks recommend the tiny tasting room at **Porter Creek Winery** (8735 Westside Rd., 707/433-6321, www.portercreekvineyards.com, 10:30am-4:30pm daily,

Healdsburg and Vicinity

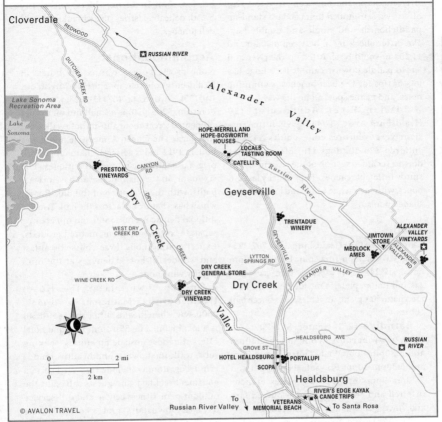

$15), which casual tasters might otherwise miss. Turn onto the dirt driveway, pass the farm-style house (the owner's family home), and park in front of a small converted shed—the tasting room. Porter Creek's wines are almost all reds, made from grapes grown organically within sight of the tasting room.

Sports and Recreation

Wine Country Bikes (61 Front St., 707/473-0610, www.winecountrybikes.com, 9am-5pm daily, rentals $39-145/day, tours $139) is on the square in downtown Healdsburg. Its Classic Wine Tour pedals through the Dry Creek region, where you'll stop and taste wine, take walks in vineyards, and learn more about the history of wine. For independent souls who prefer to carve their own routes, Wine Country Bikes also rents road bikes, tandem bikes, and hybrids ($39-145/day).

The Russian River provides water-related recreation opportunities. On the south side of town is **Healdsburg Veterans Memorial Beach** (13839 Old Redwood Hwy., 707/433-1625, http://parks.sonomacounty.ca.gov, sunrise-sunset daily, parking $7), a stretch of sandy and rocky shoreline along the river with a swimming area and a few concessions.

The **River's Edge Kayak & Canoe Trips** (13840 Healdsburg Ave., 707/433-7247, www. riversedgekayakandcanoe.com, trips $50-120) offers two self-guided tours aboard stand-up paddleboards and single and double kayaks. After checking in between 8:30am and 11:30am, you'll be shuttled up the river and left to paddle downstream. River's Edge has lots of tips for the best beaches, swimming holes, and picnic spots along the way.

Russian River Adventures (20 Healdsburg Ave., 707/433-5599, http://russianriveradventures.com, adults $45-60, children $25-30, dogs $10) offers paddles down a secluded section of the river in stable, sturdy inflatable canoes. Trips usually last 2-6 hours, with little white water and lots of serene shaded pools.

Food

Campo Fina (330 Healdsburg Ave., 707/395-4640, www.campo-fina.com, 11:30am-10pm daily, $17-24) serves excellent thin-crust pizzas and Italian plates. Outside, the semi-covered patio has plenty of tables, plus bocce ball courts.

Barndiva (231 Center St., 707/431-0100, www.barndiva.com, noon-2:30pm and 5:30pm-9pm Wed.-Thurs., noon-3pm and 5:30pm-10pm Fri.-Sat., 11am-2pm and 5:30pm-9pm Sun., $25-42) plates French-inspired and Sonoma County-sourced fare and vintage cocktails in a barn setting.

At **Mateo's Cocina Latina** (214 Healdsburg Ave., 707/433-1520, www.mateoscocinalatina.com, 11:30am-9pm Wed.-Fri., 9am-9pm Sat.-Sun., $17-35), the flavors of the Yucatan are served surrounded by colorful textiles and wood furniture. Order several of the finger food *tacones* or the *cochinita pibil*, a slow-roasted suckling pig and the signature dish. There is a well-balanced drink menu of a dozen microbrews, local wines, and a host of tequila cocktails.

Flying Goat Coffee (324 Center St., 707/433-3599, www.flyinggoatcoffee.com, 7am-7pm daily) serves coffee opposite the square. **Costeaux French Bakery & Café**

(417 Healdsburg Ave., 707/433-1913, www.costeaux.com, 7am-4pm Mon.-Thurs., 7am-5pm Fri.-Sat., 7am-1pm Sun., $10-14) sells crusty bread, delicate pastries, tasty breakfasts, and deli lunches.

Accommodations

None of the boutique inns and hotels in Healdsburg come cheap. The **Haydon Street Inn** (321 Haydon St., 707/433-5228, www.haydon.com, $205-450) is a small inn on a quiet residential street about a 10-minute walk from the plaza. The Queen Anne-style house was built in 1912 and is perfectly maintained with original detailing and period antiques. The six rooms in the main house all have private baths, with the exception of the Blue Room, which has a bathroom across the hall. Two additional deluxe rooms ($400 and up) are in a separate cottage on the manicured grounds. Expect a sumptuous three-course breakfast and wonderful hors d'oeuvres at the inn's nightly wine hour.

On the town plaza, the **Hotel Healdsburg** (25 Matheson St., 707/431-2800, www.hotelhealdsburg.com, $450-650) is a local icon. The 55-room boutique hotel offers the most upscale amenities, soaking tubs, walk-in showers, and beautiful modern decor. Rooms include free Wi-Fi and a gourmet breakfast, and guests can enjoy the outdoor pool, fitness center, and full-service day spa. Downstairs, grab a cocktail at the chic **Spirit Bar** (5:30pm-9:30pm Mon.-Fri., 3pm-10pm Sat.-Sun.) or a table on the leafy patio at the renowned **Dry Creek Kitchen** (707/431-0330, https://drycreekkitchen.com, 5:30pm-9:30pm Sun.-Thurs., 5:30pm-10pm Fri.-Sat., $29-38).

Transportation

Healdsburg is an easy destination, as it's about 15 miles north of Santa Rosa on U.S. 101. To reach downtown Healdsburg from U.S. 101, take exit 503 for Central Healdsburg. Healdsburg can also be accessed from Calistoga. Drive north of Calistoga on the beautiful Highway 128 for almost 20 miles. At

Jimtown, Highway 128 intersects Alexander Valley Road. Continue straight on Alexander Valley Road as Highway 128 turns right, heading north to Geyserville. In about three miles, turn left onto Healdsburg Avenue, which runs to downtown Healdsburg.

DRY CREEK VALLEY

This compact valley is home to an eclectic mix of wineries, from rustic homespun operations to the splashy newcomers.

Wineries

DRY CREEK VINEYARD

The midsize **Dry Creek Vineyard** (3770 Lambert Bridge Rd., 800/864-9463, www.drycreekvineyard.com, 10:30am-5pm daily, $15) focuses much effort within its own AVA (Dry Creek), producing many single-vineyard wines from grapes grown within a few miles of the estate. Try as many as you can in the ivy-covered tasting room, styled after a French chateau, or opt for a picnic on the grounds.

PRESTON VINEYARDS

At Lou Preston's idiosyncratic establishment, **Preston Vineyards** (9282 W. Dry Creek Rd., 707/433-3372, www.prestonvineyards.com, 11am-4:30pm daily, $5), homemade bread, organic vegetables, and olive oil get nearly equal attention as the wine. Inside the homespun tasting room, you'll taste some organic wine from its small portfolio dominated by Rhône varietals. The selection of locally produced foods makes this an ideal place to buy everything you need for an impromptu picnic next to the bocce courts.

Food

The ★ **Dry Creek General Store** (3495 Dry Creek Rd., 707/433-4171, http://drycreekgeneralstore1881.com, 7am-5pm Sun.-Thurs., 7am-5:30pm Fri.-Sat., $6-13) has existed since the 1880s. Inside, order a sandwich from the deli counter and then browse the collection of cookware and gourmet goodies. The **Dry Creek Bar** (3pm-close daily) is next door.

Transportation

Dry Creek Valley is five miles northwest of downtown Healdsburg across U.S. 101 via Dry Creek Road. The slower and bumpier West Dry Creek Road also travels up the valley.

GEYSERVILLE

The 20-mile-long Alexander Valley stretches from Healdsburg in the south to the small town of Cloverdale in the north. In between is the hamlet of Geyserville, home to several tasting rooms and two excellent restaurants.

Wineries

MEDLOCK AMES

Driven by a passion for wine and environmental stewardship, **Medlock Ames** (3487 Alexander Valley Rd., 707/431-8845, www.medlockames.com, 10am-4:30pm daily, tasting $15) is known for its excellent estate wines. Enjoy a tasting flight on the vine-covered patio, wine by the glass, or a wine and cheese pairing. The grounds are dotted with picnic tables, organic garden boxes, and a bocce ball court. The winery is dog- and kid-friendly and hosts live music and food trucks (10am-5pm Sun. June-Aug.) in summer.

LOCALS TASTING ROOM

The little town of Geyserville boasts a fair share of tasting rooms, but the best is **Locals Tasting Room** (Geyserville Ave. at Hwy. 128, 707/857-4900, www.tastelocalwine.com, 11am-6pm daily, free). Tasting is complimentary, with more than 40 wines available. Most of the wines hail from northern Sonoma's boutique wineries, but the overall mix is broad-ranging, from the Central Coast to Mendocino.

★ ALEXANDER VALLEY VINEYARDS

Alexander Valley Vineyards (8644 Hwy. 128, 707/433-7209 or 800/888-7209, www.avvwine.com, 10am-5pm daily, free) shares a name with the historical valley for good reason. In the 1960s the founders of the winery bought a chunk of the homestead once owned by Cyrus Alexander, the man credited with planting the valley's first vineyards in 1846.

The winery's vineyards provide the grapes for two decadent blends, Temptation Zin and Redemption Zin, and the Bordeaux-style Cyrus flagship wine. Historical sites pepper the estate, including a wooden schoolhouse built by Alexander in 1853 and the Alexander family gravesite, up the hill. Complimentary tours of the expansive wine caves are available daily at 11am and 2pm.

Food and Accommodations

The Victorian ★ **Hope-Merrill House** (21253 Geyserville Ave., 707/857-3356 or 800/825-4233, www.hope-inns.com, $141-349) has eight richly decorated guest rooms with features that range from fireplaces to whirlpool and claw-foot tubs. (The sumptuous Sterling Suite is the only room with a television.) A hearty breakfast is served in the downstairs dining room, while the outdoor saltwater pool is the perfect place to cool down on a hot day. Free wireless Internet access is available.

The **Jimtown Store** (6706 Hwy. 128, 707/433-1212, www.jimtown.com, 7:30am-3pm Sun.-Mon. and Wed.-Fri., 7:30am-4pm Sat. $7-14) has been in operation since 1895. At this old-fashioned country store with gourmet sensibility, you'll find house-made jams, condiments, penny toys, housewares, and, best of all, hot lunches. The chalkboard menu presents a tasty assortment of smoked-brisket sandwiches, chili, and buttermilk coleslaw. Enjoy table service in the back or pick up one of a box lunch to go.

Catelli's (21047 Geyserville Ave., 707/857-3471, www.mycatellis.com, 11:30am-8pm Tues.-Thurs., 11:30am-9pm Fri., noon-9pm Sat., noon-8pm Sun., $17-23) is helmed by Domenica Catelli and her brother Nick. Honoring their family's roots, but with an added dedication to healthy local food, they have created an earthy, high-quality Italian eatery geared toward sophisticated comfort food.

★ **Diavola Restaurant** (21021 Geyserville Ave., 707/814-0111, www.diavolapizzeria.com, 11:30am-9pm daily, $16-27) is a great Italian joint in a historical brick building. Centered around a wood-burning oven, this small restaurant is all about thin-crust pizzas and its house-made salumi and sausages. Diavola has a well-stocked deli case so you can take some cured meats home with you.

Transportation

Geyserville is located about 10 miles north of Healdsburg at the junction of U.S. 101 and Highway 128.

North Coast

Highlights

★ **California Coastal National Monument:** Twelve miles of stunning coastline showcase sheer cliffs, giant tide pools, and several sea arches (page 172).

★ **Mendocino:** Spend an afternoon or a weekend wandering this arts-filled community and its headlands, which jut out into the Pacific (page 179).

★ **Avenue of the Giants:** The towering coast redwoods in Humboldt Redwoods State Park are a true must-see. Simply gaze at the silent giants or head to the nearby Eel River for a quick dip (page 198).

★ **Arcata Plaza:** Arcata is Humboldt County's cultural hub, and its Arcata Plaza is a vibrant, grassy square circled by bars, bookstores, and restaurants (page 217).

★ **Trinidad:** This tiny town perched above an idyllic bay is one of the most photogenic coastal communities in the state (page 221).

★ **Prairie Creek Redwoods State Park:** With big trees, impressive wildlife, a long, lonely beach, and one-of-a-kind Fern Canyon, this park is worth a stop (page 226).

★ **Jedediah Smith Redwoods State Park:** The park showcases the rugged beauty of the North Coast with its stunning old-growth redwoods (page 229).

★ **Battery Point Lighthouse:** This lighthouse on an island off Crescent City is only accessible at low tide. If you time it right, you can take an insightful tour from the lighthouse keeper (page 231).

The rugged North Coast of California is spectacular, its wild beauty in many places almost desolate. The cliffs are forbidding, the beaches are rocky and windswept, and the surf thunders in with formidable authority.

This is not the California coast of surfer movies, though hardy souls do ride the chilly Pacific waves as far north as Crescent City.

From Bodega Bay, Highway 1 twists and turns north along hairpin curves that will take your breath away. The Sonoma and Mendocino Coasts offer lovely beaches and forests, top-notch cuisine, and a friendly, un-crowded wine region. Along the way, tiny coastal towns—Jenner, Gualala, Point Arena, Mendocino, Fort Bragg—dot the hills and valleys, beckoning travelers with bed-and-breakfasts, organic farms, and relaxing re-spites from the road. Between the towns are a wealth of coastal access areas where you can take in the striking meeting of land and sea. Inland, Mendocino's hidden wine region of-fers the rural and relaxed pace missing from that other famous wine district. Anderson Valley and Hopland can quench your thirst, whether it's for beer at the local microbrewery or wine at one of many tasting rooms. Where

Highway 1 merges with U.S. 101 is the famous Lost Coast, accessed only via steep, narrow roads or by backpacking the famous Lost Coast Trail. This is California at its wildest.

For most travelers, the North Coast means redwood country, and U.S. 101 marks the gateway to those redwoods. The famous, im-mense coastal sequoias loom along the high-way south of the old logging town of Eureka and the hip college outpost of Arcata. A pleth-ora of state and national parks lure travelers with numerous hiking trails, forested camp-grounds, kitschy tourist traps, and some of the tallest and oldest trees on the continent; you can pitch a tent in Humboldt Redwoods State Park, cruise the Avenue of the Giants, and gaze in wonder at the primordial Founders Grove. Crescent City, marking the northern terminus of the California Coast, is a seaside town known for fishing, seafood—and for surviving a tsunami.

Previous: scenic Highway 1; Avenue of the Giants. **Above:** Trinidad Memorial Lighthouse.

North Coast

BATTERY POINT LIGHTHOUSE
Crescent City
JEDEDIAH SMITH REDWOODS STATE PARK
Klamath Mountains
Six Rivers
Del Norte Coast Redwoods State Park
Del Norte County
Smith River
National
PACIFIC OCEAN
Klamath
Forest
Redwood National State Park
PRAIRE CREEK REDWOODS STATE PARK
101
Klamath River
Stone Lagoon
Orick
Humboldt Lagoons State Park
Big Lagoon
Redwood National Park
Weitchpec
Patrick's Point State Park
TRINIDAD
Trinidad
Redwood Creek
0   10 mi
0   10 km
Humboldt County
ARCATA PLAZA
COAST RANGES
Arcata
Humboldt Bay National Wildlife Complex
Eureka
Mad River
Fortuna
Ferndale
Owl Creek Ecological Reserve
Bear River
101
Humboldt Redwoods State Park
Eel River
Weott
AVENUE OF THE GIANTS
Mattole River
Lost Coast
Redway
Garberville
Shelter Cove
Richardson Grove State Park
Mattole River Ecological Reserve
Mendocino County
Sinkyone Wilderness State Park
Leggett
© AVALON TRAVEL

Sinkyone Wilderness State Park
Leggett
0   10 mi
0   10 km
Angelo Coast Range Reserve
Laytonville
MacKerricher State Park
PACIFIC OCEAN
Fort Bragg
MENDOCINO COAST BOTANICAL GARDENS
Mendocino Headlands State Park
MENDOCINO
Mendocino
Jackson Demonstration State Forest
101
Van Damme State Park
1
Willits
Manchester State Park
Anderson Valley
Mendocino County
CALIFORNIA COASTAL NATIONAL MONUMENT
128
Point Arena
Garcia River Forest
Boonville
Ukiah
20
Lake Mendocino
1
Gualala
Hopland
Lake County
Lakeport
1
Sonoma County
Salt Point State Park
Cloverdale
101
Loch Lomond
Lake Sonoma
Fort Ross State Historic Park
Jenner Headlands
Austin Creek S.R.A.
Jenner
Middletown
Sonoma Coast State Park
Windsor
Bodega Bay
Williams
Calistoga
Bodega Bay
Valley Ford
Sebastopol
Santa Rosa
Saint Helena
Marin County
Rohnert Park
Jack London State Historic Park
1
Petaluma
© AVALON TRAVEL

PLANNING YOUR TIME

If you're planning a road trip to explore the North Coast in depth and want to make stops in more than one destination, plan to spend a **full week.** Driving is the way to get from place to place, unless you're a hardcore backpacker. **Highway 1** winds along the North Coast from Bodega Bay to above Fort Bragg, where it heads east to connect with U.S. 101 at its northern terminus near Leggett. U.S. 101 then heads inland through southern Humboldt County before heading back to the coast at Eureka. North of Eureka, U.S. 101 continues through Arcata, Trinidad, and Crescent City, along with the Redwood National and State Parks.

If you are heading to Mendocino or a section of the coast north of there, take **U.S. 101,** which is a great deal faster than Highway 1, and then take one of the connector roads from U.S. 101 to Highway 1. One of the best and most scenic connector roads is **Highway 128,** which heads west off U.S. 101 at Cloverdale and passes through the scenic Anderson Valley, with its many wineries, before joining Highway 1 just south of the town of Mendocino.

Driving times on Highway 1 tend to be longer on the North Coast due to the roadway's twists, turns, and many spectacular ocean vistas. On U.S. 101 north of Leggett, expect to share the road with logging vehicles. A lot of the roads off U.S. 101 or Highway 1

are worthwhile excursions, but expect mountainous terrain.

Many Bay Area residents consider **Mendocino** ideal for a weekend getaway or romantic retreat. A **weekend** is about the perfect length of time to spend on the Mendocino Coast or in the Anderson Valley wine country. There are at least 3-4 days' worth of intriguing hikes to take in Redwood National and State Parks.

Along the **Lost Coast,** the most lodging and dining options can be found in Shelter Cove. If you want to explore the Lost Coast Trail, consider hiking it north to south, with the wind at your back. Spend the night in Ferndale or camp at the Mattole Recreation Site, where the trail begins, so that you can get an early start for the first day of backpacking.

If you're exploring the **redwood parks,** consider staying in the small towns of Arcata or Trinidad. The campgrounds at Patrick's Point State Park and Prairie Creek State Park are superb places to pitch a tent.

Summer on the North Coast has average daily temperatures in the mid-60s, which is comparable to the temps in Southern California during the winter. Expect rain on the North Coast from November to May. The chances of fog or rain are significantly lower in the **fall,** making it one of the best times to visit. Frequent visitors to the area know this, so many popular hotels book quickly for fall weekends.

Sonoma Coast

One good way to begin your meanders up the coast is to take U.S. 101 out of San Francisco as far as Petaluma, and then head west toward Highway 1. This stretch of Highway 1 is also called the Shoreline Highway. As you travel toward the coast, you'll leave urban areas behind for a while, passing through some of the most pleasant villages in California.

BODEGA BAY

Bodega Bay is popular for its coastal views, whale-watching, and seafood—but it's most famous as the filming locale of Alfred Hitchcock's *The Birds.* The town sits on the eastern side of the harbor, while Bodega Head is a peninsula that shields the bay from the ocean. The tiny town with a population of

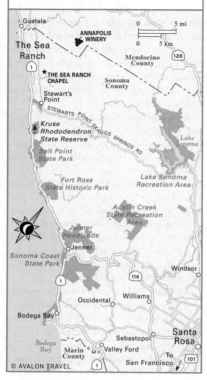

Sonoma Coast

Guatala
ANNAPOLIS WINERY
0   5 mi
0   5 km
The Sea Ranch
1
★ THE SEA RANCH CHAPEL
Mendocino County
128
Stewart's Point
Sonoma County
STEWARTS POINT SKAGGS SPRINGS RD
Kruse Rhododendron State Reserve
Salt Point State Park
Lake Sonoma
Fort Ross State Historic Park
Lake Sonoma Recreation Area
Austin Creek State Recreation Area
Jenner Headlands
Jenner
Sonoma Coast State Park
Windsor
116
Occidental
Williams
Bodega Bay
Sebastopol
Valley Ford
Santa Rosa
Bodega Bay
Marin County
1
To San Francisco
101
© AVALON TRAVEL

just over 1,000 has kite shops, marinas, and unassuming seafood restaurants. The whole town shuts down around 7pm, even on summer evenings.

Whale-Watching

The best sight you could hope to see is a close-up view of Pacific gray whales migrating home to Alaska with their newborn calves. The whales head past the area January-May on their way from their summer home off Mexico. If you're lucky, you can see them from the shore. **Bodega Head**, a promontory just north of the bay, is a place to get close to the migration route. To get to this prime spot, travel north on Highway 1 about one mile past the visitors center and turn left onto Eastshore Road; make a right at the stop sign, and then drive three more miles to the parking lot.

On weekends from January to Mother's Day weekend, volunteers from **Stewards of the Coast and Redwoods** (707/869-9177, www.stewardscr.org) are available to answer questions. Contact them for organized whale-watching tours or to learn more about their various educational programs. Or go out on a whale-watching trip with **Bodega Bay Sport Fishing** (707/875-3344, www.bodega-baysportfishing.com, Dec.-Mar., $50-60/half day) on their 60- or 65-foot boat.

Doran Regional Park

When you arrive in Bodega Bay, you'll see a sign pointing left for **Doran Regional Park** (201 Doran Beach Rd., 707/875-3540, http://parks.sonomacounty.ca.gov, 7am-sunset daily, day use $7 per vehicle). It is less than one mile down the road and worth the trip. The wide and level two-mile-long beach has a small boardwalk. You can even swim at Doran Beach; although it's cold, the water is protected from the open ocean waves, so it's much safer than most of the beaches along the coast.

Bodega Head

Bodega Bay looks like an open safety pin on maps; **Bodega Head** (3799 Westshore Rd., 707/875-3483, www.parks.ca.gov, sunrise-sunset daily, free) is the thicker side, a knob that protects the bay from the open ocean. A part of Sonoma Coast State Park, it's the best place for a hike that gives you an overview of the area. The **Bodega Head Trail** (1.9 miles, 136-foot elevation change) showcases rock arches, sandy coves, and migrating gray whales before hitting the high point and winding back to views of Doran Beach, Bodega Bay, and Bodega Harbor.

Bodega Seafood, Art, and Wine Festival

The annual **Bodega Seafood, Art, and Wine Festival** (16855 Bodega Hwy., Bodega, 707/824-8717, www.bodegaseafoodfestival.

com, Aug., adults $15-20, seniors $10-15, children 12-18 $8-10, children under 12 free) takes place the last weekend in August, combining all the best elements of the Bodega lifestyle with live music, wine-tastings, and special dinners. The proceeds benefit two worthy organizations: the Bodega Volunteer Fire Department and Stewards of the Coast and Redwoods.

Sonoma Coast State Park

Seventeen miles of coast are within **Sonoma Coast State Park** (707/875-3483, www. parks.ca.gov, sunrise-sunset daily, day use $8 per vehicle). The park's boundaries extend from Bodega Head at the south up to the Vista Trailhead, four miles north of Jenner. As you drive north along Highway 1, you'll see signs for various beaches. Although they're lovely places to walk, fish, and maybe sunbathe on the odd hot day, it is not advisable to swim here. If you go down to the water, bring your binoculars and camera. The cliffs, crags, inlets, whitecaps, mini-islands, and rock outcroppings are fascinating in any weather, and their looks change with the shifting tides and fog.

Sports and Recreation

With a usually calm bay and a protected harbor, Bodega Bay is a great place to kayak or stand-up paddleboard. Stop into the **Bodega Bay Surf Shack** (Pelican Plaza, 1400 Hwy. 1, 707/875-3944, www.bodegabaysurf.com, 10am-6pm Mon.-Fri., 9am-7pm Sat.-Sun., kayaks $45/four hours, SUPs $40/five hours) to rent your SUP or kayak, then set out in Bodega Bay, Salmon Creek, or the nearby lower portion of the Russian River. They also give private lessons ($145) and group lessons ($109) and rent surfboards ($17/day) and wetsuits ($17/day). Doran Beach has an unintimidating wave for beginners. Just north of town is Salmon Creek, a series of powerful and exposed beach breaks.

Long, rugged beaches with few people mean that the Sonoma Coast is a terrific place to go horseback riding. Just north of town at the 378-acre Chanslor Ranch, **Horse N Around Trail Rides** (2660 N. Hwy. 1, 707/875-3333, www.horsenaroundtrailrides. com, $40-250) offers 30-minute wetlands trail rides and 1.5-hour beach rides. Choose between group rides and slightly pricier private rides.

Benches overlook the water at Doran Regional Park.

Shopping

Gourmet au Bay (1412 Bay Flat Rd., 707/875-9875, www.gourmetaubay.com, 11am-8pm Thurs.-Mon., 11am-7pm Tues.-Wed., $15/ tasting) is a shop and tasting bar that offers the chance to taste wines from different vintners: some are major players in the Napa wine scene, and some are from wineries so small they don't have tasting rooms of their own. You might even get to taste the odd French or Australian wine when you "wine surf," tasting three wines poured and presented on a miniature surfboard for you to carry out to the deck to admire the view of Bodega Harbor. Inside, peruse the gift shop, which includes some local artisanal foods plus plenty of handmade ceramics and pottery and an array of toys for wine lovers.

Food

The ★ **Fishetarian Fish Market** (599 Hwy. 1, 707/875-9092, www.fishetarianfishmarket. com, 11am-7pm Fri.-Sun., 11am-6pm Mon.-Thurs., $6-15) nails the Baja-style fish taco with rockfish, a cabbage slaw, and a zingy sauce. They also do Point Reyes oysters and an award-winning clam chowder. Order at the counter above display cases of smoked salmon, oysters, and octopus salad, then dine casually inside or outside at one of the limited tables. Fishetarian has a few well-chosen craft beers on tap along with a fridge filled with bottled beers, sodas, and other cold beverages. Beware that this place closes early.

A classic and unassuming seafood spot, the **Spud Point Crab Company** (1860 Westshore Rd., 707/875-9472, www.spud-pointcrab.com, 9am-5pm daily, $7-11) sits across the street from the boats that bring in its fresh seafood. On weekdays, there can be a line out the door for the clam chowder and the crab sandwich. On crowded days, make a friend and share some space at one of the few picnic tables out front.

Right on the highway, **The Birds Café** (1407 Hwy. 1, 707/875-2900, 11:30am-6pm daily, $10) is an easy pit stop when driving through Bodega Bay. Refuel on fried artichoke tacos, fish tacos, and shrimp tacos on a large deck with views of the harbor.

Bodega Bay Lodge's **Drakes Sonoma Coast Kitchen** (Bodega Bay Lodge, 103 Hwy. 1, 707/875-3525, www.bodegabaylodge.com, 7:30am-11am and 6pm-9pm daily, $22-38) showcases Sonoma County ingredients including local artisan cheeses and wines produced by area wineries.

One of the best restaurants in the area is **Terrapin Creek** (1580 Eastshore Dr., 707/875-2700, www.terrapincreekcafe.com, 4:30pm-9pm Thurs.-Mon., $23-32) where they make creative use of the abundance of fresh seafood available and cook up tasty pasta, duck, and beef entrées.

Accommodations and Camping

The ★ **Bodega Bay Lodge & Spa** (103 Hwy. 1, 707/875-3525 or 888/875-2250, www.bode-gabaylodge.com, $279-669) is on a seven-acre property that sits high enough to overlook the bay and harbor, Doran Beach, the bird-filled marshes, and Bodega Head in the distance. Most rooms have views of the water, while all the units in the seven separate buildings have their own private balconies or terraces. Warm up on a foggy day in the heated pool, sauna, and oversized infinity soaking tub. There's a fitness center and spa in the same facility. Dine at the lodge's upscale **Drakes Sonoma Coast Kitchen** (7:30am-11am and 6pm-9pm daily, $22-40) or the casual **Drakes Fireside Lounge** (5pm-9pm daily, $6-17).

For a B&B experience, head to the **Bay Hill Mansion** (3919 Bay Hill Rd., 877/468-1588, www.bayhillmansion.com, $269-354) on the north side of Bodega Bay. Be spoiled in one of just four rooms and wake up to a family-style sit-down brunch.

Sonoma Coast State Park (707/875-3483 or 707/865-2391, www.parks.ca.gov, day use $8 per vehicle) encompasses several campgrounds along its 17-mile expanse. Both **Bodega Dunes Campground** (2485 Hwy. 1, www.reservecalifornia.com, $35) and **Wright's Beach Campground** (7095 Hwy.

1, www.reservecalifornia.com, $35-45) are developed, with hot showers and flush toilets.

Doran Regional Park (201 Doran Beach Rd., 707/565-2267, http://sonomacountycamping.org, $32-35) has 120 campsites for tents, trailers, and RVs. Amenities include restrooms with coin-operated showers.

Transportation

Bodega Bay is on Highway 1 north of Point Reyes National Seashore and west of Petaluma. From the Bay Area, it's a beautiful drive north, but the road's twists and turns require taking it slow. A faster way to get here is to take U.S. 101 north to Petaluma. Take the exit for East Washington Street and follow Bodega Avenue to Valley Ford Road, cutting across to the coast. You'll hit Bodega Bay about two miles after you pass through Valley Ford. The latter route takes about 1.5 hours, with some of the route slow and winding.

JENNER

Jenner is on Highway 1 at the mouth of the Russian River. It's a beautiful spot for a quiet honeymoon or a paddle in a kayak. **Goat Rock State Beach** (Goat Rock Rd., 707/875-3483, www.parks.ca.gov, day use $8 per vehicle) is at the mouth of the Russian River inside Sonoma Coast State Park. A colony of harbor seals breed and frolic here, and you may also see gray whales, sea otters, elephant seals, and a variety of sealife. Pets are not allowed, and swimming is prohibited.

Food and Accommodations

Both the food and the views are memorable at ★ **River's End** (11048 Hwy. 1, 707/865-2484, www.ilovesunsets.com, 11:30am-3pm and 5pm-8:30pm daily, $19-42). The restaurant is perched above the spot where the Russian River flows into the Pacific, and it's a beautiful sight to behold over seafood or filet mignon. Prices are high, but if you get a window table at sunset, you may forget that.

The renovated **Jenner Inn** (10400 Hwy. 1, 707/865-2377, www.jennerinn.com, $169-549) has a variety of quiet, beautifully furnished rooms mere steps from the river. Some rooms have hot tubs and private decks, and breakfast is included.

Fourteen miles north of Jenner is the large and luxurious **Timber Cove Inn** (21780 N. Hwy. 1, 707/847-3231 or 800/987-8319, www.timbercoveinn.com, $340-930), with a spacious bar and lounge, an oceanfront patio, rooms with spa tubs and fireplaces, and hiking trails nearby. You can't miss the inn from

Bodega Bay Lodge & Spa

the road thanks to the 93-foot-tall obelisk rising above the building. Dine on-site at Coast Kitchen (8am-11am and noon-9:30pm daily, $21-46), which pairs Sonoma wines with organic seasonal fare.

Transportation

Jenner is on the ocean along Highway 1. There is no public transportation, but it is a pretty drive from just about anywhere. The fastest route from San Francisco (about 1.75 hours) is to drive north along U.S. 101 and make a left onto Washington Street in Petaluma. Washington Street becomes Bodega Avenue and then Valley Ford Road before you make a slight left onto Highway 1 and head north toward Jenner. From Sacramento (2.5 hours) or points in the East Bay, take I-80 west and then navigate to Petaluma, where you continue west to Highway 1.

FORT ROSS STATE HISTORIC PARK

There is no historic early American figure named Ross who settled here: "Ross" is short for "Russian," and this park commemorates the history of Russian settlement on the North Coast. In the 19th century Russians came to the wilds of Alaska and worked with native Alaskans to develop a robust fur trade, harvesting seals, otters, sea lions, and land mammals for their pelts. The enterprise required sea travel as the hunters chased the animals as far as California. Eventually, a group of fur hunters and traders came ashore on what is now the Sonoma Coast and developed a fortified outpost that became known as Fort Ross State Historic Park (19005 Hwy. 1, Jenner, 707/847-3286, www.fortross.org, 10am-4:30pm Fri.-Mon., visitors center days/hours vary, parking $8). The area gradually became not only a thriving Russian-American settlement but also a center for agriculture and shipbuilding and the site of California's first windmills. Learn more at the park's large visitors center, which provides a continuous film and a roomful of exhibits.

You can walk into the reconstructed fort buildings to see how the settlers lived. The only original building still standing is the captain's quarters—a large, luxurious house for that time and place. The other buildings, including the large bunkhouse, the chapel, and the two cannon-filled blockhouses, were rebuilt using much of the original lumber used by the Russians. Be aware that a serious visit to the whole fort and the beach beyond entails a level but long walk; wear comfortable shoes and bring water.

Camping

Part of Fort Ross State Historic Park, the Reef Campground (19005 Hwy. 1, 707/847-3708, www.parks.ca.gov, Apr.-Nov., $35) has 21 first-come, first-served campsites within a small canyon winding down toward the coast. There are paths here to a couple of scenic coves.

SALT POINT STATE PARK

Stretching for miles along the Sonoma coastline, Salt Point State Park (25050 Hwy. 1, Jenner, 707/847-3221, www.parks.ca.gov, sunrise-sunset daily, $8 per vehicle) provides easy access from U.S. 101 to more than a dozen sandy state beaches. You don't have to stop at the visitors center to enjoy this park and its many beaches—just follow the signs along the highway to the turnoffs and parking lots.

If you're looking to scuba dive or free dive, head for Gerstle Cove, accessible from the visitors center just south of Salt Point proper. The cove was designated one of California's first underwater parks, and divers who can deal with the chilly water have a wonderful time exploring the diverse undersea wildlife.

Kruse Rhododendron State Reserve

For a genteel experience, head east off Highway 1 to the Kruse Rhododendron State Reserve (Hwy. 1 near milepost 43, 707/847-3221, www.parks.ca.gov, sunrise-sunset daily, free), where you can meander along the Chinese Gulf Trail in the spring, admiring the profusion of pink rhododendron flowers blooming beneath the second-growth redwood forest. If you prefer a picnic, you'll find tables at many of the beaches—though it can be quite windy in the summer.

Camping

Salt Point State Park (25050 Hwy. 1, 800/444-7275, www.reservecalifornia. com, $25-35) has scenic **Gerstle Cove Campground** on the west side of the highway and **Woodside Campground** on the eastern side.

THE SEA RANCH

The last 10 miles of the Sonoma Coast before entering Mendocino County are the property of The Sea Ranch, a private coastal community known for its distinctive buildings with wood siding and shingles. One of its structures, Condominium 1, won the American Institute of Architects Gold Medal in 1991 and is now on the National Register of Historic Places.

The community's hard-won coastal access points make The Sea Ranch a good place to take a break from driving for a short beach stroll. Visitors who want to linger here can spend the night at the Sea Ranch Lodge.

The Sea Ranch Chapel

Looking from the outside like a wooden stingray with a plume on top, **The Sea Ranch Chapel** (mile marker 55.66, Hwy. 1 at Bosun's Reach, www.thesearanchchapel.org, sunrise-sunset daily) is one of the smallest and most creatively designed places of worship that you'll ever see. Designed by architect James Hubble, this tiny building's beautiful interior has polished redwood benches, three stained glass windows, and a stone floor with an inserted mosaic, and local seashells and sea urchins are embedded throughout the structure.

Annapolis Winery

You'll find a pleasant coastal climate and a short list of classic California wines at **Annapolis Winery** (26055 Soda Springs Rd., Annapolis, 707/886-5460, www.annapoliswinery.com, noon-5pm daily, free). At this small, family-owned winery seven miles east of Sea Ranch, you can taste pinot, cabernet, zinfandel, and port, depending on what they've made this year and what's in stock. Take a glass outside to enjoy the views from the estate vineyards out over the forested mountains.

The Sea Ranch Chapel

Sports and Recreation

With its front nine holes perched above the Pacific, the **Sea Ranch Golf Links** (42000 Hwy. 1, 707/785-2468, www.searanchgolf.com, $57-67) are like the legendary golf courses at Pebble Beach except without the crowds. Designed by Robert Muir Graves, the course also allows you to putt past redwood trees.

Food and Accommodations

Situated on 52 acres of prime coastal real estate, ★ **Sea Ranch Lodge** (2.5 miles north of Stewart's Point on Hwy. 1, 707/785-2371, http://searanchlodge.com, $276-414) offers 19 rooms, all with simple 1960s throwback decor and ocean vistas that evoke paintings. Hiking trails on the grounds offer a self-guided wildflower walk and a short walk to Black Point Beach. Most rooms are equipped with gas fireplaces for those foggy days on the Sonoma Coast. Guests are treated to a complimentary hot breakfast at the lodge's **Black Point Grill** (2.5 miles north of Stewart's Point on Hwy. 1, 707/785-2371, 8am-11am and 11:30am-9pm daily, $13-27). Black Point Grill is open to the public, serving everything from burgers to local seafood in a dining area with large windows facing the sea.

Mendocino Coast

The Mendocino Coast is a popular retreat for those who've been introduced to its specific charms. On weekends, Bay Area residents flock north to their favorite hideaways to enjoy windswept beaches, secret coves, and luscious cuisine. This area is ideal for deep-sea anglers, wine aficionados, and fans of luxury spas. Art is especially prominent in the culture; from the 1960s onward, aspiring artists have found supportive communities, sales opportunities, and homes in Mendocino County, and a number of small galleries display local artwork.

Be aware that the most popular inns fill up fast many weekends year-round. Fall-winter is the high season, with the Crab Festival, the Mushroom Festival, and various harvest and after-harvest wine celebrations. If you want to stay someplace specific on the Mendocino Coast, book your room at least a month in advance for weekday stays and six months or more in advance for major festival weekends.

GUALALA

With a population of 585, Gualala (wa-LA-la) feels like a metropolis along the Highway 1 corridor in this region. While it's not the most charming coastal town, it does have some of the services other places lack.

Since 1961, the **Art in the Redwoods Festival** (46501 Gualala Rd., 707/884-1138, www.gualalaarts.org, mid-Aug., adults $6, children under 17 free) and its parent organization, Gualala Arts, have been going strong. Taking place over the course of a long weekend in mid-August, the festival features gallery exhibitions, special dinners, a champagne preview, bell ringers, a quilt raffle, and awards for the artists.

Food

Breakfast is big at **Trinks Café** (39140 Hwy. 1, 707/884-1713, http://trinkscafe.com, 7am-4pm Sat. and Mon.-Tues., 7am-4pm and 5pm-8pm Wed.-Fri., 8am-4pm Sun., $5-14), led by graduates of the California Culinary Academy. They also do lunch and dinner (Wed.-Fri.).

Locals and visitors rave about the tacos at **Patty's Tacos** (38820 S. Hwy. 1, 707/884-1789, 8am-7pm Mon.-Fri., 8am-6pm Sat., $2-12). Carne asada and carnitas are the favorite meat options. Gussy up your tacos with toppings from the salsa bar.

MendoViné (39145 S. Hwy. 1, 707/896-

2650, www.mendovinelounge.com, 6pm-9pm Thurs.-Sun., $9-12) is a wine lounge with a curated selection of local reds and whites. They also do small plates with an international flair, served up to the sounds of the occasional jazz band.

The Gualala **farmers market** (47950 Center St., 707/884-3726, www.sonoma-county.com, 9:30am-12:30pm Sat. late May-early Nov.) is at the Gualala Community Center. The **Surf** (39250 S. Hwy. 1, 707/884-4184, www.surfsuper.com, 7:30am-8pm Sat.-Wed., 7:30am-9pm Thurs.-Fri. summer; 7:30am-8pm daily winter) supermarket sells flatbread pizzas and sandwiches.

Accommodations

When it comes to food and lodging in Gualala, you're not going to hear so many of those Sonoma and Mendocino County adjectives (luxurious, elegant, pricey), but you will find choices.

For the budget-conscious, a good option is **The Surf Motel** (39170 Hwy. 1, 707/884-3571 or 888/451-7873, www.surfinngualala.com, $139-259). Only a few of the more expensive rooms have ocean views, but a full hot breakfast, flat-screen TVs with DVD players, and wireless Internet access are included for all guests.

The **Whale Watch Inn** (35100 Hwy. 1, 800/942-5342, www.whalewatchinn.com, $220-300) specializes in romance. Each of its 18 individually decorated, luxuriously appointed rooms has an ocean view and a wood-burning stove. Most also have whirlpool tubs. Every morning, a hot breakfast is delivered to your room. Explore the beach below via a staircase on the grounds.

Four miles north of Gualala, the **North Coast Country Inn** (34591 S. Hwy. 1, 707/884-4537, www.northcoastcountryinn.com, $190-245) was once part of a coastal sheep ranch. Six rooms are outfitted with antique furnishings and fireplaces; three also have kitchenettes. Mornings begin with a hot breakfast buffet. An antiques store and art gallery are on the inn's grounds.

Camping

Two nearby parks provide good camping options: **Gualala River Redwood Park** (46001 Gualala Rd., 707/884-3533, www.gualalapark.com, May-Oct., day use $5 pp, $42-49) and **Gualala Point Regional Park** (42401 Hwy. 1, 707/785-2377, http://parks.sonomacounty.ca.gov, day use $7, camping $35), one mile

Mendocino Coast

© AVALON TRAVEL

south of the town of Gualala. Both places offer access to redwoods, the ocean, and the river.

Transportation

Gualala is 115 miles north of San Francisco on Highway 1, and 60 miles south of Fort Bragg. The **Mendocino Transit Authority** (800/696-4682, http://mendocinotransit.org) has a bus line that connects Gualala to Fort Bragg.

POINT ARENA

A small coastal town 1.5 miles south of its namesake point, Point Arena might be one of the North Coast's best secrets. The town's Main Street is Highway 1, which has a couple of bars, restaurants, markets, and the Arena Theater. One mile from the downtown section is the scenic Point Arena Cove, which has a small fishing pier with rocky beaches on either side. The cove feels like the town's true center, a meeting place where fisherfolk take in the conditions of the ocean. Just north of Point Arena Cove is the California Coastal National Monument Point Arena-Stornetta Unit, a stunning coastal park.

Sights

POINT ARENA LIGHTHOUSE

Although its magnificent Fresnel lens no longer turns through the night, the **Point Arena Lighthouse** (45500 Lighthouse Rd., 707/882-2809 or 877/725-4448, www.pointarenalighthouse.com, 10am-4:30pm daily summer, 10am-3:30pm daily winter, adults $7.50, children $1) remains a Coast Guard light and fog station. But what makes this beacon special is its history. When the 1906 earthquake hit San Francisco, it jolted the land all the way up the coast, severely damaging the Point Arena Lighthouse. When the structure was rebuilt two years later, engineers devised an aboveground foundation that gives the lighthouse both its distinctive shape and additional structural stability.

The lighthouse's extensive interpretive museum, which is housed in the fog station beyond the gift shop, includes the lighthouse's Fresnel lens. Docent-led **tours** climb 145 steep steps to the top of the lighthouse and are well worth the trip, both for the views of the lighthouse from the top and for the fascinating story of its destruction and rebirth through the 1906 earthquake as told by the knowledgeable staff. Catch your breath by taking in the surrounding coastline from Manchester State Beach to the north to the California Coastal National Monument Point Arena-Stornetta Unit to the south.

B. BRYAN PRESERVE

Antelope, zebras, and giraffes wander around the 110-acre **B. Bryan Preserve** (130 Riverside Dr., 707/882-2297, http://bbryanpreserve.com, 9:30am-4pm daily Mar.-Oct., 9:30am-3pm daily Nov.-Feb., adults $35, children under 11 $20). Take a 1.5-hour tour of the preserve or choose to spend a night in one of three **lodging options** on-site ($165-235).

Recreation

★ CALIFORNIA COASTAL NATIONAL MONUMENT

The 1,655-acre **Point Arena-Stornetta Unit** of the **California Coastal National Monument** (Point Arena Cove north to Manchester State Park, 707/468-4000, www.blm.gov, sunrise-sunset daily) is like a greatest-hits compilation of the California coast: vertigo-inducing cliffs, far-ranging ocean views, sea arches, rocky points, and tide pools.

The area can be explored by eight miles of trails including a superb hike that starts from behind the Point Arena City Hall and continues 3.5 miles to Lighthouse Road. Walk another 0.5 mile on the road to visit the Point Arena Lighthouse. Parking is available at Point Arena City Hall and at the pullouts along Lighthouse Road.

SCHOONER GULCH STATE BEACH

The area around Point Arena is filled with coastal access points. A local favorite is **Schooner Gulch State Beach** (intersection of Schooner Gulch Rd. and Hwy. 1, three miles south of Point Arena, 707/937-5804, www.parks.ca.gov). From a pullout north of Schooner Gulch Bridge, trails lead to two different beaches. The southern trail leads to **Schooner Gulch Beach,** a wide, sandy expanse with rocky headlands and a stream flowing into the sea. The northern trail, though, leads to a more memorable destination: **Bowling Ball Beach.** At low tide, the ocean recedes to reveal small spherical boulders lined up in rows. The end section of the trail is steep and has a rope to help your descent. Once on the beach, hike north about 0.25 mile to find the photo-worthy sight.

Entertainment and Events

The onetime vaudeville **Arena Theater** (214 Main St., 707/882-3272, www.arenatheater. org) was also a movie palace when it opened in 1929. In the 1990s, the old theater got a facelift that returned it to its art deco glory. Today, you can see recent box-office films, new documentaries, and unusual independent films, or a live musical or theatrical show.

Right on the main drag, **215 Main** (215 Main St., 707/882-3215, http://215main.com, 3pm-10pm Sun.-Tues., 3pm-11pm Wed.-Sat.) is a venue for artists, with local art, poetry nights, live music, and Wednesday night open mics. The friendly staff pours California wines and craft beers, and there is a small bar menu.

Despite the fact that local dive bar **Sign of the Whale** (194 Main St., 707/882-2259, 2pm-10pm Sun.-Thurs., 2pm-2am Fri.-Sat., cash only) has only bottled beer, it has a surprisingly sophisticated cocktail menu. Locals hold court at the long bar, and there's a jukebox, arcade game, and two pool tables. Bar patrons can order food from the adjacent restaurant Pacific Plate.

The annual **Whale and Jazz Festival** (707/884-1138, www.gualalaarts.org/whale-jazz, Apr.) takes place around Mendocino County. Some of the nation's finest jazz performers play in a variety of venues, while the whales put on their own show out in the Pacific. Point Arena Lighthouse offers whale-watching from the shore daily, and the wineries and restaurants provide refreshment on festival evenings.

Food

Arena Market & Café (183 Main St., 707/882-3663, www.arenaorganics.org, 7am-7pm Mon.-Sat., 8am-6pm Sun.) is a co-op committed to local, sustainable, and organic food, and they do their best to compensate farmers fairly and keep money in the

NORTH COAST
MENDOCINO COAST

a cliffside trail at the Point Arena-Stornetta Unit of the California Coastal National Monument

community. Stock up on staples or sit at one of the tables out front and enjoy a cup of coffee or homemade soup. They're one of the only places in town with Wi-Fi.

The **Uneda Eat Cafe** (206 Main St., 707/882-3800, www.unedaeat.com, 5:30pm-8:30pm Wed.-Sat., $13-32, cash only) has preserved the sign of the former owner, an Italian butcher: The storefront still says "Uneda Meat Market." Now a dine-in, take-out, and catering operation run by Jill and Rob Hunter, the locavore menu offers international items like Indian-style cauliflower and clay-pot pork. The small, narrow restaurant is crowded on weekends when diners occupy the colorful tables and a small counter overlooking the kinetic kitchen.

Blue on the outside, pink on the inside, ★ **Franny's Cup and Saucer** (213 Main St., 707/882-2500, www.frannyscupandsaucer.com, 8am-4pm Wed.-Sat., $2-6, cash/check only) is whimsical and welcoming. The owners, Franny and her mother, Barbara, do all the baking—they even make truffles and candies from scratch. Heartier options include mini-pizzas, croque monsieurs, and mind-blowing bacon slippers. It's take-out only, perfect for a picnic.

Slightly north of town, **Rollerville Café** (22900 S. Hwy. 1, 707/882-2077, www.rollervillecafe.com, 8am-2pm Mon.-Thurs., 8am-7:30pm Fri.-Sun. summer, 8am-2pm Sun.-Thurs., 8am-6:30pm Fri.-Sat. winter, lunch $8-10, dinner $20-24) is a small, homey place catering to resort guests, locals, and travelers. Dinner may seem a little pricey, but lunch is available all day. Breakfast (order the crab cakes Benedict) is served until 11am.

The **Pier Chowder House & Tap Room** (790 Port Rd., 2nd fl., 707/882-3400, www.thepierchowderhouse.net, 11am-9pm daily summer, 11am-8pm Fri.-Tues. winter, $12-30) has an outside deck perfect for taking in the sunset over Point Arena's scenic cove. The menu focuses on seafood: Go for the salmon or rock cod, both caught by local anglers, when they're in season. A long bar has 31 beers on tap.

Cove Coffee and Tackle (790 Port Rd., 707/882-2665, 7am-3pm daily, $6-10) attracts locals with tasty items like "Nate's Special," an egg sandwich with pesto, cream cheese, sausage, onion, and Swiss cheese. It's the perfect place for morning coffee.

Accommodations

From 1901 to 1957, the **Coast Guard House** (695 Arena Cove, 707/882-2442 or 800/524-9320, www.coastguardhouse.com, $185-295) was a working Coast Guard lifesaving station. Now the main building hosts overnight guests who enjoy views of Point Arena Cove. Four rooms are available, including a suite with two bedrooms. Two detached cottages offer more privacy. The friendly and informative innkeepers serve a hot breakfast in the main house every morning, and restaurants are just a short walk away.

Next door to the Coast Guard House is the **Wharf Master's Inn** (785 Iverson Ave., 707/882-3171 or 800/392-4031, www.wharfmasters.com, $109-499). Many rooms have a fireplace, a two-person spa, and a private deck. Twelve of the units have ocean views. The Wharf Master's House has a kitchen and can accommodate up to eight people.

For a unique overnight, stay in the old lightkeepers' quarters at ★ **Point Arena Lighthouse** (877/725-4448, www.pointarenalighthouse.com, $150-350, cleaning fee, 2-night min. weekends). Located on a spit of land with views of the ocean, these lodging options are a real deal, especially since any room or cottage includes a free tour of the nearby lighthouse, a small bottle of wine, and chocolates. The assistant keepers' homes have three bedrooms, two baths, a kitchen, and a wood-burning fireplace. It makes a great base for exploring the North Coast.

Transportation and Services

Point Arena is 10 miles north of Gualala on Highway 1, and about 120 miles north of San Francisco.

The **Mendocino Transit Authority**

(800/696-4682, https://mendocinotransit.org, $1.50) runs the route 75 bus to connect Point Arena south to Gualala and north to Fort Bragg.

The **Coast Community Library** (225 Main St., 707/882-3114, www.coastcommunitylibrary.org, noon-6pm Mon. and Fri., 10am-6pm Tues., 10am-8pm Wed., noon-8pm Thurs., noon-3pm Sat.) offers free Internet access.

Many places in Point Arena are cash-only. The **Redwood Credit Union** (280 Main St.) has an ATM.

Manchester State Park

Seven miles north of the town of Point Arena, **Manchester State Park** (44500 Kinney Ln., Manchester, 707/882-2463, www.parks.ca.gov, day use free) is a wild place perfect for a long, solitary beach walk. The 3.5-mile-long coast is littered with bleached white driftwood and logs that lie on the dark sand like giant bones amid crashing waves. Even the water offshore is protected as part of the 3,782-acre Point Arena State Marine Reserve. At the southwestern tip of the park is Arena Rock, a nautical hazard known for sinking at least six ships before the construction of the nearby Point Arena Lighthouse to the south. Part of the 1,500 acres of onshore parkland was once a dairy ranch.

Today, there's beach, dunes, a wetlands trail, and a **campground** (Fri.-Sun. late May-early Sept., first-come, first-served, $25) with 41 sites and basic amenities, including fire pits, picnic tables, and pit toilets. Some environmental campsites in the dunes are accessible via a one-mile hike.

ELK

The town of Elk used to be called Greenwood, after the family of Caleb Greenwood, who settled here in about 1850. Details of the story vary, but it is widely believed that Caleb was part of a mission to rescue survivors of the Donner Party after their rough winter near Truckee.

Greenwood State Beach

From the mid-19th century until the 1920s, the stretch of shore at **Greenwood State Beach** (Hwy. 1, 707/937-5804, www.parks.ca.gov, visitors center 10am-4pm Wed.-Sun. Mar.-Nov.) was a stop for large ships carrying timber to points of sale in San Francisco and sometimes even China. The visitors center displays photographs and exhibits about Elk's past in the lumber business.

coastline of Manchester State Park

Greenwood State Beach is alongside the town of Elk, 10-15 miles north of Point Arena and about 17 miles south of Mendocino.

Food and Accommodations

With a perfect location in the center of town and across the street from the ocean, **Queenie's Roadhouse Café** (6061 Hwy. 1, 707/877-3285, http://queeniesroadhouse-cafe.com, 8am-3pm Thurs.-Mon., $9-18) is the place to go for hot food and a friendly atmosphere. Expect to be full for a while after leaving.

The **Beacon Light by the Sea** (7401 S. Hwy. 1, south of Elk, 707/877-3311, 5pm-11pm Fri.-Sat.) is the best bar in the area. Its colorful owner, R. D. Beacon, was born in Elk and has run the Beacon Light since 1971. He claims it's the only place you can get hard liquor for 14 miles in any direction. With 85 different brands of vodka, 20 whiskeys, and 15 tequilas, there's something for every sort of drinker. On clear days, the views stretch all the way to the Point Arena Lighthouse.

Housed in a little blue cottage attached to the resort, **Bridget Dolan's Pub & Restaurant** (5910 S. Hwy. 1, 707/877-1820, 4:30pm-8:30pm Thurs.-Mon., $9-16) is a terrific place to hole up with a draft beer on a rainy winter day or foggy summer afternoon. The tables are draped in white tablecloths and the small bar is lined with locals. The menu includes burgers, pizzas, and hearty pub fare like cottage pie.

Perched on a hillside over the stunning Greenwood State Beach cove, the ★ **Elk Cove Inn & Spa** (6300 S. Hwy. 1, 800/275-2967, www.elkcoveinn.com, $195-395) offers luxury accommodations, generous hospitality, and superb views of the nearby Pacific, studded with islands and a scattering of offshore rocks. Check-in comes with a complimentary cocktail or glass of wine and a welcome basket filled with wine, fruit, popcorn, and fresh-baked cookies. Choose from rooms in the main house, cozy cabins with an ocean view, or luxurious suites with jetted soaking tubs and private balconies or patios.

A private staircase leads down to the beach below. There's also a full-service day spa with a sauna and aromatherapy steam shower. The innkeepers make your stay top notch, from port wine and chocolates in the rooms to the big morning breakfast buffet of Southern comfort food with a glass of champagne.

The **Sacred Rock Resort** (5910 S. Hwy. 1, 707/877-3422, www.sacredrockresort.com, $138-260) has five cottages, three of which have private decks overlooking Elk Cove. Full breakfast can be delivered to your room, but there's also a lively dining room.

ALBION AND LITTLE RIVER

Tiny Albion is along Highway 1 almost 30 miles north of Point Arena and about 8 miles south of Mendocino. Little River is about five miles farther north, also on Highway 1. There is a state park and several plush places to stay.

Van Damme State Park

The centerpiece of **Van Damme State Park** (Hwy. 1, 3 miles south of Mendocino, 707/937-5804, www.parks.ca.gov, 8am-9pm daily, $8) is the **Pygmy Forest,** where you'll see a true biological rarity: mature yet tiny cypress and pine trees perpetually stunted by a combination of always-wet ground and poor soil-nutrient conditions. To get there, drive along Airport Road to the trail parking lot (opposite the county airport) and follow the wheelchair-accessible loop trail (0.25 mile, easy). You can also get there by hiking along the **Fern Canyon Trail** (7 miles round-trip, difficult).

Kayak Mendocino launches four **Sea Cave Nature Tours** (707/813-7117, www.kayakmendocino.com, 9am, 11:30am, 2pm, and sunset, $60 pp) from Van Damme State Park. No previous experience is necessary; the expert guides provide all the equipment you need and teach you how to paddle your way through the sea caves and around the harbor seals.

Food

★ **Ledford House Restaurant** (3000 N.

Hwy. 1, Albion, 707/937-0282, www.ledford-house.com, 5pm-close Wed.-Sun., $19-30) is beautiful even from a distance; you'll see it on the hill as you drive up Highway 1. With excellent food and nightly jazz performances, it's one of the true "special occasion" choices in the area. Try to reserve a table for sunset.

A fine restaurant with stunning coast views, the **5200 Restaurant & Lounge** (Heritage House Resort, 5200 N. Hwy. 1, Little River, 707/202-9000, http://heritagehouseresort.com, 8am-10:30am and 5pm-9pm Mon.-Fri., 8am-11:30am and 5pm-9pm Sat.-Sun., lounge 4pm-9pm daily, $12-33) has farm-to-fork cuisine for breakfast and dinner. The lounge has a great happy hour (4pm-6pm) in a comfortable setting that includes a fireplace, couches, and board games.

Start the day at ★ **Circa '62** (7051 N. Hwy. 1, Little River, 707/937-5525, www.schoolhousecreek.com, 8am-11am Mon. and Wed.-Fri., 8am-1pm Sat.-Sun., $9-16). Housed within a cozy blue-and-white former schoolhouse on the grounds of the Inn at Schoolhouse Creek, the building oozes charm, from its fireplace to its ocean-facing windows. Yet it's the glorious food that makes this place worthwhile. The creative, changing menu offers steak-and-egg tacos, kimchi pancakes, and a hash-brown waffle drenched in sausage gravy.

Wild Fish (7750 N. Hwy. 1, Little River, 707/937-3055, www.wild-fish.com, 11:30am-2:30pm and 5pm-9pm Sun. and Tues.-Thurs., 5pm-9pm Mon., 11:30am-2pm and 5pm-9:30pm Fri.-Sat., $28-38) utilizes local assets, from organic produce to wild-caught seafood, on an ever-changing menu. The wild king salmon and petrale sole are caught right out of Fort Bragg's Noyo Harbor.

Tucked into a corner of a convenience store, the **Little River Market Grill & Gourmet Deli** (7746 N. Hwy. 1, Little River, 707/937-5133, grill: 9am-2:50pm daily; deli: 9am-3:50pm daily, $8) is a local favorite. This better-than-average deli has a wide range of options, including burgers, pulled pork sandwiches, and fish tacos. Vegetarian options include the tasty pesto veggie and avocado sandwich. Grab a sandwich for a picnic on the coast.

Accommodations

There's no place quite like ★ **The Andiron** (6051 N. Hwy. 1, Little River, 707/937-1543, www.theandiron.com, $119-274). The one- and two-room cabins in a meadow above Highway 1 are filled with curiosities and

the steak-and-egg tacos at Circa '62

kitsch. Every room is different. One has a unique camel-shaped bar, while another has a coin-operated vibrating bed. Most have vintage board games, View-Masters, and an eclectic library of books. Standard amenities include small wooden decks and small flat-screen TVs. A hot tub is available for guests. The fun-loving owners throw happy hour parties every weekend, including "Fondue Fridays," when they also serve local beers and wines.

A longtime lodging destination, the ★ **Heritage House Resort** (5200 Hwy. 1, Little River, 707/202-9000, http://heritagehouseresort.com, $289-400) has a rich history that includes being the past hideout of bank robber "Baby Face" Nelson and the setting of the 1978 film *Same Time, Next Year*. Perched on stunning cliffs pocked with coves, the numerous buildings spread across 37 acres. The rooms are top tier: Each is enhanced by private decks, rain showers, and wood-burning or gas fireplaces. The units are priced according to proximity to the water and quality of the view. The resort has a full-service spa and restored garden.

The **Albion River Inn** (3790 N. Hwy. 1, Albion, 707/937-1919 or 800/479-7944, www. albionriverinn.com, $195-355) is a gorgeous and serene setting for an away-from-it-all vacation. This cliffside inn is all about romance. A full breakfast is included in the room rates; pets and smoking are not allowed, and there are no TVs.

The **Little River Inn** (7901 N. Hwy. 1, Little River, 707/937-5942 or 888/466-5683, www.littleriverinn.com, $205-369) appeals to coastal vacationers who like a little luxury. It has a nine-hole golf course and two lighted tennis courts. All recreation areas overlook the Pacific, which crashes on the shore just across the highway from the inn. The sprawling white Victorian house and barns hide the expansiveness of the grounds, which also have a great restaurant and a charming sea-themed bar. Relax even more at the in-house Spa at Little River Inn.

Camping

There's camping on the coast at **Van Damme State Park** (Hwy. 1, Little River, 707/937-5804, www.parks.ca.gov, reservations 800/444-7275, www.reservecalifornia.com, $35), three miles south of Mendocino. The appealing campground offers picnic tables, fire rings, and food lockers, as well as restrooms and hot showers. The park's 1,831 acres

Heritage House Resort

Mendocino

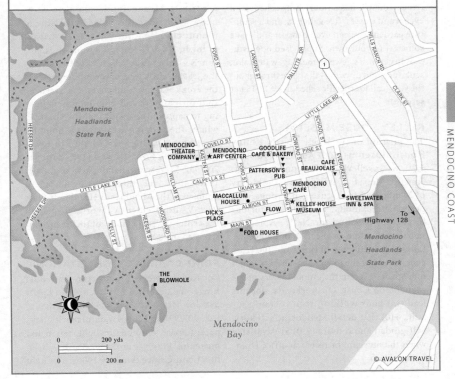

Mendocino Headlands State Park

Mendocino Headlands State Park

Mendocino Bay

MENDOCINO THEATER COMPANY

MENDOCINO ART CENTER

GOODLIFE CAFÉ & BAKERY

CAFÉ BEAUJOLAIS

PATTERSON'S PUB

MENDOCINO CAFÉ

MACCALLUM HOUSE

SWEETWATER INN & SPA

KELLEY HOUSE MUSEUM

FLOW

DICK'S PLACE

FORD HOUSE

THE BLOWHOLE

To Highway 128

© AVALON TRAVEL

include beaches as well as forest, so there's lots of natural beauty to enjoy. Reservations are strongly encouraged.

★ MENDOCINO

Perched on a headland surrounded by the Pacific, Mendocino is one of the most picturesque towns on the California coast. Quaint bed-and-breakfasts, art colonies, and local sustainable dining add to its charm, making it a favorite for romantic weekend getaways.

Once a logging town, Mendocino was reborn as an artist community in the 1950s. One of its most striking buildings is the town's Masonic Hall, dating from 1866 and adorned with a redwood statue of Father Time on its roof. Many New Englanders settled in the region in its early years. With its old water towers and historic buildings, it resembles a New England fishing village—so much so that it played one in the long-running TV series *Murder, She Wrote.* It was also a stand-in for Monterey in the 1955 James Dean film *East of Eden.*

Sights
MENDOCINO ART CENTER

The town of Mendocino has long been an inspiration and a gathering place for artists of many varieties, and the **Mendocino Art Center** (45200 Little Lake St., 707/937-5818 or 800/653-3328, www.mendocinoartcenter. org, 11am-4pm daily, donation) gives these diverse artists a community, provides them with opportunities for teaching and learning, and displays contemporary works. Since 1959, the center has offered artist workshops and retreats. Today it has a flourishing schedule of events and classes, five galleries, and a sculpture garden. You can even drop in and make some art of your own. Supervised open studios in ceramics, jewelry making, watercolor, sculpture, and drawing take place throughout the year (call for specific schedules, $12-15 per session).

KELLEY HOUSE MUSEUM
The mission of the lovely, stately **Kelley House Museum** (45007 Albion St., 707/937-5791, www.kelleyhousemuseum.org, 11am-3pm Fri.-Mon., free) is to preserve the history of Mendocino for future generations. The permanent exhibits chronicle a notorious local shipwreck and the Native American population, while a collection of photos details the town in present times and 100 years ago. Ask about the town's water-rights issues for a great lesson in the untold history of the Mendocino Coast. On weekends, docents lead two-hour **walking tours** (11am Sat.-Sun., $10) that detail Mendocino's history. Self-guided audio tours ($10) are available when the museum or research office (1pm-4pm) is open.

MENDOCINO HEADLANDS STATE PARK
No trip to Mendocino is complete without a walk along the rugged coastline of **Mendocino Headlands State Park** (west of town, 707/937-5804, www.parks.ca.gov, sunrise-sunset daily). A series of trails along the seaside cliffs west of town offer views of the area's sea caves and coves. It's a favorite spot for painters and photographers hoping to capture the majesty of the coast. In winter, the park is a great vantage point for viewing migrating gray whales. In town, the **Historic Ford House** (735 Main St., 707/937-5397, www.mendoparks.org, daily 11am-4pm, free, donations encouraged) doubles as the Mendocino Headlands State Park Visitor Center. A favorite display in the center is a scale model of the town, constructed in 1890.

POINT CABRILLO LIGHT STATION
Located between Mendocino and Fort Bragg, the beautiful **Point Cabrillo Light Station Historic Park** (45300 Lighthouse Rd., 707/937-6122, www.pointcabrillo.org, park: sunrise-sunset daily; light station and museum: 11am-4pm daily, $5) has been functioning since the early 1900s. The light

Mendocino

station was absorbed into the California State Parks system in 2002 and is currently managed by a volunteer organization, the Point Cabrillo Lightkeepers Association. Take a tour of the famous Fresnel lens, learn about the infamous *Frolic* shipwreck of 1850, and explore the tide-pool aquarium. For an overnight stay, rent the **lightkeeper's house** or two cottages on the grounds (800/262-7801, www.mendocinovacations.com, $307-1,163 2-night stays).

Entertainment and Events
BARS AND LIVE MUSIC

For a place to hunker down over a pint, head to cozy **Patterson's Pub** (10485 Lansing St., 707/937-4782, www.pattersonspub.com, 10am-midnight daily). This traditional Irish-style pub is in the former rectory of a 19th-century Catholic church. It nods to the 21st century with six plasma TVs that screen current sporting events. Order a simple, filling meal at the tables or at the bar, where you'll find 14 beers on tap, a full-fledged wine list, and liquor imported from around the world.

So where do the locals go for a drink in Mendocino? That would be **Dick's Place** (45080 Main St., 707/937-6010, 11:30am-2am daily, cash only), an old-school bar with a mounted buck head draped in Christmas lights as decor. Dick's is easy to find: Look for the only neon sign on Main Street, in the shape of a martini glass.

THEATER

The **Mendocino Theater Company** (45200 Little Lake St., 707/937-4477, www.mendocinotheatre.org, 8pm Thurs.-Sat., 2pm Sun., adults $25, students $12) offers a genuine small-theater experience. Plays are staged in the 75-seat Helen Schoeni Theater for an intimate night of live drama or comedy. The small, weathered old building exudes just the right kind of charm to draw in lovers of quirky community theater. But this little theater company has big goals, and it tends to take on thought-provoking work by contemporary playwrights.

EVENTS

For two weekends every March, the Point Cabrillo Light Station is host to the annual **Whale Festival** (707/937-6123, www.pointcabrillo.org, Mar., $5), a chance to get expert guidance as you scan the sea for migrating gray whales headed north for the summer.

In July, musicians descend on the coast for the **Mendocino Music Festival** (707/937-2044, www.mendocinomusic.com, July, prices vary). For 2.5 weeks, live performances are held at venues around the area. A centerpiece of the festival is the famed big-band concert. In addition to 13 evenings of music, there are three series of daytime concerts: piano, jazz, and village chamber concerts. No series passes are available; all events require separate tickets.

If restaurants are the heart of the Mendocino food scene, festivals are its soul. **Taste of Mendocino** (888/636-3624, http://winecrab.com) comprises a couple of subfestivals. **Mendocino Crab, Wine & Beer Days** (Jan., prices vary) offers a burst of crab-related events. The **Beer, Wine & Mushroom Festival** (Nov., prices vary) focuses on the wild mushroom season. Come for classes, tastings, and tours, learn to cook, or just eat.

Shopping

The galleries and boutiques of **Mendocino Village** are welcoming and fun, plus the whole downtown area is beautiful. It seems that every shop in the Main Street area has its own garden, and each fills with a riotous cascade of flowers in the summer.

Panache (45120 Main St., 707/937-1234, www.thepanachegallery.com, 10:30am-5pm daily) displays and sells beautiful works of art in all sorts of media—paintings, jewelry, sculpture, and art glass.

If you love fine woodworking and hand-crafted furniture, don't miss the **Highlight Gallery** (45094 Main St., 707/937-3132, www.thehighlightgallery.com, 10am-5pm daily). Its roots are in woodwork, which it maintains as a focus, although the gallery also features glasswork, ceramics, painting, and sculpture.

The **Gallery Bookshop** (Main St. and Kasten St., 707/937-2665, www.gallerybookshop.com, 9:30am-6pm Sun.-Thurs., 9:30am-9pm Fri.-Sat.) is a large store with fiction from around the world along with the works of local authors. They host an array of literary events, too.

Sports and Recreation
HIKING
Russian Gulch State Park (Hwy. 1, 2 miles north of Mendocino, 707/937-5804, www.parks.ca.gov, $8) has its own **Fern Canyon Trail** (3 miles round-trip), which winds into a second-growth redwood forest filled with lush green ferns. At the four-way junction, turn left to hike another 0.75 mile to the ever-popular waterfall. You'll likely be part of a crowd on summer weekends. Making a right at the four-way junction will take you on a three-mile loop, for a total hike of six miles that leads to the top of the attractive little waterfall. If you prefer the shore to the forest, hike west to take in the lovely, wild headlands and see blowholes, grasses, and trawlers out seeking the day's catch. The biggest attraction is the **Devil's Punchbowl,** a collapsed sea cave 100 feet across and 60 feet deep. There's also a nice beach.

KAYAKING AND STAND-UP PADDLEBOARDING
The shoreline on the Mendocino Coast is pocked with caves and coves that are ideal for kayaking or stand-up paddling. Some of the best can be accessed in the waters off Van Damme State Park. A short paddle north are some impressive sea caves that adventurous paddlers can pass through. **Kayak Mendocino** (707/813-7117, www.kayakmendocino.com, SUP rentals $25/two hours) has a bus parked by the beach that rents kayaks and SUPs. From there, guides lead SUP and kayak sea cave tours (9am, 11:30am, and 2pm daily, adults $60, children under 12 $40).

To explore the relatively sedate waters of the Big River estuary, rent an outrigger or a sailing canoe from **Catch a Canoe & Bicycles Too** (Stanford Inn, 1 S. Big River Rd., 707/937-0273, www.catchacanoe.com, 9am-5pm daily, adults $35 pp for three hours, children 6-17 $15 pp). Guided **tours** (June-Sept., $65 pp) include an estuary excursion with a naturalist and a ride on an outrigger that utilizes solar energy.

SURFING
Big River is a beach break surf spot just south of the town of Mendocino where the Big River flows into the ocean. It's a place you can check out from Highway 1, and on most days, all levels of surfers try their hand at surfing the break. More experienced surfers should try **Smuggler's Cove,** in Mendocino Bay on the south side of Big River. It's a reef break that usually only works during winter swells.

DIVING
A good spot for abalone is **The Blowhole** (end of Main St.), a favorite summer lounging spot for locals. In the water, you'll find abalone and their empty shells; colorful, tiny nudibranchs; and occasionally, overly friendly seals. The kelp beds just offshore attract divers who don't fear cold water and want to check out the complex ecosystem. Abalone is strictly regulated; most species are endangered and can't be harvested. Check with the state Department of Fish and Game (916/445-0411, www.wildlife.ca.gov) for abalone season opening and closing dates, catch limits, licensing information, and the best spots to dive each year.

SPAS
Relax on the Mendocino Coast at one of the many nearby spas. The **Sweetwater Spa & Inn** (44840 Main St., 800/300-4140, www.sweetwaterspa.com, 11am-10pm daily summer, 11am-9pm daily winter, $15-19/half hour, $18-23/hour) rents indoor hot tubs and has a range of massage services ($90-154). They also have group tub and sauna rates ($10-12). The rustic buildings and garden setting complete the experience. Appointments are required

for massage and private tubs, but walk-ins are welcome to use the communal tub and sauna.

Food

Mendocino has a weekly **farmers market** (Howard St. and Main St., www.mcfarm.org. noon-2pm Fri. May-Oct.), where you can find seasonal produce, flowers, fish, wine, honey, and more.

AMERICAN

Publications including *The Wall Street Journal* rave about **Trillium Café** (10390 Kasten St., 707/937-3200, 11:30am-2:30pm and 5:30pm-8:30pm Sun.-Thurs., 11:30am-2:30pm and 5:30pm-9pm Fri.-Sat., $22-36). The shellfish fettuccine is a favorite. Dine inside by the fireplace or out on the deck overlooking a garden where many of the restaurant's ingredients grow.

CAFES

The **Goodlife Café & Bakery** (10483 Lansing St., 707/937-0836, www.goodlifecafemendo. com, 8am-4pm daily, $5-13) is a great place for an espresso drink, a freshly made pastry, or a sandwich on delicious, pillowy focaccia. There are lots of gluten-free options as well. The busy café has seating inside and outside.

One of the most appealing and dependable places is the **Mendocino Café** (10451 Lansing St., 707/937-6141, www.mendocino-cafe.com, 11am-4pm and 5pm-9pm daily, $14-32). The café has good, simple, well-prepared food, a small kids menu, a wine list, and a beer list. Enjoy a Thai burrito, fresh local rockfish, or a steak in the warm, well-lit dining room. The café is in the gardens of Mendocino Village, and thanks to a heated patio, you can enjoy outdoor dining any time of day.

FRENCH

★ **Café Beaujolais** (961 Ukiah St., 707/937-5614, www.cafebeaujolais.com, 5:30pm-9pm Mon.-Tues., 11:30am-2:30pm and 5:30pm-9pm Wed.-Sun., $23-38) is a standout French-California restaurant in an area dense with great upscale cuisine. This charming,

out-of-the-way spot is a few blocks from the center of Mendocino Village in an old vine-covered house. Despite the white tablecloths and crystal, the atmosphere is casual at lunch and only slightly formal at dinner. The giant salads and delectable entrées are made with organic produce, humanely raised meats, and locally caught seafood. The portions are enormous, but come half-size by request. The waitstaff are friendly, helpful, and knowledgeable about the menu and wine list. Reservations are available online.

VEGETARIAN

Vegetarians and carnivores alike rave about **Ravens Restaurant** (Stanford Inn, 44850 Comptche Ukiah Rd., 0707/937-5615 or 800/331-8884, www.ravensrestaurant.com, 8am-10:30am and 5:30pm-close daily, $12-27). Inside the lodge, which is surrounded by lush organic gardens, you'll find a big, open dining room. Many of the vegetarian and vegan dishes use produce from the inn's own organic farm. At breakfast, enjoy delicious vegetarian (or vegan, with tofu) scrambles, omelets, and Florentines, complete with homemade bread and English muffins. At dinner, try one of the seasonal vegetarian entrées. The wine list reflects organic, biodynamic, and sustainable-practice wineries.

Accommodations
$150-250

The warm and welcoming ★ **Blackberry Inn** (44951 Larkin Rd., 707/937-5281 or 800/950-7806, www.blackberryinn.biz, $125-225) is in the hills beyond the center of Mendocino. The inn looks like a town from the Old West. Each of the 16 charmingly decorated rooms has a different storefront outside, including the bank, the saloon, the barbershop, and the land-grant office. Amenities include plush, comfortable bedding cozied up with colonial-style quilts, along with microwaves, fridges, and free wireless Internet. The manager-hosts are the nicest you'll find anywhere.

Sweetwater Inn & Spa (44840 Main

St., 800/300-4140, www.sweetwaterspa.com, $140-295) harks back to the days when Mendocino was a colony of starving artists. A redwood water tower was converted into a guest room, joined by a motley collection of detached cottages that guarantee privacy. Every guest room and cottage has its own style—you'll find a spiral staircase in one of the water towers, a hot tub on a redwood deck in the Garden Cottage, and fireplaces in many of the units. The eclectic decor makes each room different. Thick gardens surround the building complex, and a path leads back to the Garden Spa. The location, just past downtown on Main Street, is perfect for dining, shopping, and art walks. They also run **Sweetwater Vacation Home Rentals** (800/300-4140, http://sweetwatervacationrentals.com, $229-499), which rents apartments and home in town.

The 1882 **MacCallum House** (45020 Albion St., 800/609-0492, www.maccallumhouse.com, $169-359) is the king of luxury on the Mendocino Coast. The facility includes several properties in addition to the main building in Mendocino Village. Choose from private cottages with hot tubs, suites with jetted tubs, and rooms with opulent antique appointments. There's a two-night minimum on weekends, and a three-night minimum for most holidays. Room rates include a cooked-to-order breakfast.

The **Blue Door Inn** (10481 Howard St., 707/937-4892, www.bluedoorinn.com, $159-349) aims to spoil you. Five sleek, modern rooms come with flat-screen TVs and gas fireplaces. The two-course breakfast features homemade pastries and egg dishes.

OVER $250

Set amid redwoods, **The Stanford Inn** (44850 Comptche Ukiah Rd., 707/937-5615 or 800/331-8884, www.stanfordinn.com, $355-555) is an upscale forest lodge. The location is convenient to hiking and only a short drive from Mendocino Village and the coast. Rooms have beautiful, honey wood-paneled walls, pretty furniture, and fluffy down comforters. Amenities include a wood-burning fireplace, Internet access, a pool, sauna and hot tub, and free use of mountain bikes. Gardens surrounding the resort are perfect for strolling after a complimentary vegan breakfast at the on-site Ravens Restaurant.

A mile south of the village, the ★ **Brewery Gulch Inn** (9401 Hwy. 1, 800/578-4454, www.brewerygulchinn.com, $350-495) provides a lot of amenities to guests

the front deck of the Brewery Gulch Inn

staying in its 11 rooms, including a made-to-order hot breakfast and a light dinner buffet with wine. The rooms are modern and calming, with plush carpets, feather beds, and gas fireplaces; all have ocean views. Downstairs is a wonderful common area with a steel fireplace. Relax with a newspaper, book, or magazine from the extensive collection. There's also a collection of more than 500 DVDs to watch in the comfort of your room. Another option is the Serenity Cottage ($625/three-night minimum), a standalone oceanfront studio.

The beautifully restored 1909 **Point Cabrillo Head Lightkeeper's House** (45300 Lighthouse Rd., 707/937-5033, www.mendocinovacations.com, 2-night minimum, $307-1,163 for 2 nights) sits atop a cliff beside the Pacific, so you can watch for whales, dolphins, and seabirds without leaving the porch. Four bedrooms sleep eight people, with 4.5 baths and a very modern kitchen. Larger groups can rent two of the cottages nearby.

Transportation

It's simplest to navigate Mendocino with your own vehicle. From U.S. 101 near Cloverdale, take Highway 128 northwest for 60 miles. Highway 128 becomes Highway 1 on the coast; Mendocino is another 10 miles north. A slower, more scenic alternative is to take Highway 1 from San Francisco to Mendocino; this route takes at least 4.5 hours. Mendocino has a fairly compact downtown area, Mendocino Village, with a concentration of restaurants, shops, and inns just a few blocks from the beach.

The **Mendocino Transit Authority** (800/696-4682, http://mendocinotransit.org) operates a dozen bus routes that connect Mendocino and Fort Bragg with larger cities like Santa Rosa and Ukiah.

FORT BRAGG

Fort Bragg is the Mendocino Coast's largest city. With fast-food joints and chain hotels lining Highway 1 through town, it lacks the immediate charm of its neighbor to the south. But it does offer some great restaurants, interesting downtown shops, and proximity to coastal landmarks.

Sights
SKUNK TRAIN

The California Western Railroad, popularly called the **Skunk Train** (depot at end of Laurel St., 707/964-6371, www.skunktrain.com, 9am-3pm daily), is perfect for rail buffs and traveling families. The brightly painted trains appeal to children, and the historic aspects and scenery call to adults.

There are two rides on these restored steam locomotives. The **Northspur Flyer** (four hours, adults $84, children 2-12 $42, children under 2 $10) travels 40 miles from Fort Bragg through majestic redwood forest to the town of Willits and back. The **Pudding Creek Express** (one hour, adults $25, children 2-12 $15, children under 2 $10) does a run up to Pudding Creek. Board in either Fort Bragg or Willits and make a round-trip return to your lodgings for the night.

Another option is to take the Skunk Train to **Camp Noyo** ($100-220), a former logging camp on the Noyo River where you can bed down in a campsite or a chalet. Check the train's website for special events like a Halloween pumpkin patch excursion and a special Zombie Train.

The **Mendocino Coast Model Railroad and Navigation Company** (behind the Skunk Train Depot, www.mendorailhistory.org, 10:30am-2:30pm Wed. and Sat.-Sun, adults $5, children $3, Skunk Train ticketholders free) is an operational train yard that recreates Fort Bragg's logging past in miniature. The large room is full of noise as model trains chug, bells ding, and lumber splashes into water.

GLASS BEACH

Fascinating **Glass Beach** (Elm St. and Glass Beach Dr.) is strewn with sea glass that has been polished and smoothed by the pounding surf. At the tideline, amber, green, and clear sea glass color the shore. It's against the park rules to remove the glass, though you can take photos. The trail down to Glass Beach is short but steep and treacherous; wear good walking or hiking shoes.

TRIANGLE TATTOO MUSEUM

The **Triangle Tattoo Museum** (356B N. Main St., 707/964-8814, www.triangletattoo. com, noon-6pm daily, free) displays the implements of tattooing and photos of their results. Walk up a flight of narrow stairs and stare at the walls covered with photos of tattoos. All forms of the art are represented, from those by indigenous people to those created at carnivals and in prisons. Upstairs, glass cases display tattooing devices, some antique. More photos grace the walls of the warren of small rooms in a never-ending collage. The streetside rooms house a working tattoo parlor.

PACIFIC STAR WINERY

Pacific Star Winery (33000 N. Hwy. 1, 707/964-1155, www.pacificstarwinery.com, 11am-5pm Thurs.-Mon., tasting free) makes the most of its location 12 miles north of Fort Bragg. Barrels of wine are left out in the salt air to age, incorporating a hint of the Pacific into each vintage. Wines are tasty and reasonably priced, and you can bring your own picnic to enjoy on the nearby bluff, which overlooks the ocean.

MENDOCINO COAST BOTANICAL GARDENS

Stretching 47 acres down to the sea, **Mendocino Coast Botanical Gardens** (18220 N. Hwy. 1, 707/964-4352, www.gardenbythesea.org, 9am-5pm daily Mar.-Oct., 9am-4pm daily Nov.-Feb., adults $15, seniors $12, children 6-14 $8, children under 6 free) offer miles of walking through careful plantings and wild landscapes. The star of the gardens is the rhododendron, with 125 species on the grounds. Children can pick up "Quail Trail: A Child's Guide" and enjoy an exploratory adventure.

Entertainment and Events

The **Gloriana Musical Theatre** (Eagles Hall Theatre, 210 N. Corry St., 707/964-7469, www. gloriana.org) seeks to bring music and theater to young people, so they produce major musicals that appeal to kids, such as *Peter Pan*, while *Into the Woods* and *Chicago* appeal mostly to people past their second decade. Local performers star in the two major shows and numerous one-off performances each year.

The Mendocino Coast hosts a number of art events each year. **Art in the Gardens** (18220 N. Hwy. 1, Fort Bragg, www.gardenbythesea.org, Aug., adults $15-20, children under 16 free) takes place at the Mendocino Coast Botanical Gardens. The gardens are decked out with the finest local artwork, food, and wine, and there is music to entertain the crowds who come to eat and drink, and to view and purchase art.

North Coast Brewery Company's **Sequoia Room** (444 N. Main St., 707/964-3400, www. northcoastbrewing.com) hosts jazz shows featuring national touring acts or the local house band in a cabaret environment. The venue holds a crowd of 60 people.

Shopping

Stop in at the **Glass Beach Museum and Gift Shop** (17801 N. Hwy. 1, 707/962-0590, www.glassbeachjewelry.com, 10am-5pm daily) and you can see a wide array of found treasures; hear stories from Captain Cass, a retired sailor and expert glass scavenger; and buy sea glass set in pendants and rings.

Vintage clothing enthusiasts will love **If the Shoe Fits** (337 N. Franklin St., 707/964-2580, 11am-5:30pm Mon.-Thurs. and Sat., 11am-6pm Fri., 11am-2pm Sun.), an eclectic collection of used clothing and accessories for men and women with well-preserved, interesting pieces in good condition.

The Bookstore and Vinyl Cafe (353 Franklin St., 707/964-6559, 10:30am-5pm Mon.-Sat., 11am-3pm Sun.) is a small shop with a well-curated selection of new and used books likely to please discriminating readers. Music lovers can head upstairs where there is a selection of used records for sale.

Sports and Recreation

SPORTFISHING

The Mendocino Coast is an ideal location to watch whales do acrobatics, or to try to land the big one (salmon, halibut, rock cod, or tuna). During Dungeness crab season, you can go out on a crab boat, learn to set pots, and catch your own delectable delicacy.

Many charters leave out of Noyo Harbor in Fort Bragg. The *Trek II* (Noyo Harbor, 707/964-4550, www.anchorcharterboats. com, fishing trips $80-125, two-hour whale-watching $40) offers fishing trips and whale-watching jaunts (Dec.-May). They'll take you rockfishing in summer, crabbing in winter, and chasing after salmon and tuna in season.

The **Noyo Fishing Center** (32440 N. Harbor Dr., Noyo Harbor, 707/964-3000, www.fortbraggfishing.com, half-day fishing trips $100-250, two-hour whale-watching excursion $35) can take you out for salmon or halibut fishing. They'll help you fish for cod and various deep-sea dwellers in season. The twice-daily trips are an intimate experience, with a maximum of six passengers.

HORSEBACK RIDING

What better way to enjoy the rugged cliffs, windy beaches, and quiet forests of the coast than on the back of a horse? **Ricochet Ridge Ranch** (24201 N. U.S. 101, 707/964-9669 or 888/873-5777, www.horse-vacation.com, 9:30am, 11:30am, 1:30pm, and 3:30pm, $60) has one-hour beach trail rides departing four times daily. They also offer longer beach and trail rides, sunset beach rides, and full-fledged riding vacations by reservation.

SURFING

Just south of town is **Hare Creek** (southwest of the intersection of Hwy. 1 and Hwy. 20, north end of the Hare Creek Bridge), one of the region's most popular spots. North of town is **Virgin Creek** (1.5 miles north of Fort Bragg on Hwy. 1), another well-known break. The **Lost Surf Shack** (319 N. Franklin St., 707/961-0889, 10am-6pm daily, surfboards $25/day, wetsuits $15/day) in downtown Fort Bragg rents surfboards and wetsuits.

SPAS

The **Bamboo Garden Spa** (303 N. Main St., Ste. C, 707/962-9396, www.bamboogardenspa. com, 11:30am-8pm Tues.-Sat., massages $95-245) pampers its guests with a wide array of massage, skin, and beauty treatments.

Food

Fort Bragg hosts a **farmers market** (Franklin St. between Laurel and Pine, www.mcfarm. org, 3pm-6pm Wed. May-Oct., 3pm-5pm Nov.-Apr. inside Old Recreation Center Gym) that sells wild-caught seafood, free-range beef, and fresh-baked bread.

BAKERIES AND CAFÉS

Cowlick's Ice Cream (250 N. Main St., 707/962-9271, www.cowlicksicecream.com, 11am-9pm daily) serves delectable handmade ice cream in a variety of flavors. They even serve mushroom ice cream during the famous fall mushroom season. Get the perennial favorites such as vanilla, chocolate, coffee, and strawberry, or try a seasonal flavor (banana daiquiri, cinnamon, green tea). Ice cream from this local, family-owned chain is also sold at the **Mendocino Coast Botanical Gardens** (18220 N. Hwy. 1, 707/964-4352 ext. 20); at **Frankie's Ice Cream Parlor** (44951 Ukiah St., Mendocino, 707/937-2436, www. frankiesmendocino.com, 11am-9pm daily) in Mendocino Village; on the Skunk Train; and at **J. D. Redhouse** (212 S. Main St., Willits, 707/459-1214, 10am-6pm daily).

The **Headlands Coffeehouse** (120 Laurel St., 707/964-1987, www.headlandscoffeehouse.com, 7am-10pm Mon.-Sat., 7am-7pm Sun. summer; 7am-10pm Mon.-Sat., 7am-5pm Sun. winter) is the place to go for a cup of joe. They have 15 different self-serve roasts of coffee, as well as food ranging from breakfast burritos to paninis. There is free live music in the evenings and free Internet access (but no electrical outlets for customers).

Egghead's (326 N. Main St., 707/964-5005,

7am-2pm daily, $6-19) has been serving an enormous menu of breakfast, lunch, and brunch items to satisfy diners for more than 30 years. The menu includes every imaginable omelet combination, cinnamon raisin toast, burritos, Reuben sandwiches, and "flying-monkey potatoes," derived from the *Wizard of Oz* theme that runs through the place.

AMERICAN

The ★ **North Coast Brewing Company** (444 N. Main St., 707/964-3400, www.north-coastbrewing.com, 11:30am-9pm Sun.-Thurs., 11:30am-10pm Fri.-Sat., $15-33) serves seafood, steak, and creative salads, all washed down with a North Coast microbrew. Taste the magic in their Red Seal Ale, Old Rasputin Russian Imperial Stout, and Scrimshaw Pilsner. Sit at the cozy wooden bar in the taproom if you're here for the beer.

Jenny's Giant Burger (940 N. Main St., 707/964-2235, http://jennysgiantburger.com, 10:30am-9pm daily, $4-7) has a 1950s hamburger-stand feel. The burgers are fresh and antibiotic-free, with garden burger and veggie sandwich options. Jenny's followers are devoted, so it can get crowded, but there are a few outdoor tables, and you can always get your order to go.

ITALIAN

Small and almost always packed, the ★ **Piaci Pub & Pizzeria** (120 W. Redwood Ave., 707/961-1133, www.piacipizza.com, 11am-9:30pm Mon.-Thurs., 11am-10pm Fri.-Sat., 4pm-9:30pm Sun., $9-26) has an L-shaped bar and just a few tables, so you may share a table with some strangers. The 16 delicious pizzas range from traditional pepperoni to more creative combinations like pesto, chèvre, pears, prosciutto, and herbs. The Nonnie is a flavorful combination of prosciutto, grilled chicken, mozzarella, herbs, and a garlic sauce on a thin crust. Piaci's has an extensive list of brews, from Belgian-style beers to hearty ales.

Cucina Verona (124 E. Laurel St., 707/964-6844, www.cucinaverona.com, 8am-9pm Mon.-Thurs., 8am-9:30pm Fri.-Sat., 9am-9pm Sun., $12-35) does northern Italian food with touches of Northern California. Menu items run the gamut from butternut squash lasagna to grilled local salmon. Complement your meal with a local wine or beer. Frequent live music provides entertainment.

MEXICAN

Inside a Fort Bragg strip mall, **Los Gallitos** (130 S. Main St., 707/964-4519, 11am-8pm Mon.-Sat., 10am-7pm Sun., $7-16, cash only)

pizza at Piaci Pub & Pizzeria

doesn't look like much. But you know this is a better-than-average taqueria when the thick, fresh tortilla strips and superb salsa hit your table. Everything on the menu, from burritos to tostadas, is what you'd expect, but the attention to little details like the grilled onions and beans on the tasty carne asada torta make this place special.

SEAFOOD
With the small fishing and crabbing fleet of Fort Bragg's Noyo Harbor, it's natural that lots of seafood restaurants are clustered nearby. One spot known for its fish-and-chips is the **Sea Pal Cove Restaurant** (32390 N. Harbor Dr., 707/964-1300, 10am-11pm daily, $6-13, cash only). They also have 18 beers on tap.

THAI
Small and unassuming, **Nit's Café** (322 Main St., 707/964-7187, 11am-2pm and 5pm-9pm Tues.-Sun., $14-26, cash only) specializes in Thai and Asian fusion. Noted for its beautiful presentations of both classic and creative dishes, Nit's gets rave reviews. They have a special of the day and a fresh daily catch of the day.

Accommodations
UNDER $150
A budget option, the **Surf Motel** (1220 S. Main St., 707/964-5361, www.surfmotelfortbragg.com, $95-199) provides a bike-washing station, a fish-cleaning station, an outdoor shower for divers, a garden to stroll through, and an area set aside for horseshoes and barbecues. Your spacious modern guest room comes with breakfast, free wireless Internet access, a microwave, a fridge, and a blow dryer. The two apartments have a kitchen and room for four people.

The stately **Grey Whale Inn** (615 N. Main St., 707/964-0640 or 800/382-7244, www.greywhaleinn.com, $135-190) was once a community hospital. The blocky craftsman-style building was erected by the Union Lumber Company in 1915. Today, 13 spacious, simple rooms offer views of the water or the city. The

lovely, individually decorated rooms feature a private bath and queen or king bed, perhaps covered by an old-fashioned quilt. The inn prides itself on simplicity and friendliness, and its location in downtown Fort Bragg makes visitors feel at home walking to dinner or the beach. It also has a game room with a pool table and foosball.

$150-250
★ **Weller House** (524 Stewart St., 707/964-4415, www.wellerhouse.com, $150-320) is a picture-perfect B&B with elegant Victorian-style rooms, ocean views, and sumptuous home cooking. There are even a few secluded rooms in the old water tower. The manager, Vivien LaMothe, is a tango dancer, and the third floor of the main building—a gorgeous 1886 mansion listed on the National Register of Historic Places—is a ballroom. (There are dance events four times a week.) Weller House is one block west of Main Street and an easy walk to good restaurants and shopping.

The **Beachcomber Motel** (1111 N. Main St., 707/964-2402, www.thebeachcombermotel.com, $139-309) is just north of town right behind Pudding Creek Beach. It's one of the most pet-friendly motels along the coast. Not only are there pet-friendly rooms, but there is a dog park and suites with doggie doors that open up to a fenced-in enclosure with a doghouse. Rooms are equipped with private balconies and decks to take in the bluffs and ocean. Some units even have hot tubs. A deck on the northern end of the property has fire pits and barbecue grills. The motel rents beach cruisers for use on the Coastal Trail at adjacent MacKerricher State Park.

Next door, the ★ **Surf & Sand Lodge** (1131 N. Main St., 707/964-9383, www.surfsandlodge.com, $169-299) is the slightly more upscale sister property of the Beachcomber. Most of the rooms in the six blue buildings have views of headlands and ocean. The trails, tide pools, crashing waves, and broad beaches of MacKerricher State Park are right out front. Every room has a balcony or a porch to take in the view. Opt for a room with a Jacuzzi spa tub to soak in while looking out at the chilly Pacific.

Transportation and Services

Fort Bragg is on Highway 1; driving from San Francisco takes about four hours. The road in any direction is narrow and full of curves; be prepared to make the scenic journey part of the fun. From Willits, take Highway 20 (Fort Bragg-Willits Road) west for 30 miles. The sun pops in and out among the redwood forest and makes you want to use all the pullouts to take photos. There is no cell-phone service along this road, so fill your gas tank before the drive and allow plenty of time to travel these 30 miles.

Fort Bragg has great access to public transportation. The most enjoyable way to get here is to take the **Skunk Train** (707/964-6371, www.skunktrain.com, adults $84, children 2-12 $42, children under 2 $10) from Willits. The **Mendocino Transit Authority** (800/696-4682, http://mendocinotransit.org, $1.50-5.25) has a number of bus lines that pass through Fort Bragg. It also offers **Dial-a-Ride Curb-to-Curb Service** (707/462-3881, 7am-6pm Mon.-Fri., 10am-5pm Sat., adults $6, seniors $3, children under 6 $1.25).

The **Mendocino Coast Chamber of Commerce and Visitors Center** (217 S. Main St., 707/961-6300, www.mendocino-coast.com, 10am-5pm Mon.-Fri., 10am-3pm Sat.) also serves as the Mendocino County film office, which strongly encourages filmmaking in the area. Get the inside story on where to see the filming locations of *Summer of '42,* in which the bluffs of Fort Bragg play the role of Long Island; *East of Eden; Karate Kid III;* and *Humanoids from the Deep.*

The **Mendocino Coast District Hospital** (700 River Dr., at Cypress St., 707/961-1234, www.mcdh.org) has the nearest full-service emergency room.

MACKERRICHER STATE PARK

Three miles north of Fort Bragg, **MacKerricher State Park** (Hwy. 1, 707/964-9112, district office 707/937-5804, www.parks.ca.gov, sunrise-10pm daily, day use free) offers the small, duck-filled Cleone Lake, six miles of sandy ocean beaches, four miles of cliffs and crags, and camping. The main attraction is a gigantic, almost complete skeleton of a whale near the park entrance. If you're lucky, you can also spot live whales and harbor seals frolicking in the ocean. The coast can be rough here, so don't swim or wade unless it's what

Pudding Creek Beach in MacKerricher State Park

the locals call a "flat day"—no big waves and undertow. If the kids want to play in the water, take them to **Pudding Creek Beach** in the park, about 2.5 miles south of the campground, where they can enjoy the relatively sheltered area under the trestle bridge.

The hike to take is the **Ten Mile Beach Trail** (10 miles round-trip, moderate), starting at the Laguna Point Parking Area at the north end of Fort Bragg and running five miles up to the Ten Mile River. Most of this path is fairly level and paved. It's an easy walk, and you can turn around whenever you want. Street bikes and inline skates are also allowed.

Campground (800/444-7275, www.reservecalifornia.com, $35) reservations are recommended April 1-October 15, and they're site-specific. In winter, camping is first-come, first-served. The park has 107 sites suitable for tents and RVs (up to 35 feet) in its wooded and pleasant West Pinewood and East Pinewood Campgrounds; there are also a group campground and walk-in hike-and-bike sites. Restrooms with flush toilets as well as hot showers are provided, and each campsite has a fire ring, picnic table, and food storage locker.

WESTPORT

Westport is 16 miles north of Fort Bragg, with its own patch of ocean, a few essential services, and one lodging gem. It's the last settlement before the wild Lost Coast.

Food and Accommodations

Inside the Westport Hotel is the **Old Abalone Pub** (3892 Hwy. 1, 707/964-3688 or 877/964-3688, www.westporthotel.us, 5pm-9pm Thurs.-Fri., 3pm-9pm Sat., 10am-2pm and 5pm-9pm Sun., $10-25). Thanks to a large mirror over the bar, everyone in the dining room gets an ocean view.

The motto at the ★ **Westport Hotel** (3892 Hwy. 1, 707/964-3688 or 877/964-3688, www.westporthotel.us, $150-225) is, "At last, you've found nowhere." The Westport Hotel is marvelous and private, perfect for a honeymoon spent in luxury and comfort. Each of the six rooms has one bed and a bath with

fixtures that blend perfectly into the historic 1890 house. Some rooms have small private balconies overlooking the waves, and all guests have access to the redwood sauna. Fresh scones, fruit, and coffee are delivered to your room in the morning, and a full hot breakfast is served in the dining room.

Camping is available two miles north of Westport at **Westport-Union Landing State Beach** (Hwy. 1, 707/937-5804, www.parks.ca.gov, $25), with 86 first-come, first-served sites. There are no showers or other amenities—just the cliffs, the waves, the sunsets, and the views.

INLAND MENDOCINO COUNTY

About 60 miles east of the coast (a 1.5-hour scenic drive), Mendocino's interior valley is home to history, art, and wine. The Anderson Valley is the apex of Mendocino's wine region, the tiny town of Hopland also has its share of tasting rooms, and Ukiah is home to several microbreweries.

The interior valleys of Mendocino get hot in the summer. Bring shorts, a swimsuit, and an air-conditioned car if you plan to visit June-September.

Anderson Valley
WINERIES AND BREWERIES

The **Anderson Valley Wine Trail** (Hwy. 128) begins in Boonville and continues northwest toward the coast, with most of the wineries clustered between Boonville and Navarro.

A big name in the Anderson Valley, **Scharffenberger Cellars** (8501 Hwy. 128, Philo, 707/895-2957, www.scharffenbergercellars.com, 11am-5pm daily, $3) makes wine in Mendocino. Its tasting room is elegant and child-friendly, decorated with the work of local artists.

A broad-ranging winery with a large estate vineyard and event center, **Navarro Vineyards** (5601 Hwy. 128, Philo, 707/895-3686 or 800/537-9463, www.navarrowine.com, 8am-6pm daily summer, 8am-5pm daily winter, free) offers a range of tasty wines as

Mendocino Wine Country

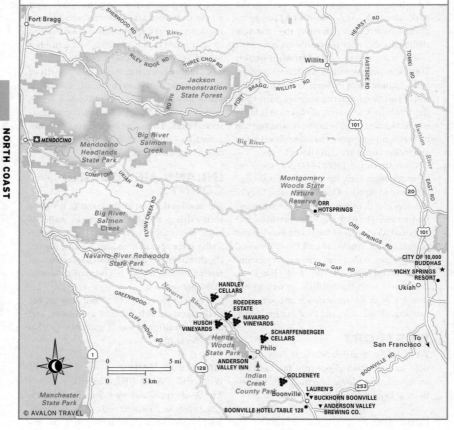

well as some interesting specialty products such as the nonalcoholic verjus.

Roederer Estate (4501 Hwy. 128, Philo, 707/895-2288, www.roedererestate.com, 11am-5pm daily, $6) sparkling wines are some of the best of the state. The large tasting room features a bar with sweeping views of the estate vineyards and huge cases filled with well-deserved awards. Pourers are knowledgeable, and you'll get to taste from magnum bottles—a rarity at any winery. Ask for a taste of Roederer's rarely seen still wines.

Handley Cellars (3151 Hwy. 128, Philo, 800/733-3151, www.handleycellars.com, 10am-6pm daily summer, 10am-5pm daily winter, free) offers a complimentary tasting of handcrafted wines. The intriguing tasting room features folk art from around the world. Books on wine are sold, especially those that focus on women making and drinking wine.

Toulouse Vineyards (8001 Hwy. 128, Philo, 707/895-2828, http://toulousevineyards. com, 11am-5pm daily) is the kind of small operation where the winemaker's dog will greet you upon arrival. Known for pinot noir, they also do a pinot gris and a Gewürztraminer.

Anderson Valley Brewing Company (17700 Hwy. 253, Boonville, 707/895-2337, www.avbc.com, 11am-6pm Sat.-Thurs., 11am-7pm Fri. summer; winter hours vary) serves up an array of microbrews that change each season and year. The warehouse-size beer hall feels like a wine-tasting room, with a bar, tables, and a good-size gift shop. A beer garden out back is comfortable in spring and fall, and the disc golf course is popular with travelers and locals.

FOOD

The Buckhorn (14081 Hwy. 128, Boonville, 707/895-3224, kitchen: 11am-9pm Mon. and Wed.-Fri., 10am-9pm Sat.-Sun., bar: 11am-11pm Sun.-Mon. and Wed.-Thurs., 11am-midnight Fri.-Sat., $11-32) has more than 40 local wines and 14 beers on tap, many from nearby Anderson Valley Brewing Company. They also do big portions of good food including burgers and hot sandwiches such as a worthwhile French dip.

Farmers markets and farm stands abound in the Anderson Valley. The **Boonville Farmers Market** (14050 Hwy. 128, Boonville, www.mcfarm.org, 10am-12:30pm Sat. May-Oct.) draws a crowd, so be prepared to hunt for parking. **Gowan's Oak Tree Farm Stand** (6600 Hwy. 128, 2.5 miles north of Philo, 707/895-3353, www.gowansoaktree.com, 8am-7pm daily June-Aug., 8am-6pm daily Sept.-Oct., 8:30am-5:30pm daily Nov.-May) belongs to the local Gowan's Oak Tree Farm and sells in-season local produce and homemade products made with the same fruits and veggies.

ACCOMMODATIONS

The **Anderson Valley Inn** (8480 Hwy. 128, Philo, 707/895-3325, www.avinn.com, $95-190), between Boonville and Philo, makes the perfect spot from which to divide your time between the Anderson Valley and the Mendocino Coast. Six small rooms are done up in bright colors, homey bedspreads, and attractive appointments. A butterfly-filled garden invites guests to sit out on the porches. Two suites have full kitchens and are perfect for longer stays. The friendly owners welcome children and dogs in the suites and can offer hints about how best to explore the region. This inn often fills quickly on summer weekends, as it's one of the best values in the region. There's a two-night minimum on weekends April-November.

The quaint **Boonville Hotel** (14050 Hwy. 128, 707/895-2210, www.boonvillehotel.com, $155-395) has a rough, weathered exterior that contrasts with the 15 contemporary rooms, each of which is bright and airy and has earth-tone furniture and mismatched decorations. Downstairs are spacious common areas and a huge garden. Amenities include a bookshop and a gift shop, a good-size bar, and a dining room. Book one of the rooms with a balcony, which comes with a hammock, or a guest room with an outdoor bathtub. Child- and pet-friendly rooms are available on request.

CAMPING

The campgrounds at **Indian Creek County Park** (Hwy. 128 at mile marker 23.48, 1 mile east of Philo, 707/463-4291, www.co.mendocino.ca.us, $25) are budget-friendly. Eight miles northwest of Boonville is **Hendy Woods State Park** (18599 Philo-Greenwood Rd., Philo, 800/444-7275, www.reservecalifornia.com, campsites $40, cabins $55), with woodsy, shaded campsites along with four rustic cabins with wood-burning stoves.

TRANSPORTATION

Highway 128 departs the Mendocino Coast approximately 10 miles south of Mendocino. From Mendocino, drive south on Highway 1 to the junction with Highway 128 and turn east. Follow Highway 128 east for 30 miles to the town of Boonville.

From Boonville, it's possible to continue east to U.S. 101, which accesses Ukiah (north) and Hopland (south).

Many of the major wine-country touring outfits operate in the Anderson Valley. **Mendo Wine Tours** (707/937-0289 or 800/609-0492, http://www.maccallumhouse.com/wine-tours, group tours $175 pp, private tours for two $500-650) is a regional specialist that offers a Lincoln Town Car for small groups and an SUV limo for groups of up to 10.

Hopland

This small farming town is on the upper section of the Russian River. The **Solar Living Center** (13771 S. U.S. 101, 707/472-2460, http://solarliving.org, 9am-6:30pm daily) is a "12-acre sustainable living demonstration site," showing, among other things, what life might be like without petroleum. Exhibits include permaculture, an organic garden, and a demonstration of solar-powered water systems. Guided **tours** (707/472-2460, 11am and 3pm Sat.-Sun. Apr.-Oct., $5/person, $10/family) are available.

The on-site **Real Goods** (707/472-2403, 10am-6pm daily summer, 10am-5pm daily winter) is also a draw for visitors; the completely recycled restrooms are worth a look. If your vehicle happens to run on biodiesel, you can fill your tank here.

WINERIES

Hopland's wineries are the perfect place to relax, enjoy sipping each vintage, and chat with the pourer, who just might be the winemaker and owner. Most of the tasting rooms are along U.S. 101, which runs through the center of town.

The star is **Brutocao Cellars** (13500 S. U.S. 101, 800/433-3689, www.brutocaocellars.com, 10am-5pm daily, free), which has vineyards that surround the town. The wide, stone-tiled tasting room and restaurant complex house exceptional wines poured by knowledgeable staff. A sizable gift shop offers gourmet goodies under the Brutocao label, and there are six regulation bocce ball courts. A second tasting room is in the Anderson Valley (7000 Hwy. 128, Philo, 800/661-2103, www.brutocaocellars.com, 10am-5pm daily, free).

Heading north, the highway passes through acres of vineyards, many of which belong to **Jeriko** (12141 Hewlett and Sturtevant Rd., 707/744-1140, www.jerikoestate.com, 10am-5pm daily summer, 11am-4pm daily winter,

$10). A glass wall exposes the barrel room, stacked high with aging wines.

FOOD

The casual **Bluebird Café & Catering Company** (13340 S. U.S. 101, 707/744-1633, 7am-2pm Wed.-Mon., $17-20) does wild game, including bison burgers. The **Hopland Tap House** (13551 S. Hwy. 101, 707/744-1255, http://hoplandtaphouse.com, noon-9pm Wed.-Sat., noon-6pm Sun., $9-14) is located within a historic brick building. The eight craft beers on tap go nicely with the small menu of burgers, hot dogs, paninis, and salads.

TRANSPORTATION

Hopland is inland on U.S. 101, about 15 miles south of Ukiah and 28 miles east of the Anderson Valley via Highway 253.

Ukiah

Ukiah's low-key, historic downtown has some worthwhile restaurants and shops. The surrounding area is home to organic wineries, the largest Buddhist monastery in the country, and historic mineral springs.

CITY OF 10,000 BUDDHAS

The **City of 10,000 Buddhas** (4951 Bodhi Way, 707/462-0939, www.cttbusa.org, 8am-6pm daily) is an active Buddhist college and monastery. The showpiece is the temple, which contains 10,000 golden Buddha statues. An extensive gift shop sells souvenirs as well as scholarly texts on Buddhism. For a treat, stop in for lunch at the **Jyun Kang Vegetarian Restaurant** (707/468-7966, 11:30am-3pm Wed.-Mon., $7), which is open to the public.

The monastery asks that guests wear modest clothing and keep their voices down out of respect for the nuns and monks who live here.

GRACE HUDSON MUSEUM AND SUN HOUSE

The **Grace Hudson Museum** (431 S. Main St., 707/467-2836, www.gracehudsonmuseum.

org, 10am-4:30pm Wed.-Sat., noon-4:30pm Sun., adults $4, seniors and students $3, family $10) focuses on the life and work of the artist Grace Hudson and her husband, Dr. John Hudson. The museum's permanent collection includes many of Grace's paintings, a number of Pomo baskets, and the works of dozens of other California artists. The 1911 craftsman-style **Sun House** (docent-guided tours available with museum ticket, noon-3pm Wed.-Sun.) was the Hudsons' home.

VICHY SPRINGS RESORT

Established in 1854, **Vichy Springs Resort** (2605 Vichy Springs Rd., 707/462-9515, www.vichysprings.com, 9am-dusk daily, baths $35/two hours, $65/day) has been patronized by Mark Twain, Jack London, Ulysses S. Grant, Teddy Roosevelt, and California governor Jerry Brown. The hot springs, mineral-heavy and naturally carbonated, closely resemble the world-famous waters of their namesake at Vichy in France and spill into indoor and outdoor concrete tubs. Services include the baths, a hot pool, and an Olympic-size swimming pool as well as a day spa. The serene 700-acre property also has 12 miles of trails.

FOOD

Local favorite **Stan's Maple Restaurant** (295 S. State St., 707/462-5221, www.stansmaplecafe.com, 7am-2pm daily, $6-14) serves tasty breakfasts and lunches. Excellent service complements good, American-style food. Shockingly good coffee is a charming final touch.

For a cool, relaxing breather on a hot day, visit one of the three locations of **Schat's Bakery Café** (www.schats.com; 113 W. Perkins St., 707/462-1670, 5:30am-6pm Mon.-Fri., 5:30am-5pm Sat.; 1255A Airport Park Blvd., 707/468-5850, 7am-8pm Mon.-Fri., 7am-7pm Sat., 8am-7pm Sun.; 1000 Hensley Creek Rd., 707/468-3145, 7am-8:15pm Mon.-Thurs., 7am-3pm Fri., $5-12) for a quick, filling sandwich on fresh-baked bread. Enjoy it in the large, airy dining room.

Ellie's Mutt Hut & Vegetarian Café
(732 S. State St., 707/468-5376, http://ellies-mutthutukiahca.com, 6:30am-8pm Mon.-Sat., $8-15) has great vegetarian entrées and an impressive hot dog list. The atmosphere is hamburger-stand casual, and the food is mostly healthy.

At **Patrona** (130 W. Standley St., 707/462-9181, www.patronarestaurant.com, 11am-9pm Mon.-Fri., 10am-9pm Sat.-Sun., $13-29), innovative California cuisine is served in a bistro-casual atmosphere by solicitous servers. The kitchen's attention to detail is impressive. The wine list features Mendocino County vintages, plus a good range of European wines.

Ukiah Brewing Company & Restaurant (102 S. State St., 707/468-5898, http://ukiahbrewing.com, 11am-9pm Sun.-Thurs., 11am-10pm Fri.-Sat., $11-28) has a wide menu that includes pizzas, sandwiches, salads, steak frites, and a chef's tasting menu, but it's the house-blended burgers on brioche buns that shine. Order the burger with bacon jam, white cheddar, and aioli. They also serve Ukiah Brewing Co. beer, which is brewed on-site.

ACCOMMODATIONS

Lodgings in Ukiah tend to be standard chain motels. Out by the airport, the **Fairfield Inn** (1140 Airport Park Blvd., 707/463-3600, www.marriott.com, $179) is a good choice, with an indoor pool and spa, a small exercise room, laundry facilities, and a generous complimentary continental breakfast. Rooms are what you'd expect: floral bedspreads, durable, nondescript carpet, and clean baths.

For a peaceful retreat, the best choice is ★ **Vichy Springs Resort** (2605 Vichy Springs Rd., 707/462-9515, www.vichysprings.com, $175-445). Rooms in the genteel and rustic inn and nearby cottages are small but comfortable, with private baths, warm bedspreads, and cool breezes; many have views of the mountains or creek. Two of the cottages date to 1852. Use of the pools and hiking trails is included in the rates, as are Internet access and a buffet breakfast.

TRANSPORTATION AND SERVICES

Ukiah is located on U.S. 101, about 15 miles north of Hopland, 22 miles east of Boonville, and 60 miles east of the Mendocino Coast.

To reach Ukiah from Boonville, turn east at the junction of Highways 128 and 253, and continue 22 miles to U.S. 101.

The Mendocino Transit Authority (800/696-4682, http://mendocinotransit.org) runs bus service throughout the county, with Ukiah as the hub; you can catch buses here and in Mendocino and Fort Bragg. Private pilots can land at Ukiah Municipal Airport (UKI, 1411 S. State St., 707/467-2817, www.cityofukiah.com).

The Ukiah Valley Medical Center (275 Hospital Dr., 707/462-3111, www.uvmc.org) has a 24-hour emergency room as part of its full-service facility.

The Redwood Coast

Of all the natural wonders California has to offer, the one that seems to inspire the purest and most unmitigated awe is the giant redwood. The coast redwood, *Sequoia sempervirens,* grows along the California coast from around Big Sur in the south and into southern Oregon in the north. Coast redwoods hold the records for the tallest trees ever recorded, and are among the world's oldest and all-around most massive living things. The two best places to experience extensive wild groves of these gargantuan treasures are Humboldt Redwoods State Park, in Humboldt County, and Redwood National and State Parks, near the north end of California around Eureka and Crescent City.

Most of the major park areas along the Redwood Coast can be accessed via U.S. 101 and U.S. 199. Follow the signs to the smaller roads that lead farther from civilization. To get to the redwood parks from the south, drive up U.S. 101 or the much slower but prettier Highway 1. The two roads merge at Leggett, north of Fort Bragg, and continue north as U.S. 101.

LEGGETT

As Highway 1 heads inland toward Leggett, the ocean views are replaced with redwoods. This part of the road is curvy, winding, and sun-dappled. It's a beautiful drive, so take it slow.

At the junction of Highway 1 and U.S. 101, you'll enter Leggett, famed for the local attraction Chandelier Drive-Thru Tree (67402 Drive-Thru Tree Rd., 707/925-6464, www.drivethrutree.com, hours and dates vary, $5). The tree opening is about six feet wide and a little over six feet high. Kids will be thrilled. And of course, there's a gift shop.

The Peg House (69501 U.S. 101, 707/925-6444, http://thepeghouse.com), which was built with pegs instead of nails, gets raves for its burgers, tri-tip, Humboldt Bay oysters, and deli sandwiches. Sometimes there is live music.

GARBERVILLE AND REDWAY

Garberville is the first real town in Humboldt County. Just three miles northwest is the slightly larger town of Redway, with just a few hundred more residents. Known as the "Gateway to the Avenue of the Giants," both towns are good places to get a meal or fill your tank with gas before heading west to the coast or north to the redwoods.

Richardson Grove State Park

Richardson Grove State Park (1600 U.S. 101, 707/247-3318, www.parks.ca.gov, daily sunrise-sunset, $8) is the first with old-growth redwoods along U.S. 101. This park has special features, like a tree you can walk through and the ninth-tallest coast redwood. The Eel River flows through the park, offering good fishing as well as camping, swimming, and hiking.

The Redwood Coast

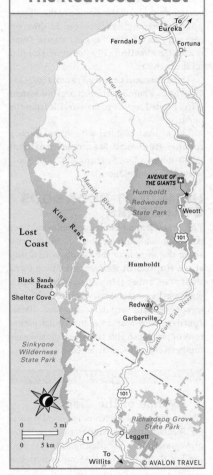

To Eureka

Ferndale

Fortuna

Bear River

AVENUE OF THE GIANTS

Humboldt Redwoods State Park

Weott

101

Mattole River

King Range

Lost Coast

Humboldt

Black Sands Beach

Shelter Cove

Redway

Garberville

South Fork Eel River

Sinkyone Wilderness State Park

101

Richardson Grove State Park

0   5 mi

0   5 km

Leggett

1

To Willits

© AVALON TRAVEL

The visitors center (May-Sept.) in the 1930s Richardson Grove Lodge has cool exhibits and a nature store. Richardson Grove State Park is seven miles south of Garberville.

Festivals and Events

The **Mateel Community Center** (59 Rusk Ln., Redway, 707/923-3368, www.mateel.org) brings music, theater, dance, comedy, film, and craft events to southern Humboldt. They also put on local annual events, including the Summer Arts & Music Festival, the Humboldt Hills Hoedown, and Winter Arts Faire.

Food

The restaurant at the ★ **Benbow Inn** (445 Lake Benbow Dr., Garberville, 707/923-2124 or 800/355-3301, www.benbowinn.com, 8am-3pm and 5pm-9:30pm daily, $19-45) serves upscale California cuisine (a vegan menu is available on request) and features an extensive wine list with many regional wineries represented. The white-tablecloth dining room is exquisite, and the expansive outdoor patio overlooking the water is the perfect place to sit as the temperature cools on a summer evening.

An easy place to stop for a pick-me-up, **Flavors Coffeehouse** (767 Redwood Dr., Garberville, 707/923-7717, 7am-7pm daily, $5-11) refuels with a menu of caffeine drinks, sandwiches, paninis, and salads. The build-your-own-grilled-cheese-sandwich option lets you add ingredients including bacon and roasted bell peppers. A good breakfast and lunch stop is the **Eel River Café** (801 Redwood Dr., 707/923-3783, 6am-2pm Tues.-Sat., $6-12), a diner with black-and-white checkerboard floors and a long counter with red stools. Try the chicken-fried steak with biscuits and gravy. You can't miss the old-school sign towering above the establishment.

You can enjoy a taste of local Humboldt-roasted coffee at **Signature Coffee** (3455 Redwood Dr., Redway, 707/923-2661, www.signaturecoffeecompany.com, 7am-5pm Mon.-Fri.), which takes pride in its organic products and sustainable practices.

Enjoy a classic roadhouse experience at **The Riverwood Inn** (2828 Avenue of the Giants, Phillipsville, 707/943-3333, https://theriverwoodinn.com, 3pm-midnight Mon.-Thurs., 11am-midnight Fri.-Sun., $80-98), six miles north of Garberville. This classic tavern was one of the few buildings that survived the Eel River flood of 1964. Come for the tasty Mexican food and stay for the live music Friday and Saturday nights. There's also five hotel rooms upstairs.

Ray's Food Place (875 Redwood Dr., 707/923-2279, www.gorays.com, 7am-11pm daily) is a supermarket in Garberville.

Accommodations

The best place to stay is the ★ **Benbow Inn** (445 Lake Benbow Dr., Garberville, 707/923-2124 or 800/355-3301, www.benbowinn.com, $195-400). A swank resort backing onto Lake Benbow, this inn has it all: a gourmet restaurant, a nine-hole golf course, an outdoor swimming pool, and a woodsy atmosphere that blends perfectly with the ancient redwood forest surrounding it. Rooms glow with dark polished woods and jewel-toned carpets. Wide king and comfy queen beds beckon guests tired after a long day of hiking in the redwoods or golfing beside the inn.

Several small motels offer reasonable rooms, and many have outdoor pools. The best of these is the **Best Western Humboldt House Inn** (701 Redwood Dr., Garberville, 707/923-2771, www.bestwestern.com, $179-239). Rooms are clean and comfortable, the pool is sparkling and cool, the breakfast is hot, and the location is convenient to restaurants and shops in Garberville. Most rooms have two queen beds.

Camping

Richardson Grove State Park (1600 U.S. 101, 800/444-7275, www.reservecalifornia. com, camping $35) has 169 campsites in three campground areas surrounded by redwoods and the Elk River.

You can park your RV year-round at the 112 sites of the posh **Benbow RV Park** (7000 Benbow Dr., Garberville, 707/923-2777, www.benbowrv.com, campsites $46-85, cabins $75-400). Premium sites come with complimentary tea and scones at the nearby Benbow Inn.

Transportation and Services

Garberville is 65 miles south of Eureka and 200 miles north of San Francisco on U.S. 101. From Garberville, take Redwood Drive just three miles to Redway. The best way to get to Humboldt Redwoods State Park is via U.S.

101. Road signs point to the Avenue of the Giants. Bicycles are not permitted on U.S. 101, but you can ride on the Avenue of the Giants.

The towns in this region can be short on necessary services such as gas stations. There is a **76 Gas Station** (790 Redwood Dr.) just off the highway.

The **Redwood County Transit** (707/443-0826, https://humboldttransit.org) bus system offers limited service to Garberville from the north.

The nearest hospital with an emergency room is **Redwood Memorial Hospital** (3300 Renner Dr., Fortuna, 707/725-3361, www.stjoehumboldt.org).

HUMBOLDT REDWOODS STATE PARK

The largest stand of unlogged redwood trees is in Humboldt, bisected by U.S. 101. A drive along the Avenue of the Giants with a stop at the **Humboldt Redwoods State Park Visitors Center** (Hwy. 254, 707/946-2263, www.parks.ca.gov or www.humboldtredwoods.org, 9am-5pm daily Apr.-Oct., 10am-4pm daily Nov.-Mar., free) and a quick nature walk or picnic can give you a taste of the lovely southern end of the coastal redwoods region.

TOP EXPERIENCE

★ Avenue of the Giants

The most famous stretch of redwood trees is the **Avenue of the Giants** (www.avenue-ofthegiants.net), paralleling U.S. 101 and the Eel River for about 33 miles between Garberville and Fortuna; look for signs on U.S. 101. Visitors drive this stretch of road and gaze in wonder at the sky-high old-growth redwoods along the way. Campgrounds and hiking trails sprout amid the trees off the road. It's easy to park your car at various points along the way and get out to walk among the giants or down to the nearby Eel River for a cool dip.

The Avenue's highest traffic volume is in July-August, when you can expect bumper-to-bumper traffic along the entire road. That's

redwood trees along the Avenue of the Giants

nature walk with helpful signs describing the denizens of the forest.

For a longer walk, try the lovely **River Trail** (Mattole Rd., 1.1 miles west of Ave. of the Giants, 7 miles round-trip, moderate) as it follows the South Fork Eel River. Check with the visitors center to be sure that the summer bridges have been installed before hiking this trail.

Hard-core hikers can get their exercise on the **Grasshopper Multiuse Trailhead** (Mattole Rd., 5.1 miles west of Ave. of the Giants), which accesses the **Johnson Camp Trail** (10.5 miles round-trip, difficult) to the abandoned cabins of railroad tie makers. Or pick another fork from the same trailhead to climb more than 3,000 feet to **Grasshopper Peak** (13.5 miles, difficult). From the peak, you can see 100 miles in any direction.

You can bring your street bike to the park and ride the Avenue of the Giants or Mattole Road. A number of the trails around Humboldt Redwoods State Park are designated multiuse, which means that mountain bikers can make the rigorous climbs and then rip their way back down.

Swimming and Kayaking

The **Eel River**'s forks meander through the Humboldt redwoods, creating great opportunities for cooling off on hot summer days. Reliably good spots include **Eagle Point,** near Hidden Valley Campground; **Gould Bar;** and **Garden Club of America Grove.** In addition to the usual precautions for river swimming, a blue-green algae (poisonous if ingested) can bloom August-September, making swimming in certain parts of the river hazardous.

Events

Humboldt Redwoods State Park is the site of a couple of excellent marathons and half-marathons. These events are also less crowded than more famous marathons, and you can camp right in the park where they begin. October has the **Humboldt Redwoods Marathon** (www.redwoodsmarathon.org, Oct., $75-95)

not necessarily a bad thing: Going slow is the best way to see the sights. But if crowds aren't your thing, visit in spring or fall, or brave the rains of winter to gain a more secluded redwood experience.

To enhance your Avenue of the Giants drive, there's an eight-stop audio tour along the route. Pick up an audio tour card at the visitors center or on either side of the drive.

Hiking and Biking

Start with the **Founder's Grove Nature Loop Trail** (0.6 mile, easy), at mile marker 20.5 on the Avenue of the Giants. This sedate, flat nature trail gives a taste of the big old-growth trees in the park. Sadly, the onetime tallest tree in the world, the Dyerville Giant, fell in 1991 at the age of about 1,600. But it's still doing its part in this astounding ecosystem, decomposing before your eyes on the forest floor and feeding new life in the forest.

Right at the visitors center, you can enjoy the **Gould Grove Nature Trail** (0.6 mile, easy), a wheelchair-accessible interpretive with a related half-marathon ($65-75) and a 5K ($25-35). The Avenue of the Giants Marathon (www.theave.org, marathon $75-95, half-marathon $65-85, 10K $40-60) is held each May.

Camping
Humboldt Redwoods State Park (707/946-2263, www.reservecalifornia. com, $35) has three developed, car-accessible campgrounds; there are also primitive backcountry campsites ($5). Each developed campground has its own entrance station, and reservations are strongly recommended, as the park is quite popular with weekend campers.

Burlington Campground (707/946-1811, year-round) is adjacent to the visitors center and is a convenient starting point for the marathons and races that traverse the park in May and October. It's shaded and comfortable, engulfed in trees, and has ample restroom facilities and hot showers. **Albee Creek** (Mattole Rd., 5 miles west of Ave. of the Giants, 707/946-2472, mid-May-mid-Oct.) offers some redwood-shaded sites and others in open meadows. ★ **Hidden Springs Campground** (Ave. of the Giants, 5 miles south of the visitors center, 707/943-3177, early May-Labor Day) is large and popular. Nearby, a trail leads to a great Eel River swimming hole. Minimalist campers will enjoy the seclusion of hike-in trail camps at **Johnson Camp** and **Grasshopper Peak**.

Equestrians can make use of the multiuse trails, and the **Cuneo Creek Horse Camp** (old homestead on Mattole Rd., 8 miles west of Ave. of the Giants, May-mid-Oct., 1 vehicle and 2 horses $35) provides a place for riders.

Transportation and Services
Humboldt Redwoods State Park is 21 miles north of Garberville on U.S. 101. The Avenue of the Giants parallels U.S. 101, and there are several marked exits along the highway to reach the scenic redwood drive.

Fill your gas tank in the nearby towns of Piercy, Garberville, Redway, Redcrest, Miranda, and Rio Dell. Markets to stock up on supplies are in Garberville, Redway, Miranda, Phillipsville, Redcrest, Myers Flat, Scotia, and Rio Dell.

The nearest hospital with an emergency room is **Redwood Memorial Hospital** (3300 Renner Dr., Fortuna, 707/725-3361, www.stjoehumboldt.org).

The Lost Coast

The Lost Coast is one of California's last undeveloped coastlines. Encompassing northern Mendocino County and southern Humboldt County, this coast is "lost" because the rugged terrain makes it impractical—some might say impossible—to build a highway here. An arduous trek along its wilderness trails is worthwhile to soak up the raw beauty of its rugged beaches.

The small fishing community of Shelter Cove is situated between the King Range Conservation Area and Sinkyone Wilderness State Park. The town has a few restaurant and lodging options and is also home to Black Sand Beach and the Cape Mendocino Lighthouse.

SINKYONE WILDERNESS STATE PARK
Encompassing the southern section of the Lost Coast, the Sinkyone Wilderness State Park (707/247-3318, www.parks.ca.gov, sunrise-sunset daily, $6) is a wild region of steep coastal mountains and surf-pounded beaches spotted with wildlife, including bears and elk. The Roosevelt elk had disappeared from the region until a herd from Prairie Creek State Park was reintroduced here. With their impressive antlers, the elk bulls usually weigh 700-1,100 pounds and can be quite a sight to see in the wild.

The Sinkyone Wilderness has a 16-mile

Lost Coast Trail that starts at Bear Harbor, south of Needle Rock, and ends at Usal Beach. This trail takes backpackers 2-3 days and has more climbing than the Lost Coast Trail to the north. The rigorous hike is mostly on bluffs above the coastline. It passes through virgin redwood groves and mixed forest with beach access at Wheeler Beach.

Needle Rock

The most easily accessible spot in the northern Sinkyone is Needle Rock, the former site of a small settlement and the current location of a park visitors center. The area's namesake rock is nearby on a black-sand beach. Visitors can camp at three environmental campsites (first-come, first-served, $25), three miles from the visitors center, as well as at an old barn (first-come, first-served, $30) close to the visitors center. Camping is done by self-registration. Needle Rock's visitors center was once a ranch house. Now it is staffed by a volunteer year-round. The visitors center has information on the region's history and various artifacts. You can also purchase maps and firewood.

To reach Needle Rock, head off U.S. 101 at the Garberville exit and take Redwood Road to Redway. Drive Briceland Road in Redway until it becomes Mendocino County Road 435. The road dead-ends into the state park. The last 3.5 miles are unpaved, steep, and narrow.

Usal Beach

At the southern tip of Sinkyone Wilderness State Park, Usal Beach is a remote, two-mile-long black-sand beach situated under cliffs bristling with massive trees. It's accessible to adventurous coastal explorers via a steep, unpaved six-mile dirt road that is not for the fainthearted or the squeamish. Passenger cars can make the drive until the winter rainy season, when four-wheel drive becomes necessary.

When you reach the beach, you can fish from shore or beachcomb the sandy expanse. Watch sea lions torpedo through the ocean

and pelicans splash into the water looking for food. Facilities include 35 primitive drive-in campsites (first come, first served, $25) with picnic tables, fire pits, and pit toilets. The rangers come here to collect the camping fees on some days, but otherwise you self-register to camp. Be aware that although firearms are not allowed in the park, locals sometimes shoot guns at night here.

From Fort Bragg, drive 25 miles north on Highway 1 to Rockport. Usal Beach is accessible from a dirt road that leaves Highway 1 three miles north of Rockport. Turn left on an unmarked road at mile marker 90.88.

SHELTER COVE

Get a taste of the Lost Coast in Shelter Cove, a fishing community with a scattering of restaurants and accommodations and access to the shoreline.

Black Sand Beach

One of the most beautiful and accessible features of the Lost Coast, the 3.5-mile Black Sand Beach (King Range National Conservation Area, www.blm.gov) is named for its unusually dark sand and stones, which contrast with the deep-blue ocean water and the towering King Range Mountains in the background. The main beach parking lot has interpretive panels about the region as well as bathrooms and a drinking fountain. It's just north of the town of Shelter Cove; to get there, follow Shelter Cove Road and then take a right onto Beach Road, which dead-ends at Black Sand Beach. The long walk across the dark sands to either Horse Creek or Gitchell Creek is relatively easy. This beach also serves as the south end of the Lost Coast Trail.

Cape Mendocino Lighthouse

At Mal Coombs Park, the 43-foot tower of the Cape Mendocino Lighthouse (www.lighthousefriends.com, tours 11am-3pm daily Memorial Day-Labor Day) is quiet and dark. It began life on Cape Mendocino—a 400-foot cliff that marks the westernmost point

Hiking the Lost Coast

Start: Mattole Beach
End: Black Sand Beach (Shelter Cove)
24 Miles One-Way / 3 Days

To fully experience one of the country's most remote and rugged coastal areas, backpackers head out on the **Lost Coast Trail.** This 24-mile beach hike stretches from the Mattole River south to Shelter Cove's Black Sand Beach. This is a once-in-a-lifetime experience that offers hiking alongside primal, mostly wild coastline, interrupted only by the abandoned Punta Gorda Lighthouse and numerous shipwrecks along the shore. Waterfalls feather the coastal bluffs, shorebirds fly above the crashing surf, sea lions congregate at the aptly named Sea Lion Gulch, and migrating whales surface along the horizon. On land, you might encounter deer and bears.

This is a strenuous hike, challenging even for experienced hikers. It demands both preparation and stamina. While scenic, the ocean along the trail is also cold, rough, and unforgiving. Use caution, as multiple people have been swept out to sea.

Planning: You can hike the trail anytime between **spring and fall.** Spring is notable for blooming wildflowers. Summer is the most crowded. Fall is the least crowded and often has the most pleasant weather. During winter, the trail can be impassable due to massive surf or flooding streams.

Most hikers start at the **Mattole River.** (Heading south, the wind is at your back, rather than in your face.) Allow **three days** and **two nights** to complete the trail, hiking around eight miles a day. Be prepared to walk on sand, cobblestones, and boulders. Plan on carrying in everything you'll need (tents, sleeping bags, equipment, food, and water). Carry it all (including any trash) back out to keep the area wild. There are creeks every 1.5-2 miles along the trail, but you need to purify the water before drinking it.

This is a wilderness hike, so there are few signs. You'll mostly just be hiking the beach except at a few spots. Two sections of the trail are impassable at high tide: The first is from Sea Lion Gulch to Randall Creek, and the second is from south of Big Flat down to Gitchell Creek. It's critical that you **consult a tide chart** and manage your time to make sure you pass through these areas of the trail during low tide.

---

of California—in 1868. In 1951 the tower was abandoned in favor of a light on a pole, and in 1999 the tower was moved to Shelter Cove, becoming a museum in 2000. When docents are available, you can take a tour of the lighthouse. The original first-order Fresnel lens is now on display in nearby Ferndale.

Sports and Recreation
HIKING

For a great hike, take the **King Crest Trail,** a mountain hike from the southern Saddle Mountain Trailhead to stunning King Peak and on to the North Slide Peak Trailhead. A good, solid, 10-mile one-day round-trip can be done from either trailhead. To reach Saddle Mountain Trailhead from Shelter Cove, drive up Shelter Cove Road and turn left onto King Peak Road. Bear left on Saddle Mountain Road and turn left on a spur road to the trailhead. Only high-clearance, four-wheel-drive vehicles are recommended.

Accessible from the Saddle Mountain Trailhead, **Buck Creek Trail** includes an infamous grade, descending more than 3,000 vertical feet on an old logging road to the beach.

An arduous but gorgeous loop trail, the eight-mile **Hidden Valley-Chinquapin-Lost Coast Loop Trail** can be done in one day, or in two days with a stop at water-accessible Nick's Camp. Access it by driving out of Shelter Cove and turning right onto Chemise Mountain Road. The trailhead will be less than a mile on your right.

Dogs are allowed on the trail as long as they are under voice control or on a leash. Dogs should be outfitted with booties so that their paws don't get scraped by the rocks on the trail.

Transportation: You'll need to park a vehicle at either end of the trail. Parking at the Mattole Trailhead is free. (There have been vehicle break-ins, so don't leave valuables in your car.) There's also free parking at Black Sand Beach at the southern end of the trail. The drive between the two trailheads is 1 hour and 45 minutes. Or leave your car in Shelter Cove and contact **Lost Coast Adventures** (707/986-9895, http://lostcoastadventures.com, $85/person) for a ride.

Permits: Hikers need a free backcountry permit that also doubles as a fire permit. Reserve a permit online at www.recreation.gov ($10) or get a permit at a self-service box at the trailheads, at the King Range office (768 Shelter Cove Rd., Whitethorn, 707/986-5400, 8am-4:30pm Mon.-Fri.), or at the Bureau of Land Management (BLM) Arcata Field Office (1695 Heindon Rd., Arcata, 707/825-2300, www.blm.gov, 7:45am-4:30pm Mon.-Fri.).

Bear canisters: Bear canisters ($5) are mandatory for storing food and scented items while on the trail. They can be rented near the Mattole Trailhead from the **Petrolia General Store** (40 Sherman Rd., Petrolia, 707/629-3694). They're also available in Shelter Cove at the BLM Whitethorn Office (768 Shelter Cove Rd., 707/986-5400,) or in Arcata at the BLM Arcata Field Office (1695 Heindon Rd., 707/825-2300).

Camping: The **Mattole Campground** (end of Lighthouse Rd., 707/825-2300, www.blm.gov, $8) has 14 first-come, first-served sites that allow you to camp near the Mattole Trailhead the night before heading out. There are no developed campgrounds or facilities along the trail. Dispersed camping is allowed at Cooksie Creek, Randall Creek, Big Creek, Big Flat Creek, Buck Creek, Shipman Creek, and Gitchell Creek.

Maps: Before heading to the area, get your hands on a copy of Wilderness Press's Lost Coast Map (www.wildernesspress.com, $7.46). Check trail conditions by visiting the U.S. Department of the Interior website (www.blm.gov) and searching "Lost Coast Trail." More information is available at the King Range Information Line (707/825-2300).

FISHING

The Lost Coast is a natural fishing haven. The harbor at Shelter Cove offers charter services for ocean fishing. Kevin Riley of **Outcast Sportfishing** (Shelter Cove, 707/223-0368, www.outcastsportfish.com, Apr.-Sept., $225 pp per day) can help plan a charter fishing trip chasing whatever is in season. The cost includes gear, tackle, and filleting and packaging your fish at the end of the day, but you must bring your own lunch. A reputable charter service is **Shelter Cove Sport Fishing** (707/923-1668, www.codking.com, fishing trips $175-250 pp), offering excursions to hunt halibut, albacore, salmon, or rockfish. The largest kayak fishing event on the west coast is **Gimme Shelter** (www.norcalkayakanglers.com, May).

SURFING

Big Flat is a legendary surf spot about eight miles north of Shelter Cove on the Lost Coast Trail. While the hike in is challenging, hardcore surfers will find it worth the effort. Local surfers are very protective of this break: Even a writer for *National Geographic Adventure* who wrote about the break refused to name it for fear of retaliation. He referred to it as "Ghost Point." Be careful: Big Flat is in the middle of nowhere, and help is a ways off.

Food

The **Delgada Pizza and Bakery** (Inn of the Lost Coast, 205 Wave St., 707/986-7672, https://innofthelostcoast.com, 4pm-9pm daily, $9-30) is the place for pizza and pasta. The appropriately named Lost Coast Pizza is a favorite. Bottled beer and wine complements your meal. This is a small place with just one table inside and three tables outside. Next door, go for coffee, breakfast, or a sandwich at the **Fish Tank Espresso Gallery** (205 Wave Dr., 707/986-7850, 7am-2pm Thurs.-Tues.).

Mario's Marina Bar (53 Machi Rd., 707/986-7600, http://mariosofsheltercove.com, 4pm-11pm Mon.-Thurs., 4pm-midnight Fri., noon-midnight Sat., 10am-11pm Sun.) is the only bar in Shelter Cove. They do a full breakfast on Sunday mornings (10am-2pm).

Accommodations

Shelter Cove offers several nice motels for those who aren't up for roughing it in the wilderness overnight. **The Tides Inn of Shelter Cove** (59 Surf Point, 707/986-7900 or 888/998-4337, www.sheltercovetidesinn.com, $170-220) has standard rooms as well as luxurious suites. The suites come with fireplaces and full kitchens. All rooms face the sea, which is only steps from the inn. The Tides Inn is within walking distance of the airstrip, local shops, and restaurants.

The **Inn of the Lost Coast** (205 Wave Dr., 707/986-7521 or 888/570-9676, www.innofthelostcoast.com, $225-345) has an array of large, airy rooms and suites with stellar views to suit even luxurious tastes. While all rooms take in the coastline, the corner king bedrooms are the most popular.

The **Cliff House at Shelter Cove** (141 Wave Dr., 707/986-7344, www.cliffhouseatsheltercove.com, $225-250) is perched atop the bluffs overlooking the black-sand beaches. Only two suites are available; they're perfect for a romantic vacation or family getaway. Each has a full kitchen, living room, bedroom, gas fireplace, and satellite TV.

Camping

There are developed campsites in the King Range National Conservation Area with amenities like restrooms, grills, fire rings, picnic tables, bear boxes, and potable water. For developed camping in Shelter Cove, the

Shelter Cove RV Campground (492 Machi Rd., Whitethorn, 707/986-7474, RVs $45, tents $35) is just feet away from the airport and has views of the ocean. They have a deli and store (grill 10am-5pm daily) on-site so you don't have to bring all your own food.

Transportation and Services

To reach Shelter Cove from U.S. 101 North, take the second Garberville exit. After exiting, look for the Shelter Cove signs and turn west on Briceland Road, which becomes Shelter Cove Road. Though the trip on Shelter Cove Road is just 23 miles, it takes an hour because it's windy and goes down to one lane at one section.

Pilots can fly into the **Shelter Cove Airport** (707/986-7447, www.sheltercove-ca.gov) if weather conditions cooperate. There are live webcams on the airport's website to check the current weather.

There are no medical facilities in Shelter Cove, but emergency services are coordinated through the **Shelter Cove Fire Department** (9126 Shelter Cove Rd., Whitethorn, 707/986-7507, www.sheltercove-ca.gov). The nearest hospital with an emergency room is **Redwood Memorial Hospital** (3300 Renner Dr., Fortuna, 707/725-3361, www.stjoehumboldt.org).

KING RANGE NATIONAL CONSERVATION AREA

The **King Range National Conservation Area** encompasses the northern section of the Lost Coast. Here, King Peak rises more than 4,000 feet from the sea in less than three miles. It's also home to the most popular version of the **Lost Coast Trail:** a 24-mile backpacking excursion along the region's wild beaches that begins at the mouth of the Mattole River and traverses beaches right by the ocean to end at Shelter Cove's Black Sand Beach.

Trails in the Kings Range National Conservation Area near Shelter Cove include **Rattlesnake Ridge, Kinsey Ridge, Spanish Ridge,** and **Lightning.** Before heading to the area, try to obtain a copy of

Wilderness Press's Lost Coast Map (www. wildernesspress.com).

Mattole Road

Mattole Road, a narrow, mostly paved two-lane road, affords views of remote ranchland, unspoiled forests, and a few short miles of barely accessible cliffs and beaches. It's one of the few paved, drivable routes that allow you to view the Lost Coast from your car (the other is Shelter Cove Road, farther south). In sunny weather, the vistas are spectacular. This road also serves as access to the even smaller tracks out to the trails and campgrounds of the Sinkyone Wilderness. The most common way to get to Mattole Road is from the Victorian village of Ferndale, where you take a right on Ocean Avenue and follow the signs toward the community of Petrolia.

Mattole Beach

At the northern end of the Lost Coast, **Mattole Beach** (end of Lighthouse Rd., 707/825-2300, www.blm.gov) is a broad length of sand that's perfect for an easy, contemplative stroll. It's also popular for picnicking and fishing. Mattole Beach is the northern entry point to the Lost Coast Trail, and the start of a shorter, six-mile round-trip day hike to the **Punta Gorda Lighthouse.** The lighthouse was built in 1911 after the coast and its rocks caused multiple shipwrecks. It was shut down in 1951 due to high maintenance costs.

To reach Mattole Beach from U.S. 101, take the Garberville, Honeydew, or Ferndale exits. Follow the signs to Petrolia on Mattole Road. Turn off Mattole Road onto Lighthouse Road, which is south of the Mattole River Bridge. Follow Lighthouse Road for five miles to the beach.

Camping

Developed campsites in the King Range National Conservation Area (no permit required) include amenities like restrooms, grills, fire rings, picnic tables, bear boxes, and potable water. Campgrounds are open year-round. Reservations are not available but the odds of getting a site are pretty good, given the small number of people who come here, even in high season. Some of the larger BLM camping areas (707/986-5400, www.ca.blm.gov) are **Wailaki** (Chemise Mountain Rd., 13 sites, $8), **Nadelos** (Chemise Mountain Rd., tents only, 8 sites, $8), **Tolkan** (King Peak Rd., 5 RV sites, 4 tent sites, $8), and **Horse Mountain** (King Peak Rd., 9 sites, no water, $5). Trailers and RVs (up to 24 feet) are allowed at most sites except Nadelos. If you are driving an RV, check road conditions beforehand.

There is a campground at **Mattole Beach** (end of Lighthouse Rd., 707/825-2300, www.blm.gov, $8) with 14 first-come, first-served sites for those who are preparing to hike the Lost Coast Trail.

FERNDALE

Ferndale was built in the 19th century by Scandinavian immigrants who came to California to farm. Little has changed since the immigrants constructed their fanciful gingerbread Victorian homes and shops. Many cows still munch grass in the dairy pastures that surround the town.

The main sight in Ferndale is the town itself, which has been designated a historical landmark. Ferndale is all Victorian, all the time: Ask about the building you're in and you'll be told all about its specific architectural style, its construction date, and its original occupants. Main Street's shops, galleries, inns, and restaurants are all set into scrupulously maintained and restored late-19th-century buildings, and even the public restrooms are housed in a small Victorian-esque structure.

Sights

The **Ferndale History Museum** (515 Shaw St., 707/786-4466, www.ferndale-museum.org, 11am-4pm Wed.-Sat., 1pm-4pm Sun., $1), one block off Main Street, tells the story of the town. Life-size dioramas depict period life in a Victorian home, and an array of antique artifacts brings history to life. Downstairs, the implements of rural coast history vividly display the reality that farmers and artisans faced in the preindustrial era. The museum owns its own seismograph and records the many earthquakes that occur near town.

To cruise farther back into the town's history, wander into the **Ferndale Cemetery** (Bluff St.). Well-tended tombstones and mausoleums wend up the hillside behind the town. Genealogists will love reading the scrupulously maintained epitaphs that tell the human history of the region.

Beaches

Ferndale locals love that they have their own beach just five miles outside of their quaint village. West of Ferndale, the **Centerville County Park and Beach** (4000 Centerville Rd., 707/445-7651, www.humboldtgov.org, 5am-11:45pm daily, free) stretches for an impressive nine miles and is home to a winter congregation of tundra swans. You can drive your four-wheel-drive vehicle on the sand, ride a horse, or build a big beach bonfire at night here.

Entertainment and Events

Ferndale is a quiet town where the sidewalks roll up early, but for visitors who like to be out after 6pm, there are a few options. The **Ferndale Repertory Theater** (447 Main St., 707/786-5483, www.ferndalerep.org, $13-18), the oldest and largest of the North Coast's community theaters, puts on a number of shows each year. Some are suitable for the whole family, like *Annie*, while others, including *In the Next Room (Or the Vibrator Play)*, feature more adult subject matter.

The Palace (353 Main St., 707/786-4165, 11am-1am Mon.-Thurs., 11am-1:30am Fri., 10am-1:30am Sat.-Sun.) is the local bar with pool tables, shuffleboard, and a jukebox.

Ferndale has hosted the **Humboldt County Fair** (1250 5th St., 707/786-9511, www.humboldtcountyfair.org, Aug., adults $8, seniors $6, children $5) since 1896. For 10 days, the old-fashioned fair hosts livestock exhibits, horse racing, competitions, a carnival, nightly musical entertainment, and a variety of shows for kids and adults.

Every Memorial Day weekend, moving sculptures race 42 miles in three days from Arcata's plaza to Ferndale's Main Street. It's the **Kinetic Grand Championship Sculpture Race** (www.kineticgrandchampionship.com, May).

Shopping

Ferndale's Main Street makes for an idyllic morning stroll. The Victorian storefronts house antiques stores, jewelry shops, clothing boutiques, and art galleries. Ferndale is also a surprisingly good place to buy a hat.

The **Golden Gait Mercantile** (421 Main St., 707/786-4891, www.goldengaitmercantile.com, 10am-5pm Mon.-Sat., noon-4pm Sun.) has it all: antiques, candies, gourmet foodstuffs, clothing, hats, souvenirs, and more. Antiques and collectibles tend to be small and reasonably priced.

Silva's Fine Jewelry (400 Ocean Ave., 707/786-4425 or 888/589-1011, www.silvasjewelry.com, 8am-9pm daily), on the bottom floor of the Victorian Inn, is not a place for the faint of wallet. But the jewels, both contemporary and antique, are classically gorgeous.

The **Blacksmith Shop** (455 Main St., 707/786-4216, www.ferndaleblacksmith.com, 9:30am-5pm daily) displays a striking collection of useful art made by top blacksmiths and glassblowers from around the country. The array of jewelry, furniture, kitchen implements, fireplace tools, and metal defies description.

Food

Tucked into the bottom floor of the Victorian Inn, the **VI Restaurant & Tavern** (400 Ocean Ave., 707/786-4950, https://victorianvillageinn.com, 8am-10am, 11:30am-3pm, and 4:30pm-9pm Tues.-Sun., 8am-10am and 4:30pm-9pm Mon., $12-36) feels like a spruced-up Western saloon. Perch yourself at the bar for casual options like fish-and-chips or sit down at a table for sophisticated dinner entrées like Portuguese paella or cold water lobster. Sundays are prime rib nights, complete with piano music.

Locals come from as far away as Eureka to dine at the restaurant at the **Hotel Ivanhoe** (315 Main St., 707/786-9000, http://hotel-ivanhoe.com, 5pm-9pm Thurs.-Sun., bar open from 4pm Thurs.-Sun., $16-37), where it's all about the hearty homemade Italian dishes and friendly personal service. A more casual Italian dining experience can be had at the **Ferndale Pizza Co.** (607 Main St., 707/786-4345, 11:30am-9pm Tues.-Thurs., 11:30am-9:30pm Fri.-Sat., noon-9pm Sun., $16-21).

For breakfast, stop in at local favorite **Poppa Joe's** (409 Main St., 707/786-4180, 6am-2pm Mon.-Fri., 6am-noon Sat.-Sun., $5.50-9). The interior is dim and narrow, but the breakfast and lunch offerings are delicious.

Valley Grocery (339 Main St., 707/786-9515, 7am-10pm daily) stocks staples and maintains a deli; it's a perfect last stop on the way out to a beach picnic. Don't forget to drop in at the heavenly candy store **Sweetness and Light** (554 Main St., 707/786-4403 or 800/547-8180, www.sweetnessandlight.com, 10am-5pm Mon.-Fri., 11am-4pm Sat.).

Accommodations

In Ferndale, lodgings tend to be Victorian-style inns, mostly bed-and-breakfasts. Guests of **The Shaw House Inn** (703 Main St., 707/786-9958 or 800/557-7429, www.shawhouse.com, $142-275) must walk a block or two to get to the heart of downtown Ferndale, but the compensation is a spacious garden on the inn's grounds. Huge shade trees and perfectly positioned garden benches make a lovely spot to sit and enjoy the serene beauty. The inn has eight rooms and three common parlor areas. A lush morning breakfast fortifies guests.

The historic ★ **Victorian Inn** (400 Ocean Ave., 707/786-4949 or 888/589-1808, www.victorianvillageinn.com, $139-359) is an imposing structure at the corner that also houses Silva's Fine Jewelry. The inn comprises 13 rooms, all decorated with antique furnishings, luxurious linens, and pretty knickknacks. For a special treat, rent the Ira Russ Suite, a spacious room with a tower alcove that takes in the town below. A full hot breakfast is served downstairs.

In a town full of history, **The Hotel Ivanhoe** (315 Main St., 707/786-9000, www.hotel-ivanhoe.com, $95-145) is the oldest extant hostelry. Plaques on the building's exterior describe its rich legacy. The four rooms are done in rich colors that evoke the Western-Victorian atmosphere of the original hotel.

An inexpensive option is **Redwood Suites** (332 Ocean Ave., 707/786-5000 or 888/589-1863, www.redwoodsuites.com, $120-185). Only a block off Main Street, the property has modern rooms that are simple but comfortable. Family suites with full kitchens are available. A stay includes a hot breakfast at the nearby Victorian Inn.

Transportation

Ferndale is not directly accessible from U.S. 101; you must get off U.S. 101 at Fernbridge and then follow Highway 211 south to Ferndale. Mattole Road leads out of town south toward the Sinkyone Wilderness area, while Centerville Road heads out to the beach. Walking provides the best views and feel of the town.

If you need medical care, the **Redwood Memorial Hospital** (3300 Renner Dr., Fortuna, 707/725-3361, www.stjoehumboldt.org) is 10 miles away in Fortuna.

Eureka

The town of Eureka began as a seaward access point to the remote gold mines of the Trinity area. Once settlers realized the value of the redwood trees, the town's logging industry was born.

Visitors can wander the town's five-block-long boardwalk on Humboldt Bay and the charming downtown shopping area, or enjoy the colorful murals and sculptures along the city streets. Outdoors enthusiasts can fish and hike, while history buffs can explore museums, Victorian mansions, and even a working Victorian-era lumber mill.

SIGHTS

For an introduction to Old Town Eureka, take a horse-drawn carriage tour of the historic district with the Old Town Carriage Co. (1st St. and F St., 646/591-2058, www.oldtowncarriageco.com, 12:30pm-6:30pm Wed.-Mon., $40-80). The carriage is usually downtown near the gazebo around the small square at 2nd and F Streets. Tours last 25 minutes, 45 minutes, or one hour.

Blue Ox Millworks and Historic Park

Blue Ox Millworks and Historic Park (1 X St., 707/444-3437 or 800/248-4259, www.blueoxmill.com, self-guided tours 9am-5pm Mon.-Fri., 9am-4pm Sat. Apr.-Nov., 9am-5pm Mon.-Fri. Nov.-Apr., adults $12, seniors $11, children $7, children under 6 free, guided tour $12.50 pp) has a working lumber mill, an upscale wood and cabinetry shop, a blacksmith forge, an old-fashioned print shop, a shipbuilding yard, a rose garden, and a historic park. It also has the world's largest collection of human-powered woodworking tools made by the historic Barnes Equipment Company. Today, the rambling buildings are filled with purchased, donated, and rehabbed tools of all kinds. Workshops feature a glassblowing kiln and a darkroom where students can learn nondigital photography methods, making their own photosensitive paper and developing black-and-white and sepia prints.

Visitors to the Blue Ox learn about the real lives and times of craftspeople of the late 1800s and early 1900s as they tour the facilities and examine the equipment. If you ask, you might be allowed to touch, and even work, a piece of wood of your own. Stop in at the gift shop—a converted lumberjack barracks—to check out the ceramics and woodwork the students have for sale.

Carson Mansion

Gables, turrets, cupolas, and pillars: the Carson Mansion (143 M St., www.ingomar.org, closed to the public) has all these architectural flourishes. The elaborate three-story, 18-room Victorian mansion was built by William Carson in 1884 and 1885 after he struck it rich in the lumber business. Almost demolished in the 1940s, it was purchased and renovated by the Ingomar Club, which now uses it for private dinner parties. It's touted as one of the most photographed buildings in the country. The building and grounds are not open to the public, but you can take photos.

Clarke Historical Museum

The privately owned Clarke Historical Museum (240 E St., 707/443-1947, www.clarkemuseum.org, 10am-6pm Tues.-Sat., 10am-3pm Sun., adults $5, families $10), housed in a regal old bank building, is dedicated to preserving the history of Eureka and the surrounding area. Changing exhibitions illuminate the Native American history of the area as well as the gold rush and logging eras. The Nealis Hall annex displays one of the best collections of Native American artifacts in the state.

Fort Humboldt State Historic Park

Established in 1853 to protect white settlers—particularly gold miners—from the local Native Americans, the original Fort Humboldt lasted only 17 years as a military installation. Today, **Fort Humboldt State Historic Park** (3431 Fort Ave., 707/445-6567, www.parks.ca.gov, 8am-5pm daily, free) gives visitors a glimpse into the lives of 19th-century soldiers and loggers. The original hospital is the only remaining building from the fort; it now serves as a museum. A gravel trail circles the grounds, where interpretive plaques depict the fort's frequently dark history. Come on the third Saturday of the month (May-Sept.) to take a five-minute ride on a steam locomotive.

Sequoia Park Zoo

The **Sequoia Park Zoo** (3414 W St., 707/441-4263, www.sequoiaparkzoo.net, 10am-5pm daily summer, 10am-5pm Tues.-Sun. winter, adults $10, seniors $7, children 3-12 $6) seeks to preserve local species and educate the public about their needs. The Secrets of the Forest exhibit recreates the ecology of a Northern California forest.

Humboldt Botanical Gardens

Humboldt Botanical Gardens (7707 Tompkins Hill Rd., 707/442-5139, www.hbgf.org, 10am-4pm Wed.-Sun. Apr.-Oct., 10am-2pm Wed.-Sat., 11am-3pm Sun. Nov.-Mar., adults $8, seniors and children $5) celebrates the ecosystems of Humboldt County. The 44-acre site includes native plants, ornamental plants, and plants that grow in riparian regions.

ENTERTAINMENT AND EVENTS
Bars

The biggest and most popular bar is the **Lost Coast Brewery & Café** (617 4th St., 707/445-4480, www.lostcoast.com, 11am-10pm Sun.-Thurs., 11am-11pm Fri.-Sat.). The tall cream-and-green building is perched by itself on the main drag, easy to spot as you pass through town. The brewery draws crowds, especially on weekends, and makes popular microbrews including Great White and Downtown Brown, which are on tap. Try the tasty brewpub-style food and a few of the delicious beers. Free tours are available at Lost Coast's off-site brewery (1600 Sunset Dr., www.lostcoast.com).

The Speakeasy (411 Opera Alley,

Humboldt Bay

© AVALON TRAVEL

Downtown Eureka

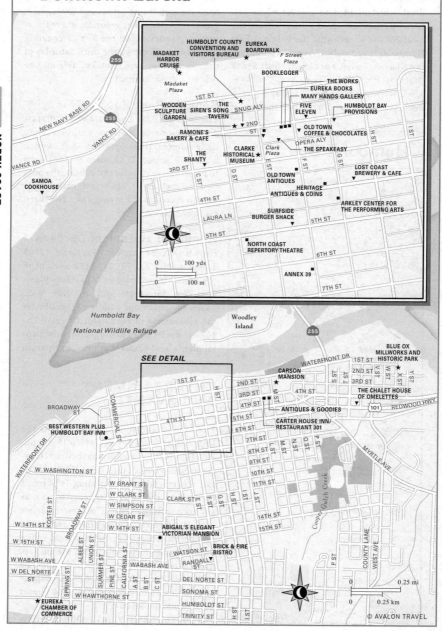

MADAKET HARBOR CRUISE

HUMBOLDT COUNTY CONVENTION AND VISITORS BUREAU

EUREKA BOARDWALK

F Street Plaza

BOOKLEGGER

THE WORKS

EUREKA BOOKS

MANY HANDS GALLERY

Madaket Plaza

1ST ST

WOODEN SCULPTURE GARDEN

THE SIREN'S SONG TAVERN

SNUG ALY

FIVE ELEVEN

HUMBOLDT BAY PROVISIONS

2ND ST

RAMONE'S BAKERY & CAFE

OLD TOWN COFFEE & CHOCOLATES

OPERA ALY

THE SPEAKEASY

Clark Plaza

THE SHANTY

CLARKE HISTORICAL MUSEUM

3RD ST

LOST COAST BREWERY & CAFE

SAMOA COOKHOUSE

OLD TOWN ANTIQUES

HERITAGE ANTIQUES & COINS

ARKLEY CENTER FOR THE PERFORMING ARTS

4TH ST

LAURA LN

SURFSIDE BURGER SHACK

5TH ST

5TH ST

NORTH COAST REPERTORY THEATRE

6TH ST

0   100 yds
0   100 m

ANNEX 39

7TH ST

Humboldt Bay National Wildlife Refuge

Woodley Island

SEE DETAIL

WATERFRONT DR

BLUE OX MILLWORKS AND HISTORIC PARK

1ST ST

2ND ST

CARSON MANSION

3RD ST

1ST ST

2ND ST

3RD ST

THE CHALET HOUSE OF OMELETTES

4TH ST

BROADWAY ST

COMMERCIAL ST

4TH ST

5TH ST

ANTIQUES & GOODIES

REDWOOD HWY

BEST WESTERN PLUS HUMBOLDT BAY INN

6TH ST

7TH ST

CARTER HOUSE INN/ RESTAURANT 301

WATERFRONT DR

W WASHINGTON ST

8TH ST

9TH ST

10TH ST

11TH ST

MYRTLE AVE

W GRANT ST

W CLARK ST

CLARK ST

W SIMPSON ST

W CEDAR ST

14TH ST

W 14TH ST

15TH ST

KOSTER ST

BROADWAY ST

SPRING ST

ALBEE ST

UNION ST

W 14TH ST

ABIGAIL'S ELEGANT VICTORIAN MANSION

W 15TH ST

WATSON ST

BRICK & FIRE BISTRO

W WABASH AVE

CALIFORNIA ST

WABASH AVE

RANDALL ST

W DEL NORTE ST

SUMMER ST

PINE ST

A ST

B ST

C ST

DEL NORTE ST

COUNTY LANE

WEST AVE

SONOMA ST

EUREKA CHAMBER OF COMMERCE

W HAWTHORNE ST

HUMBOLDT ST

TRINITY ST

0   0.25 mi
0   0.25 km

© AVALON TRAVEL

707/444-2244, 4pm-11pm Mon.-Thurs., 4pm-1am Fri.-Sat.) is the place to go for tasty cocktails. This dark, narrow bar, which sometimes has live music, serves up Southern-style drinks, including a great mint julep.

One of the best dive bars on the North Coast, **The Shanty** (213 3rd St., 707/444-2053, noon-2am Mon.-Sat., 9am-2am Sun.) impresses with friendly clientele, a superbly curated jukebox, and a lot of eclectic character. Head outdoors to play table tennis or pool or smoke a cigarette. The extended happy hour (4pm-7pm Mon.-Fri., noon-4pm Sat.-Sun.) offers top-shelf beers and liquors and rock-bottom prices.

The cool, worn-feeling Victorian space at **The Siren's Song Tavern** (325 2nd St., 707/442-8778, www.sirenssongtavern.com, 3pm-10pm Tues.-Thurs., 3pm-midnight Fri.-Sat.) hosts bands that perform on a rug in front of the window. Siren's Song has a superb craft beer list including 18 brews on tap.

Live Music

The **Arkley Center for the Performing Arts** (412 G St., 707/442-1956 or 888/859-8797, www.atlpublishing.com) is the home of the Eureka Symphony and North Coast Dance. The elegant venue, with its striking mural of musicians and dancers on the back of the building, also hosts rock, country, and jazz acts.

Events

Music lovers flock to Eureka each year for a number of big music festivals. One of the biggest is the **Redwood Coast Jazz Festival** (various venues around town, 707/445-3378, www.rcmfest.org, Apr., $25-85). For four days in spring, music lovers can enjoy every style of jazz imaginable, including Dixieland, zydeco, and big band. The festival also features dance lessons and contests.

Experience what Eureka was like during its logging heyday at the **Dolbeer Steam Donkey Days** (Fort Humboldt State Historic Park, 3431 Fort Ave., 707/445-6567, www.parks.ca.gov, Apr.). This two-day event features working logging equipment, train rides, and logging skill competitions.

The **Kinetic Grand Championship** (707/786-3443, http://kineticgrandchampionship.com, Memorial Day weekend) is a pedal-powered moving sculpture race that originates in Arcata and ends in Ferndale. The second day of this event takes place on Eureka's waterfront.

SHOPPING

Eureka boasts the largest California antiques scene north of the Bay Area. **Annex 39** (610 F St., 707/443-1323, noon-5:30pm Tues.-Sat.) specializes in vintage linens and laundry products and also has a great selection of art deco and midcentury modern pieces. **Heritage Antique & Coins** (521 4th St., 707/444-2908, 10am-5pm Tues.-Fri., 10am-3pm Sat.) is a coin shop that also carries jewelry and Native American artifacts. Generalists will love rooting through **Old Town Antiques** (318 F St., 707/442-3235, 10:30am-6pm Mon.-Sat.).

For an afternoon of shopping, head down toward the water to 2nd Street. Most of the buildings are historic, and you might find an unassuming brass plaque describing the famous brothel that once occupied what is now a toy store. Literature lovers have a nice selection of independent bookstores: **Eureka Books** (426 2nd St., 707/444-9593, www.eurekabooksellers.com, 10am-6pm daily) has a big, airy room in which to browse a selection of new and used books. **Booklegger** (402 2nd St., at E St., 707/445-1344, 10am-5:30pm Mon.-Sat., 11am-4pm Sun.) is a small but well-organized new-and-used bookshop that specializes in antique books.

Galleries and gift shops abound. **Many Hands Gallery** (438 2nd St., 707/445-0455, www.manyhandsgallery.net, 10am-9pm Mon.-Sat., 10am-6pm Sun.) represents approximately 100 local artisans and also displays work from national and international artists cooperatives, fair-trade organizations, and commercial importers. You'll find plenty of humor and whimsy, and prices range from 10 cents to $10,000.

The Works (434 2nd St., 707/442-8121, www.theworkseureka.com, 11am-6pm daily) has been providing Humboldt County music fans with vinyl records and CDs since 1971.

SPORTS AND RECREATION
Fishing

Eureka is a serious fishing destination. Oodles of both ocean- and river-fishing opportunities are available, and several fishing tournaments are held each year. In California, you must have a valid state fishing license to fish in either the ocean or the rivers. Check with your charter service or guide to be sure they provide a day license with your trip. If they don't, you will have to get your own.

For deep-sea fishing, Greenwater Fishing Adventures (707/845-9588, www. eurekafishing.net, fishing trips $170-250, crabbing $75) heads out on the 36-foot *Shellback* to catch salmon, rockfish, halibut, tuna, and crab. Full Throttle Sportfishing (601 Startare Dr., 707/498-7473, www. fullthrottlesportfishing.com, $180-275) supplies all needed tackle and can take you out to fish for salmon, rockfish, tuna, or halibut. Trips last all day, and most leave at 6:30am. If you're launching your own boat, public launches are the Samoa Boat Ramp (New Navy Base Rd., 707/445-7651, www.humboldtgov.org, 5am-11:45pm daily) and the Fields Landing Boat Ramp (Railroad Ave., 707/445-7651, www.humboldtgov.org, 5am-midnight daily).

Eureka has good spots for pier fishing. In town, try the K Street Pier, the pier at the east end of Commercial Street, or the pier at the end of Del Norte Street. Farther north, the north jetty (Hwy. 255, across Samoa Bridge) also has a public pier open for fishing.

Bird-Watching

The national, state, and county parks lacing the area are ideal bird-watching havens. The Humboldt Bay National Wildlife Refuge Complex (1020 Ranch Rd., Loleta, 707/733-5406, www.fws.gov) encompasses several wildlife-refuge sites where visitors are welcome. At the Salmon Creek Unit, you'll find the Richard J. Guadagno Headquarters and Visitors Center (8am-5pm daily), which is an excellent starting place for a number of wildlife walks. To get to the visitors center from U.S. 101, take the exit for Hookton heading north and turn left onto Eel River Drive. Take the first right onto Ranch Road, and you'll find the visitors center parking lot.

Hiking and Biking

There is a vast system of trails in the state and national parks, and the city of Eureka maintains a number of multiuse biking and hiking trails as well. Most familiar is the Old Town Boardwalk, part of the Waterfront Trail that comprises disconnected sections along Humboldt Bay. Sequoia Park Trail begins at the Sequoia Park Zoo and wends through redwood forests, past a duck pond, and through a meadow. This trail is paved and friendly for strollers and wheelchairs. The unpaved Elk River Trail (end of Hilfiker Ln.) stretches for one mile through wild meadows along the coast. Cooper Gulch Trail is more a sedate stroll than a strenuous hike, circling the Cooper Gulch park playing fields.

Kayaking, Rafting, and Stand-Up Paddleboarding

The water is cold, but getting out on it in a kayak can be exhilarating. Guided paddles, lessons, rentals, and kayak-fishing trips are available through Humboats Kayak Adventures (Woodley Island Marina, 601 Startare Dr., 707/443-5157, www.humboats. com, canoe, kayak, and SUP rentals $30-110, tours $55-95). Guides lead a huge variety of tours, from serene paddles in the harbor suitable for children to a kayaking trip among the Avenue of the Giants redwoods.

River rafters and kayakers have great opportunities for rapids fun on the inland Klamath and Trinity Rivers. Bigfoot

Rafting Company (Willow Creek, 530/629-2263, www.bigfootrafting.com, adults $89, children $79) leads half-day, full-day, and multiday trips on both rivers as well as on the Cal-Salmon and Smith Rivers. Experts can take inflatable kayaks down the Class IV rapids, while newcomers can find a gentle paddle.

Harbor Cruises

For a great introduction to Eureka and Humboldt Bay, book a tour on the *Madaket* (dock at end of C St., 707/445-1910, www.humboldtbaymaritimemuseum.com, May-Sept.), the oldest continuously operating passenger vessel in the country, with the smallest licensed bar in California. The ferry, built in 1910, offers three tours: a narrated history cruise (75 minutes, adults $22, seniors and children 13-17 $18, children 5-12 $12, children under 5 free), a cocktail cruise (one hour, $10), or a wildlife tour (1.5 hours, adults $26, seniors and children 13-17 $22, children 5-12 $12, children under 5 free). The historic cruise follows a scenic 8.5-mile loop in Humboldt Bay and the adjoining Arcata Bay. Passengers learn about the area's history and the stories behind local landmarks, and visit an egret colony.

Drag Racing

For a down-home American experience, take in a car race at the Samoa Drag Strip (New Navy Base Rd., 707/845-5755, www.samoadragstrip.com, May-Sept., adults $10, children under 13 free). The 0.25-mile track is on the Samoa Peninsula. Special nights feature Harley motorcycles or diesel trucks.

FOOD
Breakfast

One of the older restaurants in downtown Eureka, ★ The Chalet House of Omelettes (1935 5th St., 707/442-0333, http://thechaleteureka.com, 7am-3pm daily, $8-11) has been serving delicious omelets in a homey atmosphere since 1975. The build-your-own-omelet (four ingredients and three eggs, $10.25) is a favorite. The Chalet Special Omelet is recommended, filled with bacon, cheese, and avocado slices. Attentive servers fill your cup of coffee to the brim for the duration of your meal.

Bakeries and Cafés

Ramone's Bakery & Café (209 E St., 707/445-2923, http://ramonesbakery.com, 7am-6pm Mon.-Fri., 8am-5pm Sat., 8am-4pm Sun.) is a local chain, selling fresh baked

the Chalet Special Omelet at The Chalet House of Omelettes

goods and candies. Enjoy a fresh cup of coffee roasted in-house with a Danish or scone, or get a whole tart, cake, or loaf of bread to take away.

Old Town Coffee & Chocolates (211 F St., 707/445-8600, http://oldtowncoffee-eureka.com, 7am-8pm Sun.-Mon., 7am-9pm Tues.-Thurs., 7am-10pm Fri.-Sat.) does more than caffeinate their customers. They also sell chocolate and fudge made on-site, as well as bagels, waffles, wraps, and grilled cheese sandwiches. Many evenings feature live music, open mics, or book readings.

American

The ★ **Samoa Cookhouse** (511 Vance Rd., Samoa, 707/442-1659, www.samoacookhouse.net, 7am-9pm daily summer, 7am-3pm and 5pm-8pm daily winter, adults $18, children 8-11 $9) is a Eureka institution. Red-checked tablecloths cover long, rough tables to create the atmosphere of a logging-camp dining hall. All-you-can-eat meals are served family-style from huge serving platters. Diners sit on benches and pass the hearty fare down in turn. Think hunks of roast beef, mountains of mashed potatoes, and piles of cooked vegetables for lunch and dinner, or a giant plate of eggs, hash browns, sausage, and toast for breakfast. This is the place to bring your biggest appetite. After dinner, browse the small Historic Logging Museum and gift shop.

Restaurant 301 (301 L St., 800/404-1390, www.carterhouse.com, 5pm-8:30pm daily, $23-47) at the Carter House Inns seems like a big-city spot. The chef creates an ever-changing menu of delectable delicacies, along with tasting menus. Menu options include exotic duck dishes, local seafood preparations, and items from the restaurant's on-site garden. For a treat, try the wine flights suggested with the menus. Restaurant 301 is known for its extensive wine list, with more than 3,400 selections.

A turquoise floor and jade lighting give **Five Eleven** (511 2nd St., 707/268-3852, 5pm-9pm Mon.-Thurs., 5pm-9:30pm Fri.-Sat., 5pm-8pm Sun. summer; 5pm-9:30pm Fri.-Sat., 5pm-9pm Tues.-Thurs. winter; $10-35) a bold, metropolitan feel. The food changes frequently, but the Southern fried chicken and fresh oysters are staples. They also serve specialty craft cocktails, a few choice craft beers, and a wide variety of wines at the long stone bar.

The **Surfside Burger Shack** (445 5th St., 707/268-1295, 11am-7pm Sun.-Mon. and Wed.-Thurs., 11am-8pm Fri.-Sat., $6-8)

a hearty breakfast at the Samoa Cookhouse

is nowhere near the ocean, but it does have surfing decor and darn good burgers made from grass-fed Humboldt cows. The classic cheeseburger hits the spot, but the shack also gets creative with the Surfside Sunrise, a burger topped with cheese, bacon, an egg, and maple syrup.

Italian
Brick & Fire Bistro (1630 F St., 707/268-8959, www.brickandfirebistro.com, 11:30am-9pm Mon. and Wed.-Fri., 5pm-9pm Sat.-Sun., $14-22) updates Italian classics with a menu that includes fire-roasted polenta lasagna and pizzas with locally smoked salmon and quail eggs. The wild mushroom cobbler appetizer is one of the most talked-about menu items.

Seafood
Sample the products of Humboldt County at **Humboldt Bay Provisions** (205 G St., 707/672-3850, www.humboldtbayprovisions. com, 3pm-9pm daily, $10-48). Sit at the reclaimed redwood bar where you can nibble on salmon from nearby Blue Lake and slurp tasty oysters from Humboldt Bay while drinking local brews.

ACCOMMODATIONS
Under $150
Originally built by one of the town's founders, **Abigail's Elegant Victorian Mansion** (1406 C St., 707/444-3144, www.eureka-california.com, $135-145) offers an authentic Victorian experience, having retained many of the large home's original fixtures. Each of the two rooms comes with its own story and an astonishing collection of antiques; both have detached bathrooms. Guests can request a tour of Eureka in one of the inn's 1928 Fords. There are a few quirks: no reservations (rooms are first-come, first-served); no breakfast; and no credit cards (the owners only take cash).

If B&Bs aren't your style, get a room at the **Bayview Motel** (2844 Fairfield St., 707/442-1673 or 866/725-6813, www.bayviewmotel. com, $130-220). This hilltop motel has lovely views of Humboldt Bay. Rooms are spacious and decorated in elegant colors and fabrics. You'll find whirlpool suites, free Wi-Fi, cable TV, wet bars, and coffeemakers. If you're traveling with the family, rent a double suite—two rooms with an adjoining door and separate baths. Downtown Eureka is within an easy drive.

the Oasis Spa area at Best Western Plus Humboldt Bay

$150-250

The ★ **Carter House Inns** (301 L St., 800/404-1390, www.carterhouse.com, $179-595) have a range of accommodations in a cluster of butter-yellow Victorian buildings near the Carson Mansion. The main building has 23 rooms and suites, a number of which have gas fireplaces and soaking tubs. Across the street, a reproduction of a Victorian mansion has six rooms, including a family suite with two bedrooms, while **The Bell Cottage** has three rooms and a full common kitchen. For a splurge, rent **The Carter Cottage,** which has two bathrooms, a deck with a fountain, a soaking tub, and a large den and kitchen area. All guests are treated to a hot breakfast and an afternoon wine and appetizer hour. Dine at the inn's renowned Restaurant 301.

There's no place along the California coast quite like ★ **Oyster Beach** (865B New Navy Base Rd., 707/834-6555, www.humboldtbaysocialclub.com, $175-295), a set of refurbished buildings on the Samoa Peninsula. The 22-acre property has its own beach on Humboldt Bay and impressive eucalyptus groves. Five units range from The Loft, with reclaimed wood walls, to the Mid-Century Waterfront, mere feet from the bay. Just eight minutes from downtown Eureka, Oyster Beach feels like it's a world away.

★ **Best Western Plus Humboldt Bay** (232 W. 5th St., 707/443-2234, www.humboldtbayinn.com, $185-250) is a pleasant surprise. What sets it apart is its Oasis Spa Area, a tropical-themed courtyard with tiki torches, island music, fire pits, and a hot tub grotto that stand in contrast to the industrial neighborhood location. Within the enclosure are a heated pool, 24-hour fitness center, and billiards table. A complimentary continental breakfast is served daily. An unexpected amenity is an on-site limo and driver that will drive guests to any restaurant in Eureka. The rooms are modern and clean, too.

TRANSPORTATION AND SERVICES

Eureka is on U.S. 101, easily accessed by car from north or south. From Crescent City, Eureka is less than an hour's drive south on U.S. 101.

Driving is the only option if you're not staying downtown. Parking downtown is metered or free on the streets, and not too difficult to find except on holiday or event weekends.

Bus service in and around Eureka is operated by the **Humboldt Transit Authority** (HTA, http://humboldttransit.org, adults $1.70, seniors and children $1.30). The HTA's **Eureka Transit System** (ETS, 707/443-0826, https://humboldttransit.org) runs within town limits, and the **Redwood Transit System** (RTS, 707/443-0826, https://humboldttransit.org, adults $1.65-5.50, seniors and children $1.40-5) can take you around the area; it runs from Eureka north to Trinidad, south to Scotia, and east to Willow Creek.

Eureka has a small commercial airport, **California Redwood Coast-Humboldt County Airport** (ACV, 3561 Boeing Ave., McKinleyville, 707/839-5401, www.humboldtgov.org), which serves the North Coast region with expensive but convenient flights on United Airlines.

The full-service **St. Joseph Hospital** (2700 Dolbeer St., 707/445-8121, www.stjoehumboldt.org) has an emergency room and an urgent care center.

Arcata

Arcata has a distinctly small-town feel, different from its southern neighbor. The hippie daughter of blue-collar Eureka, Arcata is home to Humboldt State University. Students make up almost half of the city's population, and the town is known for its liberal politics.

Arcata has a lively arts and music scene along with a handful of restaurants that you might expect in a bigger city. It makes a great home base for exploring the wild North Coast.

SIGHTS
★ Arcata Plaza

The heart of downtown is **Arcata Plaza** (9th and G Sts., www.arcatamainstreet.com), which has been the epicenter of town since the 1850s when it was a freight and passenger stop. The park has a William McKinley statue, a couple of palm trees, and a grassy lawn where folks hang out. Circling the plaza are independent restaurants, bars, coffee shops, and stores. The plaza hosts many events, from the Saturday farmers market to the start of the annual Kinetic Grand Championship race.

Arcata Community Forest

The first city-owned forest in California, the 2,134-acre **Arcata Community Forest** (east ends of 11th St., 14th St., and California St., 707/822-5951, www.cityofarcata.org, sunrise-sunset daily) has trails winding through second-growth redwoods, open for hiking, mountain biking, and horseback riding. Just east of the city's downtown and behind Humboldt State University, the forest is an ideal place to stroll between the silent giants, many of which are cloaked in moss, and take in stumps the size of compact cars and vibrant-green waist-high ferns. The park also has a section with picnic tables and a playground.

ENTERTAINMENT AND EVENTS
Bars

A strip of dive bars lines the edge of Arcata Plaza on 9th Street. The best of the bunch, **The Alibi** (744 9th St., 707/822-3731, www.thealibi.com, 8am-2am daily), dates to the 1920s. The Alibi serves cheap, well-crafted

Arcata Plaza

cocktails with infused liquors, including a wide range of Bloody Marys. It also has an extensive breakfast, lunch, and dinner menu with specialty burgers and entrées.

The North Coast is known for its micro-brews, and **Dead Reckoning Tavern** (815 J St., 707/630-5008, 2pm-8pm Sun.-Mon., 2pm-10pm Tues.-Thurs., 2pm-11pm Fri.-Sat.) is a great place to try one. They have 34 rotating beers on tap along with one kombucha tap and a root beer tap for non-imbibers. The tavern's back room has a few arcade games and a small record store to enjoy while sipping suds.

Humboldt Brews (856 10th St., 707/826-2739, www.humboldtbrews.com, noon-11pm daily, open until 2am for live music) serves food and 25 beers on tap. This popular hang-out has a pool table and an adjacent room that serves as a concert space for midsize national jam bands, indie acts, and reggae outfits.

Richard's Goat Tavern & Tea Room (401 I St., 707/630-5000, http://richardsgoat.com, 3pm-2am Tues.-Sun., 3pm-midnight Mon.) is an oasis of culture and cocktails blocks away from the plaza's dive bar scene. The liquors are house infused, and there's craft beer on tap. The bar has its own tiny theater dubbed the Miniplex, where art house movies are screened and the occasional live act performs.

Live Music

Music legends like Elvis Costello, John Prine, Melissa Etheridge, The Growlers, and Jake Shimabukuro play at Humboldt State University's **John Van Duzer Theatre** (1 Harpst St., 707/826-4411, www.humboldt.edu). Up-and-coming acts typically perform at **The Depot** (University Center, 1 Harpst St., 707/826-4411) and the **West Gym** (top of Union St.).

Cinema

Dating to 1938, the art deco **Arcata Theatre Lounge** (1036 G St., 707/822-1220, www.arcatatheatre.com) screens movies, hosts concerts, and puts on events like Sci-Fi Pint and Pizza Night, where they show old science-fiction movies. The theater seats have been replaced by circular tables and chairs, and the full bar serves food as well as drinks.

A few blocks away, the 1914 **Minor Theatre** (1001 H St., 707/822-3456, www.minortheatre.com) is one of the oldest operating movie theaters in the country, showing independent movies as well as Hollywood films. Enjoy your film with food (from empanadas to pizza), draft beer, and wine served to your seat.

Festivals and Events

Arcata Plaza is the starting line of the **Kinetic Grand Championship** (707/786-3443, http://kineticgrandchampionship.com, Memorial Day weekend), a three-day, 42-mile race featuring human-powered art sculptures that continues to Eureka and Ferndale.

In the plaza is the annual **Arcata Main Street Oyster Festival** (707/822-4500, www.arcatamainstreet.com/oyster-fest, June), which celebrates the local Kumamoto oyster with—you guessed it—oysters. This is the largest one-day event in Humboldt County. There's live music and microbrews to enjoy with the bivalves.

SPORTS AND RECREATION

The 18-hole **Redwood Curtain Disc Golf Course** (accessible from Humboldt State University's Redwood Science Lab, though parking is only available in the lot after 5pm) winds its way through massive redwood trees. On the second hole, the tee is atop a 10-foot-high redwood stump.

For local sports action, get a ticket to see the **Humboldt Crabs** (Arcata Ball Park, F St. and 9th St., 707/840-5665, http://humboldt-crabs.com), the oldest continually active collegiate summer baseball team in the country.

Arcata Marsh and Wildlife Sanctuary

One of Arcata's most popular places to take a hike is in a section of the town's wastewater treatment facility. The **Arcata Marsh Interpretive Center** (569 S. G St.,

North Coast Breweries

California's North Coast is known for its beer. Local craft beer and microbrews are served in restaurants and line the beer aisles of local supermarkets. One way to taste these beers or sample their smaller batches is to visit a North Coast brewery.

For beer fans, the **Anderson Valley Brewing Company's Tap Room and Brewery** (17700 Hwy. 253, Boonville, 707/895-2337, www.avbc.com, 11am-6pm daily) is worth a visit. With its high ceilings and copper bar, the taproom feels more like an informal tasting room in a winery. The 20 taps serve Anderson Valley favorites like Boont Amber Ale, along with 10 rotating taps of small-batch brews, including a sour stout. Brewery tours (1:30pm and 3pm, $5) are offered when the taproom is open. You can also head outdoors to the brewery's 18-hole disc golf course (8am-6pm daily, free).

Since opening in 1988, the **North Coast Brewing Company** (444 N. Main St., Fort Bragg, 707/964-3400, www.northcoastbrewing.com, 11:30am-10pm Fri.-Sat.,

Mad River Brewing Company

11:30am-9pm Sun.-Thurs.) has expanded to a city block with the actual brewery, a brewery shop, and a taproom and grill. Head into the popular tap-room to try North Coast favorites like the Red Seal Ale or the more potent Brother Thelonious, a Belgian-style abbey ale.

If you crave sustainable suds, visit the **Eel River Brewing Company's Taproom & Grill** (1777 Alamar Way, Fortuna, 707/725-2739, http://eelriverbrewing.com, 11am-11pm daily), where you can sip organic beer made with renewable energy. Drink the Organic IPA or Organic Acai Berry Wheat Ale inside at the taproom's long wooden bar or head out to the adjacent beer garden. Tours (707/764-1772) of the brewing facilities are in the nearby town of Scotia.

The **Lost Coast Brewery & Café** (617 4th St., Eureka, 707/445-4480, www.lostcoast.com, 11am-10pm Sun.-Thurs., 11am-11pm Fri.-Sat.) feels like a local's bar and is filled with people even on weeknights. The brewery's Great White and Lost Coast Pale Ale are the most popular brews, but the smooth Downtown Brown is recommended for darker beer fans. Free half-hour tours are at their brewery (1600 Sunset Dr., Eureka, 707/267-9651).

Fifteen miles from downtown Arcata, the **Mad River Brewing Company Tasting Room** (101 Taylor Way, Blue Lake, 707/668-4151, www.madriverbrewing.com, 11:30am-9pm Sun.-Thurs., 11:30am-10pm Fri.-Sat.) is a favorite with Humboldt County beer drinkers. Not only do they brew award-winning beers like Steelhead Extra Pale Ale and Jamaica Red Ale, they also have tasty pub food, frequent live music, and an outdoor beer garden on sunny days.

A local favorite, **The Redwood Curtain Brewing Company Tasting Room** (550 S. G St., Arcata, 707/826-7222, www.redwoodcurtainbrewing.com, noon-11pm Sun.-Tues., noon-midnight Wed.-Sat.) is in an industrial park a few blocks south of downtown. This unassuming spot is the place to try their Imperial Golden Ale, their award-winning Dusseldorf Altbier, or their creative Cerise Coup, which is aged in a French oak chardonnay barrel and then infused with cherries for six months. Sit at the bar overlooking the brew room or play a game of shuffleboard.

707/826-2359, www.arcatamarsh.org, visitor center: 1pm-5pm Mon., 9am-5pm Tues.-Sun.; grounds: 4am-sunset daily) holds a small museum that explains how the city transformed an industrial wasteland into a 307-acre wildlife sanctuary using Arcata's wastewater. Hike the sanctuary's five miles of hiking and biking paths, or try to spot some of the 270 bird species that use the marsh as a migratory stop.

SHOPPING

Around Arcata Plaza and along H Street are a number of unique stores. Head into **Pacific Paradise** (1087 H St., 707/822-7143, 10am-6pm Mon.-Sat., 10:30am-5:30pm Sun.) to stock up on golf discs, hoodies, tie-dyes, and smoking equipment.

Across the street, the **Tin Can Mailman Used & Rare Books Store** (1000 H St., 707/822-1307, www.tincanbooks.com, 10am-6pm Sun.-Thurs., 10am-7pm Fri.-Sat.) crams together two floors full of used books. For the latest fiction or memoir, head to **Northtown Books** (957 H St., 707/822-2834, www.northtownbooks.com, 10am-7pm Mon.-Thurs. and Sat., 10am-9pm Fri., noon-5pm Sun.), which also has an extensive magazine collection.

Solutions (858 G St., 707/822-6972, 10am-5:30pm Mon.-Sat.) is the place to pick up hemp clothing, organic bedding, and eco-goods.

A few blocks from the plaza, **Holly Yashi** (1300 9th St., 877/607-8361, www.hollyyashi.com, 10am-6pm Mon.-Sat., noon-5pm Sun.) specializes in niobium jewelry. Niobium is a metal that gains streaks of color after being dipped in an electrically charged bath. Watch artists at work crafting the jewelry in the attached studio.

FOOD

There's a lot of water around Arcata and **Salt Fish House** (761 8th St., 707/630-5300, www.saltfishhouse.com, 11:30am-10pm Tues.-Fri., 4pm-10pm Sat.-Sun., $15-32) always has local sustainable seafood—the cod and chips are a favorite. The weekday happy hour (3pm-5pm

Mon.-Fri.) sees fish tacos, raw oysters, grilled oysters, and margaritas at nice prices.

★ **Renata's Creperie and Espresso** (1030 G St., 707/825-8783, 8am-3pm Sun.-Thurs., 8am-9pm Fri.-Sat., $4-12) is the best place to start the day. Their organic buckwheat crepes are artfully decorated with drizzled sauces and well-placed garnishes, and deliver on their promising looks with sweet and savory fillings. Expect a wait on weekends. Renata's is open for dinner on Friday and Saturday nights.

The Big Blue Café (846 G St., 707/826-7578, 8am-3pm Sun.-Thurs., 7am-3pm Fri.-Sat., $6-16) is an appropriately colored diner on Arcata Plaza with a menu that skews toward breakfast basics like omelets, French toast, and breakfast burritos. The organic house coffee is flavorful.

Abruzzi (780 7th St., 707/826-2345, www.abruzziarcata.com, 5pm-9pm Wed.-Sun., $12-40) is the place to go for fine dining. The menu includes free-range chicken dishes, seafood offerings, and classic pastas like Bolognese, primavera, and Alfredo.

A local institution for more than 30 years, ★ **Tomo Japanese Restaurant** (708 9th St., 707/822-1414, www.tomoarcata.com, 11:30am-2pm and 4pm-9pm Mon.-Sat., 4pm-9pm Sun., $10-22) serves sushi rolls and entrées that are as eclectic as its hometown. Get a spicy tofu roll or a unique locally smoked albacore roll. Tomo has a list of sakes, and there's also a full bar.

Arcata locals swear by **Taqueria La Barca** (5201 Carlson Park Dr., 707/822-6669, 10am-8pm Mon.-Fri., $7-11) for the house-made horchata, chile rellenos, and carnitas.

Stop in **Wildberries Marketplace** (747 13th St., 707/822-0095, www.wildberries.com, 6am-10pm daily) to stock up for a picnic. They also have a café, a juice bar, a coffee shop, and a farmers market (3:30pm-6:30pm Tues.). The Arcata Plaza hosts a Saturday **farmers market** (www.humfarm.org, 9am-2pm Sat. Apr.-mid-Nov., 10am-2pm Sat. mid-Nov.-Mar.) that has live music.

ACCOMMODATIONS

Downtown lodging options are limited. The **Hotel Arcata** (708 9th St., 707/826-0217, www.hotelarcata.com, $102-172) has a superb location right on the plaza. The rooms are small, but the bathrooms have claw-foot tubs outfitted with showerheads. The hallways are decorated with framed historic photos of Arcata Plaza and other local landmarks. A stay includes complimentary Wi-Fi and continental breakfast. Secure a free pass to the Arcata Community Pool from the front desk.

The Lady Anne Bed and Breakfast (902 14th St., 707/822-2797, http://ladyanne-inn.com, $150-185) has a little more character, with five rooms in an old Victorian built in 1888. All have private bathrooms, and most include gas-burning woodstoves. A music room is decorated with instruments including a piano, an accordion, and a bass guitar that guests can play. The Lady Anne serves a continental breakfast.

A few miles from the plaza, the **Best Western Arcata Inn** (4827 Valley West Blvd., 707/826-0313, http://bestwesterncalifornia.com, $101-160) is a well-regarded chain motel in the area. The rooms have satellite TV and Wi-Fi, and there's an indoor/outdoor heated swimming pool and hot tub. Fuel up with a complimentary breakfast.

TRANSPORTATION AND SERVICES

Arcata is eight miles north of Eureka on U.S. 101. Once there, it's easiest to just park your car and walk around the small city. The **Arcata & Mad River Transit System** (www.humboldttransit.org, adults $1.50, seniors and children $1.25) runs a fleet of red-and-yellow buses that travel all over Arcata.

A small commercial airport, **California Redwood Coast-Humboldt County Airport** (ACV, 3561 Boeing Ave., McKinleyville, 707/839-5401, http://humboldtgov.org) serves the region via United Airlines. Flights are expensive but convenient.

North of downtown, the **Mad River Community Hospital** (3800 Janes Rd., 707/822-3621, http://madriverhospital.com) has an emergency room and urgent care department.

Trinidad Bay

Perched on a bluff over boat-studded Trinidad Bay, Trinidad has a wealth of natural assets, including scenic headlands and wild beaches on either side of town. It also has a long history: The town was named by two Spanish Navy men who came to the area on Trinity Sunday in 1775. Right off U.S. 101, Trinidad is worth a visit, whether it's for a stop to stretch your legs or a tranquil weekend getaway.

★ TRINIDAD

With a population of just 360 people, Trinidad is one of the smallest incorporated cities in California; it's also one of the most beautiful.

Trinidad Memorial Lighthouse

Not an actual lighthouse but a replica of the one on nearby Trinidad Head, **Trinidad Memorial Lighthouse** (Trinity St. and Edwards St.) is the local photo opportunity. It was built by the Trinidad Civic Club in 1949. The small red-and-white building sits on a bluff above the bay where boats bob in the water. A marble slab and a series of plaques list names of people who have been lost at sea. To the left of the lighthouse is the old Trinidad fog bell.

Trinidad Head

A rocky promontory north of the bay, the 380-foot-high **Trinidad Head** (end of Edwards St.) affords great views of the area's beaches, bay, and town. A one-mile-long loop trail on the headlands goes under canopies of vegetation and then out to a series of clear spots with benches. A large stone cross on the west end of Trinidad Head marks where Spanish seamen initially erected a wooden cross. Below the cross is a small wooden deck where you can glimpse the top of the Trinidad Head Lighthouse. The squat lighthouse on a 175-foot-high cliff was activated in 1871. In 1914, the lighthouse made news when, according to the lighthouse keeper, a huge wave extinguished the light.

Trinidad State Beach

Below the bluffs of Trinidad Head, **Trinidad State Beach** (end of Edwards St., 707/677-3570, www.parks.ca.gov, sunrise-sunset daily, free) runs north for a mile to Elk Head. Spruce-tufted Pewetole Island and a scattering of scenic coastal islets lie offshore. The northern end has caves, an arch, and tide pools. It's a great place for a contemplative walk.

Humboldt State University Marine Laboratory

Students come to the **HSU Marine Laboratory** (570 Ewing St., 707/826-3671, www2.humboldt.edu/marinelab, 9am-4:30pm Mon.-Fri., 10am-5pm Sat.-Sun., tours by appointment, self-guided tours $1, guided tours $2) to learn about the area's coastal critters. A tour of the lab includes looks at invertebrates from nearby intertidal zones, like sea cucumbers, tube worms, giant green anemones, and red octopi. Visitors can also sign up to explore the area's tide pools with a marine naturalist ($3).

SPORTS AND RECREATION
Kayaking and Whale-Watching

Protected Trinidad Bay is an ideal spot for a scenic sea-kayaking excursion. **Humboats Kayak Adventures** (707/443-5157, www.humboats.com, $45-110) runs guided whale-watching tours in the spring and early summer when gray whales migrate right through the protected harbor area.

Sportfishing

Head out to sea with one of two Trinidad-based fishing outfits. Fish for rockfish, salmon, or Dungeness crab with **Trinidad Bay Charters** (707/499-8878, www.trinidadbaycharters.net, $120). Trips leave daily at 6:15am and 12:15pm. **Patrick's Point Charters** (707/445-4106, www.

Trinidad State Beach

patrickspointcharters.com, $120/half day) leaves out of Trinidad Harbor for rockfish, salmon, and Dungeness crab.

Surfing
South of Trinidad are some of Humboldt County's best-known surf spots. **Moonstone Beach** (3 miles south of Trinidad on Scenic Dr.) is a popular surf break where the Little River pours into Trinidad Bay. Up the road 0.5 mile, **Camel Rock** (about 2.3 miles south of Trinidad on Scenic Dr.) has right breaks that peel inside of a distinct, double-humped off-shore rock.

Salty's Supply Co. (332 Main St., 707/677-0300, https://saltystrinidad.com, 7am-6pm daily summer, 10am-6pm daily fall, 10am-5pm Tues.-Sun. winter, surfboards $30/day, wetsuits $30/day) rents surf gear along with kayaks, bikes, books, and magazines (seriously!).

FOOD
Stock up on delicious, locally smoked seafood at ★ **Katy's Smokehouse** (740 Edwards St., 707/677-0151, www.katyssmokehouse.com, 9am-6pm daily). There are smoked oysters and salmon jerky, but you can't go wrong with the smoked king salmon. It's not a sit-down restaurant, so you'll need to get your order to go.

The friendly, spunky staff at the **Beachcomber Café** (363 Trinity St., 707/677-0106, http://trinidadbeachcomber.blogspot.com, 7am-4pm Mon.-Fri., 8am-4pm Sat.-Sun.) serve coffee, cookies, paninis, and bagels. The café also has free Wi-Fi with purchase.

North of Trinidad, the ★ **Larrupin Café** (1658 Patrick's Point Dr., 707/677-0230, www.thelarrupin.com, 5pm-9pm daily, $26-50) is probably the most-loved restaurant in the area. They put their legendary mesquite barbecue sauce on everything from tofu kebabs to creole prawns and are known for their mustard dill and red sauces. Enjoy the heated patio June through September.

ACCOMMODATIONS
The only lodging in Trinidad proper is the **Trinidad Bay Bed & Breakfast** (560 Edward St., 707/677-0840, www.trinidadbaybnb.com, $300-400), across the street from the Trinidad Memorial Lighthouse. Each of the four rooms has a view of Trinidad Bay; two rooms have private entrances, and all have private bathrooms. A hot three-course breakfast is served.

Between the main section of Trinidad and

Pick up some smoked salmon at Katy's Smokehouse.

Patrick's Point State Park, The Lost Whale Bed & Breakfast Inn (3452 Patrick's Point Dr., 707/677-3425, http://lostwhaleinn.com, $275-335) has five rooms with great views of the Pacific and four with garden views. Two rooms have lofts to accommodate up to four people. There's a private trail to the beach, an oceanview hot tub, and a wood-burning sauna. A seven-course breakfast buffet is served.

The Emerald Forest (753 Patrick's Point Dr., 707/677-3554, www.cabinsintheredwoods.com, $179-349) has a variety of rustic cabins for rent. The higher-end cabins have full kitchens and amenities like wood-burning stoves. RV and tent campsites are also available ($35-48), although those at nearby Patrick's Point State Park are more spacious.

TRANSPORTATION

Trinidad is 15 miles north of Arcata on U.S. 101. Take exit 728 off the highway. The Redwood Transit System (707/443-0826, www.redwoodtransit.org, adults $3, seniors and children $2.75) has buses that connect from Arcata and Eureka to Trinidad.

Trinidad is a small city, so don't expect too many services. Most major services can be found in nearby Arcata.

PATRICK'S POINT STATE PARK

Patrick's Point State Park (4150 Patrick's Point Dr., 707/677-3570, www.parks.ca.gov, sunrise-sunset daily, day use $8) is a rambling coastal park 25 miles north of Eureka, replete with beaches, historic landmarks, trails, and campgrounds. The climate remains cool year-round, making it perfect for hiking and exploring.

Get a map and information at the Patrick's Point State Park Visitors Center (707/677-1945, 9am-5pm daily summer, 10am-4pm daily winter), immediately to the right of the entry gate. Information about nature walks and campfire programs is posted on the bulletin board.

Sights

Prominent among the local landmarks is Patrick's Point, which can be reached by a brief hike from a convenient parking lot. Adjacent to Patrick's Point in a picturesque cove is Wedding Rock, a promontory sticking out into the ocean like an upturned thumb. (People really do hike the narrow trail out to the rock to get married.)

The most fascinating area is Sumeg Village, a re-creation of a native Yurok village

Trinidad Bay Bed & Breakfast

based on an archaeological find east of here. Visitors can crawl through the perfectly round doors into semi-subterranean homes, meeting places, and storage buildings. Check out the native plant garden, a collection of local plants the Yurok people used for food, basketry, and medicine. (The local Yurok people use Sumeg Village as a gathering place; please tread lightly).

Patrick's Point has a number of accessible beaches. A steep trail leads down to Agate Beach, a wide stretch of coarse sand bordered by cliffs shot through with shining quartz veins. The semiprecious stones for which it is named really do appear here.

Hiking

Six miles of trails thread through the park, including the Rim Trail (4 miles round-trip), which will take you along the cliffs for a view of the sea and migrating whales (Sept.-Jan.,

Mar.-June). Tree lovers might prefer the Octopus Tree Trail, which provides a great view of an old-growth Sitka spruce grove.

Camping

Three campgrounds (reservations 800/444-7275, www.reservecalifornia.com, $35) have a total of 124 sites. It can be difficult to determine the difference between Agate Beach, Abalone, and Penn Creek, so get directions from the park rangers. Most campsites are pleasantly shaded by the groves of trees. All include a picnic table, fire pit, and food storage cupboard, and you'll find running water, restrooms, and showers nearby.

Transportation

Patrick's Point State Park is on the coast, 25 miles north of Eureka and 15 miles south of Orick on U.S. 101.

Redwood National and State Parks

TOP EXPERIENCE

The lands of Redwood National and State Parks (www.nps.gov/redw) meander along the coast and include three state parks—Prairie Creek Redwoods, Del Norte Coast Redwoods, and Jedediah Smith. This complex of parkland encompasses most of California's northern redwood forests. The main landmass of Redwood National Park is just south of Prairie Creek State Park along U.S. 101, stretching east from the coast and the highway.

REDWOOD NATIONAL PARK

The Thomas H. Kuchel Visitors Center (U.S. 101, west of Orick, 707/465-7765, 9am-5pm daily spring-fall, 9am-4pm daily winter) is a large facility with a ranger station, clean restrooms, and a path to the shore. Get advice, maps, backcountry permits, and books. In the summer, rangers run patio talks and coast walks that provide a great introduction

to the area for children and adults. Picnic at one of the tables outside the visitors center, or walk a short distance to Redwood Creek.

Hiking

One of the easiest, most popular ways to get close to the trees is to walk the Lady Bird Johnson Trail (Bald Hills Rd., 1.4 miles, easy). This nearly level loop provides an intimate view of the redwood and fir forests that define this region. Another easy-access trail is Trillium Falls (Davison Rd. at Elk Meadow, 2.8 miles, easy). The redwood trees along this cool, dark trail are striking, and the small waterfall is a nice treasure in the woods. This little hike is lovely any time of year but best in spring, when the water volume over the falls is at its peak.

The Lost Man Creek Trail (east of Elk Meadow, 1 mile off U.S. 101, 0.5-22 miles, easy-difficult) has it all. The first 0.5 mile is perfect for wheelchair users and families with small children. But as the trail rolls along, the grades get steeper and more challenging. Customize the length of this out-and-back trail by turning around at any time. If you reach the Lost Man Creek picnic grounds, your total round-trip distance is 22 miles with more than 3,000 feet of elevation gain and several stream crossings.

The **Redwood Creek Trail** (Bald Hills Rd. spur off U.S. 101, difficult) follows Redwood Creek for 8 miles to the **Tall Trees Grove**. If you have a shuttle car, pick up the **Tall Trees Trail** and walk another 6 miles (a total of 14 miles) to the **Dolason Prairie Trail,** which takes you back out to Bald Hills Road.

Camping

There are no designated campgrounds in Redwood National Park; free backcountry camping is allowed, but permits may be necessary. The **Elam Camp** and the **44 Camp** are both hike-in primitive campgrounds along the Dolason Prairie Trail.

Transportation

The Redwood National and State Parks line U.S. 101 from Prairie Creek Redwoods north to Jedediah Smith near Crescent City. The Thomas H. Kuchel Visitors Center at the south end of the park is 40 miles north of Eureka on U.S. 101.

★ PRAIRIE CREEK REDWOODS STATE PARK

In addition to the silent majesty of the redwoods, the 14,000 acres of **Prairie Creek Redwoods State Park** (Newton B. Drury Dr., 25 miles south of Crescent City, 707/488-2039, www.parks.ca.gov, sunrise-sunset daily, day use $8) offer miles of wild beach, roaming wildlife, and a popular hike through a one-of-a-kind fern-draped canyon.

The **Visitors Center** (Newton B. Drury Dr., 707/488-2039, 9am-5pm daily summer, 9am-4pm daily winter) includes a small interpretive museum describing the history of the redwood forests. A tiny bookshop adjoins the

Redwood National and State Parks

museum, well stocked with books describing the history, nature, and culture of the area. Many ranger-led programs originate at the visitors center, and permits are available for backcountry camping.

One of the many reasons to visit is a chance to view a herd of Roosevelt elk. This subspecies of elk can stand up to five feet high and can weigh close to 1,000 pounds. These big guys usually hang out at—where else?—the Elk Prairie, a stretch of open grassland along the highway, and off the southern end of the Newton B. Drury Drive. The best times to see the elk are early morning and around sunset. August to October is the elk mating season, when the calls of the bulls fill the air.

Newton B. Drury Scenic Parkway

A gorgeous scenic road through the redwoods, Newton B. Drury Scenic Parkway (off U.S. 101 about 5 miles south of Klamath) features old-growth trees lining the roads, a close-up view of the redwood forest ecosystem, and a grove or trailhead every hundred yards or so. The turnoff is at the Big Tree Wayside, where you can walk up to the 304-foot-high Big Tree. Follow the short, five-minute loop trail to see other giants in the area.

Gold Bluffs Beach

Gold Bluffs Beach (Davison Rd., 3 miles north of Orick off U.S. 101) is truly wild. Lonely waves pound the shore, a spiky grove of Sitka spruce tops the nearby bluffs, and herds of Roosevelt elk frequently roam the wide, salt-and-pepper-colored beach. Prospectors found gold flakes here in 1850, giving the beach its name. But the region was too remote and rugged to maintain a lucrative mining operation. Access Gold Bluffs Beach by taking Davison Road. No trailers are allowed on Davison Road.

Hiking

Perhaps the single most famous hiking trail along the redwood coast is Fern Canyon (1 mile, Davison Rd., Prairie Creek Redwoods State Park), near Gold Bluffs Beach. The unusual setting was used as a dramatic backdrop in the film *The Lost World: Jurassic Park*. This hike runs through a narrow canyon carved by Home Creek. Five-fingered ferns, sword ferns, and delicate lady ferns cascade down the steep canyon walls. Droplets from seeping water sources keep the plants alive. You can extend this hike into a longer loop (6.5 miles, moderate): When the trail intersects with James Irvine Trail, bear right and follow the spur. Bear right again onto Clintonia Trail and walk to Miners Ridge Trail. Bear right onto Miners Ridge and follow it down to the ocean. Walk 1.5 miles along Gold Bluffs Beach to complete the loop.

To get to the trailhead, take U.S. 101 three miles north of the town of Orick. At the Prairie Creek visitors center, turn west onto Davison Road (no trailers allowed) and travel two miles. This rough dirt road takes you through the campground and ends at the trailhead in 1.5 miles.

Miners Ridge and James Irvine Loop (12 miles, moderate) starts from the visitors center instead of the Fern Canyon trailhead, avoiding the rough dirt terrain of Davison Road. Start out on James Irvine Trail and bear right when you can, following the trail all the way until it joins Fern Canyon Trail. Turn left when you get to the coast and walk along Gold Bluffs Beach for 1.5 miles. Then make a left onto the Clintonia Trail and head back toward the visitors center.

The California Coastal Trail (www.californiacoastaltrail.info) runs along the park's northern coastline and can be accessed via the Ossagon Creek Trail (north end of Newton B. Drury Dr., 2 miles round-trip, moderate). It's not long, but the steep grade makes it a tough haul in spots, and the stunning trees along the way make it worth the effort.

Camping

The Elk Prairie Campground (127011 Newton B. Drury Dr., Orick, campground 707/488-2039, reservations 800/444-7275, www.reservecalifornia.com, reservations recommended Memorial Day-Labor Day, vehicles $35, hikers and cyclists $5) has 75 sites for tents or RVs and a full range of comfortable camping amenities, including showers and firewood. Several campsites are wheelchair-accessible (request at reservation). A big campfire area, an easy walk north of the campground, has evening programs put on by rangers and volunteers.

For beach camping, head to **Gold Bluffs Beach Campground** (Davison Rd., 3 miles north of Orick, www.nps.gov/redw, $35 regular sites, $20 environmental sites). There are 26 first-come, first-served sites for tents or RVs and 3 environmental sites. Amenities include flush toilets, water, solar showers, and wide ocean views. The surf can be quite dangerous here, so be extremely careful if you go in the water.

Backcountry camping is allowed in two designated camping areas: Ossagon Creek and Miners Ridge (3 sites each, $5). Permits are available at the campground kiosk or the Prairie Creek visitors center (Newton B. Drury Dr., 707/488-2171, 9am-5pm daily).

Transportation

Prairie Creek Redwoods is 50 miles north of Eureka and 25 miles south of Crescent City on U.S. 101. Newton B. Drury Drive traverses the park and can be accessed from U.S. 101 north or south.

Trees of Mystery

Generations of kids have enjoyed spotting the gigantic wooden sculptures of Paul Bunyan and his blue ox, Babe, from U.S. 101. The **Trees of Mystery** (15500 U.S. 101 N., 707/482-2251 or 800/638-3389, www.treesofmystery.net, 8am-7pm daily June-Aug., 8:30am-6:30pm daily Sept.-Oct., 9am-5pm daily Nov.-May, adults $18, seniors $14, children 6-12 $9, children under 5 free) is a great place to let the family out for some good cheesy fun. Visitors can enjoy the original Mystery Hike, the SkyTrail gondola ride through the old-growth redwoods, and the palatial gift shop. Perhaps best of all, at the left end of the gift shop is a little-known gem: the Native American museum. A large collection of artifacts from both tribes across the country and those indigenous to the redwood forests graces several crowded galleries. The restrooms here are large and well maintained, which makes Trees of Mystery a nice rest stop.

DEL NORTE COAST REDWOODS STATE PARK

Del Norte Coast Redwoods State Park (Mill Creek Campground Rd., off U.S. 101, 707/465-7335, www.parks.ca.gov, $8) encompasses a variety of ecosystems, including eight miles of wild coastline, second-growth redwood forest, and virgin old-growth forests. One of the largest in this system of parks, Del Norte is a great place to get lost in the backcountry with just your knapsack.

Del Norte state park has no visitors center, but you can get information from the **Crescent City Information Center** (1111 2nd St., Crescent City, 707/465-7306, 9am-5pm daily spring-fall, 9am-4pm Thurs.-Mon. winter).

Hiking

Several rewarding yet gentle and short excursions start and end in the Mill Creek Campground. The **Trestle Loop Trail** (1 mile, easy) begins across from the campfire center in the campground. Notice the trestles and other artifacts along the way; the loop follows the route of a defunct railroad from the logging era. Another easy stroll is the nearby **Nature Loop Trail** (1 mile, easy), which begins near the campground entrance gate. Interpretive signage teaches you about the varieties of impressive trees you'll pass.

Camping

The **Mill Creek campground** (U.S. 101, 7 miles south of Crescent City, 800/444-7275, www.reservecalifornia.com, May-Sept., vehicles $35, hikers and cyclists $5) is in an attractive setting along Mill Creek. There are 145 sites for RVs and tents, and facilities include restrooms, fire pits, and a dump station. There

California Coastal Trail

The northern section of the great California Coastal Trail (CCT, www.californiacoastaltrail.info) runs right through Del Norte Coast Redwoods State Park. The trail is reasonably well marked; look for signs with the CCT logo. The **"last chance"** section of the California Coastal Trail (Enderts Beach-Damnation Creek, 14 miles, strenuous) makes a challenging day hike. To reach the trailhead, turn west from U.S. 101 onto Enderts Beach Road in Del Norte, three miles south of Crescent City. Drive 2.3 miles to the end of the road.

The trail follows the historic route of U.S. 101 south to Enderts Beach. You'll walk through fields of wildflowers and groves of trees twisted by the wind and saltwater. Eventually, the trail climbs about 900 feet to an overlook with a great view of Enderts Beach. At just over two miles, the trail enters Del Norte Coast Redwoods State Park, where it meanders through Anson Grove's redwood, fir, and Sitka spruce trees. At 4.5 miles, cross Damnation Creek on a footbridge, and at 6.1 miles, cross the Damnation Creek Trail. (For a longer hike, take the four-mile round-trip side excursion down to the beach and back.) After seven miles, a flight of steps leads up to milepost 15.6 on U.S. 101. At this point, you can turn around and return the way you came, making for a gloriously varied day hike of about 14 miles round-trip.

One alternative is to make this a point-to-point hike, either by dropping a car off at one end to get you back at the end of the day, or by having one group of hikers start at each end of the trail and exchange keys at a central meeting point.

If you've made arrangements for a lift back at the end of the day, continue on to the DeMartin section of the Coastal Trail. From here, descend through a lush grove of ferns and take a bridge over a tributary of Wilson Creek, enjoying views of the rocky coast far below. The wildflowers continue as you enter Redwood National Park and wander through the grasslands of DeMartin Prairie. The southern trailhead (where you pick up your vehicle if you're doing the trail one-way north-south) is at the Wilson Creek Picnic Area on the east side of U.S. 101 at the north end of DeMartin Bridge.

are no designated backcountry campsites and backcountry camping is not allowed.

Transportation

Del Norte Coast Redwoods is seven miles south of Crescent City on U.S. 101. The park entrance is on Hamilton Road, east of U.S. 101.

★ JEDEDIAH SMITH REDWOODS STATE PARK

There's nowhere better to experience the majesty of the North Coast's redwoods than at Jedediah Smith Redwoods State Park (1440 U.S. 199, 9 miles east of Crescent City, 707/465-7335 or 707/458-3496, www.parks.ca.gov, sunrise-sunset daily, $8/vehicle). The most popular redwood grove in the park is the Stout Memorial Grove, a 44-acre grove of 300-foot-tall redwoods and waist-high sword

ferns. These are some of the biggest and oldest trees on the North Coast, somehow spared the loggers' saws. The quiet grove lacks visitors, since its far-north latitude makes it harder to reach than some of the other big redwood groves in California.

There are two visitors centers, about five minutes apart: Jedediah Smith Visitors Center (U.S. 101, Hiouchi, 707/465-7306, 9am-5pm daily summer) and the Hiouchi Information Center (U.S. 199, Hiouchi, 707/458-3294, 9am-5pm daily summer, 9am-4pm daily winter). Both offer information and materials about all of the nearby parks.

Hiking

The shaded trails make for wonderfully cool summer hiking. Many trails run along the river and the creeks, offering beach access and plenty of lush scenery to enjoy. The Simpson Reed Trail (U.S. 199, 6 miles east of Crescent

City, 1 mile, easy) takes you from U.S. 199 down to the banks of the Smith River.

To get a good view of the Smith River, hike the **Hiouchi Trail** (2 miles, moderate). From the Hiouchi Information Center and campgrounds on U.S. 199, cross the Summer Footbridge and then follow the river north. The Hiouchi Trail then meets the Hatton Loop Trail and leads away from the river and into the forest.

For a longer and more aggressive trek, try the **Mill Creek Trail** (7.5 miles round-trip, difficult). Start at the Summer Footbridge (seasonal) and follow the creek down to the unpaved Howland Hill Road. The trail winds through ferns, maples, pines, and stunning redwoods. (Just off the trail is the Grove of the Titans, said to be the home of the world's largest coast redwood.) There's also a pristine swimming hole with a rope swing near the southeast end of the trail.

The **Boy Scout Tree Trail** (5.2 miles, moderate) is usually quiet, with few hikers, and the gargantuan forest will make you feel truly tiny. To get to the trailhead, drive a rugged, unpaved road for a couple of miles. About three miles into the trail, you'll come to a fork. If you've got time, take both forks: first

the left, which takes you to the small, mossy, and very green Fern Falls, and then the right, which takes you to the eponymous Boy Scout Tree, one of the impressively huge redwoods. Check at the visitors center first to make sure the road to the trailhead is open.

Boating and Swimming

You'll find two boat launches in the park: one at Society Hole and one adjacent to the Summer Footbridge (winter only). Down by the River Beach Trail, you'll find **River Beach** (immediately west of the Hiouchi Information Center), a popular spot for swimming. Swimming is allowed throughout the park, but be very careful—rivers and creeks move unpredictably, and you might not notice deep holes until you're on them.

Fishing

With the Smith River and numerous feeder creeks running through Jed Smith, fishing a popular activity. Chilly winter fishing draws a surprising number of anglers to vie for king salmon up to 30 pounds and steelhead up to 20 pounds. Seasons for both species run October-February. In the summer, cast into the river to catch cutthroat trout.

Stout Memorial Grove at Jedediah Smith Redwoods State Park

Camping

The ★ **Jedediah Smith Campground** (U.S. 199, Hiouchi, 800/444-7275, www.reserveca-lifornia.com, vehicles $35, hike-in or cycle-in primitive sites $5) is beautifully situated on the banks of Smith River, with most sites near the River Beach Trail. There are 106 RV and tent sites. Facilities include restrooms, fire pits, and coin-operated showers. Reservations (accepted Memorial Day-Labor Day) are advised, especially for summer and holiday weekends.

Jedediah Smith has no designated backcountry campsites; camping outside the developed campgrounds is not allowed.

Transportation

Jedediah Smith Redwoods State Park is northeast of Crescent City along the Smith River, next door to the immense Smith River National Recreation Area (U.S. 199 west of Hiouchi). Get to the park by taking U.S. 199 nine miles east of Crescent City.

Crescent City

The northernmost city on the California coast perches on the bay that provides its name. Cool and windswept, Crescent City is a perfect place to put on a parka, stuff your hands deep into your pockets, and wander along a wide, beautiful beach. The small city also has a vibrant surf scene centered on South Beach, which frequently has good waves for longboarders.

Crescent City is also known for surviving tsunamis. In 1964, a tsunami caused by an Alaskan earthquake wiped out 29 city blocks and killed 11 people. It was the most severe tsunami on the U.S. West Coast in modern history. In 2011, a devastating earthquake in Japan resulted in a tsunami that laid waste to the city's harbor. The old, rusted warning sirens on the tops of the city's utility poles still work; when they sound, there's a chance of massive waves coming to shore.

SIGHTS
Point St. George

Wild, lonely, beautiful **Point St. George** (end of Washington Blvd., sunrise-sunset daily) epitomizes the glory of the North Coast. Walk out onto the cliffs to take in the deep blue sea, wild salt- and flower-scented air, and craggy cliffs and beaches. On a clear day, you can see all the way to Oregon. Short, steep trails lead across wild beach prairie land down to broad, flat, nearly deserted beaches. In spring and

summer, wildflowers bloom on the cliffs, and swallows nest in the cluster of buildings on the point. On rare and special clear days, you can almost make out the **St. George Reef Lighthouse** alone on its perch far out in the Pacific.

★ Battery Point Lighthouse

On an island just north of Crescent City Harbor, the **Battery Point Lighthouse** (end of A St., 707/464-3089, www.delnorte-history.org, 10am-4pm daily Apr.-Sept., 10am-4pm Sat.-Sun. Oct.-Mar. tides permitting, adults $3, children 8-15 $1) is only accessible at low tide, when a rocky spit littered with tide pools emerges, serving as a walkway for visitors. The 1856 lighthouse's current keepers reside on the island in one-month shifts; they also lead tours. You'll see a Fresnel lens and a working clock that was used by Battery Point's first lighthouse keeper. After you view the building's two residential floors, the docent leads any adventurous visitors up a metal ladder and through a small hole into the lantern room, where you'll be able to feel the heat of the still-working light just feet away. On a clear day, you'll also be able to see the pencil-like outline of the St. George Reef Lighthouse in the distance. St. George is situated on a small, wave-washed rock seven miles from shore, and its dangerous location resulted

Crescent City

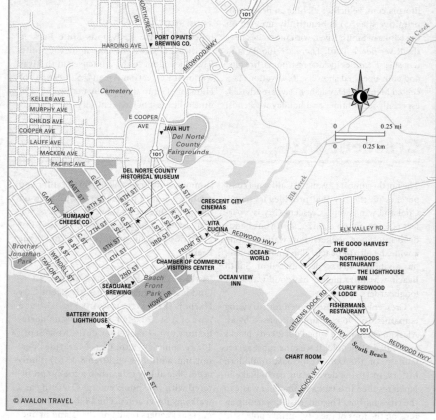

in the deaths of four keepers who worked there.

Ocean World

A great family respite is **Ocean World** (304 U.S. 101 S., 707/464-4900, www.oceanworldonline.com, 9am-6pm daily, adults $13, children 3-11 $8). Tours of the small sea park depart about every 15 minutes and last about 40 minutes. Featured attractions are the shark-petting tank, the 500,000-gallon aquarium, and the sea lion show. An immense souvenir shop sells gifts with nautical themes.

Del Norte County Historical Society Museum

The **Del Norte County Historical Society Museum** (577 H St., 707/464-3922, www.delnortehistory.org, 10am-4pm daily, free) maintains this small museum that features the local history of both the Native Americans who were once the only inhabitants of Del Norte County and the encroaching white settlers. Exhibits include the wreck of the *Brother Jonathan* at Point St. George, the story of the 1964 tsunami, and artifacts of the local Yurok and Tolowa people.

ENTERTAINMENT AND EVENTS

Port O'Pints Brewing Co. (1215 Northcrest Dr., 707/460-1154, http://portopints.com, 2pm-9pm Sun.-Thurs., 1pm-10pm Fri.-Sat.) is a small brewpub that resembles a neighborhood bar. There's an Irish feel to the place, which serves Irish red beer and features maritime decor. A sampler platter of brews is served on a ship's steering wheel. Live music on weekend nights gets the place hopping.

Take in a first-run movie at the **Crescent City Cinemas** (375 M St., 707/570-8438, www.catheatres.com).

The **Del Norte Association for Cultural Awareness** (Crescent Elk Auditorium, 994 G St., 707/464-1336, www.dnaca.net) hosts several live musical acts and other performances each year and provides a community arts calendar.

Since the early 1980s, the **Crescent City Triathlon** (707/465-3995, www.crescentcity-triathlon.com, Aug., adults $55-65, children $20-25) has challenged participants of all ages. This triathlon is a 5K run, a 500-yard swim, and a 12-mile bike ride. There's also a duathlon, which involves a run, a bike ride, and then another run; there's also a triathlon for kids that varies in intensity by age group, making it possible for anyone ages 5-12 to join the fun.

SPORTS AND RECREATION
Beaches

The sands of Crescent City are a beachcomber's paradise. **South Beach** (Hwy. 1 between Anchor Way and Sand Mine Rd.), at the south end of town, is long, wide, and flat—perfect for a romantic stroll, as long as you're bundled up. Two miles south of town, **Crescent Beach** (Enderts Rd.) is a wide, sandy strip. Down a 0.5-mile dirt trail, **Enderts Beach** (Enderts Rd.) is a superb pocket beach with a creek flowing into the ocean and an onshore rock arch.

No lifeguards patrol these beaches and swimming here is not for the faint of heart.

The water is icy cold, the shores are rocky, and undertow and rip currents are dangerous.

Bird-Watching

The diverse climates and habitats nourish a huge variety of avian residents. Right in town, check out **Battery Point Lighthouse Park** and **Point St. George.** For a rare view of an Aleutian goose or a peregrine falcon, journey to **Tolowa Dunes State Park** (1375 Elk Valley Rd., 707/465-7335, www.parks.ca.gov, sunrise-sunset daily, free), specifically the shores of Lake Earl and Kellogg Beach. South of town, **Enderts Beach** is home to another large bird habitat.

Fishing

Anglers on the North Coast can choose between excellent deep-sea fishing and exciting river trips. The Pacific yields ling cod, snapper, and salmon, while the rivers are famous for chinook (king) salmon, steelhead, and cutthroat trout. The *Tally Ho II* (Crescent City Harbor, Citizen Dock R, Slip D29, 707/464-1236, http://tally-ho-sportfishing.com, May-Oct., half-day $120 pp) is available for a variety of deep-sea fishing trips.

River fishers have a wealth of guides to choose from. **Ken Cunningham Guide Service** (50 Hunter Creek, Klamath, 707/391-7144, www.salmonslayer.net, $200-250) will take you on a full-day fishing trip; the price includes bait, tackle, and the boat.

Hiking

The redwood forests that nearly meet the wide, sandy beaches make the Crescent City area a fabulous place to hike. The hikes at **Point St. George** aren't strenuous and provide stunning views of the coastline and surrounding landscape. **Tolowa Dunes State Park** (1375 Elk Valley Rd., 707/465-7335, www.parks.ca.gov, sunrise-sunset daily, free), north of Point St. George, offers miles of trails winding through forests, across beaches, and meandering along the shores of Lake Earl.

Horseback Riding

Casual riders can enjoy a guided riding adventure through redwoods or along the ocean with **Crescent Trail Rides** (2002 Moorehead Rd., 707/951-5407, www.crescenttrailrides.com, 1.5 hours $70, 3 hours $135). **Fort Dick Stable** (2002 Moorehead Rd., 707/951-5407) offers boarding and riding lessons.

A great place to ride is **Tolowa Dunes State Park** (1375 Elk Valley Rd., 707/465-7335, www.parks.ca.gov, sunrise-sunset daily, free), which maintains 20 miles of trails accessible to horses. Serious equestrians with their own mounts can ride in to a campsite with corrals at the north end of the park off Lower Lake Road.

Surfing

Crescent City has a collection of surf breaks. Pioneering big-wave surfer Greg Noll even lives here. Just south of the harbor is the most popular break in town, **South Beach** (Hwy. 1 between Anchor Way and Sand Mine Rd.), with peeling waves perfect for longboarders and beginners. North of town, **Point St. George** (end of Washington Blvd.) has a reef and point break that comes alive during winter.

FOOD

Seafood is standard fare in Crescent City, but family restaurants and one or two ethnic eateries add some variety.

★ **SeaQuake Brewing** (400 Front St., 707/465-4444, www.seaquakebrewing.com, 3pm-10pm Tues.-Sat., $10-19) has revolutionized Crescent City's drinking and dining scene. The giant brewery and restaurant pours tasty brews, including a Citra IPA, enjoyed outside or in one of the cavernous building's two floors. The menu showcases Del Norte County's assets, from fish tacos made with locally caught rock cod, to burgers with local organic beef, to brick-oven pizzas topped with Crescent City's own Rumiano cheese. Live music on Saturday night makes this the city's ideal stop for great beer, local food, and good music.

The **Java Hut** (437 U.S. 101 N., 707/465-4439, 5am-10pm daily, $5) is a drive-through and walk-up coffee stand that serves a wide array of coffee drinks. Beware of long lines during the morning hours.

The small, family-owned, award-winning **Rumiano Cheese Co.** (511 9th St., 707/465-1535 or 866/328-2433, www.rumianocheese.com, 9:30am-5pm Mon.-Fri., 9am-3pm Sat. June-Dec., 9am-5pm Mon.-Fri. Jan.-May) has been part of Crescent City since 1921. Come to the tasting room for the cheese and stay for, well, more cheese. The dry jack cheese is a particular favorite.

Enjoy an impressive variety of fresh and healthy food at **The Good Harvest Cafe** (575 U.S. 101 S., 707/465-6028, 7:30am-9pm Mon.-Sat., 8am-8pm Sun., $10-35). It serves the best breakfast in town, with vegetarian options like tofu rancheros and veggie frittata. Steak entrées are at the pricier end of the dinner menu, which also includes burgers, pasta, vegetarian entrées, and big salads. Kitschy Native American decorations abound.

Fishermans Restaurant (700 U.S. 101 S., 707/465-3474, 6am-9pm daily, $11-26) is a casual place to grab delicious breakfasts—biscuits and gravy, pancakes, and thick, juicy bacon—and a diverse dinner menu of fresh local seafood.

The chef/owners behind **Vita Cucina** (1270 Front St., Ste. A, 707/464-1076, www.vitacucina.com, 7am-4pm Mon.-Thurs., 7am-7pm Fri., $4-15) up the city's casual dining cred with *bahn mi* sandwiches and pulled pork. On Thursday and Friday, they do pizzas, calzones, and whole smoked chickens.

For seafood at a reasonable price, the best bet is **The Chart Room** (130 Anchor Way, 707/464-5993, https://ccchartroom.com, 11am-4pm Tues., 7am-7pm Wed.-Thurs. and Sun., 7am-8pm Fri.-Sat., $10-23). It's very casual, the food is excellent, and it's right on the ocean.

Crescent City runs a **farmers market** (Del Norte County Fairgrounds, 451 U.S. 101 N., 707/464-7441, www.delnorte.org, 9am-1pm Sat. June-Oct.).

ACCOMMODATIONS

The aptly named **Curly Redwood Lodge** (701 U.S. 101 S., 707/464-2137, www.curlyredwoodlodge.com, $75-107) is constructed of a single rare curly redwood tree. You'll see the lovely color and grain of the tree in your large, simply decorated room. A 1950s feel pervades this friendly, unpretentious motel even though it offers free Wi-Fi. Some rooms even have antique TVs from the 1950s; others have flat screens.

The **Lighthouse Inn** (681 U.S. 101 S., 707/464-3993 or 877/464-3993, http://thelighthouseinncrescentcity.com, $89-145) has an elegant yet whimsical lobby to welcome guests, and the enthusiastic staff can help with restaurant recommendations and sights. Stylish appointments and bold colors grace each guest room. Corner suites with oversize whirlpool tubs make a perfect romantic retreat for couples; standard double rooms are downright cheap.

The "harbor view" inn may be a more apt name for **Ocean View Inn** (270 U.S. 101 S., 707/465-1111 or 855/623-2611, http://oceanviewinncrescentcity.com, $120-165), but the west-facing rooms do overlook a body of water. The lobby is a bit over the top with model sailboat decorations and a large mural of Crescent City's sights, but the rooms are big and worth the price. A complimentary continental breakfast is served in the morning to sweeten the deal. Pay a bit more for a two-room family suite or a room with a Jacuzzi tub and fireplace.

TRANSPORTATION

The main routes in and out of town are U.S. 101 and U.S. 199. Both are well maintained but are twisty in spots, so take care, especially at night. From San Francisco, the drive to Crescent City is about 350 miles (6.5 hours). It is 85 miles (under two hours) from Eureka north to Crescent City on U.S. 101. Traffic isn't a big issue in Crescent City, and parking is free and easy to find throughout town.

Jack McNamara Field (CEC, 250 Dale Rupert Rd., 707/464-7288, http://flycrescentcity.com) is the only airport in Crescent City. Alaska Airlines and PenAir have two daily flights to Portland, Oregon.

Redwood Coast Transit (RCT, 707/464-6400, www.redwoodcoasttransit.org, adults $1, seniors and people with disabilities $0.75) handles bus travel in Crescent City. Have exact change handy. Four in-town routes and a coastal bus from Smith River to Arcata provide ample public-transit options. Pick up a schedule at the visitors center (1001 Front St.).

Shasta and Lassen

The Northern California mountains are some of the most unspoiled areas in the state, protected by a wealth of national and state parks and forestlands.

Mounts Lassen and Shasta are the southern peaks of the Cascade Range, a string of volcanoes—some dormant, some not—that extends from northern Washington to the tip of California's Central Valley. Mount Lassen is as an active volcano; the national park that surrounds it is a hotbed of volcanic activity that includes boiling mud pots, steam vents, and sulfur springs.

North of Lassen is the stunning snow-capped peak of Mount Shasta. Shasta is a dormant volcano: it will erupt again, but probably not so soon. While the town that shares its name is easy to reach, the mountain itself is daunting to climb. Between Lassen and Mount Shasta is the resort area of Shasta Lake, which attracts boaters and water enthusiasts.

As you explore this remote area, a number of quirky places are worth a visit of their own. Go underground at Lava Beds National Monument, scale the cliffs at Castle Crags, feel the spray of McArthur-Burney Falls, and discover the shameful history of a World War II Japanese "segregation center" at Tule Lake.

PLANNING YOUR TIME

Shasta and Lassen make a fabulous weekend getaway. Mount Shasta offers fairly easy and reliable year-round access along I-5, with both winter and summer outdoor recreation. The best time to visit Mount Lassen is mid- to late summer. Lassen is in the remote eastern part of the state, and the weather can be extreme with snow as late as June. In winter, Lassen Volcanic Scenic Byway closes.

It's a 3.5- to 4-hour drive to reach the area from the San Francisco Bay Area. Redding has a municipal airport, which runs multiple trips daily to San Francisco.

Previous: Mount Shasta; Lassen Volcanic National Park. **Above:** Lake Shasta.

Highlights

★ **Bumpass Hell:** A two-mile hike leads through a hotbed of geothermal activity (page 242).

★ **Loomis Museum:** This small but lovely museum offers a history of Lassen's volcanic eruptions through a series of startling and revealing photographs (page 244).

★ **Hiking Lassen Peak:** This 10,462-foot volcano offers a rewarding hike to the top and a dramatic view below (page 245).

★ **Lake Shasta Caverns:** These wondrous caverns are filled with natural limestone, marble, and crystal-studded stalactites and stalagmites (page 257).

★ **Mount Shasta:** This dazzling glacier-topped mountain peak is truly one of the greatest visions the state has to offer (page 261).

★ **Castle Crags State Park:** A longtime favorite of rock climbers, this park offers great hiking, camping, and scenic views (page 266).

★ **McArthur-Burney Falls Memorial State Park:** This park is home to 129-foot Burney Falls, touted as California's most beautiful waterfall (page 268).

★ **Lava Beds National Monument:** With

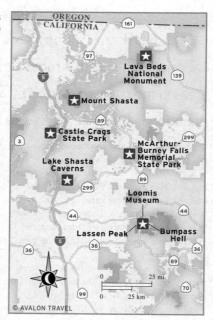

more than 700 natural caves, ancient rock art, and 14 species of bats, this strange place amazes 269).

Lassen Volcanic National Park

Lassen Volcanic National Park (530/595-4480, www.nps.gov/lavo, $25 per vehicle) is one of the remotest and most primitive national parks in the state. The paved Lassen Volcanic Scenic Byway (closed in winter) runs through the park, making it easy for summer visitors to enjoy the park's active volcanic features. The rugged weather and isolated location mean that a visit to Lassen Volcanic National Park is a trip to a largely unspoiled wilderness. Half of the park has only minimal dirt-road access, offering its rugged beauty to those willing to hike into the backcountry.

Four types of volcanoes—shield, composite, cinder cone, and plug dome—are found within the boundaries of the park. Mount Lassen, itself an active volcano, is the best example of a plug dome. It has a long record of eruptions; the last took place in 1914-1917.

PLANNING YOUR TIME

Although the park is open year-round, snow chokes the area from October until June or July, and the park road is closed. The only time to visit Lassen is in summer; most visitors arrive in August and early September. Check **road conditions** (530/595-4480, www.nps.gov/lavo) before planning a trip, even in summer.

SIGHTS

Kohm Yah-mah-nee Visitor Center

The **Kohm Yah-mah-nee Visitor Center** (Hwy. 89, 530/595-4480, www.nps.gov/lavo, 9am-5pm daily May-Oct., 9am-5pm Wed.-Sun. Nov.-Apr.) is located at the south entrance to the park and accessible in winter. Inside the LEED-certified facility are interactive exhibits on the park's geology and ecology plus a fascinating map that illuminates the volcanic features of the park. Outside are strategically placed benches to enjoy lunch or a snack while enjoying gorgeous views of the mountains. A short interpretive trail navigates paved walkways with informative signage.

The on-site **Lassen Cafe & Gift** (9am-4pm daily Apr.-mid-May. 9am-5pm daily late May-Oct.) sells souvenirs and snacks. The visitors center is convenient to Sulphur Works and the

Kohm Yah-mah-nee Visitor Center

Shasta and Lassen

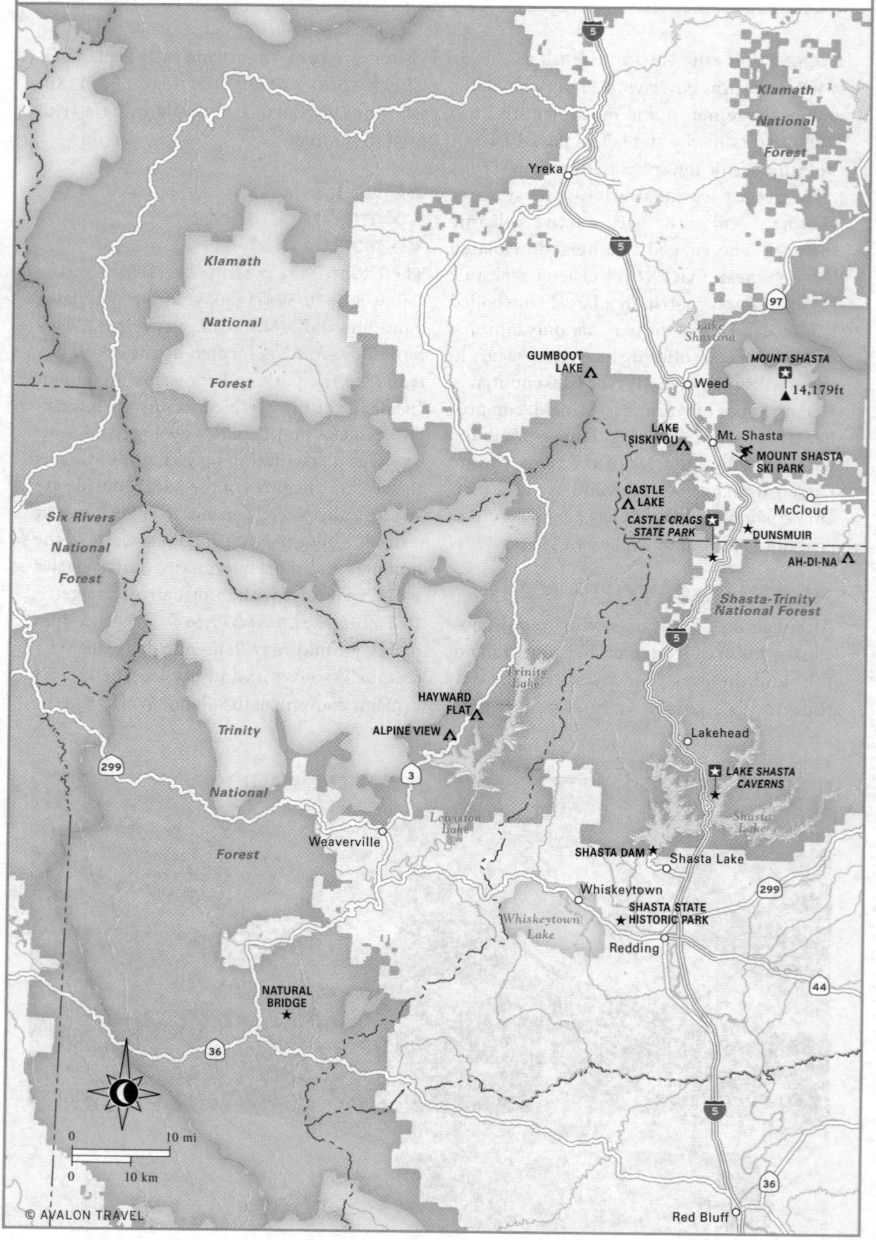

Klamath National Forest

Klamath National Forest

Yreka

5

97

GUMBOOT LAKE

MOUNT SHASTA
14,179ft

Weed

Mt. Shasta

LAKE SISKIYOU

MOUNT SHASTA SKI PARK

CASTLE LAKE

McCloud

CASTLE CRAGS STATE PARK

DUNSMUIR

AH-DI-NA

Six Rivers National Forest

Shasta-Trinity National Forest

5

Trinity Lake

HAYWARD FLAT

ALPINE VIEW

Lakehead

299

Trinity

3

Lewiston Lake

LAKE SHASTA CAVERNS

National

Shasta Lake

Forest

Weaverville

SHASTA DAM

Shasta Lake

Whiskeytown

SHASTA STATE HISTORIC PARK

Whiskeytown Lake

299

Redding

44

NATURAL BRIDGE

36

0   10 mi

0   10 km

5

36

© AVALON TRAVEL

Red Bluff

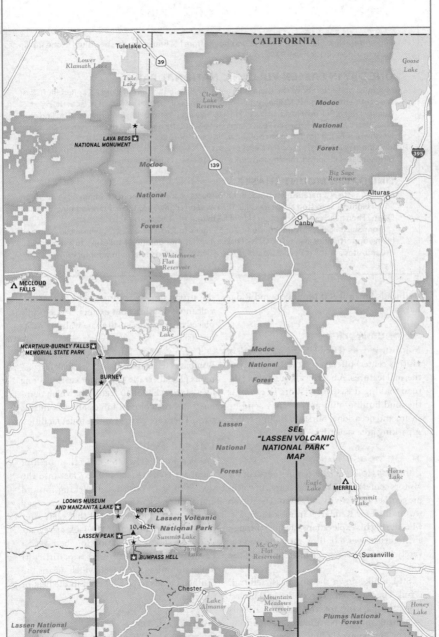

CALIFORNIA

Lower
Klamath Lake

Tulelake

39

Tule
Lake

Clear
Lake
Reservoir

Goose
Lake

Modoc

National

Forest

395

LAVA BEDS
NATIONAL MONUMENT

Modoc

139

National

Forest

Big Sage
Reservoir

Alturas

Canby

Whitehorse
Flat
Reservoir

MCCLOUD
FALLS

Big
Lake

Modoc

MCARTHUR-BURNEY FALLS
MEMORIAL STATE PARK

National

Forest

BURNEY

Lassen

SEE
"LASSEN VOLCANIC
NATIONAL PARK"
MAP

National

Horse
Lake

Eagle
Lake

MERRILL

Forest

Summit
Lake

LOOMIS MUSEUM
AND MANZANITA LAKE

HOT ROCK

Lassen Volcanic

National Park

10,462ft

Summit Lake

Mc Coy
Flat
Reservoir

Susanville

LASSEN PEAK

Juniper
Lake

BUMPASS HELL

Chester

Lake
Almanor

Mountain
Meadows
Reservoir

Honey
Lake

Lassen National
Forest

Plumas National
Forest

Two Days in Shasta and Lassen

Redding and Red Bluff are the best access points from I-5. Both areas can be visited in one trip by making a loop via Highway 89.

ONE DAY IN LASSEN VOLCANIC NATIONAL PARK

Mount Lassen rises above the Central Valley floor before the turnoff from I-5 at Red Bluff. Past the south entrance gate, trailheads line on both sides of Lassen Volcanic Scenic Byway (summer only). Pull over at Bumpass Hell to hike amid by smoking fumaroles and boiling mud pots. Nearby, the trail to Lassen Peak climbs steeply, but the beauty and the views make the effort worthwhile. At the north entrance of the park, learn more at Loomis Museum.

Campsites are at Manzanita Lake or Summit Lake Campgrounds. Lassen's park road is closed late fall-spring, making the park a mid- to late-summer destination.

ONE DAY IN MOUNT SHASTA

Mount Shasta is a paradise for outdoor enthusiasts year-round. From Redding, drive north on I-5 for eight miles to stop at Shasta Lake. Turn west on Highway 151 to explore looming Shasta Dam. Then head over to the other side of I-5 to tour the Lake Shasta Caverns.

From Shasta Lake, drive north on I-5 for 55 miles to Mount Shasta, where climbing and hiking opportunities await. The Gray Butte Trail is a moderate 3.4-mile hike to a small peak.

Campsites are at McBride Springs or Panther Meadows (both summer only).

---

trailheads for Brokeoff Mountain and Ridge Lakes.

Sulphur Works

Sulphur Works (Hwy. 89, one mile north of visitors center) offers a peek at Lassen's geothermal features. A boardwalk runs along the road making it easy for visitors to examine the loud boiling mud pots as they send up steam and occasional bursts of boiling water. A parking area is nearby.

★ Bumpass Hell

Bumpass Hell (Hwy. 89, 6 miles north of the visitors center) offers the largest area of volcanic geothermal activity in Lassen. The region was named for Kendall Vanhook Bumpass, who, during his explorations, stepped through a thin crust over a boiling mud pot and severely burned his leg, ultimately losing the limb.

Still, a hike down the Bumpass Hell trail is fun. The walk (3 miles round-trip, 2 hours) from the parking lot and trailhead leads to boiling mud pots, fumaroles, steaming springs, and pools of boiling water. Prepare for

the strong smell of sulfur, evidence that this volcano is anything but extinct. Strategically placed boardwalks ensure safe walking paths for visitors.

There's a spacious parking lot at the Bumpass Hell trailhead. Nearby, look for a famous glacial erratic (a boulder carried along by a glacier) about 10 feet high, which demonstrates the colossal forces at work in this park. There are also primitive toilet facilities.

Lassen Peak

Lassen Peak (Hwy. 89, 0.5 mile north of Bumpass Hell) reaches 10,457 feet into the sky. Stop at the trailhead parking lot and crane your neck to enjoy the view. The craggy broken mountain peak is all that's left after the 1915 eruption—note the lack of vegetation. The starting elevation for the Lassen Peak Trail (4.8 miles round-trip, difficult) to the summit is 8,000 feet, which means the trailhead tends to be cool even in the heat of summer.

Summit Lake

Summit Lake (Hwy. 89, 8.8 miles north of

Lassen Volcanic National Park

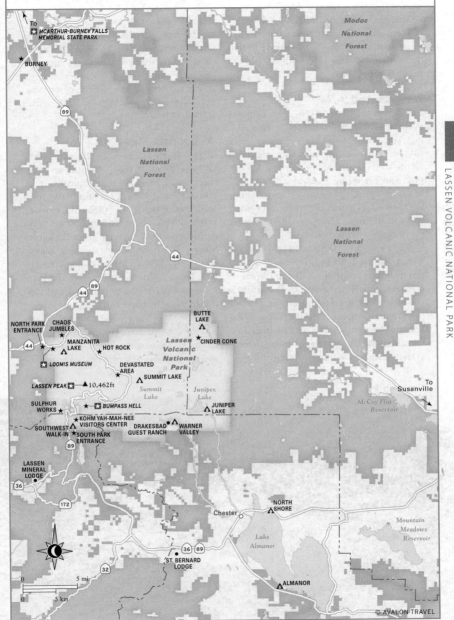

To
★ MCARTHUR-BURNEY FALLS
MEMORIAL STATE PARK

Modoc
National
Forest

★ BURNEY

89

Lassen
National
Forest

89

44

89

44

Lassen
National
Forest

44

NORTH PARK
ENTRANCE

CHAOS
JUMBLES

MANZANITA
LAKE

HOT ROCK

BUTTE
LAKE

CINDER CONE

Lassen
Volcanic
National
Park

LOOMIS MUSEUM

DEVASTATED
AREA

SUMMIT LAKE

LASSEN PEAK ▲ 10,462ft

Summit
Lake

Juniper
Lake

To
Susanville

SULPHUR
WORKS

BUMPASS HELL

JUNIPER
LAKE

McCoy Flat
Reservoir

SOUTHWEST
WALK-IN

KOHM YAH-MAH-NEE
VISITORS CENTER

SOUTH PARK
ENTRANCE

DRAKESBAD
GUEST RANCH

WARNER
VALLEY

89

LASSEN
MINERAL
LODGE

36

172

Chester

NORTH
SHORE

Mountain
Meadows
Reservoir

Lake
Almanor

32

36   89

ST. BERNARD
LODGE

ALMANOR

0   5 mi
0   5 km

© AVALON TRAVEL

Lassen Peak) attracts many campers to its two forest-shaded campgrounds. An easy walk around the lake reveals its shiny blue waters and plants that proliferate nearby. Follow one of the small trails down to the water's edge to eke out a spot on the minuscule beach. Swimming, canoeing, and fishing is permitted on Summit Lake.

Devastated Area

The **Devastated Area** (Hwy. 89, 19 miles north of visitor center) is a fascinating geologic site. When Mount Lassen blew its top in 1915, a tremendous part of the mountain and all life on its slopes were destroyed. Boiling mud and exploding gases tore off the side of Lassen's peak and killed the vegetation in the area. A hail of lava rained down, creating rocks in size from gravel to boulders across the north side of the mountain.

Today, the **Devastated Area Interpretive Trail** (0.5 mile round-trip) travels through part of the disrupted mountainside. You'll see some of the world's youngest rocks, grasses and shrubs, and tall pines. Afterward, check out the photos in the Loomis Museum, which depict the area during and immediately after the eruption for a great comparison to the spot as it looks now.

The Devastated Area offers ample parking and the walk is flat and wheelchair-accessible.

Chaos Jumbles

The broken and decimated area known as **Chaos Jumbles** (Hwy. 89, east of Manzanita Lake) was caused by a massive avalanche descending at a speed of 100 miles an hour. Today, visitors can see a wealth of new vegetation, including a variety of coniferous trees as the area recovers.

★ Loomis Museum

At the north entrance to the park is the **Loomis Museum** (Hwy. 89, near north entrance, 530/595-6140, 9am-5pm Fri.-Sun. mid-May-mid-June, 9am-5pm daily mid-June-Oct., 9am-5pm Fri.-Sun. Oct., free). Inside the historic stone museum is a wonderful opportunity to learn about the known history of Mount Lassen, focusing heavily on the 1914-1915 eruptions photographed by B. F. Loomis. Prints of those rare and stunning photos have been enlarged and captioned to create these exhibits; the museum was named for the photographer, who later became a major player in the push to make Mount Lassen a national park. This interpretive museum offers a rare chance to see the

Bumpass Hell

devastation and following stages of regrowth of the ecosystem on the volcanic slopes.

Manzanita Lake

Manzanita Lake (Hwy. 89, near north entrance) is a popular and scenic spot for camping, boating, and fishing under the watchful peak of Mount Lassen. Kayak and canoe rentals are available from the nearby **Camper Store** (530/335-7557, 9am-sunset daily in summer, first-come, first-served), along with snacks, camping supplies, and the park's only gas station.

HIKING

Hikes range from easy, interpretive day hikes along Lassen Volcanic Scenic Byway to more difficult trails that offer adventure, challenge, and solitude. The lower elevations of most trails are more than 7,000 feet above sea level. Come a day early to acclimate to the elevation.

Brokeoff Mountain

Brokeoff Mountain (Hwy. 89, road marker 2, 7.4 miles round-trip, difficult, 5-7 hours) involves a 2,600-foot ascent from a mile-high starting point, so the thin air and rigorous climb can be quite difficult due to the altitude. The reward is one of the prettiest and most serene hikes in the park, with mountain streams and stellar views over the mountains and valleys. The trailhead is near the south entrance.

Ridge Lakes

Starting from the Sulphur Works trailhead the climb to **Ridge Lakes** (2 miles round-trip, difficult, 1.5 hours) is fairly steep, but the payoff at the top is a view of two alpine lakes between Brokeoff Mountain and Mount Diller. Along the way, you'll walk through beautiful green meadows dotted with bright yellow wildflowers and then into a forest before reaching the lakes.

★ Lassen Peak Trail

The must-do hike is the **Lassen Peak Trail** (4.8 miles round-trip, difficult, 3-5 hours). The climb to the top is dramatic, challenging, and worth it. The trail gains more than 2,000 vertical feet in only 2.5 miles but is well graded with many switchbacks. Exhibits along the way explain some of the fascinating views of volcanic remains, lakes, wildlife, and rock formations. The last 0.25 mile involves some scrambling, but most of the trail is a steady upward walk. At the top, 360-degree views soak in the volcanic landscape. Look across

Lassen Peak

to the remains of the giant caldera of a huge extinct volcano, and then out north toward the Cascade Range, where you'll see Mount Shasta shining in the distance.

Kings Creek Falls Trail

The **Kings Creek Falls Trail** (Hwy. 89, road marker 32, 2.5 miles round-trip, moderate, 2 hours) starts easy. The walk travels downhill through Kings Creek Meadows to the falls, where you can admire the small cascade and pool before climbing 700 feet back up to the trailhead.

Echo and Twin Lakes

It's the length of the trail that runs from Summit Lake to **Echo and Twin Lakes** (8.8 miles round-trip, moderate, 2.5 hours) that makes it challenging. It's a pleasant and sedate two-mile walk to Echo Lake, then another two miles to Upper Twin Lake and back, with two additional miles to Lower Twin Lake. The elevation gain is only 500 feet total. Wear a swimsuit under your hiking clothes and cool off in one of the lakes before trekking back. The trailhead is at the Summit Lake Ranger Station.

Cinder Cone Trail

The dramatic **Cinder Cone Trail** (4 miles round-trip, 3 hours, strenuous) overlooks the Fantastic Lava Beds in the far northeast corner of the park. The trailhead is near Butte Lake Campground.

CAMPING

Lassen has eight campgrounds; four are accessible via the paved park road. Near the north park entrance is **Manzanita Lake Campground** (179 sites, 877/444-6777, www. recreation.gov, May-Oct., $15-26, reservations recommended), the largest campground in Lassen. The campground has flush toilets, potable running water, fire rings, and picnic tables. Sites accommodate tents and trailers (up to 40 feet; dump station available). **Cabins** (530/335-7557, www.lassenrecreation.com or www.recreation.gov, Apr.-Oct., $71-95)

are also available. A small **Camper Store** (530/335-7557, 9am-sunset daily in summer) sells camping supplies, food, snacks, and hot showers and rents canoes and kayaks for boating on the lake.

★ **Summit Lake North** and **South** (94 sites, 877/444-6777, www.recreation.gov, late June-Oct., $15-24) campgrounds are popular and reservations are recommended. The two developed campgrounds have bear lockers, fire pits, picnic tables, and an amphitheater for evening ranger programs. Summit Lake North has flush toilets and potable drinking water, but Summit Lake South has only pit toilets. Sites accommodate tents and trailers (up to 35 feet); Loops A and E are first-come, first-served.

The **Southwest Walk-In Campground** (21 sites, first-come, first-served, $10-16) is open year-round. On the east side of the Kohm Yah-mah-nee Visitor Center parking lot, the tent-only sites are accessible via a short, paved walk. Restrooms and drinking water are available at the visitor center. RVs may park in the lot.

The remaining campgrounds offer primitive facilities or are accessible via a short hike. In the remote northeast corner of the park, **Butte Lake Campground** (101 sites, 877/444-6777, www.recreation.gov, June-Oct., $15-22) has pit toilets, but no water. Sites have a fire pit and a table and accommodate trailers and RVs up to 35 feet. To get there, take Highway 44 to Butte Lake Road and drive six miles to the campground.

Juniper Lake Campground (18 sites, first-come, first-served, late June-early Oct., $12) is on the southeast side of the park at the end of a rough gravel road; RVs and trailers are not advised. The small campground beside Juniper Lake has pit toilets, bear lockers, fire pits, and tables, but no drinking water. To get there, take Highway 89/36 east to Chester. Follow signs to Juniper Lake. The last six miles is via a dirt road.

Warner Valley (17 sites, first-come, first-served, June-Oct., $16) is at the south edge of the park with pit toilets, drinking water, tables, and fire pits at each tent-only site. RVs and trailers are not allowed. The campground is 17 miles north of Chester. At the Warner Valley Ranger Station, follow the rough gravel road for one mile.

ACCOMMODATIONS

★ **Drakesbad Guest Ranch** (Warner Valley Rd., Chester 866/999-0914, www.drakesbad.com, June-Oct., $317-384) is the only lodging in Lassen Volcanic National Park. Sitting in a mountain meadow surrounded by forest and snowcapped mountains, the ranch has horse stables, a swimming pool, fishing opportunities, hiking trails, and activities for the kids. Rates include meals.

TRANSPORTATION

Lassen Volcanic National Park is three hours north of Sacramento on I-5. At the town of Red Bluff, exit I-5 onto Highway 36 and drive east for 43 miles. Turn left onto Highway 89, which serves as the main park road. In winter (Nov.-May), Highway 89 closes until June or July. The only gas station is near the Manzanita Lake Camper Store (24 hours daily, pay by credit card).

The nearest airports are in Redding, Sacramento, and Reno. There is no public transportation within the park.

HIGHWAY 89/36 EAST

South of Lassen, Highway 89/36 leads east past tiny towns and into the Lake Almanor Basin (www.lakealmanorarea.com).

Mineral

There's not much in Mineral except for the Lassen Mineral Lodge (Hwy. 36, 530/595-4422, www.minerallodge.com, May-early Nov., $90-115). The 20 small, motel rooms have fridges, but lack TVs, telephones, or frills of any kind. The Kitchenette Queen room sleeps four and is ideal for families. The lodge operates a well-stocked general store and the Mineral Lodge Restaurant (8am-8pm daily summer, 8am-6pm Sat.-Sun. winter, $10-23).

Mineral lies nine miles south of Lassen's Kohm Yah-mah-nee Visitor Center along Highway 36.

Chester

The tiny town of Chester sits between Lassen and the shores of beautiful Lake Almanor. Lumber and tourism keep the lights on in Chester, and the lake attracts a number of

Drakesbad Guest Ranch

recreation lovers drawn by the area's natural beauty.

LAKE ALMANOR

With 52 miles of shoreline, **Lake Almanor** offers ample swimming, boating, and kayaking with boat launches on the west side of the lake. The paved **Lake Almanor Recreation Trail** (11 miles one-way, easy) weaves through forest and along the shore with views of the mountains.

Several campgrounds surround the lake. The **North Shore Campground** (541 Catfish Beach Rd., 530/258-3376, www.northshorecampground.com, May-Oct., $36-46 two-night min.) has two boat docks, plus canoe, kayak, and SUP rentals, a playground, a general store, flush toilets, and showers. The campground is on Highway 89/36, two miles east of Chester.

Popular **Almanor Campground** (Almanor Dr. W., 530/258-2141, www.recreation.gov, late May-early Sept., $15-18) sits on the west shore of the lake with 104 family-friendly sites for tents and RVs (no hookups). Facilities include picnic tables, fire rings, drinking water, vault toilets, and a boat ramp. To reach the campground, turn right on Highway 89 two miles west of Chester and drive six miles to Almanor Drive West.

FOOD AND ACCOMMODATIONS

★ **St. Bernard Lodge** (44801 Hwy. 36/89, Mill Creek, 530/258-3382, www.stbernardlodge.com, $99-106) has seven rooms with no TVs and bathrooms across the hall. Hearty meals are served in the downstairs dining room (breakfast is included in the rate). The friendly and knowledgeable owner will point you to hiking trails and can offer tips for stops on the way out of town.

GETTING THERE

Chester lies 30 miles northeast of Mineral along Highway 36. From Chester, Warner Valley Road leads north to the Warner Valley and Juniper Lake areas of Lassen National Park.

Susanville

The small town of Susanville is the seat of Lassen County. Located on the Susan River, Susanville has a certain Old West charm.

LASSEN HISTORICAL MUSEUM

"Susanville ephemera" is on display at the **Lassen Historical Museum** (115 N. Weatherlow St., 530/257-3292, 10am-4pm Mon.-Fri., 11am-2pm Sat. summer; 10am-2pm Tues.-Fri., 10am-1pm Sat. winter, free). The cabin next door, Roop's Fort, was built in 1854 and remains lovingly cared for by the local historical society. It was once a trading post on the Emigrant Trail to the West.

BIZZ JOHNSON NATIONAL RECREATION TRAIL

The 25.4-mile **Bizz Johnson National Recreation Trail** (530/257-0456, www.bizzjohnsontrail.com) departs from the **Susanville Depot Trailhead Visitors Center and Museum** (601 Richmond Rd., 530/257-3252, 1pm-4pm Fri., 8am-3pm Sat., free). A favorite with hikers and cyclists, the paved trail winds along the Susan River following the Fernley and Lassen Branch Line of the former Southern Pacific Railroad route. At the depot visitors center you'll find trail maps, exhibits, and a bookstore.

EAGLE LAKE

The second-largest natural lake in California, **Eagle Lake** (530/257-4188, www.fs.usda.gov) gets its name from the large population of nesting bald and golden eagles but is best known for its trophy trout. On the south shore of Eagle Lake, the **Merrill Campground** (877/444-6777, www.recreation.gov, May-Sept., $20) has 45 sites for tents and RVs (hookups) and some walk-in sites. Facilities include laundry, showers, and a general store. Eagle Lake is 15 miles north of Susanville on Highway 139.

FOOD AND ACCOMMODATIONS

The 1862 **Lassen Ale Works at the Pioneer Saloon** (724 Main St., 530/257-7666, www.

lassenaleworks.com, 4pm-10pm Mon., 11am-10pm Tues.-Thurs., 11am-11pm Fri.-Sat., $10-25) adds a touch of swagger to Susanville's Old West vibe. The bar serves eight house beers on tap, plus seasonal brews and cocktails, plus a pub menu of comfort food. The brewery has a second location, **Lassen Ale Works at the Boardroom** (702-000 Johnstonville Rd., 530/257-4443, www.lassenaleworks.com, 3pm-9pm Wed.-Thurs., noon-9pm Fri.-Sun., $13-15), which serves a slimmed-down menu of salads, pizza, and pints.

For a hearty breakfast or burrito, swing by **El Tepeyac Grille** (1700 Main St., 530/257-7220, 7am-9pm Mon.-Wed., 7am-9:30pm Thurs.-Sat., 7am-7pm Sun., $8-25), a locally owned café with a loyal following.

The River Inn (1710 Main St., 530/257-6051, $60-82) is a simple motel with neat guest rooms and a helpful and pleasant staff. Located near several restaurants, this place is a bargain that is hard to beat.

GETTING THERE
Susanville sits 35 miles east of Chester on Highway 36 at its convergence with Highway 139.

HIGHWAY 89 SOUTH TO TAHOE
From Chester, Highway 89 follows the path of the railroad south, crisscrossing over the Feather River and climbing into the Sierra to Lake Tahoe. This scenic highway offers mining towns, campgrounds, and off-the-beaten-path excursions—plus solitude, even on busy summer weekends.

Quincy
The North Fork of the Feather River is the dividing line between the Cascades and the Sierra. The river gains momentum at the intersection of Highways 89 and 70 in Quincy, where it plunges down a deep and spectacular river gorge on the way to Lake Oroville. Quincy is the Plumas County seat.

FOOD AND ACCOMMODATIONS
Patti's Thunder Café (557 Lawrence St., 530/283-3300, 7am-2pm daily, $5-15) serves espresso and breakfast in a flower-filled building that looks as old as the town.

At **Sweet Lorraine's** (384 W. Main St., 530/283-5300, lunch 11:30am-2pm Tues.-Fri., dinner 5pm-8pm Tues.-Sat., $10-24), an eclectic mix of comfort food and international flavors are offered in a historic building with an outdoor patio.

Ada's Place (562 Jackson St., 530/283-1954, www.adasplace.com, $110-145) is the place to stay in Quincy. The four remodeled cottages exude charm and comfort.

Bucks Lake
In summer, cool off at **Bucks Lake** (530/283-2050, www.fs.usda.gov), a popular place to fish, swim, water-ski, and windsurf. In winter, there's snowshoeing and snowmobiling.

Six campgrounds encircle the lake; the largest is **Whitehorse Campground** (877/444-6777, www.reserveamerica.com, May-Oct., $20-25), along one of the lake's tributaries. The **Lakeshore Resort** (530/283-2848, http://www.buckslakeshore.com) is close to the marina and has cabins ($125-235), a general store, a restaurant ($10-24), and a full bar.

Bucks Lake is about 20 miles west of Quincy along Bucks Lake Road.

Graeagle
Highway 89 runs right past **The Millpond** (http://playgraeagle.com), where families swim and tube in summer while surrounded by tall pines. More kid-friendly fun is found at the **Graeagle Stables** (Hwy. 89, 530/836-0430, www.reidhorse.com, May-Sept., $20-52, reservations required), which offers pony rides and guided horseback riding near The Millpond and Gold Lake.

PLUMAS-EUREKA STATE PARK
Plumas-Eureka State Park (310 Johnsonville Rd., Blairsden, 530/836-2380, www.parks.ca.gov, sunrise-sunset daily,

free) preserves the region's mining history with two historical stamp mills, a blacksmith shop, and a museum (8:30am-4pm daily Memorial Day-Labor Day, by donation) housed in a former bunkhouse for gold miners. Camping (800/444-7275, www.reservecalifornia.com, $35) is available in one of 67 sites.

The park is five miles west of Graeagle on Highway 89.

FOOD AND ACCOMMODATIONS

Two restaurants are under the same roof. The Grizzly Grill (250 Bonta St., Blairsden, 530/836-1300, www.grizzlygrill.com, 5pm-9pm daily summer, hours vary fall and spring, $22-30) specializes in fancy dinners while the Mountain Cuisine (530/836-4646, www.mountaincuisine.com, 11:30am-3pm Tues.-Sun., $6-9) serves breakfast and lunch.

The Mill Works (7539 Hwy. 89, Graeagle, 530/826-2828, www.graeaglemillworks.com, 7am-5pm Sun.-Thurs., 7am-7pm Fri.-Sat., $7-14) serves coffee, sweets, and sandwiches, with barbecue on weekends (4pm-7pm Fri.-Sat.). At the edge of the lake, kids line up at the Graeagle Outpost (11 Hwy. 89, Graeagle, 530/836-2414, 7am-4pm daily summer, $5-15) for hot dogs and soft-serve ice cream.

The Chalet View Lodge (72056 Hwy. 70, Graeagle, 530/832-5528, www.chaletviewlodge.com, $105-255) is a lovely place to stay in the area, with 51 rooms, suites, and cabins. Amenities include a restaurant, a spa and swimming pool, a nine-hole golf course, an on-site taproom, and free Wi-Fi and continental breakfast. Pets ($25) are permitted.

Peaceful Gold Lake Campground (530/836-2575, www.fs.usda.gov, June-Sept., $10) is in the beautiful Lakes Basin Recreation Area with 37 first-come, first-served sites. There are pit toilets, but no drinking water. From Graeagle, take Highway 89 south for two miles, then continue south on Gold Lake Highway for 10 miles.

Sierraville

Sierraville is a ranch town 24 miles north of Truckee known for its hot springs.

SIERRA HOT SPRINGS

Soak in natural hot springs overlooking Sierra cattle country at Sierra Hot Springs (521 Campbell Hot Springs Rd., 530/994-3773, www.sierrahotsprings.org). The membership fee ($5 monthly, $20 annual) permits access to a large outdoor swimming pool, plus indoor cold and hot pools, and a dry sauna. All pools are clothing-optional.

Accommodations are in the Main Lodge (dorms $50-61, private room $72-121) and the historical Globe Hotel ($72-121). Both have shared bathrooms, full kitchens for guest use, and Internet access. Room fees include soaking in the springs. The campground ($28-33) is a great and affordable way to enjoy the springs. Cookstoves and fires are not allowed; use the kitchen in the Main Lodge or dine on-site at the Philosophy Café (5pm-8:30pm Fri. and Mon., 12:30pm-3:30pm and 5pm-8:30pm Sat.-Sun., $19-21).

FOOD AND ACCOMMODATIONS

Steak fajitas pair well with a margarita at the excellent Los Hermanos (100 S. Lincoln St., 530/994-1058, 11am-9pm Tues.-Sun., $10-17). Grab breakfast or a burger at The Fork & Horn (101 E. Main St., 530/994-1070, www.forknhorn.com, 8am-2pm Fri.-Tues., $9-15).

The Lower Little Truckee Campground (Hwy. 89, 530/994-3401, www.fs.usda.gov, reservations 877/444-6777 or www.recreation.gov, Apr.-Oct., $20) has 11 sites with picnic tables, fire rings, pit toilets, and drinking water. The campground is 12 miles south of Sierraville on Highway 89 in the Tahoe National Forest.

Stay at the Calpine Lookout (877/444-6777 or www.reserveamerica.com, $45), which was used as a forest-fire lookout until 1975. From Sierraville, take Highway 89 north for nine miles to Calpine.

Redding and Vicinity

Redding is the gateway town to the region with gas, groceries, food, shops, and a few sights. Lassen Volcanic National Park is 50 miles east via Highway 44, while Shasta Lake and Mount Shasta are a straight shot north on I-5.

TURTLE BAY AND SUNDIAL BRIDGE

Turtle Bay Exploration Park (844 Sundial Bridge Dr., 530/243-8850 or 800/887-8532, www.turtlebay.org, 8:30am-4pm Wed.-Fri., 10am-4pm Sat.-Sun., adults $16, children 4-15 $12, under four free) is a 300-acre park that straddles the Sacramento River and provides a cool break from the summer heat. Stroll the paved trails, tour the museum exhibits, explore the aquarium, or picnic in the gardens.

The spectacular **Sundial Bridge** (daily 24 hours, free) spans the river, linking the park campuses. Designed by Santiago Calatrava, the bridge features a single large pylon structure that anchors suspension cables as they fan out over the bridge. Made from 200 tons of green glass, strips of granite, and ceramic tiles from Spain, the striking bridge is also one of the largest sundials in the world.

The **Museum Store and Coffee Bar** (8:30am-5pm Mon.-Sat., 9:30am-5pm Sun.) serves sandwiches, snacks, and bottled water. Parking is free and restrooms are available in the museum and gardens. Pets are not allowed.

FOOD AND ACCOMMODATIONS

Jack's Grill (1743 California St., 530/241-9705, www.jacksgrillredding.com, 5pm-11pm Mon.-Sat., $19-38) is an old-school bar serving steaks, beer, wine, and cocktails. The smoky atmosphere can keep some folks away.

Locals love **Janya's Thai Cuisine** (630 N. Market St., 530/243-7682, www. janyas-thaicuisine.com, 11am-2:30pm and 4pm-9pm Tues.-Fri., 11:30am-9pm Sat.-Sun., $9-18) for traditional Thai food and simple but charming decor.

Bartels Giant Burger (18509 Lake Blvd. E., 530/243-7313, www.bartelsgiantburger. com, 10am-9pm Mon.-Sat., 11:30am-9pm Sun., $5-9) has plenty of fans. Enjoy your burger with lots of onions and special sauce.

From the Hearth Artisan Bakery (1427 Market St., 530/768-1306, www.fthcafe.com, 7am-9pm Mon.-Sat., 7am-6pm Sun., $4-10) offers homemade sourdough bread, pastries, hearty breakfast plates, hot and cold sandwiches, salads, and rice bowls.

For a motor lodge with local flavor, stay at the **Thunderbird Lodge** (1350 Pine St., 530/243-5422, www.thunderbirdlodgeredding.com, $61-150) near downtown. Expect the standard amenities with a splash of style, plus a pool. Some rooms have kitchenettes.

The **Bridge House Bed and Breakfast** (1455 Riverside Dr., 530/247-7177, www. bridgehousebb.com, $119-189) is a distinctive yellow house with a steeply pitched roof along the Sacramento River. Two charming rooms have TVs, spa bathrobes, and lots of amenities. Four additional (and comfy) rooms are next door in **The Puente,** owned by the same innkeepers.

TRANSPORTATION AND SERVICES

Redding is about 160 miles (3 hours) north of Sacramento on I-5. The town is easy to navigate by car and parking is plentiful and free.

The **Redding Municipal Airport** (RDD, 6751 Woodrum Circle, 530/224-4320, www. ci.redding.ca.us) offers flights on United Express, which runs multiple daily nonstops from San Francisco. **Avis** (530/221-2855 or 800/331-1212, www.avis.com), **Budget** (530/225-8652 or 800/527-7000, www.budget.com), and **Hertz** (530/221-4620 or

800/654-3131, www.hertz.com) have car rental outposts at the airport.

Redding has the only major medical services available in the region. **Mercy Medical Center Redding** (2175 Rosaline Ave., 530/225-7200, www.redding.mercy.org) has a 24-hour emergency room with a full trauma center.

RED BLUFF

The small city of Red Bluff sits 30 miles south of Redding on I-5. The south entrance of Lassen Volcanic National Park is one hour east along Highway 36.

Red Bluff Recreation Area

The **Red Bluff Recreation Area** (530/934-3316, www.fs.usda.gov) houses the trailhead for the **Shasta View Trail** (2 miles, easy), a mostly flat loop that delivers the views it promises. Bird-watching is a big attraction, and the park is home to great blue herons, egrets, great horned owls, wood ducks, Anna's hummingbirds, and other species as well as bobcats, western pond turtles, Pacific tree frogs, opossums, and woodchucks. The visitors center doubles as the **Sacramento River Discovery Center** (1000 Sale Ln., 530/527-1196, www.sacramentoriverdiscoverycenter.com, 9am-3pm Tues.-Sat.).

Food and Accommodations

From the Hearth (638 Washington St., 530/727-0616, www.fthcafe.com, 7am-8pm Mon.-Sat., 7am-6pm Sun., $8-15) serves the best morning coffee and pastry in Red Bluff, plus excellent bread, hearty breakfasts, and an array of hot and cold sandwiches.

The Green Barn (5 Chestnut Ave., 530/527-3161, www.greenbarnsteakhouse.com, 11:30am-8pm Mon.-Thurs., 11:30am-9pm Fri., 4pm-9pm Sat., $10-34) has been satisfying locals since 1959. Inside the warm, mellow atmosphere, dine on aged steaks and divine homemade sticky buns.

2 Buds BBQ (592 Antelope Blvd., 530/528-0799, 11am-6pm Mon.-Thurs., 11am-8pm Fri.-Sat., $9-12) is a hole-in-the-wall that earns raves for its ranch-style barbecue and baked beans. Grab a table beneath the elk head mounted on the wall and order the house tritip or pulled pork sandwich.

Los Mariachis (604 Main St., 530/529-5154, 9am-9pm Mon.-Fri., 9am-9:30pm Sat.-Sun., $12-17) serves traditional Mexican fare along with American-style burgers and sandwiches. They also serve huevos rancheros and Spanish omelets for breakfast.

The **Super 8** (30 Gilmore Rd., 530/529-2028, www.wyndhamhotels.com, $57-110) is right off I-5, across the river from Red Bluff's downtown. A step up, the **Best Western Antelope Inn and Suites** (203 Antelope Blvd., 530/527-8882 or 800/780-7234, $103-133) offers a pool, a complimentary hot breakfast, in-room coffeemaker, and is dog-friendly.

RVers can park their rigs at the upscale **Durango RV Resort** (100 Lake Ave., 866/770-7001, www.durangorvresorts.com, $55-60), which has a lap pool, a sauna, free wireless Internet access, paddle tennis, bocce ball courts, two laundries, a lodge and concession center, and facilities to wash your dog *and* your vehicle.

Sycamore Grove Campground (Sale Ln., 530/934-3316, www.fs.usda.gov, reservations 877/444-6777, www.recreation.gov, Mar.-Nov., $16-30) has 30 sites for tents and trailers, plus flush toilets, potable water, and coin-operated showers.

HIGHWAY 299

Shasta State Historic Park

Shasta State Historic Park (15312 Hwy. 299, 530/243-8194, www.parks.ca.gov, 10am-5pm Thurs.-Sun.) is all that remains of historic Shasta City, a bustling gold-mining boomtown of the 19th century. Brick ruins and storefronts line the road and invite exploration of the open-air park.

Stop in at the visitors center in the **Courthouse Museum** to learn the town's story and visit the jail and gallows. A path weaves through the ruins to the **Litsch General Store,** a meticulously recreated general store. History comes alive next door at the **Blumb Bakery;** on weekends, docents often bake bread in the 1870s re-created oven.

The park is six miles west of Redding on Highway 299.

Whiskeytown National Recreation Area

Whiskeytown National Recreation Area (Hwy. 299 and John F. Kennedy Memorial Dr., 530/246-1225, www.nps.gov/whis, $10 day-use fee) offers 39,000 acres of wilderness for hiking, biking, and water sports. Exhibits at the **Whiskeytown Visitors Center** (10am-4pm daily Labor Day-Memorial Day) illuminate the area's history as a gold-mining destination. It's a good place to get maps, advice, and information about camping, hiking, and tours in the park.

WHISKEYTOWN LAKE

Whiskeytown Lake is the centerpiece of this delightful outdoor playground. Thirty miles of shoreline offer plenty of room to fish, waterski, boat, kayak, canoe, and swim.

The hike to 220-foot **Whiskeytown Falls** (3.4 miles, moderate) is one of four great waterfall hikes in the park. While popular, it's not an easy hike and steep in places. Group hikes are sometimes offered from the visitors center. Access is via the James K. Carr Trail.

On the north side of the lake is the **Oak Bottom Marina** (12485 Hwy. 299 W., 530/359-2008, www.whiskeytownmarinas. com, year-round). Its small **store** (530/359-2269, 11am-6pm daily, $30-72) rents kayaks, canoes, and stand-up paddleboards plus tubes, wakeboards, ski boats, and water skis. A **campground** ($14-26) offers 94 tent and 22 RV sites.

In season, rangers lead 2.5-hour **kayak tours** (530/246-1225, 9:30am and 5:30pm daily summer) and moonlight tours (call for hours).

Whiskeytown Lake is just 10 miles west of Redding on Highway 299.

Weaverville

Weaverville is a charming community filled with a few shops and casual places to grab a bite to eat. The Joss House Chinese temple sits in the heart of the historic town and makes for a unique experience.

Weaverville is 50 miles west of Redding on Highway 299. The drive takes about an hour.

Whiskeytown Lake

Side Trip to Chico

Home to a California State University Campus, the community of Chico is a thriving college town with outstanding urban parks, charming tree-lined streets, and a surprisingly rich dining scene.

BIDWELL PARK

The land for **Bidwell Park** (530/896-7899, http://ccnaturecenter.org) was donated in 1905 by John and Annie Bidwell, the town's first and most prominent citizens. Their elegantly preserved 26-room Victorian home is part of the **Bidwell Mansion State Historic Park** (525 Esplanade, 530/895-6144, www.parks.ca.gov, visitors center 11am-5pm Sat.-Mon., tours 11am-4pm Sat.-Mon., adults $6, children 5-17 $3).

Bidwell Park boasts 3,670 acres in two sections: an undeveloped Upper Park in the Sierra Nevada foothills and Lower Park, which follows Chico Creek into downtown. Here you'll find the creek-fed Sycamore Pool; **Caper Acres** (9am-sunset Tues.-Sun., free), a children's play area; and the **Chico Creek Nature Center** (1968 E. 8th St., 530/891-4671, 11am-3pm Wed.-Sat., adults $4, children $2). Picnic tables provide a cool place to picnic in the summer. Paved biking paths weave through the park. **North Rim Adventure Sports** (178 E. 2nd Ave., 530/345-2453, http://northrimadventure.com, 9:30am-6pm Mon.-Sat., 11am-4pm Sun.) rents bikes and sells backcountry gear.

FOOD AND ACCOMMODATIONS

The hearty and eclectic sushi menu at **Raw Bar** (346 Broadway, 530/897-0626, www.rawbarchico. com, 11:30am-9pm Mon.-Thurs., 11:30am-10pm Fri.-Sat., 5pm-9pm Sun., $10-20) challenges the palate while filling the stomach.

Head to **Upper Crust Bakery** (130 Main St., 530/895-3866, www.uppercrustchico.com, 6am-7pm Mon.-Sat., 6:30am-4pm Sun., $5-9) for soups, sandwiches, salads, espresso, and wickedly good sweets.

The **Sierra Nevada Brewing Company** (1075 E. 20th St., 530/345-2739, www.sierranevada.com, 11am-9pm Sun.-Thurs., 11am-10pm Fri.-Sat., $13-30) serves its original creation, Sierra Nevada Pale Ale, along with an eclectic menu (pizza, ramen, steak) equal in excellence to its craft

JOSS HOUSE STATE HISTORIC PARK

The oldest, continually used Chinese temple in California is the **Weaverville Joss House State Historic Park** (Hwy. 299 and Oregon St., 530/623-5284, www.parks. ca.gov, 10am-5pm Thurs.-Sun., adults $4, children 6-17 $2). The Taoist house of worship is also a museum with displays of Chinese art, mining tools, and weapons used in the 1854 Tong War. Joss House, or the Temple of the Forest beneath the Clouds, was erected in 1874 as a replacement for a previous incarnation that was lost in a fire. Admission includes a tour of the temple (hourly 10am-4pm).

TRINITY ALPS WILDERNESS

Between Redding and the coast lie the **Trinity Alps,** a subrange within the Klamath Mountains. The area is known for its unique alpine flora, ice fields, and glaciers, all of which are encompassed by the 517,000-acre **Trinity Alps Wilderness** (530/226-2500 or 530/623-2121, www.fs.usda.gov), the second-largest wilderness area in the state. The highest point is Thompson Peak (8,994-9,002 feet, record varies), which has a 15-acre glacier on the north side.

Lewiston Lake

Lewiston Lake is an artificial reservoir

Autumn in Chico

brews. Sign up for a free tour or pay for the three-hour Beer Geek Tour (530/899-4776, www. sierranevada.com, $45).

On Saturday, stop at the Chico Farmers Market (2nd St. and Wall St., 530/893-3276, http:// chicofarmersmarket.com, 7am-1pm Sat.) where the bounty of the Sacramento Valley is proudly on display.

Skip the standard big chains and opt for more charm and a great downtown location at the Hotel Diamond (220 W. 4th St., 866/993-3100, https://hoteldiamondchico.com, $134-161).

GETTING THERE
Chico is 90 miles north of Sacramento and 43 miles south of Red Bluff on Highway 99.

created by a dam on the Trinity River. It's a pretty lake with a surface area of 750 acres popular for canoeing and fly-fishing. There is one boat launch at Pine Cove at the midsection of the lake.

Lewiston Lake is less than two miles north of the town of Lewiston, east of Weaverville.

Trinity Lake
Formed by Trinity Dam, Trinity Lake is one of California's largest reservoirs, with 145 miles of shoreline and a capacity of about 2.5 million acre-feet. Most people value this large lake as an aquatic playground, and it's particularly popular for water-skiing and houseboating.

The lake has two marinas. Trinity Alps Marina (1 Fairview Marina Rd., 530/286-2282, www.trinityalpsmarina.com) rents houseboats ($386-768 per day, two-night minimum), ski boats, and pontoon boats ($40-350). A store sells provisions, camp fuel, and firewood.

Trinity Lake Marina (Cedar Stock Rd., 530/286-2225 or 800/709-7814, www.trinity-lakeresort.com) has a general store and cabins ($98-265/night, $625-1,722/week). The marina offers 50-foot houseboat rentals (Apr.-Oct., $580-1,200 per day) and also rents Jet Skis ($75/hour, $325-375/day), fishing boats ($35-50/hour, $100-195/day), and pontoon boats ($495-525/day).

Trinity Lake can be found along Highway 3 at the east edge of the Trinity Alps, north of Lewiston Lake and Weaverville.

Hiking

The Granite Peak Trail (9 miles round-trip) gains more than 4,000 feet of elevation on its way to Granite Peak. From the summit, you can survey vast areas of the Trinity Alps plus Trinity Lake, Mount Shasta, and Mount Lassen. To reach the trailhead from Weaverville, drive north on Highway 3 to the signed Stoney Ridge Trailhead. Shortly after the sign, turn left onto Granite Peak Road (Forest Rd. 35N28Y) and continue three miles until you reach a spacious turnaround area and park.

The Canyon Creek Lakes Trail (16 miles, difficult) is one of the most beautiful trails in Trinity Alps. Canyon Creek climbs 3,100 feet in eight miles, passing four spectacular waterfalls before reaching the end in a chain of two lakes rimmed by high granite. Its popularity is evident by the number of hikers, but the beauty compensates for the lack of solitude. To reach the trailhead, drive west on Highway 299 and turn north on Canyon Creek Road. Continue 13 miles to the trailhead.

Backpacking

The Trinity Alps are largely a backpacking destination. Overnight backpacking permits are required (for camping and camp stoves) and available in front of the Weaverville Ranger Station (360 Main St., 530/623-2121, www.fs.usda.gov, 8am-4:30pm Mon.-Fri.).

The Stuart Fork Trail (2-4 days) leads to beautiful Emerald and Sapphire Lakes in the heart of the Trinity Alps. The entire trail is approximately 30 miles out and back with 3,000-4,000 feet of elevation gain. The trailhead is north of Weaverville; take Highway 3 north for 13 miles until it becomes Trinity Lake Boulevard. Turn left onto Trinity Alps Road and continue 2.5 miles to the Bridge Camp Trailhead.

Fishing

Trinity and Lewiston Lakes are good places to catch rainbow trout, brown trout, and small-mouth bass. Fishing licenses are required; prices and requirements vary. For information, contact the California Department of Fish and Game (601 Locust St., Redding, 530/225-2300, www.wildlife.ca.gov, 8am-4:30pm Mon.-Fri.).

To tag along with a local expert, book a trip with Scott Stratton at Trinity River Adventures (361 Ponderosa Pines Rd., Lewiston, 530/623-4179, www.trinityriveradventures.com, $450 per day for 1-2 people). Lunch and fly-fishing instruction are included.

Rafting

Some of the best white-water rafting is on the Trinity River. Trinity River Rafting (530/623-3033 or 800/307-4837, www.trinity-riverrafting.com, guided trips $65-95 per day) offers half- and full-day trips on the Trinity River. Select from a placid Class I-II float suitable for the family to a Class IV-V run for experienced rafters only.

Bigfoot Rafting Company (530/629-2263, www.bigfootrafting.com, $69-89) also has half-and full-day trips on the Trinity. Bigfoot showcases a depth of knowledge about the rivers it runs—your guide will know a great deal about the history and natural surroundings and, as a bonus, can cook up fabulous meals on the full-day trips.

Camping

Several campsites border Trinity Lake. The largest is Hayward Flat Campground (Hwy. 3, www.fs.usda.gov, 877/444-6777, www.recreation.gov, mid-May-mid-Sept., $18-30). The 98 sites are popular with families with RVs, who enjoy the proximity to the water. Expect flush toilets, drinking water, and plenty of generator and powerboat noise. It's 15 miles north of Weaverville.

Pretty Alpine View Campground (Guy Covington Dr., www.fs.usda.gov, 877/444-6777, www.recreation.gov, mid-May-mid-Sept., $23-35) sits on a sheltered arm of Trinity Lake. The 53-site campground has drinking water, flush toilets, and a view of Granite

Peak. It's near Highway 3, 25 miles north of Weaverville.

Transportation

Highway 299 (Trinity River Scenic Byway) stretches west from Redding through Whiskeytown and Weaverville. In Weaverville, Highway 3 runs north-south through the Trinity Alps region and past Trinity and Lewiston Lakes.

Shasta Lake

Shasta Lake is fed by three major rivers—the Sacramento, the Pit, and the McCloud (plus Squaw Creek)—and each arm of the lake is named after its river. The lake has 29,500 acres of surface area altogether and it's 517 feet deep when full. With 369 miles of shoreline, there are lots of great places for camping in a tent or an RV, as well as hiking and wildlife-viewing. The lake's unusual layout makes it all the more fun for house boating, waterskiing, fishing, swimming, canoeing, and wakeboarding.

Surrounding the lake are marinas, campgrounds, resorts, cabins, general stores, boat rentals, and restaurants. At the south side of the lake is the tiny city of Shasta Lake; to the north is Lakehead, right on I-5.

SIGHTS
★ Lake Shasta Caverns

Summer visitors can find themselves longing for cool air—hard to come by in August. The best natural air-conditioning in the region is inside the cool **Lake Shasta Caverns** (20359 Shasta Caverns Rd., Lakehead, 800/795-2283, www.lakeshastacaverns.com, 9am-4pm daily Memorial Day-Labor Day, 9am-3pm daily Apr.-May and Sept., 10am, noon, and 2pm daily Oct.-Mar., adults $26, children 3-15 $15). Half-day **tours** depart from Caverns Park and include a ride across the lake aboard a ferry, then a bus ride 800 feet up to the cavern entrance with spectacular views.

At the cavern entrance, you'll climb a series of natural limestone and marble stairs into the

Shasta Lake

mountain. Inside, amazing formations spring from the walls, the ceiling, and the floor; delicate stalactites, drapes, pancakes, and ribbons of "cave bacon" decorate each space. The caverns remain cold year-round; bring a jacket or sweater for the tour.

Shasta Caverns also offers a **Lake Shasta Dinner Cruise** (530/238-2752 or 800/795-2283, www.lakeshastadinnercruises.com, 6:30pm-8:30pm Fri.-Sat. May-Sept., adults $75, children 2-12 $40, reservations required).

Shasta Caverns is 17 miles north of Redding on I-5, exit 695.

Shasta Dam

Completed in 1945, **Shasta Dam** (16349 Shasta Dam Blvd., Shasta Lake, 530/275-4463, www.usbr.gov, 8am-5pm daily) is a massive concrete dam that is second in size only to Hoover Dam. At 60 stories high and weighing 30 billion pounds, it is an impressive sight. The walk across Shasta Dam is beautiful at sunset, taking in the views of the lake and Mount Shasta.

From the visitors center, one-hour **tours** (9am, 10:15am, 11:30am, 1pm, 2:15pm, and 3:30pm daily Memorial Day-Labor Day; 9am, 11am, 1pm, and 3pm daily Labor Day-Memorial Day, free) offer a broad view of

Shasta Lake. Tours are first-come, first-served and limited to 40 people; arrive 30 minutes before start time.

To get to Shasta Dam, take I-5 to exit 685 onto Shasta Dam Boulevard. Drive west six miles on Highway 151 to the Shasta Dam visitors center.

MARINAS

Marinas along the shores of Shasta Lake provide all the rentals and services you'll need. The biggest houseboat marina is **Holiday Harbor** (20061 Shasta Caverns Rd., 530/238-2383 or 800/776-2628, https://lakeshasta.com). Holiday Harbor rents midsize houseboats ($488-697 for two nights), plus Jet Skis, paddleboards, wakeboards, fishing boats, and ski boats. Facilities include a gas dock, a convenience store with ice and swimsuits, and a boat launch (free with moorage or houseboat rental). Holiday Harbor is accessed from I-5 toward the south end of the lake near the Shasta Caverns gift shop and loading dock.

Packers Bay Marina (16814 Packers Bay Rd., Lakehead, 800/595-3359, www.packersbay.com) is small independent operator that rents large houseboats ($1,515-4,620, 3-night min., sleeps up to 16). No pets are allowed. To reach Packers Bay, get off I-5 northbound at

Lake Shasta Caverns

the Shasta Caverns/O'Brien Road exit. Then get back onto I-5 southbound to the Packers Bay Road exit.

Bridge Bay Resort Marina (10300 Bridge Bay Rd., Redding, 530/275-3021 or 800/752-9669, www.bridgebayhouseboats.com) is the largest marina on Shasta Lake. The full-scale resort has a large rental fleet that includes small-medium houseboats ($1,050-2,750 two-night min.), Jet Skis ($150-300), patio boats ($75-225), fishing boats ($40-100), and ski boats ($125-300). Three docks are available, plus a restaurant and a lodge ($75-220). The Courtesy Dock next to the launch ramp is open to the public.

Silverthorn Resort (16250 Silverthorn Rd., Redding, 800/332-3044, www.silverthornresort.com, $594-1,194 per week, houseboats $4,990-8,490 for 7 nights) is situated on the secluded Pit River Arm. The McCloud Arm and the Squaw Creek Arm adjoin this marina. Silverthorn Resort has a floating recreation area and houseboat rentals ($990-2,890 3-day minimum), plus patio party boats and smaller craft ($75-550 for up to 8 hours).

FOOD

Bridge Bay Resort (10300 Bridge Bay Rd., Redding, 800/752-9669, www. bridgebayhouseboats.com, 9am-9pm Mon.-Thurs., 8am-10pm Fri.-Sun. May-Oct., 4pm-9pm Thurs.-Sun. Nov.-Mar., 8am-9pm Thurs.-Sun. Apr., $13-28) has a casual dining room that's perfect for lakeside vacationers. The lengthy menu has plenty of American favorites. Seating is on the porch or inside with views of Shasta Lake through the large windows. Upstairs is a **lounge,** with its own views.

On the east side of the lake, Silverthorn Resort has the best (and only) pizza at the **Silverthorn Pizza and Pub** (16250 Silverthorn Rd., Redding, 800/332-3044, www.silverthornresort.com, 4pm-9pm Thurs., 2pm-midnight Fri., noon-midnight Sat., noon-9pm Sun. late May-early Sept., $8-20). This casual eatery offers ice-cold beer and piping-hot pizzas. A huge deck overlooking the lake lures people out for cocktails.

In the little city of Shasta Lake, you'll find fast food as well as one local place with a little character, The **Old Mill Eatery and Smokehouse** (4132 Shasta Dam Blvd., Shasta Lake, 530/275-0515, 7am-8pm Sun.-Thurs., 7am-9pm Fri.-Sat., $9-26) is noted for its large portions (hamburgers, omelets, and barbecue), its low prices, and its friendly hometown atmosphere inside a log cabin.

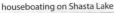
houseboating on Shasta Lake

Lakeshore Villa Market (20750 Lakeshore Dr., Lakehead, 530/238-8615, 7am-9pm Mon.-Thurs., 7am-10pm Fri.-Sun.) has food, plus basic camping, fishing, and outdoor recreation supplies for visitors at the north end of the lake.

ACCOMMODATIONS

Fawndale Lodge & RV Park (15215 Fawndale Rd., 530/275-8000, www.fawndale.com, $63-123) offers comfortable lodge rooms and cabins. Though you can't see the lake from the lodge, the surrounding forest has charm, and the garden and pool offer beauty. Rooms include a fridge, and a microwave; suites have full kitchens, sleeping space for six, and air-conditioning. Tent campers are welcome at Fawndale ($18-21), and full-hookup RV spots ($30) are available.

Toward the north end of the lake, the 10-room Shasta Lake Motel (20714 Lakeshore Dr., Lakehead, 530/238-2545 or 886/355-8189, www.shastalakemotel.com, $55-150) is a favorite for regular visitors. You'll get air-conditioning, cable TV, microwave, and coffeemaker, or pay more for a full kitchenette. Enjoy the motel pool or walk down to the shores of the lake. The motel is only a few minutes off I-5.

The ★ Bridge Bay Resort (10300 Bridge Bay Rd., Redding, 800/752-9669, www.sevencrown.com, $75-220) has one of the best locations of any resort here, right where the big I-5 bridge crosses the lake. It's close to the center of the lake's arms, making its full-service marina a perfect spot from which to launch a boat. Bridge Bay also includes a restaurant and a store with groceries, souvenirs, and bait and tackle. The lodgings aren't terribly stylish; rooms are decorated with particle-board furniture and generic prints. But this is a cheerful, family-friendly place—many of the rooms sleep 4-6, and some have full kitchens.

On the tip of a small peninsula in the Pit River Arm, the Silverthorn Resort (16250 Silverthorn Rd., Redding, 800/332-3044, www.silverthornresort.com, $99-199 per night, $594-1,194 per week) has phenomenal views from the common areas and guest cabins. Cabins rent by the week in summer and require a three-day minimum the rest of the year. Each cabin sleeps 4-6 people (the large family cabin can handle 8) and includes a full kitchen with a full-size fridge. Bedrooms are small but cute, and the atmosphere is woodsy and restful. A small grocery store and a "Pizza and Pub" room offer easy shopping and dining on-site.

CAMPING

The U.S. Forest Service rents ★ Hirz Mountain Lookout Tower (information 530/275-1587, reservations 877/444-6777, www.recreation.gov, May-mid-Oct., up to 4 people $75), located in the Shasta-Trinity National Forest. This 20-foot tower is on top of a 3,540-foot peak, so the views are phenomenal. In addition to the vast overview of the McCloud Arm, you can see both Mount Lassen and Mount Shasta. Getting here is a little tricky. Drive 5 miles down a dirt road (Forest Rd. 35N04) in a high-clearance 4WD vehicle, then walk the last 0.25 mile, and climb a couple of flights of metal steps to the tower.

One of the best places for camping in the vicinity of Shasta Lake is the Hirz Bay Campground (Gilman Rd., 877/444-6777, www.recreation.gov, reservations accepted mid-May-mid-Sept., $20-35). This 42-site Forest Service campground has amenities such as flush toilets, picnic tables, and paved parking. It also offers easy access to the lake via the Hirz Bay boat ramp and is 20 miles northeast of Redding.

TRANSPORTATION AND SERVICES

Shasta Lake is easily accessed by car via I-5, 8.5 miles north of Redding. Bridge Bay is a popular spot on due to its proximity and easy access to I-5; it's seven miles north of the town of Shasta Lake off I-5. Lakehead and the Sacramento Arm north are off I-5, 20 miles north of the town of Shasta Lake.

Mount Shasta and Vicinity

One of the most iconic natural formations in the United States, Mount Shasta is stunning from every angle at any time of day. The mountain is surrounded by equally memorable landscape including **Castle Crags State Park,** the roiling **McArthur-Burney Falls,** and otherworldly **Lava Beds National Monument.** Scattered throughout the region are equally picturesque mountain towns like the Mount Shasta City and Dunsmuir that will cap an already perfect getaway. The region is a must for hikers, boaters, skiers, anglers, and others who revel in the outdoors.

TOP EXPERIENCE

★ MOUNT SHASTA

Mount Shasta is a tremendous dormant volcano that last erupted in 1786. Although it may someday erupt again, for now it's a delightful playground and a magnetic attraction. At 14,162 feet, Mount Shasta is the 49th highest peak in the country, the fifth highest in California, and the second-tallest volcano in the Cascade Range. It has a 17-mile perimeter and stands pretty much alone, with no close neighbors of anywhere near similar stature. In winter, snow covers much of the mountain; in summer a series of glaciers makes the mountain appear white and glistening.

Hiking

In the summer, some of the best hiking can be found on and around Mount Shasta. This beautiful region abounds with waterfalls, pine forests, rivers, streams, and fascinating geology. Trails depart from either the Bunny Flat or Panther Meadow trailheads on the Washington/Everitt Memorial Highway.

For more information, visit the **Ranger Station** (204 W. Alma St., Mt. Shasta, 530/926-4511, www.fs.usda.gov, 8:30am-4:30pm Mon.-Fri. Sept.-May, 8:30am-4:30pm Mon.-Sat. June-Aug.).

GRAY BUTTE

The day hike to **Gray Butte** (3.4 miles round-trip, moderate) leads to an intermediate peak on the south slope of the mountain. The trail runs east across Panther Meadow and into

Mount Shasta

the nearby forest. At the first fork in the trail (just past 0.5 mile), turn right. In 1.5 miles, you'll come to a saddle. From the saddle, bear right again to reach (or scramble) to the peak of Gray Butte in less than 0.25 mile. On a clear day you can see all the way to Castle Crags, Mount Eddy, and Lassen Peak. Return the same way.

The trailhead is at Panther Meadows Campground, 13.5 miles along Everitt Memorial Highway.

GREEN BUTTE RIDGE

The **Green Butte Ridge Trail** (4.4 miles round-trip, difficult) is a tough climb that gains 2,250 feet, but the views (and relative solitude) are worth it. From the huge rock outcropping known as Green Butte, you'll see Lake Siskiyou and Castle Crags beyond. The trailhead is at Bunny Flat off Everitt Memorial Highway.

LAKE SISKIYOU TRAIL

The gently undulating **Lake Siskiyou Trail** (W.A. Barr Rd., 7 miles round-trip, easy) circumnavigates the spectacular Lake Siskiyou with changing perspectives on the nearby mountains, bridges, and shorelines. To reach the main trailhead from the town of Mount Shasta, head west on Hatchery Lane and take South Old Stage Road to W. A. Barr Road. Continue until you see signs for Lake Siskiyou Trail.

MOUNT EDDY

The steep trail up **Mount Eddy** (11 miles round-trip, difficult) reaches a 9,000-foot peak, where you can check out the highlights of the Cascade Range: Mount Shasta, Mount Lassen, the Trinity Alps, and even Mount McLoughlin in Oregon. The start of the trail is mostly mild climbing with some shade. The last 0.8 mile is the hard part: a series of steep, exposed switchbacks guaranteed to give you a workout. The reward is worth it: You'll soon be on the mountaintop with exceptional views.

The hike starts from the Deadfall Lake

trailhead. To get there, take north I-5 to Weed and exit at Edgewood. Cross under the freeway to Old Highway 99 and head south to Stewart Springs Road. Continue to Forest Road 17 (Parks Creek Rd.) and turn right. Drive nine miles to the trailhead. Bring plenty of water.

Climbing

Climbers come to tackle Shasta's majestic 14,162-foot peak. However, less than one-third of the 15,000 intrepid mountaineers who try to conquer Mount Shasta each year actually make it to the top. Shasta's steep and rocky slopes, its long-lasting snow-fields, and the icy glaciers that persist year-round make this a difficult climb. The thin air at this altitude also makes breathing a challenge.

The climbing season is June-August. While not technical, all routes to the top are arduous and require crampons and an ice ax, plus navigating scree, snow, ice, and dislodged boulders. A detailed map and permit are required ($20) from the **Ranger Station** (204 W. Alma St., Mt. Shasta, 530/926-4511, www.fs.usda.gov, 8:30am-4:30pm Mon.-Fri. Sept.-May, 8:30am-4:30pm Mon.-Sat., June-Aug.). For more information, contact the **Mount Shasta Climbing Advisory** (530/926-4511, www.shastaavalanche.org).

GUIDES

Shasta Mountain Guides (Mount Shasta, 530/926-3117, www.shastaguides.com, $695-895 pp) has been taking climbers to the top for decades. Join one of its scheduled group trips or call to arrange a custom expedition. Snowboard and backcountry ski tours ($145-695 pp, min. 2 people) are also available.

Sierra Wilderness Seminars (210 E. Lake St., 888/797-6867, www.swsmtns.com, $695-770 pp) leads groups of up to eight people up Mount Shasta. Start with one of the company's one-day courses, such as the Ice Ax Clinic ($145), which teaches basic snow-climbing techniques. Or make a weekend of it by combining this with the Basic

Mountaineering Clinic ($165). All clinics and climbs take place on Mount Shasta.

Fishing

Almost all the major rivers and feeder streams running through the Mount Shasta region are open for fishing. You can tie your fly on and cast into the McCloud, Sacramento, and Trinity Rivers, among many others. These rivers carry salmon, steelhead, and trout.

GUIDES

Guide services can take you out to the perfect fishing holes. For fly-fishing or scenic rafting tours, call **Jack Trout International Fly Fishing Guide Service** (530/926-4540, www.jacktrout.com, $400 for 2 people, $25 gear rentals). Jack will take you out on the McCloud, Klamath, Upper and Lower Sacramento, Pit, or Trinity Rivers, or to Hat Creek. All gear is included, and Jack brings a gourmet barbecue lunch to enjoy by the river. Bring a California fishing license, available online (www.dfg.ca.gov).

Outdoor Adventures Sport Fishing (530/221-6151 or 800/670-4448, www.sacriverguide.com, by appointment only, $175-600 pp/day) takes anglers on fly-fishing drift trips on the Sacramento and Trinity Rivers. Guides specialize in fishing for salmon, trout, and steelhead; they'll also take you on a jet-boat trip on Shasta Lake to catch salmon and trout.

Rafting

River Dancers (530/925-0237, www.riverdancers.com, adults $75-$98, children under 12 $70-$88) is a local outfit that offers rafting trips on the Sacramento River between Mount Shasta and Lake Shasta. You'll get a customized trip with a series of Class III rapids. Half- and full-day trips are available. All trips include lunch with a choice of kayaks.

Mountain Biking

Mount Shasta Ski Park (Ski Park Hwy., off Hwy. 89, 530/926-8610, www.skipark.com, adults $20-32, children 9-12 $10-16) is the place to go for mountain biking. The 1,200-foot descent from the top of Mount Marmot can be taken on single-track, irrigated trail, or dirt road. Or simply hop on the ski lift to the top for a scenic ride.

Horseback Riding

Rockin Maddy Ranch (11921 Cram Gulch Rd., Yreka, 530/340-2100, www.rockinmaddyranch.com, year-round by reservation, $55-75pp 2 hrs., $175 pp one day, $85) offers a popular two-hour Shasta View trail ride for ages 12 and up. The ranch also has 30-minute pony rides ($30) for younger ones in tow.

Winter Sports

In winter, Mount Shasta is a haven for downhill and cross-country skiers, snowboarders, and snowshoers. Some people like to go to the back side of the mountain (the "bowl"), climb as high as they can with skis strapped to their backpacks, and then ski down.

From the **Bunny Flat Trailhead** (6,900 feet), families with children can bring plastic sleds, hike a little up the mountain, and then let everyone sled down.

Mount Shasta Ski Park (Ski Park Hwy., off Hwy. 89, 530/926-8610, www.skipark.com, adults $49-65, children 8-12 and seniors $40-45, children under 8 $20-25) has 425 skiable acres, three chairlifts, and two carpet lifts. Nearly half of the downhill runs are open for night skiing (call for hours), and the Marmot lift in the beginner area makes a perfect spot for new skiers.

Cross-country skiers can get their fix at the **Mount Shasta Nordic Center** (Ski Park Hwy., 530/925-3494 or 530/925-3495, www.mtshastanordic.org, 9am-4pm Thurs.-Sun. late Dec.-mid-Apr., adults $17, seniors $15, youth $9, children under 8 free) with about 16 miles of groomed trails for cross-country skiing. There's ample backcountry to explore off-trail. Snowshoers are allowed on the groomed trails as long as they stay to the side. Ski and snowshoe rentals and lessons are available.

Camping

Shasta-Trinity National Forest manages two

campgrounds on Mount Shasta. Both are popular and fill quickly on summer weekends. Reservations are not accepted.

McBride Springs (10 sites, first-come, first-served, late May-Oct., $10) is on the mountain at 5,000 feet, just four miles from Mount Shasta City. Facilities include drinking water, vault toilets, and picnic tables.

★ **Panther Meadows** (Everitt Memorial Hwy., 15 sites, first-come, first-served, mid-July-Nov., free) is 14 miles northeast of Mount Shasta City at an elevation of 7,500 feet on the slopes of Mount Shasta. Due to the high elevation, it can be cold at night and snowed-in well into summer. Sites at this walk-in campground are only 100-500 feet from the parking lot. Facilities include picnic tables, fire rings, and vault toilets; bring your own water. This is the most popular campground on Mount Shasta and the maximum stay is three nights.

Dispersed camping is allowed throughout the Shasta-Trinity National Forest. A wilderness permit is required on Mount Shasta; all campers need a campfire permit (free), available at the **Mount Shasta Ranger Station** (204 W. Alma St., 530/926-4511, www.fs.usda.gov, 8am-4:30pm Mon.-Fri. Sept.-May, 8am-4:30pm Mon.-Sat. June-Aug.).

MOUNT SHASTA CITY

The charming town of Mount Shasta City is full of local businesses, quirky shops, and excellent outdoor stores. Most are located down Mount Shasta Boulevard.

At the north end of town, **Mount Shasta City Park** (1315 Nixon Rd., 530/926-2494, http://msrec.org) is home to play structures, wending paths, and the crystal-clear headwaters of the Sacramento River. Fill your canteens here before heading up the mountain.

Food

Breakfast and lunch are available at **Seven Suns Coffee and Café** (1011 S. Mt. Shasta Blvd., 530/926-9701, 6am-4pm daily, $8-13), which serves baked goods, burritos, wraps, and salads. The café makes coffee and espresso drinks and sells beans by the pound. There's a

spacious porch with umbrella-shaded tables, but the prime spot is the two small tables on the front sidewalk.

The best baked goods in town come from **The Oven Bakery** (214 N. Mt. Shasta Blvd., 530/926-0960, www.theoven-bakery.com, 7:30am-noon Mon. and Wed., 7:30am-5pm Tues. and Thurs., 7:30am-noon, 5pm-7pm Fri., 2pm-5pm Sun.). Sit down in the storefront and enjoy a hot scone and a cup of coffee while bread bakes in the background. The bakery also serves mouthwatering pizzas on Friday night ($24).

Housed inside an old railroad station, the retro **Burger Express Frosty & Grill** (415 N. Mt. Shasta Blvd., 530/926-3950, 11am-6:30pm Mon.-Fri., 11am-5:30pm Sat., noon-4pm Sun., $7-21) serves burgers and hot dogs, shakes, sundaes, and soft-serve ice cream. With great 1950s-style red stools and tables, a cheerful red-and-white counter, and a checkerboard floor, the place feels delightfully old-fashioned.

Casa Ramos (1136 S. Mt. Shasta Blvd., 530/926-0250, www.casaramos.net, 11am-9pm daily, $9-23) is a small chain of local Mexican family restaurants. This incarnation is particularly cheerful and welcoming. Prices are a bit spendy, but portions are ample and also include steak, chicken, and cheeseburgers.

Loaded with charm, ★ **Lily's** (1013 S. Mt. Shasta Blvd., 530/962-3372, www.lilysrestaurant.com, 8am-2pm, 5pm-9pm daily, $12-28) is a cottage turned restaurant serving fresh California food in big portions using local ingredients. On sunny days select a table on the front brick patio surrounded by flowers and hanging ivy.

Stock up at **Mount Shasta Super Market** (112 E. Alma St., 530/926-2212, 8am-8pm Mon.-Sat., 9am-7pm Sun.), which sells ice, organic produce, camping supplies, delicious deli sandwiches, and even barbecue on the weekend. **Mountain Song Natural Foods** (314 N. Mt. Shasta Blvd., 530/926-3391, 10am-5pm Mon.-Sat., noon-3pm Sun.) sells health food, including trail mix, homemade bread from The Oven Bakery, and local beans from Northbound Coffee Roasters. The **farmers market** (N. Mt. Shasta Blvd., 530/436-2532, www.mtshastafarmersmarket.com, 3:30pm-6pm Mon. May-mid-Oct.) is a treat.

Accommodations

Mount Shasta has a surprising array of independent and economy lodging. **Finlandia Hotel and Lodge** (1621 S. Mt. Shasta Blvd., 530/926-5596, www.finlandiamotelandlodge.com, $65-119) offers comfortable, pet-friendly rooms with microwaves and refrigerators, cable TV, and access to an outdoor spa. The lodge ($200-250) can sleep up to eight people; amenities include three bedrooms, a fully equipped kitchen, a sauna, an outdoor spa, and wood-burning fireplace crafted out of lava rock.

★ **Mount Shasta Ranch Bed & Breakfast** (1008 W. A. Barr Rd., 530/926-3870, www.stayinshasta.com, $85-150) has homey luxury slightly out of town. The budget-friendly rooms in the Carriage House offer small spaces, queen beds, and shared baths. The separate Cottage ($200-225) has two bedrooms that can sleep up to eight. All rooms include a full country breakfast.

The cute **Dream Inn** (326 Chestnut St., 530/926-1536 or 877/375-4744, www.dreaminnmtshastacity.com, $80-160) offers bed-and-breakfast accommodations at the base of the mountain. Four small upstairs rooms have shared baths. Downstairs, a large, white, antique bedroom has a private bath and a view of Mount Eddy. Next door, two large suites share space in a Spanish adobe-style house; each has its own living space, bath, and homelike decor. Rooms at the Dream Inn include a daily full breakfast.

Cold Creek Inn (724 N. Mt. Shasta Blvd., 530/926-9851 or 800/292-9421, www.coldcreekinn.com, $79-149) is a small motel with 19 simple but comfortable rooms and suites; some with mountain views. Amenities include free wireless Internet access, cable TV, a coffeemaker, and a continental breakfast with organic coffee. All rooms are nonsmoking, and pets are welcome.

The white farmhouse exterior of the ★ **Shasta Mount Inn Retreat & Spa** (203 Birch St., 530/261-1926, www.shastamountinn.com, $150-175) fits perfectly into its mountain setting. Each of the four rooms ooze country charm and modern comforts with private baths and a memory-foam mattress. In the morning, head downstairs for a continental breakfast and a cup of organic coffee.

Lily's is one of Mount Shasta's best restaurants.

There are on-site massage services and a barrel-shaped redwood sauna.

Tree House (111 Morgan Way, 530/926-3101, www.bestwesterncalifornia.com, $160-250) is a full-service Best Western Plus Hotel with an indoor pool, a hot tub, and a fitness center. Rooms include microwaves, fridges, and wireless Internet access. The on-site **Tree House Restaurant** (www.treehouserestaurantmtshasta.com, 6:30am-10am and 5pm-9pm daily, $11-29) serves breakfast and dinner; **Cooper's Bar & Grill** (11am-10pm daily, $7-13) serves tacos, burgers, flatbread, cocktails, wine, and beer.

For spacious grounds, beautiful scenery, spa treatments, and a golf course, stay at the **Mount Shasta Resort** (1000 Siskiyou Lake Blvd., 800/958-3363, www.mtshastaresort.com, $159-359). A variety of accommodations include rooms with a fireplace and a jetted tub to a two-room lakeside suite. Amenities are typically upscale.

Camping

If the campgrounds on Mount Shasta are full, there are several options on the west side of I-5.

Lake Siskiyou Beach and Camp (4239 W. A. Barr Rd., 530/926-2618 or 888/926-2618, www.lakesiskiyouresort.com, Apr.-Oct.) has hundreds of tent ($20) and RV sites ($26-29) with partial and full hookups as well as cabins ($65-250). Amenities include a beach, boat and equipment rentals, a **Splash Zone** water park for kids ($8/hour, $15/4 hours), canoe, kayak, and paddleboard rentals, a **Snack Shack** (10am-6pm daily Memorial Day-Labor Day), and the on-site **Lake Sis Grille & Brew** (530/926-1865, 8am-9pm Sun.-Thurs., 8am-10pm Fri.-Sat. Memorial Day-Labor Day, $10-15). The resort is right on the shore of Lake Siskiyou, three miles west of Mount Shasta City.

Pitch a tent in one of the four primitive campsites on **Gumboot Lake** (Forest Rd. 26, 530/926-4511, www.fs.usda.gov, first-come, first-served, June-Oct., free). Facilities include fire rings and a vault toilet; there are no picnic tables or drinking water. A campfire permit is required. Gumboot Lake is 12 miles west of Mount Shasta City. Contact the Forest Service for directions.

Castle Lake Campground (Castle Lake Rd., 530/926-4511, www.fs.usda.gov, first-come, first-served, May-Nov., free) offers six primitive campsites on Castle Lake with picnic tables, fire rings, and vault toilets; there is no drinking water. There is a three-night stay limit. The campground is nine miles southwest of Mount Shasta City. To get here, take W.A. Barr Road to the southern point of Lake Siskiyou. Follow Castle Lake Road for seven miles to the lake.

Transportation and Services

Mount Shasta is 62 miles north of Redding on I-5. The **Mount Shasta Ranger Station** (204 W. Alma St., 530/926-4511, www.fs.usda.gov, 8am-4:30pm Mon.-Fri. Sept.-May, 8am-4:30pm Mon.-Sat. June-Aug.) is the place to go for wilderness permits, trail advice, maps, and directions.

Mercy Medical Center Mount Shasta (914 Pine St., Mount Shasta City, 855/401-2285, www.mercymtshasta.org) has a 24-hour emergency room and a walk-in clinic (530/926-7131, 9am-5pm Mon.-Fri.).

★ CASTLE CRAGS STATE PARK

Castle Crags State Park (20022 Castle Creek Rd., Castella, 530/235-2684, www.parks.ca.gov, $8 per vehicle) has 4,350 acres of land, 28 miles of hiking trails, and some very dramatic granite peaks and cliffs. It is a wonderful destination and a convenient place to camp near Mount Shasta or Shasta Lake. You can fish and swim in the Sacramento River, climb the spectacular 6,000-foot crags, take a variety of hikes, or just enjoy stunning views of Shasta and other nearby mountains and ranges.

Hiking

From the Vista Point parking lot, **Vista Point** (0.25 mile) is a paved walk to a spectacular overlook with views all around. Use the Vista Point parking lot to access the Crags Trailhead to hike the strenuous **Crags Trail to Castle Dome** (5.5 miles round-trip, 3.5 hours). It's a steep climb with memorable views along the way. About 2 miles along the trail is a sign for Indian Springs, a 0.25-mile jaunt off the main path.

Rock Climbing

Castle Crags has more than 40 established rock climbing routes plus plenty of wide, open formations for explorers who prefer to make their own paths. You can tackle domes, spires, and walls of granite that reach 6,000 feet into the sky. Some favorite climbs at Castle Crags are the **Cosmic Wall** on **Mount Hubris**, **Castle Dome**, and **Six Toe Crack**.

Camping

The **campground** (www.reservecalifornia.com, May-Sept.; first-come, first-served Oct.-Apr.; $25) is split into two loops. Along Vista Point Road on the west side of I-5 are 64 developed sites with showers, water, and flush toilets. East of I-5, along the Sacramento River, are 12 environmental sites ($15) available year-round on a first-come, first-served basis. Some sites close to the freeway can be loud, but others are tucked deep enough in the pines to feel miles away from civilization.

Transportation

Castle Crags is 16 miles south of the city of Mount Shasta. From I-5, take exit 724 and turn left onto Castle Creek Road.

DUNSMUIR

Less than six miles north of Castle Crags, the Victorian railroad town of Dunsmuir offers a scenic stopover along I-5.

Food

Dunsmuir is a great place to grab a bite. Overlooking the train yard, **The Wheelhouse** (5841 Sacramento Ave., 530/678-3502, www.thewheelhousedunsmuir.com, 7am-3pm Wed.-Thurs. and Sun., 7am-8pm Fri.-Sat., $9-20) is the place for a pastry with morning espresso, *and* a beer with sliders. There is even a wide selection of board games.

Chase your hike with a locally brewed craft beer at the **Dunsmuir Brewery Works** (5701 Dunsmuir Ave., 530/235-1900, 11am-10pm daily June-Aug., 11am-9pm Tues.-Sun. Sept.-May, $11-13). Beers like the End of the Line Canadian Dark Ale, Blood Sweat & Tears IPA, and the light Steam of Jefferson, pair well with the menu of burgers, fish tacos, sausages, and salads. There is a kid's menu and several vegetarian options.

You'll find a variety of Mexican standards at **La Perla de Nayarit** (5855 Dunsmuir Ave., 530/235-7060, 11am-9pm Sun.-Thurs., 11am-9:30pm Fri.-Sat., $6-16), including fajitas, tacos, tamales, and enchiladas in a bright and charming interior. There's a kid's menu and burgers are available.

Accommodations

Train enthusiasts will love **Railroad Park Resort** (100 Railroad Park Rd., 530/235-4440, www.rrpark.com, $145-175), where a collection of cabooses are now private lodgings. The antique train cars have been overhauled with pine panel walls, floral comforters, refrigerators, coffeemakers, free wireless Internet, and full bathrooms that include claw-foot tubs. Cabins ($145-175), RV ($37-47), and tent ($29-39) sites are also available. A vintage dining car serves as the on-site **restaurant** (530/235-4611, 8am-11am and 4pm-10pm daily, $11-28), serving American favorites (burgers, rib roast, pasta, country-fried chicken) surrounded by railroad memorabilia.

Rooms at **Dunsmuir Lodge** (6604 Dunsmuir Ave., 530/235-2884, https://dunsmuirlodge.com, $59-153) are loaded with charm and feature homemade quilts, log beds, and windows that open onto forest and mountains. Amenities include wireless Internet, refrigerators, and cable TV. Pets are welcome ($10).

Transportation

Dunsmuir is 54 miles north of Redding along I-5 and nine miles south of Mount Shasta City.

MCCLOUD

The small town of McCloud is best known for the famous falls that share its name.

McCloud Falls

Located on the McCloud River, **McCloud Falls** (McCloud Ranger Station, 2019 Forest Rd., 530/964-2184,www.fs.usda.gov, 8am-4:30pm Mon.-Fri.) is a series of three waterfalls, each breathtaking. At Lower McCloud Falls, roiling white water pours over a 30-foot rock wall into an aerated river pool below. Middle McCloud Falls resembles a tiny Niagara, a level fall of water that's wider than it is tall. Upper McCloud Falls cascades briefly but powerfully into a chilly pool that doubles as a swimming hole.

To see all three falls, hike the **Loop Trail** (3.5 mile) or drive the paved road for 10 miles along the river, linking the overlooks of Middle and Upper Falls.

To get here from I-5 near Mount Shasta City, follow Highway 89 east for five miles past the town of McCloud. Look for signs to Fowlers Camp and Lower McCloud Falls. In one mile you'll come to the Lower Falls picnic area and parking lot.

Camping

The McCloud area has several campgrounds with access to the McCloud River. At the base of the falls, popular **Fowlers Camp** (530/964-2184, www.fs.usda.gov, mid Apr.-mid-Oct., $15) has 39 first-come, first-served sites at 3,400 feet in elevation on the Upper McCloud River. Facilities include picnic tables, fire rings, vault toilets, and drinking water.

Cattle Camp (530/964-2184, www.fs.usda.gov, 27 sites, Apr.-Nov., $15) is the second campground on the Upper McCloud River, with 27 first-come, first-served, sites. Facilities include picnic tables, fire rings, vault toilets, and drinking water. Cattle Camp is at 3,700 feet elevation, next to the popular Cattle

McArthur-Burney Falls Memorial State Park

Camp Swimming Hole. From McCloud, drive 10 miles east on Highway 89.

Ah-Di-Na (530/964-2184, www.fs.usda.gov, Apr.-Nov., $10) is a remote campground with 16 first-come, first-served sites at 2,300 feet on the Lower McCloud River. Facilities include picnic tables, flush toilets, and drinking water. The campground is 10 miles south of McCloud via a rough dirt road. To get there, follow the signs on Highway 89 near the Ranger Station.

Transportation

The town of McCloud is about 11 miles east of Mount Shasta City along Highway 89. The McCloud River area is 5.5 miles farther east along Highway 89.

★ MCARTHUR-BURNEY FALLS MEMORIAL STATE PARK

Halfway between Mount Lassen and Mount Shasta, **McArthur-Burney Falls Memorial State Park** (24898 Hwy. 89,

Burney, 530/335-2777, www.parks.ca.gov, $8) is often billed as the most beautiful waterfall in California. Fed by underground springs, Burney Falls flows year-round and requires only a short stroll from the parking lot. The **Falls Loop Trail** (1 mile, easy/moderate) goes from the base of the falls, down Burney Creek, and then up to the top of the 129-foot falls.

Lake Britton, at the north end of the park, has sandy beaches, a boat launch, and picnic areas. A concessionaire (530/335-5713) rents boats ($50-115/hour, $170-420/4 hours, $320-800/8 hours) and canoes, kayaks, and paddle-boards (all $25/hour) at the dock.

Camping

McArthur-Burney Falls **campground** (24898 Hwy. 89, Burney, 800/444-7275, www. reservecalifornia.com, year-round, $35) has 102 reservable campsites, three primitive hike-in/bike-in sites, and 24 cabins ($105) with heaters and platform beds. Facilities include restrooms with flush toilets, showers, picnic tables, and fire rings.

Transportation

McArthur-Burney Falls Memorial State Park is on Highway 89 near Burney. From Mount Shasta City, follow Highway 89 southeast for 53 miles. From Redding, take Highway 299 east for about 60 miles to Burney, and then head north on Highway 89 for six miles.

★ LAVA BEDS NATIONAL MONUMENT

Lava Beds National Monument (Hill Rd., 530/667-8113, www.nps.gov/labe, $20) is delightfully under-visited, no doubt owing to its remote location. This fascinating 47,000-acre park has Native American petroglyphs, a series of deep and twisting "tube" caves, primordial piles of lava, and an abundance of wildlife. It is a mother lode of history, nature, and awe-inspiring sights.

The lava beds were the site of the Modoc War of 1872-1873, when Captain Jack and his tribe used the tunnels as a stronghold for the Modoc people, eluding capture by the U.S.

Army for five months. Among the battle sites, hiking trails, and high-desert wilderness are more than 700 caves created by underground lava flows. Some caves have been developed for fairly easy access—outfitted with ladders, walkways, and lights—while others remain in their original condition.

Caving

The **visitors center** (530/667-8113, 8am-5:30pm daily late June-Aug., 9am-4:30pm daily Sept.-Nov. and Mar.-May, 10am-4pm daily Dec.-Feb.) recommends bringing up to three flashlights per person to explore the caves, as well as caving or bicycle helmets (it's easy to hit your head on the low ceilings of the caves). For the more challenging caves, gloves, knee pads, a cave map, and a compass are also recommended.

However, you don't necessarily need a lot of equipment to visit the caves here. The short, paved **Cave Loop Road** (2.25 miles, open 8am-5pm daily) leads past 13 different caves—their cool rocky entrances are fascinating. Three more caves are accessible via a short hiker-only trail beside the visitors center. The park recommends **Mushpot Cave** (770 feet) as an introductory cave; it's well-lit and easy to get into.

To learn more about the caves, book a tour. The **Fern Cave Tour** (2pm Sat. June-Sept., one hour, moderate) highlights the cave's unique plant and animal life, as well as its Native American art. In winter and spring, join the **Crystal Ice Cave Tour** (1pm Sat., Jan.-Mar., 3 hours, difficult), which explores the most spectacular ice formations found in the caves. **Reservations** (877/444-6777, www.recreation.gov, $1.50) are required and can be made three weeks in advance. Visitors must bring a flashlight and helmet.

Hiking

In addition to the numerous caves are 13 hiking trails. One of the best-known trails is **Captain Jack's Stronghold** (1.5 miles, moderate); the interpretive signage will help you understand the contentious history of this

Side Trip to Tule Lake

Near the very tip of California is large and lovely Tule Lake, visible from a long distance across the high-desert landscape. Although the lake you see today is still beautiful, blue, and deep, it is much smaller than it used to be. One of the early projects of the U.S. Bureau of Reclamation was to "reclaim" the land beneath Tule Lake and Lower Klamath Lake and make it available for homesteading. What was once underwater, and later homestead land, is now mostly farmland.

You can still see some striking evidence of the lake's original size from **Petroglyph Point,** a section of Lava Beds National Monument located east of the lake and separate from the main lava beds area. Along **Petroglyph Point Trail,** you may wonder how the ancient markings on the rock walls high above got up there. Tule Lake was much bigger 5,000-6,000 years ago, and what is now hot, dry land was all underwater. The Modoc artists simply steered their boats to the edge of the lake and worked on the lakeshore rock face—now far out of reach.

From 1942 to 1946 Tule Lake was the name of one of the 10 internment camps where Japanese Americans were held during World War II. In commemoration of the events that went on here and in the other camps, in December 2008 a total of nine sites were made into one national monument, collectively called the **Tule Lake Unit, World War II Valor in the Pacific National Monument** (530/260-0537, www.nps.gov/tule). This is the site of the largest and most controversial of the internment locations, where a "segregation center" stayed open even after the war, incarcerating Japanese Americans who had given unsatisfactory answers to the infamous loyalty questionnaire.

The temporary **visitors center** (800 Main St., 530/260-0537, 8:30am-5pm daily Memorial Day-Labor Day) is in the Tulelake-Butte Valley Fairgrounds Museum (530/667-5312, 9:30am-4:30pm Mon.-Fri.). Take a tour (530/260-0537, 1pm Sat. late May-early Sept., hours vary early Sept.-late May) of the very interesting **Tule Lake Segregation Center's** jail and **Camp Tulelake.** The visitors center at Lava Beds National Monument (530/667-8113) can arrange tours during the off-season.

---

area. Start at the visitors center and take the park's main road seven miles north to reach the trailhead.

The wide, easy **Schonchin Butte Trail** (1.4 miles round-trip, moderate) leads to a working fire tower on top of a cinder cone along a trail built by the Civilian Conservation Corps (CCC) in 1939-1941. To get to the Schonchin Butte Trail from the visitors center, turn left onto the main park road and drive 3.2 miles to the trail sign on the right. From here, it's a 0.5-mile drive on a gravel road to the parking area.

For many, hiking the **Big Nasty Trail** (2 miles round-trip, easy/moderate) may be may be irresistible. This loop starts at the Mammoth Crater and offers wonderful views, particularly at sunset. To reach it, head south on the dirt road toward Hidden Valley north of the visitors center.

To really stretch your legs, take the **Three Sisters Trail** (7.5 miles, easy-moderate), which starts from the campground and follows a series of collapsed lava tubes through juniper and sagebrush. Turn this a 10-mile loop by turning left onto Lyons Trail. At Skull Cave, take another left onto the Missing Link Trail and another turn onto Bunchgrass Trail back to the campground.

Camping

The **Indian Well** (43 sites, first-come, first-served, $10) campground is close to the visitors center with potable water, modern restrooms with flush toilets (no showers), and an amphitheater. Don't expect much shade at the campsites, however. One of the best features are the picnic tables built by hand out of local lava stone by the CCC in the 1930s.

Transportation

Lava Beds National Monument is in the

remote northeastern corner of the state, about 70 miles northeast of Mount Shasta City. To get here from I-5, take U.S. 97 north at Weed and drive 50 miles north. At the state line north of Dorris, turn east onto Highway 161. Continue 16 miles east on Highway 161 to Hill Road, then turn right (south), and drive 9 miles to the park entrance.

Plan at least two hours for the drive from Weed. Note that U.S. 97 gets snow at high elevations. Don't count on any cell phone service and gas up before you leave I-5.

YREKA

With a population of more than 7,000, Yreka offers some standard chain motels, a few B&Bs, and a few places to eat.

Black Bear Diner (1795 S. Main St., 530/842-9324, www.blackbeardiner.com, 6am-10pm daily, $8-17) serves a hearty

breakfast, lunch, or dinner when everything else is closed. For more local color, try **Poor George's** (100 N. Main St., 530/842-4664, 7am-11pm daily, $8-20) for real country atmosphere, homemade food, and large portions. For a local grass-fed burger and brew, stop at the **Etna Brewing Tap House** (231 W. Miner St., 530/841-0370, www.etnabrew.com, 11am-8pm Tues.-Thurs., 11am-8:30pm Fri.-Sat., $8-11) in a historic building downtown. The menu is filled with wraps, specialty sandwiches, and comfort food, plus an extensive kid's menu.

Best Western Miner's Inn (122 E. Miner St., 530/842-4355 or 800/780-7234, www.bestwesterncalifornia.com, $99) offers a dependable night's sleep.

Transportation
Yreka is on I-5 near the California/Oregon border, 40 miles north of Mount Shasta.

Lake Tahoe

Sparkling blue Lake Tahoe sits surrounded by mountains, lakes, ski resorts, hiking trails, hot springs, charming mountain towns, casinos, and a varied wilderness.

The Tahoe area has an international reputation as a skiing paradise, with some of the finest ski resorts in the nation and many opportunities for skiers, snowboarders, cross-country skiers, and snowshoers.

Tahoe is even more crowded in summer, when vacationers come to bask in the perfect weather, either lakeside or exploring the endless backcountry. Tahoe is a delight for wakeboarders, water-skiers, campers, hikers, bikers, and families to swim, sun, play in the sand, rent kayaks, or just relax in a beautiful place. Even its historic sites tend to be the estates and retreats of the vacationers of previous generations.

Californians often refer to Lake Tahoe simply as Tahoe, but the locals get more specific—it's all about the North Shore, with ski resorts; the South Shore, with its sprawling town; and East Shore, with glittering casinos just across the state line in Nevada.

PLANNING YOUR TIME

Lake Tahoe lies at an altitude of 5,000-7,000 feet and is usually accessible year-round. Weekend jaunts are popular, but one- to two-week vacations also are common. It's possible to drive all the way around the lake, stopping at both the South and North Shores and enjoying the attractions and natural beauty of both California and Nevada.

Most people come for the winter snow. The North Shore has the most downhill ski resorts, many of which are clustered near Truckee. In winter, I-80 and U.S. 50 into Tahoe can close during major storms, and smaller roads surrounding the lake can shut down for weeks. Check traffic reports for information about road closures and alternate routes and carry snow chains in your vehicle at all times.

Summers (June-Aug.) are usually sunny and clear, with average highs around 80°F and nights getting down to the 40s.

Previous: summer in Lake Tahoe; Emerald Bay in early spring. **Above:** Lake Tahoe in relief.

Look for ★ to find recommended
sights, activities, dining, and lodging.

Highlights

★ **Heavenly Gondola:** Ride the gondola at Heavenly ski resort with views from 9,123 feet (page 277).

★ **Tallac Historic Site:** Explore the grounds of these grand estates along the edge of Lake Tahoe (page 277).

★ **Emerald Bay:** The most beautiful section of the "Most Beautiful Drive in America," Emerald Bay sparkles year-round (page 279).

★ **Tahoe Rim Trail:** This 165-mile trail circumnavigates the lake, with multiple access points (page 282).

★ **Ed Z'berg Sugar Pine Point State Park:** Visit one of the state's best parks and ski on trails from the 1960 Olympics (page 292).

★ **Aerial Tram at Squaw Valley:** Take the breathtaking Aerial Tram to 8,200 feet above Squaw Valley (page 295).

★ **Downhill Skiing and Snowboarding:** Tahoe's North Shore resorts offer the best slopes for winter fun (page 295).

★ **Donner Memorial State Park:** Donner offers a lake that's perfect for recreation, along with interpretive trails and monuments

illuminating one of the most compelling stories of the American West (page 303).

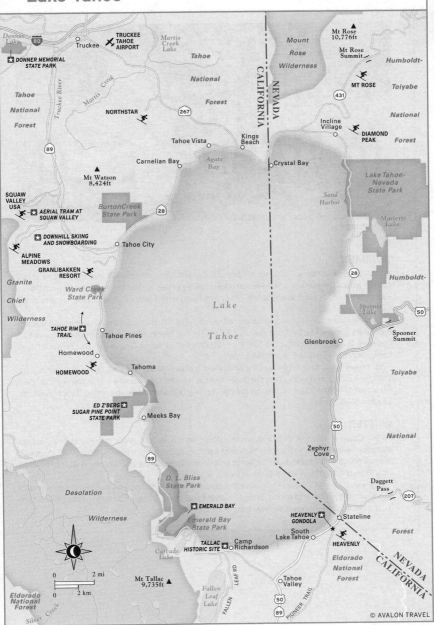

Lake Tahoe

Donner Lake

Truckee

DONNER MEMORIAL STATE PARK

TRUCKEE TAHOE AIRPORT

Martis Creek Lake

Tahoe

Tahoe National Forest

Martis Creek

Truckee River

Tahoe National Forest

NORTHSTAR

267

Tahoe Vista

Kings Beach

Carnelian Bay

Agate Bay

Crystal Bay

Mt Watson 8,424ft

SQUAW VALLEY USA

AERIAL TRAM AT SQUAW VALLEY

DOWNHILL SKIING AND SNOWBOARDING

Burton Creek State Park

28

Tahoe City

ALPINE MEADOWS

GRANLIBAKKEN RESORT

Granite Chief Wilderness

Ward Creek State Park

TAHOE RIM TRAIL

Tahoe Pines

Homewood

HOMEWOOD

Tahoma

ED Z'BERG SUGAR PINE POINT STATE PARK

Meeks Bay

89

Lake Tahoe

Glenbrook

Mount Rose Wilderness

Mt Rose 10,776ft

Mt Rose Summit

Humboldt-

MT ROSE

431

Toiyabe

Incline Village

DIAMOND PEAK

National

Forest

Crystal Bay

Lake Tahoe-Nevada State Park

Sand Harbor

Marlette Lake

Humboldt-

Spooner Lake

28

50

Spooner Summit

Toiyabe

50

Zephyr Cove

Daggett Pass

207

National

Desolation Wilderness

D. L. Bliss State Park

EMERALD BAY

Emerald Bay State Park

Cascade Lake

TALLAC HISTORIC SITE

Camp Richardson

HEAVENLY GONDOLA

Stateline

South Lake Tahoe

HEAVENLY

Forest

Eldorado National Forest

NEVADA

CALIFORNIA

Mt Tallac 9,735ft

Fallen Leaf Lake

LEAF RD

FALLEN

Tahoe Valley

50

89

PIONEER TRAIL

Eldorado National Forest

Silver Creek

CALIFORNIA

NEVADA

0   2 mi
0   2 km

© AVALON TRAVEL

One Day in Tahoe

Vikingsholm Castle

SUMMER

U.S. 50 enters the Tahoe region on the popular South Shore of Lake Tahoe. Stop at one of the casinos across the Nevada state line or take in the lay of the land on the Heavenly Gondola. Highway 89 heads west to glittering Emerald Bay, where you can hike the Rubicon Trail to Vikingsholm Castle.

Continue north on Highway 89 to reach the North and West Shores, which hold Tahoe's legendary appeal. The lively center of Tahoe City has plenty of restaurants, hotels, and campgrounds. Spend the night at the Sunnyside Resort in Tahoe City, or camp at General Creek Campground in Sugar Pine Point State Park.

In the morning, take Highway 89 east toward Truckee. Along the way, take a stroll along the Truckee River and shop along the main street in Truckee. On your way home, stop by Donner Memorial State Park. Although the park history tells a grim tale, the hiking trails around the lake are quite beautiful.

WINTER

Nothing says winter like sliding down the slopes at Tahoe. Numerous ski resorts line the lake and mountains. Heavenly rules the roost on the South Shore, while Squaw Valley draws in snowboarders and skiers on the North and West Shores. Cross-country skiers should head to Royal Gorge in the Truckee-Donner area.

Highway 89 and U.S. 50 are the main arteries to the Tahoe area, and they can become congested and blocked by snow into spring. Bring tire chains and plenty of patience—in inclement weather, it can take up to eight hours to drive here from San Francisco.

South Shore

The South Shore will likely be your point of entry on U.S. 50 to the town of South Lake Tahoe, filled with basic services such as supermarkets, banks, drugstores, plus lively restaurants and bars, upscale lodging options, and lovely beaches. Just west of the California-Nevada border is the ski resort of Heavenly Village, jam-packed in summer and winter. Heading east on U.S. 50, the town of South Lake Tahoe becomes Stateline, Nevada, with barely a sign announcing the transition.

SIGHTS

★ Heavenly Gondola

The ride up the **Heavenly Gondola** (4080 Lake Tahoe Blvd., 775/586-7000, www.skiheavenly.com, 9am-4pm Mon.-Fri., 8:30am-4pm Fri.-Sun. and holidays in winter; 10am-5pm daily in summer; adults $55, seniors and children 13-18 $40, children 5-12 $30) is a must in any season. The gondola travels 2.4 miles up the mountain to an elevation of 9,123 feet, stopping at an observation deck along the way. From here, you can view the whole of Lake Tahoe and the surrounding Desolation Wilderness. At the top, you can climb a ropes course, ride a zipline, or take a hike.

★ Tallac Historic Site

The **Tallac Historic Site** (Hwy. 89, 3.1 miles north of U.S. 50, 530/543-2600 or 530/541-5227, www.fs.usda.gov or www.tahoeheritage.org, daily, free) is a 74-acre complex that encompasses three grand summer estates. Built between 1870 and the 1920s, the Baldwin, Heller, and Pope estates are beautifully preserved, showcasing the architecture of their day and the beauty of the natural surroundings. All three line the lake and are linked by a wending nature trail.

In total, the site encompasses 33 buildings, including three mansions, plus a working **blacksmith shop** (10am-4pm daily summer) and an **artist workshop** (10am-3pm daily July-Sept.), with many docent-led tours and living history events.

In winter, the Tallac buildings are closed, but the grounds are a great spot for cross-country skiing and snowshoeing.

BALDWIN ESTATE

The **Baldwin Museum** (10am-4pm daily May-Sept., free) is on the Baldwin Estate and features exhibits about the local Washoe people and the importance of Lucky Baldwin to the history of California. Explore the Washoe medicine garden and the cedar bark tepee then follow the trail south to the Pope Estate.

POPE ESTATE

Tour the interior of the 1894 **Pope Mansion** (530/541-5227, www.tahoeheritage.org, call for times and reservations, adults $10, children 6-12 $5, children under 5 free) or sign up for children's activities, like the "Kitchen Kids" workshop (children 6-12, 1pm Wed. and Fri. June- Aug., $10), where kids can learn to cook using old-fashioned recipes in the Pope Estate kitchen.

HELLER ESTATE

The **Heller Estate** (530/541-4975, www.valhallatahoe.com), called Valhalla by its original owners, was set aside to showcase the art and music of the Tahoe region. The Heller boathouse has been converted into a 164-seat theater where concerts and plays are presented in summer. Smaller cabins on the grounds serve as summer galleries for photographers and local artists.

Taylor Creek

Taylor Creek (Hwy. 89, 3 miles north of South Lake Tahoe, 530/543-2600, www.fs.usda.gov) is a small recreation area next to the Tallac Historic Site surrounded by wetlands with nature trails, beach access, and

South Shore

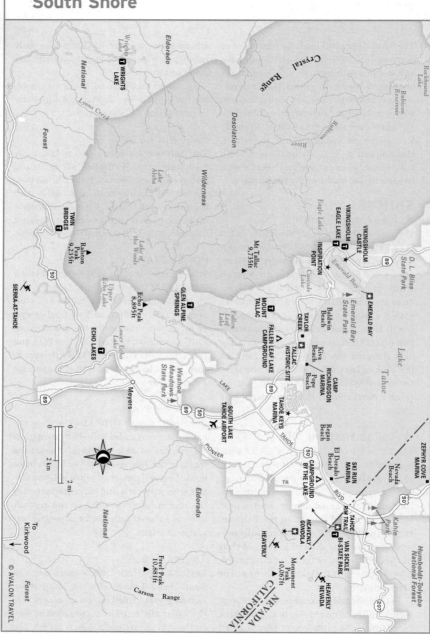

© AVALON TRAVEL

picnicking. The **visitors center** (9am-4pm daily late May-Oct.) has exhibits on the area's ecology and a little gift store. Follow the **Rainbow Trail** 0.25-mile to the **Stream Profile Chamber,** a literal look into the underwater world of Taylor Creek.

In summer, the **Tahoe Heritage Foundation** (www.tahoeheritage.org) offers a robust naturalist program in the amphitheater with evening talks about bats, astronomy, and historic figures like Mark Twain and John C. Frémont. The biggest show, however, is on the Taylor Creek Bridge in October when the kokanee salmon spawn, a unique and colorful sight.

TOP EXPERIENCE

★ Emerald Bay

North of South Lake Tahoe, Highway 89 passes through Emerald Bay State Park. Pull over at one of the several scenic overlooks, such as **Inspiration Point** (10 miles north of South Lake Tahoe) for views you won't want to miss.

The parks are extremely popular, particularly on summer weekends. To avoid congestion, take the **Emerald Bay Shuttle** (TTD Route 30, 530/541-7149, www.

tahoetransportation.org, 8:30am-5:30pm daily late June-mid-July, Fri.-Mon. mid-July-early-Sept., Sat.-Sun. Sept., $2), a pleasant open-air trolley that runs hourly between the South Y Transit Center in South Lake and Tahoe City, making multiple stops along the way.

EMERALD BAY STATE PARK
Emerald Bay State Park (Hwy. 89, 530/541-3030 or 530/525-3345, www.parks.ca.gov, $10) was designated an "underwater" state park in 1994. Its above the water attractions encompasses the historical Vikingsholm mansion; Fannette Island (mid-June-Feb.), the only island in Lake Tahoe; the Eagle Point Campground; and a boat-in campground on the north side of the bay. In addition, there are miles of hiking trails, including the **Rubicon Trail,** from Emerald Bay State Park to nearby D. L. Bliss State Park.

VIKINGSHOLM CASTLE
The elegant Scandinavian-style **Vikingsholm Castle** (530/525-9498, www.vikingsholm. org or www.parks.ca.gov) is an architectural gem. Built by a Swedish architect in 1929, the castle-like mansion is composed of granite boulders and includes towers, hand-cut

Emerald Bay

timbers, and sod roofs green with growing grass. The interior is furnished with authentic Scandinavian period reproductions. Visitors can enjoy the beach, the grounds, and the exterior; the mansion is only accessible on by **tour** (10:30am-3:30pm daily late May-Sept., adults $10, children 7-17 $8). The mansion may be reached via a steep one-mile trail from the Vikingsholm parking lot north of the Emerald Bay Overlook (Hwy. 89, $10) down to the beach.

D. L. BLISS STATE PARK
D. L. Bliss State Park (Hwy. 89, 2 miles north of Emerald Bay, 530/525-3345 or 530/525-7277, www.parks.ca.gov, spring-fall, $10) adjoins Emerald Bay State Park to create 1,830 acres of parkland on the most scenic stretch of Lake Tahoe. D. L. Bliss has some of the best views in Tahoe, plus the popular Lester and Calawee Cove Beaches, three campgrounds, and the **Rubicon-Lighthouse Trail,** which extends the length of both parks.

SPORTS AND RECREATION
Downhill Skiing and Snowboarding
HEAVENLY
The queen bee of the resorts is **Heavenly** (Wildwood Rd. and Saddle Rd., 775/586-7000, www.skiheavenly.com, adults $85-125, youth 13-18 $70-102, children 5-12 $47-68, seniors $90-102). At 10,067 feet, Heavenly offers the highest elevation of any mountain in Tahoe. The ski resort has 97 trails, 28 lifts, two terrain parks, one of the best tubing hills in the country, and plenty of backcountry.

Four base areas surround the mountain: two are in South Lake Tahoe, while the other two are in Stateline, Nevada. Closest to the lakeshore, the base area at **Heavenly Village** (4080 Lake Tahoe Blvd.) includes access to the gondola, but has limited parking. The **California Base Lodge** (3869 Saddle Rd.) is further inland with parking, ski lessons, plenty of dining options, and ski runs for all levels.

Stagecoach Lodge (375 Quaking Aspen Ln.) and **Boulder Lodge** (140 S. Benjamin Dr.) are in nearby Stateline, Nevada. Boulder caters to beginners, while the smaller Stagecoach services intermediate skiers.

Lift lines can be long and crowded on weekends and holidays. **BlueGo Shuttle** (530/541-7149, www.tahoetransportation. org, free) picks up at major lodging areas and drops skiers off at any of Heavenly's four lodges.

Sierra-at-Tahoe
For a smaller and less-crowded experience, **Sierra-at-Tahoe** (1111 Sierra-at-Tahoe Rd., Twin Bridges, 530/659-7453, www.sierraat-tahoe.com, adults $99-104, seniors $69-73, youth 13-22 $89-94, children 5-12 $39-43, under 5 free) has plenty of long, sweeping advanced runs as well as good intermediate tracks. Eight different eateries are on the mountain.

Cross-Country Skiing and Snowshoeing
Two state-designated **Sno-Parks** (916/324-4442, www.ohv.parks.ca.gov, $5 daily, $25 all-season) offer trailheads ideal for cross-country skiing and snowshoeing. **Echo Lake** (Echo Lake Rd., Echo Pass, 530/573-2600, www.fs.usda.gov) offers backcountry skiing, while **Taylor Creek** (Hwy. 89, 530/543-2600, www.fs.usda.gov or www.parks.ca.gov) is an uncongested but populous area with flat-marked trails.

Parking passes are required and available at the **Explore Tahoe Visitor Center** (4114 Lake Tahoe Blvd., 530/542-4637, www.cityofslt.us, 9am-5pm daily), the **Tahoe Roadrunner** gas station (2933 U.S. 50, 530/577-6946, 6am-10pm Sun.-Thurs., 6am-11pm Fri.-Sat.), and online (www.ohv.parks.ca.gov).

Sections of the beautiful **Tahoe Rim Trail** (775/298-4485, www.tahoerimtrail.org) can be ideal for snowshoeing, depending on conditions. The best section in South Lake is easily accessed behind Heavenly Village at

Van Sickle Bi-State Park (30 Lake Pkwy., 775/831-0494, http://parks.nv.gov). In winter, the Tahoe Rim Trail Association (775/298-4485, www.tahoerimtrail.org, Jan.-Mar.) offers guided snowshoe hikes.

Sledding and Snow Play

The Tube & Saucer Hill at Hansen's Resort (1360 Ski Run Blvd., 530/544-3361, www.hansensresort.com, 9am-5pm daily mid-Dec.-Mar., $20 first hour, $15 each additional hour, children under 4 free, cash only) is an annual favorite. Hansen's offers constructed runs roughly 400 feet long and the hourly rate includes the use of a Hansen's saucer or tube. The resort also has a snack bar.

Adventure Mountain Lake Tahoe (21200 U.S. 50, Echo Summit, 530/659-7217, http://adventuremountaintahoe.com, 10am-4:30pm Mon.-Fri., 9am-4:30pm Sat.-Sun., Dec.-Apr., $35 per vehicle) is a privately operated sno-park with six groomed sledding runs as well as a few other cross-country skiing and snowshoeing trails. In addition to a lodge with a fireplace and café, you'll also find equipment rentals including sleds (two-person sled $12/day, inner tube $25/two hours, $30/day) and snowshoes with poles ($18 per day). It's cash only at the entrance gate, but the lodge does take credit cards.

Sleigh Rides

Nothing says winter like a being bundled up in a horse-drawn sleigh. Borges Sleigh Rides (775/588-2953, www.sleighride.com, adults $50, children 11-18 $45, children 11 and under $20) offers hour-long rides in South Lake Tahoe.

Winter Sleigh Rides at the Camp Richardson Corral (Hwy. 89, 530/541-3113 or 877/541-3113, www.camprichardsoncorral.com, hours vary Dec.-Feb., adults $35, children under 3 free, reservations required) run along the lake and are capped with hot cocoa and hot apple cider.

Ice-Skating

Lace up your skates at the picturesque open-air ice rink in the heart of Heavenly Village (4080 Lake Tahoe Blvd., 530/542-4230, www.skiheavenly.com, noon-9pm Mon.-Thurs., noon-11pm Fri.-Sat., noon-8pm Sun., adults $25, children under 13 $20). Your pass includes skate rental and in-and-out access all day long.

Beaches

Expansive beaches line the base of Lake Tahoe. Popular El Dorado Beach (1004 Lakeview Ave., www.cityofslt.us, 530/542-6056), also known as Lakeview Commons, has a boat launch, fantastic barbecue and picnic area, kayak and SUP rentals, and a large expanse of sand.

Three popular public beaches lie north of the "Y" (U.S. 50 and Hwy. 89). Pope Beach (Hwy. 89, 530/543-2600, www.fs.usda.gov, $8) is a family favorite thanks to its easy parking and shelter from the wind. Kiva Beach (Hwy. 89, 530/543-2600, www.fs.usda.gov) sits at the mouth of Taylor Creek and requires a small hike from the parking lot, but the seclusion and sandy stretch are worth it. Baldwin Beach (Hwy. 89, 530/543-2600, www.fs.usda.gov, $8) is popular with windsurfers and families; the parking lot fills quickly on weekends.

Water Sports

The clear waters of Lake Tahoe are irresistible to water-skiers, wakeboarders, Jet Skiers, and kayakers.

MARINAS

There are five marinas in South Lake. Full-service Tahoe Keys Marina (2435 Venice Dr. E., 530/541-2155, www.tahoekeysmarina.net) is the largest, selling gas, providing launch access, and renting slips as well as offering boat rentals and charter fishing trips. The other marinas include Ski Run Marina (900 Ski Run Blvd., 530/544-9500), the small Lakeside Marina (4041 Lakeshore Blvd., 530/541-9800), Timber Cove Marina (3411 Lake Tahoe Blvd., 530/544-2942), and Camp Richardson (1900 Jameson Beach Rd., 530/542-6570, www.camprichardson.com).

RENTALS

Tahoe Keys Boat & Charter Rentals (2435 Venice Dr. E., 530/544-8888, www.tahoe-sports.com) operates out of both the Tahoe Keys and Ski Run marinas. They rent power-boats ($447-747/half day, $894-1,494/full day), Jet Skis ($417/half day, $834/full day), kayaks ($60-105/half day, $80-140/full day), stand-up paddleboards ($60/half day, $80/full day), and parasails ($35-95).

Action Sports (https://action-waters-ports.com) rents boats ($465-762/half-day, $930-1,524/full day), Jet Skis ($119-135/hour), kayaks ($25-35/hour, $40-60/2 hours, $65-85/4 hours), and stand-up paddleboards ($30/hour, $50/2 hours, $80/4 hours). Parasailing ($20-95) is also available. A water taxi (adults $15/one-way, $25/round-trip, children $10/one-way $15/round-trip) runs between Lakeside Marina, Timber Cove, and Camp Richardson marinas.

Kayak Tahoe (530/544-2011, www.kay-aktahoe.com) rents kayaks ($25-35/hour, $35-55/2 hours, $65-85/day) and stand-up paddleboards ($25/hour, $35/2 hours, $65/day) at Pope Beach, Baldwin Beach, and Vikingsholm in Emerald Bay. The company also offers guided kayak tours of Emerald Bay (4.5 hours, $70, 6 hours, $90), stopping at Vikingsholm and Fannette Island. The Sunset Tour (2 hours, $50) and Upper Truckee River Tour (3 hours, $55) both depart out of Timber Cove Marina.

CRUISE

The 1.5-hour **Rum Runner Emerald Bay Cruise** (530/542-6572, https://action-waters-ports.com, 1pm, 3:30pm, and 5:30pm daily summer, adults $59, children $29) and a three-hour cruise and tour of **Vikingsholm** (adults $79, children under 13 $39) operate out of the Camp Richardson marina.

Fishing

Several companies offer charter fishing trips on Lake Tahoe. **Tahoe Sport Fishing** (Ski Run Marina, 530/541-5448, www.tahoesport-fishing.com, $115-125) offers morning and afternoon fishing trips with bait and tackle, cleaning and bagging services, and cold beer and soda on board.

Tahoe Fly Fishing Outfitters (2705 Lake Tahoe Blvd., 530/541-8208, www.tahoeflyfish-ing.com, $225-575) can take you on an expert-guided fly-fishing or spin-fishing trip on one of the smaller lakes, Walker River, Carson River, Truckee and Little Truckee Rivers, or the Pleasant Valley Fly Fishing Preserve.

Hiking and Biking

Around the lake, easy, accessible nature trails include those at the **Tallac Historic Site** (Hwy. 89, 530/543-2600 or 530/541-5227, www.fs.usda.gov or http://www.tahoeheritage.org) and **Taylor Creek** (Hwy. 89, 530/543-2600, www.fs.usda.gov).

Cyclists will enjoy the serene and flat expanses of the paved **multiuse trails** parallel-ing U.S. 50 and Highway 89. Beginning near Stateline, a municipal bike trail runs eight miles to the west side of town. Another picks up less than one mile northwest of the Y inter-section and follows Highway 89 through the woods past Baldwin Beach. The two paths are connected by bike lanes and bike routes. Maps are available from the **Lake Tahoe Bicycle Coalition** (775/298-0273, www.tahoebike.org).

★ TAHOE RIM TRAIL

The 165-mile **Tahoe Rim Trail** (775/298-4485, www.tahoerimtrail.org) is easily ac-cessed from the trailhead at **Van Sickle Bi-State Park** (30 Lake Pkwy., 775/831-0494, http://parks.nv.gov). A moderate 2.5-mile round-trip hike is rewarded with beauti-ful views and a waterfall. Popular day hikes from the **Big Meadow Trailhead** (Hwy. 89, 5.3 miles south of the U.S. 50 and Highway 89 junction in Meyers) include an easy 1.2-mile round-trip hike to wildflower-filled Big Meadow and a moderate 6.4-miles round-trip to Round Lake.

Much of the Tahoe Rim Trail is not open to bicycles. One segment that *is* is the five miles from Big Meadow to Echo Summit and Echo

Lake. The trail starts heading south but soon turns northwest to Echo Summit and then Echo Lake. Near the lake, a sign warns that the trail is about to join the Pacific Crest Trail and cyclists must turn around for a 10-mile round-trip ride.

DESOLATION WILDERNESS

The **Desolation Wilderness** (530/543-2600, www.fs.usda.gov) is a federally designated wilderness area spanning nearly 64,000 acres. **Permits** (available at the trailheads, free) are required for all hikers, and backcountry **reservations** (877/444-6777, www.recreation.gov, reservation fee $6/party, overnight permit fee $5-10/night) are required for all overnight campers.

Several trailheads between Camp Richardson and D. L. Bliss State Park provide relatively easy access to the area. The **Glen Alpine Trailhead** (Fallen Leaf Lake Rd.) is the beginning of two beautiful and easy miles of the **Fallen Leaf Trail** along the edge of Tahoe's beautiful second-largest lake.

Take the southern spur of the **Glen Alpine Springs/Falls Trail** to Grass Lake (2.5 miles one-way, moderate). Along the way you'll pass the spectacular 65-foot Glen Alpine Falls and the remains of one of Tahoe's oldest resorts, some of which was designed by Bernard Maybeck.

Peak-baggers can tackle the **Mount Tallac Loop** (11.6 miles round-trip, difficult). Past the Glen Alpine Falls and ruins, the trail rises out of Glen Alpine Canyon and beyond Gilmore Lake. Switchbacks lined with wildflowers cheer the strenuous climb to 9,735-foot Mount Tallac.

The quickest way into the Desolation Wilderness is the **Lower Echo Lakes Trailhead** (Johnson Pass Rd., off Hwy. 50 near Echo Summit, 530/543-2600, www.fs.usda.gov), thanks to **Echo Chalet Water Taxi** (9900 Echo Lakes Rd., Echo Lakes, 530/659-7207, www.echochalet.com, $14 one-way). The on-demand water taxi ferries hikers from Lower Echo Lake to the edge of Upper Echo Lake, cutting three miles off the backcountry trek. The trail leads to a myriad of small alpine lakes including Tamarack Lake, Lucille and Margery Lakes, Lake in the Woods, and Aloha Lake. All are easy-to-moderate hikes ranging 2-4 miles from the taxi drop-off (3.8-6 miles from the trailhead).

EMERALD BAY STATE PARK

Emerald Bay State Park is a treasure trove of hiking trails. From the Eagle Point Campground, the **Rubicon Trail** (1.7 miles) departs near the amphitheater and leads to Vikingsholm. The well-marked trail features undulating terrain, shade, and gorgeous views. Along the way, you'll pass a spur to take in Lower Eagle Falls before reaching the sandy beach at Vikingsholm. Bring a bathing suit to take a dip in the very cold, but beautiful, bay. The Rubicon Trail runs 4.5 miles along the shoreline of Emerald Bay to the northern edge of D. L. Bliss State Park.

The **Eagle Falls Trailhead** (Hwy. 89, 530/543-2600, www.fs.usda.gov), across from the Vikingsholm parking lot, offers access to a number of great day hikes and entrance into the Desolation Wilderness. One of the most popular treks is the **Eagle Falls Trail** to Eagle Lake (2 miles round-trip, moderate). The gorgeous alpine lake rewards with equally gorgeous views of Emerald Bay. At the trailhead, opt for the scenic spur to make this a longer and more challenging loop or continue on to the even more stunning **Velma Lakes** (10 miles round-trip, moderate). Day hikers must fill out a wilderness permit, available at the trailhead.

The best waterfall in Tahoe is accessed from the **Bayview Trailhead** (Hwy. 89, 530/543-2600, www.fs.usda.gov) in the Bayview Campground opposite the Inspiration Point parking lot. Keep left to reach the 200-foot **Cascade Falls** (2 miles round-trip, easy) that pours into Cascade Lake. Bearing right at the trailhead will reward you with **Granite Lake** (4 miles round-trip, moderate to strenuous) after some steep switchbacks.

D. L. BLISS STATE PARK

Within **D. L. Bliss State Park** (Hwy. 89, 530/525-3345 or 530/525-7277, www.parks. ca.gov, spring-fall, $10), the **Rubicon-Lighthouse Trail** (4.5 miles one-way, easy) leads to Rubicon Point's lighthouse. Take a short portion of this trail from Calawee Cove Beach to the lookout at Rubicon Point, or walk farther to see the lighthouse. For a longer adventure, follow the Rubicon Trail to its end point at Upper Eagle Point Campground in Emerald Bay State Park.

On the west side of D. L. Bliss is a short, self-guided **nature trail** (0.5 mile) to Balancing Rock. Along the way, numbered signs illuminate the history and geology of the area.

Horseback Riding

The **Camp Richardson Corral** (Emerald Bay Rd., 530/541-3113 or 877/541-3113, www. camprichardsoncorral.com, $50-168) offers trail rides to explore the surrounding meadows and forest or a ride with a steak dinner included ($65-105). For the little ones, Camp Richardson also provides pony rides (children 5 and under $10) and a 40-minute hay wagon ride for the whole family ($35 pp).

Golf

The championship George Fazio course at **Edgewood Tahoe** (100 Lake Pkwy., Stateline, NV, 775/588-2787 or 888/881-8659, www.edgewoodtahoe.com, $110-260) is one of the top courses in the West. Walking the course, you'll enjoy wonderful views of the lake and mountains; several holes are right on the shore of Lake Tahoe. The rather hefty greens fees include a golf cart; you can also rent clubs and hire a caddie. After your game, enjoy lunch and a stiff drink at the **Brooks' Bar & Deck** (11am-9pm Thurs.-Mon.).

Tahoe Paradise Golf Course (3021 U.S. 50, 530/577-2121, www.tahoeparadisegc.com, $20-62) offers a pleasant course as well as pleasantly low greens fees. Pretty mountain views run along the pine tree-dotted 18-hole, moderate golf course that provides a good

game for beginners and intermediates. It also has a pro shop, a practice area, and a modest snack bar with hot dogs and beer.

The **Lake Tahoe Golf Course** (2500 Emerald Bay Rd., 530/577-0788, www.laketahoegc.com, $39-89) offers a full-service restaurant and bar, cart service on the 18-hole course, a grass driving range, pros and a pro shop, and gorgeous views. To save money, go for the "super twilight" (from 4pm, $39) price for 18 holes and a cart.

ENTERTAINMENT AND EVENTS

Nightlife

The casinos over the Nevada border in Stateline dominate the bar scene in South Lake, but there are plenty of places on the California side. The most popular dive bar is **Whiskey Dick's Saloon** (2660 Lake Tahoe Blvd., 530/544-3425, noon-2am daily, cover varies), which hosts live music several times a week.

In summer, locals and tourists crowd the outdoor tables at the **Brewery at Lake Tahoe** (3542 Lake Tahoe Blvd., 530/544-2739, www.brewerylaketahoe.com, 11am-9pm daily, $13-27) for a pint of their signature Bad Ass Ale and the popular Washoe Wheat Ale. The Brewery is known for its pizza, pasta, salads, salmon, steaks, and barbecued ribs.

Casinos

Across the Nevada state line, casinos attract a young crowd looking for a lively, hip night out. The gaming floor of the **MontBleu Resort Casino & Spa** (55 U.S. 50, Stateline, NV, 775/588-3515 or 800/648-3353, www.montbleuresort.com) is great fun on weekend evenings, with youthful gamblers enjoying free drinks as they hammer the slots. You'll find full-fledged table games of the Vegas variety: craps, roulette, blackjack, and Texas hold 'em, among others. For late-night entertainment, **The Opal Ultralounge** (10pm-dawn Thurs.-Sat., cover $10-20) includes expert mash-up DJs, resident body painters (midnight Thurs.-Sat.), and go-go dancers (11:30pm Thurs.-Sat.).

The Best of Tahoe Outdoor Recreation

Mount Tallac

Whether you're a skier, hiker, swimmer, or sunbather, Tahoe offers endless opportunities for a vacation of a lifetime. Here is a list of the best of the best.

BEST SKIING

Seasoned skiers can challenge their skills on the Olympic slopes of Squaw Valley and Alpine on West Shore, and at the divine Heavenly on South Shore. Beginners and families will best get their ski legs at the Boreal, Soda Springs, and Tahoe Donner.

BEST CROSS-COUNTRY

For solitude and scenery in Tahoe's winter wonderland, take to the trails of Ed Z'berg Sugar Pine Point where Olympians competed for gold; the expansive Tahoe Meadows on Mount Rose; and at the Royal Gorge Cross Country Ski Resort, Tahoe's only resort devoted entirely to cross-country skiing.

BEST BEACHES

Dive into Tahoe's crystal-clear waters at Pope, Kiva, and Baldwin beaches, three South Shore beaches popular with windsurfers, families, and nature lovers; the boulder-strewn beaches of the West Shore's Ed Z'berg Sugar Pine Point and Sand Harbor on the East Shore; and the sandy stretches of Nevada Beach and those along the lovely Meeks Bay.

BEST HIKING

Head for the hills on the 165-mile Tahoe Rim Trail, which encircles the entire lake through six counties in California and Nevada, one state park, three national forests, and three wilderness areas. Take one of the trails in Emerald Bay skirting the lake or that travel deep into the Desolation Wilderness. Find a chain of alpine lakes on the other end of the Echo Lake ferry. Climb the peak of Mount Tallac where the 360-degree views take your breath away.

The **MontBleu Showroom** draws live performers, including occasional big names like Snoop Dogg and K.C. and the Sunshine Band.

Gamblers should bring their frequent-player cards to **Harrah's Lake Tahoe** (15 U.S. 50, Stateline, NV, 800/427-7247, www.caesars.com/harrahs-tahoe), which has all the Vegas gaming favorites—classic craps, rapid roulette, plus Keno pads and monitors all over the place. The atmosphere is a bit more classic casino, with dim lights in the evening and a warren of slot machines that make it easy to get lost. A favorite local's nightclub is **PEEK at Harrah's** (775/586-6705, 10:30pm-4am Fri.-Sat., $10-25 cover), a late-night watering hole featuring in-house and guest DJs.

For an evening of laughs, **The Improv at Harveys** (18 U.S. 50, Stateline, NV, 775/588-6611 or 800/786-8202, www.caesars.com/harveys-tahoe, $20-35) is the place where many of today's major comedy stars honed their acts—come see who'll be famous next.

Smaller and less flashy, **Lakeside Inn and Casino** (168 U.S. 50, Stateline, NV, 775/588-7777 or 800/624-7980, www.lakesideinn.com) looks more like a mountain lodge than a high-rise gaming emporium, but it has won the most votes for Best Casino, Loosest Slots, and Friendliest Casino Employees. The casino offers all the usual games and machines, and it is particularly welcoming for beginners.

SHOPPING

In Lake Tahoe, shopping generally means gear and rentals. Along the main drag, **Tahoe Sports Limited** (4000 Lake Tahoe Blvd., 530/542-4000, www.tahoesportsltd.com, 9am-7pm daily) is the largest outdoor store in South Lake Tahoe. You'll find locals tuning, repairing, and renting their gear at **Shoreline of Tahoe** (259 Kingsbury Grade, Stateline, NV, 775/588-8777, http://shorelineoftahoe.com, 10am-6pm daily), which also rents bikes and sells clothing. **Rainbow Mountain** (1133 Ski Run Blvd., 530/541-7470 or 800/619-7470, www.rainbowskirental.com, 7am-9pm daily) shares space with **Powder House Ski & Snowboard** (530/542-6222,

www.tahoepowderhouse.com, 7am-9pm daily), which leases gear and rents pants and jackets for adults and kids.

Rentals generally run $30-45/day for a ski package ($15-27/day for kids), $30-50/day for snowboards ($20-30/day for kids), and $16-27/day cross-country skis. Shoreline has slightly better deals.

Shoreline and Rainbow/Powder House have multiple locations throughout South Shore, including near the gondola in the **Heavenly Village** (1001 Heavenly Village Way, www.theshopsatheavenly.com). In the Village, you'll also find **Patagonia** (530/542-3385, www.patagonia.com, 10am-6pm Sun.-Thurs., 10am-8pm Fri.-Sat.), as well as the lovely **Village Toys** (530/541-6600, www.villagetoys.com, 10am-6pm daily) and the crafty **On Tahoe Time** (530/541-3588, http://ontahoetime.com, 10am-8pm Sun.-Thurs., 10am-10pm Fri.-Sat.) for gifts or keepsakes.

FOOD
South Lake Tahoe

For a classic American breakfast, it's tough to do better than the ★ **Original Red Hut Café** (2723 Lake Tahoe Blvd., 530/541-9024, www.redhutcafe.com, 6am-2pm daily, $10-13). This down-home waffle spot serves classic crispy-thin waffles, plus biscuits and gravy, omelets, and plenty more. Locals recommend the waffle sandwich, a complete breakfast in a single dish. Expect to wait for a table or a seat at the counter on weekend mornings, as this spot is very popular. If you can't get in, try the less-crowded **New Red Hut Café** (3660 Lake Tahoe Blvd., 530/544-1595, 6am-10pm daily), which opens for dinner and has a soda fountain.

Step back into ski vacations of yore at **Heidi's** (3485 Lake Tahoe Blvd., 530/544-8113, http://heidislaketahoe.com, 7am-2pm daily, $9-16), where big plates of pancakes and stick-to-your-ribs egg dishes are served with bottomless cups of coffee in a kitschy 1960s-era Swiss chalet. There's also burgers and a variety of lunch options.

For a great combination of delicious healthy

food and budget dining, check out **Sprouts Café** (3123 Harrison Ave., 530/541-6969, 8am-9pm daily, $9-11). This cute, casual walk-up eatery offers ultra-healthy dishes made with fresh, mostly organic ingredients. Breakfast is served all day, and the lunch and dinner menus run to several pages. Choose among salads, burritos, rice bowls, and tasty vegetarian and vegan desserts.

★ **Freshies Restaurant & Bar** (3330 Lake Tahoe Blvd., http://freshiestahoe.com, 530/542-3630, www.freshiestahoe.com, 11:30am-9pm daily, $15-18) is an unassuming local spot with great food and plenty of veggie options. This small, popular Hawaiian-themed restaurant has been voted the "Best Place for Dinner" and "Best Place for Lunch" by the *Tahoe Daily Tribune*. The main dining room is accessed through a mall, but the best way to experience Freshies is to go to the side entrance and add your name to the list for a rooftop table, where you can see the lake.

Blue Angel Café (1132 Ski Run Blvd., 530/544-6544, www.blueangelcafe.com, 11am-9pm daily, $14-23) has a globe-trotting menu with a distinct West Coast flavor. Try one of the amazing pizzas or opt for a bowl of cioppino or vegan Thai curry. The cozy café is set up the hill from the lake in a wooded neighborhood with tons of charm.

Nepheles (1169 Ski Run Blvd., 530/544-8130, www.nepheles.com, daily by reservation, $26-41), boasts a *Wine Spectator* Award of Excellence and a creative California cuisine menu. It's the perfect place for a romantic dinner or a celebration of any kind. Next door, **Café Fiore** (1169 Ski Run Blvd., 530/541-2908, www.cafefiore.com, 5:30pm-10pm daily, $18-35) shares Nepheles' intimate atmosphere, but with a more casual bistro vibe. Inside the chalet-like interior, you'll find upscale Italian fare and a fabulous wine list.

Off the Hook Sushi (2660 Lake Tahoe Blvd., 530/544-5599, www.offthehooksushi.com, 4:30pm-9:30pm Mon.-Fri., 5pm-9:30pm Sat., 5pm-9pm Sun, $14-23) serves good rolls and fresh *nigiri* at reasonable prices in a small setting.

At the more refined **Kalani's** (1001 Heavenly Village Way, 530/544-6100, www.kalanis.com, 5pm-9pm Mon.-Fri., 11am-3pm and 5pm-9pm Sat.-Sun., $18-65), the sushi and Pacific Rim fusion food are just as good. The restaurant earned a nod from *Wine Spectator* for its inventive menu of subtly spiced salmon, mahimahi, sushi, barbecued ribs, and house specialties like the *kalua* smoked pork quesadilla and Portuguese bean soup. Come for happy hour (4pm-6pm daily) in Kalani's Puka Lounge, which serves wine, sake, cocktails, and sushi.

Everyone loves **Base Camp Pizza** (1001 Heavenly Village Way, 530/544-2273, http://basecamppizzaco.com, 11am-9:30pm Mon.-Thurs., 11am-10pm Fri.-Sun., $14-25). There are games for kids, live music and brews for adults, and a crowd-pleasing menu of pizzas (including gluten-free), pasta appetizers, soups, and salads, plus a kid's menu.

Patio dining at swank **Jimmy's** (4104 Lakeshore Blvd., 530/541-5263 or 855/700-5263, http://thelandingtahoe.com, 7am-3pm and 5pm-9pm Sun.-Thurs., 7am-3pm and 5pm-10pm Fri.-Sat., $24-49) comes with lake views and a fire pit at the Landing Resort and Spa. Small, mostly Greek, plates are designed to be shared; larger plates are typical California cuisine. Pair your meal with a bottle of wine from the restaurant's large collection or a specialty cocktail.

One of the area's best restaurants is the ★ **Beacon Bar & Grill** (Camp Richardson, 1900 Jameson Beach Rd., 530/541-0630, www.camprichardson.com, 11:30am-9:30pm Mon.-Fri., 11am-9:30pm Sat.-Sun., $14-40). In addition to excellent food (filet mignon, fresh seafood, and a great spinach salad), the Beacon offers a beachfront patio and live music.

Stateline

The **Ciera Steak + Chophouse at the MontBleu** (55 U.S. 50, Stateline, NV, 775/588-3515 or 888/829-7630, www.montbleuresort.com, 5:30pm-10pm Wed.-Sun., $28-60) is the only AAA Four Diamond Restaurant in

Lake Tahoe. Inside the dimly lit modern restaurant, plenty of steak and seafood options satisfy big appetites. At the end of your meal, enjoy a complimentary dish of chocolate-covered strawberries atop a frothing container of dry ice and a selection of deliciously flavored whipped creams to accompany your coffee.

Out of the casino fray, My Thai & Noodle (177 Hwy. 50, Stateline, NV, 775/586-8757, www.mythainoodle.com, 11am-3pm and 4:30pm-9:30pm daily, $11-17) serves authentic Thai food in a bright festive atmosphere. Expect the standard curry and noodle favorites with lots of veggie options.

One of the best dining experiences is at ★ Edgewood Tahoe Restaurant (100 Lake Pkwy., Stateline, NV, 775/588-2787, www.edgewoodtahoe.com, 5pm-9pm Wed.-Sun., $30-44). Big plates of steak, elk chops, and sea bass are served in a setting reminiscent of Michael Corleone's lakeside estate. For dessert, try the nightly crème brûlée. Slightly more business casual dining can be found at the resort's Bistro (7am-9pm Sun.-Thurs., 7am-10pm Fri.-Sat., $17-34), which serves equally good food inside or out on the patio.

ACCOMMODATIONS
$100-150

South Lake Tahoe has basic motels that offer a room for the night without breaking the bank. Midsummer rates, however, can rival resort prices. Most bargain accommodations are clustered near the state line, in a little neighborhood between Lake Tahoe Boulevard and the lake. Some have seen better days, while others are a hip version of the motor lodge. All are within easy walking distance of the Heavenly Village and the Stateline casinos.

The Coachman Hotel (4100 Pine Blvd., South Lake Tahoe, 530/545-6460, https://coachmantahoe.com, $109-279) has small rooms, custom furniture, a minimal Euro-lodge aesthetic, and heated toilet seats. It also offers free Wi-Fi, a pool and hot tub, complimentary breakfast, and a hip bar serving wine, beer, and espresso.

Basecamp (4143 Cedar Ave., South Lake Tahoe, 530/208-0180, https://basecamptahoesouth.com, $99-125) has plenty of offbeat sleeping arrangements (in-room bunk beds, tents) for casual groups and young couples. Pluses include a bright modern look, a beer garden that serves continental breakfast, and a short five-minute walk to the casinos. On the minus side, Basecamp is dangerously close to party noise.

Away from the South Lake party scene, the Apex Inn (1171 Emerald Bay Rd., South Lake Tahoe, 530/541-2940, reservations 800/755-8246, www.apexinntahoe.com, $35-149) offers the winning combination of a good location and rates on par with camping. It has free Internet access and an in-room coffeemaker.

On the west end of town, the 200-room Beach Retreat & Lodge at Tahoe (3411 Lake Tahoe Blvd., South Lake Tahoe, 530/541-6722 or 800/972-8558, www.tahoebeachretreat.com, $119-269) is surprisingly inexpensive for its lakefront location. Expect standard amenities, though some rooms have fireplaces.

★ Camp Richardson (1900 Jameson Beach Rd., South Lake Tahoe, 530/541-1801 or 800/544-1801, www.camprichardson.com, $90-262) is a full-spectrum resort with multiple accommodations including 27 hotel rooms ($90-145) with rustic furnishings and private baths. The 38 individual cabins can sleep up to eight and include full kitchens and linens but no TVs or phones. There is also a campground and an RV Village (late May-Oct., $45-50) with 115 sites. Rates include use of the beach, the lounge, and the marina. Facilities include the excellent Beacon Bar & Grill, a general store, ice-cream parlor, deli, and a coffee shop. Cross-country ski and snowshoe rentals are available in winter, with paddleboats, kayaks, and bikes in summer.

Over $150

Surrounded by motor lodges and hotels, Seven Seas Inn (4145 Manzanita Ave., South Lake Tahoe, 530/544-7031, www.7seasinn.com, $155-170) stands out as a bed-and-breakfast. Rooms range from economy kings to suites; some have fireplaces. Rates include a hearty breakfast buffet, complimentary Wi-Fi, and an outdoor hot tub. The inn is in easy walking distance to Stateline and Heavenly Village.

On the road to Heavenly, the lovely, large ★ Black Bear Lodge (1202 Ski Run Blvd., South Lake Tahoe, 530/544-4451, www.tahoeblackbear.com, $159-409) features lodgepole pine and river rock, which blend in with the surrounding nature. A giant fireplace dominates the great room, and smaller but equally cozy river-rock fireplaces are in each of the five upstairs lodge rooms. Four additional cabins dot the property. All accommodations feature king beds, plush private baths, free Internet access, and an energy-building breakfast.

Cabin and Condo Rentals

Condos are a popular option for longer stays, particularly for families and groups of friends. The Marriott Timber Lodge (4100 Lake Tahoe Blvd., South Lake Tahoe, 530/542-6600) has about 40 condos just steps away from the Heavenly Gondola. Studios ($160-225) and three-bedroom units ($280-1,200, sleeps up to 14) have full kitchens, multiple bathrooms, plenty of beds, TV, and wireless Internet.

Spruce Grove Cabins (3599-3605 Spruce Ave., South Lake Tahoe, 530/802-2343, www.sprucegrovetahoe.com, $70-280) offers seven cabins with a gay- and dog-friendly Tahoe vacation experience. The one- and two-bedroom cabins have full kitchens, dining rooms, and living rooms decorated in a wilderness-based theme. The lodge also operates a number of larger vacation rentals ($119-2,000) throughout South Lake Tahoe.

The Lodge at Lake Tahoe (3840 Pioneer Trail, South Lake Tahoe, 530/541-6226 or 866/469-8222, www.lodgeatlaketahoe.com, $135-192) has studios, one- and two-bedroom suites. The smallest studios have only kitchenettes, but the larger condos offer fully equipped kitchens. Complex amenities include a summertime pool and spa, a swing set,

a horseshoe pit, outdoor barbecues near the pool area, and a coin-operated laundry room.

Families should book one of the six cabins at Hansen's Resort (1360 Ski Run Blvd., South Lake Tahoe, 530/544-3361, www.hansensresort.com, $125-300). Most cabins sleep up to four guests and have a refrigerator, microwave, a separate sitting room, a fireplace, and wireless Internet. The biggest bonus is the 400-foot-long sledding run just outside your door.

Casino Hotels

Tahoe's casino hotels are some of the spiffiest places to stay on the Nevada side, offering upscale attractive hotel rooms often at lower than expected rates. Smoking and nonsmoking rooms are available.

The most popular casino resort is Harrah's (15 U.S. 50, Stateline, NV, 800/427-7247, www.caesars.com/harrahs-tahoe, $95-589), with ritzy accommodations and easy access to Heavenly and other South Shore ski resorts in winter and the lakeshore in summer. The high-rise hotel has more than 500 rooms; premium rooms provide excellent views of the lake and the mountains.

With 437 rooms, MontBleu Resort Casino & Spa (55 U.S. 50, Stateline, NV, 775/588-3515, www.montbleuresort.com, $115-335 summer) offers a range of affordable choices. For luxury, try a Tahoe Suite, which includes two bedrooms, a wet bar, walk-in shower, and two-person hot tub in the bedroom. The walls are paper thin—bring earplugs. Free wireless Internet access is also available.

CAMPING

Camping at Lake Tahoe in the summer is easy and gorgeous. June-August, the weather is usually perfect and the prices are reasonable, with campsites minutes from trails or beaches.

Two great state parks have gorgeous campgrounds and require advanced reservations. Emerald Bay State Park (Hwy. 89, 800/444-7275, www.reservecalifornia.com, $35) has the 100-site Eagle Point Campground and a boat-in campground (July-Sept.) on the north side of the bay. Campsites include fire rings, and restrooms and showers are available in the park.

★ **D. L. Bliss State Park** (Hwy. 89, 800/444-7275, www.reservecalifornia.com, May-Sept., $35-45) has 150 sites; beachfront campsites have a premium price of $45, and they're worth it. All campsites have picnic tables, bear-proof food lockers, and grills. Hot showers, flush toilets, and potable water are available in the park.

Camp Richardson Resort (1900 Jameson Beach Rd., 530/541-1801 or 800/544-1801, www.camprichardson.com, $45-50) offers sites for tents, campers, and RVs. Amenities include a beach, a group recreation area, and a marina. On-site facilities include the Beacon Bar & Grill and the Mountain Sports Center.

The U.S. Forest Service runs 206 sites at **Fallen Leaf Lake Campground** (Fallen Leaf Lake Rd., 877/444-6777, www.recreation.gov, mid-May-mid-Oct., $32-34). RVs up to 40 feet are welcome, though there are no hookups or dump stations. Each campsite has a barbecue grill, a picnic table, and a fire ring. Six yurts are also available and sleep up to six people. There are modern baths with flush toilets, and some restrooms have free showers. The campground is 0.25-mile north of Fallen Leaf Lake.

The **Tahoe Valley RV Resort** (1175 Melba Dr., South Lake Tahoe, 530/541-2222 or 877/570-2267, www.rvonthego.com, $47-85) has 439 sites that can accommodate small tents to big-rig RVs with water, electric, and cable TV hookups. Cabins ($160-250) are also available and sleep six. Tall pine trees give each site some shade and privacy. Amenities include tennis courts, a swimming pool, an ice-cream parlor serving Tahoe Creamery products, activities for children and families, a dog run, and free wireless Internet access.

The **Campground by the Lake** (1150 Rufus Allen Blvd., South Lake Tahoe, 800/444-7275, www.reserveamerica.com) has 162 campsites ($30-46) that can accommodate

tents and RVs, plus tent cabins and standard cabins ($79-81). Bathrooms with flush toilets and showers are available.

TRANSPORTATION AND SERVICES

Air

The nearest airports are **Reno-Tahoe International Airport** (RNO, 2001 E. Plumb Ln., Reno, NV, 775/328-6400, www.renoairport.com) and **Sacramento International Airport** (SMF, 6900 Airport Blvd., Sacramento, 916/929-5411, www.sacramento.aero). Both are served by several major airlines.

Car

U.S. 50 is the main route to South Lake Tahoe from Sacramento (100 miles, 2 hours) and San Francisco (190 miles, 3.5 hours). **Highway 89** joins U.S. 50 southwest of downtown at what locals call the "Y." From the Y, Highway 89 travels the west side of Lake Tahoe to Tahoe City and to Truckee on I-80. The city of South Lake clusters along South Lake Tahoe Boulevard, with Heavenly Village and the casinos straddling the Nevada border at Stateline.

Train

The **Amtrak's** *Capital Corridor* (800/872-7245, www.amtrak.com, $55 one-way) route runs from Emeryville to Sacramento, followed by a bus to South Lake Tahoe for a total trip of 4.5 hours.

Bus

The **Tahoe Transportation District** (TTD, 530/541-7149, www.tahoetransportation.org, adults $2 one-way, $5 day pass) runs several bus routes. Routes 50 and 53 (6:45am-midnight daily) zigzag through South Lake from Stateline to the junction of U.S. 50 and Highway 89. Route 23 (7am-1am daily) climbs from Heavenly Village to the Heavenly Stagecoach and Boulder lodges. The **Emerald Bay Shuttle** (8:30am-5:30pm daily late June-mid-July, Fri.-Mon. mid-July-early Sept.,

Sat.-Sun. mid-late Sept.) runs hourly between South Y Transit Center and Tahoe City.

Bike

South Lake Tahoe is very bikeable, thanks to relatively flat terrain and paved bike paths and lanes from Stateline nearly to Emerald Bay. Maps and information are available at **Lake Tahoe Bicycle Coalition** (775/298-0273, www.tahoebike.org). Rent bikes at **Shoreline of Tahoe** (259 Kingsbury Grade, Stateline, NV, 775/588-8777, http://shorelineoftahoe. com, 10am-6pm daily, road bike $26/half day, $40/full day, mountain bike $36/half day, $50/ full day).

Services

For medical attention, **Barton Memorial Hospital** (2170 South Ave., South Lake Tahoe, 530/541-3420, www.bartonhealth.org) has an emergency room, or go to the **Tahoe Urgent Care Center** (2130 Lake Tahoe Blvd., South Lake Tahoe, 530/541-3277, www.tahoeurgent-care.com, 8am-5:30pm daily).

HIGHWAY 88 AND CARSON PASS

Along Carson Pass on Highway 88 you'll find plenty of skiing, snowshoeing, hiking, and mountain biking, plus camping and hot springs.

To reach Carson Pass from South Lake Tahoe, take U.S.50/Highway 89 south and continue on Highway 89 after the split at Meyers. Highway 89 intersects with Highway 88 at Pickett's Junction, 11 miles south.

Hope Valley

South of Luther Pass, Highway 89 meets Highway 88 at Hope Valley, a favorite place to strap on cross-country skis. Park in the lot of the **Hope Valley Sno-Park** (Highway 88 at Blue Lakes Rd., 775/882-2766, http://ohv. parks.ca.gov, $5) and enjoy the beautiful flat terrain. At Pickett's Junction, **Hope Valley Outdoors** (http://hopevalleycrosscountry. com) rents snowshoes and cross-country skis (adults $20-33, kids $10-15) and offers ski

and telemark lessons ($40-80) and ski tours (2 hours $80). Cash or check only.

Kirkwood

Kirkwood (1501 Kirkwood Meadows Dr., off Hwy. 88, Kirkwood, 209/258-6000, www. kirkwood.com, 9am-4pm daily Dec.-Apr., adults $83, seniors and youth 13-18 $75, children 5-12 $61) is a popular mid-tier ski resort with dozens of downhill runs, plus pipes, beginner terrain, and outdoor sound systems. Kirkwood offers food and lodging ($109-160) with three restaurants, including the historic **Kirkwood Inn & Saloon** (209/258-7304) at the entrance on Highway 88.

For a more sedate adventure, check out **Cross Country and Snowshoe Center** (Hwy. 88 before Kirkwood, 209/258-7248, adults $30, youth and seniors $23, children $14), where you can get passes to the labyrinth of groomed trails, plus rentals, tours, and lessons.

In summer, Kirkwood's trails offer fabulous mountain biking, with two lifts on weekends in summer (adults $31-41, teens 13-18 $27-32, children 5-12 $20-27). **Kirkwood Mountain Sports** (209/258-7240, 9:30am-4:30pm Sat.-Sun. July-Aug.) rents high-end mountain bikes (adults $72-99, children $32-39) plus gear. Other summer activities include disc golf, fishing at nearby Caples Lake and Silver Lake, and guided horseback rides with **Kirkwood Sierra Outfitters** (209/258-7433, www.kirkwoodsierraoutfitters.com, $105/2 hours).

Mokelumne Wilderness

The Mokelumne Wilderness is an accessible and relatively uncrowded place to explore the High Sierra. Several multiday treks depart from trailheads off Highway 88, including the **Pacific Crest Trail** (www.pcta.org), which crosses the highway at Carson Pass.

For something less arduous, hike to **Lake Margaret** (4.6 miles round-trip, easy; off Hwy. 88, 209/295-4251, www.fs.usda.gov). Gaining only 500 feet in elevation, this gentle trail passes small lakes, wildflowers, and climbs over a granite slab to arrive at Lake Margaret, ideal for swimming and sunbathing.

Charming **Woods Lake** (off Hwy. 88, 209/295-4251, www.fs.usda.gov, $24) is a wonderful place to camp, with 25 first-come, first-served sites and vault toilets. From here, the **Winnemucca Lake and Round Top Loop** (6.6 miles, moderate) follows a forested trail to alpine Winnemucca Lake; take the right fork to Round Top Lake. If your calves can take it, climb the knife edge up and back to Round Top, then take the Lost Cabin Mine Trail down to Woods Lake.

Kit Carson

The **Kit Carson** area is a wonderful place to stay, particularly for families. Large Silver Lake offers two campgrounds with great swimming, boating, and hiking. **Silver Lake West** (530/622-4513, www.eid.org, mid-May-mid-Oct., $30) has 42 first-come, first-served sites, vault toilets, food lockers, and fire rings. **Silver Lake East** (877/444-6777, www.recreation.gov, June-mid-Oct., $24-48) has 48 sites that accommodate tents and RVs, with vault toilets, food lockers, and fire rings.

The delightfully rustic **Kit Carson Lodge** (32161 Kit Carson Rd., Kit Carson, 209/258-8500, www.kitcarsonlodge.com) rents rooms and cabins with an on-site restaurant (7am-9pm Thurs.-Tues., $22-30, reservations recommended) that serves surprisingly good upscale food.

Markleeville

East of Carson Pass, the charming town **Markleeville** (Hwy. 89) is a popular stop. The biggest draw is **Grover Hot Springs** (Hot Springs Rd., www.parks.ca.gov, adults $10, children $5) located in a beautiful mountain meadow with two pools—one hot and one cold—fed by nearby mineral springs. The park has a **campground** (summer reservations 800/444-7275, www.reservecalifornia.com, $35-45; winter first-come, first-served, $25) with 75 sites, bear lockers, grills, flush toilets, and showers.

North and West Shores

The North and West Shores are often considered the most desirable areas of Lake Tahoe, filled with ski resorts, beachfront property, and tall pines. **Tahoe City** is the main town and hub of activity on the West Shore, with good restaurants, bars, shops, and a sparkling waterfront.

Strung along the lake are the smaller vacation and residential communities of **Lake Forest, Sunnyside, Tahoe Pines, Homewood,** and **Tahoma. Kings Beach** sits at the north end of the lake with a small main street, a public beach, a few restaurants, and a scrappier vibe.

North along Highway 89, **The Village at Squaw Valley** is the base for the famous ski resort. The small upscale town is designed to mimic a European alpine village. Here you'll find boutiques, galleries, restaurants, snack bars, and coffee shops plus the spectacular Aerial Tram.

SIGHTS
★ Ed Z'berg Sugar Pine Point State Park

Ed Z'berg Sugar Pine Point State Park (7360 Hwy. 89, Tahoma, 530/525-7982, www.parks.ca.gov, $10) sits right on Lake Tahoe with a sandy beach for lounging in summer and a hill perfect for sledding in winter. Several interpretive trails line the lake, including the **General Creek Trail,** which stretches three miles west. The park also has water sports rentals and a scenic campground.

Historic buildings add character to the already beautiful location. The 1903 **Ehrman Mansion** (530/583-9911, www.sierrastateparks.org, 10:30am-3:30pm daily late May-late Sept., adults $10, children 7-17 $8, children under 7 free) is a beautifully preserved 12,000-square-foot house that is open for tours in summer.

Eagle Rock

Eagle Rock (mile markers 67 and 68 on Hwy. 89, Tahoe Pines) is a popular spot to take in the beauty of Lake Tahoe. A moderate, 20-minute hike leads to the top of this 200-foot volcanic outcropping. Parking is in the small dirt lot on the west side Highway 89, on the south side of the rock near Blackwood Creek.

Fanny Bridge

Named for a Paiute chief who guided an emigrant party in 1844, the Truckee River is the only outlet of Lake Tahoe. Beginning its 121-mile run from the West Shore, the river travels northeast, through Truckee and down the east side of the Sierra. At the historic **Fanny Bridge** in Tahoe City, you can lean over (hence the name of the bridge) and watch the waters depart. As the river moves north, rafting and tubing opportunities become available in summer. The rushing water is a beautiful companion along the multiuse trails that line its banks.

Gatekeeper's Museum and Marion Steinbach Indian Basket Museum

Lovely three-acre William B. Layton Park is home to 28 native plants and trees and the charming **Gatekeeper's Museum and Marion Steinbach Indian Basket Museum** (130 West Lake Blvd., Tahoe City, 530/583-1762, www.northtahoemuseums.org, 11-4pm Wed.-Sun.). Together, they offer an in-depth history of society around the lake. Transcribed oral histories, photographs, dolls, costumes, and many other artifacts are displayed in pine-and-glass cases that match the galleries' wooden floors. Authentic Native American artifacts include a large collection of baskets and caps made of willow, tule, and pine needles. There are more than 800 baskets on display from 85 tribes of North America. Skiing and sports enthusiasts will enjoy the exhibits on Sierra ski history and the 1960 Winter Olympics.

Watson Cabin

The **Watson Cabin** (560 North Lake Blvd., Tahoe City, 530/583-8717, www.northtahoe-museums.org, noon-4pm Thurs.-Sun. July-Sept.) is a log cabin that was built in 1909 by Robert Watson as a private family residence

Ehrman Mansion in Ed Z'berg Sugar Pine Point State Park

North and West Shores

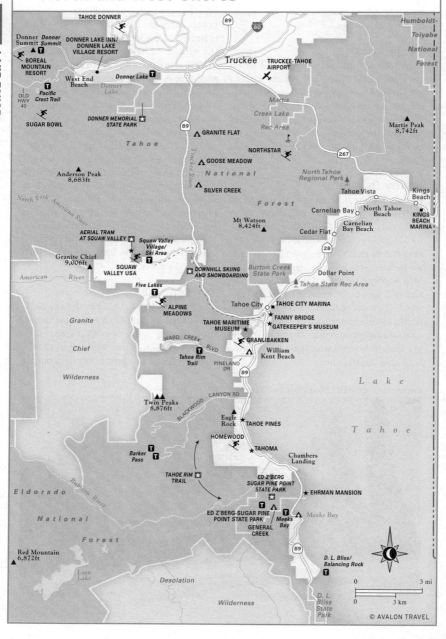

TAHOE DONNER

Humboldt-Toiyabe National Forest

Donner Summit · *Donner Summit*

DONNER LAKE INN/ DONNER LAKE VILLAGE RESORT

BOREAL MOUNTAIN RESORT

West End Beach · *Donner Lake* · *Donner Lake*

Truckee

TRUCKEE-TAHOE AIRPORT

OLD HWY 40 · *Pacific Crest Trail*

SUGAR BOWL

DONNER MEMORIAL STATE PARK

Tahoe

Martis Creek Lake Rec Area

Martis Peak 8,742ft

GRANITE FLAT

NORTHSTAR

GOOSE MEADOW

National

SILVER CREEK

North Tahoe Regional Park

Anderson Peak 8,683ft

Truckee River

Forest

Tahoe Vista

Kings Beach

KINGS BEACH MARINA

North Fork American River

Mt Watson 8,424ft

Carnelian Bay · North Tahoe Beach

Carnelian Bay Beach

Cedar Flat

AERIAL TRAM AT SQUAW VALLEY · Squaw Valley Village/ Ski Area

Granite Chief 9,006ft

SQUAW VALLEY USA

DOWNHILL SKIING AND SNOWBOARDING

Burton Creek State Park

Dollar Point

Tahoe State Rec Area

American River

Five Lakes

ALPINE MEADOWS

Tahoe City

TAHOE CITY MARINA

FANNY BRIDGE

GATEKEEPER'S MUSEUM

TAHOE MARITIME MUSEUM

Granite

WARD CREEK BLVD

Tahoe Rim Trail

GRANLIBAKKEN

William Kent Beach

Chief

PINELAND DR

Wilderness

CANYON RD

Lake

Twin Peaks 8,876ft

BLACKWOOD

Eagle Rock

TAHOE PINES

Tahoe

HOMEWOOD

TAHOMA

Chambers Landing

Barker Pass

Rubicon River

TAHOE RIM TRAIL

ED Z'BERG SUGAR PINE POINT STATE PARK

EHRMAN MANSION

Eldorado

ED Z'BERG-SUGAR PINE POINT STATE PARK

Meeks Bay

National

GENERAL CREEK

Meeks Bay

Red Mountain 6,872ft

Forest

D. L. Bliss/ Balancing Rock

Loon Lake

Desolation

0   3 mi
0   3 km

D. L. Bliss State Park

Wilderness

© AVALON TRAVEL

for his son and daughter-in-law. The cabin became a museum in the early 1970s and is still on the original site. Inside are diorama displays of pioneer life in early Lake Tahoe.

Tahoe Maritime Museum

Learn about the maritime history of Lake Tahoe and marvel at the beauty and craftsmanship of the historic boats, engines, and ephemera on display at the lovely **Tahoe Maritime Museum** (401 W. Lake Blvd., Tahoe City, 530/525-9253, www.tahoemaritimemuseum.org, 10am-4:30pm Thurs.-Tues., adults $5, children under 13 free). The museum's facility matches the beauty of its collection.

★ Aerial Tram at Squaw Valley

The **Aerial Tram at Squaw Valley** (1990 Squaw Peak Rd., Olympic Valley, 800/403-0206, www.squawalpine.com, 9am-4pm daily winter and summer, Sat.-Sun. spring and fall, adults $46-55, children 5-17 $25-30, children under 5 free) offers a spectacular ride up to High Camp at 8,200 feet in elevation where you can play disc golf, roller-skate, swim, soak in a hot tub, hike, or just enjoy the tremendous views. In summer, there's often live music at the base of the mountain, plus various special events year-round for adults and kids.

SPORTS AND RECREATION
★ Downhill Skiing and Snowboarding
SQUAW VALLEY

Squaw Valley (1960 Squaw Valley Rd., Olympic Valley, 800/403-0206, www.squawalpine.com, adults $129, seniors and youth 13-17 $112, children 5-12 $78) was the headquarters for alpine sports during the 1960 Winter Olympics. Today it is one of the most popular ski resorts in California, with every amenity and plenty of activities, from geocaching to ziplining, but skiing and snowboarding remain the primary pursuits. Squaw Valley has a great ski school with plenty of fun for new

skiers and boarders of all ages along with a wide selection of intermediate slopes. Some slopes are long, perfect for skiers who want to spend more time on the snow than on the lifts. But the jewels of Squaw are the many black-diamond and double-black-diamond slopes and the two terrain parks. During the day, especially weekends and holidays, expect long lines at the lifts, crowds in the nice, big locker rooms, and still more crowds at the numerous restaurants and cafes.

ALPINE MEADOWS

Alpine Meadows (2600 Alpine Meadows Rd., Tahoe City, 800/403-0206, www.squawalpine.com, adults $129, seniors and youth 13-17 $112, children 5-12 $78) is a sprawling resort with a full range of trails, an all-day every-day ski school, and rental equipment. Beginner skiers will enjoy the scenic network of green trails, and intermediate skiers will have a great time coming off the Summit Six or the Roundhouse Express chairlifts. Alpine also devotes considerable space to what it refers to as "Adventure Ski Zones," large clusters of black-diamond and double-black-diamond bowls and runs intended for expert skiers only. Thirteen lifts serve the mountains, including three high-speed chairs. Squaw and Alpine are jointly owned, with package passes to both resorts.

GRANLIBAKKEN

Granlibakken (725 Granlibakken Rd., Tahoe City, 530/583-4242 or 800/543-3221, www.granlibakken.com, lift tickets adults $17.50-35, children under 13 $12.50-25, lodging $165-665) is a lovely historical resort that dates back to the turn-of-the-20th century. Granlibakken offers some downhill skiing, but those who crave the excitement of bigger mountains should sleep here and take advantage of the package deals at other resorts, which include discount lift tickets and shuttle transportation to one of seven other ski areas. Accommodations range from standard rooms to townhouses that sleep eight. With several dining options, a large outdoor pool and hot tub, an on-site spa, hiking, cross-country ski trails, and one of the best-groomed sledding hills anywhere, this is an ideal spot for family vacations.

HOMEWOOD

If ever there was a mom-and-pop ski slope, **Homewood** (5145 W. Lake Blvd., Homewood, 530/525-2992, www.skihomewood.com, adults $89, children $49) is it. This small and affordable spot has 64 mostly intermediate runs, all with fantastic views and a thick forest. Protected from the heaviest winds during big storms, Homewood is often open when Squaw and Alpine are closed.

Cross-Country Skiing and Snowshoeing

One of the best cross-country ski trails for beginners is the **General Creek Trail** (Sugar Pine Point State Park, Hwy. 89, Tahoma, 530/525-7982, www.parks.ca.gov, $10), also known as the 1960 Winter Olympiad X-C Ski Trail. The trailhead is located near campsite 148. Signs and a trail map help explain a little about the trail's Olympic history. The amazingly beautiful trail is largely flat, so it's not too challenging for most skiers. Glide silently through the woods for as long as you like then turn around before you get too tired. Snowshoers are welcome but must stay out of the ski tracks.

Blackwood Canyon (Hwy. 89, 530/543-2600, www.fs.usda.gov) is a state-designated **Sno-Park** (916/324-4442, www.ohv.parks.ca.gov, $5/day, $25 all-season). Trail use requires a permit, available online (www.ohv.parks.ca.gov) or at **Tahoe Dave's Skis & Boards** (590-600 N. Lake Blvd., Tahoe City, 530/583-6415, http://tahoedaves.com, 10am-5pm Sun.-Fri., 10am-6pm Sat.). Snowmobiles are also allowed on the trail.

The nonprofit **Tahoe XC** (925 Country Club Dr., Tahoe City, 530/583-5475, www.tahoexc.org, 8:30am-3pm daily, adults $20-29, children under 19 free, dogs $5) has 24 groomed trails, three warming huts, rentals (adults $22-26, children 13-18 $18-22, children under 13 $14-18), a ski school (10:30am and 1:30pm daily, adults $55-60, children 13-17 $50-55, children under 13 $30-35), and a café (11:30am-4pm Fri.-Sun. mid-Dec-Mar., $5-8).

Sledding and Snow Play

Tahoe City Winter Sports Park (251 N. Lake Blvd., Tahoe City, 530/583-1516, http://

Homewood

wintersportspark.com, 10am-5pm Mon.-Fri., 9am-5pm Sat.-Sun., adults $12-40, children under 13 $12-35) has sledding, cross-country skiing, snowshoeing, and ice-skating (10am-8pm daily, $12, $18 with rentals). To warm up, duck into Café Zenon (530/583-1517, www.cafezenon.com, 11am-9pm Mon.-Fri., 9am-9pm Sat.-Sun., $9-21) for a beignet and an espresso.

Granlibakken (725 Granlibakken Rd., Tahoe City, 530/583-4242 or 800/543-3221, www.granlibakken.com, 9am-4pm daily, $16 per day) is a great place for sledding down the machine-groomed mountain on saucers (included).

Beaches

Several beaches line the beautiful West Shore. The four-acre Common's Beach (400 N. Lake Blvd., Tahoe City, www.tahoecitypud.com) is a popular local gathering spot with two playgrounds, barbecues, a grassy picnic area, an amphitheater, and kayak and SUP rentals. A municipal bike path runs along the edge; in summer, there are free concerts on Sunday afternoons and free movies Wednesday nights.

A large municipal beach is at King's Beach (8318 N. Lake Blvd., Kings Beach, 530/523-3203, www.parks.ca.gov, 6am-10pm daily, parking $10 May-Sept., $5 Oct.-Apr.) where you'll find picnic tables and barbecues, a playground, a boat ramp, and kayak and SUP rentals. Nearby, the North Tahoe Beach (Hwy. 28 at Hwy. 267, 530/721-0694, www.parks.ca.gov, 6am-10pm daily, free) has a beautiful grassy picnic area and access to a small sandy beach.

The prettiest beaches are found farther south at Ed Z'berg Sugar Pine Point State Park (7360 Hwy. 89, Tahoma, 530/525-7982, www.parks.ca.gov, $10) where families love to jump off and swim around the boulder-strewn beach. Meeks Bay (2 miles south of Tahoma, 530/543-2600, www.fs.usda.gov, $8) has a long sandy beach bordering the pretty bay.

Water Sports

RENTALS

Nearly every beach has its own concessionaire that rents kayaks and stand-up paddleboards. West Shore Sports (530/525-9920, www.westshoresports.com) at the north end of Ed Z'berg Sugar Pine Point State Park rents kayaks ($59-85/half day, $75-99/full day) and SUPs ($59-75/half day, $75-90/full day). The company also has locations in Homewood (5395 W. Lake Blvd., Homewood, 530/525-9920) and Sunnyside (1785 W. Lake Blvd., Tahoe City, 530/583-9920, www.westshoresports.com).

Tahoe City Kayak and Paddleboard (Commons Beach, 521 N. Lake Blvd., Tahoe City, 530/581-4336, http://tahoecitykayak.com, 9:30am-5:30pm daily May-Oct., $25/hour, $80/full day) rents kayaks and paddleboards and offers kayak tours in summer.

Kings Beach Tahoe Paddle and Oar (8299 N. Lake Blvd., Kings Beach, 530/581-3029, http://tahoepaddle.com, 9am-5pm daily, $25/hour, $100/day) rents kayaks and paddleboards and leads tours around Crystal Bay and Sand Harbor ($110-140 pp).

RAFTING

Rafting and inner tubing on the Truckee River is a popular summer activity. Most locals put in at 64-Acres Park (165 W. Lake Blvd., www.tahoecitypud.com, parking free), just south of the Y, then float down to just before River Ranch (2285 River Rd., Tahoe City, 530/583-4264, http://riverranchlodge.com) at the Highway 89 intersection with Alpine Meadows Road. You may have to dodge boulders in addition to partying college students, but the scenery and modest thrills are worth it.

Truckee River Rafting Company (2200 River Rd., Tahoe City, 530/583-0123, https://truckeeriverraft.com, adults $40, children $35, no children under 2) can set you up for a three-hour self-guided tour down a five-mile stretch of the Truckee River, with a shuttle back.

Hiking and Biking

Sugar Pine Point State Park (Hwy. 89, Tahoma, 530/525-7982, www.parks. ca.gov, $10) is a beautiful place to hike. For a simple stroll, take the **Edward F. Dolder Nature Trail** (1.5 miles, easy) off the paved Rod Beaudry Trail, which circles the Z'berg Preserve with views of the subalpine meadow and wildlife habitats. Pass by trees, a sandy beach, and the world's highest-elevation operating navigational lighthouse, the Sugar Pine Point Lighthouse.

Departing from the General Creek Campground (near site 148), the **General Creek Trail** marches to lovely lily pad-strewn **Lily Pond** (6.5 miles round-trip, easy-moderate). About 1.5 miles from the campground, a wooden bridge curves left across General Creek offering a turnaround point back to the trailhead for a total of three miles.

The **Meeks Bay Trailhead** (Hwy. 89, Tahoma, 530/543-2600, www.fs.usda. gov, permit required), opposite Meeks Bay Resort, leads to a series of alpine lakes in the Desolation Wilderness. Take the **Tahoe Yosemite Trail** to Lake Genevieve (3 miles one-way, moderate) or continue to any of the five small lakes along the next four miles.

Three major trailheads access the 165-mile **Tahoe Rim Trail** (775/298-4485, www.tahoerimtrail.org).

The Barker Pass Trailhead leads to **Barker Pass** (Blackwood Canyon Rd. off Highway 89) for a moderate four-mile round-trip hike. The famous **Pacific Crest Trail** (916/285-1846, www.pcta.org) joins the Tahoe Rim Trail at Barker Pass and runs concurrent with it for the next 50 miles into the Desolation Wilderness.

The Tahoe Rim Trail crosses Highway 89 in Tahoe City at the **64 Acres** and **Fairway Drive Trailheads** near Fanny Bridge. The 20-mile stretch between Fairway Drive Trailhead and the northern trailhead at **Brockway Summit** (off Hwy. 267, four miles north of Kings Beach) is open to mountain bikes and is a popular, if jarring ride.

A more strenuous ride is the **Stanford Rock Loop** (2255 W. Lake Blvd., Sunnyside; 14 miles, strenuous), which departs from a parking lot on Highway 89 (3.5 miles south of Tahoe City on Ward Creek-Stanford Connector). Turn left onto Stanford Rock Trail for a hard, technical climb that rewards with fantastic views before the steep descent.

For easy terrain and great views, the paved-boardwalk **Lakeside Trail** (1 mile) is a great place for a stroll or a bike ride. The larger 19-mile trail network follows Highway 89 from Squaw Valley down to Sugar Pine Point and north of Tahoe City to Dollar Point. It's a popular and easy way to get around the West Shore.

BIKE RENTALS

West Shore Sports (5395 W. Lake Blvd., Homewood, 530/525-9920; 1785 W. Lake Blvd., Tahoe City, 530/583-9920; www.westshoresports.com) rents bikes ($30-75/half day, $40-100/day), including electric, mountain, kids, and tandem bikes, plus doggie and kid trailers. The staff can help you plan your route and provides bike maps.

Fishing

Catching dinner can be a scenic adventure with **Mickey's Big Mack Charters** (Sierra Boat Company, Hwy. 28, Carnelian Bay, 530/546-4444 or 800/877-1462, www.mickeysbigmack.com, 5 hours $90 pp). Their 43-foot fishing boat operates twice daily: once in the early morning and again for a late-afternoon sunset cruise. The on-board cabin and restroom add comfort to the trip as you fish for mackinaw, rainbow, and brown trout. Mack sells fishing licenses ($15) and supplies all gear; bring your own food and drinks.

Ropes Course

For aerial fun, try a ropes course with **Tahoe Treetop Adventures** (530/581-7563, www. tahoetreetop.com, adults $50-60, children 5-12 $40-50). Three locations offer beginner and advanced courses with plenty of tree platforms, bridges, and ziplines. Courses last between 2-2.5 hours. Visit them at **Tahoe**

Vista Treetop (6600 Donner Rd., Tahoe Vista) south of Kings Beach; Squaw Valley Treetop (1901 Chamonix Pl., Tahoe City) near the Olympic Village; and Tahoe City Treetop (725 Granlibakken Rd., Tahoe City, 530/583-4242 or 800/543-3221, www.granlibakken.com), behind the Granlibakken Resort.

SHOPPING

For the best rental prices go to West Shore Sports (5395 W. Lake Blvd., Homewood, 530/525-9920, www.westshoresports.com, ski/snowboard adults $29-59/day, children $14-29/day, cross-country skis $12-18/day, snowshoes $11-22/day), or visit the second location in Sunnyside (1785 W. Lake Blvd., Tahoe City, 530/583-9920, www.westshoresports.com).

Tahoe Dave's Skis & Boards (590-600 N. Lake Blvd., Tahoe City, 530/583-6415, http://tahoedaves.com, 10am-5pm Sun.-Fri., 10am-6pm Sat., ski/snowboard adults $32-54/day, children $16-31/day, cross-country skis $18-22/day, snowshoes $15-23/day) has a great selection of skis and snowboards at four locations: Tahoe City, Kings Beach, Olympic Valley, and Truckee.

Alpenglow Sports (415 N. Lake Blvd., Tahoe City, 530/583-6917, www.alpenglowsports.com, 10am-6pm Mon.-Fri., 9am-6pm Sat.-Sun.) sells high-quality skiing, climbing, and mountaineering gear for serious backcountry enthusiasts.

Tahoe-themed gifts and jewelry are at Trunk Show (475 N. Lake Blvd., Tahoe City, 530/584-7554, 10:30am-6pm Wed.-Mon.). Locally made art and gifts are across the street at the ARTisan Shop (380 N. Lake Blvd., Tahoe City, 530/581-2787, www.northtahoearts.com, 11am-4pm daily), run by the nonprofit North Tahoe Arts.

FOOD
Tahoma and Homewood

Good pizza, good beer, and a casual vibe come together at West Shore Pizza (7000 W. Lake Blvd., Tahoma, 530/525-4771, www.westshorepizzatahoe.com, 4pm-9pm Mon.-Thurs.,

4pm-10pm Fri., noon-10pm Sat., noon-9pm Sun., $10-21). You'll find small gourmet twists to standard pizza selections tossed on housemade dough. Next door, Where We Met (7000 W. Lake Blvd., Tahoma, 530/525-1371, 7:30am-7:30pm Sun.-Fri., 7:30am-9pm Sat., $5) serves espresso and wonderful homemade gelato that changes daily.

The classy West Shore Café (noon-9pm daily summer, 5pm-9pm daily fall-spring, $18-40) features a West Shore Burger that you'll be talking about when you get home. On the back patio, watch the sun set over the lake.

Tahoe City

Fuel up for a day on the lake at the Fire Sign Café (1785 W. Lake Blvd., 530/583-0871, 7am-3pm daily, $10-15), a favorite with locals. This breakfast-and-lunch spot serves an enormous menu of hearty fare. Choose from whole-grain waffles with fruit, a kielbasa omelet, crepes, or blueberry coffee cake, plus a huge and affordable kids menu. Expect to wait for a table on weekends.

Grab a quick bite at Syd's Bagelry & Espresso (550 N. Lake Blvd., 530/584-2384, 7am-4pm daily, $5-8), where you can also check email thanks to Syd's free wireless Internet access.

The Blue Agave (425 N. Lake Blvd., 530/583-8113, www.tahoeblueagave.com, 11:30am-9pm daily, $12-32) is the place to go for Mexican food. It's located in the Tahoe Inn, which was built circa 1934 and has a long history involving gold miners, bootleggers, and film stars. The ample and delicious food is current and draws loyal patrons from all over.

Beer and pub food is the specialty at the Tahoe Mountain Brewing Company (475 N. Lake Blvd., 530/581-4677, noon-8pm Sun.-Thurs., noon-9pm Fri.-Sat., $12-18). Order the fish tacos and a Paddleboard Pale Ale while watching the game on TV. Or take a table outside and enjoy the Tahoe sunshine over a Dragon Double IPA with a house-smoked brisket pastrami sandwich.

The Bridgetender Tavern and Grill (65

W. Lake Blvd., 530/583-3341, www.tahoe-bridgetender.com, 11am-11pm Mon.-Thurs., 11am-midnight Fri., 8am-midnight Sat., 8am-11pm Sun., $10-12) is a favorite spot for a burger and a beer. Located on the Truckee River south of Fanny Bridge, the Bridgetender is known for its creekside dinning in summer. In winter, the bar fills with seasonal ski workers.

Along the Truckee River, the ★ **River Grill** (55 West Lake Blvd., 530/581-2644, www.rivergrilltahoe.com, 5pm-close daily, $21-34) is the spot for a more refined evening out. Take a table on the heated rustic wooden porch to enjoy the river view while listening to live music or sit indoors in the casually elegant dining room complete with a fireplace. Happy hour (5pm-6:30pm daily) features discounted drinks and food in the bar and at the outdoor fire pit.

An ideal spot for a delicious dinner and lake views is ★ **Christy Hill Lakeside Bistro** (115 Grove St., 530/583-8551, www.christyhill.com, 5pm-9:30pm daily, $27-34) and its outdoor **Sand Bar** (beer and wine only) on the back deck. Entrées range from fresh cannelloni with homemade lemon ricotta to Moroccan-spiced lamb loin.

Wolfdale's (640 N. Lake Blvd., 530/583-5700, www.wolfdales.com, 5:30pm-10pm Wed.-Mon., $16-36) has been serving "cuisine unique" dishes that fuse Asian and Western ingredients since 1978. The small seasonal menu is heavy on seafood, but also includes tasty beef and game meats in season.

For a light meal and a fabulous sunset, end your day at the **Sunnyside Resort** (1850 W. Lake Blvd., Sunnyside, 530/583-7200, www.sunnysidetahoe.com, 4pm-9pm daily, $15-33). The patio has an expansive view of the lake and the mountains beyond. The dining menu is brief (favorites include fish tacos and a flat-iron steak), but the wine, beer, and cocktail menu is long.

Stock up at **New Moon Natural Market** (505 W. Lake Blvd., 530/583-7426, 9am-7pm Mon.-Sat., 10am-6pm Sun.), which has a great selection of groceries and natural food, including a deli counter that makes a wide range of sandwiches. Gourmet goodies line the shelves at the upscale **West Shore Market** (1780 W. Lake Blvd., 530/584-2475, 7am-8pm daily). You'll find yummy sandwiches in the deli daily and flatbread pizza out of a wood-fired oven at night.

Kings Beach

For breakfast, head to cute **Log Cabin Café** (8692 N. Lake Blvd., 530/546-7109, www.log-cabinbreakfast.com, 7am-2pm Thurs.-Sun., $10-16), which earns rave reviews for its Benedicts, waffles, and outdoor patio. Nearby, **Jason's Beachside Grille** (8338 N. Lake Blvd., 530/546-3315, http://jasonsbeachside-grille.com, 11am-10pm daily, $13-39) serves big plates of American food that pair well with beer, cocktails, live music, and outdoor seating beneath the pines.

ACCOMMODATIONS
Tahoma and Homewood

For homey cabin living on the West Shore, you can't beat **The Tahoma Lodge** (7018 Westlake Blvd., Tahoma, 844/755-2226, www.tahomalodge.com, $150-280), a series of seven distinctive cabins that sleep 2-6 people. Each cabin has a kitchen with picnic tables and barbecues, and there's a heated outdoor swimming pool. In winter, you'll appreciate the fireplace in each unit and the outdoor hot tub.

Cedar Crest Cottages (4815 W. Lake Blvd., Homewood, 530/412-9222, www.cedar-crestcottages.com, $229-653) is a collection of nine stylish one-, two-, three-, and four-bedroom cabins. Full kitchens, comfortable living spaces, and a modern sensibility make this lodge stand out.

For a special vacation, stay at the **West Shore Inn** (5160 W. Lake Blvd., Homewood, 530/525-5200, www.westshorecafe.com, $149-1,699). Each of the four suites (sleeps 4), two rooms, and two villas (sleeps 6) has distinctive luxury, with balconies, lake views, leather sofas, fireplaces, and flat-screen TVs. A freshly baked continental breakfast is included in the suites and rooms, as is use of the inn's fleet of bicycles, kayaks, and paddleboards.

Tahoe City

The cozy rooms at **Mother Nature's Inn** (551 N. Lake Blvd., 530/581-4278 or 800/558-4278, www.mothernaturesinn.com, $65-155) are decorated with Tahoe-themed art and tchotchkes. All rooms have private baths, fridges, and coffeemakers. Pets are welcome ($15 fee). The inn is a few steps from the lakeshore and downtown Tahoe City.

The **Pepper Tree Inn** (645 N. Lake Blvd., 530/583-3711, www.peppertreetahoe.com, $111-156) is an above-average hotel with whirlpool tubs and cable TV, plus an outdoor swimming pool and free wireless Internet access. It has a great location across the street from the lake, the Lakeside Trail, and is near some of the best restaurants in Tahoe City.

Hip and affordable digs are at **Basecamp Hotel** (955 N. Lake Blvd., 530/580-8430, $100-135). Bunk beds, a minimalist style, and a lobby bar that serves microbrews and grilled-cheese sandwiches will appeal to the younger set, as will the daily continental breakfast and evening s'mores.

For those looking to splurge, book at stay at the **Sunnyside Resort** (1850 W. Lake Blvd., 530/583-7200, www.sunnysidetahoe.com, $150-450). Brightly decorated rooms feature views of the lake or the forest; some rooms have fireplaces or private decks. The on-site **restaurant** (4pm-9pm daily, $15-33) is a local favorite known for great views and food to match.

Kings Beach

Kings Beach is long on standard-issue motels, but short on charming inns and cool economy lodging. One exception is the **Hostel Tahoe** (8931 N. Lake Blvd., 530/546-3266, http://hosteltahoe.com, dorm $33, double room $65, family room $75). The double and family rooms (sleeps 4) have private bathrooms, and all come with bedding, towels, weekend breakfast, loaner bikes, and use of a communal kitchen.

Olympic Valley

For the ultimate convenience in ski vacations, book a room or condo at **The Village at Squaw Valley** (1750 Village East Rd., 866/818-6963, www.squawalpine.com, $160-590) and never leave the vicinity of the lifts. Rooms come with few amenities aside from those of the resort, but the elegant and modern condos range from compact studios perfect for singles or couples to three-bedroom homes that sleep up to eight. They have full kitchens, as well as a living room with a TV, and maybe a fireplace, and a dining table. Included in the price is use of the Village's eight outdoor hot tubs, five saunas, five fitness rooms, laundry facilities, and heated underground parking garage. Stay in Building 5; it has the clearest view of the mountain and the most comfortable amenities.

There are more than half a dozen restaurants, snack bars, and coffee shops offering sushi, pizza, expensive wine, and more. **Fireside Pizza Co.** (1985 Squaw Valley Rd., 530/584-6150, www.firesidepizza.com, 11am-9pm Sun.-Thurs., 11am-10pm Fri.-Sat., $15-26) is a favorite with a good selection of pizzas, pastas, soup, sandwiches, and kid-friendly options.

Six Peaks Grille (400 Squaw Creek Rd., 530/581-6621, 5:30pm-9:30pm Wed.-Sun., $24-48) is a fancy steak house with prices nearly as high as the mountains it overlooks. For a crisp salad or a relaxing espresso, you can't beat **CoffeeBar** (1750 Village East Rd., 530/589-4200, www.coffeebartruckee.com, 7am-7pm daily, $7-9). Expect lots of space, free wireless Internet access, and good food—homemade baked goods, crepes, panini, salads, and breakfast calzones, plus coffee (of course), and a small wine and beer menu.

CAMPING

The place to camp on the West Shore is ★ **General Creek Campground** at Ed Z'berg Sugar Pine Point State Park (7360 Hwy. 89, Tahoma, 800/444-7275, www.

reservecalifornia.com, $25-35). Every site has a picnic table, a charcoal grill, ample space for a tent or camper, coin-operated showers, and plenty of beautiful scenery plus beach and trail access. The campground gets crowded in midsummer; make reservations in advance.

The Washoe Tribe runs the **Meeks Bay Resort** (7941 Hwy. 89, Tahoma, 530/525-6946 or 877/326-3357, www.meeksbayresort.com, May-Oct., tent sites $20-30, RV sites $30-50). The 14 tent sites and 23 RV sites all have a two-night minimum; pets are not allowed. The resort features a sandy beach and a marina and hiking trails across Highway 89 that lead into the Desolation Wilderness.

William Kent Beach and Campground (Hwy. 89, 877/444-6777, www.recreation.gov, mid-May-mid-Oct., $30) has 95 sites suitable for tents or campers with flush toilets and bear lockers, but no showers or electrical hookups. There is easy beach access and trees provide some shade and privacy while helping to cut down the road noise.

Tahoe State Recreation Area (Hwy. 28, 800/444-7275, www.reservecalifornia.com, late May-early Sept., $35) has 23 sites and coin-operated showers; walk to the lake or to the shops of Tahoe City.

Lake Forest Campground (2504-2540 Lake Forest Rd., 530/583-3796, www.tahoe-citypud.com, mid-May-early Oct., $20) has 20 first-come, first-served; RVs up to 25 feet are welcome, though there are no hookups. Facilities include drinking water, vault toilets, picnic tables, and a boat ramp.

TRANSPORTATION AND SERVICES
Car

Highway 89 runs 15 miles from Truckee to Tahoe City, traveling the western length of the lake to South Lake Tahoe. North of Tahoe City, Highway 28 passes through Kings Beach, connecting to Truckee via Highway 267. The most common route to Tahoe City is to take I-80 to Truckee, then head south on Highway 89. Plan anywhere from 3-5 hours for the drive.

Train
Amtrak's *California Zephyr* (800/872-7245, www.amtrak.com, $49 one-way) arrives at least once daily from the San Francisco Bay Area and Sacramento, as does the *Capital Corridor* train/bus combo. The latter is a reliably faster trip of 4.5 hours.

Bus
In Truckee, the Highway 89 mainline **Tahoe Area Regional Transit** (TART, 530/550-1212 or 800/736-6365, www.laketahoetransit.com, adults $1.75 one-way, 24-hour pass $3.50) bus runs to Squaw or Tahoe City. TART also runs reasonably reliable bus service from Tahoma on the West Shore to Incline Village, Nevada, with many stops along the way.

The **Night Rider bus** (866/216-5222, http://www.laketahoetransit.com, 6pm-10pm daily, free) picks up once TART is done for the night, linking Squaw Valley, Tahoe City, Northstar, Kings Beach, Granlibakken, Sunnyside, Homewood, and Tahoma.

Shuttles
In summer, traffic is legendary around the lake. Consider taking the **Emerald Bay Shuttle** (TTD Route 30, 530/541-7149, www.tahoetransportation.org, 8:30am-5:30pm daily late June-mid-July, Fri.-Mon. mid-July-early-Sept., Sat.-Sun. Sept., $2), a pleasant open-air trolley that runs hourly between Tahoe City and South Lake with multiple stops along the way.

Squaw and Alpine run **free ski shuttles** (http://squawalpine.com, 800/736-6365) around the North and West Shore on winter weekends.

Bike
Avoid the car traffic on the 19-mile, paved **Lakeside Bike Trail,** which follows the lake from Sugar Pine Point to just north of Tahoe City and along the Truckee River and Highway 89 to Squaw Valley.

Services
For medical attention on the North Shore,

the **Tahoe Forest Hospital** (10121 Pine Ave., Truckee, 530/587-6011, www.tfhd.com) has a full-service emergency room. **Incline Village Community Hospital** (880 Alder Ave., Incline Village, NV, 775/833-4100 or 800/419-2627, www.tfhd.com) is the place to go for help on the Nevada side. The hospital has a 24-hour emergency room.

Truckee-Donner

Truckee is a historical old railroad town that really has no off-season. Storefronts line the main street, Donner Pass Road, offering ski rentals, a bite to eat, and places to stay. Parking is hard to find and expensive and there are long lines at restaurants, but this small mountain town has its charms.

West of Truckee, **Donner Summit** (Donner Pass Rd., I-80, www.exploredonner-summit.com or www.donnersummithistori-calsociety.org) is the 7,000-foot pass notorious for trapping the Donner party. It offers a stunning view of Donner Lake and the surrounding area from the Donner Summit Bridge on Donner Pass Road and is a favorite among hikers and climbers. At the base of the pass is **Donner Lake,** home to boating, swimming, and fishing.

SIGHTS
★ **Donner Memorial State Park**

In April 1846, 25 members of the Donner party, who had left Springfield, Illinois, on their way to new lives in California, stopped to repair their wagons in the fall after being slowed down by an ill-fated shortcut through Hastings Cutoff. It was only October when they got here, but a blizzard hit hard. Some of the party ended up staying the whole winter, and some, as you may know, never left.

Donner Memorial State Park (12593 Donner Pass Rd., off I-80, 530/582-7892, www.parks.ca.gov, daily year-round, $8) offers a much easier way to experience the lush beauty that the Donner party was heading to California to find. Near the entrance to the park is the **Pioneer Monument,** a massive structure celebrating the courage and spirit of

the Donners and others who made their way west in harder times.

The **visitors center** (10am-5pm daily year-round) offers uplifting information about the human and natural history of the area. The 0.5-mile **Nature Trail** is an easy self-guided trek through a forest of Jeffrey and lodgepole pines. The trail leads to a large boulder that served as a back wall to one of the cabins built during the Donner party's layover here in the winter of 1846-1847. A moving plaque lists those who perished and those who survived. It is all that remains of the settlement; the following season, the army burned all evidence of the tragedy.

The park has a campground near Donner Lake. The **Lakeside Interpretive Trail** is strung with picnic tables and a great way to enjoy close-up views of the lake.

Old Jail Museum

Built in 1875, the **Old Jail Museum** (10142 Jibboom St., Truckee, 530/582-0893, www.truckeehistory.org, 10am-4pm Sat.-Sun. late May-Sept., donation $2) housed prisoners continually until 1964. "Baby Face" Nelson and "Machine Gun" Kelly are among the notorious outlaws believed to have spent time here. Today, it has historical exhibits and information, with docents from the local Truckee-Donner Historical Society.

SPORTS AND RECREATION
Downhill Skiing and Snowboarding

The Truckee Basin is famous for its ability to capture the big storms of the Sierra, turning them into great blankets of snow that average

Truckee-Donner

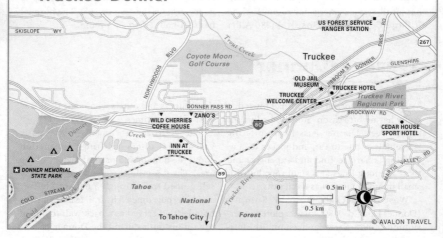

35-40 feet deep. It has the highest concentration of ski parks.

NORTHSTAR CALIFORNIA

Northstar California Resort (5001 Northstar Dr., Truckee, 530/562-1010 or 800/466-6784, www.northstarattahoe.com, adults $103, teens 13-18 $84, children 5-12 $61) is a bit less crowded than the big resorts. Beginners can head up the mountain and still find slopes running gently all the way back to the village. Slow Zones provide good spots for young children and wobbly adults. Intermediate runs crisscross the front of the mountain. The back is reserved for black-diamond skiers, although adventurous intermediates can test their ski legs here.

SUGAR BOWL

A great mid-tier ski area, **Sugar Bowl** (629 Sugar Bowl Rd., Norden, 530/426-9000, www.sugarbowl.com, adults $95-120, seniors and children 13-22 $79-99, children 6-12 $56-70, children under 6 free) has lots of skiable snow spread across a wide area and plenty of vertical drop to satisfy skiers and boarders of all abilities. Blue- and black-diamond runs toward the top of the peaks offer intense

variety, with a smattering of double-black-diamond runs out toward the edges and down the ridges. At the base, green and blue runs make it easy for younger and less experienced athletes to have a good time in the mountains. A gondola ferries visitors from the remote parking lot up to the village. The resort's Summit Chairlift brings visitors to the top of Judah Peak for easy access to backcountry trails.

The on-site **Lodge at Sugar Bowl** (530/426-6742, www.sugarbowl.com, $259-674) allows you to ski right up to your room's door.

BOREAL MOUNTAIN RESORT

Even on weekends, the lines at **Boreal Mountain Resort** (19749 Boreal Ridge Rd., Soda Springs, 530/426-3666, www.rideboreal.com, adults $59, children 13-18 $49, children 5-12 $29, children under 5 $5) seem pleasingly short compared to the bigger resorts. Boreal is very family-friendly, with ski and snowboard lessons for beginners and a lodge where folks can relax with a cup of coffee or a drink at the Upper Deck bar. For kids, the Playland Tubing area ($49, includes tube) has two magic carpets for sledding, plus plenty of groomed lanes for a fun-filled day. Boreal is one of the few resorts to offer night skiing ($29-39).

SODA SPRINGS
Small **Soda Springs** (10244 Soda Springs Rd., Soda Springs, 530/426-3901, www.ski-sodasprings.com, 10am-4pm Thurs.-Mon., adults $50, children 13-17 $45, children 6-12 $40, children 5 and under $5) is a great family resort. Its claim to fame is tubing, included with every lift ticket, or you can buy a $34 tubing-only package. The Planet Kids area for young athletes (children under 7, $34) offers a safe place for the little ones to practice tubing, skiing, and snowboarding. Rentals and instruction are included in the price, and there are two tubing carousels to add to the thrills.

TAHOE DONNER SKI AREA
With only five lifts, including two conveyor belts and one carpet, 15 runs, and 120 skiable acres, **Tahoe Donner Ski Area** (11603 Snowpeak Way, Truckee, 530/587-9444, www.tahoedonner.com/downhill-ski, adults $54-64, youth 13-17 $44-49, children 7-12 $24-29, children under 7 free) will seem minuscule to skiers used to the big resorts. It's a great spot to bring your family, however, to get a feel for snowboarding or skiing, take lessons, and enjoy the snow in the beautiful Tahoe forest. Tahoe Donner offers lessons for children as young as age three, interchangeable lift tickets for parents, and kid-friendly items on the snack bar menu.

Cross-Country Skiing and Snowshoeing
The granddaddy of Tahoe cross-country ski areas, the **Royal Gorge Cross Country Ski Resort** (9411 Pahatsi, Soda Springs, 530/426-3871 or 800/500-3871, www.royalgorge.com, 8:30am-4pm daily winter, adults $30-39, seniors and youth 13-22 $24-30, children up to 12 free) has a truly tremendous chunk of the Sierra—6,000 acres—within its boundaries. Striving to provide a luxurious ski experience, the Royal Gorge offers food, drink, a ski school, equipment rentals, equipment care

facilities and services. With the most miles of groomed trails anywhere in the Tahoe area, Royal Gorge offers two stride tracks and a skate track on every trail to allow easy passing. It even has a surface lift for skiers who want to practice downhill technique or try telemarking.

Tahoe Donner Cross Country (15275 Alder Creek Rd., Truckee, 530/587-9484, www.tahoedonner.com/cross-country, hours vary, adults $32-37, seniors and youth 13-17 $22-27, children 7-12 $13-15, children under 7 free) offers some of the better cross-country ski action in the area. Tahoe Donner has almost 3,500 acres crisscrossed with trails ranging from easy greens all the way up through double-black-diamond trails and sets four trails aside just for snowshoers (several are open to fat bikes). A cross-country ski school introduces newcomers to the sport and helps more experienced skiers expand their skills.

Hiking
The stunning area surrounding Donner Summit is a spectacular place to hike. Donner Memorial Park has a number of relatively short, mixed-use trails. West of Donner Pass, the **Pacific Crest Trail** (PCT, Old Summit Rd., Norden, 916/285-1846, www.pcta.org, or 530/543-2600, www.fs.usda.gov) cuts across Donner Pass Road east of Norden, taking intrepid hikers to Squaw Valley (17.5 miles one-way, strenuous). You can also follow the trail north to the **Summit Lake Trail** (4 miles round-trip, easy-moderate). The trail follows the PCT east, then north under I-80, before veering left toward Summit and Warren Lakes. Traveling through fir and open expanses with great views, you'll reach the pretty alpine lake in time for a snack.

Take in the history and splendor of Donner Pass on the **Donner Summit Canyon Trail** (3.5 miles one-way, moderate), which begins at a well-marked trailhead west of Donner Lake (Donner Pass Rd., http://tdlandtrust.org, 530/582-4711). Follow the path of historic Old Highway 40 (Donner Pass Rd.) as the trail climbs up the canyon and past a beaver pond, ancient petroglyphs, the sheds of the transcontinental railroad, and the historic "China Wall." Marvel at the views of Donner Lake and the grit of the pioneers who traveled this same path 150 years ago. Parking is available at the west end of the trail (also the trailhead for the PCT).

Climbing

Donner Summit is a favorite of climbers. Scores of routes cluster around Donner Pass Road and scale up massive slabs of granite. To go with a professional, you can contact both **Alpine Skills International** (530/582-9170, www.alpineskills.com, guided climbs $149-165, families $289) and **Alpenglow Expeditions** (877/873-5376, https://alpenglowexpeditions.com, half day $299, full day $595, clinics $180-199, and families $299), which offer a variety of guided trips.

FOOD

In the historic downtown, **Jax at the Tracks** (10144 W. River St., Truckee, 530/550-7450, www.jaxtruckee.com, 7am-10pm daily, $11-20) is housed in an actual 1940s diner. It has been thoroughly fixed up to be clean, fresh, and original, serving creative California-style fare from a chef who puts his own stamp on comfort food.

The boisterous **Bar of America** (10040 Donner Pass Rd., Truckee, 530/587-2626, www.barofamerica.com, 11am-9:30pm Mon.-Thurs., 11am-10pm Fri., 10am-10pm Sat., 10am-9:30pm Sun., $14-44) is popular for its historic interior (yes, it used to be a Bank of America), wood-fired pizzas, hearty main courses, creative cocktails, and large TVs playing the current game. Reservations are recommended.

Craft beer is across the tracks at the **Alibi Ale Works** (10069 Bridge St., Truckee, 530/536-5029, www.alibialeworks.com, noon-10pm Sun.-Wed., noon-midnight Thurs.-Sat., $8-14). Nachos of all stripes and flavors (Mediterranean, Korean) fill the tiny menu. It's the perfect snack food to accompany a pitcher of classic and unusual microbrews, with the occasional live music.

Make a reservation for a special night out at **Moody's Bistro and Lounge** (10007 Bridge St., Truckee, 530/587-8688, www.moodysbistro.com, 11:30am-9pm daily, $15-44), a casual yet elegant eatery on the ground floor of the historical Truckee Hotel. A wooden bar and booths give the main lounge an old-time feel, but the white-tablecloth dining room in the back feels more classically elegant. The chef promises ingredients that are "fresh, local, seasonal, and simple," jazzed up with creative preparations.

Serious foodies make reservations at **Trokay** (10046 Donner Pass Rd., Truckee, 530/582-1040, http://restauranttrokay.com, 5:30pm-9:30pm Fri.-Tues., $24-56). Inside the chic yet "rustic" interior, the service is warm and professional, but it's the food that takes notice. To really see what the chef can do, order the prix fixe menu (5 courses, $105) or the Chef's Tasting Menu (11 courses, $210).

West of downtown, **Zano's Pizza** (11401 Donner Pass Rd., Truckee, 530/587-7411, www.zanos.net, 4pm-9pm Mon.-Wed., 11:30am-9pm Thurs.-Sun., $15-25) serves huge pizzas and tremendous salads in a big casual dining room where sports plays on TV. The full menu includes pastas and Italian entrées, but it's the thin-crust pizzas that rule.

★ **Wild Cherries Coffee House** (11429 Donner Pass Rd., Truckee, 530/582-5602, www.wildcherriescoffeehouse.com, 6am-6pm daily, $5-10) is a great spot to fuel up for a day of adventuring. The expansive menu has plenty of breakfast items, hot and cold sandwiches, salads, kid's meals, smoothies, and espresso drinks.

A moodier coffeehouse experience is at **Dark Horse Coffee Roasters** (10009 W. River St., 530/550-9239, www.darkhorsecoffeeroasters.com, 7am-5pm daily, $5-8) in an old saloon in downtown Truckee. You'll find artistically crafted espresso drinks, pastries, free Wi-Fi, occasional live music, comfy couches, and deep thinking.

ACCOMMODATIONS

Since 1934, the Sierra Club has run the **Clair Tappaan Lodge** (19940 Donner Pass Rd., Norden, 530/426-3632, www.ctl.sierraclub.org, $60-90 pp, children under 4 free), a hostel located west of Donner Summit. Basic accommodations include men's or women's dormitories, a few small rooms for couples, or larger rooms for families. Bring your own bedding and expect to share a bathroom. Meals can be included (8am and 6pm, $15), and there's a lunch-making station available at 7:30am. Communal spaces include a toasty library with a wood-burning stove, hot tub, recreation room, and extensive grounds.

In downtown Truckee, the **Truckee Hotel** (10007 Bridge St., Truckee, 530/587-4444, www.truckeehotel.com, $79-229) has welcomed guests to the North Shore since 1873. Rooms show their age, but include with their fabulous period ambience high ceilings, claw-foot tubs, and Victorian touches. Most of the 36 rooms share hall baths with either a shower or a bathtub and a privacy lock. The third- and fourth-floor rooms do not have an elevator. Breakfast is included, and the hotel houses Moody's, one of the best restaurants in town.

Low-priced accommodations around Truckee are not easy to come by, especially in ski season. The **Inn at Truckee** (11506 Deerfield Dr., Truckee, 530/587-8888 or 888/773-6888, www.innattruckee.com, $90-195) is a decent, basic hotel with affordable rates, a spa and sauna, a continental breakfast, and free wireless Internet access. The convenience to major ski areas and attractions makes it a good buy. Pets are permitted ($25 per night).

Loads of charm can be found at the **Donner Lake Inn** (10070 Gregory Place, Truckee, 530/587-5574, www.donnerlake-inn.com, $164-189), an intimate five-room B&B beside Donner Lake. Rooms have private baths with a shower, a private entrance, queen beds, a large-screen TV with a DVD player, and free wireless Internet access. The friendly and hospitable owners serve a delicious full breakfast in the dining room.

For a longer stay, try **Donner Lake Village Resort** (15695 Donner Pass Rd., Truckee, 855/979-0402 or 530/587-6081, www.donnerlakevillage.com, $181-428) on the shore of Donner Lake. Guest rooms range from motel rooms without kitchens to studios, one-bedroom, and two-bedroom condos with full kitchens. The marina at Donner Lake Village rents ski boats and fishing boats; a bait and tackle shop is across the street. A two-night minimum may be required.

The ★ **Cedar House Sport Hotel** (10918 Brockway Rd., Truckee, 530/582-5655 or 866/582-5655, www.cedarhousesporthotel.com, $170-295) is an ecolodge made in stick-frame construction from log and exposed wood shingles. Nestled among the trees, the rooms are comfortable and stylish with flat-screen TVs, private porches, coffeemakers, fridge and microwave, and soft linens. Common areas offer complimentary coffee, snacks, and hot buffet breakfast. Ask about the hot tub and for any advice for exploring the area.

CAMPING

Donner Memorial State Park (12593 Donner Pass Rd., 800/444-7275, www.reserveamerica.com, late May-Oct., $35) offers a spacious tree-filled campground with easy access to the lake, the visitors center, and hiking trails. Its 152 sites are spread across three campgrounds: Ridge Campground, Creek Campground, and Splitrock. All are near the lake and include fire rings and picnic tables, plus restrooms with showers nearby.

The **Forest Service** (877/444-6777, www.recreation.gov) maintains three campgrounds along Highway 89 between Truckee and Tahoe City: **Granite Flat** (74 sites, Hwy. 89, mid-May-Sept., $22), **Goose Meadow** (24 sites, Hwy. 89, mid-May-Sept., $23), and **Silver Creek** (27 sites, mid-May-Sept., $20), which offers potable water and vault toilets. All three campgrounds get noise from the highway as well as the gentler sounds of the nearby Truckee River.

TRANSPORTATION AND SERVICES

Truckee lies at the junction of I-80 and Highway 89 north of Lake Tahoe. Many of the ski resorts are west of Truckee on Donner Pass. Donner Pass Road runs through Truckee, linking the historic downtown, Donner Memorial State Park, and Donner Lake.

The 187-mile drive from the San Francisco Bay Area can take 3-4 hours depending on traffic. From Sacramento, it is a two-hour drive for 100 miles.

Train

Amtrak's (800/872-7245, www.amtrak. com, $49 one-way) *California Zephyr* arrives once daily from the San Francisco Bay Area and Sacramento. The trip takes 4.5-6 hours. The *Capital Corridor* train runs from Emeryville to Sacramento and is followed by a bus to Truckee for a total trip of 4.5 hours. The **Truckee train station** (10065 Donner Pass Rd., 800/872-7245) is downtown.

Public Transportation

In Truckee, the **TART** bus system (530/550-7451, www.laketahoetransit.com, one-way: adults $2.50, children 3-12 $1.50; day-pass: adults $5, children under 12 $2) runs to Donner Lake daily and to Boreal, Sugar Bowl, Soda Springs, and the North Shore in the winter.

Services

The **Tahoe Forest Hospital** (10121 Pine Ave., 530/587-6011, www.tfhd.com) has a full-service emergency room.

East Shore

Lake Tahoe straddles California and Nevada. On the South Shore, U.S. 50 moves east from South Lake Tahoe to Stateline, Nevada. On the North Shore, the intersection of Highways 28 and 267 at Crystal Bay marks the California-Nevada border crossing. The drive along the Nevada side of Lake Tahoe is beautiful, woodsy, and quiet, with few towns and stopping points along the way.

SIGHTS

Thunderbird Lodge

Thunderbird Lodge (5000 Hwy. 28, Incline Village, NV, 775/832-8750 or 800/468-2463, www.thunderbirdlodge.org, tours Tues.-Sat. mid-May-mid-Oct., adults $39, children 6-12 $19) was built in 1936 by a Tahoe resident called the Captain who intended to create a luxury hotel and casino on his vast lakeside acreage. It was one of the last great upscale residential mansions constructed beside the lake and includes several outbuildings. You can't drive directly to Thunderbird Lodge.

Instead, park at the **Crystal Bay Visitors Center** (969 Tahoe Blvd., Incline Village, NV, 775/832-1606 or 800/468-2463, www.go-tahoenorth.com, 8am-5pm Mon.-Fri., 10am-4pm Sat.-Sun.) to meet the tour guide for a one-hour walking tour of the grounds and several of the buildings. The 600-foot underground tunnel from the mansion to the boathouse and card house is one of the tour highlights, especially for kids.

SPORTS AND RECREATION

Ski Resorts

MT. ROSE

Mt. Rose (22222 Mt. Rose Hwy., Reno, NV, 775/849-0704 or 800/754-7673, www.mtrose. com, lift 9am-4pm daily winter, adults $125, children 6-15 $75, children under 6 $20) offers the most choice in terms of both variety and beginner routes, plus three terrain parks. Many different ski school packages and private lesson options are available.

East Shore

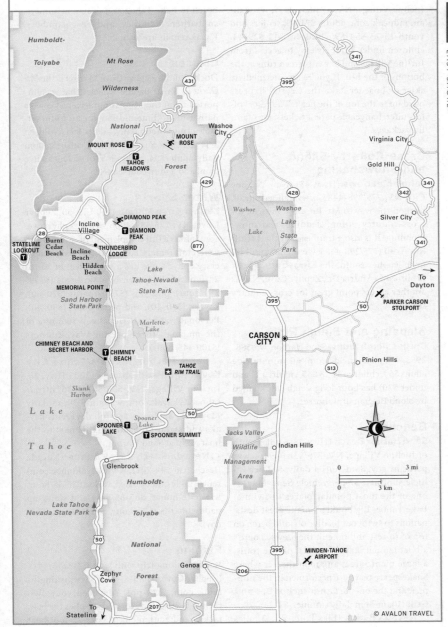

© AVALON TRAVEL

DIAMOND PEAK

Smaller **Diamond Peak** (1210 Ski Way, Incline Village, NV, 775/832-1177, www.diamondpeak.com, adults $74-89, seniors and youth 13-23 $54-69, children 7-12 $29-44, children under 7 free) is easy to access from Incline Village and has two green runs at the bottom of the hill. If you're an intermediate skier or boarder, take the Crystal Express quad up to the top of the peak. The resort offers interchangeable parent tickets, plus family packages.

Cross-Country Skiing and Snowshoeing

Tahoe Meadows (Hwy. 431, New Washoe City, NV, 775/298-4485, www.tahoerimtrail.org) on the way to Mt. Rose is a favorite for cross-country skiing, sledding, and snowmobiling. It is also a trailhead for the **Tahoe Rim Trail** (775/298-4485, www.tahoerimtrail.org). Farther south, the **Kingsbury North Trailhead** (Andria Dr., Zephyr Cove, NV) is another access point great for cross-country skiing.

Sledding and Sleigh Rides

Borges Sleigh Rides (Sand Harbor, 775/588-2953, www.sleighride.com, 60-minute ride adults $50, children 11-18 $45, children 11 and under $20) has hour-long sleigh rides pulled by blond Belgian draft horses.

Beaches

Sand Harbor Beach (Hwy. 28, 3 miles south of Incline Village, NV, 775/831-0494, www.parks.nv.gov, 8am-sunset daily, $12 per vehicle summer, $7 per vehicle Sept.-May) is one of the most popular places to swim at Lake Tahoe. Big boulders make great destinations to swim out to, dive off, and perch on top of to rest and take in the views. There's a boat launch, kayak rentals, nature trails, a large picnic area, an amphitheater where Shakespeare plays are performed in the summer, and the on-site **Sand Harbor Bar and Grill** (10am-5pm daily summer, $4-23).

Nevada Beach (Elks Point Rd., 3 miles north of Stateline, NV, 775/831-0914, www.fs.usda.gov) at Zephyr Cove is the widest beach in Lake Tahoe and draws swimmers, sunbathers, families, and beachcombers. Kayak rentals are available.

Cruises

Docked at the Zephyr Cove Marina is the *MS Dixie II,* a rear paddle-wheeler that was imported from the Mississippi River. It makes daily runs to Emerald Bay for an unforgettable cruise (noon daily, adults $64, children 3-11 $32). The Sunset Dinner Cruise (5:30pm daily, adults $94, children $40) includes a live band and a four-course meal.

Water Sports

Zephyr Cove Marina (760 U.S. 50, Zephyr Cove, NV, 775/589-4906, www.zephyrcove.com) offers a full complement of services and watercraft rentals. For skiers and wakeboarders, Zephyr Cove has a small fleet of 22- to 24-foot Sea Ray open-bow ski boats ($159-259/hour), plus skis ($20), boards ($20-60), kayaks ($30-40), and pedal boats ($30-40). Personal watercraft riders can rent one of the marina's three-person WaveRunners ($100-145/hour).

Sand Harbor Rentals/Tahoe City Kayak and Paddleboard (2005 Hwy. 28, Incline Village, NV, 530/581-4336, http://tahoecitykayak.com, 9:30am-5:30pm daily May-Oct., $25/hour, $80 full day) rents kayaks and stand-up paddleboards next to the boat ramp at Sand Harbor.

Nevada Beach Kayak Tahoe (Nevada Beach, 530/544-2011, www.kayaktahoe.com) rents single and double kayaks ($25-35/hour, $35-55/2 hours, $65-85/day) and stand-up paddleboards ($25/hour, $35/2 hours, $65/day).

Fishing

Book a fishing trip with **Nor-Cal Charters** (Zephyr Cove, 530/318-1981, www.fishingintahoe.com, $110 pp). You need your own fishing license, but Nor-Cal supplies the bait, tackle, and equipment. A cozy 22-foot boat and lots of personal attention from your guide make for an intimate angling experience.

For anglers on their own, **Spooner Lake** (U.S. 50 and Hwy. 28, 775/831-0494, www.parks.nv.gov, sunrise-sunset, $10 summer, $7 fall-spring) allows fishing year-round, including ice fishing in winter. A Nevada state fishing license is required. Hike five miles in and you'll reach **Marlette Lake,** which is full of brook, rainbow, and cutthroat trout. Marlette fishing is catch-and-release only, and the season runs July 15-September 30. For more information, visit the **Nevada Department of Wildlife** (www.ndow.org).

Horseback Riding

Sign up for a trail ride with **Zephyr Cove Resort Stables** (U.S. 50, Zephyr Cove, 775/588-5664, www.zephyrcovestable.com, 9am-5pm daily summer, 10am-4pm daily spring and fall, 1 hour $50, 1.5 hours $75, 2 hours $90). Breakfast, lunch, and dinner rides ($65-75) include a one-hour trail ride plus a meal.

Hiking and Biking

For a short walk with maximum scenery and solitude, take the moderate, mile-long hike to **Chimney Beach** (Hwy. 28, one mile south of Sand Harbor, 530/543-2600, www.fs.usda.gov). The path winds through the pines and then runs along the lake accessing three secluded beaches. To get to Chimney Beach, turn right when you reach the lake.

Near Crystal Bay is the easy-moderate, one-mile hike to the **Stateline Lookout** (Lakeshore Ave. and Forest Service Rd. 1601, Crystal Bay, NV). At the lookout, summer volunteers offer information about the region or you can take the short self-guided nature trail that runs around the lookout. The trailhead is behind the Biltmore (Lakeshore Ave.); park below the gate on Forest Service Road 1601.

In **Spooner Lake State Park** (U.S. 50 and Hwy. 28, 775/831-0494, www.parks.nv.gov, sunrise-sunset, $10 summer, $7 fall-spring), the **Marlette Lake Trail** (10 miles round-trip, moderate) slopes uphill to the Marlette Dam

on a fire road much of the way. The trail is easy to follow, and the terrain never gets too rough. For a shorter hike with less climbing, try the level **Spooner Lake Trail** (2 miles), which features interpretive signage and gets you close-up views of wildlife.

Hop on **Mount Rose/Tahoe Meadows Trailhead** (Hwy. 431, New Washoe City, NV, 530/543-2600, https://www.fs.usda.gov) and take the **Tahoe Rim Trail** to Relay Peak (10 miles round-trip, strenuous). You'll pass meadows full of wildflowers, a waterfall, and rewarding views.

Bikes can head for the **Spooner South** (Spooner Summit Rest Area, Hwy. 50, www.fs.usda.gov, 530/543-2600) and **Kingsbury North** (Andria Dr., Zephyr Cove, NV) trailheads. From the Spooner South Trailhead, it's a moderate, five-mile ride to South Camp, where you'll enjoy views of the west and the east before heading back.

The popular **Flume Trail** (14-miles one-way, moderate-difficult) departs from the **Spooner Lake Trailhead** (Spooner Lake State Park, U.S. 50 and Hwy. 28, 775/831-0494, www.parks.nv.gov) and climbs from 7,000 to 8,000 feet, ending north of Sand Harbor. The paved Lakeshore Trail connects it to Incline Village.

BIKE RENTALS

Flume Trail Mountain Bikes (1115 Tunnel Creek Rd., Incline Village, 775/298-2501, http://flumetrailtahoe.com, 8am-6pm daily May-Oct., $35-105/day) rents bikes; prices include a free shuttle to certain trailheads. Reservations are recommended and can be made by phone or online.

FOOD

Jack Rabbit Moon (893 Tahoe Blvd., Ste. 600, Incline Village, NV, 775/833-3900, www.jackrabbitmoon.com, 6pm-9:30pm Mon.-Tues., 6pm-10pm Fri.-Sat., $35-60) is a small but popular fine-dining establishment noted for its extensive wine list, fresh contemporary menu, and seafood specialties such as lobster tamales and wild salmon. Hours can fluctuate and reservations are a must, so call ahead to confirm.

At **Fredrick's Fusion Bistro** (907 Tahoe Blvd., Incline Village, NV, 775/832-3007, www.fredricksbistro.com, 5pm-9:30pm daily, $14-32), lobster dogs share a menu with surf-and-turf sushi rolls. The fusion is mostly French and Asian, but the seasonal menus make good use of fresh and local ingredients.

A good place to splurge, the **Lone Eagle Grille** (111 Country Club Dr., Incline Village, NV, 775/886-6899, www.loneeaglegrille.com, 11am-10pm Sun.-Thurs., 11am-11pm Fri.-Sat., $34-57) has an exceptional lake view. The decadent menu includes steak, lamb, and Dungeness crab, along with a superb wine list. A Lounge Menu ($14) offers a causal, yet excellent, alternative.

ACCOMMODATIONS

The East Shore has few accommodations. The **Parkside Inn at Incline** (1003 Tahoe Blvd., Incline Village, NV, 775/831-1052, www.innatincline.com, $120-199) is a modest midcentury-style motel with 38 clean rooms and adequate private baths. Amenities include an indoor pool and a hot tub (year-round), flat-screen TVs, and free wireless Internet access.

★ **Zephyr Cove Resort** (760 U.S. 50, Zephyr Cove, NV, 888/896-3830, www.zephyrcove.com, $84-289) has it all: lakefront property, lodge rooms and individual cabins, a full-service marina, winter snowmobile park, and restaurants. The four lodge rooms all have private baths. For a special treat, ask for the room with the spa tub. The 28 cabins run from cozy studios to multistory chalets that sleep up to 10 people. Inside you'll find modern furniture, phones, TVs, and wireless Internet access. Pets are welcome.

CAMPING

Spooner Lake State Park (U.S. 50 and Hwy. 28, 775/831-0494, www.parks.nv.gov, $10) has two log cabins for foot travelers: **Spooner Cabin** (Apr.-Nov.), which sleeps four, and **Wild Cat Cabin** (May-Oct. 15), which sleeps two and requires a 2.5-mile walk. Both cabins have a kitchen stove, a woodstove for heat, and compostable toilets. Rates vary seasonally; reservations must be made by email or phone. The park also has the **Marlette Peak, Hobart,** and **North Canyon Campgrounds.** All three primitive walk-in campgrounds are first-come, first-served (free).

The U.S. Forest Service **Nevada Beach Campground** (Elks Point Rd., 3 miles north of Stateline, NV, 877/444-6777, www.recreation.gov, mid-May-mid-Oct., $35-41) has 54 lakefront sites. RVs up to 45 feet are welcome, although no hookups are available. A beautiful beach, shaded campsites, drinking water, flush toilets, and convenience to both Lake Tahoe and the nightlife of Stateline are the attractions here.

TRANSPORTATION AND SERVICES

Highway 28 runs along the East Shore from Incline Village south to Spooner Lake, where it meets U.S. 50, which continues south to Stateline. There are few services.

Incline Village Community Hospital (880 Alder Ave., Incline Village, NV, 775/833-4100 or 800/419-2627, www.tfhd.com) has a 24-hour emergency room.

Sacramento and Gold Country

Look for ★ to find recommended
sights, activities, dining, and lodging.

Highlights

★ **California State Railroad Museum:**
Marvel at the gleaming locomotives and train
cars found in this gem of a museum (page 318).

★ **Capitol Building:** This building is the
epicenter for the city's political history, past and
present (page 319).

★ **Empire Mine State Historic Park:**
Stare down into mine shaft that descends 5,000
feet into the earth at the perfectly preserved site
of California's richest gold mine (page 326).

★ **Malakoff Diggins State Historic
Park:** A famed hydraulic mine is lovingly preserved at this living history museum (page 327).

★ **Marshall Gold Discovery State
Historic Park:** This is the place that started it
all—the spot where gold was discovered in 1848.
The rest is literally history (page 331).

★ **Rafting the American River:** Both
rookie and expert rafters will find opportunities
to hit the water on the American River (page
331).

★ **Apple Hill:** This 20-mile swath of grower
heaven includes dozens of orchards, vineyards,
and pit stops for dining and relaxing along the
way (page 333).

★ **Columbia State Historic Park:** This

former gold rush town is now an indoor-outdoor
museum, with exhibits, shops, and even a saloon
(page 346).

The capital of California, Sacramento is a cosmopolitan city with a friendly vibe and an energized dining and entertainment scene.

In the city's midtown, downtown, and East Sacramento neighborhoods, an urban renaissance has made this storied city into a vibrant, multicultural metropolis with cutting-edge art museums and packed bistros.

The fun continues in the Gold Country, a gorgeous 130-mile-long belt of historic parks, compelling wineries, and rugged outdoor scenery deep in the Sierra Nevada foothills. After prospectors first discovered precious metal here in 1848, California was forever changed by the gold rush and the pioneers who poured into the new state searching for riches. Today, modern-day Gold Country prospectors search for antiques, explore caves, find hole-in-the-wall eateries, sip award-winning vintages, try river-rafting, and discover luxurious inns in renovated farmhouses.

PLANNING YOUR TIME

Sacramento makes a nice day trip or weekend getaway from the Bay Area, or a fun start to a longer Gold Country and Sierra adventure. Winters are mild, but summers get blisteringly hot.

The Gold Country is too large to experience in one day; plan a weekend. Highway 49 runs more than 100 miles through the rugged Sierra foothills, with many side trips to smaller towns and specific caverns, mines, and museums along the way. With **one day,** pick a specific Gold Country town as your destination, and one or two of the major parks and attractions nearby.

In a **weekend,** you can get an overview of either the northern or southern Gold Country, driving from town to town and making short stops. The weather is best late spring to late fall.

Previous: historic Sacramento; gold panning. **Above:** Capitol Building.

Sacramento and Gold Country

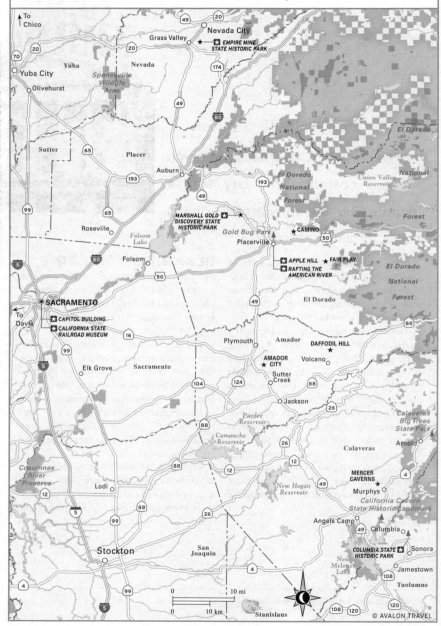

To Chico

20
49
Nevada City
Grass Valley
EMPIRE MINE STATE HISTORIC PARK

70
20
20
174
Yuba City
Yuba
Nevada
Olivehurst
Spenceville Wildlife Area
El Dorado

49

80

Sutter
65
Placer
National

193
Auburn
El Dorado
Union Valley Reservoir

49
National
Forest
Forest

65
MARSHALL GOLD DISCOVERY STATE HISTORIC PARK
Roseville
Folsom Lake
Gold Bug Park
CAMINO
99
Placerville

80
Folsom
APPLE HILL
FAIR PLAY
50
RAFTING THE AMERICAN RIVER
El Dorado

5
SACRAMENTO
National
To Davis
CAPITOL BUILDING
49
El Dorado
Forest
CALIFORNIA STATE RAILROAD MUSEUM
88
16
99
Plymouth
Amador
DAFFODIL HILL

Elk Grove
Sacramento
AMADOR CITY
Volcano
104
124
Sutter Creek
88
Jackson
26
Calaveras Big Trees State Park
Pardee Reservoir
Camanche Reservoir
Calaveras
Arnold
Cosumnes River Preserve
88
New Hogan Reservoir
MERCER CAVERNS
4
12
Lodi
88
12
49
Murphys
California Cavern State Historic Landmark
99
26
Angels Camp
49
Columbia
Stockton
San Joaquin
New Melones Lake
COLUMBIA STATE HISTORIC PARK
Sonora
4
Jamestown
108
Tuolumne
5
99
26
4
120
0   10 mi
0   10 km
108   120
Stanislaus
© AVALON TRAVEL

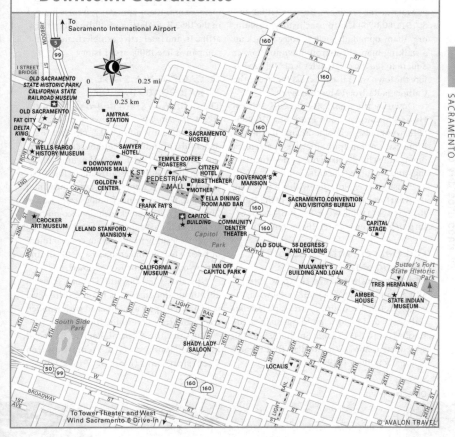

Downtown Sacramento

Sacramento

California's state capital has blossomed into a hip, thriving metropolis with an edgy art-house vibe. Old Sacramento pays homage to the city's gold rush and railroad past. The downtown area is home to the Capital Building and a flood of fabulous farm-to-fork eateries, while Midtown's beautiful tree-lined streets are lined with Victorian and Craftsman homes and tucked-away dining destinations.

SIGHTS
Old Sacramento

Sacramento became an important town as the gold rush progressed and supplies were sent up the Sacramento River from San Francisco. The most important part of the early town was the embarcadero along the river, and that's where **Old Sacramento** (http://old-sacramento.com) is today. The charming cobblestone streets and clattery wooden sidewalks pass old-time shops, restaurants, and attractions.

Start at the **Visitors Center** (1002 2nd St., 916/808-7644, http://sachistorymuseum.org, 10am-6pm daily), where you can pick up a walking map, then stroll down to Pioneer Square to see the original level of Old Sac before the town was raised. Across the street, the California Railroad Museum awaits.

Down by the wharf sits the **Old School House Museum** (1200 Front St., 916/483-8818, www.oldsacschoolhouse.org, 10am-4pm Mon.-Sat., noon-4pm Sun., free), a replica one-room schoolhouse with period furnishings and costumed docents.

Finish your exploration with a walk along the wharf and a drink on the deck of the *Delta King* **Hotel** (1000 Front St., 916/444-5464, https://deltaking.com, 11:30am-9pm daily).

Old Sacramento State Historic Park

Old Sacramento State Historic Park (J and Front Sts., 916/445-7387, www.parks.ca.gov) is filled with grassy areas, pedestrian walkways, and historic buildings such as the **Eagle Theatre** (925 Front St., 916/323-6343), a reconstruction of California's first theater originally built in 1849.

The tiny **Wells Fargo History Museum** (1000 2nd St., 916/440-4263, www.wellsfargohistory.com, 10am-5pm daily, free) is housed in the 1853 B. F. Hastings Building. Its photos, artifacts, and interactive exhibits highlight the company's late 1800s area history.

★ CALIFORNIA STATE RAILROAD MUSEUM

The **California State Railroad Museum** (125 I St., 916/445-7387, www.parks.ca.gov, 10am-5pm daily, adults $12, children 6-17 $6, children under 6 free) houses an amazing collection of artifacts and exhibits illustrating the building of railroads to the West, especially the all-important Transcontinental Railroad. The museum's fabulous collection of 21 restored rolling stock includes locomotives, freight and passenger cars, and cabooses. Imagine sleeping in a Pullman compartment or taking tea on fine china in a 1940s dining car as you wander the Roundhouse.

Upstairs, the Museum Theater shows a 20-minute documentary. On the third level is a children's play area stocked with wooden tracks and trains and a toy train gallery.

Outside, the Central Pacific Railroad Freight Depot runs a steam-powered **Excursion Train** (Front St., 916/323-9280,

Old Sacramento

hourly 11am-4pm Sat.-Sun. Apr.-Sept., adults $12, children 6-17 $6, children under 6 free) along the Sacramento River.

SACRAMENTO HISTORY MUSEUM

Located in the reconstructed 1854 City Hall and Waterworks building, the **Sacramento History Museum** (101 I St., 916/808-7059, http://sachistorymuseum.org, 10am-5pm daily, adults $8, children 6-17 $5, children under 6 free) offers in-depth exhibits on Sacramento history, the gold rush, and the area's agricultural heritage.

The museum also offers tours. On the **Gold Fever! Tour** (Sat.-Sun. Apr.-mid-Dec., adults $10, children 6-17 $6, children under 6 free), listen to tales of gold rush history and learn more about the capital's architecture. Follow the fun beneath the city's bustling streets with **Old Sacramento Underground Tours** (Sat.-Sun. Apr.-Dec., adults $15, children 6-17 $10, children under 6 free), which reveals the hidden corridors and passageways buried when the city was elevated.

★ Capitol Building

The **California State Capitol Building** (10th St. and L St., 916/324-0333, http://capitolmuseum.ca.gov, 7:30am-6pm Mon.-Fri., 9am-5pm Sat.-Sun., free) displays a grandeur befitting the great state of California. On the ground floor, the museum's magnificent collection includes California art and artifacts, oil portraits of the state's governors, two murals, and a collection of antiques. **Tours** (available hourly, free) highlight the neoclassical architecture of the building.

The capitol grounds are known as **Capital Park** and cover 40 acres. The park is filled with monuments, memorials, Native American grinding rocks, a rose garden, a cactus garden, and trees planted from around the world. Pick up a guide in the capitol visitors center (Room B-27).

Sutter's Fort State Historic Park

Sutter's Fort State Historic Park (2701 L St., 916/445-4422, www.parks.ca.gov, 10am-5pm daily, adults $5, children 6-17 $3, children under 6 free) sits on a small hill in the Midtown district. This massive white adobe fort was originally the center of John Sutter's "New Helvetia" settlement. A tour of the park begins with the mazelike museum at the entrance. Inside the fort structure, the story of John Sutter is told in photos, artifacts, and placards. After perusing the interpretive area, wander outside into the sunlight and into the fort's inner courtyard to see how the early settlers lived.

During the occasional "Hands-on History Days" (call for dates, adults $7, children 6-17 $5, children under 6 free), park staff dress in 19th-century costumes to demonstrate making rope, baking bread, and other pioneer activities of the era.

State Indian Museum State Historic Park

Adjacent to Sutter's Fort, the **State Indian Museum State Historic Park** (2618 K St., 916/324-0971, www.parks.ca.gov, 10am-5pm daily, adults $5, children 6-17 $3, children under 6 free) is dedicated to California's indigenous peoples. Their story is told through photos, tools, and cultural items such as baskets and a dugout canoe. An extensive exhibit on Ishi, the last survivor of the Yahi tribe, illustrates the tragic impact of the arrival of Europeans.

Leland Stanford Mansion

Railroad baron, former California governor, and Stanford University founder Leland Stanford and his family spent a number of years living in the capital city at what is now the **Leland Stanford Mansion State Historic Park** (800 N St., 916/324-9266, www.parks.ca.gov, 10am-5pm daily, free). Tours begin in the visitors center, next to the museum store outside the mansion. From here you'll journey inside the lavish main building, where you can admire the lovingly restored furnishings, carpets, walls, and antiques. You must be part of a tour to explore the mansion; the last tour each day starts at 4pm.

Crocker Art Museum

The **Crocker Art Museum** (216 O St., 916/808-7000, www.crockerartmuseum.org, 10am-5pm Tues.-Wed. and Fri.-Sun., 10am-9pm Thurs., adults $10, seniors and students $8, children 7-17 $5, children under 7 free) hosts centuries of fine art and historical exhibits. Notable California artists include Thomas Hill, Joan Brown, Guy Rose, and Wayne Thiebaud.

California Museum

The **California Museum** (1020 O St., 916/653-7524, www.californiamuseum.org, 10am-5pm Tues.-Sat., noon-5pm Sun., adults $9, seniors and students $7.50, children 6-17 $6.50, children under 6 free) delves into the state's history through interpretive exhibits about California Indians, missions, a California Hall of Fame (which includes Lucille Ball and poet Gary Snyder), and art installations like the Constitution Wall.

California Automobile Museum

Ogle more than 150 vintage and modern vehicles at the **California Automobile Museum** (2200 Front St., 916/442-6802, www.calautomuseum.org, 10am-5pm Wed.-Mon., adults $10, senior and students $9, children 5-17 $5, children under 5 free).

ENTERTAINMENT AND EVENTS
Nightlife

In Midtown, **Harlow's** (2708 J St., 916/441-4693, www.harlows.com, tickets $10-70, shows age 21 and over) has a sleek, urbane interior and a moneyed vibe; spiff up before rubbing elbows with the swanky crowd. Live acts range from local favorites to up-and-coming DJs. Harlow's often has a line to get in, especially if there's a show.

Mix (1525 L St., 916/442-8899, www.mixdowntown.net, hours vary Tues.-Sun.) is where the Sacramento nightlife set, well, mix. Polished wooden ceilings and wall panels give a minimalist European feel with California flair. A rooftop patio with fire pits and comfy chairs invites relaxing. Mix is popular on weekends and will have a line later in the evening.

Downtown, **Malt and Mash** (715 K St., 916/476-4403, www.maltmash.com, 4pm-midnight Tues.-Thurs. 4pm-2am Fri.-Sat.) pours pints and shots with a fun-loving Irish flair. The bar is crowded on game nights, with a small pub menu for the peckish.

The **Shady Lady Saloon** (1409 R St., 916/231-9121, http://shadyladybar.com, 11am-2am Mon.-Fri., 9am-2am Sat.-Sun.) feels like a speakeasy with a gold rush vibe. Bartenders don vintage vests and garters on their sleeves while serving libations like the White Linen or the Horse Neck. The bar also serves an upscale pub menu. Catch a variety of live acts nightly.

Midtown wine bar **58 Degrees and Holding** (1217 18th St., 916/442-5858, www.58degrees.com, 4pm-11pm Mon.-Thurs., 4pm-midnight Fri., 11am-midnight Sat, 11am-11pm Sun.) is stacked with European and Californian wines and a knowledgeable waitstaff. Choose from a variety of small upscale plates or cheese and charcuterie boards to complement your vino.

Cinema

Live music meets classic cinema at the vintage **Crest Theater** (1013 K St., 916/476-3356, www.crestsacramento.com). Behind the neon marquee, the 1912 theater both hosts live acts and shows Oscar-nominated classics like *Blade Runner.*

RECREATION

Sports lovers can catch a game at the home of the NBA Sacramento Kings, the **Golden 1 Center** (500 David J Stern Walk, 888/915-4647, https://www.golden1center.com) in downtown. The center is also a popular venue for big-name acts like Lorde and Katy Perry.

Discovery Park

Discovery Park (1600 Garden Hwy., www. regionalparks.saccounty.net, $5/vehicle) sits at the confluence of the Sacramento and American Rivers. Its 302 acres are part of the larger **American River Parkway,** which stretches 23 miles to the city of Folsom. Wending its way through wetlands and oak woodlands, is the 32-mile Jedediah Smith Memorial Trail. Cyclists, families, and dog owners all enjoy a stroll here.

FOOD

Sacramento has rechristened itself the "Farm-to-Fork Capital of America." Foodies will love the variety and quality of eateries from edgy Downtown to hip Midtown.

Bakeries and Cafés

Begin your day at **Temple Coffee Roasters** (1010 9th St., 916/443-4960, https://temple-coffee.com, 6am-6pm daily, $5-10) where minimal stylings reflect serious coffee roasting and brewing. At the hip Midtown location (2200 K St., 916/662-7625, 6am-11pm, $5-10), order coffee made by the labyrinthine Japanese Curtis Seraphim Nitrogen-infused coffee system.

For a Seattle-style coffeehouse, try ★ **Old Soul** (1716 L St., 916/443-7685, www.old-soulco.com, 6am-9pm daily, $5-8) for just tea, coffee, lattes, mochas, and great breakfasts.

American

Old Sacramento's **Fat City Bar and Café** (1001 Front St., 916/446-6768, https://fatci-tybarcafe.com, 11:30am-9pm Mon.-Thurs., 11:30am-10pm Fri., 11am-10pm Sat.-Sun., $14-26) resembles an Old West saloon from the gold-mining heyday—except you can get chow mein, tacos, meat loaf, potpie, or an enormous cheeseburger. On weekends, enjoy a mixed brunch.

★ **Mother** (1023 K St., 916/594-9812, http://mothersacramento.com, 11am-3pm and 5pm-8pm Tues.-Thurs., 11am-3pm and 5pm-9pm Fri., 5pm-9pm Sat., $12-18) is a vegetarian eatery that's more punk rock arthouse

than fixed-geared hipster. The slim and simple menu is filled with seasonal dishes both richly conceived and divinely executed. Homemade ravioli or a savory nut burger comes with beer, wine, lemonade, or kombucha. Reservations are available at this walk-up.

Mulvaney's Building & Loan (1215 19th St., 916/441-6022, www.mulvaneysbl.com, 11:30am-2:30pm and 5pm-10pm Tues.-Fri., 5pm-10pm Sat., $18-44) is an upscale eatery showcasing the best of California cuisine. The menu changes to feature local seasonal produce. The wine list offers a reasonable number of interesting vintages.

★ **Ella Dining Room and Bar** (1131 K St., 916/443-3772, www.elladiningroomand-bar.com, 11:30am-9pm Mon.-Thurs., 11:30am-10pm Fri., 5:30pm-10pm Sat., $25-55) is a downtown culinary superstar. This swanky eatery serves local, sustainably farmed fare like Scottish salmon with succotash, juniper-braised oxtail, or naturally raised trout. Book ahead on weekends to secure a table.

In Midtown, **Paragary** (1401 28th Ave., 916/457-5737, www.paragarysmidtown. com, 5pm-9pm Sun.-Thurs., 5pm-10pm Fri., 9:30am-2:30pm and 5pm-10pm Sat., 9:30am-2:30pm Sun., $19-30) is an epicurean staple. Californian cuisine meets rustic Italian fare, all served with an impressive wine list. A full bar adds color, while brunch and daily happy hours keeps it vibrant.

At **Localis** (2031 S St., 916/737-7699, www. localissacramento.com, 4pm-9pm Tues.-Thurs., 4pm-10pm Fri., 5pm-10pm Sat., 10am-2pm Sun., $25-34), all items on the slim menu are superbly hand-crafted. To savor the best of the kitchen, order the chef's five-course tasting menu ($79).

Asian

Opened by Frank Fat in 1939, **Frank Fat's** (806 L St., 916/442-7092, www.fatsrestau-rants.com, 11am-9:30pm Mon.-Thurs., 11am-10pm Fri., 5pm-10pm Sat., 4pm-9:30pm Sun., $11-35) is a legendary Sacramento institution serving authentic upscale Chinese food. The interior has a hip, cosmopolitan vibe with classy leather booths, a long shiny bar, and modern furniture.

Mexican

Both the atmosphere and the mole are authentic at **Tres Hermanas** (2416 K St., 916/443-6919, www.treshermanasonk.com, 11am-9pm Mon.-Thurs., 11am-10pm Fri., 7am-10pm Sat., 7am-8pm Sun., $10-14). The food is influenced by northern Mexican cuisine. Quesadillas, tacos, and enchiladas come heavy on herbs and veggies, with lots of pork and fish. This Midtown spot gets busy. Between 7pm and 9pm, expect a 30-minute wait.

ACCOMMODATIONS

The best bets for affordable rooms are at chain hotels, with a few exceptions.

Under $150

For budget accommodations, you can't beat the **Sacramento Hostel** (925 H St., 916/668-6631, www.norcalhostels.org/sac, $32-99) housed in the grand 1885 Llewellyn Williams Mansion. Lodgings include coed and single-sex dorms ($32-36), plus a few private rooms ($58-99). One private room includes a private bath ($89). The hostel has free wireless Internet access, laundry, on-site parking, a large shared kitchen, 24-hour guest access; bring your own linens.

The **Inn off Capitol Park** (1530 N St., 916/447-8100, www.innoffcapitolpark.com, $119-189) offers stylish accommodations within easy walking distance of the Capitol and the Sacramento Convention Center. Amenities include free Wi-Fi, and microwave and minifridges in most rooms. With only 36 rooms, this friendly boutique hotel fills fast during conventions.

$150-250

The riverboat *Delta King* (1000 Front St., 916/444-5464, http://deltaking.com, $148-230) is a hotel, restaurant, theater, and gathering space. Of the modern, elegant staterooms, the less expensive ones can be quite small, but all have private bathrooms and include a complimentary breakfast.

The best B&B in Sacramento is the 10-room ★ **Amber House** (1315 22nd St., 916/444-8085, www.amberhouse.com, $219-290), located on a quiet residential street in Midtown within walking distance of shops, restaurants, and nightlife. Rooms have either a jetted tub or a deep-soaking bathtub, comfortable beds, and top-end amenities.

The majestic art deco brownstone ★ **Citizen Hotel** (926 J St., 916/447-2700 or 877/829-2429, www.thecitizenhotel.com, $170-278) is one of downtown's most recognizable landmarks. Inside, the highly stylized retro decor includes a marble foyer and rooms with vintage pinstriped wallpaper and upholstered headboards. Amenities include a minibar, flat-screen TV, and Italian linens with services like same-day laundry, a fitness center, and valet parking ($28/day).

The swank **Sawyer Hotel** (500 J. St., 877/678-6255, www.ihg.com, $224-307) is part of the Kimpton collection. The sleek hotel has rooms with plush beds, modern decor, and sky-high views. The poolside lounge turns into the slick Revival club at night. Complimentary breakfast and central location are pluses; you must pay for parking.

TRANSPORTATION AND SERVICES

Air

Sacramento International Airport (SMF, 6900 Airport Blvd., 916/929-5411, www.sacramento.aero) is served by several major airlines.

Train and Bus

Amtrak's *Capitol Corridor* train (800/872-7245, www.amtrak.com, $31-40 one-way) runs from the Sacramento train station (401 I St.) to Oakland and San Jose several times daily. The trip takes 2-3 hours.

The **Greyhound** (420 Richards Blvd., 800/231-2222, www.greyhound.com, $7.50-48) bus station is north of downtown with service throughout the state.

Sacramento Regional Transit (SACRT,

Side Trip to Davis

Davis is home to the region's agricultural brainpower—the University of California, Davis. Known for its progressive vibe and left-leaning politics, Davis earns national recognition as a bike-friendly town with prolific and well-maintained bike paths. Downtown, boutiques and antiques stores are scattered throughout the town's shady streets.

UNIVERSITY OF CALIFORNIA, DAVIS

The University of California, Davis (1 Shields Ave., 530/752-1011, www.ucdavis.edu) first opened in 1905 as a farm school. The expansive campus is now California's largest at 5,300 acres, and has an on-site dairy and a working farm.

Oenophiles will want to stop at the Robert Mondavi Institute for Wine and Food Science (392 Old Davis Rd., 530/754-6349, http://robertmondaviinstitute.ucdavis.edu, tours $5). The sprawling agricultural complex boasts a green-certified winery, brewery, milk bottling facility, and an organic vegetable garden. Tours are available Monday-Friday.

Davis is also home to the celebrated Bohart Museum of Entomology (1124 Academic Surge, 530/752-0493, http://bohart.ucdavis.edu, 9am-noon and 1pm-5pm Mon.-Thurs., free, parking $9). With more than seven million insects, it has one of the largest collections in North America, adding 50,000 new specimens every year.

FOOD

Burgers and Brew (403 3rd St., 530/750-3600, www.burgersbrew.com, 11am-midnight Sun.-Wed., 11am-3am Thurs.-Sat., $10-17) serves big selections of both on its outdoor patio. For a glass of wine and a crepe, Crepeville (330 3rd St., 530/750-2400, 7am-11pm daily, $10) is next door and serves breakfast.

Bounty from the region's organic and community-supported farms can be found at the town's farmers market (Central Park, 3rd and C Sts., www.davisfarmersmarket.org, 8am-1pm Sat. year-round, 4:30pm-8:30pm Wed. mid-Mar.-Oct. and 2pm-6pm Nov.-mid-Mar.).

GETTING THERE

Davis is 14 miles west of Sacramento on I-80. The Richards Boulevard exit provides easy access to downtown. Amtrak (840 2nd St., 530/758-4220 or 800/872-7245, www.amtrak.com) stops several times daily in downtown Davis on the way to Oakland, San Jose, and Sacramento. Unitrans (530/752-2877, http://unitrans.ucdavis.edu, $1, children under 5 free) provides public transit around Davis and the university campus.

www.sacrt.com, adults $2.75, seniors and children 5-18 $1.35, children under 5 free, day pass $7) runs buses and a light-rail train system through downtown and Midtown.

Car

Sacramento lies at the nexus of several freeways, notably I-80 (east-west), I-5 (north-south) and U.S. 50 (east). Grid-lock traffic is legendary during commuter times and on weekends. Though it's only 90 miles north of San Francisco on I-80, the drive can take 2-4 hours depending on traffic.

Sacramento is laid out on a grid system of numbered and lettered streets, many of which are one-way. Parking is relatively easy but often metered. There are paid parking lots at the north and south ends of Old Sacramento.

Services

Sutter General Hospital (2801 L St., 916/887-1130, http://suttermedicalcenter.org) has an emergency room, or go to the emergency center run by UC Davis Medical Center (2315 Stockton Blvd., 916/734-5010).

Northern Gold Country

California's Gold Country is a great sprawling network of small towns and roads crisscrossing the Sierra Nevada Foothills where much of California's mining history began.

The Northern Gold Country extends from Nevada City south to the Shenandoah Valley. From Sacramento, I-80 leads north to the town of Auburn where Highway 49 heads north to Grass Valley and Nevada City and southeast to Placerville, Coloma, Fair Play, and the Shenandoah Valley.

AUBURN

Established in the spring of 1848, Auburn was the first mining settlement of the gold rush. Old Town Auburn (High St. and Lincoln Way) sits right off busy I-80 and showcases the town's gold rush charm.

Sights

Located on the first floor of the historical Placer County courthouse, the **Placer County Museum** (101 Maple St., 530/889-6500, www.placer.ca.gov, 10am-4pm daily, free) offers a glimpse into the town's rustic past. Exhibits span different themes and time periods in Placer County history, such as the women's jail, a recreated sheriff's office, and the stagecoach that ran from Auburn into the mountains. Free guided tours of Old Town are offered Saturday at 10am.

Auburn's gold rush history is on display at the **Gold Country Museum** (601 Lincoln Way, 530/889-6506, www.placer.ca.gov, 10:30am-4pm Tues.-Sun., free), which has a reconstructed mine, a stamp mill, an indoor panning stream, and a miner's tent.

Auburn State Recreation Area

Auburn State Recreation Area (501 El Dorado St./Hwy. 49, 530/885-4527, www.parks.ca.gov, 7am-sunset daily, $10) has more than 100 miles of trails that wind through leafy oak woodlands and past seasonal waterfalls like Codfish Falls. The area is used by hikers, joggers, mountain bikers, dirt bikers, and horseback riders. Parking is easiest at the confluence of the American River's North and Middle Forks, and it's also where most of the trails begin. This area is one of the best local places for water sports: Rafting, kayaking, and boating are all available along various stretches of the river. The river confluence has plenty of swimming holes.

Food and Accommodations

In Old Town Auburn, ★ **Carpe Vino** (1568 Lincoln Way, 530/823-0320, www.carpevinoauburn.com, 5pm-9pm Tues.-Sat., $20-33) serves dishes with sustainably grown ingredients from local farms and vendors and showcases the best of California wine. Entrées such as steak and cider-brined pork make mouths water, but the focus here is on the wine, which has a limited markup. More than 40 vintages are available by the glass. Come on Saturday (noon-10pm Tues.) for wine-tasting.

Awful Annie's (13460 Lincoln Way, 530/888-9857, www.awfulannies.com, 8am-3pm daily, $9-15) serves oversize breakfast plates of Benedicts, scrambles, and waffles, plus plenty of cold and grilled sandwiches for lunch, along with a full bar in the sunny interior.

Ikeda's (13500 Lincoln Way, 530/885-4243, www.ikedas.com, 11am-7pm Mon.-Thurs., 9am-8pm Fri.-Sun., $10-15) is a roadside burger joint and fruit stand (8am-7pm Mon.-Thurs., 8am-8pm Fri.-Sun.) that has become a de facto rest stop for travelers. Burgers, sandwiches (including the standout Dungeness crab sandwich), soft-serve ice cream, and milk shakes fill the menu, but the pies are the biggest draw.

Tio Pepe (216 Washington St., 530/888-6445, www.tiopepemex.com, 11am-9pm Sun.-Thurs., 11am-10pm Fri.-Sat., $13-15) serves hearty plates of Mexican food and colorful

Northern Gold Country

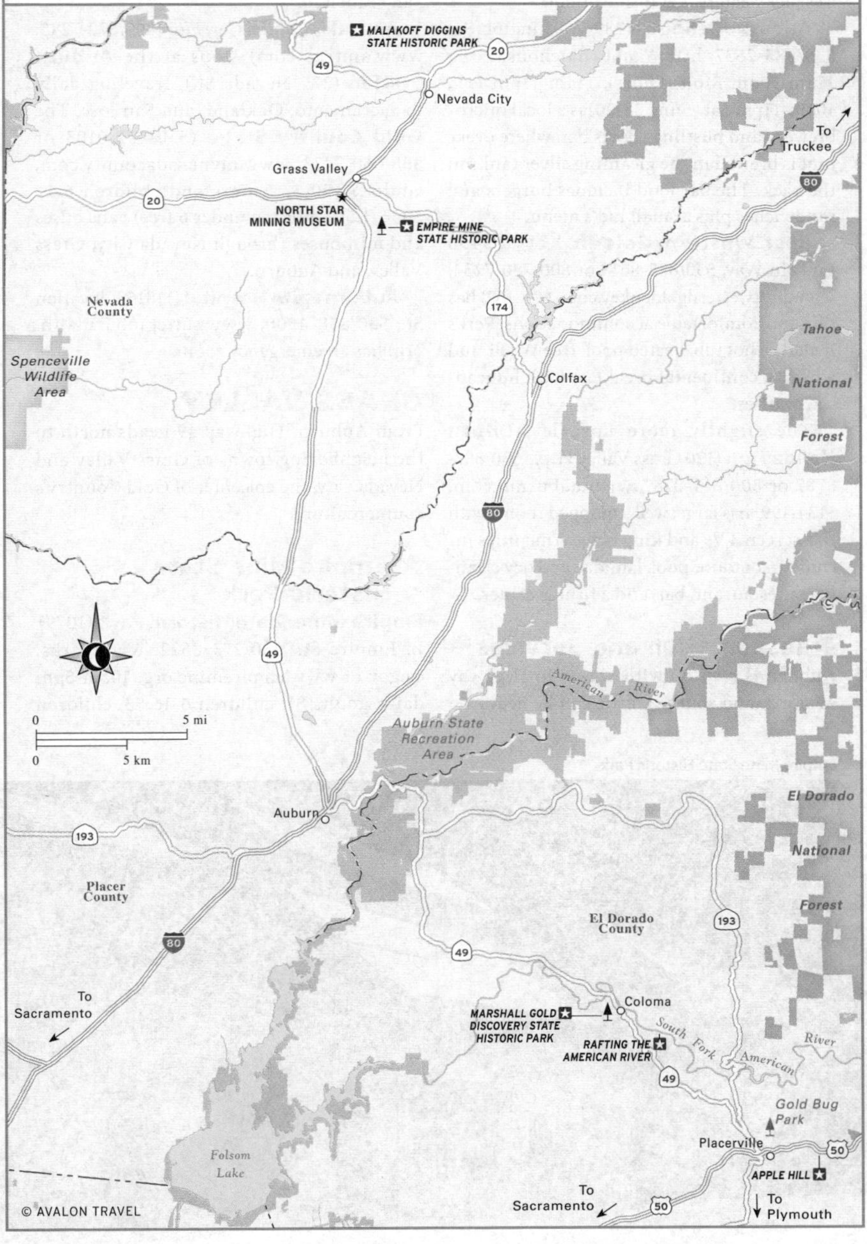

MALAKOFF DIGGINS
STATE HISTORIC PARK

20

49

Nevada City

To
Truckee

80

Grass Valley

NORTH STAR
MINING MUSEUM

EMPIRE MINE
STATE HISTORIC PARK

20

174

Nevada
County

Tahoe

Spenceville
Wildlife
Area

Colfax

National

80

Forest

American River

49

Auburn State
Recreation
Area

El Dorado

National

Placer
County

193

Forest

80

Auburn

El Dorado
County

193

To
Sacramento

49

Coloma

MARSHALL GOLD
DISCOVERY STATE
HISTORIC PARK

RAFTING THE
AMERICAN RIVER

South Fork American River

49

Gold Bug
Park

Placerville

50

Folsom
Lake

To
Sacramento

50

APPLE HILL

To
Plymouth

0   5 mi
0   5 km

© AVALON TRAVEL

margaritas inside its brightly painted interior. A variety of options (including burgers) satisfies picky eaters. Eat inside or out.

Auburn Alehouse (289 Washington St., 530/885-2537, http://auburnalehouse.com, 11am-10pm Mon.-Thurs., 11am-11pm Fri., 10am-11pm Sat.-Sun., $8-20) is a local microbrewery and bustling sports bar, where every pint is brewed in the gleaming silver tanks in the back. The bar food includes burgers and sandwiches plus a small kid's menu.

Best Western Golden Key (13450 Lincoln Way, 530/885-8611 or 800/780-7234, www.bestwesterngoldenkey.com, $98-162) has tidy and comfortable accommodations. Perks include a hot tub, heated pool, free Wi-Fi, and a hearty continental breakfast with hubcap-size waffles.

The slightly more upscale **Auburn Holiday Inn** (120 Grass Valley Hwy., 530/887-8787 or 800/814-8787, www.auburnhi.com, $134-199) has large, well-equipped rooms with flat-screen TVs and king beds. Amenities include an outdoor pool, laundry and dry cleaning, a restaurant, bar, and a fitness center.

Transportation and Services
Auburn is on I-80 with access to Highway 49 north and south. Traffic can be heavy on

weekends, especially in winter. It is 35 miles north of Sacramento and 120 miles north of San Francisco.

Amtrak's *Capitol Corridor* (800/872-7245, www.amtrak.com) stops at the **Auburn Station** (277 Nevada St.), traveling daily to Sacramento, Oakland, and San Jose. The **Gold Country Stage** (530/477-0103 or 888/660-7433, www.mynevadacounty.com, adults $1.50-3, seniors and children 6-17 $0.75-1.50, children under 6 free) runs buses and minibuses through Nevada City, Grass Valley, and Auburn.

Auburn Faith Hospital (11815 Education St., 530/888-4500, www.sutterauburnfaith. org) has an emergency room.

GRASS VALLEY
From Auburn, Highway 49 heads north to the neighboring towns of Grass Valley and Nevada City, the epicenter of Gold Country's counterculture.

★ Empire Mine State Historic Park
Empire Mine State Historic Park (10791 E. Empire St., 530/273-8522, www.parks. ca.gov or www.empiremine.org, 10am-5pm daily, adults $7, children 6-16 $3, children

Empire Mine State Historic Park

under 6 free) displays the mine's history and the struggle of the miners. The showpiece of the museum collection is the scale model of the Empire Mine and its various nearby interconnected tunnels, highlighted by audio describing parts of the overwhelmingly vast and complex underground maze. In the yard is a collection of mining tools and equipment. Chat with the resident blacksmith before peering down the track that leads to 367 miles of shafts.

Tours (daily in summer, Sat.-Sun. Sept.-May, $2) include the Mineyard and Empire Cottage and the English-style home of William Bowers Bourn Jr., designed by Willis Polk in 1897.

Nearly 14 miles of hiking trails snake through the park. The **Hardrock, Union Hill,** and **Osborn Hill Loop** trails link together from the visitors center to the remains of many hard-rock mines.

North Star Mining Museum

North Star Mining Museum (933 Allison Ranch Rd., 530/273-4255, http://nevadacountyhistory.org, 10am-4pm Wed.-Sat., noon-4pm Sun., May-Oct., donation requested) is a tribute to the industrial machinery that once powered the North Star Mine, one of California's most successful mines during the gold rush. The museum has plenty of mining relics, such as the largest Pelton wheel in the world and a working stamp mill.

★ Malakoff Diggins State Historic Park

Malakoff Diggins State Historic Park (23579 N. Bloomfield Rd., 530/265-2740, www.parks.ca.gov, sunrise-sunset daily, $5-10 vehicle) was the site of California's largest hydraulic mine. The ghostly 6,800-foot-long Diggins Pit is a chilling illustration of mining's effect on the landscape. The park encompasses more than 20 miles of hiking trails, including access to the South Yuba Trail that follows the wild Yuba River. The mining pit is best viewed from the **Diggins Loop Trail** (3 miles round-trip, easy/moderate).

The attached "ghost town" of **North Bloomfield** illustrates what life was like in this isolated mining community. The town has been carefully preserved with a recreated livery, apothecary, and general store.

The **visitors center** (10am-5pm daily Apr.-Sept.) has a great museum that digs into the environmental history of the area. Rent a pan ($1) and try your hand at finding gold at the nearby creek or hike up the hill to explore the eerily abandoned one-room schoolhouse, old cemetery, and St. Columncille's Church. **Tours** (1:30pm Apr.-Sept., free) are offered daily.

To reach the park from Nevada City, take Highway 49 north toward the town of Downieville. In 11 miles, turn right onto Tyler Foote Road and follow the center yellow line into the park. (The road name changes several times: Curzon Grade Rd., Back Bone Rd., Derbec Rd., and North Bloomfield Rd.) The park is 26 miles north of Nevada City.

South Yuba River State Park

South Yuba River State Park (17660 Pleasant Valley Rd., Penn Valley, 530/432-2546, sunrise-sunset daily, free) covers 20 miles of the Yuba River, from Malakoff Diggins State Historic Park to the covered bridge at Bridgeport, where the Yuba River crosses Highway 20. There are plenty of gold rush ruins on the river, including an old mining camp and several sections of the Virginia Turnpike, a 14-mile-long toll road. Trails follow the river leading through oak woodlands, wildflowers, and seasonal waterfalls.

In summer, the river is a popular spot to cool off, especially at the small gravel **Family Beach** (east of the covered bridge in Bridgeport). Popular access points include Highway 49, six miles north of Nevada City; Purdon Crossing (Purdon Rd.) to the east; and Edwards Crossing on North Bloomfield Road, which continues for seven bumpy dirt miles to Malakoff Diggins State Park.

A **visitors center** (11am-4pm daily summer, 11am-3pm Thurs.-Sun. fall-spring) has interpretive displays of the region's history and offers docent-led tours in spring and summer.

Entertainment and Shopping

Shops line Main and Mill Streets. Booktown Books (107 Bank St., 530/272-4655, http://booktownbooks.com, 10am-6pm Mon.-Sat., 11am-5pm Sun.) is truly the mother lode for rare and used tomes.

The historic Del Oro Theatre (165 Mill St., 530/477-9000) shows current films and blockbusters in a retro setting.

Food

The pastries at Fable Coffee (167 Mill St., 530/802-5333, www.fablecoffee.com, 7am-6pm Mon.-Thurs., 7am-7pm Fri.-Sun., $5) are just as good as the coffee.

Summer Thyme's Bakery & Deli (231 Colfax Ave., 530/273-2904, www.summerthymes.com, 6am-6pm Mon.-Fri., 6am-4pm Sat., 7am-4pm Sun., $7-15) is a bright café with house-made pastries, hot breakfasts, salads, sandwiches, and espresso drinks. There is an outdoor patio, live music on the weekends, and a play kitchen for kids.

★ Diego's (217 Colfax Ave., 530/477-1460, http://diegosrestaurant.com, 11am-9pm daily, $8-17) colorful interior complements the bright flavors and sustainable ethos of its Chilean-inspired South American menu. Choose from lamb, shrimp, steak, or tofu, plus plenty of peppers, avocado, and seasonal fruit and veggies.

Accommodations and Camping

Built in 1862, the Holbrooke Hotel (212 W. Main St., 530/273-1353 or 800/933-7077, www.holbrooke.com, $114-194) is one of the oldest lodgings in California. A host of famous 19th-century figures stayed here, including U.S. presidents Ulysses S. Grant and Grover Cleveland and writer Mark Twain. All 28 rooms include modern conveniences like a private bath with antique claw-foot tub, cable TV, updated amenities, and free Wi-Fi; some rooms have balconies or fireplaces.

The downstairs restaurant (11am-9pm daily, $14-21) serves an unpretentious lineup of fish tacos, pasta, and burgers with a late-night menu on Friday and Saturday. The saloon slings drinks and hosts live music.

Charming motel-style accommodations at Sierra Mountain Inn (816 W. Main St., Grass Valley, 530/273-8133 or 800/377-8133, www.sierramountaininn.com, $109-185) offer a romantic and relaxing option. Rooms have a quirky farmhouse feel, with plush beds, minifridges, coffeemakers, microwaves, and wireless Internet. Some rooms have complete kitchenettes. A two-night minimum is required; pets are permitted ($25 fee).

Malakoff Diggins has the small and wonderful Chute Hill Campground (800/444-7275, www.reservecalifornia.com, May-Oct., $35). The 30 sites are shaded, large, and private, and include a fire pit, bear box, and picnic tables. It's rarely crowded, even on a busy summer weekend.

Transportation and Services

In Auburn, exit onto Highway 49 west and continue 21 miles to Grass Valley. From Sacramento, the trip is 60 miles.

The Gold Country Stage (530/477-0103 or 888/660-7433, www.mynevadacounty.com, adults $1.50-3, seniors and children 6-17 $0.75-1.50, children under 6 free) runs buses and minibuses through the region.

Sierra Nevada Memorial Hospital (155 Glasson Way, 530/274-6000, www.snmh.org) has an emergency room.

NEVADA CITY

Nevada City's narrow streets lead back in time to the days of the gold rush. Most shops are on Broad and Commercial Streets. Regional theater and independent film take the stage at the Nevada Theatre (401 Broad St., 530/265-6161, www.nevadatheatre.com).

Food

★ Three Forks Bakery and Brewery (211 Commercial St., 530/470-8333, www.threeforksnc.com, 7am-10pm Mon., Wed., and Thurs., 7am-11pm Fri., 8am-11pm Sat., 8am-10pm Sun., $9-15) serves wood-fired pizza made with a wild yeast crust. The eight beers on tap include many IPAs, plus red and pale ales, stouts, and specialty seasonal brews. In the mornings, the bakery offers fabulous breads and pastries that sell out fast.

Sopa Thai (312-316 Commercial St., 530/470-0101, www.sopathai.com, 11am-3pm and 5pm-9:30pm Mon.-Fri., noon-9:30pm Sat.-Sun., $14-20) serves traditional Thai cuisine in a cozy dining room. If the weather is nice, take your curry or pad thai outside and dine in the garden out back.

At **New Moon Café** (203 York St., 530/265-6399, www.thenewmooncafe.com, 11:30am-2pm and 5pm-8pm Tues.-Fri., 5pm-8pm Sat.-Sun., $23-45), white tablecloths form a backdrop for seasonally inspired dishes such as venison with huckleberry-zinfandel sauce and roasted butternut squash crepes with kale. The lengthy wine list features vintages close to home and abroad.

The best brunch spot is the ★ **South Pine Café** (110 S. Pine St., 530/265-0260, www.southpinecafe.com, 8am-3pm daily, $8-15), with plates of tofu scramble, lobster Benedicts, chorizo breakfast tacos, and ollaliberry French toast. Lunch sees a variety of burgers, burritos, and melts. Wash it all down with fresh-pressed juice or a Bloody Mary. When this tiny spot gets crowded on weekends, try the larger Grass Valley location (102 Richardson St., 530/274-0261, 8am-3pm daily).

For espresso and some fast Wi-Fi, **Curly Wolf** (217 Broad St., 530/264-7338, 8am-midnight, $4-7) does the trick.

Accommodations

History permeates **Emma Nevada House** (528 E. Broad St., 530/265-4415, www.emmanevadahouse.com, $169-249), a large Victorian house that once belonged to the family of opera singer Emma Nevada. The six uniquely styled rooms include comfortable beds, antiques, and plush baths, some with claw-foot tubs. A multicourse gourmet breakfast is served each morning.

A short stroll from downtown, ★ **Outside Inn** (575 E. Broad St., 530/265-2233, www.outsideinn.com, $84-220) is a converted 1930s motel. Each room has a different outdoor theme, such as the Rock Climbing Suite and the romantic Creekside Hideaway cabin; some rooms have kitchenettes. The laid-back patio area includes a pool and a brick fire pit. The inn is pet-friendly ($20/night).

Transportation and Services

From I-80 in Auburn, exit onto Highway 49 west and continue 25 miles north to Nevada City. The **Gold Country Stage** (530/477-0103 or 888/660-7433, www.mynevadacounty.com, adults $1.50-3, seniors and children 6-17 $0.75-1.50, children under 6 free) runs buses and minibuses throughout the region.

DOWNIEVILLE

From Nevada City, Highway 49 climbs steadily north, where a few remote mining towns stand surrounded by the dense wilderness of the Tahoe National Forest. The largest town is Downieville at the confluence of the Downie and North Fork of the Yuba Rivers. In 1849, gold was discovered here on the North Fork of the Yuba River. One year later, there were 15 hotels and even more saloons.

History buffs should browse the collection of gold rush ephemera at the **Downieville Museum** (330 Main St., 916/289-3423, 10am-4pm daily late May-early Oct., 10am-4pm Fri.-Sat. May-Oct., donations appreciated), which is housed in an 1852 brick building that was originally a Chinese gambling house.

Mountain Biking

Mountain biking is a big draw, with scores of trails for intermediate and advanced riders. The **Downieville Downhill** is a network of several single-track trails that drops 4,400 feet over 17 miles into downtown Downieville.

Yuba Expeditions (208 Main St., 530/289-3010, www.yubaexpeditions.com, 8:30am-5:30pm Mon.-Fri. 8am-6pm

Sat.-Sun., rentals $119/day, shuttle $20) and **Downieville Outfitters** (312 Main St., 530/289-0155, www.downievilleoutfitters.com, 8am-5pm daily, rentals $70-100/day, shuttle $20) offers bike repairs, rentals, maps, and shuttles to the trailheads.

Food and Accommodations

The **Downieville Carriage House Inn** (110 Commercial St., 530/289-3573, www.downievillecarriagehouse.com, $90-195) has eight rooms with Victorian decor and private bathrooms in a historic lodge overlooking the Downie River. Some rooms use private showers down the hall, while larger rooms have TVs, minifridges and microwaves. Breakfast is included as is secured bike parking.

For the best lunch and dinner in town, go to **La Cocina de Oro** (322 Main St., Downieville, 530/289-3584, 11am-8pm Sun.-Thurs., 11am-8:30pm Fri.-Sat., $6-15). The bright, festive flavors match the bright simple decor. Snag a spot on the back patio overlooking the river.

Transportation and Services

Downieville sits squarely on Highway 49, 42 miles north and east of Nevada City. The trip takes an hour thanks to all the twists and turns. Don't except cell phone service in this remote stretch of the Sierra. While there is a **gas station** in Downieville, fill your tank before leaving Nevada City.

SIERRA CITY

Sierra City is a historic town where it feels as if it could still be the 19th century. North of town, the **Kentucky Historic Park and Museum** (100 Kentucky Mine Rd., 530/862-1310, www.sierracountyhistory.org, 10am-4pm Wed.-Sun. summer, 10am-4pm Sat.-Sun. mid-Sept.-mid-Oct., adults $2, children $0.50) preserves the area history with a museum and an old stamp mill that comes to life during **tours** (11am and 2pm, adults $7, children 7-17 $3.50, children under 7 free).

Recreation

The **Sierra Buttes Trail** (5 miles round-trip, strenuous) leads to a fire lookout at 8,587 feet. After climbing the metal stairs to the top, enjoy views of Mount Lassen, the beautiful Lakes Basin, and the deep gorge of the Yuba River. The trailhead is on Packer Lake Road (Gold Lake Hwy., 530/265-4531, www.fs.usda.gov/tahoe).

The nearby **Lakes Basin National Recreation Area** (Golden Lake Hwy., 530/836-2575, www.fs.usda.gov/plumas) is a beautiful stretch of country with 20 lakes, many accessible only by foot. The **Bear Lakes Loop** (2 miles, moderate) connects Big Bear, Little Bear, and Cub Lakes, while the trail to **Long Lake** (2.5 miles, moderate) leads to the foot of Mount Elwell. Both trails depart from Lakes Basin Campground (Elwell Lodge Rd.).

Food and Camping

Just about the only place to go in Sierra City is the cute **Red Moose Café and Inn** (224 Main St., Sierra City, 530/862-1024, http://redmoosecafe.com, 8am-2pm, $8-12), a rustic café serving hearty breakfast and lunch options.

Lakes Basin Campground (Elwell Lodge Rd., 877/444-6777, www.recreation.gov, $22-44 June-Sept.) has 24 sites with vault toilets and potable water. **Sardine Lakes Campground** (Sardine Lake Rd., 877/444-6777, www.recreation.gov, $24) is beautiful with 23 sites and swimming at nearby Sand Pond.

Transportation

Sierra City is 12 miles east of Downieville on Highway 49, and only 47 miles (1 hour) from Truckee, via highways 49 and 89.

COLOMA

East of Auburn along Highway 49, a speck found in the river at Coloma ignited the gold rush.

★ Marshall Gold Discovery State Historic Park

One day in 1848, a carpenter named James W. Marshall took a fateful stroll by the saw-mill he was building for John Sutter on the American River and found gold specks shining in the water. Marshall's discovery sparked the California gold rush, and the rest, as they say, is history.

Surrounded by a setting little changed since the time of Sutter, **Marshall Gold Discovery State Historic Park** (310 Back St., 530/622-3470, www.parks.ca.gov, 8am-8pm daily summer, 8am-5pm daily fall-spring, $8) is a rambling collection of buildings, nature trails, mining equipment, and tiny museums reflecting the ethnic diversity of the gold rush. Cedar bark tepees and grinding rocks from the area's indigenous peoples also remain in the area.

A full-size replica of **Sutter's Mill** stands near several restored historical buildings, like the tiny one-bedroom Mormon cabin, the Chinese-operated **Wah Hop** and **Man Lee** stores, the old blacksmith shop, and the **Price-Thomas** home. The **Gold Discovery Loop Trail** (3.6 miles, easy) leads to the very spot where Marshall made his discovery.

The **visitors center** (10am-5pm daily Mar.-Nov., 9am-4pm daily Nov.-Mar.) offers a quick lesson on the park's storied past. Interactive exhibits include live demonstrations (cooking or loading a wagon with mining supplies) and gold-panning lessons ($7).

TOP EXPERIENCE

★ Rafting the American River

Coloma is the white-water capital of the Gold Country. Outfitters lead trips on all three forks of the American River, including the rugged Class IV-V rapids of the North Fork and the more moderate Class III-IV white water of the Middle Fork. Rafting trips are designed for all experience levels; overnight and multiday excursions are available. The season runs April-October; trips on the North Fork run April-May or June, depending on weather and water levels.

OUTFITTERS

All-Outdoors Whitewater Rafting (800/247-2387, www.aorafting.com, $113-539) has a variety of trips from half-day, full-day, and multiday trips on the North, Middle, and South Forks of the American River to a few on the Stanislaus River in Southern Gold Country. Full-day trips on all three forks are available, as is the full-day Tom Sawyer Float Trip along the rapids-free section of the South Fork.

Beyond Limits Adventures (530/622-0553 or 800/234-7238, www.rivertrip.com, $89-300) offers half-day and one-day excursions to the North, Middle, and South Forks. Their kayak trips on the South Fork are great for kids and intermediate paddlers. The two-day trips on the South Fork include an overnight at a riverside resort.

American Whitewater Expeditions (530/642-0804 or 800/825-3205, www.americanwhitewater.com, $74-399) specializes in the American River, offering the largest variety of half-day, full-day, and multiday trips to all three forks. Expeditions come with delicious meals, friendly guides, and jaw-dropping Sierra Nevada scenery.

O.A.R.S. (209/736-4677 or 800/346-6277, www.oars.com, $110-320) guides are extremely knowledgeable and lead trips to all three forks of the American River. One-day trips are on the North or Middle Fork; half, full, or two-day trips are on the South Fork, meals included. One day trips on the Stanislaus River in Southern Gold Country are also available.

Whitewater Connection (530/622-6446, www.whitewaterconnection.com, $129-249) offers the half-, full-, and two-day trips to the North, Middle, and South Forks with great options for families. Half-day trips are on the calm "Chili Bar" section of the South Fork.

Food and Accommodations

The ★ **Argonaut** (331 Hwy. 49, 530/626-7345, http://argonautcafe.com, 8am-3pm daily, $4-12) is the best and only place to grab a bite. The homemade sandwiches, soups, and salads charm as much as the café's historic home. Vegan and gluten-free options are available as are gelato and root beer floats.

The **American River Resort** (6019 New River Rd., 530/622-6700, http://americanriverresort.com, cabins $150-250, campsites $15-25, tent cabins $79-99, RV sites $45-50) sits along the South Fork of the American River with 85 campsites (35 spots have RV hookups). Restrooms and showers are available, as is a swimming pool. The six riverside cabins have fully stocked kitchens; bring bed linens.

Transportation

Coloma is on Highway 49, 9 miles north of Placerville and 18 miles south of Auburn. There are no gas stations, and you will have no cell phone reception.

PLACERVILLE

The historic town of Placerville is a haven for antiques hunters. The town serves as jumping-off point for rafting trips, orchards, and wine-tasting. Shops and a few bars line historic Main Street downtown.

Gold Bug Park

The interpretive museum at **Gold Bug Park** (2635 Goldbug Ln., 530/642-5207, www.goldbugpark.org, 10am-4pm daily Apr.-Oct., noon-4pm Sat.-Sun. Nov.-Mar., adults $7, children 3-17 $4, children under 3 free) offers history lessons and tours of the small Hattie mine, which dates from the 1850s. This is a great stop for children, who can pan for gold (fee), don hard hats to check out the mine shaft, and learn the function of a stamp mill.

Food

The **Farm Table** (311 Main St., 530/295-8140, https://ourfarmtable.com, 11am-3pm Mon., 11am-8pm Wed., 11am-9pm Thurs.-Sat., 9am-3pm Sun., $21-39) capitalizes on a farm-to-fork emphasis with dishes of duck confit cassoulet and rabbit potpie, surrounded by seasonal veggies.

Mexican flavors are paired with craft

Placerville was also known as Hangtown.

cocktails and local wine at **Tortilla Flats** (564 Main St., 530/295-9408, www.tortillaflatscantina.com, 11:30am-8pm Sun.-Thurs., 11:30am-9pm Fri.-Sat., $9-15). The menu includes plenty of tacos, burritos, and enchiladas infused with Oaxacan flavors. Tortillas are made from scratch, as are the margaritas.

★ **The Heyday Café** (325 Main St., 530/626-9700, www.heydaycafe.com, 11am-3pm Mon., 11am-9pm Tues.-Thurs., 11am-10pm Fri.-Sat., 11am-8pm Sun., $12-26) is one of the best eateries in Placerville. The California bistro-style food fuses Asian, Italian, and Mediterranean influences. Try the bacon-artichoke-pesto pizza or the lemon salsa skewers.

Start your day at **Sweetie Pie's** (577 Main St., 530/642-0128, www.sweetiepies.biz, 6:30am-3pm Mon.-Fri., 7am-3pm Sat., 7am-1pm Sun., $9-12) with a plate of Belgian waffles, biscuits and gravy, or a turkey and asparagus scramble. Or grab a sticky bun and a cup of coffee to go.

Accommodations

Eden Vale Inn (1780 Springvale Rd., 530/621-0901, http://edenvaleinn.com, $185-448) combines a rustic foothill vibe with Napa-style luxury. Seven rooms come with gas fireplaces and lavish amenities, while five rooms have private hot tubs and enclosed patios. Don't miss the homemade breakfast buffet made from locally grown ingredients and herbs from the inn's garden. The inn is a 10-minute drive from Coloma.

The 1857 **Historic Cary House Hotel** (300 Main St., 530/622-4271, www.caryhouse.com, $130-200) is an imposing brick building in downtown Placerville. The rooms are small but bristle with character, with period antiques and old tintype photographs on the walls. In the elaborately decorated lobby, a 1920s-style elevator lifts visitors to the rooms. Amenities include Wi-Fi, continental breakfast, and cable TV. Guests frequently report ghost sightings and other strange activity—the second floor is supposedly the most haunted. Live bands play most weekends, so noise may be a factor.

Seasons Bed and Breakfast Hotel (2934 Bedford Ave., 530/626-4420, www.theseasons.net, $90-185) has five rooms scattered around the main house and two cottages that once operated as an 1859 stamp mill. All have private bathrooms, and guests enjoy a full hot breakfast each morning. The inn is pet- and child-friendly.

The **Mother Lode Motel** (1940 Broadway, 530/622-0895, www.placervillemotherlodemotel.com, $64-100) has clean and reasonably priced accommodations halfway between Placerville and Apple Hill. Modern amenities include Wi-Fi, microwaves, minifridges, and private hot tubs, as well as a decent-size pool and lounge area.

Transportation and Services

From I-80 at Auburn, drive 27 miles south on Highway 49 to Placerville. Placerville is 45 miles east of Sacramento; take U.S. 50 to the intersection of Highway 49.

For medical assistance, **Marshall Hospital** (1100 Marshall Way, 530/622-1441, www.marshallmedical.org) has an emergency room.

★ APPLE HILL

The farms of **Apple Hill** (Apple Hill Dr./Carson Rd., near Camino, 530/644-7692, www.applehill.com) produce many of the apple varieties grown in California. At some orchards you can pick your own apples in season. At others, you'll find shops stuffed with frozen homemade pies ready to be baked, as well as preserves, cookbooks, and every type of apple product imaginable. In the middle of summer, enjoy raspberries, blackberries, and blueberries. Pumpkins and Christmas trees crop up as fall slides into winter. Events and festivals draw crowds to Apple Hill, including country fair-style activities, arts and crafts shows, and tastings.

Farms

Some of the best apples are at the **Apple Pantry Farm** (2310 Hidden Valley Ln., Camino, 530/318-2834, www.applepantryfarm.com, 10am-4pm Thurs.-Sun., mid-Sept.-mid-Nov.). The farm's small store sells apples and an array of frozen uncooked pies. Next to the main store, a small trailer sells homemade pies whole or by the slice.

At **Able's Acres** (2345 Carson Rd., 530/626-0138, www.abelsappleacres.com, 8:30am-5:30pm Labor Day Weekend-Christmas), pony rides and a maze cap a day spent picking apples. Shop for local produce and gifts, or grab lunch at the grill.

One of Apple Hill's oldest farm stands is **Boa Vista** (2952 Carson Rd., 530/622-5522, www.boavista.com, 7:30am-5:30pm daily). The open-air market is stocked with apples, pies and sweets, local produce, meat, dairy, and eggs. There is even a wine-tasting bar in the back. Grab a grilled chicken sandwich followed by a slice of pie à la mode.

Wineries

The Apple Hill region is home to vineyards and award-winning wineries. Visit the elegant tasting room at **Boeger Winery** (1709 Carson Rd., 530/622-8094, www.boegerwinery.com, 10am-5pm daily, $5-15) for a reserve tasting or bring a picnic to enjoy in the redwood grove. Boeger's specializes in hearty reds with the occasional delicate white wine.

Tiny **Fenton Herriott Vineyards** (120 Jacquier Ct., Placerville, 530/642-2021, www.fentonherriott.com, 11am-5pm daily, free) makes a few hundred cases of wine annually. Stop at the tasting room for a variety of reasonably priced red wines (which you won't find retail) poured by a knowledgeable staff.

Madroña Vineyards (2560 High Hill Rd., Camino, 530/644-5948, www.madronavineyards.com, 11am-5pm daily, free) produces Rhône and Bordeaux varietals, such as barbera and cabernet franc. You'll also find a well-balanced zinfandel among nine wines in the tasting room.

Wofford Acres Vineyards (1900 Hidden Valley Ln., Camino, 530/626-6858 or 888/928-9463, www.wavwines.com, 11am-5pm Thurs.-Sun. Mar.-mid-Dec., noon-4pm Sat.-Sun. Jan.-Feb., free) is owned and operated by the Wofford family, and you're likely to run into one or more Woffords at the small tasting room. Look for low-priced but high-flavored

red table wines, red varietals, and a yummy dessert port.

★ **Lava Cap** (2221 Fruitridge Rd., Placerville, 530/621-0175, 10am-5pm daily, $5) is named for the unique volcanic soil of its vineyards, which, at 2,700 feet, are some of the highest in the state. The estate wines are aromatic and robust, with a nice minerality. Expect mostly reds on the tasting menu, along with a viognier, sauvignon blanc, and a high scoring chardonnay.

Food

Forester Pub & Grill (4110 Carson Rd., Camino, 530/644-1818, www.foresterpubandgrill.com, 11am-9pm daily, $14-26) is an English-style pub serving German-themed food like stroganoff and schnitzel, along with good American comfort food such as meat loaf. Sides include red-cabbage kraut and spätzle with gravy.

Jack Russell Farm Brewery (2380 Larsen Dr., Camino, 530/647-9420, 11am-7pm Mon.-Fri., 10am-7pm Sat.-Sun.) has nearly a dozen beers on tap, plus house-made cider and mead, in addition to local wine. Take your pleasure out onto the patio and enjoy the scenery. Food trucks often park out front on the weekend.

autumn in Apple Hill

Transportation

The Apple Hill area lines U.S. 50, east of Placerville. To get here, take U.S. 50 east from Placerville to exit 48 or 54 onto Apple Hill Drive (also known as Carson Rd.). Carson, North Canyon, Larsen, and Cable Roads have the largest clusters of farms and wineries.

To navigate the country roads and ramble of roadside farms, download a map online (www.applehill.com).

Shenandoah Valley

The Shenandoah Valley is the best-known wine region in Gold Country. Dozens of wineries are near the towns of Plymouth, Fair Play, Amador City, Sutter Creek, Jackson, and tiny Volcano. A part of the Sierra Foothills AVA, the area is best known for its jammy and robust zinfandels. In addition, you'll find plenty of gold rush history, plus a thriving outlaw culture.

To explore the mines that sprouted up here between 1848 and 1890, drive along the Sutter Creek Gold Mine Trail (www.suttercreek.org). Ruins and historical markers dot Highway 49 between Plymouth and Jackson.

PLYMOUTH

Plymouth is the gateway to the Shenandoah wine country. Near the modest Main Street are a couple of tasting rooms that are generally quiet except for the rumble of Harleys riding through town.

Nearly 1,000 different kinds of daylilies grow at the Amador Flower Farm (22001 Shenandoah School Rd., 209/245-6660, www.amadorflowerfarm.com, 9am-4pm daily Mar.-Nov., 9am-4pm Thurs.-Sun. Dec.-Feb.). Take a serene and colorful walk through the eight acres of farmland and four acres of demonstration gardens, flowers, and perennials.

Wineries

Visit the Amador Vintner's Association Visitor Center (9310 Pacific St., 209/245-6992 or 888/655-8614, 9:30am-noon Mon., Wed., and Fri., 10:30am-3pm Sat.-Sun.) for brochures, maps, directions, and advice. In town, the Amador 360 Wine Collective (18590 Hwy. 49, 209/245-6600, www.amador360.com, 11am-6pm Mon.-Fri., 10am-6pm Sat.-Sun.) offers tastings and information about smaller boutique wineries.

At Story Winery (10525 Bell Rd., 209/245-6208 or 800/713-6390, www.zin.com, noon-4pm Mon.-Thurs., 11am-5pm Fri.-Sun., free), you can taste the true history of Amador County. Some of the Story vineyards have been around for nearly 100 years and still produce grapes today. The specialty of the house is zinfandel—check out the amazing selection of old-vine single-vineyard zins.

The friendly folks at Bray Vineyards (10590 Shenandoah Rd., 209/245-6023, www.brayvineyards.com, 10am-5pm Wed.-Mon., $5) pour wines made from verdelho, tempranillo, alicante bouschet, as well as an intriguing blend of Portuguese varietals.

Deaver Vineyards (12455 Steiner Rd., 209/245-4099, www.deavervineyard.com, 10:30am-5pm daily, $5) produces a couple of white and rosé wines, some flavored sparklers, and quite a few ports, but reds are unquestionably the mainstay. Taste a range of intensely layered zins and syrahs, or the award-winning alicante bouschet.

Wilderotter Vineyard (19890 Shenandoah School Rd., 209/245-6016, www.wilderottervineyards.com, 10:30am-5pm daily, $5) started as a vineyard that sold all its grapes to various winemakers. It now bottles its own estate wine as well as a Napa cabernet and a Sonoma sparkling wine. Taste the estate zinfandel, tempranillo, barbera, syrah, and petite syrah in the new tasting room overlooking the vineyards.

Terre Rouge & Easton Wines (10801 Dickson Rd., 209/245-4277, www.

Shenandoah Valley

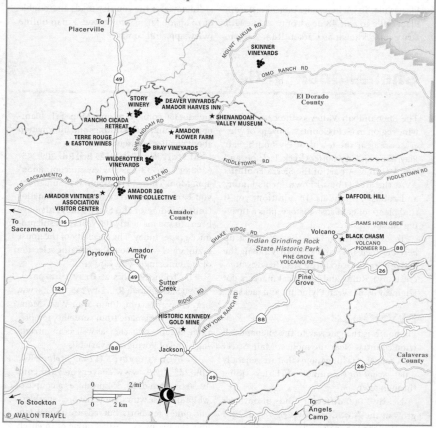

terrerougewines.com, 11am-4pm daily Sept.-Oct., 11am-4pm Thurs.-Mon. Nov.-Aug., $5) credits the volcanic soil for the quality of its 30 different wines. In the friendly tasting room, sample old vine zinfandel and barbera, as well as the delicate pinot noir and cabernet franc.

Food

Set in a modest building off Plymouth's main drag, ★ **Taste Restaurant** (9402 Main St., 209/245-3463, http://restaurant-taste.com, 5pm-9pm Mon.-Tues., and Thurs., 11:30am-2pm and 5pm-9pm Fri., 11:30am-2pm and 4:30pm-9pm Sat.-Sun., $24-42) is

Shenandoah's wine country restaurant recognized by *Wine Spectator* and *Wine Enthusiast*. Taste pairs its menus to the region's wines. Expect meat-heavy fare cooked with French precision.

Marlene and Glen's Diner (18726 Hwy. 49, 209/245-5778, 7am-2:30pm Wed.-Sun., $9-16) is a quirky roadside stop with polished chrome and red leather seats at the counter, homey curios on the wall, and heaping portions of American diner food. The service can be slow on weekends.

Amador Brewing Company (9659 Main St., Plymouth, 209/507-1900, www.

amadorbrewing.com, 2pm-8pm Fri., 11:30am-8pm Sat., 11:30am-6pm Sun.) has a local following. Inside the industrial tasting room, you'll find nearly a dozen beers on tap, including many IPAs. Outside, a rotating schedule of food trucks hawk street food.

Accommodations

The simple farmhouse ★ **Amador Harvest Inn** (12455 Steiner Rd., 800/217-2304, www.amadorharvestinn.com, $150-170) sits next to Deaver Vineyards, surrounded by trees and flowers. Inside, four rooms are decorated in a charming country style; three have private bathrooms. Guests enjoy a hot breakfast in the morning and a glass of Deaver wine in the evening.

Plymouth House Inn (9525 Main St., 209/245-3298, www.plymouthhouseinn.com, $115-180) has seven Victorian-style rooms with woodstoves, handmade antique furniture, and quilted linens, plus air-conditioning and private bathrooms. The inn has a full breakfast in the morning, a complimentary wine hour, and sits on top an old mine shaft where gold was discovered in the late 1800s. Children under 12 are not allowed.

Rancho Cicada Retreat (10001 Bell Rd., 209/245-4841 or 877/553-9481, www.ranchocicadaretreat.com, $45-166) offers both tent cabins ($45-56) and wood-sided cabins ($111-133); most share gender-divided restrooms and a communal kitchen. Two large cabins ($146-166) come with full kitchens, TVs, and linens. The main attraction is the Cosumnes River, where you can swim, float on an inner tube, and fish. Bring sleeping bags, bedding, pillows, towels, and food, plus ice chests for drinks.

Transportation

Plymouth is 20 miles south of Placerville on Highway 49. From Sacramento, take U.S. 50 to Placerville or follow Highway 16 southeast to Highway 49 and head northeast. The wineries line Shenandoah Road East. All highways are two-lane roads that can become packed on weekends.

FAIR PLAY

The Fair Play AVA appellation boasts some of the best vino in the Gold Country.

Wineries

At **Charles B. Mitchell Vineyards** (8221 Stoney Creek Rd., Fair Play, 530/620-3467, http://charlesbmitchell.com, 11am-5pm Wed.-Sun., free), you'll get a chance to sample their

Shenandoah Valley

sparkling, whites, standout zinfandels, and lush dessert ports. Opt for a barrel tasting or tour of the winery, or book ahead to bottle your own wine.

In 1860, a Scottish immigrant named James Skinner planted one of the area's first vineyards. Today, **Skinner Vineyards** (8054 Fairplay Rd., Somerset, 530/620-2220, www.skinnervineyards.com, 11am-5pm Thurs.-Mon., $10-15) is one of the top winemakers in the region. Make an appointment to taste their award-winning Rhône varietals, which include a wide variety of whites, in their relaxed tasting room.

Miraflores (2120 Four Springs Trail, Placerville, 530/647-8505, www.mirafloreswinery.com, 10am-5pm daily, free) produces muscular, focused reds from small lots of syrah and petite syrah. *Wine Spectator* has consistently scored their zinfandel at over 90 points.

Holly's Hill (3680 Leisure Ln., Placerville, 530/344-0227, 10am-5pm daily, free), makes only Rhône wines. Inside the mellow tasting room, sample their delightful viognier, granache, and mourvedre.

Food and Accommodations

Inside **Gold Vine Grill** (6028 Grizzly Flat Rd., Fair Play, 530/626-4042, www.goldvinegrill.com, 5pm-9pm Wed.-Thurs., 11am-3pm and 5pm-9pm Fri.-Sun., $17-30), gleaming wooden tables and exquisite artwork give the restaurant a stylish feel. The elegant California cuisine is mouthwateringly good.

For a quick espresso or a sandwich, stop by **Crossroads Coffee and Cafe** (6032 Grizzly Flat Rd., Somerset, 530/344-0591, 6am-3pm Fri.-Sat., 7am-1pm Sat.-Sun., $6-9). They serve a variety of breakfast dishes and sandwiches along with espresso drinks.

Lucinda's Country Inn (6701 Perry Creek Rd., Fair Play, 530/409-4169, www.lucindascountryinn.com, $160-230) welcomes visitors with five rooms, each with a fireplace, fridge, microwave, coffeemaker, and a flat-screen TV. Some rooms boast a private deck and a

two-person spa tub. A hot complimentary breakfast buffet is included.

At the **Seven-Up Guest Ranch** (8060 Fairplay Rd., Fair Play, 530/620-5450 or 800/717-5450, www.sevenupguestranch.com, $160-175), three log cabins and one main house fill a rustic property near Skinner Vineyards. Each cabin has two rooms, with private baths, a fridge, microwave, porch, and frontier charm. Breakfast is served each morning in the main house.

Transportation

Fair Play sits between Placerville and Plymouth, at the north edge of the Shenandoah Valley. From Plymouth, take Highway 16 east for 18 miles. From Placerville, follow Bucks Bar Road for 5 miles south to Somerset, then turn right on Highway 16 south.

AMADOR CITY

Amador City lies off Highway 49 north of Sutter Creek. The tiny enclave is worth the detour.

Food and Accommodations

Eating at ★ **Andrae's Bakery** (14141 Old Hwy. 49, 209/267-1352, www.andraesbakery.com, 7:30am-4pm Thurs.-Sun., $8-12) feels like eating at grandma's house. Order the gourmet sandwiches for lunch and a pastry for dessert. The cookies are dangerously good, but the seasonal scones are worth the trip.

The **Imperial Hotel** (14202 Old Hwy. 49, 209/267-9172, www.imperialamador.com, $120-195) has the brick facade and architecture of a classic 1879 Old West hotel. You'll get a true mining town experience in one of six rooms on the second floor or in one of three rooms in the 1930s cottage out back, which include private baths. Each room is a haven of peace and quiet, without TVs or phones.

The downstairs **restaurant** (dinner 5pm-9pm Tues.-Sun., brunch 9:30am-2:30pm Sat.-Sun., $14-34) serves a hot breakfast (8am-10am) included in the room rate.

SUTTER CREEK

Sutter Creek is a Gold Country gem. Most of the town structures hark back to the 19th century, and the town itself is listed as a California Historic Landmark. **Main Street** is lined with cluttered antiques shops filled with treasures great and small.

The **Monteverde Store Museum** (11A Randolph St., 209/267-1344, www.suttercreek. org, by appointment) sold staples to Sutter Creek residents for 75 years. After shopkeepers Mary and Rose Monteverde died, the city took over the building. The sisters had stipulated that it was to become a museum, and so it is—a look into the hub of town life in the 19th century.

Food

Gold Dust Pizza (20 Eureka St., 209/267-1900, 11am-8pm Mon.-Thurs., 11am-9pm Fri.-Sat., $15-25) is a local chain that serves the best pizza in Amador in one of the best settings. The pizza is heaped with toppings, and the cheese-covered breadsticks are just as famous. If the weather is nice, take a table on the outside patio.

Element (Hanford House Inn, 61 Hanford St., 209/267-0747, 8am-11am Mon. and Wed.-Fri., 8am-1pm Sat.-Sun., $9-13) serves elegant and creative breakfast and lunch items that include apple-fritter waffles, caramelized bacon, and quinoa with roasted cauliflower in a spare setting.

The polished interior of the **Hotel Sutter** (53 Main St., 209/267-0242, www.hotelsutter. com, 11am-8pm Sun.-Thurs., 11am-9pm Fri.-Sat., $13-32) reflects the food: well-prepared, meat-heavy fare. Choose from tasty burgers, savory sandwiches, or hearty dinner entrées like rack of lamb lollipops.

Provisions (78 Main St., 209/267-8034, 2pm-8pm Wed.-Fri., noon-8pm Sat., noon-6pm Sun., $8-10) is the place to stock up on supplies in Sutter Creek. Grab sandwiches, browse the eclectic foodie wares, or stay for a pint of local beer and an afternoon of live music.

Accommodations

The **Hotel Sutter** (53 Main St., 209/267-0242, www.hotelsutter.com, $121-175) was established in 1848, but its 21 rooms have since been stylishly remodeled to reflect current tastes with colorful nods to its Victorian past. Amenities include private bathrooms, flat-screen TVs, and free Wi-Fi. The on-site **restaurant** (11am-8pm Sun.-Thurs., 11am-9pm Fri.-Sat., $13-32) is a great place to grab dinner. The **Lobby Bar** (11am-9pm Sun.-Thurs., 11am-10pm Fri.-Sat.) pours craft cocktails, local wine, and cold beer.

Hanford House (61 Hanford St., 209/267-0747, www.hanfordhouse.com, $185-325) is a brick manor with nine rooms featuring flat-screen TVs, fireplaces, and stylish appointments; some rooms offer a private deck with a small hot tub. Massage and spa services are also available. Breakfast at the on-site **Element** restaurant is included in the room rate.

Each of the nine rooms at the **Grey Gables Inn** (161 Hanford St., 209/267-1039, www. greygables.com, $158-350) are named after 19th-century writers. Rooms are decked out in Victorian finery, and each has its own bathroom. The carriage house features two large suites with TVs, coffeemakers, private patios, and refrigerators. Guests enjoy a sumptuous hot breakfast each morning.

Transportation

Sutter Creek is 10 miles south of Plymouth and 5 miles north of Jackson on Highway 49. From Placerville, head south on Highway 49 for 30 miles to Sutter Creek.

JACKSON

Jackson marks the boundary between Northern and Southern Gold Country. It's the largest town in the region with a charming historic downtown that is a bit rougher around the edges. You'll find plenty of services and a few strip malls.

Historic Kennedy Gold Mine

The **Historic Kennedy Gold Mine** (12594 Kennedy Mine Rd., 209/223-9542, www.kennedygoldmine.com, 10am-3pm Sat.-Sun. Mar.-Oct., free) is a great place to learn about life in a California gold mine. The Kennedy Mine was one of the deepest hard-rock gold mines in the state, extending more than a mile into the earth.

Join a docent-led **tour** (1.5 hours, adults $10, children 6-12 $6, children under 6 free) and see the stately Mine House, marvel at the size of the head frame, and learn how a stamp mill worked to free the gold from the rocks.

Food and Accommodations

Stay in the heart of historic Jackson at the **National Hotel** (2 Water St., 209/223-0500, www.nationalhoteljackson.com, $75-250). Rooms in the historic hotel have large, comfy beds with private marble bathrooms, flat-screen TVs, and free Wi-Fi. You'll still get lace and antiques in every room and rumors of the resident ghost.

More *Californio* than gold rush, **El Campo Casa** (12548 Kennedy Flat Rd., 209/223-0100, http://elcampocasa.com, $58-118) has a mid-century motel vibe. The 15 simple rooms are somewhat spartan and the baths are a little cozy, but the rates are very affordable with access to an outdoor pool and a shady patio area.

The **Stanley's Steak House** (National Hotel, 2 Water St., 209/223-0500, www.nationalhoteljackson.com, 11am-3pm and 5pm-9pm Wed.-Thurs., 11am-3pm and 5pm-10pm Fri.-Sat., 10am-3pm and 5pm-9pm Sun., $18-44) serves hearty lunches and dinners with decadent dishes like the 35-day bourbon dry-aged steak and bacon-wrapped salads. Swing by the **bar** (11am-9pm Sun. and Wed.-Thurs., 11am-10pm Fri.-Sat.) for a true Jackson experience.

The **Mother Lode Market and Deli** (36 Main St., 209/223-0652, 8am-3:30pm Mon.-Sat., $5-8) is a local institution that serves down-home meals with some local history. Everything on the standard menu is prepared from scratch.

Transportation and Services

Jackson lies near the intersection of Highway 49 (north-south) and Highway 88 (east-west). It's 4.5 miles south of Sutter Creek and 28 miles north of Angels Camp on Highway 49. Both highways become congested in summer and on weekends.

For medical emergencies, visit **Sutter Amador Hospital** (200 Mission Blvd., 209/223-7500, www.sutteramador.org).

VOLCANO

Despite its name, tiny Volcano has no link to volcanic activity. (The miners who settled here in 1849 thought this bowl-shaped valley was formed by a volcano.) A number of gold rush buildings survive, and the entire town is listed as a California Historic Landmark.

Black Chasm Caverns

Black Chasm Caverns (15701 Volcano-Pioneer Rd., 209/296-5007, 10am-5pm daily summer, 10am-4pm daily fall and spring, 11am-3pm Mon.-Fri., 10am-4pm Sat.-Sun. winter, adults $17.50, children 12 and under $9.50) is home to an immense chasm filled with amazing calcite formations. In the Landmark Room, check out the rare helictite formations (a crystalline cave formation) that made Black Chasm famous.

Tours last 45 minutes and depart hourly from the visitors center. (Strollers or wheelchairs cannot be accommodated.)

Daffodil Hill

Each March, **Daffodil Hill** (18310 Rams Horn Grade, 209/296-7048, daily mid-Mar.-mid-Apr., free) explodes into a profusion of sunny yellow that lasts for one month. Daffodil Hill is the private working ranch of the McLaughlin family, who have been planting daffodil bulbs on their property since 1887; it now boasts approximately 300,000 blooms. Daffodil Hill is open to the public only during daffodil season. Exact opening and closing dates vary annually; call ahead to confirm. Parking can be scarce.

Indian Grinding Rock State Historic Park

Indian Grinding Rock State Historic Park (14881 Pine Grove-Volcano Rd., 209/296-7488, www.parks.ca.gov, sunrise-sunset daily, $8/vehicle) is dedicated to indigenous Californians and focuses on the history of the state before the European influx. The park celebrates the life and culture of the Northern Sierra Miwok who inhabited these foothills for centuries. The park's focal point is a huge grinding rock used by the Miwok women who lived in the adjacent meadow and forest. The dozens of divots in the rock, plus the fading petroglyphs drawn over generations, attest to the lengthy use of this chunk of marble.

Start your visit in the visitors center (10am-4pm daily), then follow the South Trail past the grinding rock to the reconstructed roundhouse, a sacred space in use by local Miwoks. Walk farther toward the Miwok village, where you can enter the dwellings to see how these native Californians once lived. For a longer hike, the North Trail winds around most of the park.

The park is 12 miles east of Jackson.

Food and Accommodations

The Union Inn and Pub (21375 Consolation St., 209/296-7711, www.volcanounion.com, $95-130) has four rooms with private bathrooms and stylish modern touches. Amenities include flat-screen TVs and radios with iPod docks; some rooms have sunken porcelain tubs. A gourmet breakfast is served daily. Children and pets are not allowed.

Some of the best food in town is served at the inn's Union Pub (5pm-8pm Mon. and Thurs., 5pm-9pm Fri., noon-9pm Sat., noon-8pm Sun., $10-29) with oyster nights, gourmet snacks, gut-busting burgers, California wine, and plenty of beer.

In operation since 1867 (and rumored to be haunted), the venerable St. George Hotel (16104 Main St., 209/296-4458, www.stgeorgevolcano.com, $75-209) has a hodgepodge of 14 second- and third-floor rooms and a bungalow in the back; only two of the rooms in the main building and the bungalow have private baths. Rooms have polished wood floors and antique-styled bedsteads.

On the ground floor of the St. George Hotel, the Whiskey Flat Saloon (4pm-close Tues.-Fri., 10am-close Sat., 9am-close Sun.) serves stiff drinks and a pub menu. The hotel restaurant (5pm-8pm Wed.-Thurs., 5pm-9pm Fri., 9am-9pm Sat., 9am-8pm Sun., $11-30) offers standard-issue burgers, chicken, and steak.

Pitch a tent at Indian Grinding Rock State Historic Park (14881 Pine Grove-Volcano Rd., Pine Grove, 800/444-7275, www.reservecalifornia.com, $30). The 22 shaded sites each have a fire pit and picnic table. Flush toilets and coin-operated showers are available.

Transportation and Services

Volcano is 12.5 miles east of Jackson along Highway 88. Take Highway 88 northeast for about nine miles; turn left on Pine Grove-Volcano Road. Volcano will appear in about three miles. Due to the higher elevation, Volcano often has heavy snowfall in winter, and chains may be required.

You won't find much in the way of services. Gas up and get cash before leaving Jackson.

Southern Gold Country

Southern Gold Country runs south from Jackson and includes the towns of Angels Camp, Murphys, Sonora, Columbia, Jamestown, and Arnold. The area is filled with caves, giant trees, excellent wine, and living history.

ANGELS CAMP

Readers of Mark Twain will recognize Angels Camp as the place where the writer first heard the tale of a frog-jumping contest that inspired his famous story "The Celebrated Jumping Frog of Calaveras County." Angels Camp remains preserved in the time of Twain and is a registered California Historic Landmark.

Angels Camp Museum and Carriage House

Inside the **Angels Camp Museum and Carriage House** (753 S. Main St., 209/736-2963, www.angelscamp.gov, 10am-4pm Wed.-Mon., adults $7, children 5-11 $3, children under 5 free), you'll see meticulously preserved artifacts of the mining era. Outside is old mining equipment, including the huge waterwheel that sits in its original location of the Angels Quartz Mine. The Carriage House shelters more than 30 horse-powered vehicles of the 19th and early 20th centuries and is the largest collection in the country. Better restored than many similar displays, the carriages and wagons here show off the elegance and function of true horse-powered transportation. History comes alive on select Saturdays when docents don period garb and demonstrate the crafts of carpentry, printing, and textile making.

Moaning Cavern

The haunting sounds of **Moaning Cavern** (5350 Moaning Cave Rd., Vallecito, 209/736-2708, www.caverntours.com, 9am-6pm daily summer, 10am-4pm Mon.-Fri. and 9am-5pm Sat.-Sun. fall, 11am-4pm Mon.-Fri.,

10am-5pm Sat.-Sun. winter, 11am-4pm Mon.-Fri., 10am-5pm Sat.-Sun. spring, adults $17.50, children 3-12 $9.50) can still be heard in this enchanting cave. Come in spring to hear Moaning Cavern's "chamber" orchestra, when rainy weather guarantees a cacophony of underground sounds.

Tours include the **Adventure Tour** (2 hours, adults and children 12 and up, $95), which navigates narrow passageways in the depths of the cavern. For thrills above ground, hop on a **zipline** ($45) or scale the 32-foot-high **climbing wall** ($5).

Calaveras County Fair and Jumping Frog Jubilee

At the **Calaveras County Fair and Jumping Frog Jubilee** (209/736-2561, www.frogtown.org, third weekend in May, adults $8-15, youth $5-10, frog jumping $5, parking $6), you'll see literally thousands of frogs leaping toward victory and a $5,000 cash prize. Other fair activities include livestock shows, baking contests, auctions, historical readings, and exhibits, plus plenty of fair food and camping.

Food and Accommodations

Mike's Pizza (294 S. Main St., 209/736-9246, www.mikespizzaangelscamp.com, 11am-9pm Mon.-Thurs., 11am-10 pm Fri.-Sun., $9-25) whips up the finest pies in town. The interior oozes an old-fashioned pizza parlor vibe with dark-paneled walls, arcade games, and glowing neon signs. There's plenty of other pub grub like burgers, pasta, and ribs, as well as a salad bar.

Crusco's (1240 S. Main St., 209/736-1440, 11:30am-9pm Thurs.-Mon., $17-32) serves hearty homemade Italian food with a Californian flair. Enjoy old-world hospitality and attentive service from the owner, who is often on hand to greet customers.

For breakfast, squeeze into tiny **Angels**

Southern Gold Country

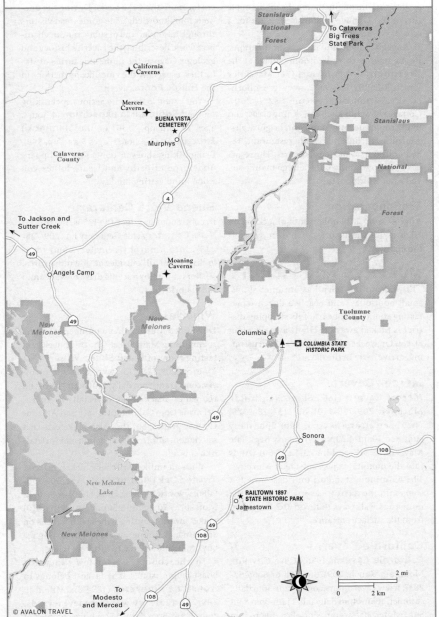

Stanislaus
National
Forest

To Calaveras
Big Trees
State Park

★ California
Caverns

4

Mercer ★
Caverns

**BUENA VISTA
CEMETERY**
★

Murphys

Stanislaus

Calaveras
County

National

4

Forest

To Jackson and
Sutter Creek

49

Moaning ★
Caverns

Angels Camp

Tuolumne
County

New
Melones

49

New
Melones

New
Melones

Columbia

★ COLUMBIA STATE
HISTORIC PARK

49

Sonora

108

49

New Melones
Lake

RAILTOWN 1897
★ STATE HISTORIC PARK
Jamestown

108

49

New Melones

108

49

To
Modesto
and Merced

0   2 mi

0   2 km

© AVALON TRAVEL

Creek Café (1246 S. Main St., 209/736-2941, 7am-2pm Fri.-Wed., $8-13) where everything on the small menu (including the divine apple turnovers) is made in-house. Prepare for a crowd on weekends.

Angels Camp is thin on accommodations. Rent a two- or three-bedroom cottage at the **Greenhorn Creek Resort** (711 McCauley Ranch Rd., 209/736-9372, www.greenhorncreekvacationcottages.com, $200-260). Cottages have full kitchens, dining areas, and living rooms decorated in light, bright styles. Amenities include an on-site restaurant, 18-hole golf course, and tennis courts. The resort has a shallow family pool, a large main pool, and a hot whirlpool tub.

Transportation

Angels Camp is 28 miles south of Jackson on Highway 49; the historic downtown is just off the highway.

MURPHYS AND VICINITY

This old mining town has antiques shops, small boutiques, and nearly a dozen wine-tasting rooms. The heart of its shopping district is tucked away off Highway 4 on Main Street. On weekends, parking can be frustrating; arrive early in the day.

Mercer Cavern

Mercer Cavern (1665 Sheep Ranch Rd., Murphys, 209/728-2101 or 415/728-2378, www.mercercaverns.com, 9am-5pm daily summer, 10am-4:30pm daily early Sept.-late May, adults $17, children 3-12 $9.50) winds into the mountains just outside of Murphys. The 45-minute standard tour descends 172 steps into the narrow cavern, crowding the numerous walkways that run 162 feet down from the surface entrance.

California Caverns

California Caverns (9565 Cave City Rd., Mountain Ranch, 209/736-2708 or 866/762-2837, www.caverntours.com, 10am-5pm daily summer, 10am-4pm daily fall, 11am-3pm Sat.-Sun. winter, 10am-4pm Mon.-Fri., 10am-5pm

Sat.-Sun. spring, adults $17.50, children 3-12 $9.50) has welcomed underground explorers for more than 150 years. During the one-hour tour, knowledgeable guides lead visitors through a wonderland of subterranean chambers while describing the cavern's history and geology. Gaze at the numerous forms of stalactites, especially the vine-like formations in the **Jungle Room** cavern.

You can also do some serious spelunking on the **Middle Earth Expedition** (4 hours, ages 16 and up, $130) or the **Mammoth Expedition** (2-3 hours, ages 8 and up, $99). Bring hiking shoes or boots for the slippery underground paths and wear clothes you won't mind getting muddy.

Buena Vista Cemetery

In continuous use since the 1850s, the **Buena Vista Cemetery** (186 Cemetery Ln., 209/728-2387, http://murphyscemetery.com) overlooks a small hill outside the downtown area. Visitors can enjoy a scenic drive or walk amid the historic rows.

Wineries

Downtown Murphys has a number of tasting rooms lining Main Street. The tiny but elegant tasting room of **Black Sheep Winery** (221 Main St., 209/728-2157, www.blacksheepwinery.com, 11am-5pm daily, $10) pours high-end red wines. Black Sheep's specialty is zinfandel made from Calaveras County and Amador County grapes, but they also make cabernet sauvignon, shiraz, and more unusual varietals like cinsault.

With an unlikely rubber-chicken mascot, **Twisted Oak Winery** (363 Main St., 209/736-9080, www.twistedoak.com, 11:30am-5:30pm Mon.-Fri., 10:30am-5:30pm Sat.-Sun., $10) makes award-winning wines with a focus on Spanish and Rhône varietals. The tasting fee buys the option to try 15 different wines.

In the countryside, a few vineyards boast major estates. The largest belongs to **Ironstone Vineyards** (1894 Six Mile Rd., 209/728-1251, www.ironstonevineyards.com, 11am-5pm daily, $5), a huge complex of vineyards, winery buildings, a museum, an amphitheater, and gardens. Inside the vast tasting room are three bars. A regular tasting includes any number of wines (most priced at $10/bottle).

Rafting

Murphys is within a short ride of the churning North Fork of the Stanislaus River, which offers intermediate-advanced white-water rafting trips through roaring Class III-IV rapids. The season runs mid-April-May, weather and river conditions permitting.

All-Outdoors Whitewater Rafting (800/247-2387, www.aorafting.com, $179) runs full-day trips on the North Fork of the Stanislaus. You can plunge through Class IV rapids with hair-raising names like Beginner's Luck, Rattlesnake, and Maycheck's Mayhem; the last rapid is a partial Class V drop. You can also take full-day and two-day trips on the calmer South Fork of the American River.

O.A.R.S. (209/736-4677 or 800/346-6277, www.oars.com, Apr.-June, $149-179) offers trips on the Stanislaus River, where it churns through Calaveras Big Trees State Park. Guides are knowledgeable and friendly; lunch is provided. O.A.R.S. also offers half-, full-, and two-day excursions on the South Fork of the American River.

Food

Grounds (402 Main St., 209/728-8663, www.groundsrestaurant.com, 7am-3pm Mon.-Tues., 7am-3pm and 5pm-8pm Wed.-Thurs., 7am-3pm and 5pm-9pm Fri.-Sat., 8am-3pm and 5pm-8pm Sun., $17-32) is one of the best places to eat in Murphys. Have an omelet for breakfast, a savory sandwich for lunch, or plates of elk, coho salmon, and mushroom risotto for dinner. The extensive wine list is filled with local selections and the full bar makes craft cocktails. Reservations are recommended.

At **V Restaurant** (Victoria Inn, 402 Main St., 209/728-0107, http://vrestaurantandbarmurphys.com, 5:30pm-8pm Wed.-Thurs., 5:30pm-9pm Fri.-Sun., $25-40) elegant upscale American fare is served in a charming atmosphere. For something more casual, the **Bistro** (11:30am-8:30pm Mon.-Wed., 8am-8:30pm Thurs.-Sun., $11-30) serves burgers, fish-and-chips, and mac and cheese for dinner, plus a variety of Benedicts with Bloody Marys for breakfast.

Murphys Pourhouse (350 Main St., 209/822-3942, 11am-8pm Sun.-Mon. and

wine country charm in Murphys

Calaveras Big Trees State Park

Highlights of **Calaveras Big Trees State Park** (1170 E. Hwy. 4, three miles east of Arnold, 209/795-2334, www.parks.ca.gov, sunrise-sunset daily, $10) include the North and South Groves of rare giant sequoia trees. The clustered **North Grove** has an easy 1.5-mile interpretive trail, while the **South Grove** offers a longer five-mile hike past the park's largest trees: the Agassiz Tree and the Palace Hotel Tree. Beyond the sequoias, you can hike and swim in 6,000 acres of pine forest crisscrossed with trails and pretty groves set up for picnicking. Take a dip in the cool, refreshing Stanislaus River running through the trees, or cast a line out to try to catch a rainbow trout.

The **visitors center** (209/795-3840, 10am-4pm daily) has trail maps, exhibits, and artifacts depicting different periods in California history. In winter, many of the roads through the park are closed.

There are two seasonal **campgrounds** (800/444-7275, www.reservecalifornia.com, $35) for tents and RVs and four **cabins** (sleeps six, $185) with full kitchens and bathrooms. The **North Grove Campground** (Apr.-Nov.) lies close to the park entrance on Highway 4 with 74 sites. **Oak Hollow Campground** (May-Oct.) is four miles inside the park with 55 sites set on a quiet hill. All campsites include a fire ring, a picnic table, and parking. Flush toilets, coin-operated showers, and drinking water are available. Reservations are accepted up to seven months in advance and are strongly recommended in summer. Off-season, campsites are first-come, first-served.

Wed.-Thurs., 11am-9pm Fri.-Sat., $8-20) has plenty of beers on tap from around California plus deli sandwiches and a kid's menu. Outdoor tables make this the place to be on sunny afternoon, and dogs are always welcome.

Accommodations

The **Victoria Inn** (402 Main St., 209/728-8933, www.victoriainn-murphys.com, $178-324) is a B&B with modern amenities and Victorian touches such as claw-foot tubs, antique furniture, and rich linens. Each of the 13 rooms has its own bathroom; some have private sitting areas, balconies, and fireplaces. Enjoy a meal downstairs at the excellent **Bistro** and **V Restaurant.**

The **Dunbar House 1880 Bed and Breakfast** (271 Jones St., 209/728-2897, www.dunbarhouse.com, $199-299) has six rooms with modern comforts and Victorian decor, plus a private bathroom; some rooms come with a secluded private patio. Enjoy a delicious hot breakfast with homemade baked goods, coffee, tea, and specially blended hot chocolate.

For a no-frills stay downtown, **Murphys Inn Motel** (76 Main St., 209/728-1818 or 888/796-1800, www.murphysinnmotel.com, $93-189) has 37 rooms; most have two queen beds furnished and decorated in a traditional style. The outdoor pool and complimentary Oreos are a bonus.

Transportation and Services

Murphys is eight miles northeast of Angels Camp along Highway 4.

COLUMBIA

Columbia is a perfectly preserved gold rush town complete with restaurants, shops, and docents dressed in period garb. It can get hot in the summer and cold in winter, and you'll be on your feet a lot, so dress accordingly.

★ Columbia State Historic Park

A walk down Main Street in **Columbia State Historic Park** (11255 Jackson St., 209/588-9128, www.parks.ca.gov, 10am-5pm daily year-round, free) is a stroll into California's boomtown past. Gold was discovered here in the spring of 1850, and the town sprang up as miners flowed in. It inevitably declined as the gold ran out; in 1945, the state took over and created the state historic park. Today, you can wander the streets, poking your head into the exhibits and shops selling an array of period and modern items. Imagine the multiculturalism of another age in the Chinese Store Exhibit or try your hand at gold panning. Or sign up for docent-led **tours** (11am daily summer, 11am Sat.-Sun. Sept.-May) to see it all.

At the **Columbia Museum** (Main St. and State St., 209/532-3184, 10am-4pm daily, free) you'll see artifacts of the mining period, from miners' equipment and clothing to household objects used by women who lived in the bustling city.

Shops

The gift shops in park's old buildings are mostly old-timey shops staffed by costumed clerks. At the **Fancy Dry Goods and Clothing Store** (22733 Main St., 209/532-1066, 10am-5pm Tues.-Sun. summer, 10am-5pm Wed.-Sun. winter), browse the "supplies" on hand like a true forty-niner, everything from bonnets and calico dresses to men's hats.

Step back in time at **Kamice's Photographic Establishment** (22729 Main St., 209/532-4861, www.photosincolumbia.com, 10am-5pm daily summer, 10am-5pm Thurs.-Mon. winter) for a sepia-toned portrait dressed like a true pioneer.

Ebler's Leather and Saddlery Emporium (22751 Main St., 209/532-1811, 10am-5pm daily) sells everything leather, from belts to slippers to saddles, as well as wool shirts, gifts and novelties, and Native American crafts.

Book lovers shouldn't pass up the **Columbia Booksellers & Stationers** (2725 Main St., 209/533-1852, www.columbiagazette.com, 10am-5pm daily), where a mix of rare and used books share the shelves with modern titles about the gold rush and the West.

Nelson's Columbia Candy Kitchen (22726 Main St., 209/532-7886, www.columbiacandykitchen.com, 9am-5pm Mon.-Fri., 9am-6pm Sat.-Sun.) has been serving candy for more than 100 years.

Food and Accommodations

Step through the swinging doors of the **Jack Douglass Saloon** (22718 Main St., 209/533-4176, 10am-6pm daily, $8-13) and order a cold beer at the bar or cool down at a table with a sarsaparilla. Hot and cold sandwiches are available. Food is also available at the **What Cheer Saloon** (209/532-1486, 11am-8pm), where burgers, beer, wine, and contemporary cocktails are served late into the night.

Columbia State Historic Park

The most popular restaurant in town is the **City Hotel Restaurant** (22768 Main St., 209/532-5964, www.cityhotelrestaurant.com, 11am-2pm and 5pm-8pm Wed.-Sun., $13-38), which serves fresh California cuisine, along with an affordable kid's menu.

After all the fun, book a room upstairs at the **City Hotel** (209/532-1479, reservations 800/444-7275 or www.reservecalifornia.com, $93-126), which has 10 antique-filled rooms, each with its own toilet and sink. Shared showers are down the hall. Near the City Hotel, three **cottages** (800/444-7275, www.reservecalifornia.com, $126-170) come with complete kitchens and bathrooms.

On the outskirts of town, **Columbia Kate's** (22727 Columbia St., 209/532-1885, www.columbiakates.com, bakery 8am-4pm daily, teahouse 11am-4pm daily, $8-13) is a cozy English-style teahouse with country hospitality. Eat a hearty lunch of sandwiches, salads, or hot comfort food like meat loaf and chicken potpie, or stop by for a full afternoon tea with scones.

Old West-style accommodations in town are at the **Fallon Hotel** (11175 Washington St., 800/444-7275, www.reservecalifornia.com, $93-126), near the park's southern boundary. The 15 cozy rooms feature Victorian-style wallpaper, handmade furniture, gold rush-era photos, double beds, sinks and toilets; showers down the hall.

Transportation

Columbia is 15 miles southeast of Angels Camp along Highway 49.

SONORA

Sonora is a gateway to Yosemite and the stunning Sonora Pass. The **Tuolumne County Museum** (158 Bradford St., 209/532-1317, www.tchistory.org, 10am-4pm Mon.-Tues. and Thurs.-Fri., 1pm-4pm Wed., 10am-3:30pm Sat., 11am-2pm Sun., donations only) in the old Sonora jailhouse houses a number of exhibits inside the jail cells. One cell has been recreated as an exhibit of what

incarceration might have been like in 19th-century Tuolumne County (hint: unpleasant).

Food and Accommodations

The ★ **Diamondback Grill** (93 S. Washington St., 209/532-6661, www.thediamondbackgrill.com, 11am-9pm Mon.-Thurs., 11am-9:30pm Fri.-Sat., 11am-8pm Sun., $11-19) serves grill food at reasonable prices. Everyone loves the burgers and the sweet potato fries, and the Asian style barbecue ribs are a treat. Fresh salads stand in for entrées, while the wine bar offers varietal flights. Expect a wait, especially on weekends.

Housed in a small historic building, **Talulah's** (13 S. Washington St., 209/532-7278, 11:30am-2:30pm and 5pm-8:30pm Tues.-Thurs., 5pm-9pm Friday, noon-3pm and 5pm-8:30pm Sat., $11-20) serves pretty plates of New American food. Expect a variety of sandwiches for lunch, including po'boys and pulled pork. Dinner is dominated by pasta and locally raised meat.

Legends (131 S. Washington St., 209/532-8120, 11am-5pm daily, $5-8) is a bookstore, coffee bar, and old-fashioned soda fountain. Grab some ice cream or an espresso while browsing rare books and antiques.

For history in your hotel room, you can't beat the **Gunn House Hotel** (286 S. Washington St., 209/532-3421, http://gunnhousehotel.com, $84-140), where a dozen rooms feature antiques, floral wallpaper, and Victorian touches. All have private bathrooms, TVs, and full heating and air-conditioning. A sumptuous Innkeeper's Breakfast buffet is included.

The **Bradford Place Inn** (56 W. Bradford St., 209/536-6075, www.bradfordplaceinn.com, $145-265) has smaller, Victorian-esque accommodations in five rooms decorated with 19th-century touches. Rooms include private baths, flat-screen TVs, and Wi-Fi. Two larger suites have fireplaces and private patios. A hot breakfast can be served on the veranda or in your room.

Side Trip: Highway 108

TWAIN HARTE

The rustic foothill hamlet of Twain Harte is an excellent day trip or overnight excursion from Sonora. A visit here is about getting away from traffic and city life to enjoy fresh, pine-scented air in the Sierra Nevada high country.

Bring your sweet tooth to brave diet-destroying menus at the Sportsman Coffee Shop (22978 Joaquin Gully Rd., 209/586-5448, www.sportsmantwainharte.com, 7am-2pm daily, $7-13). Sportsman serves up a no-nonsense breakfast with hearty omelets and buckwheat pancakes. Farm-to-fork dining is delicious at CiBO Famiglia (23036 Joaquin Gully Rd., 209/651-1101, www.cibofamiglia.com, 11:30am-2pm and 5pm-8pm Wed.-Thurs., 11:30am-2pm and 5pm-9pm Fri.-Sat., 10am-2pm and 5pm-8pm Sun., $15-32), with Italian-inspired food and a hip interior.

McCaffrey House (23251 Hwy. 108, 209/586-0757, www.mccaffreyhouse.com, $169-219) is a warm, country-style lodge with cheerful Craftsman decor and handmade Amish linens and furniture in eight rooms with private bathrooms, fireplaces, and TVs; some rooms are dog-friendly. A hot gourmet breakfast is served every morning.

Gables Cedar Creek Inn (22560 Twain Harte Dr., 209/586-3008, www.gccinn.com, $105-140) has intimate cabins tucked away in fragrant ponderosa and cedar groves. Some cabins have kitchenettes.

PINECREST LAKE

The U.S. Forest Service stocks Pinecrest Lake (Hwy. 108, 30 miles east of Sonora, www.fs.fed.us) with rainbow trout. Bring your pole and bait to the pier or launch a boat and explore the lake. The on-site Pinecrest Campground (Pinecrest Lake Rd., 877/444-6777, www.recreation.gov, May-Oct., $26) has almost 200 campsites as well as rental cabins.

DODGE RIDGE

In winter, hit the slopes at the small Dodge Ridge Ski Resort (1 Dodge Ridge Rd., Pinecrest, 209/965-3474, www.dodgeridge.com, 9am-4pm daily winter, adults $64-74, children 13-19 $52-59, children 6-12 $20-25, children under 6 free), which has beginner and advanced-beginner runs, as well as for intermediate and advanced skiers and boarders.

KENNEDY MEADOWS

At Kennedy Meadows Resort and Pack Station (Hwy. 108, Kennedy Meadows, 209/965-3911 in summer, 209/965-3900 in winter, www.kennedymeadows.com, $55–85), visitors ride on horseback through alpine meadows and forest groves on guided trips. Trips range from 75 minutes to multiday pack trips. Order a classic American breakfast, lunch, and dinner at the restaurant (6am-4pm and 5pm-9pm daily, $11-23), or book a cabin ($80-190) for a longer stay.

CAMPING

Forest Service campgrounds (Stanislaus National Forest, www.fs.usda.gov) line scenic Highway 108 all the way up to Sonora Pass. There are too many to list here, but favorites include Brightman, Dardanelle, and Boulder Flat. Highway 108 closes to snow in winter, so most campsites are first-come, first-served May-October.

GETTING THERE

Twain Harte is about 12 miles east of Sonora and Jamestown on Highway 108. Since the town is perched at an altitude of 3,600 feet, Twain Harte definitely gets a heavy dusting of snow every winter. Make sure you carry chains if traveling in this area during winter.

Transportation

Sonora is about 15 miles south of Angels Camp on Highway 49. It's near Colombia on Highway 49, just north of its intersection to Highway 108.

JAMESTOWN

Jamestown marks the southern end of the Gold Country. Its charming downtown hosts a collection of gold rush-era buildings that have made the town a California Historic Landmark.

Railtown 1897 State Historic Park

Railtown 1897 State Historic Park (10501 Reservoir Rd., 209/984-3953, www.railtown1897.org, 9:30am-4:30pm daily Apr.-Oct., 10am-3pm daily Nov.-Mar., train tickets: adults $15, children 6-17 $10, children under 6 free) is home to a working blacksmith, machine shop, and roundhouse that have been servicing trains since the turn of the last century.

The **museum** (adults $5, children 6-17 $3, children under 6 free) is located inside the old depot waiting room with artifacts and an informative video. Prize locomotives sit in the century-old **roundhouse.** Behind the roundhouse, check out the functioning turntable, then wander out to the rolling stock.

Train buffs can board a **vintage train car** (10:30am, noon, 1:30pm, and 3pm Sat.-Sun. Apr.-Oct., adults $15, youth $8) for a six-mile, 45-minute ride into the Sierra Foothills. Fares include admission to the park.

Food and Accommodations

The at-times infamous ★ **National Hotel** (18183 Main St., 209/984-3446 or 800/894-3446, www.national-hotel.com, $140-160) has operated almost continuously since 1859—whether as a hotel, a brothel, a small casino, or a Prohibition-era speakeasy. Each of the nine rooms features antique furniture and comfy linens and comforters on the one queen bed. All rooms have their own baths with a shower and access to the soaking room, which the hotel describes as its "1800s Jacuzzi." A restaurant is downstairs, and the **Gold Rush Saloon** serves up signature cocktails and wines.

More historic lodgings are just down the road at the **Jamestown Hotel** (18153 Main St., 209/984-3902, www.thejamestownhotel.com, $140-175). Built in 1919, the hotel has comfortable rooms with antiques, modern bathrooms, and free Wi-Fi. The downstairs **restaurant** (6am-10pm daily, $15-30) is a local favorite that serves American-style breakfast, lunch, and dinner. From the ornately carved **bar,** you can order one of 12 draft beers, a glass of wine, or a stiff drink.

Inside a small Victorian cottage, you'll find the **Morelia Mexican Restaurant** (18148 Main St., 209/984-1432, www.morelia-mexicanrestaurantjamestown.com, 11am-9pm Mon.-Fri., 10am-9pm Sat.-Sun., $7-17) serving a variety of tacos, burritos, and giant plates of Mexican comfort food, plus several types of tequila.

Transportation and Services

Jamestown is five miles south of Sonora on Highway 49.

Yosemite, Sequoia, and Kings Canyon

Highlights

★ **Bridalveil Fall:** It's the most monumental—and the most accessible—of Yosemite's marvelous collection of waterfalls (page 357).

★ **Half Dome:** Whether you come to scale its peak or just to see the real-life model for all those wonderful photographs, Half Dome lives up to the hype (page 360).

★ **Hiking the Mist Trail:** A hike to the top of Vernal Fall brings the valley views alive (page 361).

★ **Tuolumne Meadows:** Explore the wonders of the park's high elevations at this rare alpine meadow, where numerous hiking trails thread through Yosemite's backcountry (page 369).

★ **Mono Lake:** Stand at the edge of this immense saline lake and marvel at a unique ecosystem filled with birds, brine shrimp, and bleached tufa towers (page 379).

★ **Bodie State Historic Park:** A state of "arrested decay" has preserved this 1877 gold-mining ghost town (page 383).

★ **Devils Postpile National Monument:** A mix of volcanic heat and pressure created these near-perfect straight-sided hexagonal posts that have to be seen to be believed (page 390).

★ **General Grant Grove:** A paved walkway leads to the General Grant Tree, the world's second-largest tree and the country's only living war memorial (page 398).

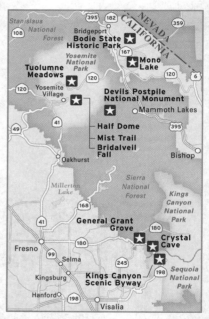

★ **Kings Canyon Scenic Byway:** Descend amid jaw-dropping scenery on this winding drive into Kings Canyon National Park (page 402).

★ **Crystal Cave:** Well-lit tunnels lead into the grand chambers of this cavern, filled with dramatic calcite formations and polished marble (page 406).

O f all the natural wonders that California has to offer, few are more iconic than the parks nestled within the Sierra Nevada.

Yosemite has been immortalized in the photographs of Ansel Adams and in the writings of naturalist John Muir who called it "the grandest of all the special temples of Nature I was ever permitted to enter." It was Muir who introduced it to President Theodore Roosevelt, which eventually resulted in Yosemite's national park designation. If this is your first visit, prepare to be overwhelmed.

South of Yosemite, Sequoia and Kings Canyon National Parks offer some of the tallest and oldest trees on earth, one of the deepest canyons in North America, plus numerous hiking trails, thriving wildlife—and smaller crowds than their famous neighbor.

East of Yosemite, the Eastern Sierra provides spectacular views of the high peaks that rise straight from the Owens Valley floor. The eerie stillness of Mono Lake and the ghost town of Bodie give visitors a taste of this high desert.

The town of Mammoth Lakes is a recreational heaven with water sports in the summer, fantastic skiing in winter, and volcanic and geologic oddities to capture the imagination. Hiking, mountain biking, fishing, backpacking, climbing and sightseeing are a great means of exploration in this area.

PLANNING YOUR TIME

Plan at least 2-3 days just in Yosemite Valley, with an excursion to Glacier Point. With a week, add Tuolumne Meadows (summer only) or Wawona. To explore the Eastern Sierra, visit in summer and plan a full weekend to explore Mono Lake and Bodie State Historic Park. Mammoth Lakes make a great ski getaway in winter, but you'll need a three-day weekend here.

Sequoia and Kings Canyon National Parks are large and spread out—to explore the parks in any depth, plan at least three days for the scenic drives past towering redwoods, plus time to hike or visit Crystal Cave.

Summer is high season in the national parks. Traffic jams and parking problems plague the parks, but Yosemite Valley provides free shuttles to popular sights and trailheads.

Previous: Yosemite's granite walls; Giant Forest Museum. **Above:** Yosemite Fall.

Yosemite National Park

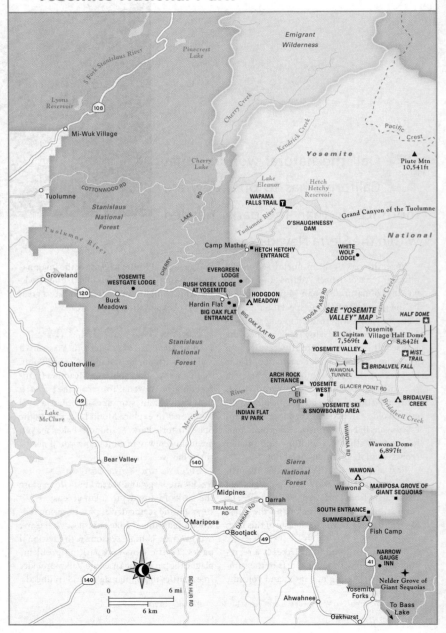

S Fork Stanislaus River

Lyons Reservoir

108

Pinecrest Lake

Emigrant Wilderness

Mi-Wuk Village

Cherry Lake

Cherry Creek

Kendrick Creek

Yosemite

Piute Mtn 10,541ft

Pacific Crest

COTTONWOOD RD

Tuolumne

Stanislaus National Forest

Tuolumne River

CHERRY LAKE RD

Lake Eleanor

Hetch Hetchy Reservoir

Tuolumne River

WAPAMA FALLS TRAIL

O'SHAUGHNESSY DAM

Grand Canyon of the Tuolumne

National

WHITE WOLF LODGE

Camp Mather

HETCH HETCHY ENTRANCE

Groveland

120

Buck Meadows

YOSEMITE WESTGATE LODGE

EVERGREEN LODGE

RUSH CREEK LODGE AT YOSEMITE

Hardin Flat

BIG OAK FLAT ENTRANCE

HODGDON MEADOW

BIG OAK FLAT RD

Stanislaus National Forest

TIOGA PASS RD

Yosemite Creek

SEE "YOSEMITE VALLEY" MAP

HALF DOME

Yosemite Village

El Capitan 7,569ft

Half Dome 8,842ft

Coulterville

49

Lake McClure

YOSEMITE VALLEY

WAWONA TUNNEL

MIST TRAIL

BRIDALVEIL FALL

ARCH ROCK ENTRANCE

River

El Portal

GLACIER POINT RD

BRIDALVEIL CREEK

Bridalveil Creek

INDIAN FLAT RV PARK

YOSEMITE WEST

YOSEMITE SKI & SNOWBOARD AREA

Bear Valley

140

Sierra National Forest

WAWONA RD

Wawona Dome 6,897ft

WAWONA

Midpines

TRIANGLE RD

Darrah

DARRAH RD

Mariposa

Bootjack

49

Wawona

MARIPOSA GROVE OF GIANT SEQUOIAS

SOUTH ENTRANCE

SUMMERDALE

Fish Camp

BEN HUR RD

NARROW GAUGE INN

41

Nelder Grove of Giant Sequoias

Ahwahnee

Yosemite Forks

To Bass Lake

Oakhurst

140

0   6 mi

0   6 km

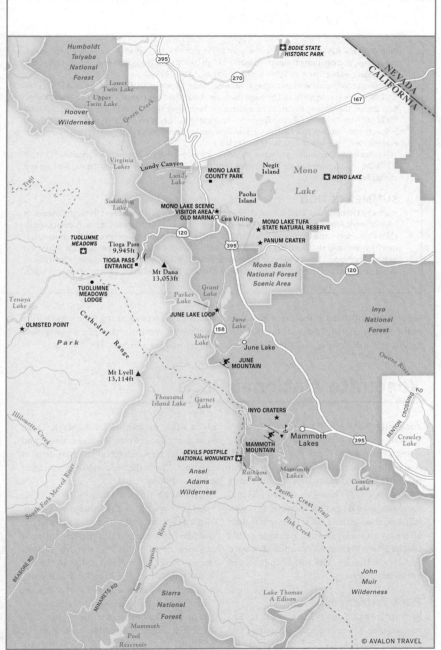

© AVALON TRAVEL

One Day in Yosemite

With only one day, concentrate on the sights in Yosemite Valley, which is accessible year-round. In summer, you can cross through Yosemite's high country via Tioga Pass Road (Hwy. 120) to the eastern side of the Sierra and view scenic sights along U.S. 395.

Yosemite National Park is most easily accessed from Highway 120 through the Big Oak Flat Entrance or via Highway 140 through the main Arch Rock entrance. Once in Yosemite Valley, hop aboard the Valley Shuttle for a scenic exploration of Bridalveil Fall, El Capitan, and Half Dome. The best way to experience Yosemite's beauty is on one of its many trails. Enjoy a leisurely stroll around Mirror Lake, scale a waterfall on the Mist Trail, or test your powers of endurance on the way to Upper Yosemite Fall.

It takes advance planning to score an overnight reservation in Yosemite Valley. Half Dome Village is your best bet for last-minute tent cabins or try one of the first-come, first-served campsites off Tioga Road.

SUMMER OPTION

Highway 120 becomes Tioga Road (open in summer only) as it heads east through Yosemite's high country. Along the way, gape at jaw-dropping vistas from Olmsted Point, gaze at crystal-clear alpine lakes and the grassy Tuolumne Meadows, and explore some of Yosemite's rugged high-elevation backcountry on a hike to Cathedral Lakes. Tioga Road peaks at Tioga Pass as it leaves the park, descending to the arid desert along U.S. 395. Here, abandoned ghost towns like Bodie State Historic Park and saline Mono Lake characterize the drier Eastern Sierra.

For fewer crowds, head to Tuolumne Meadows or the Eastern Sierra. Spring is best for waterfalls and wildflowers, and there are fewer crowds. Fall sees stunning colors and cooler weather. In winter, many parks roads close and crowds are minimal.

Yosemite National Park

Yosemite National Park (209/372-0200, www.nps.gove/yose, open daily year-round) is best known for its scenic valley, immortalized in the photographs of Ansel Adams. But the entire park and wilderness contain nearly 1,200 square miles home to alpine lakes and meadows, sequoia groves, thundering waterfalls, and sheer granite cliffs. Five park regions offer easy access for visitors: Yosemite Valley, Glacier Point, Wawona, Tuolumne Meadows, and Hetch Hetchy. The rest is rugged and beautiful wilderness.

Park Entrances

Park entrance fees ($35 per vehicle, $25 motorcycles, $20 individual) are paid at five park entrances; entrance fees are valid for seven days. In winter (Nov.-May), Tioga Road and Glacier Point Road are closed, and chains may be required on any park road at any time. Check the park website for current road conditions.

The Arch Rock Entrance (Hwy. 140, open year-round) is the most direct route into Yosemite Valley, reached via Merced and Mariposa. Lines at this popular entrance can back up 9am-5pm. Plan to arrive early in the morning (before 9am) or late in the day (after 3pm). From the Arch Rock Entrance, it's a 25-minute drive along El Portal Road to Yosemite Valley, depending on traffic.

The Big Oak Flat Entrance (Hwy. 120, open year-round) enters the park from the north, via Modesto, Manteca, and Groveland.

It is the closest entrance from the San Francisco Bay Area. Once inside the park, Highway 120 becomes Big Oak Flat Road. From the entrance, it's about 25 miles to Yosemite Valley, but allow at least 45 minutes for the drive.

The South Entrance (Hwy. 41, open year-round) enters the park from the south via Fresno and Oakhurst with immediate access to Wawona. Inside the park, Highway 41 becomes Wawona Road. Chains may be required in winter. The drive from Wawona to Yosemite Valley is about 35 miles (1.25 hours). Midway is the turn onto Glacier Point Road (closed in winter) to Glacier Point.

The Tioga Pass Entrance (Hwy. 120) is on the east side of Yosemite, 12 miles west of U.S. 395 near the town of Lee Vining. The road is called Tioga Road west of the entrance and Tioga Pass Road to the east. Tioga Pass is the only road in the park that crosses the Sierra, with access to Tuolumne Meadows. Tioga Road is closed in winter (Oct.-May or early June) from Crane Flat to Tioga Pass.

The Hetch Hetchy Entrance (off Hwy. 120, sunrise-sunset year-round) is the only road access to Hetch Hetchy Reservoir. From Highway 120, turn left (north) onto Evergreen Road before the Big Oak Flat Entrance. After about seven miles, Evergreen Road becomes Hetch Hetchy Road, which leads through the entrance and to the reservoir.

TOP EXPERIENCE

YOSEMITE VALLEY

Yosemite Valley, with its cascading waterfalls, cathedral-like granite walls, and wildflower-strewn meadows, is what most people imagine when they think of Yosemite National Park. The most visited region in the park, the valley is filled with sights, hikes, and services, in addition to historic lodging and cultural artifacts of Yosemite's previous residents and admirers.

Sights
YOSEMITE VILLAGE

Your first stop in Yosemite Valley should be the Valley Visitors Center (shuttle stops 5 and 9, off Northside Dr., 9am-5pm daily year-round), home to the Yosemite Museum and store, information, a bookstore, maps, park rangers, and a gift store. The Yosemite Valley Auditorium and Yosemite Theater share a building behind the visitors center; programs here include the John Muir Performances (7pm Wed. and Thurs. Apr.-Oct., adults $10, children under 12 free), starring Yosemite's resident actor Lee Stetson. Adjacent to the visitors center is the re-created Indian Village. The village includes different structures, including some made by the later Miwoks, who incorporated European architecture into their building techniques. Located next to the visitors center, The Ansel Adams Gallery (209/372-4413, www.anseladams.com, 9am-6pm daily) offers photography classes and showcases works of the noted photographer. Nearby is the Valley Wilderness Center (8am-5pm daily, hours vary seasonally) where backcountry hikers can pick up permits. The Yosemite Art Center (209/372-4207, 10am-2pm Mon.-Sat., open seasonally, $15) leads beginner art classes.

The village also has several dining options, parking, and the all-important public restrooms.

★ BRIDALVEIL FALL

Bridalveil Fall (Wawona Rd. and Southside Dr.) is many visitors' first introduction to Yosemite's famed collection of waterfalls. The Bridalveil Fall Trail (0.5 mile, 20 minutes) is a pleasantly sedate walk up to the fall. Although the 620-foot waterfall runs year-round, its fine mist sprays most powerfully in the spring—expect to get wet! The trailhead has its own parking area, so it's one of the first sights people come to upon entering the park.

Yosemite Valley

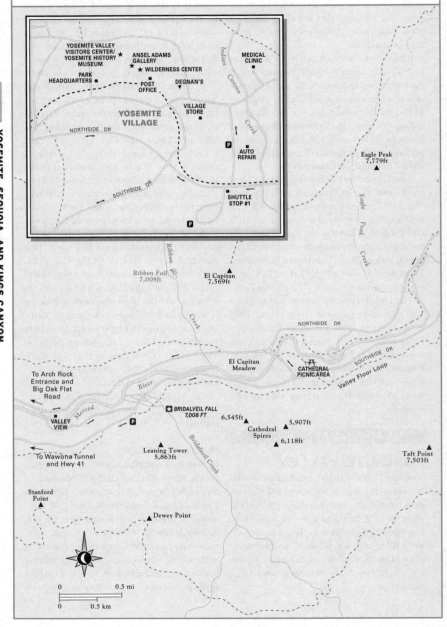

YOSEMITE VALLEY
VISITORS CENTER/
YOSEMITE HISTORY
MUSEUM

ANSEL ADAMS
GALLERY

WILDERNESS CENTER

MEDICAL
CLINIC

PARK
HEADQUARTERS

POST
OFFICE

DEGNAN'S

YOSEMITE
VILLAGE

VILLAGE
STORE

Indian Canyon

Creek

NORTHSIDE DR

P

AUTO
REPAIR

SOUTHSIDE DR

SHUTTLE
STOP #1

P

Eagle Peak
7,779ft

Eagle Peak Creek

Ribbon

Ribbon Fall
7,008ft

El Capitan
7,569ft

Creek

NORTHSIDE DR

El Capitan
Meadow

CATHEDRAL
PICNIC AREA

SOUTHSIDE DR

Valley Floor Loop

To Arch Rock
Entrance and
Big Oak Flat
Road

River

Merced

VALLEY
VIEW

P

BRIDALVEIL FALL
7,008 FT

6,545ft

Cathedral
Spires

5,907ft

6,118ft

Bridalveil Creek

To Wawona Tunnel
and Hwy 41

Leaning Tower
5,863ft

Taft Point
7,503ft

Stanford
Point

Dewey Point

0   0.5 mi

0   0.5 km

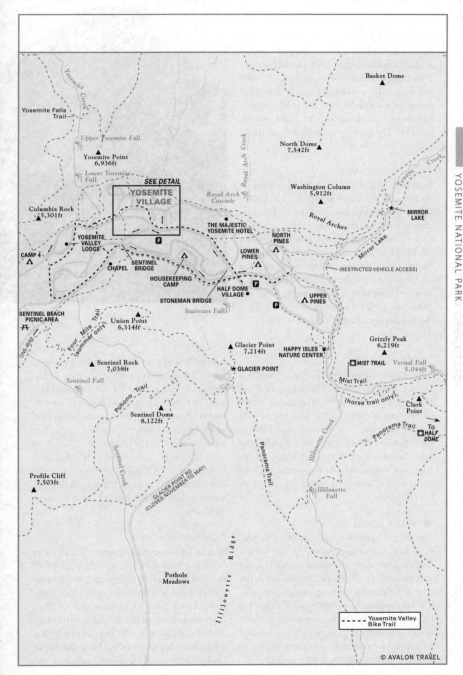

Basket Dome

Yosemite Falls Trail

Upper Yosemite Fall

Yosemite Point
6,936ft

North Dome
7,542ft

Lower Yosemite Fall

SEE DETAIL
YOSEMITE VILLAGE

Royal Arch Cascade

Washington Column
5,912ft

Columbia Rock
5,301ft

THE MAJESTIC YOSEMITE HOTEL

Royal Arches

MIRROR LAKE

YOSEMITE VALLEY LODGE

NORTH PINES

Mirror Lake

CAMP 4

LOWER PINES

CHAPEL

SENTINEL BRIDGE

HOUSEKEEPING CAMP

(RESTRICTED VEHICLE ACCESS)

STONEMAN BRIDGE

HALF DOME VILLAGE

UPPER PINES

Staircase Falls

SENTINEL BEACH PICNIC AREA

Union Point
6,314ft

Four Mile Trail (summer only)

ONE WAY

Sentinel Rock
7,038ft

Glacier Point
7,214ft

HAPPY ISLES NATURE CENTER

Grizzly Peak
6,219ft

MIST TRAIL

Vernal Fall
5,044ft

GLACIER POINT

Mist Trail

Sentinel Fall

Pohono Trail

Sentinel Dome
8,122ft

(horse trail only)

Clark Point

Panorama Trail

To HALF DOME

Illilouette Creek

Sentinel Creek

Profile Cliff
7,503ft

GLACIER POINT RD (CLOSED NOVEMBER TO MAY)

Panorama Trail

Illilouette Fall

Pothole Meadows

Illilouette Ridge

- - - Yosemite Valley Bike Trail

© AVALON TRAVEL

EL CAPITAN

On the north side of the valley is 7,569-foot El Capitan (Northside Dr., west of El Capitan Bridge), a massive hunk of Cretaceous granite. This craggy rock face rises more than 3,000 feet above the valley floor and is accessible two ways: a long hike from Upper Yosemite Fall or rock climbing the face. Most visitors, however, just gaze up adoringly from the El Capitan picnic area.

YOSEMITE FALLS

Yosemite Falls (shuttle stop 6, Northside Dr.) is actually three separate waterfalls—Upper Fall, Lower Fall, and the middle cascades. This dramatic formation together creates one of the highest waterfalls in the world. The flows are seasonal; if you visit during the fall or the winter, you'll see just a trickle of water on the rocks or nothing at all. The best time to visit is the spring, when the snowmelt swells the river above and creates the beautiful cascade that makes these falls so famous.

Half Dome

MIRROR LAKE

Mirror Lake (shuttle stop 17, end of Southside Dr., no vehicles) offers a stunningly clear reflection of the already spectacular views of Tenaya Canyon and the ubiquitous Half Dome. A short, level hiking and biking path (2 miles round-trip, 1 hour) reaches the lake. Add a few more miles (5 miles round-trip, easy to moderate) to circumnavigate the entire lake. Come early in the season before the lake dries out.

★ HALF DOME

One of the valley's most recognizable features rises high above the valley floor—Half Dome. This piece of a narrow granite ridge was polished to its smooth dome-like shape tens of millions of years ago by glaciers, giving it the appearance of half a dome. Scientists believe that Half Dome was never a whole dome—the way it appears to us now is actually its original formation. One of the best spots to view the granite giant is at Mirror Lake.

Hiking

An endless variety of hiking trails can be found in and depart from the Yosemite Valley. Stop at the visitors center (shuttle stops 5 and 9, off Northside Dr.) to ask rangers about current trail conditions, pick up maps, and fill water bottles. Many people love the valley trails, so you won't be alone.

Located near the trailhead to Mist Falls and Half Dome, The Nature Center at Happy Isles (shuttle stop 16, 9:30am-5pm daily in summer) has natural history exhibits and a bookstore.

COOK'S MEADOW

Soak in quintessential Yosemite Valley views from the easy Cook's Meadow Loop (1 mile, 30 minutes, shuttle stop 5 or 9). From the trailhead at the visitors center, you'll observe Ansel Adams's famous view of Half Dome from Sentinel Bridge and also the Royal Arches and Glacier Point. You can extend this hike into a loop (2.25 miles) by circling both Cook's and Sentinel Meadows. Trail signs, and the plethora of other hikers, make it easy to find the turns.

VALLEY LOOP TRAIL

The **Valley Loop Trail** (paved path beside Northside Dr. and Southside Dr.) traverses the El Capitan Bridge, following the path of many old wagon roads and historical trails. From the Lower Yosemite Falls trailhead (shuttle stop 6), the **half loop** (6.5 miles, 3 hours) offers a moderate half-day hike, while the **full loop** (13 miles, 6 hours) spends a full day wandering the valley. Though paved, the route can be hard to follow; pick up a map at the visitors center.

LOWER YOSEMITE FALL

The **Lower Yosemite Fall** (1.1 miles round-trip, 30 min., shuttle stop 6) trail enjoys the wondrous views of both Upper and Lower Yosemite Falls, complete with lots of cooling spray. This easy trail works well for families with children; hike in the spring or early summer, when the flow of the falls is at its peak.

YOSEMITE FALLS TRAIL

One of the most strenuous, yet most rewarding, treks is the **Yosemite Falls Trail** (7.2 miles round-trip, 6-8 hours, strenuous, shuttle stop 7). From the trailhead at Camp 4, the climb starts getting steep right away—2,700 vertical feet in just 3 miles. In one mile (and 1,000 feet), you'll reach **Columbia Rock,** with astonishing views of the valley below. Turn back here for a two-mile (2-3 hours) round-trip hike. The trail to the top of the falls is made passable with stone steps, switchbacks, and occasional railings, but much of the trail tends to be wet and slippery. Plan all day for this hike and bring plenty of water and snacks to replenish your energy for the potentially tricky climb down.

★ MIST TRAIL

Starting at the Happy Isles Nature Center (shuttle stop 16), the moderately strenuous **Mist Trail** leads over steep, slick granite—including more than 600 stairs—up to the top of **Vernal Fall** (2.4 miles round-trip, 3 hours). Your reward is the stellar view of the valley below from flat granite boulders that abut the Merced River. Hardier souls can continue another steep and strenuous 1.5-2 miles of switchbacks to the top of **Nevada Fall** (5.4 miles round-trip, 5-6 hours) and return via the John Muir Trail.

The hike to Nevada Fall gains 2,000 feet in elevation. Bring a lightweight rain jacket and expect to get wet. The Mist Trail is **closed in winter** due to ice and snow and can be dangerous in the spring months, when the river is at its peak; hikers have been lost in the waters here. Exercise caution in extreme conditions and obey all trail signage.

HALF DOME

The most famous climb in Yosemite Valley takes you to the top of monumental **Half Dome** (14-16 miles round-trip, 10-12 hours, May-Oct., shuttle stop 16). The trail follows the Mist Trail to Nevada Fall (5.4 miles) and then is signed for Half Dome. The final 400-foot ascent is via metal cables. Once you stagger to the top, you'll find a restful expanse of stone on which to enjoy the scenery.

All hikers must have a **permit** (877/444-6777, www.recreation.gov, $20 pp) to climb Half Dome. There are 300 permits issued per day; 225 permits are allotted for day hikers, and the rest are for backpackers. The park distributes permits through an online lottery starting in March. A daily permit lottery awards up to 50 permits; applications must be received two days prior to the hike day. The park's public information office (209/372-0826) can answer questions about the lottery process.

Do not attempt this trail lightly—it is not suitable for small children or anyone out of shape. Potential issues include altitude sickness, unsafe weather conditions, and physical injuries. Hikers must begin the trail *before sunrise* and turn around by 3:30pm or whenever the trail is closed. Continuing on when conditions suggest otherwise risks your life and the lives of others.

Rock Climbing

The rock climbing at Yosemite is some of the best in the world. **El Capitan,** the face of **Half Dome,** and **Sentinel Dome** in the high country draw climbers from all over. If you plan to climb one of these monuments, check with the Yosemite park rangers well in advance for necessary information and permits. Many of the spectacular ascents are not beginners' climbs. The right place to start climbing in Yosemite is the **Yosemite Mountaineering School** (209/372-8344, www.travelyosemite.com, Apr.-Oct., $143-167), where you'll find beginner, intermediate, and advanced classes for adults and children over age 10. Guided climbs, hikes, and backpacking trips are also available.

Rafting

Rafting down the Merced River is a popular activity in late spring and summer. Most put their rafts or tubes in at Stoneman Bridge and float down to Sentinel Beach. Four-person raft rentals ($29.50 pp, no children below 50 pounds) are available at the tour and activities desks at the **Yosemite Valley Lodge** (shuttle stop 7 and 8), **Half Dome Village** (shuttle stop 13), **Yosemite Village** (shuttle stop 5 and 9), and **The Majestic Yosemite Hotel** (shuttle stop 3). The price includes a shuttle back to Stoneman Bridge (departs every 30-40 minutes) or opt for just the shuttle ($5.50 pp).

Ice-Skating

Half Dome Village (end of Southside Dr., 209/372-8319, 3:30pm-9pm Mon.-Fri., noon-9pm Sat.-Sun., 9am-9pm holidays, Dec.-Mar., adults $10, children $9.50, rentals $4) has an ice-skating rink in winter.

Food

Yosemite Valley has the greatest variety of dining options in the park, from casual to fine dining. Hours vary seasonally.

YOSEMITE VILLAGE

In Yosemite Village (shuttle stop 5 and 9), **Degnan's Loft** (noon-9pm daily, $12-25)

serves artisan pizza, appetizers, beer, and wine. **Degnan's Kitchen** (7am-6pm daily year-round, $10) offers an array of sandwiches, salads, and takeout munchies. The **Village Grill Deck** (11am-6pm daily Apr.-Sept., $11-17) serves burgers, hot dogs, and veggies on an expansive outdoor deck.

HALF DOME VILLAGE

Half Dome Village (shuttle stop 13) has relatively cheap fast food. The **Village Pavilion** (7am-10am, 5:30pm-8:30pm daily, $10-12) serves breakfast and dinner and an all-inclusive barbecue menu ($22) Saturday night in the summer. Stop at **Coffee Corner** (6am-11am daily Mar.-Nov.) for a quick breakfast or ice cream in the afternoon. The **Village Bar** (11am-10pm daily Mar.-Oct.), the **Pizza Deck** (11am-10pm daily), and the **Meadow Grill** (11am-8pm daily summer, $5-7), all serve burgers, salads, and sandwiches.

YOSEMITE VALLEY LODGE

Enjoy a spectacular view of Yosemite Falls at the **Mountain Room Restaurant** (shuttle stop 7 and 8, dinner 5pm-10pm daily, brunch 9am-1pm Sun., $18-38). The glass atrium lets every table take in the view, whether you are having a burger or filet mignon. Expect upscale food accompanied by a good California wine menu and original and old-fashioned cocktails. A casual bar menu is available at the **Mountain Room Lounge** (4:30pm-11pm Mon.-Fri., noon-11pm Sat.-Sun., $8-13). The nearby **Base Camp Eatery** (6:30am-10pm daily, $8-15) offers basic meals in a cafeteria-style setting.

THE MAJESTIC YOSEMITE LODGE

The dining room at ★ **The Majestic Yosemite Lodge** (shuttle stop 3, reservations 209/372-1489, 7am-10am, 11:30am-3pm, 5:30pm-9pm Mon.-Sat., 7am-3pm and 5:30pm-9pm Sun., $27-47) enjoys a reputation for fine cuisine that stretches back to 1927. The grand dining room features expansive ceilings, wrought-iron chandeliers, and a stellar valley view. Reservations are recommended. For dinner, "resort casual" attire (semiformal) is requested. The **bar** (11:30am-11pm daily) serves wine, cocktails, and a small pub menu ($12-22), as well as coffee (7am-10:30am daily).

Accommodations

All valley lodgings, including campsites, book quickly—up to six months in advance. **Reservations** (888/413-8869, www.travelyosemite.com) are essential for overnight accommodations. All rates vary seasonally.

HOUSEKEEPING CAMP

Want to camp, but don't want to schlep all the gear? The 266 three-sided tent cabins at **Housekeeping Camp** (shuttle stop 12, mid-Apr.-early-Oct., $107-127) have cement walls, white canvas roofs, and a white canvas curtain separating the bedroom from a covered patio. Each cabin has a double bed, a bunk bed (with room for two additional cots), electrical outlets, a bear-proof food container, and an outdoor fire ring. Bring your own linens or sleeping bag. Central bathrooms with showers and towels are available.

HALF DOME VILLAGE

Half Dome Village (shuttle stop 13, daily Mar.-Nov. and Dec.-Jan.; Sat.-Sun. only Jan.-Mar.) is a sprawling array of wood and tent cabins (with or without heat, and with or without a private bath), originally created in 1899. There are 403 **Canvas Tent Cabins** ($85-143), small, wood-frame, canvas-covered structures that sleep 2-4 in a combination of single and double cot beds. A small dresser, sheets, blankets, and pillows are provided, but there is no electricity or heat. Bear-proof lockers and shared showers and restrooms are available. A few **heated tent cabins** ($115-162) are also available.

The 46 **Yosemite Cabins** ($217-237) are wood structures with private baths and 1-2 double beds that sleep up to five. There are also 14 cabins ($150-160) that share a central bathhouse. The 18 **Stoneman Standard Motel Rooms** ($235-280) sleep 2-6 and have

heat, private baths, and daily maid service. An extra charge of $10-12 applies for each person beyond the first two. There are no TVs or telephones in any of the lodgings; all are close to the food options in Half Dome Village.

YOSEMITE VALLEY LODGE

★ **Yosemite Valley Lodge** (shuttle stop 7 and 8, open year-round, from $160-270) has a perfect location near Yosemite Falls. Traditional motel-style rooms have king beds and balconies overlooking the valley. The larger Family Rooms have bunk beds and some extra space. All rooms have refrigerators, coffeemakers, TVs, and free wireless Internet. Enjoy a heated pool in the summer and a free shuttle to the Glacier Point in winter. Excellent food is just steps away at the on-site **Mountain Room Restaurant,** the **Mountain Room Lounge,** and the **Base Camp Eatery.**

THE MAJESTIC YOSEMITE HOTEL

Built as a luxury hotel in the early 1900s, the ★ **The Majestic Yosemite Hotel** (shuttle stop 3, open year-round, $325-550) boasts a gorgeous stone facade, striking stone fireplaces, and soaring ceilings in the common areas. The hotel is listed as a National Historic Landmark and combines elements of the Arts and Crafts movement with Native American art and decor. Accommodations run from standard hotel rooms to cottages and two-room suites fit for a queen (Queen Elizabeth stayed here in the 1980s). All rooms come with one king or two double beds, flat-screen TVs, phone, refrigerators, and Wi-Fi. Make dinner reservations at the stunningly elegant on-site **Dining Room** to cap the experience.

Camping

There are four campgrounds in Yosemite Valley, and they are deservedly popular. **Reservations** (877/444-6777, www.recreation.gov, Mar.-Nov.) for Upper Pines, Lower Pines, and North Pines are very competitive. At 7am (Pacific Standard Time) on the 15th of each month, campsites become available for a period up to five months in advance. A few minutes after 7am, choice sites and dates—maybe even all of them—will be gone. If you need a reservation for a specific day, get up early and call or check online diligently starting at 7am.

If you're in the valley and don't have a campsite reservation, call the **campground status line** (209/372-0266) for a recording of what's available that day. Or try one of the first-come, first-served campgrounds (but get there early).

Showers are available at **Half Dome Village** (24 hours daily year-round) and **Housekeeping Camp** (7am-10pm daily Apr.-Oct.), which also has coin-operated **laundry** (8am-10pm daily).

LOWER, UPPER, AND NORTH PINES

Sites at the **Lower Pines campground** (shuttle stop 19, 60 sites, Mar.-Oct., $26) accommodate tents and RVs up to 40 feet and include fire rings, picnic tables, a bear-proof food locker, water, flush toilets—and very little privacy. Supplies and showers are available nearby. Reservations are required and can be made up to five months in advance.

Upper Pines campground (shuttle stop 15, 238 sites, year-round, $26) is the largest campground in the valley. It lies immediately southeast of Lower Pines and is encircled by the park road. Sites accommodate tents and RVs up to 35 feet and include fire rings, picnic tables, a bear-proof food locker, water, and flush toilets. Supplies and showers are available nearby. Reservations are required and can be made up to five months in advance.

Set along the Merced River and Tenaya Creek, **North Pines** (shuttle stop 18, 81 sites, Apr.-Nov., $26) offers slightly more privacy than its Upper and Lower Pines siblings. Sites accommodate tents and RVs up to 40 feet and include fire rings, picnic tables, a bear-proof food locker, water, and flush toilets. Supplies and showers are available nearby. Reservations are required and can be made up to five months in advance.

CAMP 4

★ **Camp 4** (shuttle stop 7, 35 sites, year-round, $6 pp) sits near the foot of El Capitan and is filled with climbers. The walk-in campground only accommodates tents; no RVs or trailers are allowed. Sites include fire pits, picnic tables, and a shared bear-proof food locker. You'll find showers, food and groceries, and restrooms with water and flush toilets nearby. Pets are not permitted.

Reservations are not accepted. Spring-fall, hopeful campers must register with a park ranger. Plan to wait in line at the campground kiosk well before the ranger arrives at 8:30am. Sites are available **first-come, first-served** and hold six people each, so you may end up sharing with another party.

Transportation and Services

Yosemite Valley is about 200 miles from the San Francisco Bay Area, a drive of 4-5 hours. From the Bay Area, take I-580 east to I-205 to I-5 to Highway 120, and continue through Groveland and to the Big Oak Flat Entrance. After entering the park, it's 25 miles (45 min.) to the valley.

Valley parking lots fill by 9am on weekends and by 10am on weekdays in summer. Plan to arrive early morning or later in the afternoon, or visit other areas of the park.

SHUTTLES

In summer—especially on weekends—traffic can be slow and stressful and parking nonexistent. Use the free **Yosemite Valley shuttle** (7am-10pm daily year-round, free) to get around. The shuttle runs every 10-20 minutes, stopping at the Yosemite Valley Lodge, the Valley Visitors Center, Half Dome Village, all campgrounds, and the Happy Isles trailhead. The **El Capitan Shuttle** (9am-7pm daily mid-June-early Oct.) stops at El Capitan, the Four Mile trailhead, and the visitors center.

BIKES

The **Yosemite Valley Bike Path** (12 miles) is a mostly flat bike trail that winds across the valley floor. **Bicycle rentals** (9am-6pm daily spring-fall, $12.50/hour, $30.50/day) are available from Yosemite Valley Lodge (shuttle stop 8) and Half Dome Village (shuttle stops 13 and 20). Bikes with attached trailers ($19/hour, $56.50/day), plus wheelchairs, strollers, and electric scooters are also available.

PUBLIC TRANSIT

Yosemite Area Regional Transportation System (YARTS, 877/989-2787, www.yarts.com, $4-36) runs four seasonal routes into the valley from Merced (Hwy. 140), Fresno (Hwy. 41), Sonora (Hwy. 120), and Mammoth Lakes (Hwy. 120/395). No reservations are necessary. Buy tickets online or on the bus; children under age 12 ride free. YARTS fares include the park entrance fee. Buses run more frequently in summer, with connections to Amtrak, Greyhound, and regional airports.

SERVICES AND PROGRAMS

The **Yosemite Village Garage** (9002 Village Dr., Yosemite Village, 209/372-8320, 8am-5pm daily, towing 24 hours daily) provides towing and repairs. The nearest **gas stations** are in El Portal and at Crane Flat. **Groceries** are available at the Yosemite Village Store (8am-10pm daily), Housekeeping Camp (8am-6pm daily), and Half Dome Village (8am-8pm daily). **ATMs** are located at Yosemite and Half Dome Villages. Emergencies should be brought to **Yosemite Medical Clinic** (9000 Ahwahnee Dr., 209/372-4637, 9am-7pm daily summer, 9am-5pm Mon.-Fri. fall-spring).

The **Yosemite Conservation Heritage Center** (shuttle stop 12, 10am-4pm Wed.-Sun, 8pm Fri.-Sat.) has a library and a children's center, with free evening programs in summer.

GLACIER POINT

The drive via Glacier Point Road (16 miles from Chinquapin junction) to Glacier Point is an easy one, but the vistas down into Yosemite Valley are anything but common. The first five miles of Glacier Point Road stay open all year, except when storms make it temporarily impassable, to allow access to the ski area, but chains may be required.

Yosemite Ski & Snowboard Area

Downhill skiing at **Yosemite Ski & Snowboard Area** (209/372-8430, www.travelyosemite.com, 8:30am-4pm daily mid-Dec.-mid-Mar., adults $30-55, seniors $27-47, youth 13-17 $27-47, children 7-12 $15-32, children under 7 free) is a favorite winter activity at Yosemite. This was the first downhill ski area created in California, and it's still perfect for moderate skiing with plenty of beginner runs and classes plus enough intermediate runs to make it interesting for mid-level skiers. Ski and snowboard **lessons** (adults $80-110, youth 13-17 $75-105, children 7-12 $70-100, children 4-6 $67/one day, $87/two days) include lift tickets and rentals. All-day lift tickets ($32-55) are available online. Downhill skis ($21-37), snowboards ($21-37), and snowshoe ($18-23) rentals are also available, as is a **tubing area** (11:30am-1:30pm and 2pm-4pm daily, $17 pp).

The **Cross-Country Ski School** (www.travelyosemite.com, 8:30am-4pm daily in winter) offers access to 90 miles of marked trails with ski classes and equipment rentals, including snow camping gear.

A variety of guided cross-country ski and snowshoe tours include a **full-moon snowshoe hike** ($35, includes rentals) and an overnight trip to **Glacier Point Ski Hut** (209/372-8344, $140-200 pp).

The ski area is located along Glacier Point Road, five miles from Chinquapin junction. A free shuttle makes multiple daily runs from accommodations in Yosemite Valley.

Hiking

SENTINEL DOME AND TAFT POINT

The trail to **Sentinel Dome** (1.8 miles round-trip, 2 hours) is a surprisingly easy walk; the only steep part is climbing the dome at the end of the trail. From the trailhead (1-2 miles south of Glacier Point on Glacier Point Rd.), turn right and follow an old road through the forest to the top of the dome where you can see all the way from the High Sierra to Mount Diablo in the Bay Area.

At the same trailhead turn left instead to reach **Taft Point and the Fissures** (2.2 miles round-trip, 2 hours), which takes you along unusual rock formations called the Fissures, through the always lovely woods, and out to precarious vistas at Taft Point, 2,000 feet above the valley.

PANORAMA TRAIL
The **Panorama Trail** (8.3 miles one-way, 6-8 hours) departs from Glacier Point and follows the ridgeline to Nevada Fall, where you'll catch the Mist Trail back down to the valley. The trail changes 3,200 feet of elevation along the way with views of Illilouette Fall and Panorama Point, Half Dome, Upper and Lower Yosemite Falls. To avoid the car shuffle, consider taking the **Glacier Point Tour shuttle** (888/413-8869, www.travelyosemite.com, 8:30am and 1:30pm daily May-Nov., adults $25, seniors 62 and up $23, children 5-12 $15, children under 5 free) from the Yosemite Valley Lodge.

FOUR MILE TRAIL
Departing from Glacier Point, the **Four Mile Trail** (4.8 miles one-way, 3-4 hours) climbs down into the valley, affording an ascending series of views of Yosemite Falls and Yosemite Valley that grow more spectacular with each switchback. Take the shuttle to **Glacier Point** (888/413-8869, www.travelyosemite.com, 8:30am and 1:30pm daily May-Nov., adults $25, seniors 62 and up $23, children 5-12 $15, children under 5 free) and then hike down to make this a reasonable day hike.

Accommodations and Camping
Bridalveil Creek (110 sites, first-come, first-served, Aug.-mid-Sept., $18) has a short season because of the snow that blankets this area, but its location along Bridalveil Creek makes it an appealing spot. Sites permit tents and RVs up to 35 feet and include fire pits,

picnic tables, a shared bear-proof food locker, and a bathroom with water and flush toilets nearby. It's located midway up Glacier Point Road, eight miles from Chinquapin junction and 45 minutes south of the valley.

Yosemite West (off Henness Rd., near the Chinquapin junction, 888/967-3648, www.scenicwonders.com, $125-695) offers a range of accommodations from small cabins to condos and sprawling three-bedroom houses. All units have free wireless Internet, but you'll need to go to the valley for any groceries or services.

Transportation
Glacier Point is a one-hour drive from Yosemite Valley. From the Valley Visitors Center, drive 14 miles south to Chinquapin junction and turn left onto Glacier Point Road (closed Nov.-May). In winter (Dec.-Mar.), the first five miles of the road are plowed; however, chains may be required.

The **Glacier Point Tour shuttle** (888/413-8869, www.travelyosemite.com, 8:30am and 1:30pm daily late May-Oct., adults $25/one-way or $49/round-trip, seniors over age 62 $23/one-way or $44/round-trip, children 5-12 $15/one-way or $35 round-trip, children under 5 free) travels from the Yosemite Valley Lodge to Glacier Point Road. Purchase tickets online or on the bus (the exact cash).

WAWONA
The small town of **Wawona** is four miles north of the South Entrance to Yosemite, home to a lovely historical district, a hotel and restaurant, outdoor exhibits, and even a golf course.

Sights
The **Wawona Visitors Center at Hill's Studio** (8:30am-5pm daily May-Oct.) is housed in the former studio and gallery of Thomas Hill, a famous landscape painter from the 1800s. The visitors center is perfect for gathering information, getting free wilderness permits, and renting bear-proof canisters.

The **Pioneer Yosemite History Center** (open daily year-round) is a rambling outdoor display area housing an array of historic vehicles and many of the original structures built in the park. Pass through the covered bridge to an uncrowded stretch of land where informative placards describe the history of Yosemite National Park through its structures. In summer, take a 10-minute tour by **horse-drawn carriage** (adults $5, children 3-12 $4), or check the *Yosemite Guide* for listings of living history programs and live demonstrations.

MARIPOSA GROVE OF GIANT SEQUOIAS

The **Mariposa Grove** (Wawona Rd./Hwy. 41, 4 miles south of Wawona, closed Nov.-May) offers a rare view of giant sequoia redwoods in the park. Several trails wind throughout the grove, allowing you to see some of the most impressive trees in a mile or less. Within the grove, the **Mariposa Grove Museum** (Upper Mariposa Grove) is a replica of the cabin of Galen Clark, a former guardian of Yosemite National Park who is credited as the first nonnative to see Mariposa Grove.

Hiking

In addition to the trails in the Mariposa Grove of Giant Sequoias, there are easy walks along the **Swinging Bridge Loop** (4.8 miles, 2 hours) from the trailhead at the Pioneer Gift & Grocery.

WAWONA MEADOW LOOP

The easy **Wawona Meadow Loop** (3.5 miles, 2 hours) is a flat and uncrowded sweep around the lovely Wawona Meadow and a somewhat incongruous nine-hole golf course. This wide trail can be traversed by bike, but the pavement has eroded and there is much dirt and tree detritus. The trailhead is across Highway 41 from the Big Trees Lodge.

CHILNUALNA FALLS

The strenuous trail to **Chilnualna Falls** (8.2 miles, 5 hours) switchbacks 2,300 feet to the top of a waterfall with stunning views of Wawona below. (Avoid entering the stream during spring and summer.). The trailhead is at the Chilnualna Falls parking area at the end of Chilnualna Falls Road.

Horseback Riding

You'll find horses at **Big Trees Lodge Stable** (Pioneer Yosemite History Center, Wawona Rd., 209/375-6502, www.travelyosemite.com, tours 8am, 11am, and 2pm daily June-Sept., $65), and many travelers, too—reservations are strongly recommended. From Wawona you can take a sedate two-hour ride around the historical wagon trail with views of Wawona Meadow and Wawona Dome.

Food and Accommodations

The charming **Big Trees Lodge** (888/413-8869, www.travelyosemite.com, Mar.-Nov. and mid-Dec.-early Jan., $150-220) opened in 1879 and has been a Yosemite institution ever since. The green-and-white hotel complex includes a wraparound porch and on-site dining. Rooms (with bath and without) come complete with Victorian wallpaper, antique furniture, and a lack of in-room TVs and telephones. In the summer, take advantage of the outdoor pool or the nine-hole golf course ($21.50-41.50).

The ★ **dining room** (209/375-1425, 7am-10am, 11am-3pm, 5pm-9pm daily Mar.-Nov. and mid-Dec.-early Jan., $21-31) serves upscale California cuisine in a large white dining room. Reservations are not accepted; you may have to wait for a table on weekends. The **lounge** (5pm-9:30pm daily Mar.-Nov. and mid-Dec.-early Jan.) serves cocktails and a modest bar menu. On Saturday night (7pm-9pm in summer, adults $22-27.50, children 3-12 $12.50, children under 3 free), the lodge fires up the barbecue and guests enjoy heaping plates of meat, coleslaw, baked beans, watermelon, apple pie, and iced tea.

Camping

Lovely and forested **Wawona Campground** (877/444-6777, www.recreation.gov, 93 sites, reservations required Apr.-Oct., $26; first-come, first-served Oct.-mid-Apr., $18), one mile north of Wawona, welcomes tent campers, RVs (no hookups), and even has two equestrian sites. Amenities include drinking water, fire rings, picnic tables, and food lockers; there are no showers.

Transportation

The **South Entrance** (Hwy. 41, year-round) is four miles south of Wawona. From Wawona, it's a 1.5-hour drive north to Yosemite Valley. **Yosemite Area Regional Transportation System** (YARTS, 877/989-2787, www.yarts.com, mid-May-mid-Sept., $8-15/one-way, $15-30 round-trip) runs daily buses between Fresno and Yosemite Valley, stopping at Wawona in summer.

TIOGA PASS AND TUOLUMNE MEADOWS

Tioga Road (Hwy. 120, June-Oct.) crosses Yosemite's High Sierra for 39 miles from Crane Flat (Big Oak Flat Rd.) to Tioga Pass and U.S. 395 in the Eastern Sierra. Along the way, turnouts allow exploration of giant sequoias, mammoth monoliths, expansive alpine meadows, and jewel-like lakes and jaw-dropping views. The region has spectacular hikes into the backcountry, several campgrounds, a few restaurants, and a cozy lodge. A shuttle (June-mid-Sept., free) allows visitors to park the car and focus on the views.

Sights

Midway along Tioga Road, the **Tuolumne Meadows Visitors Center** (shuttle stop 6, 9am-5pm daily June-Sept.) is the place to stop for information, maps, trail conditions, and ranger talks and guided walks.

OLMSTED POINT

From **Olmsted Point** (shuttle stop 12), jaw-dropping views of the High Sierra unfold, including the back of Half Dome. A short 0.5-mile walk from the parking lot shows off Clouds Rest in all its grandeur, as Half Dome peeks out behind it. A number of large glacial erratic boulders litter the parking area and draw almost as many visitors as the point itself.

TENAYA LAKE

Jewel-like **Tenaya Lake** (shuttle stops 10, 9) sits nestled in a deep granite valley. From the parking lot, an easy trail (2 miles round-trip) passes both sunny beaches and forest before

Tenaya Lake

hugging the granite cliffs on the southern edge of the lake.

POTHOLE DOME

Pothole Dome (shuttle stop 8) is a bubble of solid granite, where a scramble to the top reveals views of Tuolumne Meadows.

★ TUOLUMNE MEADOWS

In tones of brilliant green, the waving grasses of **Tuolumne Meadows** (shuttle stop 6) offer a rare peek at a fragile alpine meadow that supports a variety of wildlife. Park at the visitors center (shuttle stop 6) and get out for a quiet, contemplative view of the meadows along the short, easy trail to **Soda Springs and Parsons Lodge** (1.5 miles, 1 hour). From the trailhead at **Lembert Dome** (shuttle stop 4), the trail leads past a carbonated spring to the historical **Parsons Lodge** (10am-4pm daily in season) before ending at the Tuolumne Meadows Visitors Center.

Hiking

Hiking the high-elevation trails in this region may literally take your breath away. Allow time to acclimate and drink plenty of water. Trailheads are listed west to east along Tioga Road. For wilderness permits, safety, and trip planning, visit the **Tuolumne Meadows Wilderness Center** (shuttle stop 3, 8am-5pm daily June-Sept.).

TUOLUMNE GROVE OF GIANT SEQUOIAS

If you're aching to see some giant trees, try the **Tuolumne Grove of Giant Sequoias** (2 miles round-trip, moderate). The trailhead and parking are at the junction of Tioga Road and Big Oak Flat Road. This hike takes you down 500 vertical feet into the grove, which contains roughly 25 mature giant sequoias. (You do have to climb back up the hill to get to your car.)

To stretch your legs further, drive past the junction of Tioga and Big Oak Flat Road west to the south side trailhead of **Merced Grove** (3 miles round-trip, moderate). The trails drops 1.5 miles (making it a long and strenuous return climb), but you'll be treated to the least visited (and quietest) sequoia grove in the park.

NORTH DOME

For an unusual look at a Yosemite classic, take the moderate **North Dome Trail** (9 miles, 4-5 hours) through the woods out to the dome, where you'll get to stare eye level at the face

Tuolumne Meadows

Tuolomne Meadows and Tioga Pass

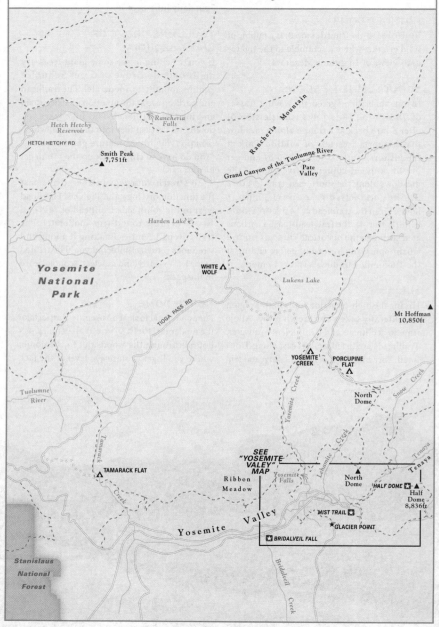

Hetch Hetchy
Reservoir

HETCH HETCHY RD

Rancheria
Falls

Smith Peak
7,751ft

Rancheria Mountain

Grand Canyon of the Tuolumne River

Pate
Valley

Harden Lake

Yosemite
National
Park

WHITE
WOLF

Lukens Lake

Mt Hoffman
10,850ft

Tioga Pass Rd

YOSEMITE
CREEK

PORCUPINE
FLAT

Snow Creek

Tuolumne
River

North
Dome

Tamarack

TAMARACK FLAT

Yosemite Creek

Lehamite Creek

SEE
"YOSEMITE
VALEY"
MAP

Ribbon
Meadow

Yosemite
Falls

North
Dome

Tenaya

Tenaya Creek

HALF DOME

Half
Dome
8,836ft

Valley

Creek

MIST TRAIL

Yosemite

Valley

GLACIER POINT

BRIDALVEIL FALL

Stanislaus
National
Forest

Bridalveil Creek

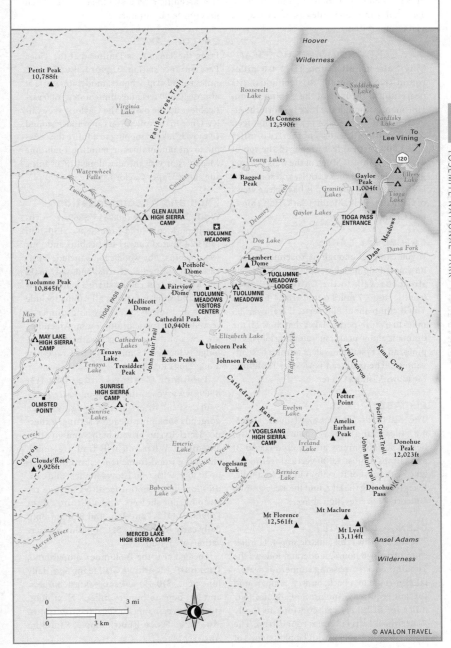

Hoover
Wilderness

Pettit Peak
10,788ft

Virginia
Lake

Roosevelt
Lake

Saddlebag
Lake

Gardisky
Lake

Mt Conness
12,590ft

To
Lee Vining

120

Waterwheel
Falls

Conness Creek

Young Lakes

Ragged
Peak

Delaney Creek

Granite
Lakes

Gaylor
Peak
11,004ft

Ellery
Lake

Pacific Crest Trail

Tuolumne River

GLEN AULIN
HIGH SIERRA
CAMP

Gaylor Lakes

TIOGA PASS
ENTRANCE

Tioga
Lake

Dana
Meadows

TUOLUMNE
MEADOWS

Dog Lake

Dana Fork

Tuolumne Peak
10,845ft

Pothole
Dome

Lembert
Dome

TUOLUMNE
MEADOWS
LODGE

May
Lake

Fairview
Dome

Medlicott
Dome

TIOGA PASS RD

TUOLUMNE
MEADOWS VISITORS
CENTER

TUOLUMNE
MEADOWS

Lyell Fork

Kuna Crest

MAY LAKE
HIGH SIERRA
CAMP

Cathedral
Lakes

Cathedral Peak
10,940ft

Elizabeth Lake

Lyell Canyon

John Muir Trail

Tenaya
Lake

Tresidder
Peak

Echo Peaks

Unicorn Peak

Johnson Peak

Rafferty Creek

SUNRISE
HIGH SIERRA
CAMP

Sunrise
Lakes

Cathedral Range

Potter
Point

Pacific Crest Trail

OLMSTED
POINT

Creek

Evelyn
Lake

Amelia
Earhart
Peak

John Muir Trail

Donohue
Peak
12,023ft

Clouds Rest
9,926ft

Canyon

VOGELSANG
HIGH SIERRA
CAMP

Ireland
Lake

Emeric
Lake

Fletcher Creek

Vogelsang
Peak

Bernice
Lake

Donohue
Pass

Babcock
Lake

Lewis Creek

Mt Florence
12,561ft

Mt Maclure

MERCED LAKE
HIGH SIERRA
CAMP

Mt Lyell
13,114ft

Ansel Adams

Merced River

Wilderness

0   3 mi

0   3 km

© AVALON TRAVEL

of Half Dome and Clouds Rest just beyond. The trailhead is one mile east of Porcupine Flat Campground.

MAY LAKE AND MOUNT HOFFMAN

May Lake (shuttle stop 11, 2.4-6 miles round-trip, moderate to strenuous) sits peacefully at the base of the sloping Mount Hoffman. Although the hike is short, the elevation gain to the lake is a steep 500 feet. A difficult trail leads another two miles and 2,000 vertical feet higher to the top of Mount Hoffman. Much of the walk is along granite slabs and rocky trails, and some of it is cross-country, but you'll have clear views of Cathedral Peak, Mount Clark, Half Dome, and Clouds Rest.

CATHEDRAL LAKES

If you can't get enough of Yosemite's granite-framed alpine lakes, take the moderately strenuous walk to the Cathedral Lakes (shuttle stop 7, 7 miles round-trip, 4-6 hours). You'll climb about 800 vertical feet over 3.5 miles to picture-perfect lakes that show off the dramatic alpine peaks, surrounding lodgepole pines, and crystalline waters to their best advantage. The trailhead is west of Tuolumne Meadows Visitors Center.

ELIZABETH LAKE

The trail to Elizabeth Lake (shuttle stop 5, 4.8 miles round-trip, 4-5 hours, moderate) begins at Tuolumne Campground (Loop B) and climbs almost 1,000 vertical feet to the lake, with most of the climb in the first mile. Evergreens ring the lake, and the steep granite Unicorn Peak rises high above.

GLEN AULIN TRAIL

The Glen Aulin Trail (shuttle stop 4, 11 miles round-trip, 6-8 hours, moderate) follows the Tuolumne River, passing numerous waterfalls en-route to a backcountry campground (permit required). Tuolumne Falls lies four miles in; fit hikers can continue to lovely Waterwheel Falls (18 miles round-trip). The trail is steep and rocky, with fabulous views of

the cascading river along the trail, but it can get crowded in summer.

GAYLOR LAKES

From the Tioga Pass Trailhead at the Tioga Pass entrance station, Gaylor Lakes Trail (2 miles round-trip, 2 hours, moderate) starts at almost 10,000 feet and climbs a steep 600 vertical feet up the pass to the Gaylor Lakes valley. Once in the valley, you can wander around five lovely lakes, stopping to admire the views out to the mountains surrounding Tuolumne Meadows or visit the abandoned 1870s mine site above Upper Gaylor Lake.

Food and Accommodations

White Wolf Lodge (888/413-8869, www.yosemitepark.com, mid-June-Sept., $130-160) rents 24 heated canvas-tent cabins and four wood cabins. The wood cabins include a private bath, limited electricity, and daily maid service. The tent cabins share a central restroom and shower facility; all cabins include linens and towels. Breakfast and dinner is served in the rustic dining room. Amenities are few, but the scenery is breathtaking. The lodge is located 15 miles east of Crane Flat along Tioga Road.

Tuolumne Meadows Lodge (888/413-8869, www.yosemitepark.com, early June-Sept., $125) offers rustic lodgings in a gorgeous subalpine meadow setting. Expect no electricity, no private baths, and no other amenities. What you will find are small, charming wood-frame tent cabins that sleep up to four, with woodstoves for heat and candles for light. Central facilities include restrooms, hot showers, and a dining room (209/372-8413, 7am-9pm and 5:30pm-8pm daily early June-Sept., $11-30); dinner reservations are required.

Located near the Tuolumne Campground, Tuolumne Meadows Grill (8am-6pm daily June-Sept., $10-15) serves breakfast, burgers, and hot dogs to hungry hikers. Next door, stock up on camping staples at the Tuolumne Meadows Store (shuttle stop 5, 8am-8pm Aug.-Sept.).

Camping

Seven campgrounds line Tioga Road. **Reservations** (877/444-6777, www.recreation.gov) are accepted for Hodgdon Meadow, Crane Flat, and Tuolumne Meadows and usually book far in advance April-September. The remaining campgrounds are first-come, first-served with limited amenities. The closest showers are in Yosemite Valley.

HODGDON MEADOW

Directly past the Big Oak Flat Entrance Station, **Hodgdon Meadow** (Hwy. 120, 105 sites, reservations required Apr.-Oct., $26; first-come, first-served Oct.-Apr., $18) can be an excellent choice for those who arrive Friday night. At 4,900 feet, the campground accommodates tents or RVs (no hookups) with fire rings, picnic tables, bear-proof food lockers, drinking water, and flush toilets. Supplies are available at Crane Flat. Pets are permitted.

CRANE FLAT

Crane Flat (Big Oak Flat and Tioga Rds., 166 sites, reservations required, June-Oct., $26) is 17 miles north of Yosemite Valley at 6,200 feet elevation. The campground accommodates tent and RVs up to 35 feet (no hookups), with fire rings, picnic tables, bear-proof food lockers, drinking water, and flush toilets. Supplies are available at the Crane Flat gas station and store. Pets are permitted.

TAMARACK FLAT

Tamarack Flat (Tioga Rd., 52 sites, first-come, first-served, June-Oct., $12) is a primitive tent-only campground at 6,300 feet elevation. Sites include picnic tables and bear-proof food lockers. There are pit toilets, but no drinking water; bring or filter your own.

WHITE WOLF

White Wolf (Tioga Rd., 74 sites, first-come, first-served, July-Sept., $18) is at 8,000 feet. Sites accommodate tents and RVs up to 27 feet and include fire pits and picnic tables; there are bear-proof food lockers, water, and flush toilets. Pets are permitted. The turnoff is on the left, down a narrow side road.

YOSEMITE CREEK AND PORCUPINE FLAT

West of Olmsted Point, **Yosemite Creek** (75 sites, first-come, first-served, July-Sept., $12) and **Porcupine Flat** (52 sites, first-come, first-served, July-mid-Oct., $12) are primitive tent-only campgrounds with fire pits, picnic

tent cabins at Tuolumne Meadows Lodge

tables, and bear-proof food lockers. There is no drinking water and only vault toilets.

TUOLUMNE MEADOWS

★ **Tuolumne Meadows** (Tioga Rd., June-Sept., $26) is one of the largest campgrounds in the park with 304 sites, and it can fill every night. Half of the sites are available by reservation; the remaining half are first-come, first-served. Sites with fire rings and picnic tables accommodate tents and RVs up to 35 feet (no hookups). There are bear-proof food lockers, drinking water, and flush toilets. Tuolumne Meadows is at about 8,600 feet elevation, so it can get chilly even in summer. Leashed pets are permitted.

HIGH SIERRA CAMPS

To spend days in the backcountry without hauling all your gear, book an overnight stay at one of the five ★ **High Sierra Camps** (888/413-8869, www.travelyosemite.com, late-June-early Sept., adults $147-155, children 7-12 $78-83). The camps at **Merced Lake, Vogelsang, Glen Aulin, May Lake,** and **Sunrise Camp** are all accessible via a 6-10-mile hike from their respective trailheads.

All offer tent cabins and include a family-style breakfast and dinner, plus boxed lunches for the next day's adventure. There's no electricity in the cabins and you'll need to bring your own linens. Showers and laundry are available at May Lake, Sunrise, and Merced; flush toilets are available at Glen Aulin, May Lake, and Merced. It's also possible to link a multiday hiking trip from one camp to another (each are 8-10 miles apart).

Reservations are by lottery only; applications are accepted in October for the following summer. You must submit an application to join the lottery; even if you win a spot, there's no guarantee you'll get your preferred dates. A "Meals Only" reservation option allows backpackers with wilderness permits to dine at the camp (adults $85, children 7-12 $38).

Five- and seven-day **guided trips** (adults $710-1,059, children 7-12 $382-571) are also available.

Transportation
CAR

Tioga Road (Hwy. 120, summer only) runs 39 miles from Crane Flat to Tioga Pass, the east entrance, where it becomes Tioga Pass Road. **The road is open only in summer.** To check weather conditions and road closures, call 209/372-0200.

From the west, Highway 120 becomes Big Oak Flat Road at the Big Oak Flat entrance. In nine miles, at Crane Flat junction, turn left onto Tioga Road. The Tuolumne Meadows Visitors Center is 38 miles west. To get to Tioga Road from Yosemite Valley, take Northside Road to Big Oak Flat Road. At the Tioga Road junction, turn east.

SHUTTLES

In summer, the **Tuolumne Meadows Shuttle** (209/372-1172, www.nps.gov/yose, 7am-7pm daily, June-Sept., $1-18) runs along Tioga Road between Olmsted Point and Tuolumne Meadows Lodge, with service farther east to Mono Pass and Tioga Pass.

The **Yosemite Valley to Tuolumne Meadows Hikers Bus** (209/372-1240, www.travelyosemite.com, Aug.-early-Sept., adults $5-23, children 5-12 $2.50-11.50, children under 5 free) departs Yosemite Valley around 8am to arrive in Tuolumne Meadows by 10:30am; the return trip departs Tuolumne Meadows at 2pm. Pick up tickets at the Yosemite Valley Lodge, then hop onboard at one of 10 stops; exact fare is required.

BUS

Yosemite Area Regional Transportation System (YARTS, 877/989-2787, www.yarts.com, Sat.-Sun. June and Sept., daily July-Aug., $6-18 one-way, $12-36 round-trip) runs a Highway 120 East bus from Yosemite Village to Mammoth Lakes in the Eastern Sierra, stopping at Crane Flat, White Wolf Lodge, and Tuolumne Meadows.

HETCH HETCHY

John Muir once proclaimed the undammed **Hetch Hetchy Valley** (open sunrise-sunset year-round) equal in beauty to Yosemite Valley. At less than 4,000 feet in elevation, Hetch Hetchy is one of the lowest parts of Yosemite; it gets less snow and has a longer hiking season than many other areas of the park. It's also warmer here in summer, so bring plenty of water and keep an eye out for poison oak.

O'SHAUGHNESSY DAM

Located north of Highway 120 in Hetch Hetchy, the winding valley is now home to the O'Shaughnessy Dam, completed in 1923 to provide water for San Francisco. The massive, curved gravity dam backs the Tuolumne River into the Hetch Hetchy Reservoir. The dam stands 426 feet high, and 900 feet long, holding 1,972 acres of surface area of water, at a maximum depth of 312 feet, with capacity of 117 billion gallons. The water is deep and blue, and the gushing waterfalls along the sides of the valley are gorgeous.

Hiking

TUEEULALA AND WAPAMA FALLS

The moderate hike along the Wapama Falls Trail (5 miles round-trip, 2 hours) begins by crossing O'Shaughnessy Dam and walking through a tunnel to follow the shore of the reservoir. At a trail junction, veer right to stay on the Wapama Falls Trail. You'll pass Tueeulala Falls first, set back in the hillside, before reaching powerful Wapama Falls. Note that the footbridge over Wapama Falls may close in high-water years.

RANCHERIA FALLS

From Wapama Falls, the Wapama Falls Trail continues to Rancheria Falls (13.4-mile round-trip, 6-8 hours), which can be reached as a long, moderately strenuous day hike with an elevation gain of about 700 feet. Large granite slabs beside the waterfall make a great place to stop for lunch. Or turn this into an overnight trip with a backcountry reservation at Rancheria Falls Camp (wilderness permit and reservation required).

CARLON FALLS

The trailhead to Carlon Falls (4 miles, 2 hours, easy) begins outside the Yosemite park boundaries in the Stanislaus National Forest. From the Carlon Day Use Area, the trail enters the park to follow the South Fork of the Tuolumne River. At the end of one brief uphill climb is the lovely Carlon Falls, a year-round waterfall.

To reach to the trailhead from Highway 120, turn north on Evergreen Road and drive one mile to the Carlon Day Use Area. Past the bridge is a pullout on the right with room for a few cars.

Accommodations and Camping

One mile from the Hetch Hetchy Entrance, the ★ Evergreen Lodge (33160 Evergreen Rd., Groveland, 209/379-2606, www.evergreenlodge.com, $105-455) rents 88 cabins in a variety of styles and sizes. The lodge has a summer camp atmosphere, albeit a gorgeous one, with plenty of organized activities. Dining options include the Main Lodge (7am-10:30am, noon-3pm, and 5pm-9pm daily, $23-32); the Tavern (noon-2am daily), which serves lunch, dinner, and drinks with live music and a pool table; the Pool Bar (hours vary), which has sandwiches, pizza, ice cream, and cocktails; and the General Store (hours vary), which sells snacks and groceries, plus breakfast and espresso to go.

There are no developed campgrounds in Hetch Hetchy. The Hetch Hetchy Backpacker Campground ($6 pp, year-round) provides overnight campsites for backpackers with wilderness permits in the area; campers may stay one day before and one day after their permitted backpacking trip.

Transportation

Hetch Hetchy is in the northwest corner of Yosemite National Park. The Hetch Hetchy Entrance is about 10 miles north of the Big Oak Flat Entrance on Highway 120. From Highway 120, take the Hetch Hetchy turnoff

Hetch Hetchy

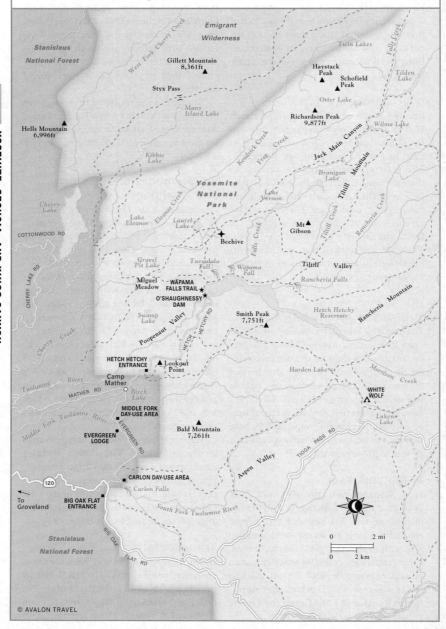

© AVALON TRAVEL

north onto Evergreen Road, and continue 7.2 miles to Camp Mather. Turn right onto Hetch Hetchy Road and proceed another 16 miles through the entrance gate. There is a parking lot near O'Shaughnessy Dam.

Hetch Hetchy Road is open 7am-9pm daily May 1 through Labor Day. It takes about 1-1.5 hours to reach Hetch Hetchy from Yosemite Valley, a distance of about 40 miles.

GATEWAYS TO YOSEMITE

Groveland (Hwy. 120)

Highway 120 winds through Groveland, 26 miles west of the Big Oak Flat Entrance to Yosemite National Park. It is a perfect place to stop for gas, food, coffee, and a place to sleep.

FOOD

En-route to Groveland, the **Priest Station Café** (16756 Old Priest Grade, Big Oak Flat, 209/962-1888, http://prieststation.com, 11am-3pm Mon.-Thurs., 8am-8pm Fri.-Sun., $9-22) serves burgers, steaks, beer, and some vegan dishes on its outdoor patio overlooking Old Priest Grade.

The place to drink is the **Iron Door Saloon** (18761 Main St., 209/962-8904, 7am-1am daily $9-25), which has been slinging drinks for more than 150 years. A local's spot, the Iron Door also serves breakfast, lunch, and dinner.

Across the way is **Cocina Michoacana** (18730 Main St., Groveland, 209/962-6651, 10am-10pm daily, $12-17), which serves filling Mexican food.

Turn north off Main Street to reach **Two Guys Pizza Pies** (18955 Ferretti Rd., 209/962-4897, 11am-10pm daily, $11-30), where delicious piping-hot pizzas are served inside or out with a generous salad bar.

ACCOMMODATIONS

The colorful **Yosemite International Hostel** (8605 Main. St., 209/962-0365, www.yosemitehostels.com, dorm room $28-38 pp, private room $36-53) offers dorm rooms with shared bathrooms and private rooms with

bathrooms; all rooms include linens and use of the communal kitchen.

The historical ★ **Groveland Hotel** (18767 Main St., 209/962-4000, www.groveland.com, $133-255), built in 1849, captures Groveland's Victorian past. The hotel's 17 rooms are furnished in modern decor with down comforters, flat-screen HDTVs, and private bathrooms. Amenities include a hot buffet breakfast, free wireless Internet, and an open-door policy for dogs.

Yosemite Riverside Inn (11399 Cherry Lake Rd., 209/962-7408 or 800/626-7408, www.yosemiteriversideinn.com, $69-295) sits 11 miles west of the Big Oak Flat Entrance and offers affordable motel-style rooms, cabins with full kitchens, and large suites designed to accommodate families.

The **Yosemite Westgate Lodge** (7633 Hwy. 120, 800/253-9673 or 209/962-5281, www.yosemitewestgate.com, $89-235) has 48 nonsmoking and pet-free rooms, a heated pool, spa, and a playground.

Less than one mile from the park entrance, **Rush Creek Lodge at Yosemite** (34001 Hwy. 120, $236-530) has 143 lodge rooms, including large villas, set amid wooded grounds with a saltwater pool, a poolside cafe, two hot tubs, **a restaurant** (7am-10:30am, noon-4pm, and 5pm-9pm daily, $16-20), a full bar that also serves food, and a general store.

Mariposa (Hwy. 140)

Plenty of chain motels fill the tiny town of Mariposa, about 30 miles west of the Arch Rock Entrance (and 40 miles west of Yosemite Valley).

FOOD

Grab breakfast at the **Sugar Pine Café** (5038 Hwy. 140, 209/742-7793, 7am-3pm daily, $6-12), a preserved-in-amber 1940s diner. If you're around for dinner, **1850 Brewing Company** (5114 Hwy. 140, 209/966-2229, www.1850restaurant.com, 11am-9pm daily, $17-30), the new hot spot in town, delivers an array of comfort food alongside pints of their original brews.

ACCOMMODATIONS

In town, **River Rock Inn** (4993 7th St., 209/966-5793, www.riverrockmariposa.com, $67-160) is a quirky, whimsical motel with unusually decorated rooms.

A few miles closer to the park, the **Yosemite Bug Rustic Mountain Resort** (6979 Hwy. 140, Midpines, 209/966-6666 or 866/826-7108, www.yosemitebug.com) is part hostel, part rustic lodge with five hostel dormitories ($26-35), private rooms ($60-175, some with private baths), attractively appointed tent cabins ($40-80) with beds and down comforters, and cabins ($60-135) with private baths. The on-site **June Bug Cafe** (7am-11pm daily, $8-24) serves comfort food (vegan and vegetarian available) in a warm and friendly dining room. The **Yosemite Health Spa** (10am-10pm daily) offers a sauna, hot tub, and massage downstairs.

El Portal (Hwy. 140)

El Portal is less than 4 miles from the Arch Rock Entrance and just 15 miles from Yosemite Valley.

FOOD AND ACCOMMODATIONS

The **Yosemite View Lodge** (11136 Hwy. 140, 209/379-2681, www.stayyosemiteviewlodge.com, $189-399) lies only two miles from the park. The 336-room complex borders the Merced River and offers standard hotel rooms, suites with kitchenettes, plus multiple pools and spas. The on-site **River Restaurant and Lounge** (209/379-2183, 7am-9am, 5:30pm-8:30pm daily, $15-32) serves American food plus beer and wine overlooking the Merced River. The adjacent **Parkside Pizza** (5:30pm-9:30pm daily Apr.-Oct.) is the place to grab a pie. The hotel is conveniently located along the YART bus line.

Indian Flat RV Park (9988 Hwy. 140, 209/379-2339, www.indianflatrvpark.com) is a full-service resort with everything from tent ($20-30) and RV sites ($37-48, some hookups) to tent cabins ($59-139) and cottages ($85-289) with kitchenettes. Showers are available ($3 for nonguests), and the lodge next door allows use of its outdoor pool. Indian Flat is relatively small (25 RV sites, 25 tent sites); reservations are strongly recommended May-September. Pets are permitted ($5 fee).

Oakhurst (Hwy. 41)

Oakhurst lies less than 15 miles from the South Entrance of Yosemite National Park.

FOOD AND ACCOMMODATIONS

The **Best Western Plus Yosemite Gateway Inn** (40530 Hwy. 41, 559/683-2378 or 888/256-8042, www.yosemitegatewayinn.com, $149-159) offers better-than-average chain motel rooms in addition to two-room suites. Amenities include indoor and outdoor pools and hot tubs, free wireless Internet, and an on-site **restaurant** (5pm-9pm daily, $14-24) with a complimentary breakfast (6:30am-10am daily).

The **Oakhurst Lodge** (40302 Hwy. 41, 559/683-4417 or 800/655-6343, www.theoakhurstlodge.com, $80-185) has 33 modest rooms with queen beds within walking distance of shops and restaurants. The pet-friendly lodge also offers a complimentary buffet breakfast.

The elegant **Chateau du Sureau** (48688 Victoria Ln., 559/683-6860, www.chateausureau.com, $346-625) is a breathtakingly beautiful lodge with 10 rooms, turrets, a spa, and the excellent **Erna's Elderberry House** (559/683-6800, www.elderberryhouse.com, dinner 5:30pm-8pm daily, brunch 11am-1pm Sun., $112). Dine on the five-course tasting menu or opt for a bite in the more casual **Cellar** (5pm-8pm Fri.-Sat., $7-15).

South Gate Brewing Company (40233 Enterprise Dr., 559/692-2739, 11am-9pm Mon.-Sat., 10am-9pm Sun., $12-16) pairs burgers and beers. **Taqueria Plazuelas** (40015 Hwy. 49, 559/658-7771, 11am-8:30pm Mon.-Sat., $7-20) is a hole-in-the-wall that trades ambience for homemade tortillas, mole, and tender *carne asada*.

Fish Camp (Hwy. 41)

Fish Camp is 40 miles from Yosemite Valley

via the South Entrance, a little over an hour's drive.

ACCOMMODATIONS AND FOOD
The **Narrow Gauge Inn** (48571 Hwy. 41, 559/683-7720, www.narrowgaugeinn.com, $109-248) is a charming 26-room mountain inn with woodsy nonsmoking rooms, outdoor seating, a complimentary breakfast, and an on-site restaurant (5:30pm-9:30pm daily summer, $18-32). East of Fish Camp, check in to the **White Chief Mountain Lodge** (7776 White Chief Mountain Rd., 209/742-7777, www.whitechiefmountainlodge.com, Apr.-Dec., $116-179), with basic rooms, small TVs, and wireless Internet.

The **Tenaya Lodge** (1122 Hwy. 41, 559/683-6555 or 866/771-9629, www.tenayalodge.com, $169-540) offers plush lodge-style accommodations: choose from rooms in the lodge or one of the three dozen cottages. Tenaya Lodge focuses on guest care, offering a pool, full-service spa, and organized activities. There are five dining venues on-site: **Sierra Restaurant** (6:30am-11am and 6pm-10pm daily, $13-35), which serves big plates of expensive food; the casual **Jackalope's Bar and Grill** (7am-11pm daily, $13-20); **Timberloft Pizzeria** (5pm-10pm daily, $16-25); and the **Harvest and Grounds Deli,** ideal for coffee and a boxed lunch to go.

One mile south of the South Entrance, the small **Summerdale Campground** (Hwy. 41, 877/444-6777, www.recreation.gov, May-Sept., $30-32) is a lovely spot with 26 campsites and a strict limit on RV size (24 feet). Sites have a fire ring and a grill with plenty of shade, vault toilets, and a water spigot (filter all water). There is a two-night minimum on weekends and a three-night minimum on holiday weekends.

The Eastern Sierra

East of Yosemite, the Sierra slope dramatically down into the Great Basin along U.S. 395. The Eastern Sierra is dry and sparse, home to volcanic formations and geological oddities, ghost towns and ski areas, and outstanding recreation.

Tioga Pass (Hwy. 120, $35 park entrance fee) provides a convenient route between Yosemite and the Eastern Sierra, but only from June to September. The rest of the year, travelers can only access U.S. 395 from the north via Reno or Tahoe.

LEE VINING AND VICINITY
The town of Lee Vining sits on the eastern edge of Yosemite National Park. Founded in 1852 as a mining camp, the small town sits on the shores of Mono Lake and provides a convenient stopover for trips to Bodie State Historic Park, Mammoth Lakes, and Bishop. Stop at the **Mono Lake Committee** **Information Center & Bookstore** (U.S. 395 and 3rd St., 760/647-6595, 9am-5pm daily) for maps, brochures, and information.

★ Mono Lake
Unusual and beautiful, **Mono Lake** is home to a body of water that is 2.5 times saltier than the ocean and 1,000 times more alkaline. Over time, the lake has collected huge stores of calcium carbonate, which solidifies into bleached and strange-looking tufa towers. The lake surrounds two large islands: **Negit Island,** a volcanic cinder cone and nesting area for California gulls, and **Paoha Island,** which was created when volcanic activity pushed sediment from the bottom of the lake up above the surface.

The **South Tufa** area of **Mono Lake Tufa State Natural Reserve** (off Hwy. 120, 11 miles east of Lee Vining, 760/647-6331, www.parks.ca.gov, $3) is one of the best places to view the spectacular tufa towers. A one-mile interpretive trail (southeast of the visitors center, adjacent to Navy Beach) winds through the South Tufa area; panels describe the natural history of the area and the formations. In summer, naturalists lead a one-mile, one-hour walking tour (10am, 1pm, and 6pm daily summer, free) around South Tufa. Departing from Navy Beach, Caldera Kayak Tours (760/934-1691, www.calderakayak.com, $75) offer a four-hour paddle around the lake, a natural history lesson, a break for lunch, and a stop at the one of the islands.

Mono Lake County Park (off U.S. 395, 5 miles north of Lee Vining) offers lake access, a picnic area, a playground, and boardwalk trail where docents lead birding walks (8am Fri. and Sun., mid-May-Labor Day, free). The county park offers access for boating, swimming, and kayaking.

Learn more about the lake at excellent Mono Basin National Forest Scenic Area Visitor Center (U.S. 395, 0.5 mile north of Lee Vining, 760/647-3044, www.fs.usda.gov, 8am-5pm daily summer, 9am-4:30pm Thurs.-Mon. spring-fall), where you'll find interactive exhibits, a bookstore, and a helpful staff. A 1.5-mile trail leads to the Old Marina, where a series of trails reach the lake and tufa towers, including a wheelchair-accessible boardwalk trail.

Mono Craters

South of Mono Lake, the Mono Craters offer ample hiking. Panum Crater is the youngest (600 years old) and most accessible. Climb to the top via the Panum Crater Loop Trail (3.5 miles, round-trip, moderate). Guided hikes (10am Sat.-Sun. summer) are also available. The trailhead is off Highway 120, five miles south of Lee Vining.

Food

The place to eat in Lee Vining is at the ★ Whoa Nellie Deli (22 Vista Point Dr., Hwy. 120 and U.S. 395, 760/647-1088, www.whoanelliedeli.com, 6:30am-9pm daily late Apr.-Oct., $10-20) inside the Tioga Gas Mart at the Mobile Gas Station. The deli serves excellent fish tacos, buffalo meat loaf, and pizza, best enjoyed with pitchers of beer and margaritas. Seating is available inside or snag an outside table for a view of Mono Lake. On-site is a large grocery store and gift shop and the clean restrooms. Expect to wait in line as this is a popular place.

Morning coffee comes with flowers and sunshine at the Latte Da Coffee Café (El

Mono Lake Tufa State Natural Reserve

The Eastern Sierra

To Bridgeport

395

NEVADA
CALIFORNIA

270

BODIE STATE HISTORIC PARK

167

Green Creek

Lower Twin Lake

Upper Twin Lake

GREEN CREEK RD

Dunderberg Creek

Conway Summit 8,138ft

Mono Basin National Forest Scenic Area

Green Lake

Nutter Lake
Gilman Lake
Trumbull Lake
Moat Lake

West Lake

East Lake

Hoover Lakes

VIRGINIA LAKES RD

Mono Lake Tufa State Reserve

Summit Lake

Virginia Lakes

Excelsior Mtn 12,446ft

LUNDY LAKE RD

Lundy Lake

Mill Creek

Mono City

Black Point

Negit Island

Mono Lake

McCabe Lakes

Blue Lake

Crystal Lake

Mono Lake County Park

MONO BASIN SCENIC AREA VISITOR CENTER/ OLD MARINA

Paoha Island

Saddlebag Lake

Oneida Lake

Lee Vining

MONO LAKE

Hoover Wilderness

TIOGA PASS RESORT
Tioga Pass 9,945ft

Ellery Lake

Tioga Lake

120

Lee Vining Creek

Panum Crater

NAVY BEACH/ SOUTH TUFA NATURAL RESERVE

TIOGA PASS ENTRANCE

Gibbs Canyon Creek

395

Mono Craters

120

To Yosemite Valley

Mt Dana 13,053ft

Walker Creek

Walker Creek

Crater Mtn 9,172ft

Pacific Crest Trail

Sardine Lake

JUNE LAKE LOOP

Inyo National Forest

Yosemite National Park

Parker Creek

Parker Lake

Grant Lake

June Lake Junction

Koip Peak 12,979ft

Alger Lakes

Silver Lake

June Lake

158

Gull Lake

June Lake

Owens River

Mt Lyell 13,114ft

Waugh Lake

Gem Lake

Agnew Lake

JUNE MOUNTAIN

Deadman Creek

Thousand Island Lake

North Fork San Joaquin River

Garnet Lake

Middle Fork San Joaquin River

Minaret Vista

Mammoth Lakes

To Bishop and Ancient Bristlecone Pine Forest

395

203

0   2 mi
0   2 km

Minarets 12,281ft

MAMMOTH MOUNTAIN

MAMMOTH LAKES BASIN

Sadler Peak 10,567ft

Mammoth Lakes

Convict Lake

DEVILS POSTPILE NATIONAL MONUMENT

© AVALON TRAVEL

Mono Motel, 1 3rd St. at U.S. 395, 760/647-6310, www.elmonomotel.com, 7am-8pm daily summer, $6). For breakfast, order homemade granola or a filling breakfast sandwich served on house-made focaccia. Dine on the front porch or out back in the flower garden.

A classic American diner, **Nicely's** (U.S. 395 and 4th St., Lee Vining, 760/647-6477, 7am-9pm daily summer, 7am-8pm daily winter, $9-23) offers friendly service and familiar food. Inside, you'll find a large dining room with half-circle booths upholstered in cheerful red vinyl. Portions are more than generous. Nicely's has longer hours and a longer season than most places in the area. This is a good place for comfort foods like burgers, fries, and macaroni and cheese.

If you're looking for a Wild West atmosphere and a good spicy sauce, have lunch or dinner at **Bodie Mike's Barbecue** (51357 U.S. 395 at 4th St., Lee Vining, 760/647-6432, 11:30am-10pm daily June-Sept., $7-26). Use your fingers to dig into barbecued ribs, chicken, beef, brisket, and more. Red-checked tablecloths, and local patrons in cowboy boots completes your dining experience. Don't expect the fastest service in the world. At the back of the dining room is the entrance to a small, dark bar populated by locals.

Pop into **Mono Cone** (51508 U.S. 395, 760/647-6606, 11am-7pm daily summer, 11am-6pm spring and fall, $5-11, cash only), where you can get mouthwatering burgers, fries, and soft-serve ice cream, but figure on waiting in line at this popular little roadside shack. Indoor and outdoor seating is available.

A great place for a to-go breakfast or lunch is the **Mono Market** (51303 U.S. 395, 760/647-1010, 7am-9pm daily summer, 7am-8pm daily winter, $3-6). Breakfast sandwiches and pastries are made fresh daily, as are the sandwiches, wraps, and larger entrées you can carry out for lunch or dinner. There's also a full-service grocery store.

Accommodations

Lee Vining has a variety of affordable independent lodging options. **Yosemite Gateway Motel** (51340 U.S. 395, 760/647-6467, www.yosemitegatewaymotel.com, $89-259) is only 14 miles from Yosemite's east entrance. The rustic board-and-batten exterior is modern inside with gleaming wood, furnishings, and clean baths. TVs and Internet access provide entertainment on chilly evenings, and the suites add extra comfort for families.

For clean, comfortable, affordable lodgings, try **Murphey's Motel** (51493 U.S. 395, 760/647-6316 or 800/334-6316, www.murpheysyosemite.com, $68-145). Open year-round, this motel provides everything from small rooms with double beds to rooms that sleep six; some rooms even have kitchens. A central location in downtown Lee Vining makes dining and shopping convenient. Guests enjoy Wi-Fi and TVs.

El Mono Motel (1 3rd St. at U.S. 395, 760/647-6310, www.elmonomotel.com, late May-Oct., depending on weather, $76-103 shared bath, $96-106 private bath) offers comfy beds and clean rooms at very reasonable prices. Enjoy the location in downtown Lee Vining and start each morning with a fresh cup of organic coffee from the on-site café (7am-8pm daily summer).

At the junction of Highway 120 and U.S. 395, stay at the comfortable and affordable **Lake View Lodge** (51285 U.S. 395, 760/647-6543 or 800/990-6614, www.bw-lakeviewlodge.com, cabins $169-338, rooms $116-180). The lodge rents cottages (summer only) and motel rooms (year-round); some rooms have porches and kitchens. All rooms have cable TV; Internet access is available, if spotty. The **Epic Café** (349 Lee Vining Ave., 760/965-6282, http://epiccafesierra.com, 7am-9pm Mon.-Sat. Apr.-Oct., $8-13) serves a breakfast, lunch, and dinner plus beer and wine.

The **Tioga Lodge at Mono Lake** (54411 U.S. 395, 619/320-8868 or 760/647-6423, www.tiogalodgeatmonolake.com, late May-mid-Oct., $129-189) offers unobstructed views of the lake. Opened in 1897, the charming lodge is a collection of cabins—some old, some dragged from the ghost town of Bodie.

All have been redone with rustic charm and comfortable amenities, including private bathrooms. There is wireless Internet, but no TVs. The only drawback is it's a busy location on U.S. 395. The on-site **Hammond Station Restaurant** (7:30am-10:30am, 5:30pm-9:30pm daily mid-June-early Oct., $9-25) serves excellent food, including vegan, gluten-free, and dairy-free options. The hotel is a short drive from Lee Vining.

Camping

Campgrounds line Highway 120 east of Yosemite in the **Inyo National Forest** (760/873-2400, www.fs.fed.us/r5/inyo): **Tioga Lake** (13 sites, $22), **Ellery Lake** (12 sites, $22), **Big Bend** (17 sites, $22) at the end of Poole Power Plant Road, and **Aspen Grove** (45 sites, $14), also along Poole Power Plant Road. All campgrounds are first-come, first-served and have vault toilets, bear lockers, fire pits. The campgrounds close in winter.

Transportation

Lee Vining is north of the junction of Highway 120 (Tioga Pass Rd.) and U.S. 395, which runs north-south from Reno to Bishop. In summer, when Tioga Pass is open, it's possible to drive east through Yosemite on Highway 120 to reach the Eastern Sierra. A park entrance fee is required and traffic congestion is common.

Sonora Pass (Hwy. 108) offers an alternative route in summer (and without the park fee). Both passes are typically open May-November and close in winter. When the passes are closed, access the Eastern Sierra via Highway 50 from South Lake Tahoe or I-80 from Reno.

Yosemite Area Regional Transportation System (YARTS, 877/989-2787, www.yarts.com, Sat.-Sun. June and Sept., daily July-Aug., $6-18 one-way, $12-36 round-trip) runs a Highway 120 East bus from Yosemite Village to Mammoth Lakes in the Eastern Sierra, stopping at Crane Flat, White Wolf Lodge, Tuolumne Meadows, and Lee Vining.

★ BODIE STATE HISTORIC PARK

Bodie State Historic Park (Hwy. 270, 760/647-6445, www.parks.ca.gov, 9am-6pm daily mid-Mar.-Oct., 9am-4pm daily Nov.-mid-Mar., hours vary in winter, adults $8, children 4-17 $5, children under 3 free, cash/check only) is the largest and best-preserved ghost town in California. The rough town of Bodie sprang up around a gold mine in 1877. It quickly rose to a population of more than 7,000 people, supporting 30 mines, 60 saloons, a dedicated Chinatown, a red-light district, and a very busy funeral parlor. The boom didn't last; by the turn the 19th century, its population had dwindled to a few hardy souls. By the 1940s mining had dried up, and the remote location and lack of viable industry led to Bodie's desertion.

Today, the town is preserved in a state of "arrested decay." Houses and buildings stand exactly as lived in when the town was abandoned: dusty broken furniture, peeling wallpaper, table settings, trash and all. Peer in through the windows of the schoolhouse, fire station, and the Methodist church. It can take a full day to explore the town on foot; bring a bike to see it all.

At the park entrance, purchase a self-guided tour map ($2) for detailed information on the buildings. The **visitors center** (9am-6pm daily mid-Mar.-Oct.) is located in the Miners' Union Hall, where you'll also find a gift shop, a museum, and **tours** (11am, 1pm, and 3pm daily late May-early Sept., $6) to the Stamp Mill. There are restrooms in the park, but no other services.

Transportation

Bodie State Historic Park is 30 miles northeast of Lee Vining. Take U.S. 395 north to Highway 270 and turn east. Drive 10 miles to the end of the paved road and then continue another 3 miles on a rough dirt-and-gravel road to the ghost town and parking area. The road is closed in winter. Plan to gas up in Lee Vining and bring plenty of food and water with you.

JUNE LAKE

As U.S. 395 heads south of Lee Vining, it passes through narrow valleys and four subalpine lakes best explored via the June Lake Loop (Hwy. 158). The 16-mile scenic drive takes in Gull Lake, Silver Lake, Grant Lake, and June Lake. Each lake is unique, but Silver Lake—surrounded by granite cliffs and aspens—and June Lake are the most popular.

Silver Lake is home to the bustling Silver Lake Resort (6957 Hwy. 158, 760/648-7525, http://silverlakeresort.net), which offers plenty of opportunities for fishing and boating (rentals: $10-18/hour, $39-45/half-day, $49-55/full-day) and horseback riding (760/648-7701 in summer, 760/872-4038 in winter, https://frontierpacktrain.com, $40/hour, $75/half-day, $120/full-day).

June Lake has a wide sandy beach, perfect for picnics, plus swimming, kayaking, and paddleboarding (rentals 760/924-3075, www.mammothkayaks.com, 10am-3pm daily July-Labor Day, $25/hour). East of June Lake, the loop returns to U.S. 395, 20 miles north of Mammoth Lakes.

Winter Sports

June Mountain Ski Resort (3819 Hwy. 158, 760/648-7733 or 888/586-3686, www.junemountain.com, lifts 8am-4pm daily Dec.-Apr., adults $69-109, seniors and children 13-18 $57-89, children 12 and under free) offers seven lifts (two quads, four doubles, and a carpet) and more than 2,500 feet of vertical drop on 1,400 skiable acres. The resort caters to beginners and intermediate skiers, and 80 percent of its trails are green or blue. Rentals and lessons are available. June Mountain Ski Resort is about four miles west of U.S. 395.

Food and Accommodations

Near the ski resort, the Double Eagle Resort and Spa (5587 Hwy. 158, 760/648-7004, www.doubleeagle.com, open year-round, $199-649) has 15 two-bedroom cabins ($279-349) that sleep six; all come with decks and fully equipped kitchens. The 16 luxurious lodge rooms ($199-229) come with coffee service, free Internet access, a refrigerator, and whirlpool tubs. There's also a sprawling guest-house ($599-649) that sleeps 12. The on-site Creekside Spa includes an indoor pool and a fitness center, and the resort has the Eagle's Landing Restaurant (7:30am-9pm daily, $11-25).

Silver Lake Resort (6957 Hwy. 158,

Bodie State Historic Park

760/648-7525, http://silverlakeresort.net) has a full-service RV park ($38) with 17 cabins ($190-295). Each cabin is like a small house, with a full kitchen, bathroom, linens, and modern furnishings. Laundry facilities are available. Visitors can grab a bite at the on-site **Café** (7am-2pm, $8-13), which serves chili, burgers, and sandwiches. The adjacent **General Store** (7am-7pm) sells limited groceries and camping supplies.

Camping

The U.S. Forest Service maintains several popular campgrounds along the June Lake Loop in the Inyo National Forest. Sites tend to be small; some border the lakes while others sit next to Highway 158. The pretty **Silver Lake Campground** (Hwy. 158, 877/444-6777, www.recreation.gov, mid-Apr.-mid-Nov., $23) is 7 miles west of U.S. 395. Many of the 63 sites are on the shore of lovely Silver Lake.

Near June Lake, **Oh! Ridge Campground** (North Shore Dr. off Hwy. 158, 877/444-6777, www.recreation.gov, mid-Apr.-mid-Nov, $28) is the largest campground with 143 sites. Though it's not on the lake (and has little shade), the campground is close to the family-friendly beach. Both campgrounds have bear-proof food lockers, picnic tables, and fire rings, with flush toilets, and drinking water. Small stores are nearby.

Transportation

June Lake is 14 miles south of Lee Vining on U.S. 395 and 20 miles north of Mammoth Lakes. From U.S. 395, turn west onto Highway 158 to drive the loop.

MAMMOTH LAKES

Mammoth Lakes has it all. There's camping, swimming, boating, fishing, hiking, and mountain biking in summer; skiing, cross country skiing, and snowshoeing in winter. From the center of town, Lake Mary Road leads to the Lakes Basin while Minaret Summit Road (Hwy. 203) heads north to Mammoth Mountain's Main Lodge and Devils Postpile National Monument.

The unpretentious town is loosely organized, with strip malls along each corridor. The hub of visitor activity is the **Village at Mammoth** (6201 Minaret Rd., 760/924-1575, www.villageatmammoth.com), with lodging, dining, and shopping organized around a central pedestrian plaza. In summer, the plaza erupts with outdoor seating, live music, and festivals.

June Lake

Side Trip: Hoover Wilderness

The **Hoover Wilderness** (www.fs.usda.gov) is a 128,421-acre section of Mono County within the Inyo and Humboldt-Toiyabe National Forests. The wilderness extends into the Ansel Adams Wilderness and Tioga Pass to the south and the Emigrant Wilderness and Sonora Pass to the north, with plenty of hiking and camping in between. Permits and information are at the **Bridgeport Ranger Station** (75694 U.S. 395, Bridgeport, 760/932-7070, 8am-4:30pm daily summer, 8am-4:30pm Mon.-Fri. winter) and at the **Mono Basin National Forest Scenic Area Visitor Center** (U.S. 395, 0.5 mile north of Lee Vining, 760/647-3044, 8am-5pm daily summer, 9am-4:30pm Thurs.-Mon. spring-fall, closed Dec.-Mar.).

TRAVERTINE HOT SPRINGS

Travertine Hot Springs (www.monocounty.org) is a naturally occurring series of spring-fed pools hidden in the hills. One of the pools has a concrete bottom, added by human hands, while the rest are the way nature made them, with uneven rocky sides. The springs can be slippery with moss or smelly from sulfur, but if you like to relax outdoors in a peaceful setting (especially under a full moon) this is a memorable experience.

To find the springs, drive north from Lee Vining on U.S. 395. In about 24 miles, just south of the town of Bridgeport, look for a ranger station on the right-hand side of the road, signed "Animal Shelter." Turn right at the sign onto Jack Sawyer Road. In a few hundred yards, turn left onto a dirt road and continue one mile to the springs.

HIKING

There are several trailheads to the east of U.S. 395 between Lee Vining and Bridgeport. Trails here quickly climb through the high desert to subalpine lakes and peaks, including the spectacular Sawtooth Ridge, which separates Yosemite National Park from the Hoover Wilderness.

Lundy Canyon Trail (4.4-10 miles round-trip, moderately strenuous) gains more than 2,000 feet of elevation. You'll cross Mill Creek, pass a trappers cabin, a couple beaver ponds, two waterfalls, and plenty of alpine lakes. Lake Helen, 3.3 miles from the trailhead, is a good place to turn around. The trailhead is seven miles north of Lee Vining, and seven west of U.S. 395 along Lundy Canyon Road.

Virginia Lakes Trail (6.2 miles round-trip, moderately strenuous) climbs from the trailhead

---

In winter, the **Village Gondola** (7:45am-5pm, free) ferries skiers to Canyon Lodge, one of the main lodges of the mountain.

The **Panorama Gondola** (8:30am-4pm daily winter, adult $29, seniors and children 13-18 $24, children under 13 free; 9am-4:30pm daily June-Sept., adults $23, seniors and children 13-18 $19, children under 13 free) runs from the Main Lodge of Mammoth Mountain to McCoy Station, where you can enjoy views from 11,053 feet. After the 20-minute ride to the top, visit the **Eleven53 Interpretive Center and Cafe** (10am-3pm Fri.-Sun., $6-18) for lunch.

Skiing

A number of cross-country ski trails are managed by the Forest Service. **Shady Rest Trails** (Sawmill Cutoff Rd.) is a group of beginner loops near the **Mammoth Lakes Welcome Center** (2510 Main St./Hwy. 203, 760/924-5500 or 888/466-2666, www.visitmammoth.com, 8am-5pm daily).

MAMMOTH MOUNTAIN

The premier downhill skiing and snowboarding mountain is, aptly, **Mammoth Mountain** (10001 Minaret Rd., 760/934-2571 or 800/626-6684, www.mammothmountain.com, lifts at 9,500 feet to a two-mile wide basin of eight small alpine lakes. You'll reach the first three lakes after a mere 1.4 miles. Push on for another 1.8 miles (not so easy at this altitude) and reach the 11,100 pass at Summit Lake, framed by the dramatic Sawtooth Ridge. Take in the view and enjoy a picnic before returning down the trail. The trailhead is 14 miles north of Lee Vining along U.S. 395, At Virginia Lakes Road, turn west and drive to the Big Virginia Lake Day Use Area.

CAMPING

Camping requires a wilderness permit ($3 reservation fee), available at the Bridgeport Ranger Station (75694 U.S. 395, Bridgeport, 760/932-7070, www.fs.usda.gov, 8am-4:30pm daily summer, 8am-4:30pm Mon.-Fri. winter). Self-register when the station is closed. The Forest Service enforces permit quotas in this part of the Hoover Wilderness from the end of June through September 15; permits are available on a first-come, first-served basis when quotas are in effect. There are no quotas for the parts of the wilderness in the Inyo National Forest. Visitors can obtain a permit upon arrival; reservations are not required. For more information about wilderness permits, contact the Inyo National Forest Permit Reservation Line (760/873-2483, 8am-4:30pm daily summer, 8am-4:30pm Mon.-Fri. winter).

FOOD AND ACCOMMODATIONS

The town of Bridgeport provides services to the region. The Bridgeport Inn (205 Main St., 760/932-7380, www.thebridgeportinn.com, 7am-9pm daily, mid-Mar.-mid-Nov., $10-30) offers a genteel dining experience in a historical inn with a variety of rooms ($49-89). For casual dining, try Rhinos Bar & Grille (226 Main St., 760/932-7345, 8am-8:30pm daily, $10-25) or the Three95 Mexican Café (21 Hayes St., 760/616-4829, 7am-2pm Sun.-Fri., 7am-8pm Fri.-Sat., $5-13), the most-raved about Mexican restaurant on U.S. 395.

GETTING THERE

The Hoover Wilderness lies southeast of Bridgeport. Access is off U.S. 395 north of Lee Vining via Lundy Canyon and Virginia Lakes Roads. The town of Bridgeport is 25 miles north of Lee Vining along U.S. 395. The Sonora Pass (Hwy. 108, closed in winter) intersects U.S. 395 at Bridgeport.

8:30am-4pm daily, adults $127-159, seniors and children 13-18 $104-130, children 5-12 $51-64). Whether you're completely new to downhill thrills or a seasoned expert looking for different terrain, you'll find something great on Mammoth Mountain. More than two dozen lifts, including three gondolas and 10 express quads, take you up 3,100 vertical feet to the 3,500 acres of skiable and snowboardable terrain; there are also three pipes. The Mountain Center (760/924-7057 or 800/626-6684, www. mammothmountain.com, 9am-6pm daily summer and winter) rents equipment, offers lessons, and sells lift and shuttle tickets.

Mammoth Mountain has four base lodges: the Main Lodge (10001 Minaret Rd./Highway 203); The Mill (Minaret Rd./ Highway 203), one mile before the Main Lodge; the large Canyon Lodge (1000 Canyon Blvd.) on the west edge of town; and the smaller Eagle Lodge (4000 Majestic Pines Dr.), home to gentle terrain ideal for beginners and families. Along Minaret Road, between the village and Main Lodge, Woolly's Tube Park and Snow Play (760/934-7533, www.mammothmountain.com, 10am-5pm daily, $20-41), has six groomed slopes for tubing, a tube lift, and a snack bar.

TAMARACK CROSS-COUNTRY SKI CENTER

Tamarack Cross-Country Ski Center (163 Twin Lakes Rd., 760/934-2442, www.tamaracklodge.com, 8:30am-5pm daily mid-Nov.-Apr., adults $20-29, youth age 13-22 and seniors $17-23, children age 12 and younger $5) offers 19 miles of groomed cross-country ski tracks, some with groomed skating lanes, for all abilities and levels. Snowshoe and cross-country rentals ($24-29) and lessons ($32-87) are available as are naturalist-led **snowshoe tours** (10:30am Fri.-Sun., free). The center is run by Mammoth Mountain, but located at Tamarack Lodge, which has a restaurant, a lounge, and a bar. A **shuttle** (8:30am-5:15pm daily late Jan.-mid-Apr., free) runs from the village.

Hiking

Hiking in the area includes trails in **Devils Postpile National Monument** (Minaret Vista Rd., 760/934-2289, www.nps.gov/depo, mid-June-mid-Oct., adults $7, children 3-15 $4), as well as the **John Muir Trail** (www.johnmuirtrail.org) and the **Pacific Crest Trail** (www.pcta.org), which intersect in the park. Backpacking permits (free) are required and are available at the **Mammoth Lakes Welcome Center** (2510 Main St./Hwy. 203, 760/924-5500 or 888/466-2666, www.visitmammoth.com, 8am-5pm daily). May-November a quota system is in place and a **reservation** (760/873-2483, www.fs.usda.gov or www.recreation.gov, $15 pp) is required.

West of Mammoth Lakes is the **Lakes Basin.** From the trailhead at Horseshoe Lake (end of Lake Mary Rd.), seeping carbon dioxide has bleached the soil and surrounding trees a spectral white. Pass through the ghostly forest to reach lovely **McCloud Lake** (1.8 miles one-way, easy-moderate) or continue to the **Red Cones Loop** (6.7 miles round-trip, moderate), which climbs over Mammoth Pass to Crater Meadow. In early summer, don't miss the trail to **Emerald Lake and Sky Meadows** (4 miles round-trip, easy), when wildflower blooms are surrounded by permanent snowfields and granite cliffs. The trailhead is at Lake Mary.

Biking

In summer, ski trails transform into mountain biking paths. The **Mammoth Mountain Bike Park** (10001 Minaret Rd., 760/934-2571 or 800/626-6684, www.mammothmountain.com, 8am-6pm daily in summer, trails: adults $17, children $6; trail, gondola, and shuttle: adults $49, children $24) has nearly 90 miles of bike trails accessible by shuttle and gondola. The **Mammoth Adventure Center** (in the Main Lodge, 8am-6pm daily June-Sept.) sells tickets, rents bikes, and offers lesson and clinics ($50-169). The **Mountain Center** (The Village, 6201 Minaret Rd., 760/924-7057 or 800/626-6684, www.mammothmountain.com, 9am-6pm daily summer and winter) sells bikes, gear, and tickets, with rentals and repairs.

Most trails in the surrounding **Inyo National Forest** (760/873-2400, www.fs.usda.gov) are open to mountain bikes, including those around **Horseshoe Lake** (Lake Mary Rd.) and the **Shady Rest Trails** (Sawmill Cutoff Rd.). Paved bike trails weave through downtown, into the Lakes Basin, and along the **Mammoth Scenic Loop.**

Footloose Sports (3034 Main St., 760/934-2400, www.footloosesports.com, 8am-8pm daily) is an excellent bike shop with a knowledgeable staff. Rentals are available.

Horseback Riding

Perhaps the most traditional way to explore the Eastern Sierra is on the back of a horse or mule. From the **McGee Creek Pack Station** (2990 McGee Creek Rd., Crowley Lake, June-Sept. 760/935-4324, Oct.-May 760/878-2207, www.mcgeecreekpackstation.com, $40/hour, $140/full day), 10 miles south of Mammoth Lakes on U.S. 395, you can ride into McGee Canyon, a little-visited wilderness area. Standard rides range from one hour to a full day, but McGee's specialty is multiday and pack trips.

Food

Mammoth has a variety of food options. The best breakfast is at the homey ★ **Good Life Café** (126 Old Mammoth Rd., 760/934-1734, http://mammothgoodlifecafe.com, 6:30am-9pm daily, $8-14) with stick-to-the-ribs breakfast plates and bottomless cups of coffee. At lunch and dinner, you'll find equally hearty sandwiches, salads, wraps, burritos, and burgers, plus beer and wine.

Sports fans love **Slocums** (3221 Main St., 760/934-7647, www.slocums.com, 4pm-10pm Mon.-Sat., $13-33). The bar has craft beer on tap, plenty of TVs, big plates of American comfort food, and a friendly vibe. Happy hour starts at 4pm.

Hopheads will gravitate to the ★ **Eatery By Bleu at Mammoth Brewing Company** (18 Lake Mary Rd., 760/934-7141, www.mammothbrewingco.com, noon-8:30pm Mon.-Thurs., 11:30am-9:30pm Fri., 10am-9:30pm Sat., 10am-8:30pm Sun., $9-25). Standard pub grub gets a new twist with dishes like flatbread pizzas, lobster corn dogs, and Irish Caesar salad. Order a pint of the crisp and malty Golden Trout Pilsner or go for the hoppy Epic IPA. The party spills out onto the patio/beer garden in summer.

Reserve a special night out at **The Lakeside Restaurant** (Tamarack Lodge, 163 Twin Lakes Rd., 760/934-2442, www.mammothmountain.com, 5:30pm-9pm daily, $35-55) on the edge of Twin Lakes, where you'll savor plates of elk and Muscovy duck as the snow falls outside.

Skadi (94 Berner St., 760/914-0962, www.skadirestaurant.com, 5pm-9pm Wed.-Mon., $30-38) serves a menu of "alpine cuisine," a creative mix of Scandinavian, French, and even Japanese flavors. Seats fill fast in this tiny restaurant dressed in Danish minimalism. Make reservations in advance.

The Village (6201 Minaret Rd., 760/924-1575, www.villageatmammoth.com) has several dining options. For killer Mexican food, step into the cavernous **Gomez Restaurant and Tequileria** (760/924-2693, www.gomezs.com, 11:30am-9pm daily, $11-33). Latin fusion food is served alongside signature Mammoth Margaritas and 500 bottles of tequila.

At the **Side Door Bistro** (760/934-5200, www.sidedoormammoth.com, 11am-9pm daily, $8-18), crepes and panini fill the menu of this French-style wine bar.

For a quick bite on the go, **Old New York Deli and Bakery** (760/934-3354, www.oldnewyork.com, 6am-4pm daily, $5-10) sells an assortment of freshly made bagels, salads, and sandwiches.

Accommodations

Two hotels dominate The Village at Mammoth, with easy access to the slopes. Accommodations at **The Village Lodge** (1111 Forest Tr., 760/934-1982 or 800/626-6684, www.thevillagelodgemammoth.com, $299-599) range from studios to three-bedroom condos. All come with full kitchens, gas fireplaces, and access to the lodge's fitness centers, heated pool, and spa. The **Westin Monache Resort** (50 Hillside Dr., 760/934-0400 or 888/627-8154, www.westinmammoth.com, $250-800) offers studio and two-bedroom condos.

Budget options in Mammoth include the **Innsbruck Lodge** (913 Forest Tr., 760/934-3035, www.innsbrucklodge.com, $80-295), with economy rooms and access to the on-site whirlpool tub. The quiet location is on the ski area shuttle route and within walking distance to the restaurants and village attractions. The no-frills **Sierra Lodge** (3540 Main St., 760/934-8881 or 800/356-5711, www.sierralodge.com, $89-199) offers reasonably priced rooms right on the ski shuttle line. Rooms are nonsmoking with kitchenettes and plenty of space for gear. Breakfast, cable TV, and Internet access are included.

Cross-country ski right to your door at the **Tamarack Lodge & Resort** (163 Twin Lakes Rd., 760/934-2442, www.tamaracklodge.com, $109-749). The 11 lodge rooms and 35 cabins range from studios to three-bedroom units that sleep up to nine. Tamarack's rustic atmosphere includes fireplaces and woodstoves, but no televisions.

The ornately carved Austria Hof (924 Canyon Blvd., 760/934-2764 or 866/662-6668, www.austriahof.com, $124-200) offers motel rooms with stylish American appointments. It's adjacent to Canyon Lodge and the free gondola to the village.

The Mammoth Mountain Inn (Main Lodge, 10400 Minaret Rd., 760/934-2581 or 800/626-6684, www.themammothmountain-inn.com, $169-399) offers accommodations from standard hotel rooms to two-bedroom condos. Amenities include a fitness room, child care, access to the Panorama Gondola, and the on-site Mountainside Bar & Grill (760/934-0601, 7am-10am and 5pm-9pm daily, $16-31).

Near the Eagle Lodge, the ★ Juniper Springs Resort (4000 Meridian Blvd., 760/924-1102 or 800/626-6684, www.juni-perspringsmammoth.com, $179-600) has 284 accommodations that range from hotel rooms to large townhomes. Consistent with Mammoth Mountain lodging, amenities are generous and include a game room, fitness center, easy access to the slopes, and the on-site Daily Grind (6:30am-1pm daily summer, 6:30am-11pm daily winter) coffee shop.

Camping

Five first-come, first-served Forest Service campgrounds line Minaret Road: Agnew Meadows (21 sites, $23), Upper Soda Springs (28 sites, $23), Pumice Flat (17 sites, $23), Minaret Falls (27 sites, $23), and Reds Meadow (52 sites, $23). Agnew Meadows and Minaret Falls are prettiest, but all have access to hiking trails. Some campgrounds accommodate RVs. Facilities include vault toilets, potable water, fire rings, and bear lockers. The campgrounds are located past the entrance to Devils Postpile, and a shuttle fee ($10) is required.

The Lakes Basin has five lakeside campgrounds that are open June-mid-September. Three campgrounds accept reservations (877/444-6777, www.recreation.gov), while the other two are first-come, first-served. All campgrounds have fire rings, bear boxes,

flush toilets, access to showers, proximity to groceries and bike trails.

Close to downtown, Twin Lakes Campground ($24) has 92 sites with flush toilets and access to fishing, a boat launch, and services at the Tamarack Lodge. On the north shore of Lake Mary, Lake Mary Campground ($24) has 48 sites with flush toilets and boating and fishing access. On the south side of Lake Mary is ★ Coldwater Campground ($24) with 77 sites in a narrow valley between Coldwater and Mammoth Creeks. Pine City (10 sites, $24) and Lake George (15 sites, $24) are first-come, first-served campgrounds on Lake Mary.

Transportation

The town of Mammoth Lakes is west of U.S. 395 along Highway 203. It is almost 30 miles south of Lee Vining. The high-elevation area receives snow in winter; carry tire chains in your vehicle. For weather and road conditions, call Caltrans (800/427-7623).

In summer, the Yosemite Area Regional Transportation System (YARTS, 877/989-2787, www.yarts.com, June-Aug., $6-18 one-way, $12-36 round-trip) runs buses from Mammoth Lakes to Yosemite Valley with stops at Lee Vining and Tuolumne Meadows.

The Mammoth Yosemite Airport (MMH, 1200 Airport Rd., 760/934-3813, www.ci.mammoth-lakes.ca.us) is served by Alaska Airlines with daily flights from San Diego, Los Angeles, and San Francisco.

In Mammoth, the Eastern Sierra Transit Authority (ESTA, 760/924-3184 or 760/934-2517, www.estransit.com) operates free local bus service around Mammoth Lakes. In winter, the agency also runs a shuttle to the June Mountain Ski Resort (3819 Hwy. 158, 760/648-7733 or 888/586-3686, www.junemountain.com).

★ DEVILS POSTPILE NATIONAL MONUMENT

Devils Postpile National Monument (Minaret Vista Rd., 760/934-2289, www.

Inyo Craters

A geologic side trip from Mammoth Lakes, the **Inyo Craters** (Mammoth Scenic Loop, 760/873-2400, www.fs.usda.gov) were created by explosions of steam around 1350. Two of the three craters are about 200 feet deep and are so large that they have lakes inside them. The third crater is smaller, but all are worth seeing. They are located off Mammoth Scenic Route (Dry Creek Rd.) almost six miles north of the town of Mammoth Lakes. At the sign for the Inyo Craters, about 3 miles from Highway 203, turn left and drive about 1.3 more miles on a dirt road (not plowed, or advised, in winter). Park in the lot and walk 0.3 mile to the crater site.

nps.gov/depo, mid-June-mid-Oct., adults $7, children $4) is named for the strange natural rock formation called the Devils Postpile—straight-sided hexagonal posts created by volcanic heat and pressure. The formation stands 60 feet high, some of it curved, other parts splintered to unusual effect. To learn more about the region's geology, join one of the guided **ranger walks** (11am daily summer), which start from the ranger station (shuttle stop 6).

Within the monument, hikes lead to serene meadows and thundering waterfalls. The popular trail to **Rainbow Falls** (shuttle stop 6 or 9, 2.5 miles one-way, easy) ends at a beautiful crystalline fall that cascades 101 feet to a pool, throwing up stunning rainbows of mist. To escape the crowds, hike to the **Minaret Falls** (shuttle stop 6, 1.4 miles one-way, easy-moderate), which lies outside the monument boundary.

Accommodations and Camping
Red's Meadow Resort & Pack Station (760/934-2345, www.redsmeadow.com) offers the only accommodations inside the monument. Mountain cabins ($200) have electricity, a cook range and fridge, kitchenware, heat,

bathrooms, and linens; cabins sleep six and have a three-night minimum July-August. Motel rooms ($110) have private bathrooms. Two hiker cabins ($55 pp) with bunk beds offer lodging for JMT/PCT thru-hikers; showers are included in the rate. The on-site **Mule House Café** (7am-7pm daily, $11-30) serves breakfast, lunch, and dinner (make reservations by 4pm). A **general store** (7am-7pm daily) sells food, beer, ice, and camping supplies. The resorts also offers horseback rides and pack trips into the Sierra.

The monument's **campground** (mid-June-mid-Oct., $20) offers 20 first-come, first-served sites that accommodate tents and RVs up to 20 feet. Facilities include flush toilets, drinking water, and bear-proof food lockers. Sites fill on weekends in summer. Five other Forest Service campsites line Minaret Road outside the monument boundaries.

Transportation
Devils Postpile National Monument is 13 miles east of Mammoth Lakes along Minaret Road. The road is closed late October to mid-June. In summer, visitors must park at the Main Lodge near the Mammoth Mountain ski area (10001 Minaret Rd.) and enter the monument via **shuttle bus** (7am-7pm daily mid-June-early Sept., $7 adults, $4 children). Shuttle tickets are available at the Mammoth Mountain Adventure Center adjacent to the shuttle. Visitors who arrive before 7am or after 7pm, or who have overnight reservations at Red's Meadow Resort or one of the campgrounds, may drive their cars into the park for a fee ($10).

BISHOP AND VICINITY
Bishop is the largest city in Inyo County. It sits at the north end the Owens Valley, framed by the White Mountains to the east and the towering Sierra to the west.

Bishop is a friendly town with a mixed community of Native Americans, conservative farm families, and those who relish Bishop's proximity to climbing and the great outdoors. The main street offers multiple hotel and dining options, as well as ample places to rent equipment and seek advice.

Laws Railroad Museum and Historic Site

A bit of history lives on at the **Laws Railroad Museum and Historic Site** (Silver Canyon Rd., off U.S. 6, 760/873-5950, www.laws-museum.org, 10am-4pm daily, donation). The historical village encompasses artifacts from the area's history, including original houses with period furniture and a number of railroad cars, including a self-propelled Death Valley Car from 1927 and a caboose that dates to 1883. The museum is 4.5 miles north of Bishop off U.S. 395.

Hiking

West of Bishop, Highway 168 runs to Bishop Canyon where three forks of Bishops Creek draw anglers, hikers, and backpackers. The **Lake Sabrina Trail** (6 miles round-trip, moderate) starts at Lake Sabrina and leads to Blue Lake, one of a series of alpine lakes beneath 13,000-foot-high granite peaks. The climb to Blue Lake takes 1.5 hours with an elevation gain of 1,200 feet. Donkey and Baboon Lakes lie 1.5 miles beyond. Lake Sabrina is 20 miles east of Bishop along Highway 168.

It's 10 long, uphill miles to Bishops Pass on the eastern border of Kings Canyon National Park from the trailhead at South Lake, a stunning lake boxed in by walls of granite. For a day hike, follow the main trail, keeping left, to Long Lake and **Bishop Lake** (end of South Lake Rd., 9 miles round-trip, strenuous) or veer right to **Treasure Lakes** (6 miles round-trip, moderate).

Climbing

Bishop is a big destination for rock climbing. Popular places to climb include **The Buttermilks** (Buttermilk Rd., off Hwy. 168, west of Bishop), a jumble of 30 plus erratic boulders, and the **Volcanic Tablelands** (Pleasant Valley Rd., off Hwy. 6, north of Bishop), a 300-foot-high volcanic plateau, which includes the Happy and Sad Boulders.

Sierra Mountain Guides (312 N. Main St., 760/648-1122, www.sierramtnguides.com) and **Sierra Mountain Center** (200 S. Main St., 760/873-8526, www.sierramountaincenter.com) both offer climbing lessons and guided trips, in addition to ice climbing, mountaineering programs, avalanche courses, and guided backpacking treks. Nearby, the excellent **Eastside Sports** (224 N. Main St., 760/873-7520, http://eastsidesports.com,

Devils Postpile National Monument

9am-6pm Mon.-Fri., 9am-9pm Sat.-Sun.) sells gear and can offer advice, maps, and local expertise.

Fishing
Bishop offers fishing along the Owens River and along the South Fork of Bishops Creek. **Lake Sabrina** (20 miles east of Bishop along Hwy. 168) and **South Lake** (15 miles east of Bishop along Hwy. 168) have boat launches.

Sierra Trout Magnet (2272 N. Sierra Hwy., 760/873-0010, http://sierratroutmagnet.com, 8am-2pm Sun.-Wed., 8am-5pm Thurs.-Sat.) specializes in fly-fishing and offers guided trips, as well as equipment, tackle, and advice.

Hot Springs
A short drive outside Bishop, **Keough's Hot Springs** (800 Keough Hot Springs Rd., 760/872-4670, www.keoughshotsprings.com, open year-round, 11am-7pm Mon., Wed.-Thurs., 11am-8pm Fri., 9am-8pm Sat., 9am-7pm Sun., adults $12, children 3-12 $7, children under 3 $4) has a kitschy charm to go with its relaxing hot springs. Soak in the 100-by-30-foot warm pool or the smaller hot pool; both are heated by natural hot mineral springs.

Horseback Riding
Rainbow Pack Outfitters (5845 South Lake Rd., 760/873-8877, http://rainbow.zb-net.com) offers a wide range of options for horse lovers. At the stables, small children can enjoy their "Li'l Cowpoke" ride ($20) on a pony or horse with an expert leading. Options for bigger kids and adults include the Rainbow Meadow Ride (1 hour, $40), the South Lake Vista Ride (2 hours, $60), the Long Lake Scenic Ride (4 hours, $80), the All-day Ride (9am-5pm, $125), and the All-day Fishing Ride (9am-5pm, $150), which is a mini-pack trip. Rainbow provides service into the John Muir Wilderness, the Inyo National Forest, and Sequoia and Kings Canyon National Parks.

Food and Accommodations
The **Looney Bean** (399 N. Main St., 760/873-3311, www.looneybean.com, 5:30am-6pm daily) serves espresso, bagel sandwiches, and premade salads and sandwiches amid local art with free Wi-Fi and an easygoing vibe. **Black Sheep Coffee Roasters** (232 N. Main St., 6:30am-6pm Mon.-Thurs, 6:30am-7pm Fri.-Sat., 7am-6pm Sun.) serves excellent, award-winning artisan coffee in a narrow white-brick space.

Erick Schat's Bakkerÿ (763 N. Main St., 760/873-7156 or 866/323-5854, http://schats-bakery.com, 6am-6pm daily, $6-10) is famous for the simple shepherd bread that it has been selling since 1938. Today, the bakery also makes delectable sweets, to-die-for cinnamon rolls, and limitless varieties of pastries. In the next room, a **sandwich bar** (7am-3pm Mon.-Thurs., 7am-3:30pm Fri.-Sat., 7am-5pm Sun.) serves hearty soups, salads, and sandwiches.

★ **Mountain Rambler Brewery** (186 S. Main St., 760/258-1348, www.mountainramblerbrewery.com, 11:30am-10:30pm Sun.-Thurs., 11:30am-11:30pm Fri.-Sat., $8-11) serves a simple menu of tacos, flatbreads, burgers, and vegetarian meal options that pair nicely with their craft beer, enjoyed in a warm and sophisticated interior.

Ambient music and posted drumming hours indicate that the ★ **Hostel California** (213 Academy Ave., 760/399-6316, www.the-hostelcalifornia.com, dorm room $25-35, private room $60-170) caters to the climbing set, but the cheerful hostel is welcoming to all. Common areas include a giant kitchen, a living room, and dining room. Accommodations are in dorms or private rooms with their own bathrooms. Linens are provided.

Handsome **Creekside Inn** (725 N. Main St., 760/872-3044, www.bishopcreeksideinn.com, $129-199) has rooms with modern amenities, including flat-screen TVs, coffeemakers, and semiprivate patios. Bishop Creek snakes through the lovely grounds. A hot breakfast is included in the rate.

Keough's Hot Springs (800 Keough Hot Springs Rd., 760/872-4670, www.

keoughshotsprings.com) offers a range of accommodations for overnight relaxing after a soak in their hot springs. Choose from "dry" tent or RV sites ($28), campsites with water and electricity ($33), four tent cabins ($90-105), or two mobile homes ($130-140) that sleep four and have full kitchens. Keough's is six miles south of Bishop on U.S. 395.

Along Bishop Creek, **Bishop Creek Lodge** (2100 S. Lake Rd., 760/873-4484, www.bishopcreekresort.com, $119-270, Apr.-Oct.) rents cabins and has a café and general store. Farther along the road, **Parchers Resort** (5001 S. Lake Dr., 760/873-4177, www.parchersresort.net, $145-310) has a variety of cabins, as well as RV sites; most cabins include showers, heat, running water, and linens.

Camping

Forest Service (760/873-2400, www.fs.usda. gov) campgrounds line Bishop Creek. Along South Lake Road, off Highway 168, **Four Jeffrey Campground** (877/444-6777, www. recreation.gov, May-Oct., $26) has 106 sites with potable water and flush toilets. Nearby, **Willow** (7 sites, $23) and **Mountain Glen** (5 sites, $23) are both first-come, first-served with vault toilets, but no potable water.

Near pretty Lake Sabrina, **Sabrina Campground** (760/873-2400, www.fs.usda. gov, May-Sept., $26) sits at 9,300 feet elevation with 18 first-come, first-served sites, vault toilets, and easy access to hiking trails. It's 18 miles west of Bishop along Highway 168.

Showers ($6) are available for purchase at Bishop Creek Lodge and Parchers Resort.

Transportation and Services

Bishop is at the junction of U.S. 395 and U.S. 6, 40 miles south of Mammoth. Set at an elevation of 4,000 feet, the area does not receive as much snow as Mammoth, but it's still a good idea to carry tire chains in winter. Bishop is the best place to fill your gas tank, as services are few and far between. Cell phone reception is minimal.

Stop at the **White Mountain Ranger**

Ancient Bristlecone Pine Forest

Station (798 N. Main St., 760/873-2500, www.fs.usda.gov, 8am-5pm daily summer, 8:30am-4:30pm Mon.-Fri. fall-spring) for tips, permits, and maps to the area.

ANCIENT BRISTLECONE PINE FOREST

The **Ancient Bristlecone Pine Forest** (www.fs.usda.gov/inyo) lies at 11,000 feet in the heart of the White Mountains, via a steep and narrow drive 23 miles east of Big Pine. The forest is home to the world's oldest trees, gnarled and twisted bristlecone pines that are thousands of years old. Stop at the **visitors center** (760/873-2500, 10am-5pm daily summer, 10am-5pm Sat.-Sun. spring and fall, $3 pp or $6/car) to pick up trail guide and maps, then visit the nearby **Schulman Grove.** The grove can be explored via the **Discovery Trail** (1 mile round-trip, easy), but opt for the longer **Methuselah Loop** (4.5 miles round-trip, moderate), named for the 4,850-year-old Methuselah tree (the tree is unmarked and its location secret).

Hiking Mount Whitney

One of the most famous climbing or backpacking trips in California is Mount Whitney (www.nps.gov/seki). At 14,500 feet, Whitney is the highest peak in the continental United States, and this must-do trek draws intrepid hikers and climbers from around the world. Whitney also marks the southern end of the John Muir Trail and makes for a dramatic end or beginning for thru-hikers doing the whole trail.

Mount Whitney sits on the eastern border of Sequoia National Park and Inyo National Forest, west of the town of Lone Pine, which is the main departure point for the popular hike to the top. From the trailhead on Whitney Portal Road (13 miles west of Lone Pine), the trail climbs 11 miles to the peak of Whitney, with an elevation gain of 6,131 feet over one vertical mile. While it's possible to hike to the top of Mount Whitney and back in one day, it's not fun nor advisable. If you attempt to bag this peak, apply for an overnight wilderness permit to break the trek up into two days.

Permits (www.fs.fed.us/r5/inyo, $15) are required for anyone entering the Mount Whitney Zone—even day hikers. May-October, there's a quota for hikers; those who want to hike must enter the permit lottery (Feb. 1-Mar. 15) in order to have a good chance of getting a permit for the following summer. After April 1, permits are first-come, first-served; November-April, a permit is still required, but there are no quotas in place.

For more information, contact the Inyo National Forest (760/873-2483, www.recreation.gov). Permits must be picked up in person at the Eastern Sierra Interagency Visitors Center (U.S. 395 and Hwy. 136, 760/876-6200, www.fs.fed.us/r5/inyo, 8am-5pm daily). During the off-season, you can self-register for a permit if the visitors center is closed.

The nearest campground is the 43-site Whitney Portal (end of Whitney Portal Rd., 877/444-6777, www.recreation.gov, late Apr.-late Oct., $24), 13 miles west of Lone Pine in the Inyo National Forest. To stay closer to the summit, try for the 10 walk-in sites near the Mount Whitney trailhead (760/873-2400, www.fs.usda.gov, first-come, first-served, one-night limit, $12).

The second notable grove is the Patriarch Grove, home of the Patriarch Tree—the world's largest bristlecone pine. A self-guided nature trail wanders among the scrubby trees. The Patriarch Grove is 12 miles north of Schulman on an unpaved dirt road that can be unsafe for passenger vehicles.

Camping

Several first-come, first-served campgrounds line White Mountain Road. Grandview Campground (www.fs.usda.gov/inyo, $5) is five miles from Schulman Grove at 8,600 feet. There are 23 sites with picnic tables, fire grills, and vault toilets; there is no drinking water.

Transportation

The Ancient Bristlecone Pine Forest is a one-hour drive southeast of Bishop. From U.S. 395, drive 15.5 miles south to Big Pine and turn left (east) onto Highway 168. Follow Highway 168 for 13 miles to White Mountain Road. Turn left (north) and drive 14 miles to the visitors center in Schulman Grove. Two miles south of the Schulman Grove, the road closes in the winter. There are no services; gas up in Bishop before the drive.

Sequoia and Kings Canyon

Sequoia and Kings Canyon (559/565-3341, www.nps.gov/seki, open year-round, $30/vehicle, $25 motorcycles, $15 bike or on foot) encompass more than 864,000 acres of this dramatic landscape and include two distinct parks, a forest, and a monument: Kings Canyon National Park to the north, Sequoia National Park to the south, Sequoia National Forest surrounding much of the parkland, and Giant Sequoia National Monument, a subset of the national forest to the south and west of the parks. Sequoia and Kings Canyon are jointly administered by the National Park Service.

Generals Highway is the main road running north-south through the two parks; it connects Highway 180 (Kings Canyon National Park) in the north to Highway 198 (Sequoia National Park) in the south. The steep, narrow, twisting mountain road can be treacherous in bad weather and road construction may also create delays. The maximum allowed RV length on Generals Highway is 22 feet, and trailers are not permitted. Neither RVs nor trailers are permitted on Mineral King Road or Moro Rock-Crescent Meadow Road. Plan at least an hour to drive the road.

Park Entrances

There are three entrances to Sequoia and Kings Canyon National Parks located on the western side of the park. There is no access from the east and no road that traverses the Sierra.

The **Big Stump Entrance** (Hwy. 180) comes into the park from the west and is the most direct route to Kings Canyon National Park. From the entrance station, stay left on Highway 180 and continue 3.5 miles to Grant Grove Village. To reach Sequoia National Park, turn right onto Generals Highway and head south.

The **Ash Mountain Entrance** (Hwy. 198) enters Sequoia National Park from the south. Inside the park, Highway 198 becomes Generals Highway North. The drive can be slow thanks to a combination of heavy traffic (especially in summer) and road construction. In winter, the Ash Mountain Entrance is plowed before the Big Stump Entrance. Call (559/565-3341 or 800/427-7623) to check road conditions.

The **Lookout Point Entrance** (Mineral King Rd. ay Hwy. 198, Apr.-Oct.) accesses the remote Mineral King area of Sequoia National Park. Mineral King Road is narrow, winding, and closed in winter (Nov.-May). RVs and trailers are not advised.

SHUTTLE

A free **shuttle** (877/287-4453, www.sequioashuttle.com, 8am-6:30pm daily late May-Sept.) stops at the Lodgepole Visitor Center, Wuksachi Lodge, Giant Forest Museum, and Moro Rock.

GENERALS HIGHWAY

This twisty, mountainous stretch of **Highway 198** connects Kings Canyon in the north to Sequoia National Park south, passing through segments of Giant Sequoia National Monument and Sequoia National Forest along its 32 miles.

Pullouts along Generals Highway provide access to hiking trails, lodges, and scenic overlooks. At **Kings Canyon Overlook** (7 miles south of the Grant Grove), views look east over the rugged Kings Canyon. Stop at **Redwood Mountain Overlook** (6 miles south of Grant Grove) to peer over the world's largest grove of giant sequoias.

GRANT GROVE

The Grant Grove area of Kings Canyon National Park is three miles east of the Big Stump Entrance on Highway 180. The hub of Grant Grove Village has a visitors center,

Sequoia and Kings Canyon

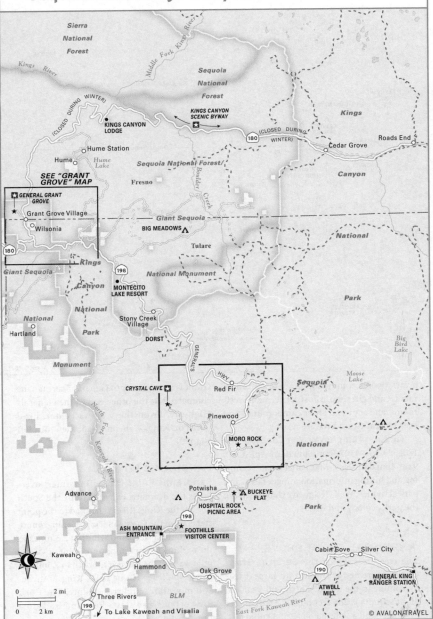

Sierra National Forest

Kings River

Middle Fork Kings River

Sequoia National Forest

KINGS CANYON SCENIC BYWAY

Kings

(CLOSED DURING WINTER)

KINGS CANYON LODGE

Hume Station

Hume

Hume Lake

Sequoia National Forest

Boulder Creek

180 (CLOSED DURING WINTER)

Cedar Grove

Roads End

Canyon

SEE "GRANT GROVE" MAP

Fresno

GENERAL GRANT GROVE

Grant Grove Village

Wilsonia

180

Giant Sequoia

BIG MEADOWS

Tulare

National

Kings

Giant Sequoia

198

MONTECITO LAKE RESORT

National Monument

Park

National

Canyon

Hartland

Park

Stony Creek Village

DORST

GENERALS

Big Bird Lake

Monument

North Fork Kaweah River

CRYSTAL CAVE

HWY

Red Fir

Sequoia

Moose Lake

Pinewood

MORO ROCK

National

Advance

Potwisha

HOSPITAL ROCK PICNIC AREA

BUCKEYE FLAT

Park

ASH MOUNTAIN ENTRANCE

198

FOOTHILLS VISITOR CENTER

Cabin Cove

Silver City

Kaweah

Hammond

Oak Grove

190

MINERAL KING RANGER STATION

ATWELL MILL

0   2 mi
0   2 km

Three Rivers

198

To Lake Kaweah and Visalia

BLM

East Fork Kaweah River

© AVALON TRAVEL

Grant Grove

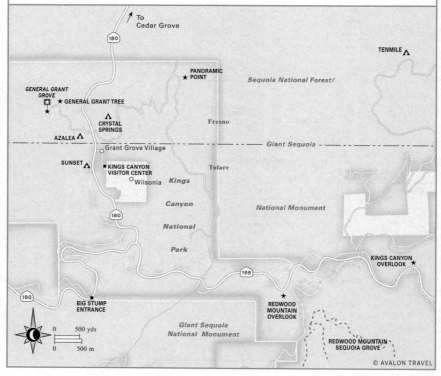

To Cedar Grove

180

TENMILE

PANORAMIC POINT

Sequoia National Forest/

GENERAL GRANT GROVE

★ GENERAL GRANT TREE

CRYSTAL SPRINGS

Fresno

AZALEA

SUNSET

Grant Grove Village

Giant Sequoia

KINGS CANYON VISITOR CENTER

Wilsonia

Tulare

Kings

Canyon

National

Park

National Monument

KINGS CANYON OVERLOOK ★

198

180

BIG STUMP ENTRANCE

REDWOOD MOUNTAIN OVERLOOK

Giant Sequoia National Monument

REDWOOD MOUNTAIN SEQUOIA GROVE

0   500 yds

0   500 m

© AVALON TRAVEL

a variety of accommodations, a restaurant, a market and gift shop, a post office, public restrooms, and showers. Three campgrounds and the General Grant Tree are nearby.

The **Kings Canyon Visitor Center** (Hwy. 180, 559/565-4307, 9am-5pm daily Apr.-Oct., 9am-4pm daily Nov.-Mar.) offers maps, camping and hiking information, ranger talks, and park activities. Well-designed exhibits explore the park ecology and history.

Sights

★ GENERAL GRANT GROVE

The tree after which the **General Grant Grove** is named is the second-largest tree by volume in the world. This 1,700-year-old giant sequoia is 268 feet tall with a diameter of 40 feet and a volume of 46,608 cubic feet.

Grant is second only to General Sherman, its compatriot at the other end of the Generals Highway. From the visitors center, head north on Kings Canyon Road, then turn left (signed).

PANORAMIC POINT

Panoramic Point (closed in winter) overlooks the dramatic canyon cut by the South Fork of the Kings River. The road to the point starts from the Crystal Springs Campground, then climbs a steep and winding 2.3 miles to the parking lot for Panoramic Point. It's 0.25-mile walk to the ridge at more than 7,500 feet where you'll see Hume Lake, Kings Canyon, and mountains and trees galore. The **Park Ridge Trail** also starts here and leads to a fire lookout.

General Grant Grove

Hiking
BIG STUMP TRAIL

Immediately inside the Big Stump Entrance, less than a mile west of the junction of Highway 180 and the Generals Highway, the **Big Stump Trail** (2 miles round-trip, easy) weaves through a grove that was heavily logged in the late 19th century. You'll be able to get close to a couple giant sequoias that were spared, climb on those that weren't (including the Mark Twain stump, the remains of a 26-foot-wide tree that was cut in 1891), and see the imprint of the lumber mill that was once here.

GENERAL GRANT GROVE

General Grant Grove is home to dozens of giant sequoias. The largest of these is the General Grant Tree, which truly lives up to its hype. The **General Grant Tree Trail** (0.3 mile, easy) leads past many other stunning sights on the way to and from its namesake tree in just a short distance. Along this trail is the **Fallen Monarch,** an immense tree lying

on its side and hollowed out in the middle, the 1872 **Gamlin Cabin,** used as the living quarters for the first ranger stationed here, and the **Centennial Stump,** so large that whole Sunday school classes have stood on top of it.

The General Grant Tree Trail is a paved, short, and easy walk and is accessible for wheelchairs. Trail guides ($1.50) are available at the trailhead, which has a large parking lot with restrooms. From the visitors center, head north on Kings Canyon Road, then turn left (signed).

The **North Grove and Dead Giant Loop** (3 miles, easy) takes you to the Dead Giant, a first-growth giant sequoia that was most likely killed by loggers who tried, and failed, to cut it for lumber. The trail continues to an overlook of Sequoia Lake, actually an old mill pond from the logging days. The trailhead starts from the lower end of the General Grant Tree parking area.

SUNSET TRAIL

For a longer, more demanding day hike, check out the **Sunset Trail** (6 miles, strenuous). From the visitors center, cross Kings Canyon Road, entering the Sunset Campground (the trail leaves the campground at site 118). After 1.25 miles, follow the South Boundary Trail for 0.25 mile to Voila Falls. Then, on the Sunset Trail, hike downhill to Ella Falls. Altogether, you'll climb about 1,400 vertical feet round-trip through magnificent mixed forests. To return to the trailhead, either head back the way you came or follow the fire road north to the General Grant Tree trailhead.

PARK RIDGE TRAIL

Enjoy views of the eastern park from the **Park Ridge Trail** (4.7 miles, easy). There's little elevation change on this walk, and much of it is on a wide, easy-to-follow fire road, but the altitude can make it a little challenging. The trailhead is located at the parking lot for Panoramic Point, 2.5 miles east of Grant Grove Village. The road to the point is closed in winter.

REDWOOD CANYON

Redwood Canyon is home to the largest grove of giant sequoias in the world. The 16 miles of trails within the canyon make it a good place to wander around and see the trees up close. At the trailhead, turn left to begin the **Hart Tree and Fallen Goliath Loop** (6.5 miles, easy). This trek leads across Redwood Creek and past the former logging site of Barton's Post Camp. About halfway around the loop, you'll come to a short spur trail that takes you to the Hart Tree, the largest in the grove and the 25th-largest known in the world. Fallen Goliath, a little farther along, is another impressive sight, even lying down.

To get here, take Generals Highway seven miles south of Grant Grove Village. At the sign for Redwood Canyon, turn right onto the dirt road and travel two miles to the end of the road where there is ample room for parking.

BUENA VISTA PEAK

Opposite the Kings Canyon Overlook, **Buena Vista Peak** (2 miles, easy) is an ideal spot to gaze out at the Western Divide, Mineral King, Farewell Gap, and a sea of conifers. Park at the Buena Vista trailhead. It sits opposite the highway from the overlook and six miles south of Grant Grove.

BIG BALDY

Big Baldy (4 miles, easy-moderate) is a popular out-and-back hike with an elevation gain of only 1,000 feet over two miles. It's one of the most rewarding hikes in the park, considering the relatively small effort you have to expend for the major views. From the granite summit of Big Baldy, you'll be able to see far into Redwood Canyon, plus the High Sierra Peaks and the Great Western Divide. The trailhead and parking area are along the Generals Highway, eight miles south of Grant Grove.

Horseback Riding

Grant Grove Stables (Grant Grove, 559/335-9292 in summer, 559/799-7247 off-season, June-Sept., $40-75) leads guided trail rides through the North Grove, Lion Meadow, and along Dead Giant Loop.

Food

The **Grant Grove Restaurant** (Grant Grove Village, Hwy. 180, 559/335-5500, www.visitsequoia.com, 7am-10am, 11:30am-3:30pm, 5pm-9pm daily, $12-30) serves surprisingly good food in a casual yet beautiful dining room. Order the giant Grant Grove bacon cheeseburger and a pint of Tioga Sequoia Firefall Red Ale and enjoy the views of the back meadow through floor-to-ceiling windows.

Snacks and camping supplies are sold at the **Grant Grove Market** (Grant Grove Village, Hwy. 180, 8am-8pm daily), with a gift store next door.

Accommodations
GRANT GROVE VILLAGE

★ **Grant Grove Cabins** (Grant Grove Village, open seasonally) offer an array of lodging styles at a variety of prices. The economy option is in the 17 **tent cabins** (May-Oct., $62-89), which are short on amenities, with no electricity or heat and with shared central baths. The so-called **camp cabins** (May-Nov., $89-110) are at the low end of the fully enclosed cabins. They have solid walls and 2-3 double beds, plus electricity, a propane heater, and daily maid service, but no private baths. **Rustic cabins** (May-Nov., $99-110) come with at least two double beds and have carpets and insulation. The **bath cabins** (year-round, $129-140) have all of the amenities, plus private baths with a tub and shower.

John Muir Lodge (Grant Grove Village, open year-round, $111-240) shares a woodsy aesthetic and excellent accommodations. The 36 rooms feature queen or king beds, flat-screen TVs, local art, and porches with chairs or rockers that enjoy views into the forest. John Muir Lodge is two stories with no elevator.

Lodging **reservations** (866/807-3598, www.visitsequoia.com) in Grant Grove can fill 4-6 months in advance.

ALONG GENERALS HIGHWAY

In Giant Sequoia National Monument, **Montecito Sequoia Lodge** (63410 Generals Hwy., 559/565-3388 or 800/227-9900, www.mslodge.com, mid-Aug.-May, $139-318, meals included) is a rustic full-service resort on Generals Highway south of Grant Grove. Accommodations include lodge rooms with private baths, suites that sleep up to six (some with private decks), cabins with private decks and baths, and rustic cabins with electricity and shared bathhouses. In summer, Montecito operates primarily as a family camp, but it is available to non-campers. The lodge is 11.7 miles south along Generals Highway.

Stony Creek Resort (559/565-3388 or 877/828-1440, www.sequoia-kingscanyon.com, May-early Oct., $209-239) is located in the Sequoia National Forest of the Giant Sequoia National Monument. It has 11 modest hotel rooms with private baths. Facilities include a **pizzeria** (4pm-6:30pm daily in season, $10-25), a market and gift shop (7am-8pm daily), a coin laundry (9am-6pm daily), showers (9am-6pm daily, $4), an ATM, and a gas station (with credit card 24 hours daily). The resort is 13 miles south of Grant Grove on Generals Highway.

Camping
GRANT GROVE VILLAGE

Three campsites cluster around Grant Grove Village. Campers can make reservations at **Sunset** (156 sites, 877/444-6777, www.recreation.gov, summer only, $22), while sites at ★ **Azalea** (110 sites, year-round, $18) are first-come first-serve. **Crystal Springs** (49 sites, summer only, $18) is on the east side on the road toward Panorama Point. Its wide, flat sites offer little privacy, but are great for groups (7-19 people, $50). Each campground comes with picnic tables, fire rings, bear lockers, drinking water, and restrooms with flush toilets. Showers are available at Grant Grove Village. Campgrounds fill all weekends in July-August. Opening and closing dates vary seasonally; call 559/565-3341 to confirm.

HUME LAKE

The **Hume Lake Ranger District** is home to three Forest Service campgrounds. **Hume Lake** (Hume Lake Rd., 877/444-6777, www.recreation.gov, May-Sept., $25) sits on the shore of Hume Lake with 74 sites and flush toilets. Groceries, gas, and laundry are nearby. Tiny **Landslide Campground** (Tenmile Rd., summer only, $21) has nine first-come, first-served sites with vault toilets, but no potable water. **Tenmile** (Tenmile Rd., 877/444-6777, www.recreation.gov, May-Sept., $21) is close to Generals Highway with 13 sites that allow RVs up to 22 feet long. It has vault toilets but no drinking water.

Hume Lake is 3.6 miles southeast of Highway 180 (past Grant Grove). The campgrounds are located along Hume Lake Road and Tenmile Road. The road between Hume Lake and Generals Highway is closed in winter.

Princess Campground (Hwy. 180, 877/444-6777, www.recreation.gov, June-Sept., $25) lies four miles west of Hume Lake with 88 sites, vault toilets, and an RV dump station. It is part of Giant Sequoia National Monument (559/338-2251, www.fs.fed.us/r5/sequoia) and is six miles north of Grant Grove Village.

ALONG GENERALS HIGHWAY

Several campgrounds are scattered along south Generals Highway.

Eight miles south of Grant Grove, Big Meadows Road leads to **Horse Camp** (5 sites, first-come first-served, June-Sept., free) and **Big Meadows** (45 sites, 877/444-6777, www.recreation.gov, June-Sept., $21-46). Both Forest Service campgrounds have grills, food lockers, and vault toilets, but no potable water.

Stony Creek Campground (Generals Highway, 877/444-6777, www.recreation.gov, May-Oct., $25) has 49 tent and RV sites with fire rings, flush toilets, drinking water, and food lockers. Nearby **Upper Stony Creek Campground** ($21) has 18 sites with fire rings, picnic tables, water, and pit toilets. Both

Forest Service campgrounds are convenient to Stony Creek Resort. Stony Creek is 14 miles southeast of Grant Grove.

In Sequoia National Park, **Dorst Creek Campground** (877/444-6777, www.recreation.gov, late June-early Sept., $22) has 212 sites with flush toilets, drinking water, picnic tables, fire rings, food lockers, and a dump station. Dorst is one of the larger campgrounds and accommodates RVs. Sites fill fast in summer. It's six miles north of Wuksachi Village.

Transportation and Services

Grant Grove is located in Kings Canyon National Park, four miles east of the Big Stump Entrance on Highway 180. Grant Grove Village has ATMs, groceries, and coin-operated showers.

There are no gas stations inside the national park boundaries. There is a gas station at **Hume Lake Market** (559/305-7770, 9am-5pm daily, shorter hours in winter). **Stony Creek Resort** (559/565-3388, www.sequoia-kingscanyon.com, mid-May-mid-Oct.), 13 miles south of Grant Grove, has showers, laundry, a market, and a gas station (24 hours with credit card).

CEDAR GROVE

Cedar Grove sits in the heart of the glacially carved Kings Canyon at the end of the Kings Canyon Scenic Byway, 30 miles northeast of Grant Grove on Highway 180. In winter, the road closes from the junction with Generals Highway, near the Princess Campground in Sequoia National Forest.

The centerpiece of **Cedar Grove Village** (8am-9pm daily summer, 8am-8pm daily spring and fall) is the **Cedar Grove Lodge** (559/565-0100, May-Oct.). Other services in the village include a **snack bar** (7:30am-10:30am, 11:30am-2:30pm, 5pm-8pm daily), gift shop, small market, laundry, showers, and an ATM. Located next to the Sentinel Campground near Cedar Grove Village, the **Cedar Grove Visitor Center** (559/565-3793, 9am-5pm daily mid-May-late Sept.) has books, maps, first aid, and park rangers.

★ Kings Canyon Scenic Byway

The section of Highway 180 from Grant Grove through Cedar Grove is known as the **Kings Canyon Scenic Byway,** and it offers tremendous views of the vast canyons that give the park its name. The drive

Kings Canyon

starts at 6,600 feet at Grant Grove, weaving down as far as 3,000 feet around Convict Flat before climbing back up to 5,000 feet before its terminus at Roads End. Much of the road passes through Sequoia National Forest. It reenters Kings Canyon National Park six miles east of Convict Flat. Along the way, you'll be treated to dramatic vistas, narrow passageways, heart-stopping precipices, rushing rivers, and granite monoliths. Though curvy, the road is not treacherous, but it is essential to maintain a reasonable-to-slow speed. Ample roadside pullouts are available on both sides of the highway, so you'll find it easy to stop for photos along the way.

One mile east of Cedar Grove Village, pull over at **Canyon View** to admire the glacier-carved canyon.

Less than one mile down the road is the small but picturesque **Knapp's Cabin.** It was built in the 1920s by George Knapp, a Santa Barbara businessman who stored his extensive fishing gear here.

In three miles, Highway 180 hits **Roads End,** where trails lead into the park's panoply of canyons, forests, and lakes. The rustic **Roads End Permit Station** (7am-3:30pm daily late May-late Sept.) is the place to get your wilderness permit and to talk to the rangers about trail conditions, recommended routes, and food storage regulations before your backcountry adventure.

Hiking

SHEEP CREEK CASCADE

The hike to **Sheep Creek** (Sheep Creek Trailhead, 2 miles, 1.5 hours, moderate) ascends 600 vertical feet along the Don Cecil Trail to a picturesque shaded glen that's perfect for picnicking amid the serene surroundings.

DON CECIL-LOOKOUT PEAK

From the Don Cecil Trailhead, the **Don Cecil Trail to Lookout Peak** (13 miles round-trip, strenuous) is one of the more challenging day hikes. You'll climb 4,000 feet to the top where

views stretch into the Sequoia wilderness. (The trail passes through areas recovering from the 2015 Rough Fire.)

ROARING RIVER FALLS

The short and easy stroll to **Roaring River Falls** (less than 0.25 mile) is under a canopy of trees, making it cool in summer. Just looking at the falls feels refreshing after driving the Generals Highway. From here, the easy **River Trail** (1.6 miles) leads to Zumwalt Meadow and all the way to Roads End (2.7 miles). The parking area is three miles east of Cedar Grove Village.

ZUMWALT MEADOW

The **Zumwalt Meadow Trail** (1.5 miles, easy) leads past granite walls and through lush meadows through a grove of heavenly smelling incense cedar and pine trees along the Kings River. The trailhead parking lot is one mile west of Roads End. The boardwalk trail remains under repair following the 2017 floods.

MIST FALLS

The **Mist Falls Trail** (8 miles round-trip, moderate-strenuous) is a popular jumping-off point for backpackers destined for the Kings Canyon backcountry. You can hike to Mist Falls and back or keep going all the way to Paradise Valley (14 miles, strenuous). Plan for dust and heat on the first couple of miles of the trail and then steep switchbacks up 1,500 vertical feet to the falls. Park at the Roads End trailhead.

Backpacking

Backcountry wilderness permits are required year-round for overnight hikes. Permits are available at the **Roads End Permit Station** (7am-3:30pm daily late May-late Sept, $15 pp). From late May through late September, a trail quota is in place; applications are accepted started in March. Permits ($15) must be picked up at the permit station. From October to early May, permits are free.

Horseback Riding

Cedar Grove Pack Station (1 mile east of Cedar Grove Village, summer 559/565-3464, off-season 559/337-2413, www.nps.gov/seki, May-mid-Oct., weather permitting) offers customized backcountry horseback riding trips for up to two weeks. Guides will provide the food and do the cooking, bring all the gear (except your sleeping bag), and take care of the horses along the way. The minimum for backcountry pack trips ($250/day pp) is three days for four people. Short trips in the Cedar Grove area include one-hour ($40) and two-hour ($75) excursions along the Kings River, a half-day ride to Mist Falls or the Kings Canyon Overlook ($100), and an all-day trip ($150). Reservations are required for multiday trips.

Food and Accommodations

Cedar Grove Lodge (Cedar Grove Village, 866/807-3598 or 877/436-9615, May-Oct., $119-160) has 21 rooms with two queen beds and private baths; some rooms have private patios and a minifridge. The no-frills **Cedar Grove Grill** (7:30am-10:30am, 11:30am-2:30pm, 5pm-8pm daily mid-May-late Oct., $8-22) serves hamburgers and other items. The nearby **Cedar Grove Market and Gift Shop** (7am-9pm daily, mid-May-late Oct.) sells sandwiches, supplies, and souvenirs.

Camping

The **Sentinel Campground** (Cedar Grove Village, 877/444-6777, www.recreation.gov, May-Nov., $18-22) is the largest campground with 82 sites. Reservations are accepted in summer, but sites are first-come, first-served in spring and fall. The campground is conveniently close to showers, a market, a restaurant, and the visitors center.

Less than one mile away, **Canyon View** (May-Sept., $40-60) has 16 reservable group sites (no RVs or trailers), while **Moraine** (May-Sept., $18) offers 121 first-come, first-served sites. Close to the park entrance,

Sheep Creek (May-Nov., $18) has 111 first-come, first-served sites. All campgrounds have drinking water, flush toilets, and food lockers.

Convict Flat (Hwy. 180, 559/338-2251, www.fs.fed.us, summer only, free) is a Forest Service campground with five primitive, first-come, first-served sites with vault toilets but no drinking water. It's six miles north of Cedar Grove.

Transportation and Services

Cedar Grove is 30 miles northeast of Grant Grove on Highway 180, less than 35 miles from the Big Stump Entrance to Kings Canyon. Only the first six miles of the road are open in winter. Road opening and closing dates vary depending on snowfall, and chains can be required at any time. Call the park (559/565-3341) to confirm conditions.

Cedar Grove Village has ATMs, pay phones, and coin-operated showers and laundry. There is no gas or cell service.

TOP EXPERIENCE

GIANT FOREST AND LODGEPOLE

Visitors short on time should focus their visit on the Lodgepole and Giant Forest area. Located at the midpoint along the Generals Highway in Sequoia National Park, the Giant Forest is home to a grove of giant sequoias that covers 1,880 acres with a network of more than 40 hiking trails. The Lodgepole Village complex provides a hub of visitor services for enjoying it all.

The **Lodgepole Visitor Center** (559/565-4436, 8am-4:30pm daily May-Oct.) provides books, maps, and souvenirs; you can also join a ranger talk or walk. Wilderness permits (summer $15, off-season free) are available inside (self-register outside when closed). You'll also find camping, groceries, food, and **Crystal Cave tour tickets** (daily mid-May-late Oct.).

Giant Forest and Lodgepole

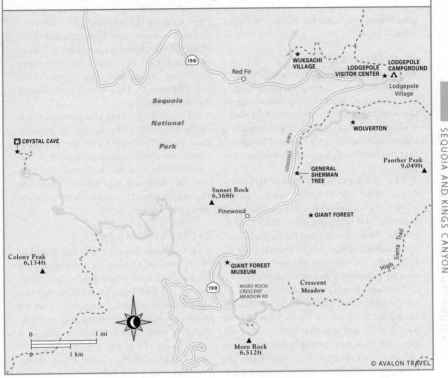

Sights
WOLVERTON

The **Wolverton Picnic Area** (Generals Hwy.) is two miles north of the General Sherman Tree. The wide-open spaces offer plenty of room for picnicking in the summer and sledding in winter.

GIANT FOREST MUSEUM

The **Giant Forest Museum** (Generals Hwy., 559/565-4480, 9am-5pm daily) is a lively place full of giant sequoias and touchable exhibits that provide context to all the facts and figures about these trees. You'll learn how the park used to look and why many of the buildings have been removed to make way for more trees. Numerous hikes branch out into the

Giant Forest Sequoia Grove. **Crystal Cave tour tickets** (from 9am daily Nov.) are also sold here after the Lodgepole Visitor Center closes for the winter.

THE GENERAL SHERMAN TREE

The **General Sherman Tree** (Wolverton Rd., off Generals Hwy., 4 miles north of the Giant Forest Museum) is, by sheer volume of wood, the largest tree known on earth. It's an easy 0.5-mile downhill walk down from the parking lot or from the shuttle stop at Wolverton Road. When you get to the viewing area, you'll find masses of people paying their respects. This enormous attraction can get crowded on summer weekends, so if you're able to visit on a weekday, or early in the morning, you may enjoy the experience even more.

The trailhead and parking area are at the grove's north end near the Wolverton Picnic Area.

★ CRYSTAL CAVE

Magical **Crystal Cave** (Generals Hwy., 3 miles south of the General Sherman Tree) is one of the most beautiful of the 200 or so caves that occur naturally in the park. Its immense underground rooms are filled with sparkling stalagmites and stalactites made of limestone that has metamorphosed into marble over time.

The **Sequoia Natural History Association** (559/565-3759, www.sequoia-history.org) offers 50-minute guided tours (daily late May-late Sept., adults $16, children 5-12 $8, children under 5 $5) of Crystal Cave. A more challenging 1.5-hour tour ($18, age 12 and older only) takes you deeper into the caverns for a detailed lesson on the cave's history and geology. Serious spelunkers can sign up for the **Wild Cave Tour** (559/565-4222, age 16 and up, $135), a 4- to 6-hour crawl off the well-lit trails and into the depths of Crystal Cave. You must be in good physical condition to join this expedition. The shorter **Junior Caver Tour** (2.5 hours, $30) provides a good introduction. Caving gear is provided.

Tickets are available at the Giant Forest Museum (Generals Hwy., 559/565-4480, 9am-5pm daily), the Foothills Visitor Center (Hwy. 198, 559/565-4212, 8am-4:30pm daily), and online (www.recreation.gov). Ticket sales close 90 minutes before the day's final tour.

The long and winding dirt road to the cave parking lot can take more than an hour from either visitors center (no trailers or RVs over 22 feet). Tours fill quickly; get tickets early in the morning or a day in advance. In summer, book tours one month in advance.

MORO ROCK

The granite dome of **Moro Rock** stands starkly alone in the middle of the landscape, providing an amazing vantage point for much of the park. For maximum impact, park in the lot at the base of the rock and climb the 400 steps to the top, a distance of about 0.25 mile. The stairs are solid, and there are handrails all along the way. You'll want to take it slow, in any case; the entire route is filled with photo ops as you look down on the canyons of the Great Western Divide and across the peaks of the Sierra Nevada.

To reach the parking area from Generals Highway, take Moro Rock/Crescent Meadow Road south. There are restrooms and interpretive signage in the large parking lot. A free **shuttle** (9am-6pm Fri.-Sat., 8am-6pm Sat.-Sun., late May-mid-Sept.) runs in summer. The road is closed to vehicles summer weekends and holidays.

CRESCENT MEADOW

A sort of oasis beside at the south end of Giant Forest, **Crescent Meadow** is a bright-green and yellow plain, thick with grasses and teeming with wildlife. You can walk around the whole meadow in about an hour, watching for all manner of birds, squirrels, chipmunks, marmots, and even black bears. To reach the parking area from Generals Highway, take Moro Rock/Crescent Meadow Road south, past Moro Rock to the road's terminus. A free **shuttle** (9am-6pm Fri.-Sat., 8am-6pm Sat.-Sun., late May-mid-Sept) runs in summer. The road is closed to private vehicles summer weekends and holidays.

Hiking
LITTLE BALDY

How can you resist a hike to a granite formation called **Little Baldy** (3.5 miles round-trip)? This moderate climb takes you up about 700 feet to the top of the granite dome. Look down from the peak, which tops out at over 8,000 feet, over the Giant Forest and Moro Rock, and snap a few photos. The trailhead is nine miles north of the General Sherman Tree on Generals Highway.

TOKOPAH FALLS

To cool off, head for **Tokopah Falls** (3.4 miles round-trip, easy). Early summer, when the flow is at its peak, is the best time to trek out the almost two miles along the Marble Fork of the Kaweah River to this fantastic 1,200-foot waterfall. The trailhead is near Marble Fork Bridge in Lodgepole Campground.

CONGRESS TRAIL

From the trailhead at the General Sherman Tree, the **Congress Trail** (2.9 miles round-trip, easy-moderate) weaves through many of the park's most famous giant sequoias—Chief Sequoyah, General Lee, and President McKinley—as well as the House and Senate Groups. Much of the trail is paved and wheelchair accessible, interrupted only by the stairs back to the trailhead. Handicapped parking is available at a small parking area along the Generals Highway. In summer, a shuttle makes stops here. The trailhead is in the parking lot for the General Sherman Tree off Wolverton Road.

BIG TREES TRAIL

The **Big Trees Trail** (1.2 miles, easy) starts from the Giant Forest Museum and navigates a level path through the Round Meadow. Interpretive panels make this a fun walk for kids, and the paved boardwalk is wheelchair accessible. Accessible parking is available at the Big Trees trailhead. Otherwise, park at the Giant Forest Museum and follow the hike from the Trail Center trailhead.

HAZELWOOD AND HUCKLEBERRY MEADOW LOOP

From the Giant Forest Museum, the **Hazelwood** and the **Huckleberry Meadow Loop** (4.5 miles round-trip, easy) starts on the Hazelwood Nature Trail, where signs describe the history of humans' relationship with the giant sequoia trees. Then, take the Alta Trail to the Huckleberry Meadow Loop, which passes the 1880s Squatter Cabin, one of the oldest structures in the park. A spur leads the second-largest tree in the world, the Washington Tree.

CRESCENT MEADOW-LOG MEADOW LOOP TRAIL

The **Crescent Meadow-Log Meadow Loop Trail** (1.6 miles, easy) is a short loop that lets you experience more wildflowers and forest. From the Crescent Meadow parking lot and picnic area, the trail leads past Tharp's Log, the park's oldest shelter, within a hollowed out log. Follow the High Sierra Trail to its intersection with the Crescent Meadow Loop (watch for signs for Tharp's Log). Then, take the Tharp's Log Trail north to its namesake along Log Meadow. Explore the "cabin," then turn west to visit the Chimney Tree at the northern edge of Crescent Meadow. Follow the Crescent Meadow Loop south to return to the parking area.

Food and Accommodations

Built in 1999, the ★ **Wuksachi Lodge** (64740 Wuksachi Way, 877/436-9615 or 866/807-3598, www.visitsequoia.com, $154-325) offers the most luxurious accommodations inside the parks. Rooms are scattered in smaller lodges around Wuksachi Village and are decorated with colorful Native American textiles and Craftsman touches. Amenities include a coffeemaker, fridge, ski racks, daily maid service, and Internet access.

At the Wuksachi Lodge, the excellent ★ **Peaks Restaurant** (559/565-4070, www.visitsequoia.com, 7am-10am, 11am-2:30pm, 4:30pm-8:30pm daily, $12-37) serves hearty entrées, grass-fed burgers, and cocktails next to picture windows that frame forest views. A kid's menu and boxed lunches ($9-13) are available. Make dinner reservations on summer weekends.

The **Lodgepole Market Center** (Lodgepole Village, 559/565-3301, 8am-9pm May-Aug., 9am-6pm Sept.-Oct., 8:30am-6:30pm Sat.-Sun. Nov.-Apr.) sells basic groceries and camping supplies. The **Watchtower Deli** (559/565-3301, 11am-6pm daily early May-late Oct.) has premade sandwiches, salads, and wraps, and plenty of snacks. The Harrison Grill (9am-11am and 11:30am-6pm daily) serves pizza, hamburgers, and hot dogs.

Camping

At the end of Lodgepole Village, the Lodgepole Campground (877/444-6777, www.recreation.gov, May-Sept., $22) straddles the Kaweah River. The campground has 214 shady sites set amid rocky terrain. Facilities include flush toilets, picnic tables, food storage, and a dump station. It's close to showers, laundry, and groceries in the village. From October through April, 16 walk-in tent sites are first-come, first-served.

Transportation and Services

Lodgepole is on Generals Highway 22 miles north of the Ash Mountain (south) Entrance and 27 miles south of the Big Stump (northwest) Entrance. It takes about an hour to drive to Lodgepole from either entrance. Wuksachi Village is just two miles northwest of Lodgepole, and the General Sherman Tree parking lot is 2.5 miles south of Lodgepole, off Wolverton Road.

Lodgepole Village (559/565-3301) is the visitor hub with a market, restaurants, a gift shop, coin laundry and showers (7am-1pm and 3pm-9pm daily early May-late Oct., 8am-1pm and 3pm-6pm daily late Mar.-early May), ATM, shuttle services, a post office, and pay phones. There is no cell service. Many facilities close in winter.

FOOTHILLS

The Foothills area of Sequoia National Park is in the south part of the park, with lower elevations and drier, snow-free weather. It is accessed from the Ash Mountain Entrance on Highway 198, east of Three Rivers.

The Foothills Visitor Center (Hwy. 198, 559/565-4212, 8am-4:30pm daily) is one mile north of the Ash Mountain Entrance and serves as the park headquarters with a bookstore, exhibits, and ranger talks and walks. You can also buy Crystal Cave tickets or pick up a wilderness permit (late May-late Sept., $15 for up to 15 people).

Pull over at the Hospital Rock Picnic Area (near Buckeye Flat) to see Native American pictographs and grinding holes across the road.

Hiking
MARBLE FALLS TRAIL

For a vigorous adventure with a big payoff, take the Marble Falls Trail (7.8 miles, moderate-strenuous) to Marble Falls. This hike starts in the Potwisha Campground near site 14. Start out on a forest road, and you'll soon see a sign directing you to keep left; the way then becomes more trail-like, winding upward through the woods. After 2.5 miles, you'll emerge from the trees for sweeping views of the canyons around you and the water below. In four miles or less you'll come to Marble Falls. The falls are beautiful, noisy, and dramatic, and you'll see why they got their name—the viewpoint actually looks like a very large slab of white marble.

PARADISE CREEK

A nice, short nature walk in the Foothills area starts in Buckeye Flat Campground and leads alongside Paradise Creek (3 miles, easy). Start by crossing the footbridge near campsite 28 and then bear right to follow the trail beside the creek. The Middle Fork of the Kaweah River heads off to the left. In about 1.5 miles the trail will start to peter out. At that point, turn around and return the same way. No day parking is allowed at Buckeye Flat; park at Hospital Rock Picnic Area and walk about a mile on a paved road to Buckeye Flat.

Camping

Potwisha (42 sites, 877/444-6777, www.recreation.gov, year-round, $22) is on the Kaweah River, about four miles north of the Ash Mountain Entrance. Amenities include flush toilets, drinking water, a dump station, and bear-proof containers.

Just a few miles farther north along Generals Highway, on a little spur to the east, you'll find **Buckeye Flat** (28 sites, 877/444-6777, www.recreation.gov, May-Sept., $22) in a lovely spot along the Kaweah River. This tent-only campground has flush toilets; it does not accommodate RVs or trailers.

At the southern end of the park, **South Fork** (10 sites, year-round, $12) is a tent-only campground 13 miles off Highway 198 on South Fork Drive near Three Rivers. The campground is first-come, first-served with pit toilets and bear-proof containers, but no drinking water.

Transportation
The Foothills area is easily accessed from the south via Highway 198; it's the first part of the park you encounter after the Ash Mountain Entrance.

MINERAL KING
The **Mineral King area** (Mineral King Rd., closed in winter) of Sequoia National Park encompasses the highest elevation reachable by car. The subalpine landscape is filled with dense forests with outcroppings of shale and granite with few examples of human intervention: the Mineral King Ranger Station, the Silver City Mountain Resort, a few private cabins, and two campgrounds (Atwell Mill and Cold Springs). The nearest food and gas are in the town of Three Rivers, and the 24-mile road to get there takes at least 1.5 hours to drive in good weather. The one-lane road is open to two-way traffic, so expect to pull over and wait now and then. Mineral King Road is 24 miles east of Highway 198.

The **Mineral King Ranger Station** (Mineral King Rd., 559/565-3768, 8am-4pm daily May-Sept.) is located near the end of Mineral King Road, beyond the Silver City Resort and close to Cold Springs Campground. You can get information and wilderness permits here, and there is a self-service **wilderness permit box** ($15 summer, free winter).

Hiking
Many hikes begin in Mineral King Valley,

and you can visit a number of charming alpine lakes if you're up for a hike of 7-12 miles. However, at 7,500 feet elevation, hikes in the Mineral King area are demanding and strenuous. Bring lots of water and honestly gauge the fitness level of yourself and others before hitting the trail. Mosquitoes can be a problem.

A good place to start walking in Mineral King is the **Cold Springs Nature Trail** (1 mile). This easy interpretive walk describes and displays the natural wonders and the formation of the valley.

TIMBER GAP
The **Timber Gap Trail** (4 miles round-trip) follows an old mining road through a forest of red fir trees. You'll enjoy pretty views out to Alta Peak and the Middle Fork of the Kaweah River. Remember that you're at over 7,500 feet in elevation, so you may feel you're getting a workout even on this short hike.

MONARCH LAKES
Upper and Lower Monarch Lakes (8.5 miles round-trip) sit nestled beneath majestic Sawtooth Peak. The trek is mostly flat and easy walking through forest and meadows, with views of the Great Divide. Bring a picnic to enjoy beside the lakes.

EAGLE AND MOSQUITO LAKES
Plan to spend all day on the hike out to **Eagle and Mosquito Lakes** (7 miles round-trip), which lie in the backcountry beyond the Mineral Creek Ranger Station. The Eagle and Mosquito Lakes trailhead is at the end of Mineral King Road. From the trailhead, climb two miles up Mineral King Valley to Eagle Basin. Where the trail splits, head left to Eagle Lake (3.4 miles from trailhead) or right to Mosquito Lake (3.6 miles from trailhead).

WHITE CHIEF TRAIL
The **White Chief Trail** (5.8 miles round-trip) begins at the Eagle and Mosquito Lakes trailhead at the end of Mineral King Road. The trail leads to the abandoned mine site at White Chief Bowl. It's a fairly steep climb at

times, but the rewards include scenic views of the Mineral King Valley and a look at some remnants from the area's mining history, including the Crabtree Cabin, which dates to the 1870s.

Food and Accommodations

Silver City Mountain Resort (Mineral King Rd., 559/561-3223, www.silvercityresort.com, May-mid-Oct., $110-410) is a privately owned resort on national park land. The resort has 13 different cabins. The economical "historical cabins" built in the 1930s have propane lighting, refrigerators, and stoves with bathrooms nearby. The "family cabins" sleep up to five people and have propane, plus a toilet but no shower. The studios sleep 2, have a large deck and full bathrooms, and come with a complimentary breakfast. The more modern "chalets" are outfitted with decks, fireplaces, showers, phones, full kitchens, and outstanding mountain views. Wi-Fi is included in the rates.

Most cabins come with a kitchen. The **Silver City Restaurant** (8am-8pm Thurs.-Mon., $12-20) is the only place to get food . . . and pie (9am-5pm Tues.-Wed.).

Camping

There are two campgrounds in the Mineral King area: **Atwell Mill** (21 sites, May-Oct., $12) and **Cold Springs** (40 sites, May-Oct., $12). Both are first-come, first-served and have vault toilets. If you want showers or food, you can drive to Silver City, 0.5 mile east of Atwell Mill and 2.5 miles west of Cold Springs. Both campgrounds have drinking water available May-mid-October. The water is turned off the rest of the year. The Mineral King Ranger Station is located beside the Cold Springs campground.

Transportation

To get to Mineral King, approach Sequoia National Park from the south on Highway 198. Instead of entering the park, make a right turn onto Mineral King Road, two miles before the Ash Mountain Entrance, and drive 25 miles east. It will take about 45 minutes to come to the end of this narrow, winding road; trailers and RVs are not allowed. Along the way, you will enter the boundaries of Sequoia National Park through the small Lookout Point Entrance (May-Oct., $30) and pay the entrance fee at a self-serve station. November-April, the gate is locked for the season.

Monterey and Big Sur

Look for ★ to find recommended sights, activities, dining, and lodging.

Highlights

★ **Santa Cruz Beach Boardwalk:** With thrill rides, carnival games, and retro-cool live music, this is the best old-time boardwalk in the state (page 415).

★ **Surfing in Santa Cruz:** If there's anywhere in Northern California to don a wetsuit and go surfing, it's Santa Cruz. Breaks range from easy-rolling beginner waves at **Cowell's Beach** to more powerful breakers at **Steamer Lane** (page 423).

★ **Elkhorn Slough:** There's no better place to view the marine mammals of Monterey Bay than from a kayak in the Elkhorn Slough (page 428).

★ **Monterey Bay Aquarium:** This mammoth aquarium astonishes with a vast array of sealife and exhibits on the local ecosystem (page 430).

★ **Scuba Diving, Kayaking, and Stand-Up Paddleboarding:** Experience Monterey Bay's calm water and unique wildlife by getting into the water (page 436).

★ **Carmel Beach:** A great place for a stroll, a surf, or a picnic, this is one of the finest beaches on Monterey Bay (page 450).

★ **Point Lobos State Natural Reserve:** The crown jewel of California's impressive state park system has pocket coves, tide pools, forests of Monterey cypress, and diverse marine and terrestrial wildlife (page 451).

★ **Point Sur Light Station:** Crowning a 361-foot-high rock towering above the sea, this lighthouse is arguably California's most stunning light station (page 461).

★ **Pfeiffer Beach:** With rock formations

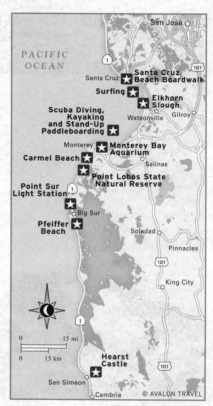

offshore and purple sand, Pfeiffer Beach is one of Big Sur's most picturesque spots (page 465).

★ **Hearst Castle:** Newspaper magnate William Randolph Hearst's 56-bedroom mansion is the closest thing that the United States has to a castle (page 478).

The wild and rugged Central Coast provides ample opportunities to explore marine ecosystems, historic sights, and charming small towns. It's a favorite getaway for locals as much as visitors.

Monterey Bay is the largest marine sanctuary in the country. Dive into its pristine waters to explore swaying kelp forests, or visit the famous aquarium for close-up views of local sea creatures. Santa Cruz is home to a seaside amusement park that offers roller coasters, bumper cars, and family-friendly beaches. Victorian architecture and butterfly migrations are the draws at Pacific Grove. Exclusive Pebble Beach offers some of the most-photographed scenery in the state. Artsy Carmel-by-the-Sea is an idyllic village gently descending to a white-sand beach. Inland Carmel Valley offers a burgeoning wine industry with enough tasting rooms to fill a long, relaxing afternoon.

Big Sur's 90 miles of rugged coastline begin just south of Carmel and stretch south to San Simeon. Here, the mountains rise up suddenly and drop just as dramatically into the sea. Highway 1 twists and turns like a two-lane snake, trying to keep up with the land- and seascape.

South of Big Sur, San Simeon is home to one of California's biggest attractions: the magnificent Hearst Castle, a monument to the incredible wealth of newspaper magnate William Randolph Hearst. Farther south, Cambria has a pleasant downtown and Moonstone Beach, where you can pick up pieces of the gemstone right off the sand.

PLANNING YOUR TIME

For a relaxed weekend without much travel, focus your trip on Santa Cruz or the Monterey Peninsula. If you've got more than a couple of days, start in either Santa Cruz or Monterey and work your way down the coast.

Many people drive through Big Sur in one day, taking Highway 1 south from Carmel and pulling off at the road's many turnouts. Outdoors enthusiasts who want to *really* experience Big Sur will need at least a couple of

---

Previous: Bixby Bridge in Big Sur; Tide pooling is popular along the rich Monterey Bay. **Above:** the Chairoplane at the Santa Cruz Beach Boardwalk.

Monterey and Big Sur

Big Basin Redwoods State Park
Bonny Doon
Felton
Davenport
Scotts Valley
17
Forest of Nisene Marks
Santa Cruz
Capitola
SANTA CRUZ BEACH BOARDWALK
SURFING
La Selva
Beach
Watsonville
152
Monterey Bay
Moss Landing
129
SCUBA DIVING, KAYAKING, AND STAND-UP PADDLEBOARDING
MONTEREY BAY AQUARIUM
Castroville
156
101
Marina
183
ELKHORN SLOUGH
Pacific Grove
Sand City
Salinas
CARMEL BEACH
Monterey
Seaside
POINT LOBOS NATURAL RESERVE
Carmel
68
Garrapata State Park
Carmel Valley Village
POINT SUR LIGHT STATION
G17
101
Andrew Molera SP
G16
Gonzales
Big Sur
PFEIFFER BEACH
Los Padres National Forest
Soledad
John Little SR
Ventana Wilderness
Greenfield
Lopez Pt
Lucia
Limekiln SP
KIRK CREEK
King City
PLASKETT CREEK
FORT
Jade Cove RA
HUNTER
Cape San Martin
TREEBONES RESORT
LIGGET
0   5 mi
0   5 km
Pacific Ocean
HEARST CASTLE
Lake San Antonio
San Simeon
Lake Nacimiento
CAMP ROBERTS MILITARY RES
San Simeon State Park
Cambria
San Miguel
© AVALON TRAVEL

days. The **Big Sur Valley** (26 miles south of Carmel) is a good place to stay for a great outdoors experience and amenities such as restaurants and lodging. The valley is also home to **Pfeiffer Big Sur State Park,** which has more than 200 campsites. The south coast toward San Simeon has fewer amenities; there are a few campgrounds, the Treebones Resort, and Hearst Castle.

Summer is the busy season; reservations are essential for hotels and campsites. Monterey Bay's summer fog catches a lot of visitors off guard. Santa Cruz is warmer than the Monterey Peninsula, but it, too, has its number of foggy summer days. If you crave sun, spend an afternoon in Carmel Valley, which is inland enough to dodge the coastal fog. **Fall** is the ideal time for a trip to the area, with warmer temperatures and fewer crowds (and less fog).

Highway 1 connects Santa Cruz south to Carmel. (In morning and afternoon rush hour, the Santa Cruz section of Highway 1 can be jammed.) South of Santa Cruz, Highway 1 becomes a two-lane road near Moss Landing, about midway to Monterey; expect backups on busy weekends. The Highway 1 traffic generally lightens up around Monterey, although it can be slow on summer weekday afternoons. Mountainous Highway 17 connects San Jose to Santa Cruz and is known for heavy traffic, sharp turns, and frequent accidents.

A trip to Big Sur involves planning—secure supplies and get gas in advance. Big Sur does have a few markets and gas stations, but you will pay a premium for both. Landslides, bridge failures, and wildfires can all close Highway 1 through Big Sur at any time. Check road and weather conditions.

Santa Cruz

Nowhere else can you find another town that has embraced the radical fringe of the nation and made it into a municipal-cultural statement like Santa Cruz. Most visitors come to hit the Boardwalk and the beaches, while locals tend to hang out on Pacific Avenue and stroll on West Cliff. The east side of town has fewer attractions for visitors but offers a vibrant surf scene around Pleasure Point.

Outside Santa Cruz, several tiny towns blend into an appealing beachside suburbia. Aptos, Capitola, and Soquel lie south along the coast with their own shopping districts, restaurants, and lodgings, as well as charming beaches as nice to visit as their northern neighbors.

SIGHTS
★ Santa Cruz Beach Boardwalk

The **Santa Cruz Beach Boardwalk** (400 Beach St., 831/423-5590, www.beachboardwalk.com, hours vary daily mid-May-Aug., open Sat.-Sun. and holidays Sept.-late May, weather permitting, parking $15-40) has a rare appeal that beckons to young children, too-cool teenagers, and adults of all ages. The amusement park rambles along each side of the south end of the Boardwalk. Entry is free, but you must buy either per-ride tickets ($4-7 per ride) or an all-day rides wristband ($28-36). The Giant Dipper is an old-school wooden roller coaster that opened in 1924 and still gives riders a thrill. The Double Shot shoots riders up a 125-foot tower for great views before free-falling straight down. The Boardwalk also offers several kids' rides.

At the north end of the Boardwalk, choose between the lure of prizes from the traditional midway games and the large arcade. Stairs lead down to the broad, sandy beach below the Boardwalk, which gets crowded in the summer. During summer, the Boardwalk puts on free Friday-night concerts on the beach featuring retro acts like Warrant and A Flock of Seagulls.

Monterey Bay National Marine Sanctuary Exploration Center

The **Monterey Bay National Marine Sanctuary Exploration Center** (35 Pacific Ave., 831/421-9993, https://montereybay.noaa.gov, 10am-5pm Wed.-Sun., free) teaches visitors about the protected waters off Santa Cruz and Monterey. Just across the street from Cowell's Beach and the Santa Cruz Wharf, this two-story facility built and operated by the National Oceanic and Atmospheric Administration (NOAA) has exhibits on the water quality, geology, and marine life of the continental United States' largest marine sanctuary. Highlights include a 15-minute film screened upstairs and an interactive exhibit where visitors get to control a remote operational vehicle (ROV) with an attached camera in a large aquarium. Downstairs is a gift shop. The center also practices environmental sensitivity: The building is built from mostly recycled or reused construction waste and runs on solar power.

Santa Cruz Mission

Believe it or not, weird and funky Santa Cruz started out as a mission town. **Santa Cruz Mission State Historic Park** (130 Emmet St., 831/425-5849, www.parks.ca.park, 10am-4pm Mon. and Thurs.-Sat., noon-4pm Sun.) is devoted to interpreting one of the later California missions, dedicated in 1791. Today, the attractive white building with its classic red-tiled roof welcomes parishioners to the active Holy Cross church and visitors to the historic museum areas of the old mission. (The building is not the original complex built in the 18th century, but a replica built in the 1930s.) Stop in at the Galeria, which houses the mission gift shop and a stunning collection of religious vestments.

Santa Cruz

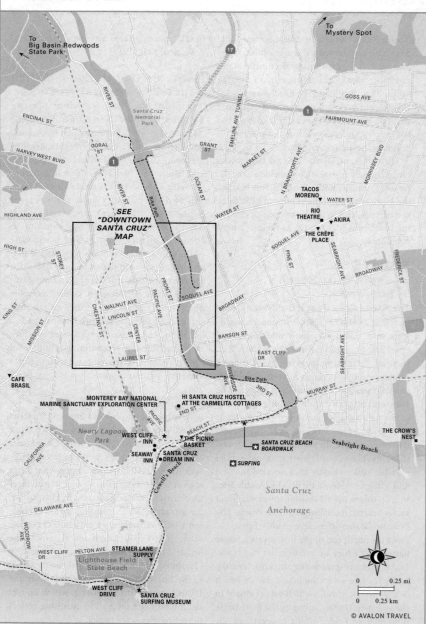

To Big Basin Redwoods State Park

To Mystery Spot

ENCINAL ST

HARVEY WEST BLVD

DORAL ST

RIVER ST

Santa Cruz Memorial Park

GRANT ST

OCEAN ST

EMELINE AVE TUNNEL

MARKET ST

17

GOSS AVE

1

FAIRMOUNT AVE

HIGHLAND AVE

HIGH ST

STOREY ST

KING ST

MISSION ST

Bike Path

SEE "DOWNTOWN SANTA CRUZ" MAP

WALNUT AVE

LINCOLN ST

CENTER ST

CHESTNUT ST

PACIFIC AVE

FRONT ST

LAUREL ST

SOQUEL AVE

WATER ST

N BRANCIFORTE AVE

TACOS MORENO

WATER ST

RIO THEATRE

AKIRA

THE CRÊPE PLACE

SOQUEL AVE

PINE ST

SEABRIGHT AVE

MORRISSET BLVD

FREDERICK ST

BROADWAY

BARSON ST

EAST CLIFF DR

Bike Path

RIVERSIDE AVE

3RD ST

SEABRIGHT AVE

MURRAY ST

CAFE BRASIL

MONTEREY BAY NATIONAL MARINE SANCTUARY EXPLORATION CENTER

PACIFIC AVE

Neary Lagoon Park

2ND ST

HI SANTA CRUZ HOSTEL AT THE CARMELITA COTTAGES

BEACH ST

WEST CLIFF INN

THE PICNIC BASKET

SANTA CRUZ BEACH BOARDWALK

THE CROW'S NEST

Seabright Beach

CALIFORNIA AVE

SEAWAY INN

SANTA CRUZ DREAM INN

Cowell's Beach

SURFING

Santa Cruz Anchorage

DELAWARE AVE

WOODROW AVE

WEST CLIFF DR

PELTON AVE

STEAMER LANE SUPPLY

Lighthouse Field State Beach

WEST CLIFF DRIVE

SANTA CRUZ SURFING MUSEUM

0   0.25 mi

0   0.25 km

© AVALON TRAVEL

Seymour Marine Discovery Center

The **Long Marine Laboratory** is worthwhile for people interested in sea creatures and marine issues. The large, attractive complex at the end of Delaware Avenue sits on the edge of the cliff overlooking the ocean—convenient for the research done primarily by students and faculty of University of California, Santa Cruz.

The **Seymour Marine Discovery Center** (100 Shaffer Rd., 831/459-3800, http://seymourcenter.ucsc.edu, 10am-5pm Tues.-Sun., adults $8, seniors, students, and children $6) is the part of the lab that's open to the public. Outside the door, a blue whale skeleton lights up at night. Inside is a marine laboratory similar to those used by scientists elsewhere in the complex. The aquariums showcase fascinating creatures including monkeyface eels and speckled sand dabs, while displays highlight environmental issues like shark finning. Kids love the touch tanks; check out the seasonal tank that contains the wildlife that's swimming around outside in the bay. **Tours** run at 11am, 1pm, 2pm, and 3pm each day; sign up an hour in advance to be sure of getting a slot.

University of California, Santa Cruz

The **University of California, Santa Cruz** (UCSC, 1156 High St., 831/459-0111, www.ucsc.edu) might be the most beautiful college campus in the country. Set in the hills above downtown Santa Cruz, the classrooms and dorms sit underneath groves of coast redwoods, among tangles of ferns and vines that are home to woodland creatures. The Office of Admissions (Cook House, 9am-4pm Mon.-Fri.) provides **self-guided tour maps.**

The UCSC campus has some other natural wonders: caves, which are in a gulch behind Porter and Kresge Colleges. **Porter Cave** is the easiest to find and the best for beginning spelunkers. Enter the subterranean chamber by descending a 20-foot steel ladder. The cave can get quite muddy, so wear clothes you don't mind getting dirty. To find the cave, go behind Porter College and follow the trail across the meadow and into the trees. Then head right alongside Empire Grade Road. Look for a concrete block that marks the cave opening. Bring a flashlight.

Santa Cruz Surfing Museum

The tiny **Santa Cruz Surfing Museum**

Santa Cruz Beach Boardwalk

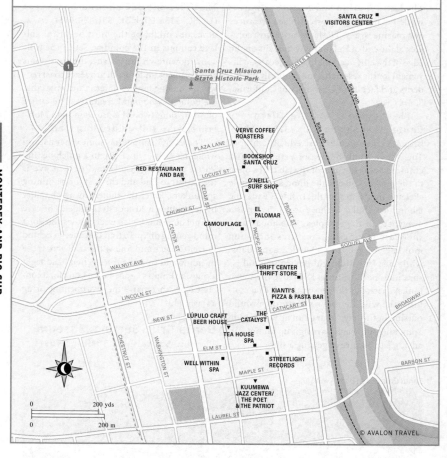

Downtown Santa Cruz

SANTA CRUZ VISITORS CENTER

WATER ST

Bike Path

Santa Cruz Mission State Historic Park

1

VERVE COFFEE ROASTERS

PLAZA LANE

BOOKSHOP SANTA CRUZ

RED RESTAURANT AND BAR

LOCUST ST

O'NEILL SURF SHOP

CEDAR ST

CHURCH ST

EL PALOMAR

CAMOUFLAGE

CENTER ST

PACIFIC AVE

FRONT ST

SOQUEL AVE

WALNUT AVE

THRIFT CENTER THRIFT STORE

LINCOLN ST

KIANTI'S PIZZA & PASTA BAR

BROADWAY

CATHCART ST

NEW ST

CHESTNUT ST

WASHINGTON ST

LÚPULO CRAFT BEER HOUSE

THE CATALYST

TEA HOUSE SPA

ELM ST

WELL WITHIN SPA

STREETLIGHT RECORDS

BARSON ST

MAPLE ST

KUUMBWA JAZZ CENTER/ THE POET & THE PATRIOT

LAUREL ST

0   200 yds
0   200 m

(1701 W. Cliff Dr., 831/420-6289, www.cityof-santacruz.com, 10am-5pm Thurs.-Tues. July 4-early Sept.; noon-4pm Thurs.-Mon. early Sept.-July 3, by donation) is housed within a still-operating lighthouse. Opened in 1986, it is the world's first museum dedicated to the sport. Run by the Santa Cruz Surfing Club Preservation Society, the one-room museum has pictures of Santa Cruz's surfing culture from the 1930s to the present. One haunting display on shark attacks includes a local surfboard with bite marks from a great white shark.

Wilder Ranch State Park

North of Santa Cruz's city limits, the land on both sides of Highway 1 suddenly gives way to farmland perched atop coastal terraces. The best place to get a feel for this stretch of coastline is to visit **Wilder Ranch State Park** (1401 Coast Rd., 831/423-9703, www. parks.ca.gov, 8am-sunset daily, $10/vehicle).

Visitors can step back in time and discover what it was like to live on this ranch through its many living-history demonstrations. Annual events include gardening demonstrations and the Old-Fashioned Independence Day Celebration.

At the **Wilder Visitor Center & Store** (Thurs.-Sun. 10am-4pm), you can get a primer on the park's cultural and natural history. Explore the park's natural beauty via the **Old Cove Landing Trail** (2.5 miles), a flat, easy hike to the wildlife-rich coastline. The east side of the park is popular with mountain bikers for its beginner to intermediate climbs with coastal views. The **Wilder Ridge Loop** provides a good introduction to the park's trails, while the **Enchanted Loop** traverses more technical terrain.

Wilder Ranch State Park is less than a 10-minute drive from downtown Santa Cruz. From Mission Street, which doubles as Highway 1 through town, head north for less than three miles.

The Forest of Nisene Marks State Park

The Forest of Nisene Marks State Park (four miles north of Aptos on Aptos Creek Rd., 831/763-7062, www.parks.ca.gov,

sunrise-sunset daily, $8/vehicle) was once the site of serious logging operations but is now shaded by second-growth redwoods. Mountain bikers can ride the fire road through the center of the park, while hikers can explore more than 30 miles of trails. The popular **Loma Prieta Grade Trail** (6 miles round-trip) follows an old railway bed to the remnants of a lumber camp.

The Mystery Spot

Santa Cruz has its own kitschy tourist trap: **The Mystery Spot** (465 Mystery Spot Rd., 831/423-8897, www.mysteryspot.com, 10am-6pm Mon.-Fri., 10am-8pm Sat.-Sun. summer, 10am-4pm daily winter, adults $8, children under 3 free, $5 parking), a tiny piece of land just outside of Santa Cruz where gravity fails. Balls roll uphill and people can stand off the side of a wall. It may be an area of spatial distortion where the laws of physics don't apply . . . or it may be a collection of optical illusions.

ENTERTAINMENT AND EVENTS
Bars and Clubs

Lovers of libations should grab a drink at **Red Restaurant and Bar** (200 Locust St.,

the Santa Cruz Surfing Museum

831/425-1913, www.redrestaurantandbar.com, 5pm-1:30am daily), upstairs in the historic Santa Cruz Hotel Building. Creative cocktails include signature creations like the Jean Grey, a mix of house-infused Earl Grey organic gin, lemon, and simple syrup. They also have a nice selection of 30 craft and Belgian beers on tap. With its dark wood paneling and burgundy barstools, Red feels like an old speakeasy. It also serves a comprehensive late-night menu until 1am for those who need some food to soak up their alcohol.

The Crêpe Place (1134 Soquel Ave., 831/429-6994, http://thecrepeplace.com, Mon.-Thurs. 11am-midnight, Fri. 11am-1am, Sat.-Sun. 9am-midnight) has recently emerged as a hangout for the hipster crowd, who are drawn in by the high-profile indie rock acts and popular Bay Area bands that perform in its intimate front room. There is also outdoor seating and a comprehensive menu of creative crepes.

Beer fans should make their way to the **Lúpulo Craft Beer House** (233 Cathcart St., 831/454-8306, www.lupulosc.com, 11:30am-10pm Mon.-Thurs., 11:30am-11:30pm Fri., 11am-11:30pm Sat., 11am-10pm Sun.). A small drinking establishment with a hip industrial feel, Lúpulo has 16 rotating craft beers on tap and over 300 types of bottled beer to consume on premises or take to go. There is also a small-bites menu featuring tacos, salads, and sandwiches. This husband-and-wife-owned business also conducts brewing demos, tastings, and other beer-related events.

Set in an alley, **The Poet & The Patriot** (320 Cedar St., 831/426-8620, daily 1pm-2am) is a popular watering hole that was opened by a Santa Cruz politician and playwright. The bar has two main rooms including one where there is frequently live music and another one that has four regulation dartboards. Both rooms feature framed memorabilia on the walls and banners on the ceiling.

Live Music

The Catalyst (1011 Pacific Ave., 831/423-1338, www.catalystclub.com), right down-

town on Pacific Avenue, hosts a variety of reggae, rap, and punk acts from Snoop Dogg to Agent Orange. Check the calendar when you buy tickets—some shows are 21 and over. The 800-person main concert hall is a standing-room-only space, while the balconies offer seating. The bar sits downstairs adjacent to the concert space. The vibe tends to be low-key, but it depends on the night and the event. The **Catalyst Atrium,** a smaller room in the same building, snags some superb national touring bands. Buy tickets online or by phone; purchasing in advance is recommended, especially for national acts.

The Crow's Nest (2218 E. Cliff Dr., 831/476-4560, www.crowsnest-santacruz.com) is as a venue for all kinds of live musical acts. Rock, soul, reggae, and funk bands typically play Tuesday-Saturday. Sundays are live comedy evenings, and Tuesdays are reggae jam nights.

A former 1940s movie house, the **Rio Theatre** (1205 Soquel Ave., 831/423-8209, www.riotheatre.com) hosts everything from film festivals to performances by international touring acts like Ladysmith Black Mambazo and Built to Spill. Check the theater's website for a full list of upcoming events.

Named one of the great jazz venues in the world by *Downbeat Magazine*, the **Kuumbwa Jazz Center** (320 Cedar St., 831/427-2227, http://kuumbwajazz.org) is a 200-seat treasure of a venue. It puts on 120 intimate concerts a year, aided by a superb sound and lighting setup. Past performers have included Bobby Hutcherson, Pharaoh Sanders, Christian McBride, and David Grisman.

Breweries

Since 2013, Santa Cruz's craft brewing scene has exploded. Sample Santa Cruz's suds by booking a seat on the **Brew Cruz** (831/222-0120, www.scbrewcruz.com, $69 pp), an army-green bus with a refrigerated cooler on board. The bus stops at three local breweries over a four-hour period.

One of the city's best breweries is

Discretion Brewing (2703 41st Ave., Ste. A, Soquel, 831/316-0662, www.discretionbrewing.com, 11:30am-9pm daily). Their tasting menu includes the award-winning and widely popular Uncle Dave's Rye IPA and Oh Black Lager. The indoor and outdoor space also serves farm-to-table comfort food.

Comedy

For a good laugh in Santa Cruz, **The Crow's Nest** (2218 East Cliff Dr., 831/476-4560, www.crowsnest-santacruz.com) hosts a weekly **stand-up comedy show** (Sun. 9pm, $7). Because the show runs on Sunday nights, The Crow's Nest takes advantage of the opportunity to hire big-name comics who have been in San Francisco or San Jose for weekend engagements. This lets folks see headliners in a more casual setting for a fraction of the cost of the big-city clubs. The Crow's Nest, with its great views out over the Pacific, also has a full bar and restaurant. Enjoy drinks and dinner while you get your giggle on.

Theater

When the long-running Shakespeare Santa Cruz went belly-up in 2013, the nonprofit **Santa Cruz Shakespeare** (The Sinsheimer-Stanley Festival Glen, UCSC Performing Arts Center, Meyer Dr., 831/460-6396, box office 831/460-6399, www.santacruzshakespeare.org, July-Aug., adults $40-52, seniors and military $36-48, children 18 and under $16, previews $20) was formed in 2014 so Bard lovers could still get their fix. Recent productions, presented in The Grove at DeLaveaga Park (501 Upper Park Rd.) have included *A Midsummer Night's Dream* and *Hamlet*.

SHOPPING

Santa Cruz's bustling downtown is centered on **Pacific Avenue** (Water St. to Laurel St.). At the north end, shoppers peruse antiques, clothing, and kitchenware. In the middle, grab a cappuccino, a cocktail, or a bite to eat in one of the many independent eateries. At the (slightly seedy) south end, visitors can purchase body jewelry or tattoos. The sidewalks are often jammed with shoppers, street performers, panhandlers, and sightseers. It's a good idea to park in one of the structures a block or two off Pacific Avenue and walk.

Bookshop Santa Cruz (1520 Pacific Ave., 831/423-0900, www.bookshopsantacruz.com, Sun.-Thurs. 9am-10pm, Fri.-Sat. 9am-11pm) is a superb independent bookstore that hosts regular readings by literary heavy hitters like Jonathan Franzen and Daniel Handler. Browse new books and used books, as well as an extensive collection of magazines.

Santa Cruz's Jack O'Neill is credited with making cold-water surfing possible with the invention of the wetsuit. His **O'Neill Surf Shop** (110 Cooper St., 831/469-4377, 10am-9pm Sun.-Thurs., 10am-10pm Fri.-Sat. summer; 10am-8pm Sun.-Thurs., 10am-9pm Fri.-Sat. winter) specializes in surfboards, brand-name clothing, and, of course, wetsuits.

One of the largest secondhand-clothing shops sits only a block off Pacific Avenue—the **Thrift Center Thrift Store** (504 Front St., 831/429-6975, Mon.-Sat. 9am-8pm, Sun. 10am-6pm). This big, somewhat dingy retail space offers a wide array of cheap secondhand clothes.

Camouflage (1329 Pacific Ave., 831/423-7613, www.shopcamoflauge.com, 10am-10pm Mon.-Sat., 10am-8pm Sun.) is an independent, family-owned, and women-friendly adult store. The first room contains mostly lingerie and tame items. Walk through the narrow black-curtained passage and you'll find the *other* room, which is filled with grown-up toys.

Stop in to **Streetlight Records** (939 Pacific Ave., 831/421-9200, www.streetlightrecords.com, Sun.-Mon. noon-8pm, Tues.-Thurs. 11am-9pm, Fri.-Sat. 11am-10pm) to pick up the latest music. With records and turntables making a serious comeback, Streetlight is also the place in Santa Cruz to find new and used vinyl.

SPORTS AND RECREATION
Beaches
NATURAL BRIDGES STATE BEACH

At the tip of the West Side, picturesque **Natural Bridges State Beach** (2531 W. Cliff Dr., 831/423-4609, www.parks.ca.gov, 8am-sunset daily, $10) has a beach that doesn't stretch wide but falls back deep, crossed by a creek that feeds into the sea. An inconsistent break makes surfing at Natural Bridges fun on occasion, while the near-constant winds bring out windsurfers every weekend. Hardy sun-worshippers brave the breezes, bringing out their beach blankets, umbrellas, and sunscreen on rare sunny days (usually in late spring and fall). A wooded picnic area has tables and grills for small and larger parties. The park's Monarch butterfly preserve is where the migrating insects take over the eucalyptus grove during the fall and winter months. Rangers offer guided tours of the tide pools that range out to the west side of the beach. Access is by a scrambling short hike (0.25-0.5 mile) on the rocky cliffs.

COWELL'S BEACH

Cowell's Beach (350 W. Cliff Dr.) is where lots of beginning surfers rode their first waves.

This West Side beach sits right at a crook in the coastline that joins with underwater features to create a reliable small break that lures new surfers by the dozens.

SEABRIGHT BEACH

At the south end of Santa Cruz, down by the harbor, beachgoers flock to **Seabright Beach** (E. Cliff Dr. at Seabright Ave., 831/427-4868, www.thatsmypark.org, 6am-10pm daily, free). This miles-long stretch of sand, protected by the cliffs from the worst winds, is a favorite retreat for sunbathers and loungers. While there's little in the way of facilities, there is soft sand, plenty of room to play football or set up a volleyball net, and, of course, easy access to the chilly Pacific Ocean. There's no surfing here—Seabright has a shore break that delights skim-boarders but makes wave riding impossible. Beach fires are allowed in fire rings.

NEW BRIGHTON STATE BEACH

One of the most popular sandy spots is **New Brighton State Beach** (1500 Park Ave., Capitola, 831/464-6330, www.thatsmypark.org, 8am-sunset daily, $10/vehicle). This forest-backed beach has everything: a strip of sand perfect for lounging and swimming,

Natural Bridges State Beach

a forest-shaded campground for both tents and RVs, hiking trails, and ranger-led nature programs. New Brighton can get crowded on sunny summer days, but it's nothing like the wall-to-wall people of the popular Southern California beaches.

SEACLIFF STATE BEACH

Seacliff State Beach (1500 Park Ave., Capitola, 831/685-6500, www.parks.ca.gov, 8am-sunset daily, $10/vehicle) is known as the final resting place of the *SS Palo Alto,* a concrete ship that was once an amusement park. The vessel is visible, but inaccessible. The surrounding beach makes a fine sunning and swimming spot.

★ Surfing

The coastline of Santa Cruz has more than its share of great surf breaks. The water is cold, demanding full wetsuits year-round, and the shoreline is rough and rocky.

The best place for beginners is **Cowell's** (stairs at W. Cliff Dr. and Cowell's Beach). The waves rarely get huge, and they typically provide long, mellow rides, perfect for surfers just getting their balance. Because the Cowell's break is acknowledged as the newbie spot, the often-sizable crowd tends to be polite to newcomers and visitors.

For more advanced surfers looking for smaller crowds in the water, **Manresa State Beach** (San Andreas Rd., Aptos, 831/724-3750, www.parks.ca.gov, 8am-sunset daily, $10/vehicle) is a nice beach break south of Santa Cruz. Manresa is several minutes' drive toward Aptos. During summer, it's a great place to surf and then recline on the beach.

Visitors who know their surfing lore will want to surf the more famous spots along the Santa Cruz shore. **Pleasure Point** (between 32nd Ave. and 41st Ave.) encompasses a number of different breaks. You may have heard of **The Hook** (steps at 41st Ave.), a well-known, experienced longboarder's paradise. But don't mistake The Hook for a beginner's break; the locals feel protective of the waves here and aren't always friendly toward inexperienced tourists. The break at **36th and East Cliff** (steps at 36th Ave.) can be a better place to go on weekdays—on the weekends, the intense crowding makes catching your own wave a challenge. Up at **30th and East Cliff** (steps at 36th Ave.), you'll find shortboarders catching larger, long peeling sets if there is a swell in the water.

The most famous break in all of Santa Cruz can also be the most hostile to newcomers. **Steamer Lane** (W. Cliff Dr. between Cowell's and the Santa Cruz Surfing Museum) has a fiercely protective crew of locals. But if you're experienced and there's a swell coming in, Steamer Lane can have some of the best waves on the California coast.

Yes, you can learn to surf in Santa Cruz. Check out either **Club Ed Surf School and Camps** (831/464-0177, https://club-ed.com, beginner group lesson $90 pp, beginner/private lessons for children $120/hour) or the **Richard Schmidt School** (849 Almar Ave., 831/423-0928, www.richardschmidt.com, 2-hour class $90 pp, private lessons $100-180/hour) to sign up for lessons.

Stand-Up Paddleboarding

Stand-up paddleboarders vie for waves with surfers at Pleasure Point and can also be found in the Santa Cruz waters with less wave action. **Covewater Paddle Surf** (726 Water St., 831/600-7230, www.covewatersup.com, 2-hour lesson $65) conducts beginner stand-up paddleboarding (SUP) classes in the relatively calm waters of the Santa Cruz Harbor. They also rent paddleboards ($40/two hours, $75/all day).

Hiking and Biking

Winding **West Cliff Drive** has a full-fledged sidewalk trail running its length on the ocean side; it's the town's favorite walking, dog walking, jogging, skating, scootering, and biking route. Start at Santa Cruz Municipal Wharf and go 2.75 miles to Natural Bridges State Beach (the west end of West Cliff). You'll pass the *To Honor Surfing* statue along with views of the ocean studded with sea stacks. Watch for fellow path-users, as it can get crowded.

To rent a bike, head to **Pacific Ave Cycles** (320-322 Pacific Ave., 831/471-2453, 10am-6pm daily, hourly $8-15, daily $25-45). The small shop with single- and multiple-speed bikes is just a few blocks east of the start of West Cliff Drive.

Spas

The **Tea House Spa** (112 Elm St., 831/426-9700, www.teahousespa.com, 11am-11pm Mon.-Thurs., 11am-midnight Fri.-Sun., spa rooms $12-35/hour, massages $55-140) is a half-block off Pacific Avenue and offers private hot tubs with views of a bamboo garden. It's not fancy, but the tubs will warm you up and mellow you out. The **Well Within Spa** (417 Cedar St., 831/458-9355, http://wellwithinspa.com, 11am-midnight daily) has indoor spa rooms and outdoor spas ($16-47/hour) and offers massages ($50-115).

FOOD
California Cuisine

The **Shadowbrook Restaurant** (1750 Wharf Rd., Capitola, 831/475-1511, www.shadowbrook-capitola.com, 5pm-8:45pm Mon.-Fri., 4:30pm-9:45pm Sat., 4:30pm-8:45pm Sun., $20-55) is where to celebrate a special occasion. The adventure begins with a cable car ride down to the restaurant, which is perched on a steep slope above Soquel Creek. Entrées include a slow-roasted, bone-in pork prime rib, a one-pound surf-and-turf dish, and several vegetarian options. If you're staying within a three-mile radius of the restaurant, you can be shuttled to the restaurant in a 1950 Dodge (free, tips appreciated). Reserve a ride when you make dinner reservations.

Breakfast

Just a few feet away from legendary surf spot Steamer Lane, the ★ **Steamer Lane Supply** (698 W. Cliff Dr., 831/621-7361, http://steamerlanesc.com, 7:30am-sunset daily, $4-10) has everything a surfer needs before hitting the waves: hot coffee, breakfast quesadillas, surf

wax, surf leashes, and more. This small, take-out concession stand within Lighthouse Field State Park is an ideal place to take in the surf by Santa Cruz's West Cliff Drive. On Saturday and Sunday, they do fish tacos from a food truck.

Coffee and Bakeries

For a casual sandwich or pastry, head to **Kelly's French Bakery** (402 Ingalls St., 831/423-9059, www.kellysfrenchbakery.com, 7am-7pm daily, $8-20). This popular bakery makes its home in an old industrial warehouse-style space, and its domed shape constructed out of corrugated metal looks like anything but a restaurant. It has both indoor and outdoor seating, and serves full breakfasts and luncheon sandwiches.

★ **Verve Coffee Roasters** (1540 Pacific Ave., 831/600-7784, www.vervecoffeeroasters.com, 6:30am-9pm daily) offers a hip, open space with lots of windows at the eastern edge of Pacific Avenue. Order a drink at the counter and then grab a seat in this frequently crowded coffee shop. They also have locations on the East Side (846 41st Ave., 831/475-7776, 6am-8pm daily; 104 Bronson St., Ste. 19, 831/471-8469, 6am-5pm daily).

Italian

Kianti's Pizza & Pasta Bar (1100 Pacific Ave., 831/469-4400, www.kiantis.com, 11am-10pm Mon.-Fri., 10am-10pm Sat.-Sun., $13-21) draws in crowds with pastas, pizzas, and salads. Pizza toppings range from traditional Italian ingredients to more creative options (one pie is covered with seasoned beef, lettuce, tomato, avocado, and tortilla chips). Kianti's full bar and outdoor seating area are right on Pacific Avenue.

Japanese

South of downtown, **Akira** (1222 Soquel Ave., 831/600-7093, www.akirasantacruz.com, 11am-11pm daily, $6-21) is a modern sushi bar with interesting creations. Some rolls employ unconventional ingredients like skirt steak and spicy truffled shoestring yams; more traditional rolls are served at the sushi bar or tableside. Akira's happy hour (4pm-6pm and 9:30pm-10:30pm daily) offers appetizers to go with your beer, sake, or wine.

Mexican

At **El Palomar** (1336 Pacific Ave., 831/425-7575, http://elpalomarsantacruz.com, 11am-9pm Mon.-Wed., 11am-10pm Thurs., 11am-10:30pm Fri., 10am-10:30pm Sat., 10am-9pm Sun., $13-27), enjoy shrimp enchiladas or chicken mole while a roving mariachi band plays. Jose's Special Appetizer can be a light meal for two. The informal taco bar is great for a quick bite and drink. El Palomar also has a happy hour (3pm-6pm Mon.-Fri.).

Sandwiches

Just feet from the Santa Cruz Beach Boardwalk is a casual eatery with a simple menu that utilizes locally sourced, tasty goodness: ★ **The Picnic Basket** (125 Beach St., 831/427-9946, http://thepicnicbasketsc.com, 7am-9pm daily summer, 7am-4pm daily winter, $3-9). Its attention to detail shines through even on a simple turkey, cheese, and avocado sandwich. Options include breakfast items, salads, mac and cheese, and local beer and wine.

South American

Cafe Brasil (1410 Mission St., 831/429-1855, www.cafebrasil.us, 8am-3pm daily, $6-11) serves up the Brazilian fare its name promises. Thanks to a building painted jungle green with bright yellow and blue trim, you can't miss this totally Santa Cruz breakfast and lunch joint. In the morning, the fare runs to omelets and Brazilian specialties. Lunch includes pressed sandwiches, meat and tofu dishes, and Brazilian house specials.

ACCOMMODATIONS
Under $150

The **Hostelling International Santa Cruz Hostel** (321 Main St., 831/423-8304, www.hi-santacruz.org, dorm beds $28, private rooms $48-113) offers the area's only budget lodging. The historic cottages, just two blocks from the Santa Cruz Beach Boardwalk, are clean, cheap, friendly, and close to Cowell's Beach. There's a big, homey kitchen open for guest use and a garden, outdoor deck, free linens, laundry facilities, and a free Internet kiosk. The hostel is closed 11am-5pm daily, so there is no access to guest rooms or indoor common areas. Guests are allowed to leave their luggage inside or in outdoor lockers.

a sandwich from The Picnic Basket

$150-250

The ★ **West Cliff Inn** (174 W. Cliff Dr., 831/457-2200, www.westcliffinn.com, $209-399) is a gleaming white mansion topping the hill above Cowell's Beach and the Boardwalk. This three-story historic landmark was constructed back in 1877 and was the first of the bluff's Millionaires' Row residences. The nine rooms in the main house have stunning white-marble bathrooms, some of which have oversize soaking tubs. The more moderately priced and pet-friendly Little Beach Bungalow is behind the main house. Fill up on a morning breakfast buffet and an afternoon wine and appetizer hour. The inn's veranda and second-floor balcony provide wonderful views.

The ★ **Seaway Inn** (176 W. Cliff Dr., 831/471-9004, www.seawayinn.com, $204-330) offers a night's stay across from Cowell's Beach. Rooms are clean, but not fancy, and have a shared patio or deck with chairs; the bathrooms are small. The 18 units in the main building have TVs with DVD players, microwaves, and mini-fridges. Family suites accommodate up to five adults. The complimentary breakfast boasts make-your-own waffles. The friendly staff also operate a nearby building that has five studio apartments, each with a full kitchen. Pets are welcome ($15 for the first night, $5 each additional night).

Over $250

Perched over Cowell's Beach and the Santa Cruz Wharf, **Santa Cruz Dream Inn** (175 W. Cliff Dr., 831/426-4330, www.dreaminnsantacruz.com, $421-669) has 165 rooms with striking ocean views and either a private balcony or a shared common patio. The retro-chic rooms match perfectly with the vibrant colors of the nearby Boardwalk. The Dream Inn's sundeck is right on Cowell's Beach; among the inn's amenities are a heated swimming pool, a large hot tub, and a poolside bar.

The **Ocean Echo Inn & Beach Cottages** (410 Johans Beach Dr., 831/462-4192, www.oceanecho.com, $375-630) is a secluded gem on the East Side, just 53 footsteps down to a locals' pocket beach. The inn's water tower, chicken coop, and carriage house have all been converted into cozy cottages. There are 15 units, including the cottages and inn rooms (11 have full kitchens), and multiple decks along with a Ping-Pong table and grills. A modest continental breakfast is put out in the morning.

The Seaway Inn is one of Santa Cruz's best overnight bargains.

TRANSPORTATION AND SERVICES

Navigating the winding, broken-up streets of this oddly shaped town isn't for the faint of heart. Highway 1 (Mission St. on the West Side) is the main artery through Santa Cruz down to Capitola, Soquel, and Aptos. Highway 1 at the interchange to Highway 17 is a parking lot most of the time.

Car

From San Francisco, Santa Cruz is 75 miles south, about 1.5 hours away. Take either **U.S. 101** or I-280 south (101 can be slightly faster, but less scenic and more prone to traffic) to **Highway 17** toward Santa Cruz. Most locals take this 50-mile-per-hour corridor fast—probably faster than they should. Each year, several people die in accidents on Highway 17, so keep to the right and take it slow, no matter what the traffic to the left of you is doing. Check traffic reports before you head out; Highway 17 is known as one of the worst commuting roads in the Bay Area, and weekend beach traffic in the summer jams up fast in both directions.

For a more leisurely drive, opt for two-lane **Highway 1.** Once in town, Highway 1 becomes Mission Street on the West Side and acts as the main artery through Santa Cruz and down to Capitola, Soquel, Aptos, and coastal points farther south.

Another option for a more leisurely drive is two-lane **Highway 9.** The tight curves and endless switchbacks will keep you at a reasonable speed; use the turnouts to let the locals pass and watch for bicyclists and motorcyclists.

Parking in Santa Cruz can be challenging. Downtown, head straight for the parking structures one block away from Pacific Avenue on either side. They're much easier to deal with than trying to find street parking. The same goes for the beach and Boardwalk areas. At the Boardwalk, just pay the fee to park in the big parking lot adjacent to the attractions. You'll save an hour and a possible car break-in or theft trying to find street parking in the sketchy neighborhoods that surround the Boardwalk.

Public Transit

Buses are run by the **Santa Cruz Metro** (831/425-8600 www.scmtd.com, adults $2 per ride, passes available). In the summer, take advantage of the **Santa Cruz Trolley** (831/420-5150, http://santacruztrolley.com, noon-8pm daily late May-early Sept., $0.25). The vintage trolley car connects the Boardwalk and downtown via a three-stop route running every 15-20 minutes.

Services

To pick up a map of Santa Cruz, hit the **Santa Cruz County Visitors Center** (303 Water St., Ste. 100, 800/833-3494, www.santacruz.org, 9am-noon and 1pm-4pm Mon.-Fri., 11am-3pm Sat.-Sun.) or stop by the **Downtown Information Kiosk** (1130 Pacific Ave., K2, 831/332-7422 Ext. 2, www.downtownsantacruz.com, 11am-6pm Sun.-Thurs., 11am-8pm Fri.-Sat.). Medical treatment is available at **Dominican Hospital** (1555 Soquel Ave., 855/489-4580).

Moss Landing

Moss Landing is a picturesque, working fishing village (just ignore the rising smokestacks of the towering Moss Landing Power Plant). The main drag, Moss Landing Road, has a scattering of antiques stores and art galleries, and Moss Landing Harbor is home to a fleet of fishing vessels. To the south, Salinas River State Beach offers miles of wild, undeveloped shoreline. North of the inlet, Zmudowski State Beach is popular with local surfers during the winter months. Offshore, the Monterey Submarine Canyon is one of North America's

Side Trip: Santa Cruz Mountains

North of Santa Cruz, Highway 9 snakes through redwood-dense mountains lined with the towns of **Felton, Ben Lomond,** and **Boulder Creek.** Along the way are several stellar state parks.

Henry Cowell Redwoods State Park (101 N. Big Trees Park Rd., Felton, 831/335-4598, www.parks.ca.gov) encompasses old-growth redwoods and waterfalls, and offers 20 miles of trails as well as campsites (Apr.-Oct.).

At **Roaring Camp Railroads** (5401 Graham Hill Rd., Felton, 831/335-4484, www.roaring-camp.com, 9am-5pm daily), antique steam engines wind through the Santa Cruz Mountains, over trestles and beneath towering redwoods, on hour-long tours.

Big Basin Redwoods State Park (21600 Big Basin Way, Boulder Creek, 831/338-8860, www.parks.ca.gov, $10) is home to the largest continuous stand of old-growth coast redwoods south of San Francisco and owes this distinction to becoming California's first state park in 1902. Big Basin has 80 miles of trails. One of the most popular hikes is to **Berry Creek Falls** (12 miles, strenuous), a series of four waterfalls cascading through old-growth redwoods. Campsites and tent cabins are available, as are backpacking sites. Reservations can be made by phone or online (800/444-7275, www.reservecalifornia.com).

Big Basin is 25 miles northeast of Santa Cruz near the intersections of Highways 35 and 9. The main entrance is seven miles down Highway 236. Boulder Creek is the closest town, nine miles south on Highway 9.

largest submarine canyons. It's the reason that the Moss Landing Marine Laboratories and Monterey Bay Aquarium Research Institute have local addresses.

SIGHTS
★ Elkhorn Slough

Elkhorn Slough is the second-largest section of tidal salt marsh in California after San Francisco Bay. The estuary hosts an amazing amount of wildlife that includes marine mammals and over 340 bird species, which makes it one of the state's best birding spots. The best way to explore the slough is by kayak, where you can view rafts of lounging sea otters and a barking rookery of California sea lions from water level. In Moss Landing's North Harbor, which connects to the slough, **Monterey Bay Kayaks** (2390 Hwy. 1, 831/373-5357, www.montereybaykayaks.com, 9am-7pm daily summer, 9am-6pm daily spring and fall, 9am-5pm winter, SUP rental $35/day) rents kayak ($30-35/day) and has a range of guided tours ($45-80), from a 1.5-hour paddle around the harbor to monthly full-moon tours.

Elkhorn Slough Safari (Moss Landing Harbor, Dock A, 7881 Sandholdt Rd.,

831/633-5555, www.elkhornslough.com, adults $38, children $28, seniors $35) offers a 1.5- to 2-hour tour of the estuary by boat.

ENTERTAINMENT AND EVENTS

The **Moss Landing Inn** (7902 Hwy. 1, 831/633-9803, http://wenchilada.com, 1pm-2am Mon.-Thurs., noon-2am Fri.-Sun.) is a dive bar where dollar bills hang off the ceiling. Spend a few hours getting acquainted with the local characters. It's connected to The Whole Enchilada restaurant and offers live music on weekends.

On the last Sunday of July, Moss Landing is flooded with antiques enthusiasts for the annual **Moss Landing Antique Street Fair** (831/633-4501, www.mosslandingchamber.com, July, adults $5, children under 12 free). The giant outdoor antiques market has more than 200 booths selling collectibles; other booths serve local foods.

SHOPPING

Located behind the Haute Enchilada Café, the **Haute Enchilada Gallery** (7902 Moss Landing Rd., 831/633-3743, www.

hauteenchilada.com, 11am-5pm daily) has multiple rooms filled with sculptures, watercolors, woodworks, and ceramic items. **Driftwood** (8071-B Moss Landing Rd., 831/632-2800, www.driftwoodstore.com, noon-5pm Sun.-Thurs., 11am-6pm Fri.-Sat.) bills itself as an "artisan gift boutique." Expect hipster-approved jewelry, home furnishings, and candles.

SPORTS AND RECREATION
Beaches

Just north of Moss Landing's harbor, **Moss Landing State Beach** (Jetty Rd., 831/649-2836, www.parks.ca.gov, 8am-sunset daily) and **Zmudowski State Beach** (20 miles north of Monterey on Hwy. 1, 831/649-2836, www.parks.ca.gov, 8am-sunset daily) stretch for miles. They're mostly enjoyed by locals who fish, surf, or ride horses on the beach. To get to the beaches from Highway 1, take Struve Road and turn onto Giberson Road.

Just south of Moss Landing is the **Salinas River State Beach** (Potrero Rd., 831/649-2836, www.parks.ca.gov, 8am-sunset daily). Expect some serenity among a few horseback riders or anglers.

Whale-Watching

For a glimpse of gray whales or orcas, catch a ride with **Sanctuary Cruises** (7881 Sandholt Rd., 831/350-4090, www.sanctuarycruises. com, adults $55, children under 13 $45). Running on biodiesel, the 43-foot ocean vessel *Sanctuary* takes passengers out daily for 4-5-hour cruises. **Blue Ocean Whale Watch** (7881 Sandholt Rd., 831/600-5103, www.blueoceanwhalewatch.com, adults $50, children 4-12 $40) heads into the bay for 3-4-hour whale-watching expeditions.

Fishing

Anglers can cast a line for rockfish, lingcod, salmon, halibut, or albacore on the 50-foot *Kahuna,* run by **Kahuna Sportfishing** (7881 Sandholdt Rd., 831/633-2564, www.kahunasportfishing.com, $85-180 per person).

FOOD

Moss Landing is best known for its seafood restaurants. The most popular is ★ **Phil's Fish Market** (7600 Sandholt Rd., 831/633-2152, www.philsfishmarket.com, fish market: 8:30am-8pm daily in summer, 8:30am-7pm Sun.-Wed., 8:30am-8pm Thurs.-Sat. in winter; eatery: 10am-9pm daily in summer, 10am-8pm Sun.-Wed., 10am-9pm Thurs.-Sat. in winter, $9-26), known for its cioppino—a hearty Italian American seafood stew that includes clams, mussels, fish, Dungeness crab, prawns, and scallops. A heaping bowl comes with salad and garlic bread, while blackened sea scallops are served in a lemon-caper butter sauce. This informal market/eatery has a bluegrass band playing Monday-Thursday nights.

The Whole Enchilada (7902 Hwy. 1, 831/633-3038, http://wenchilada.com, 11:30am-8:15pm daily, $10-24) does seafood with a Mexican slant. Dine on seafood enchiladas, Mexican-style cioppino, or chile relleno stuffed with crab, shrimp, and cheese in the brightly colored dining room or on the outdoor patio.

Part art gallery, part eatery, fanciful **Haute Enchilada Café & Galleries** (7902 Moss Landing Rd., 831/633-5843, www.hauteenchilada.com, 11am-9pm daily, $17-26) serves Peruvian empanadas and skirt steaks in Oaxacan black bean sauce.

ACCOMMODATIONS AND CAMPING

The ★ **Captain's Inn** (8122 Moss Landing Rd., 831/633-5550, www.captainsinn.com, $188-287) is the perfect place to spend an evening in the fishing village. Rooms are in two buildings: a historic structure, once the site of the Pacific Coast Steamship Company, and the Boathouse, where every room has a superb view of the nearby tidal marsh. Wildlife watchers might be able to catch a glimpse of marine mammals or birds in the nearby tidal marsh, while maritime fans will love the bed sets crafted out of boat parts. Wake up to a home-cooked breakfast that can be taken to-go.

The **Monterey Dunes Company** (407 Moss Landing Rd., 831/633-4883 or 800/553-8637, www.montereydunes.com, from $733/night) rents 2-4-bedroom homes on the beach south of Moss Landing. Guests have access to the development's tennis courts, swimming pool, saunas, and hot tub.

The **Moss Landing KOA Express** (7905 Sandholt Rd., 831/633-6800 or 800/562-3390, https://koa.com, $75-85) has almost 50 RV sites right in the Moss Landing Harbor area.

TRANSPORTATION

Moss Landing is 25 miles south of Santa Cruz and 15 miles north of Monterey on Highway 1.

Monterey

Monterey has roots as a fishing town. Native Americans were the first to ply the bay's waters, and fishing became an economic driver with the arrival of European settlers in the 19th century. Author John Steinbeck immortalized this unglamorous industry in his novel *Cannery Row*. Monterey's blue-collar past is still evident in its architecture, even though the cannery workers have been replaced by visiting tourists.

There are two main sections of Monterey: the old downtown area and "New Monterey," which includes Cannery Row and the Monterey Aquarium. The old downtown is situated around Alvarado Street and includes the historic adobes that make up Monterey State Historic Park. New Monterey bustles with tourists during the summer. The six blocks of Cannery Row are packed with businesses, including the must-see Monterey Bay Aquarium, seafood restaurants, shops, galleries, and wine-tasting rooms. One way to get from one section to the other is to walk the Monterey Bay Coastal Recreation Trail, a paved path that runs right along a stretch of coastline.

SIGHTS
Cannery Row

Cannery Row (www.canneryrow.com) did once look and feel as John Steinbeck described it in his famed novel of the same name. In the 1930s and 1940s, fishing boats docked here and offloaded their catches straight into the huge, warehouse-like cannery buildings.

But overfishing took its toll, and by the late 1950s Cannery Row was deserted. A slow renaissance began in the 1960s, driven by new interest in preserving the historic integrity of the area, as well as by a few savvy entrepreneurs who understood the value of beachfront property. Today, what was once a worker's wharf is now an enclave of boutique hotels, big seafood restaurants, and souvenir stores selling T-shirts adorned with sea otters. Cannery Row is anchored at one end by the aquarium and runs for several blocks that include a beach; it then leads into the Monterey Harbor area.

TOP EXPERIENCE

★ Monterey Bay Aquarium

The **Monterey Bay Aquarium** (886 Cannery Row, 831/648-4800, www.montereybayaquarium.org, 9:30am-6pm daily, adults $50, seniors and students $40, children 3-12 $30) displays a dazzling array of local sealife. First-class exhibits include the Kelp Forest, which mimics the environment just outside; the Open Sea exhibit, with its deepwater tank that's home to giant bluefin tuna and hammerhead sharks; Wild About Otters, which gives an up-close view of rescued otters; and the Jellies Experience, which illuminates the delicate creatures. Check the feeding schedules when you arrive, and show up in advance to get a good spot near the critters for the show. The aquarium is wildly popular, and in the summer, the crowds can be

Monterey Bay

To San Jose

Henry W. Coe

State Park

Coyote
Reservoir

UC
SANTA CRUZ

THE
MYSTERY SPOT

The Forest of
Nisene Marks
State Park

Natural Bridge
State Park

Santa
Cruz

Soquel

1

Capitola

Aptos

101

Gilroy

152

GILROY
HISTORICAL
MUSEUM

SANTA CRUZ
SURFING MUSEUM

Seabright
Beach

PLEASURE
POINT

Rio Del Mar

SANTA CRUZ BEACH
BOARDWALK

Manresa State
Beach

La Selva Beach

To
I-5

SURFING IN
SANTA CRUZ

152

Manresa State Beach

Watsonville

129

25

156

Sunset State Beach

1

Palm Beach

Monterey
Bay

ELKHORN SLOUGH

Moss Landing

156

San Juan
Bautista

156

Hollister

101

G1

25

Fort Ord Dunes
State Park

183

SCUBA DIVING,
KAYAKING, AND STAND-UP
PADDLEBOARDING

Marina

101

Pacific
Grove

MONTEREY
BAY AQUARIUM

1

Salinas

17-MILE
DRIVE

Monterey

Sand
City

G17

CARMEL
BEACH

DEL MONTE
GOLF COURSE

MAZDA RACEWAY
LAGUNA SECA

Spreckels

Pebble Beach

Jack Peak's
County Park

68

G17

POINT LOBOS STATE
NATURAL RESERVE

101

0   5 mi

0   5 km

G16

Carmel
Valley

Carmel Valley

CARMEL VALLEY

Gonzales

Pinnacles
National
Park

Los

CACHAGUA RD

Salinas

River

101

Padres

National

1

TASSAJARA RD

G17

Soledad

To POINT SUR LIGHT STATION

PFEIFFER BEACH, and

HEARST CASTLE

Forest

G16

To
San Luis Obispo

146

© AVALON TRAVEL

Cannery Row

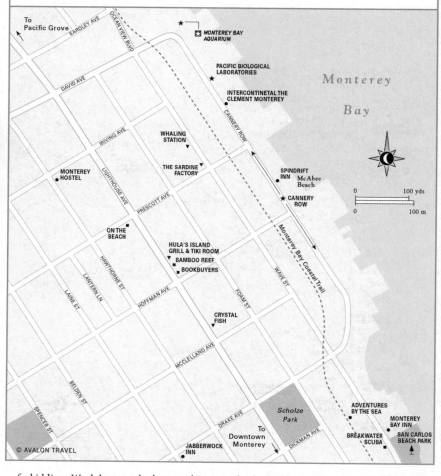

© AVALON TRAVEL

forbidding. Weekdays can be less crushing (though you'll run into school groups much of the year), and the off-season is always a better time to visit. Most exhibits at the aquarium are wheelchair-accessible.

Monterey State Historic Park

Monterey State Historic Park (20 Custom House Plaza, 831/649-2907, www.parks. ca.gov, 9am-5pm daily May-Sept., 10am-4pm daily Oct.-Apr., free) pays homage to the long

and colorful history of the city of Monterey. This busy port town acted as the capital of California when it was under Spanish and Mexican rule. Today, the park is a collection of old buildings scattered about downtown Monterey, and it provides a peek into the city as it was in the mid-19th century.

Built in 1827, the **Custom House** (east of Fisherman's Wharf, 10am-4pm daily, $5) is the oldest government building still standing in the state. Wander the adobe building and

Downtown Monterey

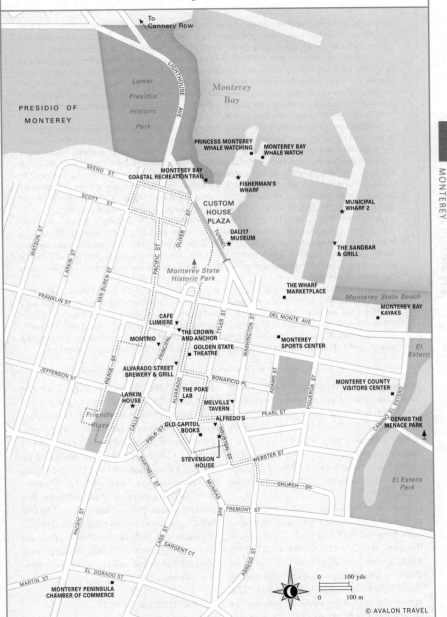

To Cannery Row

Monterey Bay

PRESIDIO OF MONTEREY

Lower Presidio Historic Park

LIGHTHOUSE AVE

SEENO ST

SCOTT ST

WATSON ST

LARKIN ST

VAN BUREN ST

PACIFIC ST

OLIVER ST

PRINCESS MONTEREY WHALE WATCHING

MONTEREY BAY WHALE WATCH

MONTEREY BAY COASTAL RECREATION TRAIL

FISHERMAN'S WHARF

CUSTOM HOUSE PLAZA

MUNICIPAL WHARF 2

DALI17 MUSEUM

TUNNEL

Monterey State Historic Park

THE SANDBAR & GRILL

FRANKLIN ST

THE WHARF MARKETPLACE

Monterey State Beach

DEL MONTE AVE

MONTEREY BAY KAYAKS

CAFE LUMIERE

PIERCE ST

MONTRIO

PRINCIPAL ST

TYLER ST

WASHINGTON ST

THE CROWN AND ANCHOR

GOLDEN STATE THEATRE

MONTEREY SPORTS CENTER

ADAMS ST

FIGUEROA ST

El Estero

JEFFERSON ST

ALVARADO STREET BREWERY & GRILL

ALVARADO ST

BONAFICIO PL

MONTEREY COUNTY VISITORS CENTER

LARKIN HOUSE

CALLE PRINCIPAL

THE POKE LAB

POLK ST

MELVILLE TAVERN

PEARL ST

CAMINO EL ESTERO

Friendly Plaza

OLD CAPITOL BOOKS

ALFREDO'S

HOUSTON ST

DENNIS THE MENACE PARK

HARTNELL ST

STEVENSON HOUSE

WEBSTER ST

El Estero Park

CHURCH ST

MUNRAS AVE

FREMONT ST

PACIFIC ST

CASS ST

SARGENT CT

ABREGO ST

MARTIN ST

EL DORADO ST

MONTEREY PENINSULA CHAMBER OF COMMERCE

0   100 yds

0   100 m

© AVALON TRAVEL

Steinbeck's Legacy

John Ernst Steinbeck was born in Salinas, California, in 1902 and grew up in its tiny, isolated agricultural community. He somehow managed to escape life as a farmer, a sardine fisherman, or a fish canner, and ended up living the glamorous life of a writer for his too-short 66 years.

Steinbeck's experiences in the Salinas Valley farming community and in the fishing town of Monterey informed many of his novels. The best known of these is *Cannery Row*, but *Tortilla Flat* is also set in working-class Monterey (though no one knows exactly where the fictional "Tortilla Flat" neighborhood was supposed to be). The Pulitzer Prize-winning novel *The Grapes of Wrath* takes more of its inspiration from the Salinas Valley. Steinbeck used the valley as a model for farming in the Dust Bowl during the Great Depression.

Steinbeck was fascinated by the plight of workingmen and women; his novels and stories generally depict ordinary folks going through tough and terrible times. Steinbeck lived and worked through the Great Depression, thus it's not surprising that many of his stories do *not* feature happy Hollywood endings. Steinbeck was a realist in almost all of his novels, portraying the good, the bad, and the ugly of human life and society. His work gained almost immediate respect: In addition to his Pulitzer, Steinbeck also won the Nobel Prize for Literature in 1962. Almost every American high school student from the 1950s onward has read at least one of Steinbeck's novels or short stories; his body of work forms part of the enduring American literary canon.

As the birthplace of California's most illustrious literary son in the 20th century, Salinas became equally famous for spawning the author and inspiring his work. You'll find a variety of Steinbeck maps online (www.mtycounty.com) that offer self-guided tours of the regions made famous by his various novels. Poor Steinbeck's name is taken in vain all over now-commercial Cannery Row, where even the cheesy wax museum tries to draw customers in by claiming kinship with the legendary author.

Serious scholars of Steinbeck prefer the **National Steinbeck Center** (1 Main St., 831/796-3833, www.steinbeck.org, 10am-5pm daily, $11) and the **Steinbeck House** (132 Central Ave., 831/424-2735, www.steinbeckhouse.com, monthly tours: 11pm-1pm Sun. May-Sept., $10), both in the still-agricultural town of Salinas. And if the museums aren't enough, plan to be in Monterey County in early August for the annual **Steinbeck Festival** (www.steinbeck.org), a big shindig put on by the Steinbeck Center that celebrates the great man's life and works in fine style.

check out the artifacts on display, meant to resemble the building's goods when it was under Mexican rule. On the nearby plaza, enter the first floor of the **Pacific House Museum** (hours and days vary seasonally) to see a range of Monterey's history from the Native Californians to the American Period. The second floor has a plethora of Native American artifacts.

The other buildings that compose the park were built mostly with adobe and/or brick between 1834 and 1847. These include the **Casa del Oro** (210 Oliver St., 831/649-3364, 11am-3pm Thurs.-Sun.); the **First Brick House** (10am-4pm daily); the **Larkin House** (464 Calle Principal, 831/649-7172, private tours: $75 for up to 12 people); the **Old Whaling Station** (391 Decatur St.,

831/375-5356, 10am-2pm Tues.-Fri.); the **Sherman Quarters** (closed to the public); and the **Stevenson House** (530 Houston St., hours and days vary seasonally), once a temporary residence of Robert Louis Stevenson.

For an introduction to the park and its history, take a **guided tour** (Pacific House Museum, hours and days vary, $5). The one-hour walk includes the Pacific House, the Custom House, the First Brick House, the Old Whaling Station (with its whalebone sidewalk out front), California's First Theatre, Casa del Oro, and the Memory Garden. A **cell phone tour** (831/998-9458) offers a two-minute rundown on each building.

Fisherman's Wharf

Monterey's scenic harbor is a great place

to stroll along the shore, spot marine life, and explore the area's three wharves. Most popular is **Fisherman's Wharf** (1 Old Fisherman's Wharf, 831/238-0777, www.montereywharf.com, hours vary daily, free), which hosts a collection of seafood restaurants, touristy gift shops, and whale-watching boats. It has also been featured in the HBO series *Big Little Lies.*

The **Coast Guard Pier,** a 1,700-foot-long breakwater on the north end of the harbor, is one of Monterey's best wildlife-viewing areas. Look for sea lions and harbor seals as you walk out on the structure.

Municipal Wharf II is on the eastern edge of the harbor. It still has working fishing operations along with a few wholesale fish companies, a couple of restaurants, an abalone farm underneath its deck, and fine views of the harbor and nearby Del Monte Beach.

Dalí 17 Museum

One does not usually associate Salvador Dalí with Monterey; however, in 1941 the artist lived at Monterey's Hotel Del Monte, where he threw a legendary, surreal party. The **Dalí 17 Museum** (5 Custom House Plaza, 831/372-2608, www.dali17.com, 10am-5pm Sun.-Thurs., 10am-6pm Fri.-Sat., adults $20, seniors and students $16, children 6-17 $10, children under 6 free) has the second-largest collection of his works in the country, including 557 lithographs and 230 originals. Take a stroll through the two-floor museum, which portrays well this one-of-a-kind artist and his many quirks.

Dennis the Menace Park

The brainchild of Hank Ketcham, the creator of the *Dennis the Menace* comic strip, **Dennis the Menace Park** (777 Pearl St., 831/646-3860, 10am-dusk daily May-Sept., 10am-dusk Wed.-Mon Sept.-May) opened in 1956. The park has a nine-foot climbing wall, a suspension bridge, curvy slides, brightly colored jungle gyms, and a (fenced-in, nonworking) locomotive, as well as a bronze sculpture of the little menace near the entrance.

ENTERTAINMENT AND EVENTS
Bars and Clubs

Descending into **The Crown & Anchor** (150 W. Franklin St., 831/649-6496, www.crownandanchor.net, 11am-1:30am daily) feels a bit like entering a ship's hold. Along with the maritime theme, The Crown & Anchor serves up 20 international beers on tap. They

Monterey Bay Aquarium

also have good pub fare, including cottage pies and curries; the curry fries are a local favorite.

Microbrew fans should make for ★ **Alvarado Street Brewery & Grill** (426 Alvarado St., 831/655-2337, www.alvaradostreetbrewery.com, 11:30am-10pm Sun.-Thurs., 11:30am-11pm Fri.-Sat.). The boisterous, big modern space has more than 20 beers on tap, including their own sours, ales, and Mai Tai PA, a Great American Beer Festival gold-medal winner. Enjoy sipping the tasty brews out front on their sidewalk patio or in the beer garden in back.

A distinct stone building just a couple of blocks off Alvarado Street, **Alfredo's Cantina** (266 Pearl St., 831/375-0655, 10am-midnight Sun.-Thurs., 10am-2am Fri.-Sat., cash only) is a cozy dive bar. This comfortable drinking establishment has dim lighting, a gas fireplace, cheap drinks, and a good jukebox.

Live Music

Downtown Monterey's historic **Golden State Theatre** (417 Alvarado St., 831/649-1070, www.goldenstatetheatre.com) hosts live music, a speaker series, and dance, comedy, and theater productions. The theater dates to 1926 and was designed to resemble a Moorish castle. Performers have included music legends like Patti Smith, Willie Nelson, and "Weird Al" Yankovic.

Festivals and Events

The annual **Monterey Wine Festival** (Custom House Plaza, 360/693-6023, http://montereywine.com, June) celebrates wine with a generous helping of food on the side. The outdoor festival is the perfect introduction to Monterey and Carmel wineries, many of which have not yet hit the "big time" in major wine magazines. It is also, incongruously, home to the West Coast Chowder Competition.

One of the biggest music festivals in California is the **Monterey Jazz Festival** (Monterey County Fairgrounds, 2004 Fairground Rd., 831/373-3366, www.montereyjazzfestival.org, Sept.). As the site of the longest-running jazz festival on earth, Monterey attracts 500 artists from around the world to the fest's eight stages. Past acts to grace the stage include Herbie Hancock, Booker T. Jones, and The Roots.

Monterey Car Week (www.seemonterey.com, Aug.) lures car enthusiasts to the Monterey Peninsula for seven days of car shows, races, and high-end automobile auctions. An event with a big sense of humor, the **Concours d'Lemons** (Seaside City Hall, 440 Harcourt Ave., Seaside, https://24hoursoflemons.com, Aug.) showcases clunkers, junkers, and automotive oddities.

SPORTS AND RECREATION

★ Scuba Diving

There's one great place to get certified in scuba diving: Monterey Bay. Accordingly, dozens of dive schools cluster in and around the city of Monterey. Locals' favorite **Bamboo Reef** (614 Lighthouse Ave., 831/372-1685, www.bambooreef.com, 9am-6pm Mon.-Fri., 7am-6pm Sat.-Sun.) offers scuba lessons and rents equipment just a few blocks from popular dive spots, including Breakwater Cove. The aquamarine storefront has been helping people get underwater since 1980.

Aquarius Dive Shop (2040 Del Monte Ave., 831/375-1933, www.aquariusdivers.com, 9am-6pm Mon.-Thurs., 9am-7pm Fri., 7am-7pm Sat., 7am-6pm Sun.) offers air and nitrox fills, equipment rental, and certification courses, and can help book a trip on a local dive boat. Aquarius works with five boats to create great trips for divers of all interests and ability levels. Call 831/657-1020 for local dive conditions.

★ Kayaking and Stand-Up Paddleboarding

The coast off Monterey is an ideal place for paddling: It is less exposed than other spots along the coast, and if the swells are big, you can duck into Monterey Harbor and paddle past moored boats and harbor seals. When

Sea Sanctuary

Monterey Bay is in a federally protected marine area known as the Monterey Bay National Marine Sanctuary (MBNMS). Designated a sanctuary in 1992, the protected waters stretch far past the confines of Monterey Bay to a northern boundary seven miles north of the Golden Gate Bridge and a southern boundary at Cambria in San Luis Obispo. The sanctuary was created for resource protection, education, public use, and research. The MBNMS is the reason so many marine research facilities, including the Long Marine Laboratory, the Monterey Bay Marine Laboratory, and the Moss Landing Marine Laboratories, dot the Monterey Bay shoreline.

Among the many marine treasures of the MBNMS is the Monterey Bay Submarine Canyon, which is right offshore of the fishing village of Moss Landing. The canyon is similar in size to the Grand Canyon and has a rim-to-floor depth of 5,577 feet. In 2009, the MBNMS expanded to include another fascinating underwater geographical feature: the Davidson Seamount. Located 80 miles southwest of Monterey, the undersea mountain rises an impressive 7,480 feet, yet its summit is still 4,101 feet below the ocean's surface.

the surf is manageable, the paddle from San Carlos Beach to the aquarium and back (1.16 miles round-trip) guarantees you will see an otter or a harbor seal. Note that Monterey Bay National Marine Sanctuary regulations require all paddlers to stay 150 feet from all sea otters, sea lions, and harbor seals.

Adventures by the Sea (299 Cannery Row, 831/372-1807, www.adventuresbythe-sea.com, 9am-8pm daily summer, 9am-5pm daily winter, kayak tours $60-85 pp, kayak rentals $35/day, SUP rentals $50/day) rents kayaks and SUPs and lets you choose your own route around the Monterey Bay kelp forest. Adventures also offers tours (2.5 hours, 10am and 2pm daily in summer) from Cannery Row. Guides can tell you all about the wildlife you'll see: harbor seals, sea otters, pelicans, gulls, and maybe even a whale in the winter. The tandem sit-on-top kayaks make it a great experience for children. They also run a tour of Stillwater Cove at Pebble Beach. Reservations are recommended for all tours. The company has other locations in Monterey (685 Cannery Row, 32 Cannery Row, and 210 Alvarado St.).

Rent a kayak or SUP from **Monterey Bay Kayaks** (693 Del Monte Ave., 831/373-5357, www.montereybaykayaks.com, 9am-7pm daily summer, 9am-6pm daily spring, 9am-5pm daily fall/winter; kayak tours $450-100,

kayak rentals $30-50 pp, SUP rentals $35 pp) and paddle into the bay from the beach just south of the Municipal Wharf. Tours include kayak fishing, Sunday sunrise excursions, and a Point Lobos paddle. There's also a branch in Moss Landing on the Elkhorn Slough.

Whale-Watching

Whales pass quite near the shores of Monterey year-round. Although you can sometimes even see them from the beach, boats can take you out for a closer look. The area hosts many humpbacks, blue whales, and gray whales, plus the occasional killer whale, minke whale, fin whale, and pod of dolphins. Bring your own binoculars for a better view, but the experienced boat captains will do all they can to get you as close as possible to the whales and dolphins. Most tours last 2-3 hours and leave from Fisherman's Wharf.

Monterey Bay Whale Watch (84 Fisherman's Wharf, 831/375-4658, www.montereybaywhalewatch.com, adults $40-145, children 4-12 $29-39, children under 4 $15) leaves from an easy-to-find red building on Fisherman's Wharf and runs tours in every season. You must make a reservation in advance, even for regularly scheduled tours. Afternoon tours are available.

Princess Monterey Whale Watching (96 Fisherman's Wharf, 831/372-2203, www.

montereywhalewatching.com, adults $45-65, children 3-11 $35-55) prides itself on its knowledgeable guides and its comfortable, spacious cruising vessels. It costs a bit extra to secure a space on the ship's upper deck. The *Princess Monterey* offers morning and afternoon tours, and you can buy tickets online or by phone.

Fast Raft Ocean Safaris (Monterey Harbor and Moss Landing Harbor, 408/659-3900, www.fastraft.com, $150/pp) offers an intimate way to explore the coast and wildlife. The "fast raft" is a 33-foot-long inflatable boat with a rigid hull that accommodates six passengers. The outfit does whale-watching trips out of Moss Landing and coastal safaris that depart from Monterey and head south to Pebble Beach's Stillwater Cove and Point Lobos. Note that the fast raft does not have a restroom.

Fishing

J&M Sport Fishing (66 Fisherman's Wharf, 831/372-7440 or 800/251-7440, https://jmsportfishing.com, $80-90) took over the longtime Randy's Fishing fleet. The new operation leaves shore for salmon, rock cod, and a fishing/crabbing combo trip.

To catch your own seafood, head out with **Westwind Charter Sport Fishing & Excursions** (66 Fisherman's Wharf, 831/392-7867, http://montereysportfishing.com). Depending on what's in season, you can catch salmon ($650/up to four people), rock cod, lingcod, or halibut ($550/up to four people).

Hiking

The 18-mile paved **Monterey Bay Coastal Recreation Trail** (831/646-3866, https://monterey.org) stretches from Pacific Grove north to the town of Castroville. The most scenic section is from Monterey Harbor down to Pacific Grove's Lovers Point Park. It's a great way to take in Monterey's coastline, sea otters, and harbor seals.

Jack's Peak County Park (25020 Jacks Peak Park Rd., 831/775-4895, www.co.monterey.ca.us, 10am-close daily, $4-5) is home to the highest point on the Monterey Peninsula. The park has picnic sites and 8.5 miles of walking paths, including the 0.8-mile-long **Skyline Trail.** The trail passes through a rare Monterey pine forest and offers glimpses of fossils from the Miocene epoch before reaching the summit, which offers an overview of the whole peninsula.

Fort Ord Dunes State Park was home to a U.S. Army post from 1917 to 1994,

the Monterey Bay Coastal Recreation Trail

(831/649-2836, www.parks.ca.gov, 8am-sunset daily, free). Across the park, paths lead to remnants of the military past plus four miles of beach access. To get there from Monterey, head north on Highway 1 and take the Lightfighter Drive exit. Turn left onto 2nd Avenue and then take a left on Divarty Street. Turn right on 1st Avenue and follow the signs to the park entrance at the 8th Street Bridge over Highway 1.

Golf

The **Monterey Pines Golf Course** (Fairground Rd. and Garden Rd., 831/656-2167, www.montereypeninsulagolf.com, Mon.-Fri. $18-34, Sat.-Sun. $20-37) is a beginner-friendly 18 holes next to the Monterey County Fairgrounds. The Pebble Beach Company manages the **Del Monte Golf Course** (1300 Sylvan Rd., 800/654-9300, www.montereypeninsulagolf.com, $110), an 18-hole course that claims to be the oldest continuously operating course west of the Mississippi.

Motor Sports

The **Mazda Raceway Laguna Seca** (1021 Monterey-Salinas Hwy., 831/242-8200, www.mazdaraceway.com) is one of the country's premier road-racing venues. You can see historic auto races, superbikes, speed festivals, and an array of Grand Prix events. Laguna Seca also hosts innumerable auto clubs and small sports car and stock car races. The major racing season runs May-October. You can camp here, and you'll find plenty of concessions during big races.

FOOD

The Monterey Bay Seafood Watch program (www.montereybayaquarium.org) is the definitive resource for sustainable seafood, while the Salinas Valley inland hosts a number of organic farms. The primary farmers market in the county, the **Monterey Farmers Market** (Alvarado St. between Del Monte Ave. and Pearl St., 831/655-8070, www.oldmonterey. org, 4pm-7pm Tues. Oct.-Apr., 4pm-8pm Tues. May-Sept.) takes over downtown Monterey with fresh-produce vendors, restaurant stalls, jewelry booths, and live music.

Cafés

Connected to the Osio Cinemas, Monterey's art-house movie theater, **Café Lumiere** (365 Calle Principal, 831/920-2451, http://cafe-lumieremonterey.com, 7am-9pm Sun.-Thurs., 7am-10pm Fri.-Sat.) is where Monterey's old Sicilian anglers hang out in the morning while sipping coffee drinks and munching on pastries. There are a lot of tempting options behind the counter's glass case, but the café also offers breakfast, lunch, and Sunday brunch dishes. In addition, the café has weekday lunch specials including a very popular giant bowl of pho (Vietnamese noodle soup) on Thursday. The tasty coffee is from Acme Coffee Roasting Company, a local favorite.

American

Inside an old brick firehouse, **Montrio** (414 Calle Principal, 831/648-8880, www.montrio.com, 4:30pm-close daily, $19-46) is an elegantly casual Monterey eatery. The ever-changing menu includes meat and seafood entrées, but Montrio is also an ideal place for a lighter dinner. Dine inside under ceilings decorated with art that resembles clouds, or out front on the patio. Executive chef Tony Baker is known for his dry-cured bacon. Happy Hour (4:30pm-6:30pm daily, $6.50) is worth a visit for cocktails and well-priced snacks.

A cozy locals' spot in a brick building a block off Alvarado Street, ★ **Melville Tavern** (484 Washington St., 831/643-9525, www.melvilletav.com, 11am-9pm Mon.-Fri., 10:30am-9pm Sat.-Sun., $11-30) does a bit less damage on the wallet. The straightforward but well-executed menu of sandwiches, salads, tacos, and a green chile cheeseburger will hit the spot. There's a nicely curated mix of beers on tap and wine by the glass or the bottle (look for the $3 beer of the week and the $6 wine of the week).

Seafood

On weekends, there is typically a line out the door at **Monterey's Fish House** (2114 Del Monte Ave., 831/373-4647, http://monterey-fishhouse.com, 11:30am-2:30pm and 5pm-9:30pm Mon.-Fri., 5pm-9:30pm Sat.-Sun., $11-30), one of the peninsula's most popular seafood restaurants with a fun, old-school Italian vibe. Inside, expect attentive service and fresh seafood including snapper, albacore tuna, and calamari fished right out of the bay.

The Sandbar & Grill (Municipal Wharf II, 831/373-2818, www.sandbarandgrillmonterey.com, 11am-9pm Mon.-Sat., 10:30am-9pm Sun., $12-30) has the best fried calamari around. They are also known for their fresh sand dabs and Dungeness crab sandwich with bacon. The restaurant hangs off the Municipal Wharf over Monterey Harbor.

For a South Pacific spin on seafood, head to ★ **Hula's Island Grill & Tiki Room** (622 Lighthouse Ave., 831/655-4852, www.hulas-tiki.com, 4pm-9:30pm Mon., 11:30am-9:30pm Tues.-Thurs., 11:30am-10pm Fri.-Sat., 4pm-9pm Sun., $12-23). Hula's is Monterey's most fun casual restaurant, with tasty and sometimes imaginative food. In addition to fresh fish and a range of tacos, the menu has land-based fare like Jamaican jerk chicken. The happy hours (4pm-6pm Sun.-Mon., 2pm-9:30pm Tues., 2pm-6pm Wed.-Sat.) feature tiki drinks and pupus (appetizers) for just six bucks a pop.

The Sardine Factory (701 Wave St., 831/373-3775, http://sardinefactory.com, 5pm-10:30pm Sun.-Thurs., 5pm-11pm Fri.-Sat., $26-59) is the area's iconic seafood and steak house. Its abalone bisque was served at one of President Ronald Reagan's inaugural dinners, and part of Clint Eastwood's directorial debut *Play Misty for Me* was filmed in the restaurant. This place oozes old-school cool, complete with a piano player in the lounge (Tues.-Sat.). The menu includes pasta, steak, and wild abalone medallions. Ask for a tour of the building, which has a glass-domed conservatory and an exclusive wine cellar that feels transported from a European castle.

★ **The Poke Lab** (475 Alvarado St., 831/200-3474, www.thepokelab.com, 11am-8pm daily, $11-15) dishes up poke (raw seafood) salads in a fast-casual setting. There may be a line out the door for the small eatery's build-your-own poke bowls or the namesake bowl (spicy tuna, ahi tuna, salmon, avocado, and toppings on sushi rice, brown rice, or salad).

the giant beached boat outside of The Sardine Factory

Steak House

The Whaling Station (763 Wave St., 831/373-3778, www.whalingstation.net, 5pm-9pm Sun.-Thurs., 5pm-10:30pm Fri.-Sat., $24-58) has been a local institution since 1970. Waiters present different cuts of meat on a tray and answer questions about the best qualities of each piece. Options include a New York steak, beef Wellington, and red-wine braised beef short ribs. Non-beef items include rack of lamb, seafood, and pasta. The moderately priced bar menu offers a steak sandwich or a burger made with ground filet mignon.

Sushi

Fresh seafood and creative rolls make **Crystal Fish** (514 Lighthouse Ave., 831/649-3474, http://crystalfishmonterey.com, 11:30am-2pm and 5pm-9:30pm Mon.-Thurs., 11:30am-2pm and 5pm-10pm Fri., 1pm-10pm Sat., 1pm-9:30pm Sun., $14-27) the Monterey go-to for sushi. There's not a lot of ambience, but there are a lot of rolls, including fresh salmon, tuna, eel, octopus, calamari, and unusual ingredients like asparagus and eggplant.

ACCOMMODATIONS
Under $150

The **Monterey Hostel** (778 Hawthorne St., 831/649-0375, http://montereyhostel.org, dorm bed $39, private room $139-184, family room $174-184) offers inexpensive accommodations within walking distance of the major attractions of Monterey. Accommodations include a men's dorm room, women's dorm room, private rooms, a five-person family room, and a coed dorm room with 16 beds; linens are included. A self-service laundry is within walking distance. Common areas include a large, fully stocked kitchen and spaces with couches and a piano. The kitchen serves a free pancake breakfast every morning.

$150-250

Jabberwock Inn (598 Laine St., 831/372-4777, www.jabberwockinn.com, $209-599)

is named after a nonsense poem written by Lewis Carroll as part of his novel *Through the Looking Glass*. Despite its name, the amenities of this comfortable former convent turned eight-room bed-and-breakfast are no-nonsense. The common area has a covered wraparound sun porch with views of Monterey Bay and two fireplaces. There are no TVs or telephones. Breakfasts are tasty and filling, while the innkeepers are warm and knowledgeable. Perks include free parking and late-afternoon wine and appetizers, along with evening milk and cookies. The B&B is just a short walk to Cannery Row, the aquarium, and Lighthouse Avenue.

The ★ **Spindrift Inn** (652 Cannery Row, 831/646-8900, www.spindriftinn.com, $239-529) is a boutique hotel towering above the golden sand and clear green waters of scenic McAbee Beach. This 45-room establishment has been called the country's most romantic hotel. Most of the hardwood-floored rooms have wood-burning fireplaces and full or half canopy beds. The very friendly staff serves a wine and cheese reception daily (4:30pm-6pm) and delivers a complimentary continental breakfast to your room.

The greatest asset of **Monterey Tides** (2600 Sand Dunes Rd., 831/394-3321 or 800/242-8627, https://www.jdvhotels.com, $200-400) is its proximity to the sand and surf. The four-story building sits right over Monterey State Beach; 102 of its 196 rooms face Monterey Bay. At night, take in the tapered triangle of lights on the Monterey peninsula from the wooden patios off the hotel's lobby. There's a heated pool (year-round) alongside a spa, and bikes and stand-up paddleboards are available for rent. The lobby bar, Bar Sebastian, and the top-floor Vizcaino restaurant have stellar views to accompany meals and drinks. The hotel also offers something most don't: fires on the beach (firewood, $25; bonfire kit with s'mores, $30).

Over $250

Luxury hotel **InterContinental The Clement Monterey** (750 Cannery Row,

831/375-4500, www.ictheclementmonterey.com, $250-850) has a can't-be-beat location just a splash away from the bay and aquarium. The hotel has 208 rooms and 12 luxury suites decorated with tasteful Asian elements such as a bonsai tree, a tiny Zen garden, and live orchids. Most of the bathrooms have a separate soaking tub and walk-in shower. Oceanside rooms have views of the bay, while units on the other side of Cannery Row have fireplaces. There are a lot of amenities, including a fitness room, an outdoor whirlpool, The Spa (831/642-2075, 9am-7pm daily, massages $80-175), The C Restaurant & Bar (831/375-4800, 6:30am-10pm daily, $29-58), a sliver of an outdoor pool to swim laps in, and an artsy, jellyfish-inspired staircase connecting the first and second floors.

Located between San Carlos Beach and Cannery Row, the ★ Monterey Bay Inn (242 Cannery Row, 831/373-6242 or 800/424-6242, www.montereybayinn.com, $309-600) has oceanfront rooms with private balconies that overlook Monterey Bay and in-room binoculars for spotting wildlife. The hotel's rooftop hot tub offers another vantage point to take in the action offshore. Enjoy a continental breakfast delivered to your room in the morning and cookies in the evening.

Camping

One mile up a hill from downtown Monterey, the 50-acre Veterans Memorial Park (Via Del Rey and Veterans Dr., 831/646-3865, www.monterey.org, $30/single vehicle, $38/ two vehicles) has 40 first-come, first-served campsites with views of Monterey Bay.

TRANSPORTATION AND SERVICES

Most visitors drive into Monterey via scenic Highway 1. Inland, U.S. 101 allows access into Salinas from the north and south. From Salinas, Highway 68 travels west into Monterey.

For a more leisurely ride, Amtrak's Coast Starlight train (11 Station Pl., Salinas, 10am-2pm and 3pm-8pm daily) travels through Salinas.

The Greyhound bus station (3 Station Pl., Salinas, 831/424-4418, www.greyhound.com, 9am-noon and 1pm-4pm Mon.-Sat.) is 18.5 miles east of Monterey. To get to Monterey, walk two blocks to the Salinas Transit Center (110 Salinas St., 888/678-2871, https://mst.org) and hop on a Monterey-Salinas Transit bus to the coast.

In Monterey, take advantage of the free Monterey Trolley (Waterfront Area Visitor Express, 888/678-2871, https://mst.org, hours vary daily late May-early Sept., 10am-7pm Sat.-Sun. early Sept.-late May), which loops between downtown Monterey and the aquarium. Monterey-Salinas Transit (888/678-2871, www.mst.org, $1.25-2.50) has routes throughout Monterey.

For medical needs, the Community Hospital of the Monterey Peninsula (CHOMP, 23625 Holman Hwy., 831/624-5311 or 888/452-4667, www.chomp.org) provides emergency services to the area.

Pacific Grove

Sandwiched between historic Monterey and exclusive Pebble Beach, Pacific Grove makes a fine base for exploring the peninsula. It's also worth a visit for its colorful turn-of-the-20th-century Victorian homes and its striking strand of coastline. Founded in 1875 as a Methodist summer retreat, this quiet city is perfect for a relaxing afternoon of strolling among the yellow, purple, and green Victorian homes and cottages on Lighthouse Avenue. (There's a different Lighthouse Avenue in adjacent Monterey.)

Pacific Grove's "Poor Man's 17-Mile Drive" winds around a piece of coastal real estate

Local Favorites

While the Monterey Bay Aquarium and the Santa Cruz Beach Boardwalk draw many visitors to the coast, lesser-known attractions appeal to adventurous travelers.

Walking around Monterey's Cannery Row today, it's hard to imagine this was once a rough and tumble neighborhood filled with sardine canneries. Not much remains from those days, with the exception of the **Pacific Biological Laboratories** (800 Cannery Row, 831/646-5648, www.monterey.org, free tours monthly), the former residence and workplace of Ed Ricketts, one of Cannery Row's most colorful characters. (Ricketts was the basis for the character Doc in the John Steinbeck novel *Cannery Row*.) The city-owned property opens to the public once a month for free tours.

The **Land of the Medicine Buddha** (5800 Prescott Ave., Soquel, 831/462-8383, http://landofmedicinebuddha.org, 7am-8pm Mon.-Fri., noon-8pm Sun., donations appreciated) is a Buddhist meditation and retreat center in the Santa Cruz foothills. Visitors can wander the grounds of the 108-acre facility to spin an ornate prayer wheel or enjoy a contemplative walk on Eight Verses Trail, which features eight Buddhist verses posted at signs along the path.

Founded in 1797, the **Mission San Juan Bautista** (406 2nd St., San Juan Bautista, 831/623-4528, http://oldmissionsjb.org, 9:30am-4:30pm daily) was the 15th in California's chain of missions. Visitors can stroll the grounds and explore the many buildings; there is a small museum and gift shop, as well as daily tours. Adjoining the mission is the **San Juan Bautista State Historic Park** (2nd St. at Washington and Mariposa Sts., 831/623-4881, www.parks.ca.gov, 10am-4:30pm daily).

About a one-hour drive inland from Monterey, **Pinnacles National Park** (5000 Hwy. 146, Paicines, 831/389-4486, www.nps.gov/pinn, 7:30am-8pm daily, $25 entrance fee) is a wonderland of rock spires and caves, with California condors sailing overhead. Take a satisfying day hike or spend the night in the campground on the east side of the park.

between Lover's Point Park and Asilomar Beach that's almost as striking as Pebble Beach's 17-Mile Drive. Start on Ocean View Boulevard by Lover's Point and continue onto Sunset Drive to get the full experience. In the spring, flowering ice plant right along the road adds a riot of color to the landscape.

SIGHTS
Lover's Point Park

Aptly named **Lover's Point Park** (Ocean View Blvd. and 17th St., 831/648-3100, www.cityofpacificgrove.org) is one of the area's most popular wedding sites. A finger of land with a jumble of rocks at its northernmost point, Lover's Point offers expansive views of the interior section of Monterey Bay. The park also has a sheltered pocket beach that is ideal for a dip. A kelp forest right offshore offers a superb spot for snorkelers to get a feel for Monterey Bay's impressive underwater ecosystem. During summer, an old-fashioned

hamburger stand operates above the beach, and a vendor rents kayaks, bikes, and snorkeling equipment.

Point Pinos Lighthouse

Surrounded by a golf course, **Point Pinos Lighthouse** (80 Asilomar Ave. between Lighthouse Ave. and Del Monte Ave., 831/648-3176, www.pointpinoslighthouse.org, 1pm-4pm Thurs.-Mon., adults $2, children $1) is the oldest continuously operating lighthouse on the West Coast, in service since 1855. Point Pinos is also notable for the two female lighthouse keepers who served there during its long history. The light was automated in 1975, but it is still an active aid to local marine navigation. Lighthouse lovers will enjoy walking through the building's two floors and cellar.

Monarch Grove Sanctuary

Pacific Grove is also known as "Butterfly Town U.S.A." An impressive migration of

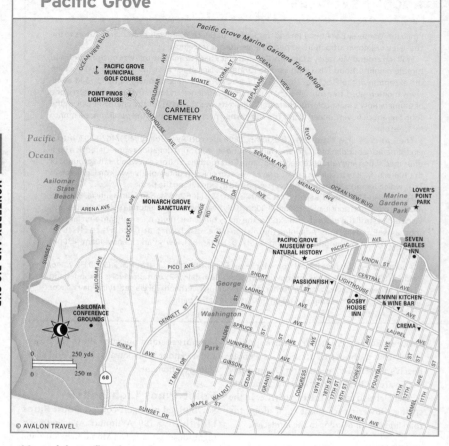

Pacific Grove

Pacific Ocean

PACIFIC GROVE MUNICIPAL GOLF COURSE

POINT PINOS LIGHTHOUSE ★

EL CARMELO CEMETERY

Pacific Grove Marine Gardens Fish Refuge

OCEAN VIEW BLVD

ASILOMAR AVE

MONTE

CORAL ST

OCEAN

BLVD

ESPLANADE

VIEW

BLVD

LIGHTHOUSE AVE

SEAPALM AVE

JEWELL DR

MERMAID AVE

AVE

OCEAN VIEW BLVD

Marine Gardens Park

LOVER'S POINT PARK ★

Asilomar State Beach

ARENA AVE

SUNSET DR

ASILOMAR AVE

CROCKER AVE

MONARCH GROVE SANCTUARY ★

RIDGE RD

17 MILE DR

PACIFIC GROVE MUSEUM OF NATURAL HISTORY ★

PACIFIC

AVE

UNION ST

CENTRAL

SEVEN GABLES INN ●

PICO AVE

SHORT ST

PASSIONFISH ▼

LIGHTHOUSE

AVE

JENINNI KITCHEN & WINE BAR ▼

George

LAUREL

GOSBY HOUSE INN ●

ASILOMAR CONFERENCE GROUNDS ●

DENNETT ST

Washington

PINE

AVE

AVE

CREMA ▼

LAUREL

SPRUCE ST

AVE

ST

SINEX AVE

17 MILE DR

Park

ALDER ST

JUNIPERO

GIBSON

AVE

CEDAR

GRANITE AVE

CONGRESS AVE

19TH ST

18TH ST

17TH ST

16TH ST

FOREST AVE

FOUNTAIN AVE

13TH ST

12TH ST

11TH ST

AVE

0   250 yds

0   250 m

68

SUNSET DR

MAPLE ST

WALNUT ST

SINEX AVE

CARMEL AVE

© AVALON TRAVEL

Monarch butterflies descends on the town each year. The small **Monarch Grove Sanctuary** (Ridge Rd. between Lighthouse Ave. and Short St., 831/648-5716, www.cityof-pacificgrove.org, free) offers stands of euca-lyptus and pine trees that are cloaked with colorful insects during the migration period (Oct.-Feb.). The best time to visit is in the early afternoon, when sunlight illuminates the butterflies and docents can answer your questions.

Asilomar State Beach

One of the Monterey Peninsula's most popular beaches, **Asilomar State Beach** (Sunset Dr., 831/646-6440, www.parks.ca.gov) draws beachgoers, walkers, and surfers. The beach is a narrow, one-mile-long strip of coastline with a boardwalk trail on the dunes behind it. Keep walking on the trail to get to nearby Pebble Beach.

Right across Sunset Drive, visitors can explore the **Asilomar Dunes Natural Preserve** and the **Asilomar Conference Grounds** (800 Asilomar Ave., 831/372-8016, www.visitasilomar.com). The dunes pre-serve is 25 acres of restored sand dune eco-system that can be accessed via a 0.25-mile boardwalk. The conference grounds are shaded by Monterey pines and studded with arts and crafts-style structures designed by Hearst Castle architect Julia Morgan. Enjoy the facilities, including the Phoebe A. Hearst Social Hall, which has pool tables, a fireplace, and some comfy seats. One-hour **ranger-guided tours** of the grounds (831/646-6443) focus on the architecture, the dunes, the forest, and the coast.

To reach Asilomar, take the Route 68 West exit off Highway 1 and turn left onto Sunset Drive.

Pacific Grove Museum of Natural History

Stop into the **Pacific Grove Museum of Natural History** (165 Forest Ave., 831/648-5716, www.pgmuseum.org, 10am-5pm Tues.-Sun., adults $9, military, students, and children $6) and learn how to identify the animal and plant species of the Monterey Peninsula. The museum provides a fairly comprehensive overview of the region's biodiversity. One room is dedicated to feathered friends and includes 300 mounted birds found around the county, among them the gigantic California condor. Other rooms highlight large terrestrial mammals (mountain lions, bears) and whales. There's also a space devoted to the Monarch butterfly. Out front is a life-sized gray whale statue, while out back is a native plant garden.

ENTERTAINMENT AND EVENTS

A couple of family-friendly annual events occur in "America's Last Hometown." Recalling another era, Pacific Grove's **Good Old Days** (831/373-3304, www.pacificgrove.org, Apr.) is a weekend of good clean fun that includes a parade, a quilt show, pony rides, and live entertainment. For more than 70 years, kids have been getting dressed up like butterflies at the **Butterfly Parade and Bazaar** (www.pacificgrove.org, first Sat. of Oct.), which welcomes the wintering Monarch butterflies to the area every fall.

SPORTS AND RECREATION
Scuba Diving and Snorkeling

Some of the best scuba diving and snorkeling spots lie off Pacific Grove. **Lover's Point Park** (Ocean View Blvd. and 17th St., novice to advanced, 10-40 feet) has a protected cove and kelp forest right off its shores. The cove's protected, sandy beach makes an easy entry point for scuba divers and snorkelers. A few blocks away, **Otter Cove** (Ocean View Blvd. and Sea Palm Ave., novice to advanced, 10-60 feet) is a dive spot best explored during days of calm seas. One of the highlights is an underwater pinnacle that rises from 50 feet to just 18 feet below the surface. Nearby **Coral Street Cove** (Coral St. and Ocean View Blvd., advanced, 20-50 feet) is known for its fish population.

For equipment, visit **Bamboo Reef** (614 Lighthouse Ave., 831/372-1685, www.bambooreef.com, 9am-6pm Mon.-Fri., 7am-6pm Sat.-Sun.), **Aquarius Dive Shop** (2040 Del Monte Ave., 831/375-1933, www.aquariusdivers.com, 9am-6pm Mon.-Fri., 7am-6pm Sat.-Sun.), or **Breakwater Scuba** (225 Cannery Row, Monterey, 831/717-4546, http://breakwaterscuba.com, 9am-6pm Mon.-Fri., 7am-6pm Sat.-Sun.).

Surfing

During the summer and fall, clean swells produce fun waves at **Asilomar State Beach** (Sunset Dr., 831/646-6440, www.parks.ca.gov), making it one of the peninsula's most popular surf spots. Winter produces big, often dangerous swells, so stay out of the water during that time of the year. To get there, take the Route 68 West exit off Highway 1 and turn left onto Sunset Drive.

During big swells, **Lovers Point** (Ocean View Blvd. and 17th St.) turns into a nice left. There are some rocks in the lineup, so it is probably best that first-timers go out with someone who knows the break.

On the Beach (693 Lighthouse Ave., Monterey, 831/646-9283, http://onthebeachsurfshop.com, 10am-6pm Sun.-Thurs.,

10am-7pm Fri.-Sat., surfboard rental $30/day, wetsuit rental $15/day) rents boards and wetsuits.

Golf

The **Pacific Grove Golf Links** (77 Asilomar Blvd., 831/648-5775, www.playpacificgrove.com, daily sunrise-sunset, Mon.-Thurs. $46, Fri.-Sun. and holidays $52) doesn't have the acclaim of the nearby Pebble Beach courses, but it's on a similarly gorgeous length of coastline just a few miles away.

FOOD
American

★ **Crema** (481 Lighthouse Ave., 831/324-0347, http://cremapg.com, 7am-4pm daily, $7-15) is a gourmet comfort food restaurant in a multilevel building that feels like someone's house. Dine on oversize burgers or chicken sandwiches beside a fireplace or a piano. They also offer a stout beer float (stout beer, ice cream, and espresso) and weekend pitchers of mimosas and sangria.

Crema offers gourmet comfort food.

In the cavernous American Tin Cannery shopping mall, **First Awakenings** (125 Oceanview Blvd., 831/372-1125, www.first-awakenings.net, 7am-2pm Mon.-Fri., 7am-2:30pm Sat.-Sun., $6-12) serves oversize versions of classic breakfast fare including huevos rancheros, eggs Benedict, crepes, and omelets. Locals frequently vote this place the county's top breakfast spot. On sunny days, dine outside on the large patio while surrounded by the sounds of nearby Monterey Bay.

Italian

Il Vecchio (110 Central Ave., 831/324-4282, noon-1:30pm and 5pm-9pm Mon.-Thurs., noon-1:30pm and 5pm-9:30pm Fri., 5pm-9:30pm Sat., 5pm-9pm Sun., $13-22) is a Pacific Grove favorite. The name Il Vecchio means "the old" and refers to traditional Italian fare like gnocchi with pesto. They make their pasta daily and offer traditional Italian takes on meats and seafood. Mondays are Piatti at Vecchio (5pm-9pm, $18), where you can sample three popular dishes in smaller portions. The Lunch for the Workers Special (noon-1:30pm Mon.-Fri., $9) offers diners a salad and two pastas.

Mediterranean

The **Jeninni Kitchen & Wine Bar** (542 Lighthouse Ave., 831/920-2662, 4pm-close Thurs.-Tues., $18-30) has elevated Pacific Grove's dining scene. The menu changes frequently, but the wagyu bullfighter's steak and the eggplant fries are favorites. Sit in the dining area in the front of the building or walk up a few stairs to the bar area for small plates, wine, and craft beers.

Seafood

One of the Monterey Peninsula's most lauded seafood restaurants is ★ **Passionfish** (701 Lighthouse Ave., 831/655-3311, www.passionfish.net, Sun.-Thurs. 5pm-9pm, Fri.-Sat. 5pm-10pm, $16-36), which is on a mission to spread the gospel about sustainable seafood. Passionfish does great food, especially creative and flavorful sustainable seafood. Their menu starts with a nice scallop appetizer and includes seared albacore tuna in a bacon sauce or basil-stuffed rainbow trout entrées. They are also known for their extensive, moderately priced wine list. The knowledgeable waitstaff could teach a course on seafood.

ACCOMMODATIONS

Pacific Grove is known for bed-and-breakfasts in nice Victorian buildings.

Under $150

The ★ **Gosby House Inn** (643 Lighthouse Ave., 800/527-8828, www.gosbyhouseinn. com, $125-280) has been taking care of visitors since the 1880s. The white-and-yellow Queen Anne-style Victorian, which sits on downtown Pacific Grove's main street, is a welcome cross between a boutique hotel and a B&B. Amenities include free Wi-Fi, flat-screen TVs in most rooms, and a complimentary breakfast. The photo- and antique-heavy main house has 22 rooms, some with gas fireplaces. The two deluxe rooms in the adjacent Carriage House have a balcony, a gas fireplace, a roomy bathroom, and a nice-sized soaking tub.

$150-250

Staying overnight at the ★ **Asilomar Conference Grounds** (804 Crocker Ave., 831/372-8016, www.visitasilomar.com, $190-335) can feel like going back to summer camp. Common areas on the 107 acres include the Phoebe Apperson Hearst Social Hall, where visitors can relax by a roaring fire or play pool at one of two billiards tables. Accommodations range from historic rooms to family cottages to modern rooms with a view of nearby Asilomar Beach, but purposefully lack TVs and telephones. Rooms with an ocean view and a fireplace are definitely recommended. The lodging hosts a multitude of conferences, so expect to see corporate types walking through the forests of Monterey pine, Monterey cypress, and coast live oaks.

The **Old St. Angela Inn** (321 Central Ave., 831/372-3246, www.oldstangelainn.com,

$165-290) spoils with cozy accommodations, a friendly staff, and terrific food. The nine homey rooms have pine antiques, live plants, and comfortable beds. Comfy common areas are downstairs, while out back is a brick patio area with a fire pit and a waterfall fountain. One of the best features of The Old St. Angela Inn is its house-made food. Afternoon teatime offers wine, a dessert, and an appetizer. The scrumptious breakfast includes yogurt, granola, muffins, and a hot sweet or savory item.

One of the finest and most notable Queen Anne Victorian buildings is the dark green and white **Green Gables Inn** (301 Ocean View Blvd., 831/375-2095 or 800/722-1774, www.greengablesinnpg.com, $169-309). The main building, which was built in 1888, has a downstairs common area with ocean views—it's the place to stay, with a throwback feel and antique furnishings. Behind the main inn, the Carriage House has five spacious rooms, all with a gas fireplace, a jetted tub, and ocean views. The inn offers afternoon wine and appetizers, a morning breakfast buffet, and a few bikes that can be borrowed for a spin on the nearby Monterey Bay Coastal Recreation Trail.

Over $250

The most striking bed-and-breakfast on the Pacific Grove coast, the **Seven Gables Inn** (555 Ocean View Blvd., 831/372-4341, www. sevengablesinn.com, $329-469) is perched just feet away from Lover's Point. Every room has superb ocean views. Decorated with antique furniture and artwork, the inn is for those who want to step back in time and experience ornate Victorian- and Edwardian-style lodging.

TRANSPORTATION AND SERVICES

Most visitors drive into the area via scenic Highway 1. From Highway 1, take the Route 68 West exit to reach downtown Pacific Grove. For medical needs, the **Community Hospital of the Monterey Peninsula** (CHOMP, 23625 Holman Hwy., 831/624-5311 or 888/452-4667, www.chomp.org) in Monterey provides emergency services to the area.

Pebble Beach

Between Pacific Grove and Carmel, the gated community of Pebble Beach lays claim to some of the Monterey Peninsula's best and highest-priced real estate. Pebble Beach is famous for the scenic 17-Mile Drive and its collection of high-end resorts, restaurants, spas, and golf courses, owned by the Pebble Beach Company, a partnership that included golf legend Arnold Palmer and film legend Clint Eastwood. Pebble Beach also hosts the annual **AT&T Pebble Beach National Pro-Am** (831/649-1533, www.attpbgolf.com, Feb., event prices vary)., a charity golf tournament that pairs professional golfers with celebrities.

SIGHTS
17-Mile Drive

The best way to take in the stunning scenery of Pebble Beach is the **17-Mile Drive** ($10.25/vehicle). Pay the fee at the gatehouse and receive a map of the drive that describes the parks and sights you'll pass along the winding coastal road: the much-photographed Lone Cypress, the beaches of Spanish Bay, and Pebble Beach's golf course, resort, and housing complex. If you're in a hurry, you can get from one end of the 17-Mile Drive to the other in 20 minutes. But go slowly and stop often to enjoy the natural beauty of the area. Plenty of turnouts let you stop to take photos, and you can picnic at many of the beaches; most have basic restroom facilities and ample parking lots. The only food and gas are at the Inn at Spanish Bay and the Lodge at Pebble Beach.

SPORTS AND RECREATION

Spa at Pebble Beach (1518 Cypress Dr., 831/649-7615 or 800/877-0597, www.pebblebeach.com, 8:30am-7:30pm daily, $165-470) has specialty massages for golfers before or after a day on the greens.

Biking

Traveling the **17-Mile Drive** by bike means you don't have to pay the $10 vehicle admission fee. It's also a great bike route. Expect fairly flat terrain with lots of twists and turns, and a ride that runs . . . about 17 miles. Foggy conditions can make this ride a bit slick in the summer, but spring and fall weather are perfect for pedaling.

Bay Bikes (3600 The Barnyard Shopping Center, Carmel, 831/655-2453, www.baybikes.com, 10am-5pm Sun.-Mon., 10am-6pm Tues.-Fri., 9am-6pm Sat., $8-16/hour, $24-48/four hours) is the closest place to rent a cruiser, hybrid bike, road bike, or tandem.

Golf

Golf has been a major pastime here since the late 19th century; today avid golfers come from around the world to tee off (and pay $200 or more for a single round of golf). The 18-hole, par-72 **Spyglass Hill** (1700 17-Mile Dr., 800/654-9300, www.pebblebeach.com, $395) gets its name from the Robert Louis Stevenson Novel *Treasure Island*. Spyglass Hill boasts some of the most challenging play in this golf course-laden region. Expect a few bogeys, and tee off from the championship level at your own (ego's) risk.

A favorite with the Pebble Beach crowd is the famed 18-hole, par-72 **Poppy Hills Golf Course** (3200 Lopez Rd., 831/622-8239, www.poppyhillsgolf.com, $210). Poppy Hills shares amenities with the other Pebble Beach golf courses. Expect the same level of care and devotion to the maintenance of the course and your experience as a player.

The **Pebble Beach Golf Links** (1700 17-Mile Dr., 800/877-0597, www.pebblebeach.com, $495) has been called the nation's best golf course by *Golf Digest*. The high ranking might have something to do with the fact that some of the fairways are perched above the Pacific Ocean. The course will host its sixth men's U.S. Open championship in 2019 and is one of three courses utilized during the popular AT&T Pro-Am.

Less pricey than the Pebble Beach Golf Links, **The Links at Spanish Bay** (2700 17-Mile Dr., 831/647-7495 or 800/877-0597, $155-270) is on native sand dune habitat. Due to the environmental sensitivity of the grounds, the course caps the number of players and spectators on the greens.

FOOD AND ACCOMMODATIONS

You need to drop some serious money to stay in Pebble Beach. To experience the luxury of Pebble Beach without spending your savings, consider having lunch, dinner, or a drink here and then head back to a less expensive lodging in nearby Pacific Grove or Monterey.

The Hawaiian fusion cuisine of celebrity chef Roy Yamaguchi takes center stage at **Roy's at Pebble Beach** (The Inn at Spanish Bay, 2700 17-Mile Dr., 831/647-7423, www.pebblebeach.com, 6:30am-10pm daily, $27-50). Island-inspired dishes include seafood and sushi, all with an Asian flair. Head to **Peppoli** (The Inn at Spanish Bay, 2700 17-Mile Dr., 831/647-7433, www.pebblebeach.com, 6pm-10pm daily, $25-110) for a hearty Italian dinner of gnocchi with black truffle cream sauce or seared local halibut.

The Bench Restaurant (The Lodge at Pebble Beach, 1700 17-Mile Dr., 800/654-9300, 11am-10pm daily, $25-36) overlooks the famed 18th hole of the Pebble Beach Golf Links. The chef employs wood-roasting and open-flame cooking techniques to create wood-fired Brussels sprouts and grilled steaks. **The Tap Room** (The Lodge at Pebble

Beach, 1700 17-Mile Dr., 831/625-8535, 11am-midnight daily, $22-79) bar serves burgers, bratwurst, Wagyu beef filet mignon, and fresh Maine lobster (the prime rib chili is worth your time), and 14 beers on tap at an inflated price ($10.75). Bill Murray is an occasional customer.

Porter's in the Forest (3200 Lopez Rd., 831/622-8240, http://poppyhillsgolf.com/porters, 6am-6pm daily, $13-25), beside the Poppy Hills Golf Course, serves ingenious twists on clubhouse fare with items like a Korean Philly cheesesteak and carne asada fries. They serve breakfast, lunch, and a twilight menu.

Expect luxury amenities at **The Lodge at Pebble Beach** (1700 17-Mile Dr., 831/647-7500 or 800/654-9300, www.pebblebeach.com, $900-4,400), by the 18th hole of the Pebble Beach Golf Links. Most rooms and suites have wood-burning fireplaces as well as private patios or balconies. Some high-end rooms have their own spas. A stay includes access to The Beach & Tennis Club, which has a heated outdoor pool, a whirlpool spa, and a tennis pavilion. **The Inn at Spanish Bay** (2700 17-Mile Dr., 831/647-7500 or 800/654-9300, www.pebblebeach.com, $790-4,450) has rooms with fireplaces and decks or patios. There's also a fitness center and tennis pavilion on-site.

TRANSPORTATION

Pebble Beach is a gated community and entry requires a fee ($10.25). There are several gates to get into Pebble Beach, including three in Pacific Grove and one in Carmel. You can get the fee waived if you are dining at a Pebble Beach restaurant. Just make a reservation and tell the guard at the entry gate.

Carmel-by-the-Sea

There are no addresses in Carmel-by-the-Sea (frequently referred to as simply Carmel). There are lots of trees and no streetlights, and street signs are wooden posts with names written perpendicularly, to be read while walking along the sidewalk, rather than driving down the street. There's little to do at night. These are a few clues as to how this village facing the Pacific Ocean maintains its lost-in-time charm.

Formerly a Bohemian enclave where local poets George Sterling and Robinson Jeffers hung out with literary heavyweights including Jack London and Mary Austin, Carmel-by-the-Sea is now a popular vacation spot for the moneyed, the artistic, and the romantic. People come to enjoy the small coastal town's almost European appeal. They stroll its sidewalks, peering into the windows of upscale shops and art galleries that showcase the work of sculptors, plein air painters, and photographers. Between the galleries are some of the region's most revered restaurants. The main thoroughfare, Ocean Avenue, slopes down to Carmel Beach, one of the finest on the Monterey Peninsula.

The old-world charms of Carmel can make it a little confusing for drivers. Because there are no addresses, locations are sometimes given via directions, for example: on 7th Avenue between San Carlos and Dolores Streets; or the northwest corner of Ocean Avenue. The town is compact, laid out on a plain grid system, so you're better off getting out of your car and walking anyway. Expect to share everything from Carmel's sidewalks to its restaurants with our canine friends. Carmel is very pro-pup.

SIGHTS
★ Carmel Beach

Carmel Beach (Ocean Ave., 831/624-4909, http://ci.carmel.ca.us/carmel, 6am-10pm daily) is one of the Monterey Bay region's best beaches. Under a bluff dotted with twisted, skeletal cypress trees, it's a long, white, sandy beach that borders a usually clear blue-green Pacific. In the distance to the south, Point Lobos juts out from the land like a pointing

the white sand of Carmel Beach

finger, while just north of the beach, the green-as-billiard-table-felt golf courses cloak the grounds of nearby Pebble Beach. Like most of Carmel, Carmel Beach is very dog friendly. On any given day, all sorts of canines fetch, sniff, and run on the white sand.

One of the best places to access the beach is at the west end of Ocean Avenue. There's a parking lot here, along with four beach volleyball courts, a wooden observation deck, and restrooms.

For surfers, Carmel Beach is one of the Monterey area's most consistent breaks.

Carmel Mission

San Carlos Borromeo de Carmelo Mission (3080 Rio Rd., 831/624-1271, www.carmelmission.org, 9:30am-7pm daily, adults $6.50, seniors $4, children $2) was Father Junípero Serra's favorite among his California mission churches. He lived, worked, and died here; visitors can see a replica of his cell. An active Catholic parish remains part of the complex, so please be respectful when taking the self-guided tour. The rambling buildings and courtyard gardens show some wear, but restoration work makes them attractive and eminently visitor friendly.

The Carmel Mission has a small memorial museum in a building off the second courtyard that shows a slice of the lives of the 18th- and 19th-century friars. The highlight is the church with its gilded altar front, its shrine to the Virgin Mary, the grave of Junípero Serra, and an ancillary chapel dedicated to his memory. Round out your visit by walking the gardens to admire the flowers and fountains and to read the grave markers in the small cemetery.

Tor House

Local poet Robinson Jeffers penned nature poems to the uncompromising beauty of Carmel Point and nearby Big Sur. He built this rugged-looking castle on the Carmel coast in 1919. Jefffers named it **Tor House** (26304 Ocean View Ave., 831/624-1813, www.torhouse.org, tours 10am-3pm Fri.-Sat.,

adults $10, students $5) after its rocky setting, and he added the majestic Hawk Tower a year later.

Volunteer docents offer tours of the property that include a walk through the original home, which was hand built by Jeffers with giant stones. The poet once hosted luminaries like Ansel Adams, Charlie Chaplin, Edna St. Vincent Millay, and Dylan Thomas within the dining room, which offers fine views of Carmel Point and Point Lobos. The highlight of the tour is a visit to **Hawk Tower,** a four-story stone structure crowned with an open-air turret.

★ Point Lobos State Natural Reserve

Said to be the inspiration behind the setting of Robert Louis Stevenson's *Treasure Island,* **Point Lobos State Natural Reserve** (Hwy. 1, three miles south of Carmel, 831/624-4909, www.parks.ca.gov and www.pointlobos.org, 8am-7pm daily spring-fall, 8am-sunset daily winter, $10) is a wonderland of coves, hills, and jumbled rocks. The reserve's Cypress Grove Trail winds through a forest of antler-like Monterey cypress trees that are cloaked in striking red algae.

Point Lobos offers a lesson on the region's fishing history in the **Whaler's Cabin** (9am-5pm daily, staff permitting), a small wooden structure that was built by Chinese fishermen in the 1850s. Half of the reserve is underwater, open for scuba divers who want to explore the 70-foot-high kelp forests just offshore. The parking lots in Point Lobos tend to fill up on crowded weekends; park on nearby Highway 1 and walk in to the park during these times.

WINERIES

The town of Carmel (www.carmelcalifornia.org) has wine-tasting rooms in its downtown area. At the wooden slab bar in the sleek **Caraccioli Cellars Tasting Room** (Dolores St. between Ocean and 7th Aves., 831/622-7722, www.caracciolicellars.com, 2pm-7pm Mon.-Thurs., 11am-10pm Fri.-Sat., 11am-7pm

Carmel-by-the-Sea

1ST AVE

17-MILE DRIVE

2ND AVE

2ND AVE

SANTA RITA ST

CARMEL WAY

Pebble Beach Golf Course

3RD AVE

4TH AVE

3RD AVE

2ND AVE

N CASANOVA ST

MONTE VERDE ST

LINCOLN ST

DOLORES ST

SAN CARLOS ST

MISSION ST

JUNIPERO ST

TORRES ST

SANTA FE ST

PALOU AV

LOPEZ AVE

N CAMINO REAL

N SAN ANTONIO AVE

N CARMELO ST

CASANOVA

5TH AVE

CARMEL VISITOR CENTER

KATY'S PLACE

STARLIGHT 65 ROOFTOP TERRACE AT VESUVIO

CARMEL ART ASSOCIATION

EM-LE'S

AKAONI

BRUNO'S MARKET

To CA-1

LOBOS LODGE

6TH AVE

OCEAN AVE

CARMEL VALLEY ROASTING COMPANY

DAMETRA CAFÉ

Carmel Plaza

MOUNTAIN VIEW AVE

CARMEL BAY COMPANY

SALUMERIA LUCA

7TH AVE

BICYCLETTE

TUCK BOX

Carmel Bay

7TH AVE

THE FOREST THEATER

CYPRESS INN

8TH AVE

VIZCAINO AVE

LA PLAYA HOTEL

GOLDEN BOUGH PLAHOUSE

SCENIC RD

SAN ANTONIO AVE

CAMINO REAL

CASANOVA ST

9TH AVE

SUNSET CENTER

MONTE VERDE ST

LINCOLN ST

DOLORES ST

SAN CARLOS ST

MISSION ST

CARMELO ST

10TH AVE

CARMEL BEACH

11TH AVE

TORRES ST

12TH AVE

0   500 yds

0   500 m

13TH AVE

JUNIPERO ST

Mission

Trail

SANTA LUCIA AVE

Park

SCENIC RD

BAY VIEW AVE

SAN ANTONIO AVE

14TH AVE

FRANCISCAN WAY

RIO RD

15TH AVE

LASUEN DR

CARMELO ST

WALKER AVE

CARMEL MISSION

SCENIC RD

OCEAN VIEW AVE

ISABELLA AVE

VALLEY VIEW AVE

16TH AVE

16TH AVE

MISSION RANCH RESTAURANT AT MISSION RANCH

STEWART WAY

RIO AVE

SCENIC RD

17TH AVE

Carmel River State Beach

Sun., $10-15), taste wines made from pinot noir and chardonnay grapes. They also pour a brut and a brut rosé.

The family-owned **De Tierra Vineyards Tasting Room** (Mission St. and 5th Ave., 831/622-9704, www.detierra.com, 2pm-8pm Tues.-Thurs., noon-8pm Fri.-Sun. summer; 2pm-7pm Tues.-Thurs., noon-8pm, Fri.-Sun. winter, $10-15) has a rosé, syrah, merlot, chardonnay, red blend, riesling, and a pinot noir. A chalkboard lists a cheese and chocolate plate menu.

Grammy Award-winning composer Alan Silvestri makes wines in Carmel Valley. They can be sampled in the **Silvestri Tasting Room** (7th Ave. between Dolores and San Carlos Sts., 831/625-0111, www.silvestrivineyards.com, noon-7pm daily, $10-15).

Taste the wares at **Scheid Vineyards Carmel-by-the-Sea Tasting Room** (San Carlos St. and 9th Ave., 831/656-9463, www.scheidvineyards.com, noon-6pm Sun.-Thurs., noon-7pm Fri.-Sat., $10-20), a clean, friendly space.

ENTERTAINMENT AND EVENTS
Bars and Clubs
Barmel (San Carlos St. between Ocean Ave.

and 7th Ave., 831/626-3400, 2:30pm-midnight daily) has live music Thursday-Saturday with a DJ on weekend nights.

Live Music
The **Chamber Music Monterey Bay** (831/625-2212, www.chambermusicmonterey-bay.org) society brings talented ensembles and soloists from around the world to perform on the lovely Central Coast. String quartets rule the small stage. Shows are performed at the **Sunset Cultural Center** (San Carlos St. at 9th Ave., 831/620-2048, www.sunsetcenter.org), a state-of-the-art performing center with more than 700 seats. Chamber Music Monterey Bay reserves up-front seats for children and their adult companions.

Theater
The **Pacific Repertory Theater** (831/622-0100, www.pacrep.org, adults $15-39, seniors $15-28, military, students, and teachers $10-15, children $7.50) is the only professional theater company on the Monterey Peninsula. Shows travel the region, but most are in the **Golden Bough Playhouse** (Monte Verde St. and 8th Ave.), the company's home theater. Other venues include the **The Forest Theater** (Mountain View St. and Santa Rita

Point Lobos State Natural Reserve

St.) and the **Circle Theater** (Casanova St. between 8th and 9th Aves.) within the Golden Bough complex. The company puts on dramas, comedies, and musicals both new and classic. Buy tickets online or by phone to guarantee a seat.

Festivals and Events

One of the biggest events of the year is the **Carmel Art Festival** (Devendorf Park at Mission St., www.carmelartfestivalcalifornia.com, May). This three-day event celebrates visual arts in all media with shows by internationally acclaimed artists at galleries, parks, and other venues all across town. This wonderful festival also sponsors here-and-now contests, including the prestigious plein air (outdoor painting) competition. A wealth of children's activities help even the youngest festivalgoers become budding artists.

One of the most prestigious festivals in Northern California is the **Carmel Bach Festival** (831/624-1521, www.bachfestival.org, July). For 15 days each July, Carmel-by-the-Sea and its surrounding towns host dozens of classical concerts. You can also hear Mozart, Vivaldi, Handel, and other heavyweights of Bach's era. Concerts and recitals take place every day of the week.

SHOPPING

It is easy to spend an afternoon poking into Carmel's many art galleries. Sample Carmel's art scene at the monthly **Carmel Art Walk** (www.carmelartwalk.com, 5pm-8pm second Sat. of the month), a self-guided tour of the town's art galleries. Talk to the artists, sip wine, and listen to live music.

The paintings at the **Joaquin Turner Gallery** (Dolores St. between 5th and 6th Sts., 831/869-5564, www.joaquinturnergallery.com, 11am-5pm Thurs.-Mon., by appointment Tues.-Wed.) are a nod to the works of early-20th-century Monterey Peninsula artists.

At the **Steven Whyte Sculpture Gallery** (Dolores St. between 5th and 6th Sts.,

831/620-1917, www.stevenwhytesculptor.com, 9:30am-4pm Mon. and Wed.-Thurs., 9:30am-5pm Fri., 10am-5pm Sat., 10:30am-4pm Sun.), you can watch the artist create amazing life-size sculptures in his open studio.

One of the best galleries in town is the **Weston Gallery** (6th Ave., 831/624-4453, www.westongallery.com, 11am-5pm Tues.-Sun.), which highlights the photographic work of 20th-century masters including Ansel Adams, Diane Arbus, Robert Mapplethorpe, and Edward Weston.

A tiny art gallery owned by two local photographers, **Exposed** (Carmel Sq., San Carlos St. and 7th Ave., 831/238-0127, http://gallery-exposed.blogspot.com, 1pm-3pm Sat., 5pm-8pm first Fri. of the month) is worth a peek.

Carmel Plaza (Ocean Ave. and Mission St., 831/624-0138, www.carmelplaza.com, 10am-6pm Mon.-Sat., 11am-5pm Sun.) is an outdoor mall with luxury fashion shops like Tiffany & Co. as well as the hip clothing chain Anthropologie.

Don't miss locally owned establishment **The Cheese Shop** (800/828-9463, www.thecheeseshopinc.com, 10am-6pm Mon.-Sat., 11am-5:30pm Sun.), which sells delicacies like cave-aged gruyère cheese.

SPORTS AND RECREATION

Carmel Beach (Ocean Ave., 831/624-4909, 6am-10pm daily) has some of the area's most consistent beach breaks. Being a beach break, the sandbars shift, so the best spot on the beach frequently changes. The waves are usually at their finest from spring to late summer. The winds blow out a lot of area breaks in the spring, but Carmel Beach really comes alive during this time of year.

Carmel Surf Lessons (831/915-4065, www.carmelsurflessons.com) can teach you to surf at Carmel Beach. **On the Beach** (693 Lighthouse Ave., Monterey, 831/646-9283, http://onthebeachsurfshop.com, 10am-6pm Sun.-Thurs., 10am-7pm Fri.-Sat., surfboard rental $30/day, wetsuit rental $15/day) rents boards and wetsuits.

FOOD
American

★ **Carmel Belle** (Doud Craft Studios, Ocean Ave. and San Carlos St., 831/624-1600, www.carmelbelle.com, 8am-6pm daily, $6-15) is a little eatery with big attention to detail. The superb breakfast menu includes an open-face breakfast sandwich featuring a slab of toasted bread topped with a poached egg, strips of thick bacon, a bed of arugula, and wedges of fresh avocado. Its slow-cooked Berkshire pork sandwich with red onion-currant chutney is a perfect example of what can happen when savory meets sweet.

Aubergine (Monte Verde St. at 7th Ave., 831/624-8578, www.auberginecarmel.com, 6pm-9:30pm daily, $175) has been racking up accolades, among them coveted awards from the James Beard Foundation. The Tasting Menu includes eight courses and changes daily.

Italian

On paper, **Vesuvio** (6th Ave. and Junipero St., 831/625-1766, http://chefpepe.com, 4pm-11pm daily, $16-32) dishes out cannelloni, gnocchi, and wood-oven pizzas, but there's a lot more going on. A popular rooftop bar has fire pits, heat lamps, and love seats. There's also a great eight-ounce burger topped with caramelized onions, oozing cambozola cheese, and chipotle aioli on a house-made mini-sub roll. Order it as a "Grown-up Happy Meal" with fries and a well cocktail or glass of wine.

Mediterranean

Dametra Café (Ocean Ave. at Lincoln St., 831/622-7766, www.dametracafe.com, 11am-11pm daily, $11-27) has a wide-ranging international menu that includes the all-American cheeseburger and Italian dishes like spaghetti alla Bolognese. Still, it's best to go with the lively restaurant's signature Mediterranean food. The Greek chicken kebab is a revelation with two chicken-and-vegetable kebabs drizzled with aioli sauce over yellow rice and a Greek salad. The owner and his staff have been known to serenade evening diners.

Mexican

★ **Cultura Comida y Bebida** (Dolores St. between 5th and 6th Sts., 831/250-7005, www.culturacarmel.com, 5:30pm-midnight Mon.-Fri., 10:30am-midnight Sat.-Sun., $18-28) satisfies adventurous diners with superb upscale Mexican cuisine. Try the *chapulines* (toasted grasshoppers) appetizer or skip ahead to the relleno-style abalone. The restaurant's large mescal menu offers the smoky spirit in cocktails or one-ounce pours. The late-night menu (10pm-midnight daily) includes $2 street tacos.

Seafood

The **Flying Fish Grill** (Mission St. between Ocean Ave. and 7th Ave., 831/625-1962, http://flyingfishgrill.com, 5pm-10pm daily, $21-36) serves Japanese-style seafood with a California twist. Entrées include rare, peppered ahi and black bean halibut. You might even be able to score a market-price meal of Monterey abalone. Relax over your meal in the dimly lit, wood-walled establishment.

Sushi

Akaoni (Mission St. and 6th Ave., 831/620-1516, 5:30pm-8:30pm Mon.-Tues., 11:30am-1pm and 5:30pm-8:30pm Wed.-Sat., $7-40) is a superb hole-in-the-wall sushi restaurant. Sit at the bar (or one of the few tables) and order tempura-fried oysters, soft-shell crab rolls, and an unagi donburi (eel bowl). Daily specials showcase the freshest seafood including items flown in from Japan. Adventurous diners can opt for the live Monterey spot prawn.

ACCOMMODATIONS
$150-250

Just two blocks from the beach, the ★ **Lamp Lighter Inn** (Ocean Ave. and Camino Real, 831/624-7372 or 888/375-0770, www.carmel-lamplighter.com, $225-425) has 11 rooms in five cottages with a comfortable, beachy decor. The cottages encircle a courtyard area that has two fire pits. Guests are treated to an afternoon wine and cheese reception and a morning continental breakfast. This is a pet-friendly property; two of the units have fenced-in backyards.

Outside of downtown Carmel, **Mission Ranch** (26270 Dolores St., 831/624-6436, www.missionranchcarmel.com, $165-380) is a sprawling old ranch complex with views of sheep-filled pastures and Point Lobos in the distance. If you get a glimpse of Mission Ranch's owner, it might just make your day: It's none other than Hollywood icon and former Carmel-by-the-Sea mayor Clint Eastwood. On the grounds is a restaurant with a nightly sing-along piano bar.

Over $250

Touted by *Architectural Digest,* **Tradewinds Carmel** (Mission St. and 3rd Ave., 831/624-2776, www.tradewindscarmel.com, $250-550) brings a touch of the Far East to California. The 28 serene hotel rooms are decorated with Asian antiquities and live orchids. Outside, the grounds have a water fountain that passes through bamboo shoots and horsetails along with a meditation garden, where an oversize Buddha head overlooks a trio of cascading pools. A continental breakfast includes French pastries and fruit.

Coachman's Inn (San Carlos St. and 8th Ave., 831/624-6421, www.coachmansinn.com, $249-329) is a small downtown motel with 30

clean, well-appointed rooms. The rooms have large flat screens, mini-fridges, microwaves, and Keurig coffeemakers. Some also have gas fireplaces and jetted spa tubs. A stay includes access to a hot tub, sauna, and exercise bike. The inn's staff will deliver a light continental breakfast to your room ($10).

The initial structure at ★ **La Playa Carmel** (Camino Real at 8th Ave., 831/293-6100 or 800/582-8900, www.laplayahotel.com, $399-849) was a mansion built for a member of the Ghirardelli family. It still has many features from an earlier era, including the dark, wood-walled bar, stained glass windows, and a tiled staircase. Half of the 75 rooms at La Playa look out onto nearby Carmel Beach, only two blocks away. Wander the grounds and stop by the library, the heated outdoor pool, and the courtyard with its oversize chessboard. The staff will treat you to an afternoon wine reception, a dessert of fresh-baked cookies, and a champagne breakfast with made-to-order omelets and waffles.

The landmark **Cypress Inn** (Lincoln St. and 7th Ave., 831/624-3871 or 800/443-7443, www.cypress-inn.com, $279-699) welcomes human and canine guests in a white, ornate Mediterranean-inspired building. This is one of the most pro-pup hotels in the state.

La Playa Carmel

They have dog cookies at the desk, water bowls are situated around the hotel, and they provide dog beds and dog towels by request. The rooms come with complimentary cream sherry, fruit, and snacks for guests, while some also have fireplaces and/or jetted tubs. Human visitors are treated to a breakfast that includes several hot items.

TRANSPORTATION

The quick way to get to Carmel from the north or the south is via Highway 1. From Highway 1, take Ocean Avenue into the middle of downtown Carmel.

There are no street addresses in Carmel-by-the-Sea, so pay close attention to the street names and the block you're on. To make things even more fun, street signs can be difficult to see in the mature foliage, and a dearth of streetlights can make signs nearly impossible to find at night. Show up during the day to get the lay of the land before trying to navigate after dark.

The nearest major medical center is in Monterey at the **Community Hospital of the Monterey Peninsula** (CHOMP, 23625 Holman Hwy., Monterey, 831/624-5311, www.chomp.org).

Carmel Valley

The landscape changes quickly as you leave the coast. You'll see the mountains rising above you, as well as farms, ranches, and orchards. Thirteen miles east of Highway 1 is the unincorporated Carmel Valley Village. In the small strip of businesses hugging Carmel Valley Road is a collection of wineries, tasting rooms, restaurants, and even an Old West saloon.

SIGHTS
Earthbound Farm

One of the largest purveyors of organic produce in the United States, Earthbound Farm began at **Earthbound Farm's Farm Stand** (7250 Carmel Valley Rd., 831/625-6219, www.earthboundfarm.com, 8am-6:30pm Mon.-Sat., 9am-6pm Sun.). This 2.5-acre farm and roadside stand offers visitors easy access to the company's smallish facility in the Carmel Valley. Browse a variety of organic fruits, veggies, and flowers or ramble the fields, checking out the chamomile labyrinth and the kids' garden (yes, your kids can look *and* touch). Select and harvest your own fresh herbs from the cut-your-own-herb garden, or purchase delicious prepared organic dishes at the farm stand. Scheduled walks offer a guided tour of the fields.

WINERIES

This small, charming wine region makes for a perfect wine-tasting day trip from Carmel, Monterey, or Big Sur. Small crowds, light traffic, and meaningful tasting experiences categorize this area, which still has many family-owned wineries.

The **Bernardus Winery** (5 W. Carmel Valley Rd., 831/298-8021 or 800/223-2533, www.bernardus.com, 11am-5pm daily, tasting $15-35) sits on a vineyard estate that also hosts a luxurious lodge and gourmet restaurant. Bernardus creates a small list of wines, but the pride of the winery is the Bordeaux-style blended red Marinus Vineyard wine. Other varietals (chardonnay, pinot noir, and sauvignon blanc) come from cool coastal vineyards.

Tiny **Parsonage Village Vineyard** (19 E. Carmel Valley Rd., 831/659-7322, www.parsonagewine.com, 11am-5pm daily, tasting $10-20) has a tasting room in a little strip of shops, the space glowing with light that bounces off the copper of the bar. At the bar, you'll taste wonderful syrahs, hearty cabernet sauvignons, and surprisingly deep and complex blends—the Snosrap (that's Parsons spelled backward) table wine is inexpensive and incredibly tasty.

In the same strip of wineries, the **Cima**

Carmel Valley

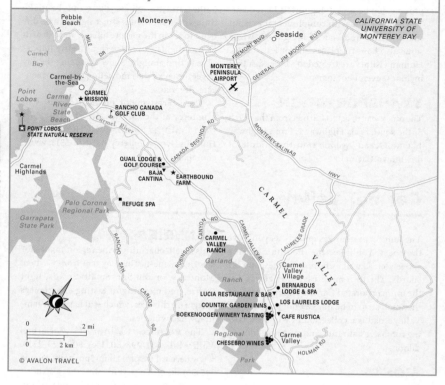

Pebble Beach
Monterey
Seaside
CALIFORNIA STATE UNIVERSITY OF MONTEREY BAY
17
MILE DR
FREMONT BLVD
JIM MOORE BLVD
GENERAL
Carmel Bay
MONTEREY PENINSULA AIRPORT
Carmel-by-the-Sea
Point Lobos
Carmel River State Beach
★ CARMEL MISSION
RANCHO CANADA GOLF CLUB
Carmel River
POINT LOBOS STATE NATURAL RESERVE
CANADA SEGUNDA RD
MONTEREY-SALINAS
HWY
Carmel Highlands
QUAIL LODGE & GOLF COURSE
BAJA CANTINA
★ EARTHBOUND FARM
C A R M E L
Palo Corona Regional Park
REFUGE SPA
Garrapata State Park
ROBINSON CANYON RD
CARMEL VALLEY BLVD
LAURELES GRADE
V A L L E Y
RANCHO SAN CARLOS RD
CARMEL VALLEY RANCH
Garland Ranch
Carmel Valley Village
BERNARDUS LODGE & SPA
LUCIA RESTAURANT & BAR
LOS LAURELES LODGE
COUNTRY GARDEN INNS
CAFE RUSTICA
BOEKENOOGEN WINERY TASTING
Regional
CHESEBRO WINES
Carmel Valley
HOLMAN RD
Park
0 2 mi
0 2 km
© AVALON TRAVEL

Collina (19 E. Carmel Valley Rd., Ste. A, 831/620-0645, http://cimacollina.com, noon-6pm daily, tasting $5) tasting room looks like a farmhouse with a front porch. Inside, enjoy pinot noir, chardonnay, sauvignon blanc, pinot blanc, and Cima Collina wines like the Howlin' Good Red.

A smaller, well-regarded Carmel winery, **Heller Estate Organic Vineyards** (69 W. Carmel Valley Rd., 831/659-6220, www.heller-estate.com, 11am-5pm daily, tasting $15-18) is a completely organic winery that uses natural methods, including predatory wasps, to rid the vineyard of pests rather than resorting to chemical-laden sprays. After visiting the tasting room, sit outdoors in Heller's sculpture garden.

Folktale Winery and Vineyards (8940 Carmel Valley Rd., 831/293-7500, www.folktalewinery.com, 11am-8pm daily, tasting $20) aims to be "an extension of your backyard" with bocce, horseshoes, and cornhole. Winery events include yoga, stand-up comedy, and concerts featuring musical acts like Lukas Nelson.

Talbott Vineyards (25 Pilot Rd., 831/659-3500, www.talbottvineyards.com, 11am-5pm daily, tasting $10-15) utilizes two vineyards 18 miles apart to produce their chardonnays and pinot noirs. At the Carmel Valley tasting room, they pour six of their chardonnays and six of their pinot noirs alongside an impressive collection of vintage motorcycles. There's another tasting room near Salinas (1380 River

Rd., 831/675-0942, 11am-4:30pm Thurs.-Mon., tasting $10-15).

The **Boekenoogen Vineyard & Winery** (24 W. Carmel Valley Rd., 831/659-4215, www.boekenoogenwines.com, 11am-5pm daily, tasting $15-20) tasting room offers pinot noirs, chardonnays, and syrahs, as well as a garden patio for those sunny Carmel Valley afternoons.

One fun way to get around the wineries is to hitch a ride on the **Happy Trails Wagon Tour** (831/970-8198, http://carmelvalleyhappytrailswagontours.com, noon-4pm Wed.-Sun., adult $25, child $10). Cowboy Pete pulls a 10-passenger wagon behind an antique tractor to wineries and restaurants in the immediate area.

Carmel Valley Village shows off its local wines and locally produced art at the daylong **Carmel Valley Art & Wine Celebration** (831/659-4000, www.carmelvalleychamber.com, June, free).

SPORTS AND RECREATION
Hiking
The 4,462-acre **Garland Ranch Regional Park** (700 W. Carmel Valley Rd., 831/372-3196, www.mprpd.org, sunrise-sunset daily, free) boasts the best hiking trails in Carmel Valley. The **Lupine Loop** (1.4 miles, easy) is a level, dog-friendly trail that circles a flat part of the park, while **Snively's Ridge Trail-Sky Loop** (6 miles, difficult) involves a very steep hike to a ridge that offers views of the ocean and mountains. The **Mesa Trail** (1.6 miles, moderately strenuous) climbs to a saddle with valley views and a small pond.

Golf
The **Quail Lodge Golf Club** (8505 Valley Greens Dr., 866/675-1101, www.quaillodge.com, $185) has an 18-hole course with 10 lakes, as well as an academy to improve your game.

Spas
Sprawled over two acres in the shadow of the Santa Lucia Mountains, **Refuge Spa** (27300 Rancho Carlos Rd., 831/620-7360, www.refuge.com, 10am-10pm daily, admission $49, treatments $129-239) features warm waterfalls tumbling into soaking pools and two kinds of cold plunge pools. Don't miss the eucalyptus steam room, where a potent cloud of steam will purge all of your body's impurities.

FOOD
Led by revered local chef Cal Stamenov, the **Lucia Restaurant & Bar** (Bernardus Lodge & Spa, 415 W. Carmel Valley Rd., 831/658-3400, www.bernarduslodge.com, 7am-2:30pm and 5pm-9pm daily, $21-62) uses herbs from the garden out front and serves wines created from the adjacent vineyard. The menu features meat-centric dishes, while oenophiles should consider wine pairings, including the superb Bernardus Pisoni pinot noir and the Bernardus Ingrid's chardonnay. The knowledgeable and friendly staff will properly guide you.

With a large outdoor dining area, **Café Rustica** (10 Del Fino Pl., 831/659-4444, www.caferusticacarmel.com, 11am-2:30pm and 5pm-9pm Tues.-Sun., $13-30) is known for its nightly fish specials and herb-roasted half chicken.

Sip a wide range of tasty, intoxicating margaritas on the large wooden deck at ★ **Baja Cantina** (7166 Carmel Valley Rd., 831/625-2252, www.carmelcantina.com, 11:30am-11pm Mon.-Fri., 11am-midnight Sat.-Sun., $13-20). The menu includes hearty Americanized Mexican cuisine, like rosemary chicken burritos and wild mushroom and spinach enchiladas. The nachos have so much baked cheese that they resemble a casserole.

The Running Iron Restaurant & Saloon (24 E. Carmel Valley Rd., 831/659-4633, www.runningironrestaurantandsaloon.com, 11am-9pm daily, $12-25) keeps Carmel Valley's cowboy culture alive in the face of all the area's wineries. Named for a type of branding iron, The Running Iron is decorated with cowboy memorabilia. Enjoy stick-to-yer-ribs fare and a full bar at this classic California saloon.

ACCOMMODATIONS

Country Garden Inns (102 W. Carmel Valley Rd., 831/659-5361, www.countrygardeninns.com, $179-249) offers a perfect spot to rest and relax. Composed of two inns, the Acacia and the Hidden Valley, this small B&Bs offers French country-style charm in the violet and taupe rooms, as well as a pool, a self-serve breakfast bar, and strolling gardens. Rooms run from romantic king-bed studios to big family suites; most sleep at least four people (with daybeds in the window nooks).

Hosting guests on and off since 1915, the former ranch at **Los Laureles Lodge** (313 W. Carmel Valley Rd., 831/659-2233, www.loslaureles.com, $160-290, three-bedroom house $650) can put you up in a room, a honeymoon cottage, or a three-bedroom house. Enjoy the property's restaurant, saloon, and, most of all, its swimming pool and adjacent pool bar.

The spacious suites at the 500-acre ★ **Carmel Valley Ranch** (1 Old Ranch Rd., 831/625-9500, www.carmelvalleyranch.com, $430-800) are 650-1,200-square feet and have fireplaces and decks. An activity calendar comes with your stay and includes everything from a beekeeping class to nightly s'mores over an open fire. Don't miss the amazing pool deck with a saltwater swimming pool and an infinity pool hot tub that overlooks some beautiful oak trees and the resort's vineyard.

TRANSPORTATION

From Highway 1 south of Monterey, take Carmel Valley Road east for 13 miles to Carmel Valley Village, where most of the area's restaurants and wineries are.

Big Sur

Big Sur welcomes many types of visitors. Nature lovers come to camp and hike the pristine wilderness areas, to don thick wetsuits and surf often-deserted beaches, and even to hunt for jade in rocky coves. On the other hand, some of the wealthiest people from California visit to relax at unbelievably posh hotels and spas with dazzling views of the ocean. Whether you prefer a low-cost camping trip or a luxury resort, Big Sur offers its beauty and charm to all. Part of that charm is Big Sur's determination to remain peacefully apart from the Information Age (this means that your cell phones may not work in many parts of Big Sur).

TOP EXPERIENCE

BIG SUR COAST HIGHWAY

Even if you're not up to tackling the endless hiking trails and deep wilderness backcountry of Big Sur, you can still get a good sense of the glory of this region just by driving through it. The **Big Sur Coast Highway,** a 90-mile stretch of Highway 1, is quite simply one of the most picturesque roads in the country. A two-lane road, Highway 1 twists and turns with Big Sur's jagged coastline, running along precipitous cliffs and rocky beaches, through dense redwood forests, over historic bridges, and past innumerable parks. In winter, you might spot migrating whales offshore spouting fountains of air and water, while spring finds yucca plants feathering the hillsides and wildflowers coloring the landscape. Construction on this stretch of road was completed in the 1930s, connecting Cambria to Carmel.

Start out at either town and spend a whole day making your way to the other end of the road. The road has plenty of wide turnouts set into picturesque cliffs to make it easy to stop to admire the glittering ocean and stunning wooded cliffs running right out to the water. (Please use the turnouts to park, rather than looking away from the road.) Bring a camera as you'll want to take photos every mile for hours on end. Be aware that there can be frequent highway delays due to road construction.

At time of publication, a very large landslide had closed Highway 1 at the southern end of Big Sur between Gorda and Ragged Point. The road is expected to reopen in late summer 2018.

Garrapata State Park

Garrapata State Park (Hwy. 1, 6.7 miles south of Carmel, 831/624-4909, www.parks.ca.gov, 8am-sunset daily, free) has most of the features that make Big Sur such a famed destination for outdoor enthusiasts: redwood trees, rocky headlands, pocket beaches, and ocean vistas from steep hills and mountains. **Garrapata Beach** is northern Big Sur's finest, with two miles of coastline.

At time of publication, the eastern section of the park remained closed following the 2016 Soberanes Fire.

HIKING

The **Soberanes Point Trail** (2 miles round-trip) is a mild hike up and around the park's rocky headlands. Stroll along the beach, scramble up the cliffs for a better view of the ocean, or check out the seals, sea otters, and sea lions near Soberanes Point. In winter, grab a pair of binoculars to look for migrating gray whales passing close to shore.

Bixby Bridge

Bixby Bridge (Hwy. 1, 15 miles south of Carmel) is one of the most-photographed bridges in the nation. The picturesque, open-spandrel arched cement bridge was built in the early 1930s as part of the massive government works project that completed Highway 1 through Big Sur. Pull out north of the bridge to take photos or just look out at the attractive span and Bixby Creek flowing into the Pacific far below. Get another great view of the bridge by driving a few hundred feet down the dirt Old Coast Road, which is on the bridge's northeast side.

★ Point Sur Light Station

Sitting lonely and isolated out on its cliff, the **Point Sur Light Station** (Hwy. 1, 19 miles

Big Sur coast

Big Sur

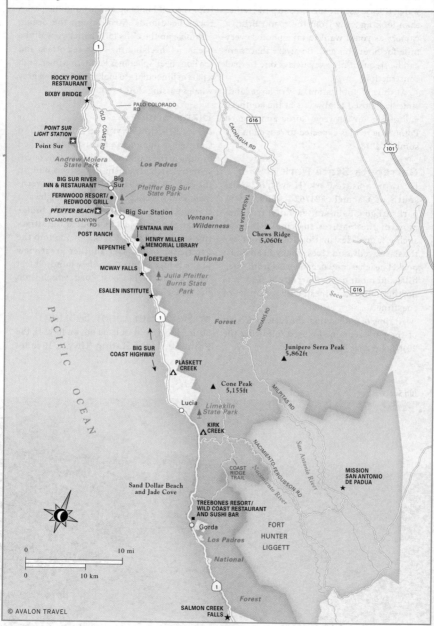

ROCKY POINT
RESTAURANT
BIXBY BRIDGE

PALO COLORADO
RD

G16

CACHAGUA
RD

101

POINT SUR
LIGHT STATION
Point Sur

OLD COAST RD

Andrew Molera
State Park

Los Padres

BIG SUR RIVER
INN & RESTAURANT

Big
Sur

Pfeiffer Big Sur
State Park

FERNWOOD RESORT/
REDWOOD GRILL

PFEIFFER BEACH

SYCAMORE CANYON
RD

Big Sur Station

TASSAJARA RD

POST RANCH

VENTANA INN

Ventana
Wilderness

Chews Ridge
5,060ft

HENRY MILLER
MEMORIAL LIBRARY

NEPENTHE

DEETJEN'S

National

MCWAY FALLS

Julia Pfeiffer
Burns State
Park

G16

ESALEN INSTITUTE

Seco

1

Forest

PACIFIC

OCEAN

BIG SUR
COAST HIGHWAY

Junipero Serra Peak
5,862ft

PLASKETT
CREEK

INDIAN RD

Cone Peak
5,155ft

MILPITAS RD

Lucia

Limekiln
State Park

San Antonio River

KIRK
CREEK

NACIMIENTO-FERGUSSON RD

Nacimiento River

MISSION
SAN ANTONIO
DE PADUA

COAST
RIDGE
TRAIL

Sand Dollar Beach
and Jade Cove

TREEBONES RESORT/
WILD COAST RESTAURANT
AND SUSHI BAR

FORT
HUNTER
LIGGETT

Gorda

Los Padres

0   10 mi

National

0   10 km

Forest

© AVALON TRAVEL

SALMON CREEK
FALLS

south of Carmel, 831/625-4419, www.point-sur.org, tours: 1pm Wed., 10am Sat.-Sun. Oct.-Mar.; 10am and 2pm Wed. and Sat., 10am Sun., Apr.-Sept., adults $15, children $5) crowns the 361-foot-high volcanic rock Point Sur. It's the only complete 19th-century light station in California that you can visit, and even here access is severely limited. First lit in 1889, this now fully automated light station still provides navigational aid to ships off the coast.

TOURS

Take one of the **moonlight tours** (call 831/625-4419 for information) to learn about the haunted history of the light station buildings.

You can't make a reservation for a Point Sur tour, so just show up and park your car off Highway 1 on the west side by the farm gate. Your guide will meet you there and lead you up the paved road 0.5 mile to the light station. Once there, you'll climb the stairs up to the light, explore the restored keepers' homes and service buildings, and walk out to the cliff edge. Expect to see a great variety of flora and fauna, from brilliant wildflowers in the spring to gray whales in the winter to flocks of pelicans flying in formation at any time of year. Dress in layers; it can be sunny and hot or foggy and cold, winter or summer, and sometimes both on the same tour! Tours last three hours and require more than a mile of walking, with a bit of slope, and more than 100 stairs.

If you need special assistance for your tour or have questions about accessibility, call 831/649-2836 as far in advance as possible of your visit to make arrangements.

Andrew Molera State Park

Andrew Molera State Park (Hwy. 1, 21 miles south of Carmel, 831/667-2315, www.parks.ca.gov, sunrise-sunset daily, $10/vehicle) has several hiking trails that run down to the beach and up into the forest along the river.

At the park entrance, you'll find bathrooms but no drinking water or food concessions.

HIKING

The beach is a one-mile walk down the easy, multiuse **Trail Camp Beach Trail** (2 miles round-trip, easy). From there, climb out to the headlands on the **Headlands Trail** (0.5 mile round-trip, easy) for a beautiful view of the Big Sur River emptying into the sea. In the distance is Pico Blanco, one of the region's

Bixby Bridge

most distinctive mountains, rising like a pyramid from behind a ridgeline. For a better look at the river, take the flat, moderate **Bobcat Trail** (5.5 miles round-trip, easy) and perhaps a few of its ancillary loops. You'll walk right along the riverbank, enjoying the local microhabitats.

For a longer and more difficult trek up the mountains and down to the beach, the **Ridge Trail and Panorama Trail Loop** (8 miles round-trip, moderate) is one of the best coastal hikes in Big Sur. Start at the parking lot on the **Creamery Meadow Beach Trail,** then make a left onto the long and fairly steep **Ridge Trail** to get a sense of the local ecosystem. Then turn right onto the **Panorama Trail,** which has sweeping views of the coast, including Molera Point and Point Sur, as it runs down to the coastal scrublands. Take the small **Spring Trail** (0.2 mile round-trip, easy) down a driftwood-littered gully to a scenic stretch of beach. Hike back out and take a left connecting to the **Bluffs Trail,** which takes you back to Creamery Meadow along the top of a marine terrace.

Pfeiffer Big Sur State Park

The most developed park in Big Sur, **Pfeiffer**

Big Sur State Park (Hwy. 1, 26 miles south of Carmel, 831/667-2315, www.parks.ca.gov, sunrise-sunset daily, $10/vehicle) is home to a lodge, a restaurant and café, hiking trails, and lovely redwood-shaded **campsites**. This is one of the best parks in the area to see Big Sur's redwoods and a great place to dip into the cool Big Sur River.

HIKING

Pfeiffer Big Sur has the tiny **Ernst Ewoldsen Memorial Nature Center** (open seasonally), which features taxidermy examples of local wildlife. The historic **Homestead Cabin,** off the Big Sur Gorge Trail, was once the home of part of the Pfeiffer family, who were the first European immigrants to settle in Big Sur.

The **Nature Trail** (0.7 mile round-trip, easy) leaves from Big Sur Lodge and provides an introduction to the park's natural assets. No bikes or horses are allowed on trails in this park, which makes it quite peaceful for hikers.

The **Buzzard's Roost Trail** (3 miles round-trip, moderate) explores the park's west side. Climb from the river's edge through redwoods and oak trees on the way up to the summit of Pfeiffer Ridge, where you'll have a view of the coastline.

Point Sur Light Station

Big Sur Station

The ranger station at **Big Sur Station** (Hwy. 1, 27 miles south of Carmel, 831/667-2315, 9am-4pm daily) offers maps and brochures for all the major parks and trails of Big Sur, plus a minimal bookshop. This is where the trailhead for the popular backcountry **Pine Ridge Trail** is located. Get a free backcountry fire permit as well as pay for Pine Ridge Trailhead parking.

★ Pfeiffer Beach

Pfeiffer Beach (end of Sycamore Canyon Rd., http://campone.com, 9am-8pm daily, $10/vehicle) is one of the coastline's most picturesque spots. This frequently windswept beach has two looming rock formations right where the beach meets the surf, and both of these rocks have holes that look like doorways, allowing waves and sunlight to pass through. Occasionally, purple sand colors the beach; it is eroded manganese garnet from the bluffs above. It can be incredibly windy here some days.

GETTING THERE

Getting to Pfeiffer Beach is a bit tricky. It is at the end of the second paved right south of the Big Sur Station. Motorists (no motor homes) must then travel down a narrow, windy, two-mile road before reaching the entrance booth and the beach's parking lot. It's part of the adventure. This road gets very busy during the summer and on weekends. Plan a trip to Pfeiffer Beach when it's less busy. Otherwise, the two-mile drive might take a lot longer than expected.

Henry Miller Memorial Library

Henry Miller lived and wrote in Big Sur for 18 years, and his 1957 novel *Big Sur and the Oranges of Hieronymus Bosch* describes his time here. Today, the **Henry Miller Memorial Library** (Hwy. 1, 31 miles south of Carmel, 831/667-2574, www.henrymiller.org, 10am-5pm Wed.-Mon., free) celebrates the life and work of Miller and his brethren in this quirky community center, museum, coffee shop, and gathering place. Inside is a well-curated bookstore featuring the works of Miller as well as other authors like Jack Kerouac and Richard Brautigan. The small redwood-shaded lawn hosts concerts and literary events. During summer, the library puts on an international short-film series every Thursday night.

MONTEREY AND BIG SUR

BIG SUR

beach off Highway 1

Julia Pfeiffer Burns State Park

One of Big Sur's best postcard-perfect views can be attained at **Julia Pfeiffer Burns State Park** (Hwy. 1, 37 miles south of Carmel, 831/667-2315, www.parks.ca.gov, sunrise-sunset daily, $10/vehicle)—the scenic, if crowded, walk to McWay Falls. To get to the stunning view of **McWay Falls,** take the **Overlook Trail** (0.6 mile round-trip) along a level, wheelchair-accessible boardwalk. Stroll under the highway, past the Pelton wheelhouse, and out to the observation deck. The 80-foot-high waterfall cascades year-round off a cliff and onto the beach of a remote cove, where the water wets the sand and trickles out into the sea. You'll look down on a pristine and empty stretch of sand—there's no way down to the cove that is even remotely safe.

HIKING

The west side of the road is where you pick up the **Partington Cove Trail** (2 miles round-trip, easy), an underrated walk that goes to a striking, narrow coastal inlet. It begins as a steep dirt road and continues through a 60-foot-long tunnel blasted into the rock. The trail arrives at a cove where John Partington used to ship out the tanbark trees that he had harvested in the canyon above. There is a bench at the end of the trail with views of the cove and the coastline to the south. To reach the trailhead from the north, drive nine miles south of Pfeiffer Big Sur State Park on Highway 1. Look for a big bend in the road to the east with dirt pullouts on either side. Park here and then begin your hike where the gated road departs from the west side.

The **Waters Trail** (1.2 miles one-way, easy) connects the Tanbark Trail to the Ewoldsen Trail. Begin either at the main park entrance—where you'll find the trailhead off the Ewoldsen Trail—or start from the Tanbark Trail. The path cuts across the hillside while offering postcard-worthy coastal views along most of its route. In the spring, this area is painted purple by fields of flowering lupine. Unless you use two cars, you will have to walk

McWay Falls at Julia Pfeiffer Burns State Park

along the highway a short distance to return to your vehicle. This hike is worth all of the effort.

Limekiln State Park

The 716-acre **Limekiln State Park** (Hwy. 1, 56 miles south of Carmel, 805/434-1996, www.parks.ca.gov, 8am-sunset daily, $10/vehicle) is home to redwoods, an impressive waterfall, a campground, ruins from the region's rugged past, and a nice beach on the stunning coastline. The park is named for four large, rusted limekilns accessed via the **Limekiln Trail.** From 1887 to 1890, the Rockland Lime and Lumber Company extracted and processed the land's limestone rock deposits in kilns, which used hot wood fires to purify the stones.

It's worth hiking the trail to **Limekiln Falls,** a 100-foot-high waterfall that splashes down a rock face in two distinct prongs. A sandy stretch of beach is littered with boulders, with the Limekiln Creek Bridge as a backdrop. A single picnic table plopped in the sand provides a terrific place for lunch. The park also has a **campground** with 32 sites.

Nacimiento-Fergusson Road

The only road that traverses Big Sur's Santa Lucia Mountains, the **Nacimiento-Fergusson Road** (58 miles south of Carmel) offers spectacular coastal views to those who are willing to wind their way up this twisty, paved, 1.5-lane road. Simply drive a few miles up to get an eyeful of the expansive Pacific Ocean or to climb above Big Sur's summer fog. It also heads in and out of infrequent redwood forests on the way up. The road connects Highway 1 to U.S. 101, passing through Fort Hunter Liggett army base on its journey.

The road is frequently closed during the winter months. It is not recommended for those who get carsick.

Sand Dollar Beach

Sand Dollar Beach (60 miles south of Carmel, www.fs.usda.gov, sunrise-sunset daily, $10/vehicle) is one of Big Sur's biggest and best beaches. This half-moon-shaped beach is tucked under cliffs that keep the wind down. Though frequently strewn with rocks, the beach is a great place to plop down for a picnic or an afternoon in the sun. From the beach, enjoy a striking view of Big Sur's south coast mountains including Cone Peak, rising like a jagged fang from a long ridgeline. A series of uncrowded beach breaks offer waves for surfers even during the flatter summer months.

The area around the parking lot has picnic tables with raised grills, pit toilets, and a pay phone. If the parking lot is full, park on the dirt pullout to the south of the entrance.

Jade Cove Recreation Area

It's easy to miss **Jade Cove Recreation Area** (Hwy. 1, 61 miles south of Carmel). A road sign marks the area, but there's not much in the way of a formal parking lot or anything else to denote the treasures of this jagged, rough part of the Big Sur coastline. Park in the dirt/gravel strip off the road and head past the fence. It's fun to read the unusual signs along the narrow, beaten path that seems to lead to the edge of a cliff. Once you get to the edge of the cliff, the short trail gets rough. It's only 0.25 mile, but it's almost straight down a rocky, slippery cliff. Don't try to climb down if you're not in reasonable physical condition, and even if you are, don't be afraid to use your hands to steady yourself. At the bottom, you'll find huge boulders and smaller rocks and very little sand. But most of all, you'll find the most amazing minerals in the boulders and rocks. Search the smaller rocks beneath your feet for chunks of sea-polished jade. If you're a hardcore rock nut, join the locals in scuba diving for jewelry-quality jade. As long as you find it in the water or below the high-tide line, it's legal for you to take whatever you find here.

Jade Cove has no water, no restrooms, no visitors center, and no services of any kind.

Salmon Creek Falls

One of the best natural attractions is **Salmon Creek Falls** (Hwy. 1, 71 miles south of Carmel). A pair of waterfalls flow year-round down rocks over 100 feet high, their streams joining halfway down. For a great perspective of the falls, take an easy 10-minute walk over a primitive trail littered with rocks fallen from the highway. The unmarked parking area is a pullout in the middle of a hairpin turn on Highway 1.

Note: At time of publication, the area south of the landslide remained blocked.

SPORTS AND RECREATION

Horseback Riding

Take a guided horseback ride into the forests or out onto the beaches of Andrew Molera State Park with **Molera Horseback Tours** (831/625-5486, http://molerahorsebacktours.com, $75). The 1-2.5-hour tours depart daily at 9am, 11am, 1pm, and 3pm. Call ahead to guarantee a spot or to book a private guided ride. Each ride begins at the modest corral area, from which you'll ride along multiuse trails through forests or meadows, or along the Big Sur River, and down to Molera Beach. There you'll guide your horse along the solid sands as you admire the beauty of the wild Pacific Ocean.

Molera Horseback Tours are suitable for children over age six and riders of all ability levels; you'll be matched to the right horse for you. All but one of the rides go down to the beach. Tours can be seasonal, so call ahead if you want to ride in the fall or winter.

Backpacking

If you long for the lonely peace of backcountry camping, the **Ventana Wilderness** (www. ventanawild.org) area is ideal for you. This area comprises the peaks of the Santa Lucia Mountains and the dense growth of the northern reaches of the Los Padres National Forest. It has 167,323 acres of steep, V-shaped canyons and mountains that rise to over 5,000 feet. You'll find many trails beyond the popular day hikes of the state parks, especially as Big Sur stretches down to the south.

One of the most popular hikes is the 10-mile-long climb on the **Pine Ridge Trail** (Big Sur Station, 0.25 mile south of Pfeiffer Big Sur State Park) to **Sykes Hot Springs,** a cluster of warm mineral pools at a backcountry camp on the Big Sur River. The trail closes periodically; check trail access and secure a campfire permit and parking pass from the Big Sur Station.

Farther south, the **Vicente Flat Trail** (4 miles south of Lucia on Hwy. 1, across from the Kirk Creek Campground, 10 miles roundtrip) heads up toward Cone Peak, the jagged mountain rising in the distance, while gaining sweeping views of the coast. Do this one as a grueling up-and-back day hike to the Vincente Flat Camp or backpack it. Check the Ventana Wilderness Alliance website (www. ventanawild.org) in advance to find reports on the conditions of the trails you've decided to tackle, and stop in at Big Sur Station to get the latest news on the backcountry areas.

Fishing

The region offers your choice of shore or river fishing. Steelhead run up the Big Sur River to spawn each year, and a limited fishing season follows them up the river into **Pfeiffer Big Sur State Park** and other accessible areas. Check with Fernwood Resort (831/667-2422, www.fernwoodbigsur.com) and the lodges around Highway 1 for the best spots this season.

The numerous creeks that feed into and out of the Big Sur River also play home to their fair share of fish. The California Department of Fish and Game (www.wildlife.ca.gov) can give you specific locations for legal fishing, season information, and rules and regulations.

If you prefer the fish from the ocean, cast off several of the beaches for the rockfish that scurry about in the near-shore reefs. **Garrapata State Beach** has a good fishing area, as do the beaches at **Sand Dollar.**

Scuba Diving

There's not much for beginner divers in Big Sur. Expect cold water and an exposure to the ocean's swells and surges. Temperatures are in the mid-50s in the shallows, dipping into the 40s as you dive deeper down. Visibility is 20-30 feet, though rough conditions can diminish this significantly; the best season for clear water is September-November.

The biggest and most interesting dive locale here is **Julia Pfeiffer Burns State Park** (Hwy. 1, 37 miles south of Carmel, 831/667-2315, www.parks.ca.gov, sunrise-sunset, $10/ vehicle). You'll need to acquire a special permit at Big Sur Station and prove your experience to dive at this protected underwater park. You enter the water from the shore, which gives you the chance to check out all the ecosystems, beginning with the busy life of the beach sands before heading out to the rocky reefs and then into the lush green kelp forests.

Divers at access-hostile **Jade Cove** (Hwy. 1, 61 miles south of Carmel) come to stalk the wily jade pebbles and rocks that cluster in this special spot. The semiprecious stone striates the coastline right here, and storms tear clumps of jade out of the

California Condors

With wings spanning 10 feet from tip to tip, the California condors soaring over the Big Sur coastline are some of the area's most impressive natural treasures. But, in 1987, there was only one bird left in the wild, and it was taken into captivity as part of a captive breeding program. The condors' population had plummeted due to their susceptibility to lead poisoning along with deaths caused by electric power lines, habitat loss, and being shot by indiscriminate humans.

Today the reintroduction of the high-flying California condor, the largest flying bird in North America, to Big Sur and the Central Coast is truly one of conservation's greatest success stories. In 1997, the Monterey County-based nonprofit Ventana Wildlife Society (VWS) began releasing the giant birds back into the wild. Currently, 70 wild condors soar above Big Sur and the surrounding area, and in 2006, a pair of condors were found nesting in the hollowed-out section of a redwood tree.

The species' recovery in the Big Sur area means that you may be able to spot a California condor flying overhead while visiting the rugged coastal region. Look for a tracking tag on the condor's wing to determine that you are actually looking at a California condor and not just a big turkey vulture. Or take a two-hour tour with the **Ventana Wildlife Society** (831/455-9514, $50/person), which uses radio telemetry to track the released birds.

cliffs and into the sea. Much of it settles just off the shore of the tiny cove, and divers hope to find jewelry-quality stones to sell for a huge profit.

If you're looking for a guided scuba dive, contact **Adventure Sports Unlimited** (303 Potrero St., Santa Cruz, 831/458-3648, https://asudoit.com, $200-918).

Bird-Watching

The Big Sur coast is home to innumerable species, from the tiniest bushtits up to grand pelicans and beyond. The most famous avian residents of this area are the rare and endangered California condors. Once upon a time, condors were all but extinct, with only a few left alive in captivity and conservationists struggling to help them breed. Today, around 70 of these birds soar above the trails and beaches of Big Sur. You might even see one swooping down low over your car as you drive down Highway 1!

The **Ventana Wildlife Society** (VWS, www.ventanaws.org) watches over many of the endangered and protected avian species in Big Sur. As part of their mission to raise awareness of the condors and many other birds, the VWS offers bird-watching expeditions.

Spas

Spa Alila at Ventana Big Sur (Ventana Big Sur, 48123 Hwy. 1, 28 miles south of Carmel, www.ventanainn.com, 10am-6:30pm daily, massages $175-615) offers a large menu of spa treatments to both hotel guests and visitors. Indulge in a soothing massage, purifying body treatment, or rejuvenating or beautifying facial. Take your spa experience a step further in true Big Sur fashion with an astrological reading, essence portrait, or a jade stone massage. Hotel guests can choose to have a spa treatment in the comfort of their own room or out on a private deck.

Across the highway from the Ventana, the **Post Ranch Inn's Spa** (Post Ranch Inn, 47900 Hwy. 1, 30 miles south of Carmel, 831/667-2200, www.postranchinn.com, 10am-7pm daily, massages $165-495) is an ultra-high-end resort spa only open to those spending the evening at the luxurious resort. Shaded by redwoods, the relaxing spa offers massages and facials along with more unique treatments including Big Sur jade stone therapy and craniosacral therapy. They also offer sessions inspired by Native American shamanism ($315-365), including a shamanic session, a fire ceremony, and a drum journey.

ENTERTAINMENT AND EVENTS

Live Music

Big Sur has become an unexpected hotbed of concerts. More than just a place to down a beer and observe the local characters, **Fernwood Tavern** (Fernwood Resort, 47200 Hwy. 1, 27 miles south of Carmel, 831/667-2422, www.fernwoodbigsur.com, 11am-11pm Sun.-Thurs., 11am-1am Fri.-Sat.) also has live music. Most of the big-name acts swing through in the summer and fall, but a wide range of regional acts perform on Saturday night starting at 10pm.

Down the road, the **Henry Miller Memorial Library** (48603 Hwy. 1, 31 miles south of Carmel, 831/667-2574, www.henrymiller.org) hosts concerts, book readings, and film screenings.

The manager of the **Big Sur River Inn** (46480 Hwy. 1, 25 miles south of Carmel, 831/667-2700, www.bigsurriverinn.com, 1pm-5pm Sun. late Apr.-early Oct.) jokes that they have been doing Sunday afternoon concerts on their back deck since "Jesus started riding a bicycle." The live music tradition here began in the 1960s with famed local act Jack Stock and the Abalone Stompers. Now mostly local jazz bands play on the restaurant's sunny deck, while a barbecue is set up on the large green lawn.

Bars

Fernwood Tavern (Fernwood Resort, 47200 Hwy. 1, 27 miles south of Carmel, 831/667-2422, www.fernwoodbigsur.com, 11am-11pm Sun.-Thurs., 11am-1am Fri.-Sat.) is a classic watering hole with redwood timbers and a fireplace that warms the place in the chilly months. Enjoy a beer or cocktail inside or out back on the deck under the redwoods.

The **Big Sur Taphouse** (47250 Hwy. 1, 29 miles south of Carmel, 831/667-2197, www.bigsurtaphouse.com, noon-10pm daily) has 10 rotating beers on tap, with a heavy emphasis on West Coast microbrews. The cozy interior has wood tables, a gas fireplace, and board games. With two big-screen TVs, the Taphouse is also a good place to catch your favorite sports team in action. Out back is a large patio with picnic tables and plenty of sun. They serve better-than-average bar food, including tacos and pork sliders.

The **Big Sur River Inn Restaurant** (46840 Hwy. 1, 831/667-2700, www.bigsurriverinn.com, 8am-11am, 11:30am-4:30pm, and 5pm-9pm daily) is a fine place for a cocktail or beer. In the late afternoon and early evening, the intimate bar area gets a fun local crowd.

Festivals and Events

The **Big Sur International Marathon** (831/625-6226, www.bsim.org, $175-200, Apr.) is one of the most popular marathons in the world, due in no small part to the scenery. Begin at the Big Sur Station and then wind, climb, and descend again on the way to Carmel's Rio Road.

Throughout the summer, the **Henry Miller Memorial Library** (48603 Hwy. 1, 831/667-2574, www.henrymiller.org, June-Aug.) hosts the **Big Sur International Short Film Screening Series,** where free films from all over the globe are shown on Thursday nights.

The **Big Sur Food & Wine Festival** (831/596-8105, www.bigsurfoodandwine.org, Nov.) celebrates cuisine and vino in stunning settings. Events include live music, dinner, and hiking with stemware.

FOOD

In Big Sur, a ready meal isn't something to take for granted. Pick up supplies in Cambria or Carmel before you enter the area to avoid paying premiums at the few mini-marts.

Casual Dining

The **Fernwood Bar & Grill** (Fernwood Resort, 47200 Hwy. 1, 27 miles south of Carmel, 831/667-2129, www.fernwoodbigsur.com, 11am-10pm daily, $10-25) looks and feels like a grill in the woods ought to. Even in the middle of the afternoon, the aging, wood-paneled interior is dimly lit and strewn with casual tables and chairs. Walk up to the counter to order tacos, burgers, or pizzas, then head to the bar to grab a soda or a beer.

One of Big Sur's most popular attractions is ★ **Nepenthe** (48510 Hwy. 1, 29 miles south of Carmel, 831/667-2345, www.nepenthebigsur.com, 11:30am-4:30pm and 5pm-10:30pm daily July 4-early Sept., 11:30am-4:30pm and 5pm-10pm daily early Sept.-early July, $15-44), a restaurant built on the site where Rita Hayworth and Orson Welles owned a cabin until 1947. The deck offers stellar views. Sit under multicolored umbrellas on long, bar-like tables with stunning south-facing views. Order a basket of fries with Nepenthe's signature Ambrosia dipping sauce and wash them down with a potent South Coast margarita. The restaurant's most popular item is the Ambrosia burger, a ground steak burger drenched in tasty Ambrosia sauce.

If there's a line, consider dining at **Café Kevah** (weather permitting, 9am-4pm daily mid-Feb.-Jan.1, $9-16), an outdoor deck below the main restaurant that serves brunch, salads, and paninis.

The **Big Sur Bakery** (47540 Hwy. 1, 29 miles south of Carmel, 831/667-0520, www.bigsurbakery.com, bakery 8am daily; restaurant dinner 5:30pm-8:30pm Wed.-Sun., $18-32) might sound like a casual establishment, and the bakery part is. Stop in beginning at 8am for a fresh-baked scone, a homemade jelly doughnut, or a flaky croissant sandwich. On the dining room side, an elegant surprise awaits. Make reservations or you might miss out on the creative wood-fired pizzas, wood-grilled meats, and seafood. At brunch, they serve their unique wood-fired bacon and three-egg breakfast pizza.

The locals know ★ **Deetjen's** (48865 Hwy. 1, 31 miles south of Carmel, 831/667-2378, www.deetjens.com, 8am-noon and 6pm-9pm daily, $10-32) for its breakfast—an almost required experience for visitors to the area. Among fanciful knickknacks and framed photos of inn founder "Grandpa" Deetjen, diners can fill up on Deetjen's popular eggs Benedict dishes or the equally worthy Deetjen's dip, a turkey and avocado sandwich with hollandaise dipping sauce. In the evening, things get darker and more romantic as entrées, including the spicy seafood paella and an oven-roasted rack of lamb, are served at your candlelit table.

If it's a warm afternoon, get a table on the sunny back deck of the ★ **Big Sur River Inn Restaurant** (46840 Hwy. 1, 25 miles south of Carmel, 831/667-2700, http://bigsurriverinn.com, 8am-11am, 11:30am-4:30pm, and

the outdoor deck at Nepenthe

5pm-9pm daily, $12-32). On summer Sundays, bands perform on the crowded deck, and you can take your libation to one of the chairs situated right in the middle of the cool Big Sur River. If it's chilly out, eat in the wood-beamed main dining room. The restaurant serves sandwiches, burgers, and fish-and-chips for lunch along with steak, ribs, seafood, and the recommended Noelle's salad at dinner. For dessert, they still do the famous apple pie that put them on the map back in the 1930s. The bar is known for its popular spicy Bloody Mary cocktails.

The unassuming **Ripplewood Café** (47047 Hwy. 1, 26 miles south of Carmel, 831/667-2242, www.ripplewoodresort. com, daily 8am-2pm, $9-16) may save the day on summer weekends when Deetjen's is flooded. Dine inside at the classic breakfast counter or on the outside brick patio among flowering plants. The breakfast menu includes pancakes, three-egg omelets, and a worthwhile chorizo and eggs. The grilled potato gratin is a highlight. Ripplewood shifts to lunch at 11:30am; offerings include sandwiches, Mexican food items, and salads.

The Big Sur Roadhouse (47080 Hwy. 1, 26 miles south of Carmel, 831/667-2370, www. glenoaksbigsur.com, 8am-2:30pm daily, $7-16) is one of the best bets for affordable, creative California dining in Big Sur for breakfast and lunch. The decor is homegrown modernism, with contemporary art hanging on the walls. The outdoor seating area has heating lamps and two fire pits. The menu skews toward Mexican items, including huevos rancheros and chilaquiles.

Oceanview Sushi Bar (Treebones Resort, 71895 Hwy. 1, 64 miles south of Carmel, 805/927-2390, 4:30pm-8pm Wed.-Sun. Mar.-Dec., $8-19) offers an intimate place to eat artfully prepared sushi. Just 10 seats are available at a redwood sushi bar within a tent-like structure. The menu includes simple rolls, garden rolls, specialty rolls, and hearty rolls designed to resemble burritos. There are two beers on tap along with sake, Japanese beer,

and California wine. Seating priority is given to Treebones' guests.

Fine Dining

Enjoy a fine gourmet dinner at **The Sur House** (Ventana Big Sur, 48123 Hwy. 1, 28 miles south of Carmel, 800/628-6500, www. ventanainn.com, 7:30am-10:30am, 11:30am-4:30pm, and 6pm-close daily, $80-90). The spacious dining room boasts a warm wood fire, an open kitchen, lodge-like wood beams, and comfortable banquettes with plenty of throw pillows. Request a table outside to enjoy stunning views on the expansive patio. Chef Paul Corsentino has upped the quality of the menu, which at times has wild boar and Monterey sardine courses. Choose an à la carte main course or go for the vegetarian or chef's tasting menus.

The **Sierra Mar** (Post Ranch Inn, 47900 Hwy. 1, 28 miles south of Carmel, 831/667-2800, www.postranchinn.com, 12:15pm-3pm and 5:30pm-9pm daily) restaurant offers a decadent four-course prix-fixe dinner menu every night ($125) or a nine-course tasting menu ($175). There's also a less formal three-course lunch ($65) every day. With floor-to-ceiling glass windows overlooking the plunging ridgeline and the Pacific below, this is a good place to schedule dinner during sunset. The daily menu rotates, but some courses have included farm-raised abalone in brown butter and a succulent short rib and beef tenderloin duo.

Markets

The best of the local markets is the ★ **Big Sur Deli** (47520 Hwy. 1, 29 miles south of Carmel, 831/667-2225, www.bigsurdeli.com, 7am-8pm daily). Very popular with locals, the deli has large, made-to-order sandwiches, burritos, tamales, tacos, and pasta salads. If the line is long at the counter, opt for a premade sandwich for a quicker exit. They also have cold drinks, wine, beer, and some basic supplies.

River Inn Big Sur General Store (46840 Hwy. 1, 25 miles south of Carmel,

831/667-2700, 11am-7pm daily) has basic supplies, along with beer and a nice selection of California wines. Even better, it has a wonderful burrito bar and smoothie counter in the back. There are also simple premade turkey and ham sandwiches in a nearby fridge for taking out on a hike or picnic.

ACCOMMODATIONS
$100-150
New Camaldoli Hermitage (Hwy. 1, 51 miles south of Carmel, 831/667-2456, www.contemplation.com, $135-291) offers a quiet stay in the mountains above Lucia. The Hermitage is home to Roman Catholic monks who offer overnight accommodations for people of any or no religious denomination. The five private hermitages are basically trailers decorated with religious iconography and outfitted with a bed, desk, bathroom, and kitchen with a gas stove. There are also nine private rooms with a half bath and garden. Male guests can stay overnight in a monk's cell within the monastic enclosure; there are also a few units outside the enclosure for groups of two guests. Meals from the monastery's kitchen are included in the price. In addition to being a unique experience, staying at the Hermitage is one of the region's best deals.

The accommodations can be rustic, but they are worth it if it's solitude you're after. Radios and musical instruments are not permitted.

$150-250
You'll find a couple of small motels along Highway 1 in the valley of Big Sur. One of the more popular is the **Fernwood Resort** (47200 Hwy. 1, 27 miles south of Carmel, 831/667-2422, www.fernwoodbigsur.com, motel rooms $155-200, cabins $250). The cluster of buildings includes a 12-room motel, a small convenience store, a restaurant, and a bar that is a gathering place for locals and a frequent host of live music. The motel units are on either side of the restaurant-bar-convenience store. The nicely priced units start at a simple queen bedroom and go up to a queen bedroom with a fireplace and a two-person hot tub on an outdoor back deck. Near the Big Sur River, the cabins have fully equipped kitchens and a refrigerator. The cabins are a good deal for groups of two to six people.

Your guest room at ★ **Deetjen's Big Sur Inn** (48865 Hwy. 1, 31 miles south of Carmel, 831/667-2378, www.deetjens.com, $155-290) will be unique, still decorated with the art and collectibles chosen and arranged by Grandpa Deetjen. The historic inn prides itself on its

Deetjen's Big Sur Inn

rustic construction, so expect thin, weathered walls, funky cabin construction, and no outdoor locks on the doors. Five rooms have shared baths, but you can request a room with private bath when you make reservations. Deetjen's prefers a serene environment and does not permit children under 12. The inn has no TVs or stereos, no phones in rooms, and no cell phone service, but you can have a night's worth of entertainment by reading your room's guest journals.

Over $250

The best part about staying at the **Big Sur Lodge** (Pfeiffer Big Sur State Park, 47225 Hwy. 1, 26 miles south of Carmel, 800/424-4787, www.bigsurlodge.com, $309-479) is leaving your room and hitting the trail. Set on a sunny knoll, the lodge has 62 units, with the majority being two-bedroom options; 12 units have kitchenettes. All rooms have a deck. There are no TVs and Internet access is an extra fee, but stays come with a pass to all of Big Sur's state parks, including Pfeiffer Big Sur State Park, Andrew Molera State Park, and Julia Pfeiffer Burns State Park. Several amenities are a short walk down from the rooms, including the **Big Sur Lodge Restaurant,** the **Deli & Café,** and the **Gift Shop & General Store.** Take advantage of the lodge's pool (9am-9pm daily Mar.-Oct.) and watch for the semi-wild turkeys that roam the property.

The **Big Sur River Inn** (46480 Hwy. 1, 25 miles south of Carmel, www.bigsurriverinn. com, $260-400) has 14 rooms on the east side of Highway 1 and six suites on the west side of the road. The east-side rooms are cozy, with knotty pine walls and small porches. The west-side suites each have two rooms, one with a king bed and the other with a trundle bed, which is good for families and small groups. The suites have decks overlooking the Big Sur River. Also on-site is a seasonally heated outdoor pool.

Filled with creative touches and thoughtful amenities, ★ **Glen Oaks Big Sur** (47080 Hwy. 1, 26 miles south of Carmel, 831/667-2105, www.glenoaksbigsur.com, $275-650)

offers the region's best lodging for the price. Its 16 units bring the motor lodge into the new millennium with heated stone bathroom floors, in-room yoga mats, spacious showers, and elegant gas fireplaces. Glen Oaks also has two cottages and eight cabins by the Big Sur River. The cabins are clean, with a modern rustic feel, and have kitchenettes along with outdoor fire pits. Guests have access to two on-site beaches on scenic sections of the Big Sur River.

At **Ventana Big Sur** (48123 Hwy. 1, 28 miles south of Carmel, 800/628-6500, www. ventanainn.com, $1,000-1,500), one of Big Sur's two luxury resorts, the panoramic views begin on the way to the parking lot. Rooms range from "modest" standard rooms—with king beds, tasteful exposed cedar walls and ceilings, and attractive green and earth-tone appointments—to gorgeous suites to multibedroom houses. The property has an infinity tub overlooking redwoods. Another option for staying at Ventana is in their Glamping Tents ($325-500), safari-style canvas tents on wooden decks with amenities including beds, electricity, and USB ports.

A night at **Post Ranch Inn** (47900 Hwy. 1, 28 miles south of Carmel, 831/667-2200 or 888/524-4787, www.postranchinn.com, $925-3,000), staring at the stars over the Pacific from one of the stainless-steel hot soaking tubs, can temporarily cause all life's worries to ebb away. Situated on a 1,200-foot-high ridgeline, the rooms at this luxury resort have striking views of the ocean or the jagged peaks of the nearby Ventana Wilderness. The units blend in with the natural environment, including the seven tree houses, which are perched 10 feet off the ground. Each one has a king bed, an old-fashioned wood-burning fireplace, a spa tub, and a private deck. Take advantage of complimentary activities including yoga classes, nature hikes, garden tours, and stargazing. Breakfast includes made-to-order omelets and French toast as well as a spread of pastries, fruit, and yogurt served in the Sierra Mar Restaurant with its stellar ocean views.

Esalen:
An Advanced California Experience

The **Esalen Institute** is known throughout California as the home of Esalen massage technique, a forerunner and cutting-edge player in ecological living, and a space to retreat from the world and build a new and better sense of self. Visitors journey from all over the state and beyond to sink into the haven that is sometimes called "The New Age Harvard."

One of the institute's biggest draws, the bathhouse, sits down a rocky path right on the edge of the cliffs overlooking the ocean. The bathhouse includes a motley collection of mineral-fed hot tubs with ocean views—choose the open-air Quiet Side or the indoor Silent Side, and then sink into the water and contemplate the Pacific Ocean's limitless expanse, meditate on a perfect sunset or arrangement of stars, or (on the Quiet Side) get to know your fellow bathers—who will be naked. Regardless of gender, marital status, or the presence of others, Esalen's bathhouse area is "clothing optional"; its philosophy puts the essence of nature above the sovereignty of humanity, and it encourages openness and sharing among its guests—to the point of chatting nude with total strangers in a smallish hot tub.

You'll also find a distinct lack of attendants to help you find your way around. Once you've parked and been given directions, it's up to you to find your way down to the cliffs. You'll have to find your own towel, ferret out a cubby for your clothes in the changing rooms, grab a shower, and then wander out to find your favorite of the hot tubs. Be sure you go all the way outside past the individual claw-foot tubs to the glorious shallow cement tubs that sit right out on the edge of the cliff with the surf crashing just below.

In addition to the nudity and new-age culture of Esalen, you'll learn that this isn't a day spa. You'll need to make an appointment for a massage (at $165 a pop), which grants you access to the hot tubs for an hour before and an hour after your 75-minute treatment session. If you just want to sit in the mineral water, you'll need to stay up late. Very late. Inexpensive ($20) open access to the Esalen tubs begins on a first-come, first-served basis at 1am and ends at 3am. Many locals consider the sleep deprivation well worth it to get the chance to enjoy the healing mineral waters and the stunning astronomical shows.

If you're not comfortable with your own nudity or that of others, you don't approve of the all-inclusive spiritual philosophy, or you find it impossible to lower your voice or stop talking for more than 10 minutes, Esalen is not for you. If you've never done anything like this before, think hard about how you'll really feel once you're in the changing area with its naked hippies wandering about. But if this description of a California experience sounds just fabulous to you, make your reservations now! **The Esalen Institute** (55000 Hwy. 1, 41 miles south of Carmel, 831/667-3000, www.esalen.org) accepts reservations by phone if necessary. Go to the website for more information.

Camping

The **Fernwood Resort** (47200 Hwy. 1, 25 miles south of Carmel, 831/667-2422, www.fernwoodbigsur.com, tent site $60, campsite with electrical hookup $80, tent cabin $110, adventure tent $150) offers a range of options. There are 66 campsites around the Big Sur River, some with electrical hookups for RVs. Fernwood also has tent cabins with room for four in a double and two twins. Bring your own linens or sleeping bags, pillows, and towels. The rustic Adventure Tents are canvas tents draped over a solid floor with fully made queen beds and electricity courtesy of an extension cord. All camping options have easy access to the river. Hot showers and restrooms are a short walk away.

The biggest and most developed campground in Big Sur is at ★ **Pfeiffer Big Sur State Park** (Hwy. 1, 26 miles south of Carmel, 800/444-7275, www.parks.ca.gov, www.reservecalifornia.com, $35-50), with more than 150 sites, each of which can handle two vehicles and eight people or an RV (maximum 32 feet, trailers maximum 27 feet, dump station on site). A grocery store and laundry facility operate within the campground, and plenty of flush toilets and hot showers are scattered throughout. In the evenings, walk down to the Campfire Center for entertaining and educational programs. Pfeiffer Big Sur fills up fast in the summer, especially on weekends. Reservations are recommended.

★ **Julia Pfeiffer Burns State Park** (Hwy. 1, 37 miles south of Carmel, 831/667-2315 or 800/444-7275, www.parks.ca.gov, www.reservecalifornia.com, $30) has two walk-in environmental campsites perched over the ocean behind McWay Falls. It's a 0.3-mile walk to these two sites, which have fire pits, picnic tables, and a shared pit toilet, but no running water. More importantly, they have some of the best views of the California coast that you can find in a developed state park campground. Fall asleep to the sound of waves crashing into the rocks below. Saddle Rock is the better of the two, but you can't go wrong with either. The sites book up far in advance, particularly in summer. Reservations can be made seven months in advance.

A popular U.S. Forest Service campground on the south coast of Big Sur, **Kirk Creek Campground** (Hwy. 1, 58 miles south of Carmel, 805/434-1996, www.recreation.gov, $25) has a great location on a bluff above the ocean. Right across the highway is the trailhead for the Vicente Flat Trail and the scenic Nacimiento-Fergusson Road. The sites have picnic tables and campfire rings with grills, while the grounds have toilets and drinking water.

Plaskett Creek Campground (Hwy. 1, 63 miles south of Carmel, 805/434-1996, www.recreation.gov, $25) is right across the highway from Sand Dollar Beach. The sites are in a grassy area under Monterey pine and cypress trees. There are picnic tables and a campfire ring with a grill at every site, along with a flush toilet and drinking water in the campground.

For the ultimate high-end California green lodging-cum-camping experience, book a yurt (a circular structure made with a wood frame covered by cloth) at the **Treebones Resort** (71895 Hwy. 1, 64 miles south of Carmel, 877/424-4787, www.treebonesresort.com, $300-420). The yurts tend to be spacious and charming, with polished wood floors, queen beds, seating areas, and outdoor decks for lounging, but they are not soundproof. There are also five walk-in campsites ($98-150 for two people, breakfast and use of

a yurt at Treebones Resort

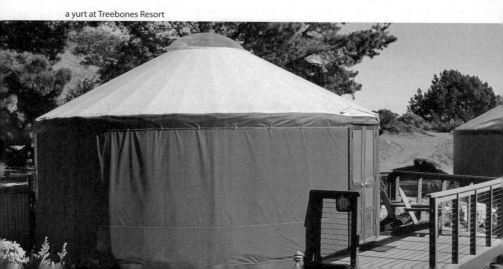

the facilities included). For a truly different experience, camp in the human nest ($175), a bundle of wood off the ground outfitted with a futon mattress, or a hand-woven twig hut ($215). Any stay includes a complimentary breakfast with make-your-own waffles. In the central lodge, you'll find nice hot showers and clean restroom facilities. There is also a heated pool with an ocean view and a hot tub on the grounds. Treebones has a couple of on-site dining options: the **Wild Coast Restaurant** and the **Oceanview Sushi Bar.**

The campgrounds at Bottchers Gap (Palo Colorado Rd., 805/434-1996, http://campone. com) and Andrew Molera State Park (CA-1, 831/667-2315, www.parks.ca.gov) remain closed due to damage from the 2016 Soberanes Fire.

TRANSPORTATION AND SERVICES

Big Sur can only be reached via Highway 1, which can have one or both lanes closed at times—especially in the winter months when rockslides occur. Check the **Caltrans** website (www.dot.ca.gov) or the **Big Sur California Blog** (www.thebigsurblog.com) for current road conditions.

It is difficult to get around Big Sur without a car. However, **Monterey-Salinas Transit** (888/678-2871, www.mst.org, daily late May-early Sept., $3.50) runs a bus route through Big Sur that stops at Nepenthe, the Big Sur River Inn, and Andrew Molera State Park as it heads to Carmel and Monterey.

Big Sur Station (Hwy. 1, 27 miles south of Carmel, 831/667-2315, 9am-4pm daily) is the closest thing to a visitors center. The staffed building offers maps and brochures for all the major parks and trails of Big Sur, plus a bookshop. This is also where the trailhead for the popular backcountry Pine Ridge Trail is located. Get a **free backcountry fire permit** as well as pay the $5 fee for the Pine Ridge Trailhead parking here.

Your **cell phone** may not work anywhere in Big Sur. The best places to get cell service are around Andrew Molera State Park and Point Sur, along with the large dirt pullout 0.25-mile south of Big Sur Station on Highway 1. Likewise, GPS units may struggle in this region. It's best to have a map in your vehicle, or pick up a free *Big Sur Guide,* which has a general map of the region.

The **Big Sur Health Center** (Hwy. 1, 24 miles south of Carmel, Big Sur, 831/667-2580, http://bigsurhealthcenter.org, 10am-1pm and 2pm-5pm Mon.-Fri.) can take care of minor medical needs, and provides an ambulance service and limited emergency care. The nearest full-service hospital is the **Community Hospital of the Monterey Peninsula** (23625 Holman Hwy., Monterey, 831/624-5311 or 888/452-4667, www.chomp.org).

San Simeon and Cambria

Cambria owes much of its prosperity to the immense tourist trap on the hill: Hearst Castle. About seven miles north in San Simeon, Hearst Castle, quite frankly, *is* San Simeon; the town grew up around it to support the overwhelming needs of its megalomaniacal owner and never-ending construction.

SAN SIMEON

The tiny town of San Simeon was founded primarily to support the construction efforts up the hill at Hearst Castle. The town dock provided a place for ships to unload tons of marble, piles of antiques, and dozens of workers. The general store and post office acted as a central gathering place for the community, and today you can still walk up its weathered wooden steps and make a purchase. Around the corner at the building's other door, buy a book of stamps or mail a letter at the tiny but operational post office.

The **William Randolph Hearst**

Memorial State Beach (750 Hearst Castle Rd., 805/927-2035, www.parks.ca.gov, dawn-dusk daily) sits in San Simeon's cute little cove and encompasses what remains of the old pier. Lie on the beach or have a picnic up on the lawn above the sand.

Housed alongside the Hearst Ranch Winery tasting room and the tiny San Simeon post office, **Sebastian's Store** (442 Slo San Simeon Rd., 805/927-3307, 11am-4pm daily, $7-12) showcases tender, juicy beef from nearby Hearst Ranch in burgers, tri-tip, and pulled pork. This is a popular place, and the sandwiches take a few minutes to prepare, so don't stop in right before your scheduled Hearst Castle tour.

★ Hearst Castle

There's nothing else in quite like **Hearst Castle** (Hwy. 1 and Hearst Castle Rd., 800/444-4445, www.hearstcastle.org, tours daily 9am-5pm, prices vary). Newspaper magnate William Randolph Hearst conceived the idea of a grand mansion in the Mediterranean style on land his parents bought along the central California coast. His memories of camping on the hills above the Pacific led him to choose the spot where the castle now stands. He hired Julia Morgan, the first female civil engineering graduate from the University of California, Berkeley, to design and build the house for him. She did a brilliant job with every detail, despite the ever-changing wishes of her employer. By way of decoration, Hearst purchased hundreds of European and Renaissance antiquities, from tiny tchotchkes to whole gilded ceilings. Hearst also adored exotic animals, and he created one of the largest private zoos in the nation on his thousands of Central Coast acres. Most of the zoo is gone now, but you can still see the occasional zebra grazing peacefully along Highway 1 south of the castle.

There are several tours to choose from, each focusing on different spaces and aspects of the castle. The **Grand Rooms Museum Tour** (45 minutes, 106 stairs, 0.6 mile, adults $25, children $12) is recommended for first-time visitors. It begins in the castle's assembly room, which is draped in Flemish tapestries, before heading into the dining room, the billiard room, and the impressive movie theater, where you'll watch a few old Hearst newsreels. The guide then lets you loose to take in the swimming pools: the indoor pool, decorated in gold and blue, and the stunning outdoor Neptune Pool.

Other tours include the upstairs suites, the cottages and kitchen, art and Hollywood themed tours, and an evening tour.

TICKETS

Reserve tour tickets in advance online (www.reservecalifornia.com, tours: adults $25-36, children $12-$18, $8 reservation fee). Pick tickets up at the visitors center 15-20 minutes before your tour starts. The visitors center has a gift shop, a restaurant, a café, and a movie theater where you can watch the much-touted film *Hearst Castle—Building the Dream,* which will give you an overview of the construction and history of the marvelous edifice, and of William Randolph Hearst's empire. (Only daytime tours offer free showings of the movie. During evening tours, a movie ticket is $6 for adults and $4 for children. To see the movie without a tour, tickets cost $10 for adults and $8 for children.)

Ticket-holders board a shuttle for the ride up the hill to the castle. (Private cars are not allowed on the roads.) Expect to walk for at least an hour on whichever tour you choose, and to climb up and down many stairs. Wheelchair-accessible Grand Rooms and Evening Tours are available for visitors with limited mobility. Strollers are not permitted. The restrooms and food concessions are in the visitors center. No food, drink, or chewing gum is allowed on any tour.

Piedras Blancas Light Station

First illuminated in 1875, the **Piedras Blancas Light Station** (tours meet at the Piedras Blancas Motel, 1.5 miles north of the light station on Hwy. 1, 805/927-7361, www.piedrasblancas.org, tours offered Tues.,

Thurs., and Sat., adults $10, children 6-17 $5, children under 6 free) and its adjacent grounds can be accessed on a two-hour tour. In 1948, a nearby earthquake caused a crack in the lighthouse tower and the removal of its first-order Fresnel lens, which was replaced with an automatic aero beacon.

Piedras Blancas Elephant Seal Rookery

Stopping at the **Piedras Blancas Elephant Seal Rookery** (Hwy. 1, 7 miles north of San Simeon, 805/924-1628, www.elephantseal. org, free) is like watching a nature documentary in real time. On this sliver of beach, up to 17,000 elephant seals rest, breed, give birth, or fight one another. The rookery is right along Highway 1; turn into the large gravel parking lot and follow the boardwalks north or south to viewing areas where informative plaques give background on the elephant seals. Volunteer docents are available to answer questions (10am-4pm daily). The beaches themselves are off-limits to humans, since they're covered in the large marine mammals. But thanks to the wheelchair-accessible boardwalks built above the beach, visitors can get just a matter of feet away from the giant creatures. In the fall, most adult seals head out to sea, returning in early to mid-December. Most of the seal births occur between the end of December and the middle of February.

CAMBRIA

Once you're through with the castle tours, a few attractions in the lower elevations beckon as well. Cambria began as, and to a certain extent still is, an artists' colony. The windswept hills and sparkling ocean provide plenty of inspiration for painters, writers, sculptors, glassblowers, and more. The small beach town becomes surprisingly spacious when you start exploring it. Plenty of visitors come here to ply Moonstone Beach, peruse the charming downtown area, and just drink in the laid-back, art-town feel.

Sights

NITT WITT RIDGE

While William Randolph Hearst built one of the most expensive homes ever seen in California, local eccentric Arthur Harold Beal (aka Captain Nit Wit or Der Tinkerpaw) got busy building the cheapest "castle" he could. **Nitt Witt Ridge** (881 Hillcrest Dr., 805/927-2690, tours by appointment, $10) is the result of five decades of scavenging trash and using it as building supplies to create a multistory

elephant seals at the Piedras Blancas Elephant Seal Rookery

home like no other on the coast. The rambling structure is made of abalone shells, used car rims, and toilet seats, among other found materials. Features like the cobblestone archways reveal a true artist's touch. Make an appointment with owner Mike O'Malley to take a tour of the property; don't just drop in.

To find Nitt Witt Ridge, drive on Cambria's Main Street toward Moonstone Beach and make a right onto Cornwall Street. Take the second right onto Hillcrest Avenue and look for the unique structure.

MOONSTONE BEACH

Known for its namesake shimmering stone, **Moonstone Beach** (Moonstone Beach Dr.) is a scenic, pebbly slice of coastline with craggy rocks offshore. Cambria's moonstones are bright, translucent pebbles that can be easiest to find at low tides and when the sun shines, highlighting their features. They are fairly easy to collect, especially after winter storms. The moonstones on Moonstone Beach are not gem quality, but they make a fun souvenir. Many Cambria boutiques and galleries carry moonstone jewelry.

A wooden boardwalk runs along the top of the bluffs above the beach. From here, take in the scenery and watch moonstone collectors with buckets wander below in the tide line. Access is at Leffingwell Landing, Moonstone Beach Drive, and Santa Rosa Creek.

Nightlife

Mozzi's (2262 Main St., 805/927-4767, http://mozzissaloon.com, 1pm-close Mon.-Fri., 11am-close Sat., noon-close Sun.) is a classic old California saloon—there's been a bar on this site since 1866. Old artifacts like lanterns and farm equipment hang from the ceiling above the long redwood bar, jukebox, and pool tables in this historic watering hole. Save some money on "Three Dollar Tuesdays" when all well drinks are just three bucks a pop.

Food

The ★ **Main Street Grill** (603 Main St., 805/927-3194, www.firestonegrill.com,

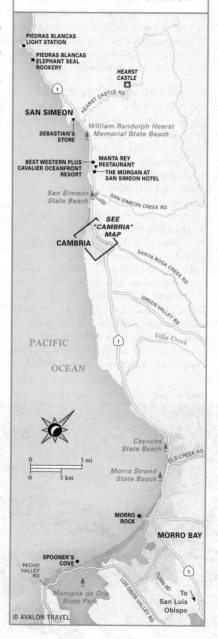

Cambria and San Simeon

PIEDRAS BLANCAS LIGHT STATION

PIEDRAS BLANCAS ELEPHANT SEAL ROOKERY

HEARST CASTLE

SAN SIMEON

HEARST CASTLE RD

SEBASTIAN'S STORE

William Randolph Hearst Memorial State Beach

BEST WESTERN PLUS CAVALIER OCEANFRONT RESORT

MANTA REY RESTAURANT
THE MORGAN AT SAN SIMEON HOTEL

San Simeon State Beach

SAN SIMEON CREEK RD

SEE "CAMBRIA" MAP

CAMBRIA

SANTA ROSA CREEK RD

GREEN VALLEY RD

Villa Creek

PACIFIC

OCEAN

0   3 mi
0   3 km

Cayucos State Beach

OLD CREEK RD

Morro Strand State Beach

MORRO ROCK

MORRO BAY

SPOONER'S COVE

PECHO VALLEY RD

Montaña de Oro State Park

LOS OSOS VALLEY RD

TURRI RD

To San Luis Obispo

© AVALON TRAVEL

Cambria

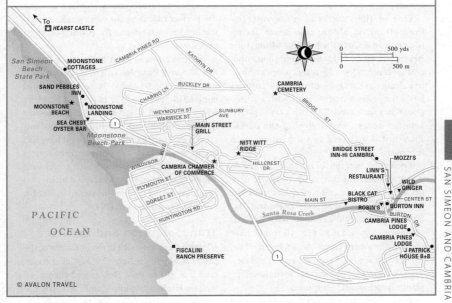

© AVALON TRAVEL

11am-9pm daily June-Aug., 11am-8pm daily Sept.-May, $4-18) is a popular eatery housed in a cavernous building. The tri-tip steak sandwich—tri-tip drenched in barbecue sauce and placed on a French roll dipped in butter—is a favorite, even though the ABC burger (avocado, bacon, and cheese) puts most burger joints to shame. The giant Cobb salad comes with lots of diced-up bacon and your choice of chicken or steak.

For a seafood dinner, head for the ★ **Sea Chest Oyster Bar** (6216 Moonstone Beach Dr., 805/927-4514, www.seachestrestaurant. com, 5:30pm-9pm Wed.-Mon., $20-30, cash only). The restaurant is in a wooden cottage with great ocean views. Framed photographs on the walls and books on bookshelves add to the homey feel of the place. No reservations are accepted, so expect a long line out the door at opening time, and prepare to get here early (or wait a long while) for one of the window-side tables. Sit at the bar to watch the cooks prepare the impressive dishes like halibut,

salmon, and cioppino, which is served in the pot in which it was cooked.

The eclectic menu at **Robin's** (4095 Burton Dr., 805/927-5007, www.robinsrestaurant.com, 11am-9pm Sun.-Thurs., 11am-9:30pm Fri.-Sat., $16-26) features cuisine from around the world, including Thai green chicken, curries, and wild prawn enchiladas, as well as flatiron steak and the signature salmon bisque, all of which are done well. The menu also has vegetarian and gluten-free dishes. The historic building has a large dining room and a deck. Expect fine service from a staff that's proud of their product.

Accommodations

Next to a church, the ★ **Bridge Street Inn-HI Cambria** (4314 Bridge St., 805/215-0724, http://bridgestreetinncambria.com, $50-90) used to be the pastor's house. Now it's a clean, cozy hostel with a dorm room and five private rooms. The kitchen has a collection of cast-iron kitchenware, and there's a volleyball court out front. There's no TV here, but they do offer Wi-Fi and an eclectic book library.

One of the cuter and more interesting options on Moonstone Beach Drive, **Moonstone Cottages** (6580 Moonstone Beach Dr., 805/927-1366, http://moonstonecottages.com, $269-389) offers peace and luxury along the sea. Each of the three cottages has a fireplace, a marble bath with a whirlpool tub, a flat-screen TV with a DVD player, Internet access, and a view of the ocean. Breakfast is delivered to your cottage each morning.

For a great selection of anything from economical standard rooms up to rustic cabins with king beds and a fireplace, pick the **Cambria Pines Lodge** (2905 Burton Dr., 805/927-4200 or 800/927-4200, www.cambriapineslodge.com, $165-365). All rooms have plenty of creature comforts, including TVs, private baths, and, in some cases, fireplaces. There's also a nice garden area with flowering plants, benches, and sculptures.

Her Castle Homestay Bed and Breakfast Inn (1978 Londonderry Ln., 805/924-1719, www.hercastle.cc, $140-170) is a bit different from your average B&B, with only two rooms available and lots of personal

attention from the owners. When you make your reservations, ask about a half-day wine tour or dinner reservations. Her Castle can be the perfect hideaway for two couples traveling together who desire the privacy of "their own house."

A stone's throw from Moonstone Beach, the ★ **Sand Pebbles Inn** (6252 Moonstone Beach Dr., 805/927-5600, www.cambriainns.com, $219-369) is a gray two-story building where the clean, tastefully decorated rooms have comfortable beds, mini-fridges, and microwaves. The six rooms facing west have full ocean views, while the bottom three rooms have patios. Expect amenities such as welcome cookies, a better-than-average continental breakfast, coffee and tea served in the lobby, and a lending library of DVDs.

Transportation and Services
Highway 1 travels south through Cambria, the prettiest way to get here. For a quicker route, take U.S. 101 to Paso Robles and then head west on Highway 46 into Cambria. If you use Cambria as a base to explore the Paso Robles wine area or Morro Bay (15 miles), a car will be necessary.

The regional bus system, the **RTA** (805/541-2228, www.slorta.org), connects San Luis

Sand Pebbles Inn

Obispo, Morro Bay, Cayucos, Cambria, and San Simeon. Fares are $1.50-3.

If you prefer to travel by rail, take **Amtrak's** *Coast Starlight* (www.amtrak.com) to either the Paso Robles or the San Luis Obispo (SLO) stations, and make arrangements to rent a car (easiest from SLO) or get alternative transportation out to the coast.

The **Cambria Public Library** (1043 Main St., 805/927-4336, www.slolibrary.org, 9am-5pm Tues.-Wed., 10am-6pm Thurs., 10am-5pm Fri.-Sat.) offers tourist information and local history, including a map for a self-guided historical walking tour.

Cambria is served by three healthcare facilities: **Twin Cities Hospital** (1100 Las Tablas Rd., Templeton, 805/434-3500, www.twincitieshospital.com) in Templeton, 25 miles inland, and **Sierra Vista Regional Medical Center** (1010 Murray Ave., San Luis Obispo, 805/546-7600, www.sierravistaregional.com) and **French Hospital** (1911 Johnson Ave., San Luis Obispo, 805/543-5353, www.dignityhealth.org), both in San Luis Obispo, 37 miles south. Cambria and San Simeon are policed by the **San Luis Obispo Sheriff's Department** (805/781-4550, www.slosheriff.org).

Background

The Landscape

GEOGRAPHY

California's geographic profile is as diverse as its population. At nearly 159,000 square miles, California is the third-largest state in the United States, stretching 770 miles from the Oregon state line to its southern border with Mexico. California includes the Sierra Nevada mountain range, numerous national parks and monuments, coastal and giant redwoods, volcanoes, the agricultural Central Valley, and the tallest mountain in the continental United States, Mount Whitney, at 14,505 feet. In addition, two major tectonic plates—the north-moving Pacific and south-moving North American Plate—give California a reputation for shaking things up a bit.

Mountain Ranges

The California coast is characterized by craggy cliffs, rocky beaches, and enormous coast redwoods (*Sequoia sempervirens*) that reach heights up to 380 feet. The coast is bounded by the aptly named Coast Range, ruggedly steep mountains formed 30 million years ago when part of the Pacific Plate jammed, folded, and compressed to form the Coast Range and Transverse Range. In addition to the Coast Range, there are two other significant high-elevation regions in the state. In the north, the Cascade Mountains evolved through volcanic activity 10 million years ago when the Juan de Fuca Plate, earth's smallest tectonic plate caught between the North American and Pacific Plates, collided with the North American Plate and was forced under the larger plate. Magma from the melting plate raised a series of mountains, including California's two active volcanoes—Mount Lassen and Mount Shasta. Mount Lassen (10,462 feet) last blew its top

in 1915; today, the surrounding park offers a glimpse into the earth's formation. Majestic Mount Shasta, along I-5 north of Redding, has not erupted in quite some time. At 14,179 feet, Mount Shasta's extreme height creates its own weather system.

To the east is the Sierra Nevada, stretching 400 miles north-south and forming the eastern spine of the state. Its peaks and valleys include Mount Whitney, Lake Tahoe, Yosemite, and the giant sequoias (*Sequoiadendron giganteum*) in Sequoia and Kings Canyon National Parks. The Sierra Nevada formed 60 million years ago when magma seeped up between the Pacific and North American Plates. It created a massive pool of granite that slowly cooled to form a batholith, a massive dome-shaped formation of intrusive igneous rock. For the past 12 million years the formation has been pushing upward.

Earthquakes and Faults

Earthquakes occur when the tectonic plates that compose the earth's crust shift along faults, the boundaries between the plates—and California's seat on the Pacific Ring of Fire is well established. The North American Plate and Pacific Plate came together about 150 million years ago, causing compression and folding of the earth's crust that created the Sierra Nevada; it eventually eroded to fill with sediments that would become the Central Valley. About 30 million years ago, a ridge of the Pacific Plate became jammed and caused the folding and compression that formed the Coast and Transverse Ranges. More importantly, the contact caused the Pacific Plate to change direction and move northward, forming the San Andreas Fault. This infamous strike-slip fault, where two

Earthquake Tips

Visitors from outside California may have the impression that big earthquakes happen here all the time. Well, that's only partly correct. Earthquakes do happen all the time, but most shakers are measurable only by sophisticated equipment and remain unfelt by most residents. According to the California Emergency Management Agency, there are some things you can do to protect yourself during an earthquake:

- Drop! Cover! Hold on! California schoolchildren learn this early on through education programs. It means that if an earthquake begins, drop to the ground. Find cover under a sturdy desk or table, or stand in a corner or doorway. Hold on to something sturdy if the ground begins to pitch.

- If you're in a high-rise building, avoid elevators, windows, and outside areas.

- If you're outside, move to a clear area away from trees, buildings, overpasses, walls, and power lines—anything that could fall on you.

- If you're in a car, pull over to the side of the road. Make sure you're not parked underneath a structure that could collapse.

- If you're inside a crowded place, do not rush to the exit. Instead, squat down and protect your head and neck with your hands and arms.

It's important to stay as calm as possible after an earthquake; the ground may start shaking again. Aftershocks, usually smaller, often follow a sizable earthquake and originate near the same location. A mild earthquake might cause anxiety, but it should not affect your travel plans aside from slight delays in public transportation and other inconveniences. A major earthquake—magnitude 4.5 and larger—is a different story, but these earthquakes are pretty uncommon (it's more likely that you'll win the state lottery than experience a major earthquake).

For more information on what to do before, during, and after an earthquake, visit the **California Emergency Management Agency** (www.caloes.ca.gov) and the **U.S. Geological Survey** (www.usgs.gov).

tectonic plates move horizontally—the North American Plate moving mostly southward and the Pacific Plate moving mostly northward—runs along the North Coast, near San Francisco, and east of Los Angeles before branching off into Mexico and the Pacific Ocean.

The plates frequently catch as they move past each other, storing energy and causing tension to build. When the plates jolt past one another, they release this energy in the form of an earthquake. The San Andreas Fault is not the only fault in California; earthquakes along numerous faults happen daily, 10,000–37,000 times each year. Most register less than magnitude 3 and go unnoticed by Californians used to the shake, rattle, and roll. However, there have been several significant earthquakes in California history.

The 1906 San Francisco earthquake had a magnitude of 7.7-8.3 and involved the "rupturing" of the northern 300 miles of the San Andreas Fault from San Juan Bautista to Cape Mendocino. The 1989 Loma Prieta earthquake, with an epicenter near Loma Prieta Peak in the Santa Cruz Mountains, was small by comparison at magnitude 6.9 and with only 25 miles of ruptured fault. California's stringent building codes, developed in the wake of deadly and destructive earthquakes, include an extensive seismic retrofit program that has brought older buildings, overpasses, bridges, and other structures up to stringent standards.

CLIMATE

Vast in size and varied in geography, California also has a vastly varied climate, from boiling heat in the Central Valley to sub-arctic temperatures at mountain summits.

Along the North Coast, the weather stays fairly constant: chilly, windy, and foggy. Summer days rarely reach 80°F, and winter rainstorms can pound the area. San Francisco shares its cool and foggy climate with temperatures in the 50s and 60s well into summer. South on the peninsula or across the Bay in Marin County and the East Bay, the temperature may rise 20-30 degrees and the fog often makes way for sun.

North of San Francisco, the Wine Country is graced with milder weather and warm summers, perfect for growing grapes. Inland, Sacramento and the Central Valley can be very hot. Daily temperatures in summer can peak well over 100°F and often worsen air quality, causing Spare the Air alerts. Winters in the Central Valley are cool and usually clear, however the nearby Sierra Nevada Foothills often receive snow in the winter, and roads can become impassable.

Expect harsh weather if you head to Yosemite, Lake Tahoe, Mount Shasta, Mount Lassen, or the Eastern Sierra in the winter. Snowfall in a 24-hour period can be measured in feet, forcing road closures and power outages that wreak havoc with travel plans. But activities such as skiing, snowboarding, sledding, snowshoeing, and snow camping abound. The short hot summers draw campers, hikers, and mountain bikers.

The Central Coast is a bit warmer than the San Francisco Bay Area, but still, expect cool temperatures and fog in summer. A chilly wind accompanies the rain in the winter, often closing mountain roads and highways, and mudslides can close Highway 1.

ENVIRONMENTAL ISSUES

Californians face several major environmental issues. The state constantly battles drought; with record-low rainfall and snow levels, water for both farms and human consumption is in short supply. Water conservation measures may be enforced at restaurants, hotels, and in state and national parks.

Exacerbated by drought conditions, the state is experiencing a proliferation of wildfires. In 2017, nearly 1,400,000 acres burned. As a result, wildfire bans may be in place in many outdoors areas and campgrounds and visitors should exercise extreme caution traveling outdoors during summer and fall.

The wildfires are fueled in part by a combination of climate change, drought, sudden oak death, bark beetle infestation, and a high density of trees. Massive swaths of the Sierra forest have been affected by several tree diseases and pathogens. While waves of tree mortality are cyclical, the current rate poses the question as to whether these forests will return to their previous state.

Water pollution is another concern. While tap water is safe to drink, recreation in bays, lakes, and rivers, as well as the Pacific Ocean, requires caution. Swimming in the Pacific Ocean may result in E. coli outbreaks. Fishing bans in bays, lakes, and rivers are often in place due to high mercury levels in sealife. Boating restrictions may be instituted to protection alpine lakes and to limit exposure to invasive zebra mussels. For restrictions and regulations, contact the **Department of Fish and Game** (916/445-0411, www.dfg.ca.gov).

Plants and Animals

PLANTS
Redwoods

A visit to California's famous redwoods should be on every traveler's list. The coast redwood (*Sequoia sempervirens*) grows along the North Coast as far south as Big Sur. Coast redwoods are characterized by their towering height, flaky red bark, and moist understory. Among the tallest trees on earth, they are also some of the oldest, with some individuals almost 2,000 years old. Coast redwoods occupy a narrow strip of coastal California, growing less than 50 miles inland to collect moisture from the ocean and fog. Their tannin-rich bark is crucial to their ability to survive wildfires and regenerate afterward. The best places to marvel at the giants are within the Redwood State and National Parks, Muir Woods, and Big Basin State Park.

The giant sequoia (*Sequoiadendron giganteum*) grows farther inland in a 260-mile belt at 3,000-8,900 feet elevation in the Sierra Nevada mountain range. Giant sequoias are the largest trees by volume on earth; they can grow to heights of 280 feet with a diameter up to 26 feet and can live for thousands of years. Giant sequoias share the ruddy bark of the coast sequoia as well as its fire-resistant qualities. The best places to see giant sequoias up close are at Sequoia and Kings Canyon National Parks, Calaveras Big Trees, and the Mariposa Grove at Yosemite National Park.

Oaks

California is home to many native oaks. The most common are the valley oak, black oak, live oak, and coastal live oak. The deciduous valley oak (*Quercus lobata*) commonly grows on slopes, valleys, and wooded foothills in the Central Valley. The black oak, also deciduous, grows throughout the foothills of the Coast Range and Sierra Nevada. The live oak habitat is in the Central Valley, while the coastal live oak occupies the Coast Range. The acorns of all these oaks were an important food supply for California's Native American population and continue to be an important food source for wildlife.

Wildflowers

California's state flower is the California poppy (*Eschscholzia californica*). The pretty little perennial grows just about everywhere, even on the sides of the busiest highways. The flowers of most California poppies are bright orange, but they also appear occasionally in white, cream, and an even deeper red-orange.

ANIMALS
Mountain Lions

Mountain lions (*Felis concolor*) are an example of powerful and potentially deadly beauty. Their solitary territorial hunting habits make them elusive, but human contact has increased as more homes are built in mountain lion habitat throughout California. Many parks in or near mountain lion territory post signs with warnings and advice: Do not run if you come across a mountain lion; instead make noise and raise and wave your arms so that you look bigger. The **California Fish and Game Department** (www.dfg.ca.gov) offers a downloadable brochure on encounters and other tips.

Black Bears

Don't take the name black bear (*Ursus americanus*) too literally. The black bear can actually have brown and even cinnamon-colored fur, sometimes with a white patch on the chest. The black bear is pretty common throughout North America, including in the forests of the Coast Range, the Sierra Nevada, and the Transverse Range. While the black bear can appear cuddly from a distance, distance is exactly what should separate bears and humans—at least 25 feet or more. These are wild animals; do not attempt to feed or approach them, and never come between a mama bear and her cubs. Bears can run up to 30 mph, and they can definitely outrun you. Campers should use bear-proof food lockers at campgrounds or a bear canister in the backcountry; never keep food or any scented products (toothpaste, energy bars, hair products) in a tent or in view inside a car. Bears can be crafty and destructive—some, especially in Yosemite National Park, have broken into cars and shredded the interiors looking for food. Bears are mostly nocturnal but can be seen out during the day, and they do not always hibernate in winter.

Tule Elk

Tule elk (*Cervus elaphus nannodes*, also known as wapiti, California elk, or dwarf elk) are the smallest elk in North America and once thrived in the Central Valley; tule elk were nearly hunted to extinction to feed gold rush settlers. There are now almost 3,000 tule elk in approximately 20 free-range and protected herds in several grassland habitats in the Central Valley and Point Reyes National Seashore. Usually pale gray, brown, or tan with thick chestnut brown necks, the male bull can grow antlers that stretch five feet or more. In the fall, the bull gives a low bellow followed by a distinctive far-carrying whistle or bugle, while the female whistles in spring. The best place to see Roosevelt Elk is in Prairie Creek Redwoods State Park, 50 miles north of Eureka.

Whales

The massive, majestic gray whale (*Eschrichtius robustus*) was once endangered, but its numbers have rebounded with international protection. The gray whale measures about 40 feet long and has mottled shades of gray with black fins; its habitat is inshore ocean waters, so there is a chance to get a glimpse at them from headlands up and down the coast. Gray whales generally migrate south along the coast November to January and are closer to shore February to June when they migrate northward. Mendocino County is a perfect place to watch the water for a glimpse of breaching whales.

Perhaps a more recognizable behemoth is the humpback whale (*Megaptera novaeangliae*). At 45-55 feet long, the humpback is the only large whale to breach regularly, then roll and crash back into the water, providing one of the best shows in nature; the whale also rolls from side to side on the surface, slapping its long flippers. Humpbacks generally stay a little farther from shore, so it may be necessary to take a whale-watching cruise to catch a glimpse of them, but their 20-foot spouts can help landlubbers spot them from shore. Look for humpbacks between April and early December off the coast near Big Sur, particularly at Julia Pfeiffer Burns State Park.

The blue whale (*Balaenoptera musculus*) is the largest animal on earth. At 70-90 feet long, the blue whale even exceeds dinosaurs in size. With a blue-gray top and a yellowish bottom, the blue whale has a heart the size of a small car and two blowholes, but alas does not breach. They can be seen June-November off the California coast, but especially at Monterey and north of Point Reyes.

Seals and Sea Lions

Watching a beach full of California sea lions (*Zalophus californianus*) sunning themselves and noisily honking away can be a pleasure. Sea lions are migratory, so they come and go at will, especially in the fall when they head to the Channel Islands for breeding. If you have a serious hankering to see California sea lions, try Pier 39 near Fisherman's Wharf or on the coast at Seal Rocks, both in San Francisco.

The massive northern elephant seal (*Mirounga angustirostris*) comes to Año Nuevo State Park December-March to breed. Considerably larger than sea lions, elephant seals can reach up to 5,000 pounds.

Sea Otters

Much higher on the cuteness scale is the sea otter (*Enhydra lutris*), which can be spotted just offshore in shallow kelp beds. Once near extinction, the endearing playful sea otter has survived. It can be a bit mesmerizing to witness a sea otter roll on its back in the water and use a rock to break open mollusks for lunch. Sea otter habitat runs mainly from Monterey Bay to Big Sur, but they have also been spotted in the waters near Mendocino.

Birds

California has a wide range of habitat with accessible food and water that makes it perfect for hundreds of bird species to nest, raise their young, or just stop over and rest during long migrations. Nearly 600 species have been spotted in California, so it may be just the place for a bird-watcher's vacation.

California's state bird is the California quail (*Callipepla californica*), found throughout the state with the exception of the southeastern deserts and mountain.

Among the most regal of California's bird species are raptors. The red-tailed hawk (*Buteo jamaicensis*) is found throughout California and frequently sighted perched in trees along the North Coast highway, in the Central Valley, and even in urban areas such as San Francisco. The red-tailed hawk features a light underbelly with a dark band and a distinctive red tail that gives the bird its name.

The California condor (*Gymnogyps californianus*) is largest land bird in North America, with a wing span of nearly 10 feet. The condor was extinct in the wild in 1987, but thanks to a successful breeding program, condors now be seen in Big Sur and Pinnacles National Monument.

Reptiles

Several varieties of rattlesnakes are indigenous to the state. The Pacific Northwest rattler makes its home in California, while more than half a dozen different rattlesnake varieties live in Southern California, including the western diamondback and the Mojave rattlesnake.

If you spot California's most infamous native reptile, keep your distance. All rattlesnakes are venomous, although death by snakebite is extremely rare in California. Most parks with known rattlesnake populations post signs alerting hikers to their presence; hikers should stay on marked trails and avoid tromping off into meadows or brush. Pay attention when hiking, especially when negotiating rocks and woodpiles, and never put a foot or a hand down in a spot you can't see first. Wear long pants and heavy hiking boots for protection from snakes as well as insects, other critters, and unfriendly plants you might encounter.

Butterflies

California's vast population of wildflowers attracts an array of gorgeous butterflies. The Monarch butterfly (*Danaus plexippus*) is emblematic of the state. These large orange-and-black butterflies have a migratory pattern that's reminiscent of birds. Starting in August, they begin migrating south to cluster in groves of eucalyptus trees. As they crowd together and close up their wings to hibernate, their dull outer wing color camouflages them as clumps of dried leaves, thus protecting them from predators. In spring, the butterflies begin to wake up, fluttering lazily in the groves for a while before flying north to seek out milkweed on which to lay their eggs. Pacific Grove, Santa Cruz, and Cambria are great places to visit these California "butterfly trees."

History and Culture

INDIGENOUS CULTURES

The diverse ecology of California allowed Native Americans to adapt to the land in various ways. Communities settled from the border of present-day Oregon south though the mountain ranges and valleys, along the coast, into the Sierra Nevada, and in the arid lands that stretch into Mexico. These groups include the Maidu, Miwok, Yurok, and Pomo. More than 100 Native American languages were spoken in California, and each had several dialects, all of which were identified with geographic areas.

Following is an overview of the groups most commonly encountered when traveling around the state.

Yurok

The Yurok people are the largest Native American population in California, and they continue to live along the Klamath River and the Humboldt County coast near Redwood National Park, north of Eureka and south of Crescent City. Spanish explorers arriving in 1775 were the Yurok's first contact with Europeans. Fur traders and trappers from the Hudson's Bay Company arrived in about 1827, but it wasn't until gold miners arrived in 1850 that the Yurok faced disease and destruction that diminished their population by 75 percent. Researchers put the 1770 population at 2,500-3,100, which dropped to 669-700 by 1910. Today, there are more than 5,000 Yurok living in California and about 6,000 in the United States overall.

Pomo

The name for the Pomo people and their language first meant "those who live at the red earth hole," possibly referring to the magnesite used for red beads or the reddish earth and clay mined in the area. It was also once the name of a village near the present-day community of Pomo in Potter Valley. The Pomo territory was large, bounded by the Pacific Ocean to the west and extending inland to Clear Lake in Lake County. Today, the territory includes present-day Santa Rosa and much of the Sonoma County wine country.

In 1800 there were 10,000-18,000 Pomo living in approximately 70 communities that spoke seven Pomo languages. But as the Pomo interacted and traded with the Russians at Fort Ross, added pressure came from the Spanish missionaries and American settlers pressing in from the south and east. European encroachment may have been the reason Pomo villages became more centralized and why many Pomo retreated to remote areas to band together in defense.

The Pomo suffered not only from lifestyle changes and loss of territory but from diseases for which they had no immunity. Missionaries, traders, and settlers brought with them measles, smallpox, and other illnesses that devastated indigenous populations. In 1850 miners began settling in the Russian River Valley, and the Lake Sonoma Valley was homesteaded. As a result, the U.S. government forced the Pomo off their land and onto reservations. Historians believe there were 3,500-5,000 Pomo in 1851, but only 777-1,200 by 1910. Today, there are nearly 9,000 Pomo living in California.

Miwok

Before contact with settlers in 1769, the Miwok people lived in small bands in separate parts of California. The Plains and Sierra Miwok lived on the Sacramento-San Joaquin Delta, parts of the San Joaquin and Sacramento Valleys, and the foothills and western slopes of the Sierra Nevada. The Coast Miwok—including the Bodega Bay Miwok and the Marin Miwok—lived in what is now Marin and southern Sonoma Counties. Lake Miwok people were found in the Clear Lake Basin of Lake County. The Bay Miwok lived in present-day Contra

Costa County. Miwok domesticated dogs and grew tobacco but otherwise depended on hunting, fishing, and gathering for food. Miwok in the Sierra exploited the California black oak for acorns, and it is believed that they cultivated the tree in parts of what is now Yosemite National Park.

Like so many indigenous people in California, the Miwok suffered after explorers, missionaries, miners, and settlers arrived. Historians estimate there were at least 11,000 Miwok in 1770, but in all four regions there were only about 671 Miwok in 1910 and 491 in 1930. Today, there are about 3,500 Miwok.

Ohlone

The Ohlone people once occupied what is now San Francisco, Berkeley, Oakland, Silicon Valley, Santa Cruz, Monterey, and the lower Salinas Valley. The Ohlone (a Miwok word meaning "western people") lived in permanent villages, only moving temporarily to gather seasonal foods such as acorns and berries. The Ohlone formed an association of about 50 different communities with an average of 200 members each. The villages interacted through trade, marriages, and ceremonies. Basket weaving, ceremonial dancing, piercings and tattoos, and general ornamentation indicated status within the community and were all part of Ohlone life. Like other Native Americans in the region, the Ohlone depended on hunting, fishing, gathering, and agrarian skills such as burning off old growth each year to get a better yield from seeds.

The Ohlone culture remained fairly stable until the first Spanish missionaries arrived to spread Christianity and to expand Spanish territorial claims. Spanish explorer Sebastián Vizcaíno reached present-day Monterey in December 1602, and the Rumsen group of Ohlone was the first they encountered. Father Junípero Serra's missionaries built seven missions on Ohlone land, and most of the Ohlone people were brought to the missions to live and work. For the next 60 years, the Ohlone suffered, as did most indigenous people at the missions. Along with the culture shock of

subjugation came the diseases for which they had no immunity—measles, smallpox, syphilis, and others. It wasn't until 1834 that the California missions were abolished and the Mexican government redistributed the mission landholdings.

The Ohlone lost the vast majority of their population between 1780 and 1850 because of disease, social upheaval from European incursion, and low birth rates. Estimates are that there were 7,000-26,000 Ohlone when Spanish soldiers and missionaries arrived, and about 3,000 in 1800 and 864-1,000 by 1852. There are 1,500-2,000 Ohlone people today.

Yokut

The Yokut people have inhabited the Central Valley for at least 8,000 years; they may even have been the first people to settle here. The Yokuts live in the San Joaquin Valley from the Sacramento-San Joaquin River Delta south to Bakersfield and east to the Sierra Foothills. Sequoia and Kings Canyon National Parks are included in this area, as are the cities of Fresno and Modesto. Like other Native Americans, the Yokuts developed water transportation, harvesting abundant tule reeds to work them into canoes.

Spanish explorers entered the valley in 1772 and found 63 different Yokut groups scattered up and down the Central Valley. Many of the Yokuts were taken to the various missions, where they suffered from European subjugation and diseases. Later, as miners entered the region, the Yokut people were forced from their lands. There may have been as many as 4,500 Yokuts when the Spaniards arrived, but the last full-blooded member of the Southern Yokuts is said to have died in 1960. In 1910, the Yokut population was a mere 600. In 2010, that number grew to 2,000.

Paiute

The Paiute people are grouped by their language—despite location, political connection, or even genetic similarity. For the Northern Paiutes and the Southern Paiutes, that language is the Numic branch of the Uto-Aztecan family of Native American languages. The Northern Paiutes live in the Great Basin; the Southern Paiutes lived in the Mojave Desert on the edge of present-day Death Valley National Park. Between the Northern Paiutes and the Southern Paiutes are the Mono Lake Northern Paiutes and the Owens Valley Paiutes.

The Northern Paiute lifestyle was well adapted to the harsh environment of the Great Basin. Each band occupied a territory usually centered around a lake or other water source that also provided fish and waterfowl. Food drives to capture rabbits and pronghorn were communal and often involved nearby bands. Piñon nuts were gathered and stored for winter, and grass seeds and roots were part of the diet. Because of their remoteness, the Northern Paiutes may have completely avoided the hardships of the mission period. Their first contact with European Americans may have occurred in 1820, but sustained contact did not happen until the 1840s; several violent confrontations over land and other conflicts occurred in this period. In the end, smallpox did more to decimate the Northern Paiutes than warfare. The Northern Paiutes established colonies that were joined by Shoshone and Washoe people and eventually received recognition by the federal government.

The Southern Paiutes were not as fortunate. The first contact with Europeans came in 1776, when the priests Silvestre Vélez de Escalante and Francisco Atanasio Domínguez met them while seeking an overland route to the California missions. The Southern Paiutes suffered slave raids by the Navajo and Ute before Europeans arrived, and the raids increased afterward. In 1851, Mormon settlers showed up and occupied local water sources, and the slave raids ended. Settlers and their agrarian practices such as cattle herding drove away game and limited the Southern Paiutes' ability to gather food, disrupting their traditional lifestyle.

Today, there are nearly 7,000 Paiutes throughout the West.

EXPLORATION

Juan Rodríguez Cabrillo, a Portuguese explorer and adventurer, was commissioned in 1542 by the viceroy of New Spain (Mexico) to sail into what is now San Diego Bay. He continued north as far as Point Reyes before heading to Santa Catalina Island in late November 1542 to winter and make repairs to his ship. On Christmas Eve, Cabrillo tripped, splintering his shin, and the injury developed gangrene. He died on January 3, 1543, and is buried on Catalina. The rest of his party arrived in Barra de Navidad on April 14, 1543. Having found no wealth, advanced Native American civilization or agriculture, or northwest passage, Portuguese interest in exploring California lapsed for more than 200 years.

Francis Drake, an English explorer, claimed a chunk of the California coast in 1579. It is thought that Drake landed somewhere along Point Reyes to make extensive repairs to his only surviving ship, *The Golden Hind*. Drakes Bay, just east of Point Reyes, is marked as the spot of his landing, but the actual location is disputed. Drake eventually left California and completed the second recorded circumnavigation of the world (Ferdinand Magellan's was the first).

THE MISSION PERIOD

In the mid-1700s, Spain pushed for colonization of Alta California, rushing to occupy North America before the British beat them to it. The effort was overly ambitious and underfunded, but missionaries started to sweep into present-day California.

The priest Junípero Serra is credited with influencing the early development of California. A Franciscan monk, Serra took an active role in bringing Christianity and European diseases to Native American people from San Diego north to Sonoma County. The Franciscan order built a string of missions; each was intended to act as a self-sufficient parish that grew its own food, maintained its own buildings, and took care of its own people. However, mission structures were limited by a lack of suitable building materials and skilled labor. Later, the forced labor of Native Americans was used to cut and haul timbers and to make adobe bricks. By the time the missions were operating, they claimed about 15 percent of the land in California, or about one million acres per mission.

Spanish soldiers used subjugation to control indigenous people, pulling them from their villages and lands to the missions. Presidios (royal forts) were built near some of the missions to establish land claims, intimidate indigenous people, and carry out the overall goal of finding wealth in the New World. The presidios housed the Spanish soldiers that accompanied the missionaries. The cities of San Francisco, Santa Barbara, San Jose, and later Santa Cruz grew from the establishment of these missions and the presidios.

In 1821, Mexico gained independence from Spain along with control of Alta California and the missions. The Franciscans resisted giving up the land and free labor, and Native Americans continued to be treated as slaves. From 1824 to 1834 the Mexican government handed out 51 land grants to colonists for land that had belonged to Native Americans and was held by nearby missions. From 1834 to 1836 the Mexican government revoked the power of the Franciscans to use Native American labor and to redistribute the vast mission landholdings.

In the 20th century, interest in the history of the missions was rekindled, and funds were invested to restore many of the churches and complexes. Today, many of the missions have been restored as Catholic parishes, with visitors centers and museum displays of various levels of quality and polish. Some have been restored as state parks.

THE BEAR FLAG REVOLT

Mexico gained independence in 1821, claiming the Spanish lands that would become California and the U.S. Southwest. Hostilities between U.S. and Mexican troops began in April 1846 when a number of U.S. Army troops in the future state of Texas were attacked and killed. The first major battle of the Mexican-American War was fought the following month, and Congress responded with a declaration of war.

Rumors of possible Mexican military action against newly arrived settlers in California led a group of 30 settlers to seize the small Sonoma garrison in 1846. The uprising became known as the Bear Flag Revolt after a hastily designed flag depicting a grizzly bear and a five-point star was raised over Sonoma as the revolutionaries declared independence from Mexico. John A. Sutter, who had received a land grant near present-day Sacramento, and his men joined and supplied the revolt.

Captain John C. Frémont, who was leading a U.S. Army Corps of Topographical Engineers Exploratory Force, returned to California when he received word that war with Mexico was imminent and a revolt had occurred. The Bear Flag Revolt was short-lived; Frémont took over the rebellion and replaced the Bear Flag with the U.S. flag. Without orders and without knowing about the declaration of war, Frémont went on to the San Francisco Presidio to spike, or disable, the cannons there. More U.S. ships, marines, and sailors arrived and took control of California ports up and down the coast. Frémont's forces grew into the California Battalion, whose members were used mainly to garrison and keep order in the rapidly surrendering towns.

THE GOLD RUSH

James Marshall was a carpenter employed by John Sutter to build a sawmill in Coloma near Placerville. Marshall made a glittery discovery on January 24, 1848, in a nearby stream: gold. Soon news spread to Sacramento and San Francisco that chunks of gold were on the riverbeds for the taking, and the gold rush was on. Thousands of people streamed into California seeking gold. After gold seekers panned streams and water-blasted hillsides for gold, the construction started on the famous hard-rock mines of California. Although panning continued, by the 1860s most of the rough men had taken jobs working in the dangerous mines. The most productive region was a swath of land nearly 200 miles long, roughly from El Dorado south to Mariposa, known as the Mother Lode or Gold Country. Mining towns such as Sonora, Volcano, Placerville, Sutter's Creek, and Nevada City swelled to huge proportions, only to shrink back into obscurity as the mines eventually closed one by one. Today, Highway 49 winds from one historic gold rush town to the next, and gold mining has mostly given way to tourism.

As American and European men came to California to seek their fortunes in gold, a few wives and children joined them, but the number of families in the average mining town was small.

Another major group of immigrants came to California from China. These immigrants quickly established a booming district (Chinatown) in the center of San Francisco. Some went to work the gold fields, while others opened businesses to service the influx of visitors. By the end of the 1850s, one-fifth of the mining communities in Southern Gold Country were Chinese.

The dramatic population boom caused by the gold rush ensured that California would be on the fast track to admission into the United States, bypassing the territorial phase. California became a state in 1850—it had gone from a Mexican province to the 31st U.S. state in little more than four years.

THE RAILROADS

California's population swelled to more than 250,000 within three years of the gold rush. To avoid the grueling cross-country trip, Eastern industrialists pushed for a railroad to open the West.

Leading the charge was engineer Theodore D. Judah. Unlike most of his contemporaries, Judah was convinced that it was possible to build a railroad across the Sierra Nevada. After lobbying Washington, D.C., he managed to convince a group of Sacramento merchants—Leland Stanford, Charles Crocker,

Collis Huntington, and Mark Hopkins—to invest in the railroad. Known as the Big Four, they incorporated the Central Pacific Railroad in 1861.

The Big Four were instrumental in developing the state railroad system from 1861 to 1900. Stanford operated a general store for miners before becoming an American tycoon, industrialist, politician, and the founder of Stanford University. Crocker founded a small independent iron forge, invested in the railroad venture, and eventually gained a controlling interest in Wells Fargo Bank before buying the rest of the bank for his son. Huntington was a Sacramento merchant who later went on to build other railroads. Hopkins was another Sacramento merchant who formed a partnership with Huntington before joining him in investing in the transcontinental railroad.

In mid-1862 President Abraham Lincoln signed the Pacific Railroad Act, giving the Central Pacific Railroad the go-ahead to build the railroad east from Sacramento and the Union Pacific Railroad to build west from Omaha. The government used land grants and government loans to fund the project. Workers for the two companies met May 10, 1869, at Promontory Summit, Utah, to complete the nation's first transcontinental railroad with a ceremonial golden spike.

THE GREAT DEPRESSION

The stock market crash of 1929 led to the Great Depression. Many property owners lost their farms and homes, and unemployment in California hit 28 percent in 1932; by 1935, about 20 percent of all Californians were on public relief.

The Great Depression transformed the nation. Beyond the economic agony was an optimism that moved people to migrate to California. Settling primarily in the Central Valley, these Midwest transplants preserved their ways and retained identities separate from other Californians. The Midwest migrant plight was captured in John Steinbeck's

1939 novel *The Grapes of Wrath*. Steinbeck, a Salinas native, gathered information by viewing firsthand the deplorable living and labor conditions under which Okie families existed. The novel was widely read and was turned into a movie in 1940. Government agencies banned the book from public schools, and libraries and large landowners campaigned to have it banned elsewhere. That effort lost steam, however, when Steinbeck won the 1940 Pulitzer Prize.

Even during the worst economic depression in U.S. history, Californians continued to build and move forward. The San Francisco-Oakland Bay Bridge was completed in 1936 and the Golden Gate Bridge in 1937, connecting the land around San Francisco Bay and putting people to work. The 1939 Golden Gate International Exposition on Treasure Island in San Francisco Bay helped show the Great Depression the door.

WORLD WAR II

During World War II, San Francisco become the point of debarkation for the Pacific Theater, and a lead producer of liberty ships and military armaments.

Unfortunately, the state was also home to a deplorable chapter in the war—the internment camps for Japanese people and Japanese Americans. In reaction to the attack on Pearl Harbor, President Franklin Roosevelt signed Executive Order 9066 in 1942, creating "military exclusion zones" for people of Japanese ancestry. Approximately 110,000 Japanese Americans were uprooted and sent to war relocation camps in desolate areas such as Manzanar, in the dry basin of the Eastern Sierra; Tulelake, in the remote northeast corner of the state; and as far away as North Dakota and Oklahoma.

In San Francisco, the immigration station on Angel Island became a deportation center in addition to interring Japanese prisoners of war. Today, examples of their carved inscriptions on the prison walls remain as part of the museum in the old barracks building.

While many Japanese-Americans were allowed to return home after the war, their homes were gone and their neighborhoods had been transformed.

THE 1960S

Few places in the country felt the impact of the radical changes of the 1960s more than California. It's arguable that the peace and free-love movements began here, probably on the campus of the indomitable University of California, Berkeley. Certainly Berkeley helped to shape and foster the culture of hippies, peaceniks, and radical politics. The college campus was the home of the Black Panthers, anti-Vietnam War sit-ins, and numerous protests for many progressive causes.

If Berkeley was the de facto home of 1960s political movements, then San Francisco was the base of its social and cultural phenomena. Free concerts in Golden Gate Park and the growing fame of the hippie community taking over a neighborhood called Haight-Ashbury drew young people from across the country. Many found themselves living on Haight Street for months and experimenting with the mind-altering chemicals emblematic of the era. The music scene became the stuff of legend. The Grateful Dead—one of the most famous and longest-lasting of the 1960s rock bands—hailed from San Francisco.

CALIFORNIA TODAY

The spectacular growth of the tech industry began in Silicon Valley. From its origin in the halls of Stanford University, the electronics industry has led to innovations in personal computers, video games, networking systems, and the Internet. Tech giants such as Hewlett-Packard, Facebook, Google, and Apple still call the Silicon Valley and San Francisco Bay Area home and the effects of this boom are felt in the region's skyrocketing cost of living.

Essentials

Getting There

AIR

Northern California is easy to fly to, particularly if you're heading for one of the major metropolitan areas. Reaching the more rural outlying regions is a bit trickier, and you'll probably find yourself driving—possibly for hours—from one of the major airports.

San Francisco's major airport is San Francisco International Airport (SFO, 780 McDonnell Rd., San Francisco, 800/435-9736, www.flysfo.com), approximately 13 miles south of the city on U.S. 101. Plan to arrive at the airport up to three hours before your flight leaves. Airport lines, especially on weekends and holidays, are notoriously long, and planes can be grounded due to fog.

To avoid the SFO crowds, consider booking a flight into one of the Bay Area's less crowded airports. Oakland International Airport (OAK, 1 Airport Dr., Oakland, 510/563-3300, www.flyoakland.com) serves the East Bay with access to San Francisco via the Bay Bridge and BART, the regional commuter train. San Jose International Airport (SJC, Airport Blvd., San Jose, 408/392-3600, www.flysanjose.com) is south of San Francisco in the heart of Silicon Valley. These airports are quite a bit smaller than SFO, but service is brisk from many U.S. destinations.

Sacramento International Airport (SMF, Airport Blvd., Sacramento, 916/929-5411, www.sacramento.aero) is a good launching point for trips in the Central Valley, Gold Country, or the Sierra Nevada and Lake Tahoe areas.

If driving long distances is not for you, Southwest Airlines (www.southwest.com, 800/435-9792) offers many affordable connecting flights among these California airports. To reach the small but user-friendly airports in Monterey, Eureka, Crescent City, and Redding from the Bay Area, check with United Airlines (www.united.com, 800/864-8331).

Airport Transportation

Several public and private transportation options can get you into San Francisco. Bay Area Rapid Transit (BART, www.bart.gov) connects directly with SFO's international terminal, providing a simple and relatively fast (under 1 hour) trip to downtown San Francisco. The BART station is an easy walk or a free shuttle ride from any point in the airport; a one-way ticket to any downtown station costs $9.65. BART also runs a line to the Oakland Airport.

Caltrain (800/660-4287, www.caltrain.com, $3-13) is a good option if you are staying farther south on the peninsula. To access Caltrain from the airport, you must first take BART to the Millbrae stop, where the two lines meet. This station is designed for folks jumping from one line to the other. Caltrain tickets range $3.75-15 one-way depending on your destination.

Shuttle vans are another cost-effective option for door-to-door service, although these make several stops along the way. From the airport to downtown San Francisco, the average one-way fare is $17-25 per person. Shuttle vans congregate on the second level of SFO above the baggage claim area for domestic flights and on the third level for international flights. Advance reservations guarantee a seat, but these aren't required and don't necessarily speed the process. Companies include: GO Lorries Shuttle (415/334-9000, www.gosfovan.com), Quake City Shuttle (415/255-4899, www.

Winter Driving

It can snow in the mountains anytime between November and April; if you plan on crossing any high passes, make sure you have tire chains in your vehicle. In winter, the mountain passes on I-5 near Mount Shasta and on I-80 to Tahoe and over the Sierra Nevada can be very hazardous and may require chains, snow tires, or both. Close to Tahoe, many roadside chain installers set up in pullouts along the side of I-80 and will install tire chains for a hefty fee. Chains can also be rented at certain automotive stores and service stations.

Road closures elsewhere in the state can be common in winter. Highway 1 along the coast can shut down because of flooding or landslides. I-5 through the Central Valley can either close or be subject to hazardous driving conditions resulting from tule fog, which can reduce visibility to only a few feet. Some highways avoid these problems altogether by closing for part of the year. Highway 120, which runs over Tioga Pass and connects Yosemite Valley with the Eastern Sierra, is generally closed November-May.

The **California Department of Transportation** (Caltrans, 800/427-7623, www.dot.ca.gov) has a very user-friendly website to check current road conditions before your trip.

quakecityshuttle.com), and **SuperShuttle** (800/258-3826, www.supershuttle.com). Quake City also services Oakland Airport and San Jose. SuperShuttle services all four major California airports.

For **taxis,** the average fare to downtown San Francisco is around $40.

TRAIN

Several long-distance **Amtrak** (800/872-7245, www.amtrak.com) trains rumble through Northern California daily. There are five train routes that serve the region: The *California Zephyr* runs from Chicago and Denver to Emeryville; the *Capitol Corridor* serves Auburn, Sacramento, Emeryville, Oakland, and San Jose and is a popular route with local commuters; the *Coast Starlight* travels down the West Coast from Seattle and Portland as far as Los Angeles; the *Pacific Surfliner* will get you to the Central Coast from Southern California; and the *San Joaquin* connects the southern Central Valley to the Bay Area. There is no train depot in San Francisco; the closest station is in Emeryville in the East Bay. Fortunately, comfortable coach buses ferry travelers to and from the Emeryville Amtrak station with many stops in downtown San Francisco.

CAR

The main transportation artery in Northern California is **I-5,** which runs north-south from Oregon through Sacramento and ending at the Mexican border.

Highway 1, also known as the Pacific Coast Highway, follows the North Coast from Leggett to San Luis Obispo on the Central Coast and points south. Running parallel and intertwining with Highway 1 for much of its length, **U.S. 101** stretches north-south from the Oregon border to Los Angeles. These alternate routes are longer but prettier than I-5.

The main east-west conduit is **I-80,** which begins as part of the Bay Bridge in San Francisco and runs east through Sacramento to Tahoe and over the Sierra into Nevada. I-80 can close because of heavy winter snows.

Highway speeds in Northern California are generally 55 mph, unless otherwise posted. Larger freeways, such as I-80 and I-5, may have posted speed limits of 65-70 mph.

California law requires that all drivers carry liability insurance for their vehicles.

Getting Around

AIR

Domestic flights can be an economical and faster option when traversing between major cities within the state. The main airports are **San Francisco International Airport** (SFO, www.flysfo.com), **Oakland International Airport** (OAK, www.flyoakland.com), **San Jose International Airport** (SJC, www.flysanjose.com), and **Sacramento International Airport** (SMF, www.sacramento.aero).

Smaller regional airports include the **Monterey Regional Airport** (MRY, www.montereyairport.com), the **Redding Municipal Airport** (RDD, www.ci.redding.ca.us), the **Mammoth-Yosemite Airport** (MMH, http://ci.mammoth-lakes.ca.us), and the **Arcata-Eureka Airport** (ACV, http://co.humboldt.ca.us/aviation).

Southwest Airlines (www.southwest.com) provides affordable flights among the larger airports, while **United Airlines** (www.united.com) has regular flights to regional airports. Geared toward commuters, flights are generally frequent but a bit pricey.

TRAIN

Amtrak (www.amtrak.com) runs several trains through the state. The *California Zephyr, Capitol Corridor, Coast Starlight, Pacific Surfliner,* and *San Joaquin* routes offer services to Auburn, Sacramento, Emeryville, Oakland, San Jose, the Central Coast, and the Central Valley. Trains are roomy, comfortable, and offer a dining car for affordable snacks and meals. While there is no train station in San Francisco, Amtrak provides bus service between downtown San Francisco and Emeryville in the East Bay, the main Amtrak hub for this part of the state.

In the San Francisco Bay Area, **Bay Area Rapid Transit** (BART) is a high-speed train that runs from San Francisco south to the airport and across to the East Bay. **Caltrain** (www.caltrain.com) is largely a commuter train that runs from San Francisco down the peninsula as far as Gilroy, south of San Jose.

BUS

The **San Francisco Station** (200 Folsom St., 415/495-1569) is a hub for **Greyhound** (800/231-2222, www.greyhound.com) bus lines serving Northern California. Other major stations include Oakland (2103 San Pablo Ave., 510/823-4730), San Jose (65 Cahill St., 408/295-4153), and Sacramento (420 Richards Blvd., 916/444-6858). Greyhound routes generally follow the major highways, traveling up U.S. 101 through Santa Rosa to Arcata, along I-5 through Redding and Mount Shasta, near I-80 to Reno, and south through San Jose to Santa Cruz. Greyhound does not go to destinations like Wine Country and Gold Country.

Megabus (https://us.megabus.com) offers low-cost, long-distance bus service from San Francisco (Townsend St. at 5th St.) to Sacramento (6740 Q St., 2 hours, $5 one-way) multiple times daily.

CAR AND RV

California is great for road trips. Scenic coastal routes such as Highway 1 and U.S. 101 are often destinations in themselves, while inland I-5 is the most direct route north-south through the state. However, traffic congestion, accidents, mudslides, fires, and snow can affect highways at any time. To explore Northern California safely, have a good map and check road conditions online with the **California Department of Transportation** (Caltrans, 800/427-7623, www.dot.ca.gov) before departure. The *Thomas Guide Road Atlas* (www.mapbooks4u.com, $15) is a reliable and detailed map and road guide and a great insurance policy against getting lost.

Larger highways like I-5 and I-80 are relatively easy to navigate, but many smaller two-lane highways that connect Northern California's rural destinations offer scenic and leisurely alternatives. Mountain passes such as I-80 to Tahoe and I-5 in the Shasta and Lassen regions may require snow tires or chains at any time. In rural areas, gas stations may be few and far between.

The left lanes of most major Bay Area freeways become **carpool lanes** during the heaviest commute times (generally 7am-10am and 3pm-7pm). Posted signs list the hours of operation, the number of people you have to have in your car to use the lanes, and the often hefty fine for violating.

Bridge tolls are charged to cross the **Bay Bridge** (westbound, $6), the **Richmond Bridge** (westbound, $6), and the **Golden Gate Bridge** (southbound, $7.75). Bay Area commuters pay electronically via **FasTrak** (www.bayareafastrak.org), a transponder in their car that deducts the toll from the user's account as they pass through the toll plaza. For those without FasTrak, the toll is collected via a bill mailed to the address listed on record with the vehicle license plate.

Car and RV Rental

Most car rental companies are located at major airports. To reserve a car in advance, contact **Budget Rent A Car** (800/527-0700, www.budget.com), **Dollar Rent A Car** (800/800-5252, www.dollar.com), **Enterprise** (800/266-9289, www.enterprise.com), or **Hertz** (800/654-3131, www.hertz.com).

To rent a car, drivers in California must be at least 21 years of age and have a valid driver's license. California law also requires that all vehicles carry liability insurance. You can purchase insurance with your rental car, but it generally costs an additional $10 per day, which can add up quickly. Most private auto insurance will also cover rental cars. Before buying rental insurance, check your car insurance policy to see if rental car coverage is included.

The average cost of a rental car is $60-120 per day or $250-600 per week; however, rates vary greatly based on the time of year and distance traveled. Weekend and summer rentals cost significantly more. Generally, it is more expensive to rent from car rental agencies at an airport. To avoid excessive rates, first plan travel to areas where a car is not required, then rent a car from an agency branch in town to explore more rural areas. Rental agencies occasionally allow vehicle drop-off at a different location from where it was picked up for an additional fee.

If you rent an RV, you won't have to worry about camping or lodging options, and many facilities, particularly farther north, accommodate RVs. However, RVs are difficult to maneuver and park, limiting your access to metropolitan areas. They are also expensive, in terms of both gas and the rental rates. Rates during the summer average $945-1,614 per week and $400-1,345 for three days, the standard minimum rental. **Cruise America** (800/671-8042, www.cruiseamerica.com) has branches in San Jose, Sacramento, San Mateo, and at SFO. **El Monte RV** (415/771-8770, www.elmonterv.com) has two locations: in Sacramento and near SFO.

Travel Tips

VISAS AND OFFICIALDOM
Passports and Visas

If visiting from another country, you must have a valid passport and a visa (https://travel.state.gov) to enter the United States. In most other countries, the local U.S. embassy should be able to provide a tourist visa.

The average fee for a visa is US$160. While a visa may be processed as quickly as 24 hours on request, plan at least a couple of weeks, as there can be unexpected delays, particularly during the busy summer season (June-Aug.).

Check with the U.S. Department of Homeland Security (www.cbp.gov) to see if you qualify for the Visa Waiver Program (www.dhs.gov/visa-waiver-program). Passport holders of certain countries can apply online with the Electronic System for Travel Authorization at least 72 hours before traveling. Have a return plane or cruise ticket to your country of origin dated less than 90 days from your date of entry. Holders of Canadian passports don't need visas or visa waivers.

Embassies

San Francisco has embassies and consulates from many countries around the globe. If you should lose your passport or find yourself in some other trouble while visiting California, contact your country's offices for assistance. To find an embassy, check online at www.state.gov, which lists the websites for all foreign embassies in the United States. A representative will be able to direct you to the nearest embassy or consulate.

Customs

Before you enter the United States from another country by sea or by air, you'll be required to fill out a customs form. Check with the U.S. embassy in your country or the Customs and Border Protection (www.cbp.gov) for an updated list of items you must declare.

If you require medication administered by injection, you must pack your syringes in a checked bag; syringes are not permitted in carry-ons coming into the United States.

Also, pack documentation describing your need for any narcotic medications you've brought with you. Failure to produce documentation for narcotics on request can result in severe penalties in the United States.

If you're driving into California along I-5 or another major highway, prepare to stop at Agricultural Inspection Stations a few miles inside the state line. You don't need to present a passport, a visa, or even a driver's license; instead, you must be prepared to present all your fruits and vegetables. California's largest economic sector is agriculture, and a number of the major crops grown here are sensitive to pests and diseases. If you've got produce, especially homegrown or from a farm stand, it could be infected by a known problem pest or disease. Expect it to be confiscated on the spot.

TOURIST INFORMATION

When visiting California, you might be tempted to stop in at one of several Golden State Welcome Centers (www.visitcwc.com) scattered throughout the state. If you're in an area that doesn't have its own visitors center, the State Welcome Center might be a useful place to pick up maps and brochures. Otherwise, stick with local, regional, and national park visitors centers, which tend to be staffed by volunteers or rangers who feel a real passion for their locale.

If you are looking for maps, almost all gas stations and drugstores sell maps both of the place you're in and of the whole state. AAA of Northern California (www.csaa.com) is the auto club for Northern California, and it offers free maps to auto club members.

Many local and regional visitors centers also offer maps, but you'll need to pay a few dollars for the bigger and better ones. But if all you need is a wine-tasting map in a known wine region, you can probably get one for free along with a few tasting coupons at the nearest regional visitors center. Basic national park maps come with your admission payment. State park maps can be free or cost a few dollars at the visitors centers.

Visit California (916/444-4429, www.visitcalifornia.com) is a nonprofit that provides helpful and free tips, information, and downloadable maps and guides.

California is in the Pacific time zone (PST and PDT) and observes daylight saving time March-November.

Money

California businesses use the U.S. dollar ($). Most businesses also accept the major credit cards Visa, MasterCard, Discover, and American Express. ATM and debit cards work at many stores and restaurants, and ATMs are available throughout the region. In remoter areas, such as Gold Country and the North Coast, some businesses may only accept cash, so don't depend entirely on your plastic.

You can change currency at any international airport in the state. Currency exchange points also crop up in downtown San Francisco and at some of the major business hotels in urban areas.

California is not a particularly expensive place to travel, but keeping an eye on your budget is still important. San Francisco and the Wine Country are the priciest regions for visitors, especially with the amount of high-quality food and luxury accommodations. Advance reservations for hotels and marquee restaurants in these areas are recommended.

Banks

As with anywhere, traveling with a huge amount of cash is not recommended, which may make frequent trips to the bank necessary. Fortunately, most destinations have at least one major bank. Usually Bank of America or Wells Fargo can be found on the main drags through towns. Banking hours tend to be 8am-5pm Monday-Friday, 9am-noon Saturday. Never count on a bank being open on Sunday or federal holidays. If you need cash when the banks are closed, there is generally a 24-hour ATM available. Furthermore, many cash-only businesses have an ATM on-site for those who don't have enough cash ready in their wallets. The unfortunate downside to this convenience is a fee of $2-4 per transaction. This also applies to ATMs at banks at which you don't have an account.

Tax

Sales tax in California varies by city and county, but the average rate is around 8.5 percent. All goods are taxable with the exception of food not eaten on the premises. For example, your bill at a restaurant will include tax, but your bill at a grocery store will not. The hotel tax is another unexpected added expense to traveling in California. Most cities have enacted a tax on hotel rooms largely to make up for budget shortfalls. As you would expect, these taxes are higher in areas more popular with visitors. In Wine Country you can expect to add an additional 12-14 percent onto your hotel bill, while in San Francisco the tax tops 15 percent. Some areas, like Eureka, have a lower hotel tax of 10 percent.

Tipping

Tipping is expected and appreciated, and a 15 percent tip for restaurants is about the norm. When ordering in bars, tip the bartender or waitstaff $1 per drink. For taxis, plan to tip 15-20 percent of the fare, or simply round the cost up to the nearest dollar. Cafés and coffee shops often have tip jars out. There is no consensus on what is appropriate when purchasing a $3 beverage. Often $0.50 is enough, depending on the quality and service.

Tipping is also expected in hotels and B&Bs; look for an envelope to tip housekeeping staff. Depending on the type of accommodations, $2-5 per night is the standard rate.

Communications and Media

The major newspaper is the *San Francisco Chronicle*. (www.sfgate.com). KQED (88.5 FM) is San Francisco's NPR radio station that can also be heard in Sacramento (89.3 FM).

California has multiple area codes throughout the state: the city of San Francisco (415); the San Francisco Bay Area (510 and 925); San Mateo County, including Palo Alto (650); San Jose (408); Monterey County (831); Wine Country and the North Coast (707); Sacramento and Gold Country (916); and Lake Tahoe (530 and 775). The 800, 866, or 888 area codes are toll-free numbers. When dialing outside the area code, dial 1, then the area code, followed by the seven-digit number.

CONDUCT AND CUSTOMS

The legal drinking age in California is 21. Expect to have your ID checked if you look under age 30, especially in bars and clubs, but also in restaurants and wineries. Most California bars and clubs close at 2am; you'll find the occasional after-hours nightspot in San Francisco.

Smoking has been banned in many places throughout California. Don't expect to find a smoking section in any restaurant or an ashtray in any bar. Smoking is illegal in all bars and clubs, but your new favorite watering hole might have an outdoor patio where smokers can huddle. Taking the ban one step further, many hotels, motels, and inns throughout Northern California are strictly nonsmoking, and you'll be subject to fees of hundreds of dollars if your room smells of smoke when you leave.

There's no smoking in any public building, and even some of the state parks don't allow cigarettes. There's often good reason for this; the fire danger in California is extreme in the summer, and one carelessly thrown butt can cause a genuine catastrophe.

In 2018, recreational marijuana was legalized in California. Users must be over age 21 in order to buy and possess marijuana. Smoking is only allowed on private property (not in public). Each individual is allowed to possess a maximum of one ounce (or eight grams) of cannabis concentrate, such as those found in edibles. Driving under the influence of marijuana is strictly prohibited; open packages must be stowed safely in the trunk.

ACCESS FOR TRAVELERS WITH DISABILITIES

Most Northern California attractions, hotels, and restaurants are accessible for travelers with disabilities. State law requires that public transportation must accommodate the special needs of travelers with disabilities and that public spaces and businesses have adequate restroom facilities and equal access. This includes national parks and historical structures, many of which have been refitted with ramps and wider doors. Most parks have one or two trails that are accessible to wheelchairs, and campgrounds often designate specific campsites that meet the Americans with Disabilities Act standards. The state of California also provides a free telephone TDD-to-voice relay service; just dial 711.

If you are traveling with a disability, there are many resources to help you plan your trip. **Access Northern California** (http://accessnca.org) is a nonprofit organization that offers general travel tips, including recommendations on accommodations, activities, parks and trails, transportation, and travel equipment. The organization also publishes the website www.wheelingcalscoast.org for those in wheelchairs visiting the California coast with information on accessible beaches and parks, historic sites, and attractions, as well as general travel resources.

Gimp-on-the-Go (www.gimponthego. com) offers general travel tips, while the **American Foundation for the Blind** (www.afb.org) message board is a good forum to discuss travel strategies for the visually impaired.

San Francisco's **Wheelchair Getaways** (800/642-2042, www.wheelchairgetaways.com, $95-110 per day) rents wheelchair-accessible vans and offers pickup and drop-off service ($100-300) from San Francisco, Oakland, San Jose, and Sacramento airports.

Scootaround (888/879-4273, www.scootaround.com, $115-215/day) rents cars, scooters, and wheelchairs to make traveling with a disability easier. Delivery is available (additional fee).

TRAVELING WITH CHILDREN

Many spots in California are ideal destinations for families with children of all ages. Amusement parks, interactive museums, zoos, parks, beaches, and playgrounds all make for family-friendly fun. On the other hand, there are a few spots in the Golden State that beckon more to adults than to children. Frankly, there aren't many family activities in Wine Country. This adult playground is all about alcoholic beverages and high-end dining. Similarly, the North Coast's focus on original art and romantic B&Bs brings out couples looking for weekend getaways rather than families. In fact, before you book a room at a B&B that you expect to share with your kids, check to be sure that the inn can accommodate extra people in the guest rooms and whether they allow guests under age 16.

WOMEN TRAVELING ALONE

California is a pretty friendly place for women traveling alone. Most of the major outdoor attractions are incredibly safe, and even many of the urban areas boast pleasant neighborhoods that welcome lone female travelers. But you'll need to take some basic precautions and pay attention to your surroundings, just as you would in any unfamiliar place. When you're walking down a city street, be alert and keep an eye on your surroundings and on anyone who might be following you. In rural areas, don't go tromping into unlit wooded areas or out into grassy fields alone at night without a flashlight; many of California's critters are nocturnal. Of course, this caution applies to men as well; mountain lions and rattlesnakes don't tend to discriminate.

SENIOR TRAVELERS

Throughout the state you'll find senior discounts nearly every place you go, including restaurants, golf courses, major attractions, and even some hotels, though the minimum age can range 50-70. Be prepared to produce ID when requesting a senior discount. You can often get additional discounts on rental cars, hotels, and tour packages as a member of AARP (888/687-2277, www.aarp.org). If you're not a member, its website can also offer helpful travel tips and advice. Elderhostel (800/454-5768, www.roadscholar.org) is another great resource for senior travelers. Dedicated to providing educational opportunities for older travelers, Elderhostel provides package trips to beautiful and interesting destinations. Called "Educational Adventures," these trips are generally 3-13 days long and emphasize history, natural history, art, music, or a combination thereof.

GAY AND LESBIAN TRAVELERS

The Golden State is a golden place for gay travel—especially in the bigger cities and even in some of the smaller towns around the state. As with much of the country, the farther you venture into rural and agricultural regions, the less likely you are to experience the liberal acceptance the state is known for.

San Francisco has the biggest and arguably best Gay Pride Festival (www.sfpride.org) in the nation, usually held on Market Street on the last weekend in June. Year-round, the Castro district offers fun of all kinds, from theater to clubs to shopping, mostly targeted at gay men but with a few places sprinkled in for lesbians. If the Castro is your primary destination, you can even find a place to stay in the middle of the action.

Santa Cruz on the Central Coast is a quirky town specially known for its lesbian-friendly culture. A relaxed vibe informs everything from underground clubs to unofficial nude beaches to live-action role-playing games in the middle of downtown. Even the lingerie and adult toy shops tend to be woman-owned and operated.

Many gay and lesbian San Francisco residents go to Guerneville for a weekend escape. This outdoorsy town on the Russian River has rustic lodges, vacation rentals, and cabins down by the river; rafting and kayaking

companies offer summertime adventures, and nearby wineries offer relaxation. The short but colorful Main Street is home to queer-friendly bars and festivals.

The oh-so-fabulous California vibe has even made it to the interior of the state—Sacramento's newly revitalized Midtown neighborhood offers a more low-key but visible gay evening scene.

Health and Safety

MEDICAL SERVICES

For an emergency anywhere in California, dial 911. Inside hotels and resorts, check your emergency number as soon as you get to your guest room. In urban and suburban areas, full-service hospitals and medical centers abound, but in remoter regions, help can be more than an hour away.

WILDERNESS SAFETY

If you're planning a backcountry expedition, follow all rules and guidelines for obtaining wilderness permits and for self-registration at trailheads. These are for your safety, letting the rangers know roughly where you plan to be and when to expect you back. National and state park visitors centers can advise in more detail on any health or wilderness alerts in the area. It is also advisable to let someone outside your party know your route and expected date of return.

Heat Exhaustion and Heatstroke

Being out in the elements can present its own set of challenges. Despite California's relatively mild climate, heat exhaustion and heatstroke can affect anyone during the hot summer months, particularly during a long strenuous hike in the sun. Common symptoms include nausea, lightheadedness, headache, or muscle cramps. Dehydration and loss of electrolytes are the common causes of heat exhaustion. If you or anyone in your group

develops any of these symptoms, get out of the sun immediately, stop all physical activity, and drink plenty of water. Heat exhaustion can be severe, and if untreated can lead to heatstroke, in which the body's core temperature reaches 105°F. Fainting, seizures, confusion, and rapid heartbeat and breathing can indicate the situation has moved beyond heat exhaustion. If you suspect this, call 911 immediately.

Hypothermia

Hypothermia is caused by prolonged exposure to cold water or weather. For many in California, this can happen on a hike or backpacking trip without sufficient rain gear, or by staying too long in the ocean or another cold body of water without a wetsuit. Symptoms include shivering, weak pulse, drowsiness, confusion, slurred speech, or stumbling. To treat hypothermia, immediately remove the wet clothing, cover the person with blankets, and feed him or her hot liquids. If symptoms don't improve, call 911.

Altitude Sickness

You don't have to be outdoors to suffer from altitude sickness. A flu-like illness, it can affect anyone who has made a quick transition from low to high elevation. It occurs most commonly above 8,000 feet, but some individuals suffer at lower elevations. Headaches are the most common symptom, followed by nausea, dizziness, fatigue, and even the swelling of hands, feet, and face. Symptoms either go away once the individual has acclimated to the thinner air and lower oxygen levels or they don't, requiring either medical attention or a return to lower elevation. To prevent altitude sickness, avoid any strenuous exercise, including hiking, for the first 24 hours of your stay. Drinking alcohol also exacerbates altitude sickness because it can cause dehydration.

Water Safety

Swimming and surfing in the Pacific Ocean should be approached with caution. Temperatures range 50-60 degrees F and prolonged exposure without a wetsuit may result in hypothermia. Sneaker waves, rip currents, and undertows are common, making even wading potentially dangerous. Before entering the water, check swim conditions at the beach and follow safety guidelines. Watch children when playing in the surf and never turn your back on the ocean.

Swift-moving rivers can be equally hazardous. Drowning is the leading cause of death in places like Kings Canyon National Park, where currents are faster than they appear and inviting rivers can quickly swell their banks with snowmelt. Check and follow park guidelines for posted warnings.

Wildlife

Many places are still wild in California, making it important to use precautions with regard to wildlife. While California no longer has any grizzly bears, black bears thrive and are often seen in the mountains foraging for food in the spring, summer, and fall. **Black bears** certainly don't have the size or reputation of grizzlies, but there is good reason to exercise caution. Never get between a bear and her cub, and if a bear sees you, identify yourself as human by waving your hands above your head, speaking in calm voice, and backing away slowly. If a bear charges, do not run. One of the best precautions against an unwanted bear encounter is to keep a clean camp, store all food in airtight bear-proof containers, and strictly follow any guidelines given by the park or rangers.

Even more common than bears are **mountain lions,** which can be found in the Sierra foothills, the Coast Range, grasslands, and forests. Because of their solitary nature, it is unlikely you will see one, even on long trips in the backcountry. Still, there are a couple things to remember. If you come across a kill, probably a large partly eaten deer, leave immediately. And if you see a mountain lion and it sees you, identify yourself as human, making your body appear as big as possible, just as with a bear. And remember: Never run. As with any cat, large or small, running triggers its hunting instincts. If a mountain lion should attack, fight back; cats don't like to get hurt.

The other treacherous critter in the backcountry is the **rattlesnake.** They can be found in summer in generally hot and dry areas from the coast to the Sierra Nevada. When hiking in this type of terrain—many parks will indicate if rattlesnakes are a problem in the area—keep your eyes on the ground and an ear out for the telltale rattle. Snakes like to warn you to keep away. The only time this is not the case is with baby rattlesnakes that have not yet developed their rattles. Unfortunately, they have developed their fangs and venom, which is particularly potent. Should you get bitten, seek immediate medical help.

Mosquitoes can be found throughout the state, particularly in the Central Valley and the Sierra Nevada. At higher elevations they can be worse, prompting many hikers and backpackers to don head nets and apply potent repellents, usually DEET. The high season for mosquitoes in this area is late spring-early summer, at the end of snowmelt when there is lots of still freshwater in which to multiply. In the Central Valley, there has been concern over West Nile virus, which can cause nausea, diarrhea, and fever for 3-6 days. In very rare cases, the illness becomes more serious, and medical attention becomes necessary.

Ticks live in many of the forests and

grasslands throughout the state, except at higher elevations. Tick season generally runs late fall-early summer. If you are hiking through brushy areas, wear pants and long-sleeve shirts. Ticks like to crawl to warm moist places (armpits are a favorite) on their host. If a tick is engorged, it can be difficult to remove. There are two main types of ticks found in Northern California: dog ticks and deer ticks. Dog ticks are larger, brown, and have a gold spot on their backs, while deer ticks are small, tear-shaped, and black. Deer ticks are known to carry Lyme disease. While Lyme disease is relatively rare in California—there are more cases in the northernmost part of the state—it is very serious. If you get bitten by a deer tick and the bite leaves a red ring, seek medical attention. Lyme disease can be successfully treated with early rounds of antibiotics.

There is only one major variety of plant in California that can cause an adverse reaction in humans if you touch the leaves or stems: poison oak, a common shrub that inhabits forests throughout the state. Poison oak has a characteristic three-leaf configuration, with scalloped leaves that are shiny green in the spring and then turn yellow, orange, and red in late summer-fall. In fall the leaves drop, leaving a cluster of innocuous-looking branches. The oil in poison oak is present year-round in both the leaves and branches. Your best protection is to wear long sleeves and long pants when hiking, no matter how hot it is. A product called Tecnu is available at most California drugstores—slather it on before you go hiking to protect yourself from poison oak. If your skin comes into contact with poison oak, expect an itchy, irritating rash. Poison oak is also extremely transferable, so avoid touching your eyes, face, or other parts of your body. Calamine lotion can help, and in extreme cases a doctor can administer cortisone to help decrease the inflammation.

CRIME AND SAFETY PRECAUTIONS

The outdoors is not the only place that harbors danger. In both rural and urban areas, theft can be a problem. When parking at a trailhead or in a park or at a beach, don't leave any valuables in the car. If you must, place them out of sight either in a locked glove box or in the trunk. The same holds true for urban areas. Furthermore, avoid keeping your wallet, camera, and other expensive items, including lots of cash, easily accessible in backpacks; keep them within your sight at all times. Certain neighborhoods in San Francisco and Oakland are best avoided at night. However, many of them, like the Mission and Tenderloin districts in San Francisco or downtown Oakland, are also home to great restaurants, clubs, and music venues. If you find yourself in these areas after dark, consider taking a cab to avoid walking blocks and blocks to get to your car or to wait for public transportation. In case of a theft or any other emergency, call 911.

Resources

Suggested Reading

FICTION

Kerouac, Jack. *Desolation Angels*. New York: Penguin, 2012.

Kerouac, Jack. *Dharma Bums*. New York: Penguin, 2006

London, Jack. *The Valley of the Moon*. Berkeley: University of California Press, 1999.

Maupin, Armistead. *Tales of the City*. New York: Harper, 2007

Stegner, Wallace. *Angle of Repose*. New York: Penguin, 1992.

Steinbeck, John. *Cannery Row*. New York: Penguin, 2002.

Steinbeck, John. *East of Eden*. New York: Penguin, 2002.

Stevenson, Robert Louis. *The Complete Short Stories of Robert Louis Stevenson: Strange Case of Dr. Jekyll and Mr. Hyde and Nineteen Other Tales*. New York: Modern Library, 2002.

FIELD GUIDES

Alden, Peter, and Fred Heath. *National Audubon Field Guide to California*. New York: Knopf, 1998.

Alt, David. *Roadside Geology of Northern and Central California*. Missoula, MT: Mountain Press, 2016.

Blackwell, Laird. *Wildflowers of California: A Month-By-Month Guide*. Berkeley: University of California Press, 2012.

Quady, David. *Birds of Northern California*. Olympia, WA: R.W. Morse Co, 2015.

HISTORY

Belden, L. Burr, and Mary DeDecker. *Death Valley to Yosemite: Frontier Mining Camps and Ghost Towns*. Bishop, CA: Spotted Dog Press, 2000.

Brands, H. W. *The Age of Gold: The California Gold Rush and the New American Dream*. New York: Anchor, 2003.

Brechin, Gray. *Imperial San Francisco: Urban Power, Earthly Ruin*. Berkeley: University of California Press, 2006.

Fradkin, Philip. *The Seven States of California: A Natural and Human History*. Berkeley: University of California Press, 1997.

Gudde, Erwin G., and William O. Bright. *California Place Names: The Origin and Etymology of Current Geographical Names*. Berkeley: University of California Press, 2010.

Gutiérrez, Ramon A., and Richard J. Orsi, eds. *Contested Eden: California Before the Gold Rush*. Berkeley: University of California Press, 1998.

Kroeber, Theodora. *Ishi in Two Worlds: A Biography of the Last Wild Indian in North America.* Berkeley: University of California Press, 2011.

Margolin, Malcolm. *The Way We Lived: California Indian Stories, Songs, and Reminiscences.* Berkeley, CA: Heyday Press, 2017.

Reisner, Marc. *Cadillac Desert: The American West and Its Disappearing Water.* New York: Penguin, 1993.

Star, Kevin. *California: A History.* New York: Modern Library, 2007.

Sullivan, Charles. *A Companion to California Wine: An Encyclopedia of Wine and Winemaking from the Mission Period to the Present.* Berkeley: University of California Press, 1998.

Talbot, David. *Season of the Witch: Enchantment, Terror, and Deliverance in the City of Love.* New York: Free Press, 2013.

NATURAL HISTORY

Bakker, Elna, and Gordy Slack. *An Island Called California.* Berkeley: University of California Press, 1985.

McPhee, John. *Assembling California.* New York: Farrar, Straus and Giroux, 1994.

Schoenherr, Allan A. *A Natural History of California.* Berkeley: University of California Press, 2017.

TRAVEL

Brown, Ann Marie. *Moon 101 Great Hikes of the San Francisco Bay Area.* Berkeley, CA: Avalon Travel, 2018.

Stienstra, Tom. *Moon California Camping.* Berkeley, CA: Avalon Travel, 2017.

Stienstra, Tom, and Ann Marie Brown. *Moon California Hiking.* Berkeley, CA: Avalon Travel, 2016.

Thornton, Stuart. *Moon Coastal California.* Berkeley, CA: Avalon Travel, 2018.

Veneman, Elizabeth Linhart. *Moon California.* Berkeley, CA: Avalon Travel, 2017.

Veneman, Elizabeth Linhart. *Moon Napa & Sonoma.* Berkeley, CA: Avalon Travel, 2017.

Internet Resources

CALIFORNIA

California Department of Transportation
www.dot.ca.gov
Contains state map and highway information.

Visit California
www.visitcalifornia.com
The official tourism site of the state of California.

REGIONAL SITES

Central Coast Regional Tourism

www.centralcoast-tourism.com
A guide to the Central Coast region, including Santa Cruz and Monterey.

Eureka-Humboldt Vistors Bureau
www.visitredwoods.com
Information about activities and events throughout Humboldt County.

NapaValley.com
www.napavalley.com
A tourism website for Napa County.

Sacramento Convention and Visitors Bureau

www.visitsacramento.com
The official website of the Sacramento Convention and Visitors Bureau.

San Francisco Travel

www.sftravel.com
The official website of the San Francisco Visitors Bureau.

Shasta and Lassen Regional Tourism

www.shastacascade.org
The California Travel and Tourism Information Network includes information and a downloadable visitors guide to Mount Shasta, Shasta Lake, Redding, and Lassen.

Visit California Gold Country

www.calgold.org
The website from the Gold Country Visitors Association, with information about Grass Valley, Nevada City, Placer County, Sacramento, and Amador County.

Visit Mendocino

www.visitmendocino.com
The website for the Mendocino County tourism board.

PARKS AND OUTDOORS

California State Parks

www.parks.ca.gov
The official website lists hours, accessibility, activities, camping areas, fees, and more information for all parks in the state system.

Lassen Volcanic National Park

www.nps.gov/lavo
The official website for Lassen Volcanic National Park.

Redwood National Park

www.nps.gov/redw
The official website for all Redwood State and National Parks.

Reserve California

www.reservecalifornia.com
The online reservation system for California State Parks.

San Francisco Golden Gate National Recreation Area

www.nps.gov/goga
Information for the national parks and recreation areas in the San Francisco Bay Area.

Sequoia and Kings Canyon National Parks

www.nps.gov/seki
The official website for Sequoia and Kings Canyon.

State of California

www.ca.gov/tourism/greatoutdoors.html
Outdoor resources for California state and government organizations. Check for information about fishing and hunting licenses, backcountry permits, boating regulations, and more.

Yosemite National Park

www.nps.gov/yose
The National Park Service website for Yosemite National Park.

Yosemite National Park Vacation and Lodging Information

www.yosemitepark.com
The concessionaire website for Yosemite National Park lodging, dining, and reservations.

Index

C

List of Maps

Photo Credits

All photos © Elizabeth Linhart Veneman except page 10 © Coleong | Dreamstime.com; page 14 © Adeliepenguin | Dreamstime.com; page 15 © Yun Gao | Dreamstime.com; page 19 © Andreykr | Dreamstime.com; page 20 © Lucidwaters | Dreamstime.com; page 22 © Andrew Zarivny/123rf.com; page 23 © Luckyphotographer | Dreamstime.com; page 25 © Thicoz | Dreamstime.com; page 27 © Mblach | Dreamstime.com; page 28 © Paulbradyphoto | Dreamstime.com; page 30 © Emersont | Dreamstime.com; page 32 © Sepavo | Dreamstime.com; page 159 © Stuart Thornton; Dreamstime.com; page 161 © Dreamstime.com; page 169 © Dreamstime.com; page 180 © Dreamstime.com; page 188 © Stuart Thornton; page 199 © Dreamstime.com; page 213 © Stuart Thornton; page 216 © Stuart Thornton; page 219 © Stuart Thornton; page 224 © Stuart Thornton; page 230 © Stuart Thornton; page 244 © Maislam | Dreamstime.com; page 245 © Miker37 | Dreamstime.com; page 258 © Mariusz Jurgielewicz/123rf.com; page 261 © Photoquest | Dreamstime.com; page 411 © Lunamarina | Dreamstime.com; page 413 © Violafattore | Dreamstime.com; page 417 © Wolterk | Dreamstime.com; page 419 © Stuart Thornton; page 422 © A4ndreas | Dreamstime.com; page 425 © Stuart Thornton; page 426 © Stuart Thornton; page 438 © Stuart Thornton; page 440 © Stuart Thornton; page 446 © Stuart Thornton; page 450 © Snovitsky | Dreamstime.com; page 453 © Kavram | Dreamstime.com; page 456 © Stuart Thornton; page 461 © Maislam | Dreamstime.com; page 463 © Stuart Thornton; page 464 © Stuart Thornton; page 465 © Azahirar | Dreamstime.com; page 466 © Luckyphotographer | Dreamstime.com; page 471 © Stuart Thornton; page 473 © Stuart Thornton; page 476 © Stuart Thornton; page 479 © Vladirochka | Dreamstime.com; page 482 © Stuart Thornton; page 497 © Masterlu | Dreamstime.com; Diomedes66 | Dreamstime.com

ACADIA
NATIONAL PARK
HILARY NANGLE

ARCHES &
CANYONLANDS
NATIONAL PARKS

BANFF
NATIONAL PARK

DEATH VALLEY
NATIONAL PARK

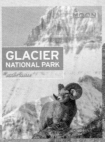

GLACIER
NATIONAL PARK

GRAND
CANYON

KATHLEEN BRYANT

GREAT SMOKY
MOUNTAINS
NATIONAL PARK

JASON FRYE

MOUNT RUSHMORE
& THE BLACK HILLS

LAURAL A. BIDWELL

ROCKY MOUNTAIN
NATIONAL PARK

ERIN ENGLISH

YELLOWSTONE
& GRAND TETON

BECKY LOMAX

YOSEMITE,
SEQUOIA &
KINGS CANYON

ANN MARIE BROWN

ZION &
BRYCE

W. C. MCRAE, JUDY JEWELL

In these books:

- Full coverage of gateway cities and towns
- Itineraries from one day to multiple weeks
- Advice on where to stay (or camp) in and around the parks

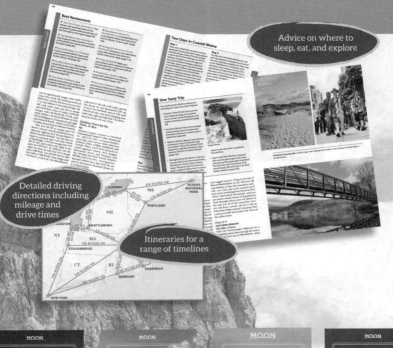

Explore California's great outdoors

101 GREAT HIKES
SAN FRANCISCO BAY AREA

MOON
CALIFORNIA CAMPING
The Complete Guide to More Than 1,400 Tent and RV Campgrounds
TOM STIENSTRA

MOON
CALIFORNIA HIKING
The Complete Guide to 1,000 of The Best Hikes in the Golden State
TOM STIENSTRA • ANN MARIE BROWN

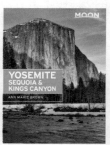

MOON
YOSEMITE SEQUOIA & KINGS CANYON
ANN MARIE BROWN

Plan a weekend adventure

MOON
LOS ANGELES

MOON
SAN DIEGO
IAN ANDERSON

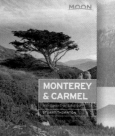

MOON
MONTEREY & CARMEL
with Santa Cruz & Big Sur
STUART THORNTON

NAPA & SONOMA

MOON
PALM SPRINGS & JOSHUA TREE

MOON
TAHOE
ANN MARIE BROWN

Or go big and go abroad

MOON
TRIP OF A LIFETIME
ANGKOR WAT

MOON
CROATIA & SLOVENIA

MOON
TRIP OF A LIFETIME
GALÁPAGOS ISLANDS

MOON
TRIP OF A LIFETIME
MACHU PICCHU

MOON
ROME, FLORENCE & VENICE

#TravelWithMoon

MAP SYMBOLS

▰▰▰	Expressway	○	City/Town	✕	Airport	⛳	Golf Course
▱▱▱	Primary Road	◉	State Capital	✕	Airfield	▯	Parking Area
▱▱	Secondary Road	⊛	National Capital	▲	Mountain	⚎	Archaeological Site
------	Unpaved Road	★	Point of Interest	+	Unique Natural Feature	♟	Church
——	Feature Trail	•	Accommodation			⬒	Gas Station
- - - -	Other Trail	▼	Restaurant/Bar	⟿	Waterfall		Glacier
··········	Ferry	▪	Other Location	♠	Park		Mangrove
▱▱▱	Pedestrian Walkway	⋀	Campground	⬛	Trailhead		Reef
▰▰▰	Stairs			⛷	Skiing Area		Swamp

CONVERSION TABLES

°C = (°F - 32) / 1.8
°F = (°C x 1.8) + 32
1 inch = 2.54 centimeters (cm)
1 foot = 0.304 meters (m)
1 yard = 0.914 meters
1 mile = 1.6093 kilometers (km)
1 km = 0.6214 miles
1 fathom = 1.8288 m
1 chain = 20.1168 m
1 furlong = 201.168 m
1 acre = 0.4047 hectares
1 sq km = 100 hectares
1 sq mile = 2.59 square km
1 ounce = 28.35 grams
1 pound = 0.4536 kilograms
1 short ton = 0.90718 metric ton
1 short ton = 2,000 pounds
1 long ton = 1.016 metric tons
1 long ton = 2,240 pounds
1 metric ton = 1,000 kilograms
1 quart = 0.94635 liters
1 US gallon = 3.7854 liters
1 Imperial gallon = 4.5459 liters
1 nautical mile = 1.852 km

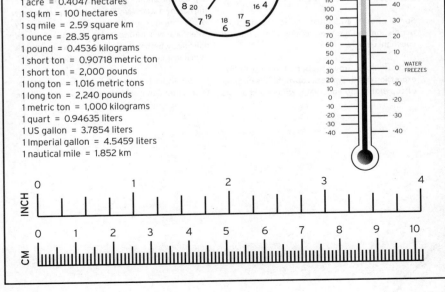

MOON NORTHERN CALIFORNIA

Avalon Travel
Hachette Book Group
1700 Fourth Street
Berkeley, CA 94710, USA
www.moon.com

Editor: Sabrina Young
Series Manager: Kathryn Ettinger
Copy Editor: Ashley Benning
Production and Graphics Coordinator: Darren Alessi
Cover Design: Faceout Studios, Charles Brock
Interior Design: Domini Dragoone
Moon Logo: Tim McGrath
Map Editor: Albert Angulo
Cartographers: Brian Shotwell, Albert Angulo,
 Karin Dahl
Proofreader: Kelly Lydick
Indexer: Greg Jewett

ISBN-13: 978-1-64049-282-0

Printing History
1st Edition — 2000
8th Edition — December 2018
5 4 3 2 1

Text © 2018 by Elizabeth Linhart Veneman and
 Avalon Travel.
Contributing Author: Stuart Thornton
Maps © 2018 by Avalon Travel.

Some photos and illustrations are used by
permission and are the property of the original
copyright owners.

Front cover photo: rock formation in Lake Tahoe
 © Hotaik Sung / Alamy Stock Photo
Back cover photo: Muir Woods National Monument
 © Layfphoto | Dreamstime.com

Printed in China by RR Donnelley.